World Histories of Crime, Culture and Violence

Series Editors
Marianna Muravyeva
University of Helsinki
Helsinki, Finland

Raisa Maria Toivo
Tampere University
Tampere, Finland

Palgrave's World Histories of Crime, Culture and Violence seeks to publish research monographs, collections of scholarly essays, multi-authored books, and Palgrave Pivots addressing themes and issues of interdisciplinary histories of crime, criminal justice, criminal policy, culture and violence globally and on a wide chronological scale (from the ancient to the modern period). It focuses on interdisciplinary studies, historically contextualized, across various cultures and spaces employing a wide range of methodologies and conceptual frameworks.

Kathy Stuart

Suicide by Proxy in Early Modern Germany

Crime, Sin and Salvation

palgrave
macmillan

Kathy Stuart
University of California, Davis
Davis, CA, USA

ISSN 2730-9630   ISSN 2730-9649 (electronic)
World Histories of Crime, Culture and Violence
ISBN 978-3-031-25243-3   ISBN 978-3-031-25244-0 (eBook)
https://doi.org/10.1007/978-3-031-25244-0

© The Editor(s) (if applicable) and The Author(s), under exclusive licence to Springer Nature Switzerland AG 2023
This work is subject to copyright. All rights are solely and exclusively licensed by the Publisher, whether the whole or part of the material is concerned, specifically the rights of translation, reprinting, reuse of illustrations, recitation, broadcasting, reproduction on microfilms or in any other physical way, and transmission or information storage and retrieval, electronic adaptation, computer software, or by similar or dissimilar methodology now known or hereafter developed.
The use of general descriptive names, registered names, trademarks, service marks, etc. in this publication does not imply, even in the absence of a specific statement, that such names are exempt from the relevant protective laws and regulations and therefore free for general use.
The publisher, the authors, and the editors are safe to assume that the advice and information in this book are believed to be true and accurate at the date of publication. Neither the publisher nor the authors or the editors give a warranty, expressed or implied, with respect to the material contained herein or for any errors or omissions that may have been made. The publisher remains neutral with regard to jurisdictional claims in published maps and institutional affiliations.

This Palgrave Macmillan imprint is published by the registered company Springer Nature Switzerland AG.
The registered company address is: Gewerbestrasse 11, 6330 Cham, Switzerland

For Louise

Acknowledgments

My friends and colleagues have been hearing about Suicide by Proxy for a long time. Now years of research in two dozen archives and libraries across Germany and Austria have culminated in this book. Throughout, I enjoyed comradery and intellectual exchange with Duane Corpis, Allyson Creasman, Alex Fisher, Helmut Graser, Mark Häberlein, Michaela Schmölz-Häberlein, Christine Johnson, Hans-Jörg Künast, H. C. Erik Midelfort, Beth Plummer, Ann Tlusty, and Wolfgang Meyer, members of our longstanding Augsburg *Archivstammtisch*. Helmut Graser and Helmut Zäh helped decipher fragmentary Latin passages.

Conversations with Ann Goldberg, David Luebke, Yair Mintzker, and David Sabean also informed this project. Joel Harrington shared with me transcriptions of two early suicides by proxy cases in Nuremberg, and Martin Scheutz alerted me to cases of suicidal iconoclasm in Vienna's house of correction. I hashed out a chapter with James Melton and Jonathan Strom at the James Allen Vann Seminar at Emory University. Mary Lindemann helped navigate the Staatsarchiv Hamburg. My colleagues at the University of California, Davis, Ali Anooshahr, David Biale, Corrie Decker, Edward Dickinson, Stacy Fahrenthold, Ellen Hartigan-O'Connor, Bill Hagen, Katie Harris, Kyu Kim, Lisa Materson, Sally McKee, Lorena Oropeza, Michael Saler, Daniel Stolzenberg, John Smolenski, and Baki Tezcan provided community and intellectual support. A special shout-out to Corrie Decker, Ann Tlusty, and Hans-Jörg Künast for their detailed feedback on the manuscript. Thank you also to my students Molly Ingram, Hunter Kiley, Pilar Svendsen, Michael Wheeler, and Collin Wonnacott for their enthusiasm and engagement. A UC President's Fellowship and sabbatical leaves enabled me to conduct the research for this book. Teaching a UC Davis Summer Abroad Program in Vienna over several years enabled me to retrace the footsteps of some of the Viennese murderous protagonists who feature in this book, my students in tow.

I could not have written this book without the substantive support by staff in numerous archives and libraries. The Wien Bibliothek stands out for the helpfulness and efficiency of its staff. Special thanks also to Michaela Laichmann and Andreas Weigl of the Wiener Stadt- und Landesarchiv, Christoph Stöttinger of the Stiftarchiv Lambach, Gergor Gatscher-Riedl of the Archiv der Marktgemeinde Perchtoldsdorf, and Josef Weichenberger of the Oberösterreichisches Landesarchiv Linz. Helga Heist, intrepid researcher of Upper Austrian history, was an invaluable guide. Wolfgang Meyer and Edeltraud Prestel of the Staats- und Stadtbibliothek Augsburg, Georg Feuerer of the Stadtarchiv Augsburg, and Wilfried Sponsel and Susanne Faul of the Stadtarchiv Nördlingen helped me unearth obscure sources and images. Emily Russell and Steven Fassioms, my editors at Palgrave Macmillan, expertly guided this book through the publication process.

I had the opportunity to present my research on "Suicide by Proxy" to a national and even international audience thanks to an invitation by Ira Glass to participate in an episode on "Loopholes" (#473) on his radio show *This American Life*. Serendipitously, two Austrian filmmakers Veronika Franz and Severin Fiala heard this broadcast. This led to a fruitful and exciting collaboration over several years. They enlisted me as a historical advisor for their forthcoming feature film, *The Devil's Bath* (*Des Teufels Bad*) (2023). The film's protagonist, the fictional suicidal child murderer Agnes Lizlfellnerin, is a composite of two historical child murderers, Agnes Catherina Schickin (Württemberg, 1704) and Eva Lizlfellnerin (Upper Austria, 1762), who both appear in the pages of this book.

Thank you also to my non-historian friends Alain Belkaious, Elke Berger, Louise Bierig, Anh Bui, Paul Eric Davis, Kristine Fowler, Jeannette Heulin, Davis Krauter, Dominique Lambert, Jim Mavrikios, Regina and Josef Merkinger, Cary Norsworthy, Frank Paré, and S. Rope Wolf. And, of course, Louise Lanoue, my partner in life, to whom this book is dedicated.

Over many years I subjected them to innumerable gruesome stories about suicidal child murderers and host desecrators over drinks, dinners, and walks. Their curiosity and engaging questions helped me figure out ways to narrate, explain, and contextualize the horrific crimes committed by suicidal perpetrators to a broader audience, to make the incomprehensible comprehensible. That, at least, was my goal.

Portions of Chaps. 1 and 2 have been published in "Suicide by Proxy: The Unintended Consequences of Public Executions in Eighteenth-Century Germany," *Central European History* 41 (2008): 413–445.

Contents

1 Introduction   1

2 Liturgies of Suicide by Proxy   37

3 "Fear God and the Court, while there is still Time." Crime and Zealous Prosecution in Early Modern Hamburg   91

4 "The Unbelievably Frequent Examples of such Murders Committed solely out of Weariness with Life." Hamburg, 1668–1810   139

5 Mary with the Axe: The Cult of the Injured Icon in Baroque Vienna   209

6 The Injured Crucifix: The Emperor's Conscience and Prisoners' Defiance   263

7 Crime and Justice in a Sacred Landscape: Vienna, 1668–1786   329

8 Conclusion: The Decline of Suicide by Proxy and its
   Historical Effacement   395

Bibliography   407

Index   449

Abbreviations

AFMV	Acta facultatis medicae Vindobonensis
DAW	Diözesanarchiv Wien
FÖWAH	Fürstliches Oettingen-Wallersteinisches Archiv, Harburg
GNM	Germanisches Nationalmuseum, Nuremberg
HAB	Herzog August Bibliothek, Wolfenbüttel
HMW	Historisches Museum der Stadt Wien
HRG	*Handwörterbuch zur deutschen Rechtsgeschichte*
HStAD	Hauptstaatsarchiv Dresden
HStAS	Hauptstaatsarchiv Stuttgart
ISG	Institut für Stadtgeschichte Frankfurt
ÖNB	Österreichische Nationalbibliothek, Vienna
OÖLA	Oberösterreichisches Landesarchiv Linz
ÖWB	Oettingen-Wallersteinische Bibliothek
StadtAN	Stadtarchiv Nürnberg
StadtBN	Stadtbibliothek Nürnberg
StAN	Staatsarchiv Nürnberg
StiftAL	Stiftsarchiv Lambach
SUBH	Staats- und Universitätsbibliothek Hamburg
SuStBA	Staats- und Stadtbibliothek Augsburg
UAW	Universitätsarchiv Wien
UBA	Universitätsbibliothek Augsburg
WB	Wien Bibliothek
WD	*Wiennerisches Diarium*
WStLA	Wiener Stadt- und Landesarchiv

List of Figures

Image 1.1	Christoph Murer, "Allegory of Good Government with Innocence," 1598. Stained glass, Nuremberg. Detail. Museen der Stadt Nürnberg, Kunstsammlungen. Inv.-Nr. 33 (MM 295). Photo: Richard Krauss	3
Image 1.2	Christoph Murer, "Politia," 1597. Stained glass, Nuremberg, Detail. Nuremberg, Museen der Stadt Nürnberg, Kunstsammlungen. Leihgabe des Freistaats Bayern. Inv. Nr. 33 (MM 296). Photo Credits: Kunstsammlungen der Stadt Nürnberg. Photo: Richard Krauss	5
Image 1.3	*Darstellung der Grausamen Mordthat der Maria Anna Mayrinn ledig Stands 23. Jahr alt von Oberhausen.* Munich: [1783]. Engraving. StadtAA, Strafamt Nr. 162	10
Image 2.1	Urs Graf d. Ä. *Richtstätte*. Pen and ink drawing. 1512. The ALBERTINA Museum, Vienna. Inv. Nr. 3050	39
Image 2.2	Hans Bützer's petition to the Duke of Württemberg. Hauptstaatsarchiv Stuttgart, A 209 Bü 166	50
Image 2.3	Roman soldier stabbing an Infant. Figurine in "Rinner Krippe: Bethlehemitischer Kindermord." Rinn in Tirol, c. 1760. Volkskunde Museum Wien, Vienna. Photo: Birgit & Peter Kainz, facsimile digital. ÖMV/35.899	56
Image 2.4	Anderl von Rinn. Engraving, 1724. Volkskunde Museum Wien, Vienna. ÖMV/34.467	61
Image 2.5	Knife. 1731. Stadtarchiv Nördlingen. R 39 F2 Fasc 9 Selbstmord, Ao 1731	78

Image 2.6	*InfantICIDa aVgVstUs*, Kunstsammlungen und Museen Augsburg. Inv. Nr. G9740	86
Image 2.7	*Die allhier in Augsburg Ao. 1740 d. 14. Martii von seinem eignen Vatter grausam ermordete Unschuld Maria Magdalen Bertzin....* Engraving. 1740. Staats- und Stadtbibliothek Augsburg: Graph 29/120	87
Image 2.8	*Hinrichtung der Maria Elisabetha Beckensteinerin.... 20 Martii 1742....* Engraving. 1740. Staats- und Stadtbibliothek Augsburg: Graph 29/123	88
Image 3.1	"Van pynlikē sakē dat hogeste belangende." Miniature. Hamburg *Stadtrecht*, 1497. Hamburg Staatsarchiv, 111-1 Senat Cl. VII Lit. La Nr. 2 Vol. 1c, f. 250v	100
Image 3.2	"Hamburgum," Map (Detail), in Georg Braun and Franz Hogenberg, *Civitates Orbis Terrarum*, vol. 4. Cologne: 1588. Staats- und Universitätsbibliothek Hamburg, Signatur Kt H 202	112
Image 3.3	Execution of Cord Jastram and Hieronimus Schnitger, 1687. Engraving (Detail). "Außführung Cord Jastrams und Hieronymi Schnitgers." Hamburg Staatsarchiv, A 320/22	114
Image 4.1	"Method of Punishing the Idle at the Poor House at Hamburgh." 1778. Wellcome Collection 43268i	151
Image 4.2	Soldiers disciplined by riding "the wooden horse." Engraving. Hanns Friedrich von Fleming, *Der Vollkommene Teutsche Soldat* (Leipzig: Johann Christian Martini, 1726), 184–185. ETH-Bibliothek Zürich, Rar 9315	153
Image 4.3	Frontispiece. Gerhard Hackmann, *Catechismus-Schule: Darinn Die Jugend in den Häuptstücken unserer wahren Christlichen Religion/ ...unterrichtet wird*. Hamburg: Werner, 1641. Forschungbibliothek Gotha, Signatur Theol 8° 00371/09	156
Image 4.4	Title page. *Ausführlicher Bericht/ Derer in Hamburg hingerichteten Missethäters* ([Hamburg], c. 1720). Hamburg Staatsarchiv, 111-1, Senat, CI.VII, Lit, Mb, No.3, Vol. 1	174
Image 5.1	Trinity Column, Vienna, 1693 (Detail). Photo by author	225
Image 5.2	Emperor Joseph I Venerates the Sacrament, 1701. Engraving by Christoph Weigel (after Caspar Luyken). The ALBERTINA Museum, Vienna. Historische Blätter Wien 8, Joseph I	227

Image 5.3	"Prospect des Grabens." Engraving by Georg Daniel Heumann after Salomon Kleiner, in Salomon Kleiner, *Vera Et Accurata Delineatio Omnium Templorum et Coenobiorum Quae tam in Caesarea Urbe ac Sede Vienna Austriae, quam in circumjacentibus Suburbys ejus reperiuntur*. Vol. 2, *Abbildung der keysserl. Burg und Lust-Häuser*. (Augsburg: Johann Adreas Pfeffel, 1725), plate 99	230
Image 5.4	Devotional image of the Marian icon Maria Grünberg. Engraving, early eighteenth century. *Das wundertthaetige Bildnis Maria bei den Franziskanern*. Volkskunde Museum Wien, Vienna. AÖMV13.888	234
Image 5.5	Maria Grünberg, or "Mary with the Axe", Marian icon above the high altar in the Franciskanerkircher, Vienna. Photo by author	235
Image 5.6	Priest leads procession bringing last rites to dying parishioner. "Prospect des Gräfflich Kaysersteinischen Hauses" (Detail). Engraving by J. A. Corvinus after Sal. Kleiner. In Salomon Kleiner, *Vera Et Accurata Delineatio Omnium Templorum et Coenobiorum Quae tam in Caesarea Urbe ac Sede Vienna Austriae, quam in circumjacentibus [circumiacentibus] Suburbijs [Suburbiis] ejus [eius] reperiuntur*. Vol 3. *Das florirende vermehrte Wien*. (Augsburg: Johann Adreas Pfeffel, 1733), plate 211	240
Image 5.7	"Der aergerlicher Laesterer des Hochheiligsten Sacraments." Engraving. In Mathias Fuhrmann, *Alt- und Neues Wien, Oder Dieser Kayserlich- und Ertz-Lands-Fürstlichen Residentz-Stadt Chronologisch- und Historische Beschreibung*. Vol. 2. (Vienna: Johann Baptist Prasser, 1739), with p. 807	244
Image 5.8	*Eygentlicher Bericht/Was massen der getrauffte/ jedoch wider vom Christenthumb abgefallene Jud/ zu Wien den 22. Augusti 1642...verurtheilt/...wegen der grausamen Gotteslästerung/... vollzogen worden*. Photo: Wien Museum, Gerichtswesen 1642, IN52093 M. 790	248
Image 5.9	*Zerschneiden Zweymahl die Hl. Hostia...* Kaberger-Ketzerbilder, 18th century. Stiftarchiv Schlierbach, Image 10. Photo: OÖLKG/Ernst Grilnberger	256
Image 5.10	"Abbildung der wunderbaren H. Hostien zu Wolfsberg in Kaernten." Engraving. Volkskundemuseum Wien, Vienna, AÖMV/13.808	261

xviii LIST OF FIGURES

Image 6.1	*Jüdische neue Zeitung vom Marsch aus Wien...* (s.l., s.d). Vertreibung der Juden aus Wien 1670. Copperplate Engraving. Photo: Wien Museum. In. Nr. 199198	265
Image 6.2	Emperor Leopold I's signature under the imperial privilege founding the house of correction, 1671. Wiener Stadt und Landesarchiv, Hauptarchivsakten, Privilegien 77, f. 13	266
Image 6.3	Apotheosis of Emperor Leopold I. Frontispiece to 1671 imperial privilege authorizing the founding of the house of correction. Wiener Stadt und Landesarchiv, Hauptarchivsakten, Privilegien 77	267
Image 6.4	Vienna's House of Correction. Water coloring, c. 1850. Photo: Wien Museum. In. Nr. 15069, C. N. 231 (= Leopoldgasse Nr. 32) (Das alte Zuchthaus)	272
Image 6.5	Execution of Catherina Jacobin, Vienna, 1769. Engraving. In *Todesurtheil einer ledigen Weibperson, Namens Catherina J....* Wienbibliothek im Rathaus, C-39975/1769	283
Image 6.6	The ravenstone outside the Scottish Gate, c. 1760. Anonymous Pen and Ink Drawing. The ALBERTINA Museum, Inv. 7377, Ansichten (Vues) Wien, äussere Bezirke 2: Das Hochgericht gegen die Rossau hin	294
Image 6.7	Drawing of instruments of execution included in court records concerning Joseph Zeitler, executed 1719 in the territory of the Benedictine Abbey of Lambach for church robbery. Stiftarchiv Lambach, Criminalia 377, Joseph Zeitler, 1719	304
Image 6.8	Nicolaus Starck's signature under his *Urfehde* of 17 December 1756. Wiener Stadt und Landesarchiv, Handschriften A 19, fol. 142r	309
Image 6.9	Depiction of blasphemy in Joos de Damhouder, *Praxis rerum criminalium: Gründlicher Bericht und anweisung, Welcher massen in Rechtfärtigung Peinlicher sachen, nach gemeynen beschriebenen Rechten vor und in Gerichten ordentlich zuhandeln* (Franckfurt am Mayn: Johann Wolfius, 1571), 102v. Bayerische Staatsbibliothek München, 4 Crim. 41	323
Image 6.10	Depiction of blasphemy in Joos de Damhouder, *Praxis rerum criminalium: Gründlicher Bericht und anweisung, Welcher massen in Rechtfärtigung Peinlicher sachen, nach gemeynen beschriebenen Rechten vor und in Gerichten ordentlich zuhandeln* (Franckfurt am Mayn: Nicolaus Basseus, 1581), 92. Staatliche Bibliothek Regensburg, 999/2 Jur.353.	324

LIST OF FIGURES   xix

Image 7.1	Edict on Child Murders. "Wie es mit Bestrafung des Kinder-Mords zu halten," 22 March 1706. Archiv der Marktgemeinde Perchtoldsdorf, Patente, Karton 344	339
Image 7.2	Anonymous photo of the "Wheel Cross" (Räderkreuz), Column with Pieta adjacent to execution site on the Wienerberg, taken 1868 prior to its demolition. "Mariensäule an der Triesterstraße vor der Matzleinsdorfer[linie] b[eim] Richtplatz." Photo: Wien Museum, Inv. Nr. 78.369/1, 10	341
Image 7.3	Parcel map showing execution sites on the Vienna Mountain, c. 1730. Wiener Stadt- und Landesarchiv, Pläne und Karten: Sammelband, P1, Pläne und Karten, 50, Gegend vor der Martleinsdorfer Linie	343
Image 7.4	Execution of Catherina Jacobin, Vienna, 1769. Engraving. In *Todesurtheil einer ledigen Weibperson, Namens Catherina J.*… Wienbibliothek im Rathaus, C-39975/1769	349
Image 7.5	Frontispiece, in "Verzeichnis deren von einer Hochlöblichen Privilegierten Kays. Königl. Todtenbruderschaft übernohmenen Malleficanten." Wienbibliothek im Rathaus, HIN-19008	362
Image 7.6	Frontispiece, in *Probatica Piscina del Purgatorio Situata Fra Li Sacri Monti Austriaci* (Vienna: Maria Rittia Vedova, 1638). National Library of the Czech Republic, Prague, Shelf Mark 36 E 000081	365
Image 7.7	Execution Procession departing from Vienna's prison, Engraving by Johann August Corvinus after Salomon Kleiner, in Salomon Kleiner, *Vera Et Accurata Delineatio Omnium Templorum et Coenobiorum Quae tam in Caesarea Urbe ac Sede Vienna Austriae, quam in circumjacentibus Suburbys ejus reperiuntur*, vol. 1. (Augsburg: Johann Adreas Pfeffel, 1724), plate 41	373
Image 7.8	"Wahrhafte Bildnuß Francisci Nadasti wegen aufrührerischem Meineid in dem Rathaus zu Wien enthaupt den 30. April 1671." Engraving (Detail). Photo: Wien Museum. Inv. Nr. 37988	378

Image 7.9　　Procession of a Confraternity. "Prospect des Hoch-Gräffl. Traunischen Gebäudes in der Herren-Gassen." Engraving by J. A. Corvinus after Sal. Kleiner. In Salomon Kleiner, *Vera Et Accurata Delineatio Omnium Templorum et Coenobiorum Quae tam in Caesarea Urbe ac Sede Vienna Austriae, quam in circumjacentibus [circumiacentibus] Suburbijs [Suburbiis] ejus [eius] reperiuntur.* Vol 3. *Das florirende vermehrte Wien.* (Augsburg: Johann Adreas Pfeffel, 1733), plate 202　　380

Image 7.10　　The Poor Sinners' Graveyard. "Prospect des Bürgerl. Hospitals-Gotts-Acker nebst der Capelle St. Rochi, vor dem Kärnter Thor. a. S. Caroli Borromaei Kirche." Engraving by J. A. Corvinus after Sal. Kleiner. In Salomon Kleiner, *Vera Et Accurata Delineatio Omnium Templorum et Coenobiorum Quae tam in Caesarea Urbe ac Sede Vienna Austriae, quam in circumjacentibus [circumiacentibus] Suburbijs [Suburbiis] ejus [eius] reperiuntur.* Vol. 4. *Des florirenden vermehrten Wiens fernere Befolgung.* Plate 47　　382

CHAPTER 1

Introduction

In 1598 the Swiss artist Christoph Murer completed a stained-glass window for the city hall of the Lutheran free imperial city of Nuremberg. An allegory of good government, it was one in a cycle of four windows commissioned by Nuremberg's patrician city councilors. This window and its companion pieces fell within the genre of "Images of Justice" that hung in court rooms and city council chambers throughout Europe. City governments commissioned the art works and set the iconographical program to communicate their ideology of governance.[1] Murer's windows expressed the self-image of Nuremberg councilmen as benevolent and vigilant city fathers and protectors of the innocent. The 1598 window centers on a naked, golden-haired, baby boy chained to a marble slab, resembling a sacrificial altar.[2] The boy, a personification of Innocence, is under threat by a knife-wielding Jew to his left, clearly identified by the circular badge on his shoulder. This was the yellow circle, the traditional stigma symbol Jews were required to wear since the late Middle Ages. To the baby's right is an

---

[1] Katja Sperling, "Christoph Murers Glasgemälde für den Rat und für Patrizierfamilien der Stadt Nürnberg." (Master's thesis, Friedrich-Alexander-Universität Erlangen-Nürnberg, 1991), 61. On "Images of Justice," see Wolfgang Schild, "Gerechtigkeitsbilder," in *Recht und Gerechtigkeit im Spiegel der europäischen Kunst*, eds. Wolfgang Pleister and Wolfgang Schild (Cologne: DuMont Buchverlag, 1988), 86-171.

[2] Charles Zika, *The Appearance of Witchcraft: Print and Visual Culture in sixteenth-century Europe* (London: Routledge, 2007), 233.

© The Author(s), under exclusive license to Springer Nature Switzerland AG 2023
K. Stuart, *Suicide by Proxy in Early Modern Germany*, World Histories of Crime, Culture and Violence, https://doi.org/10.1007/978-3-031-25244-0_1

old hag, the stereotypical witch, topless, her withered breasts sagging, her unkempt hair hanging freely. The witch grabs the child by the hair, holding him prone for the Jew's knife. Behind the witch, a soldier thrusts his halberd toward the child. These are the vices of avarice (the Jew), envy (the witch), and war (the soldier). The Jew represented more than avarice, of course. To any early modern viewer, the Jew with a knife evoked the specter of Jewish ritual murder. This was an iconography with which Murer's Nuremberg patrons were thoroughly familiar. Perhaps the most iconic representation of Jewish ritual murder ever created was produced in Nuremberg just over a century earlier. Schedel's *World Chronicle*, published 1493, includes a richly detailed image of the alleged martyrdom of Simon of Trent in 1475, the case after which all subsequent accusations of Jewish ritual murder were modeled.[3]

Murer's work portrays an infernal alliance between the blood-thirsty Jew and the child-murdering witch. Behind the aggressors to the left, a crowned figure, a negligent king, shirks his responsibility as ruler by covering his eyes so as not to see the horrible scene unfolding before him. He too will be held to account for his dereliction of duty. Truth thrones above this scene. She holds a book with the words "The Word of God endures forever" (Isaiah 40:8), the bible verse that became the logo of the Protestant Reformation.[4] This was a declaration of Nuremberg's Lutheran identity. Truth is assisted by Justice, sword, scales and orb in hand, and by Peace, who stand to the left and right of the city's coat of arms. The virtues collectively represent the wise governance of Nuremberg's city

---

[3] Hartmut Schedel, *Weltchronik* (Nuremberg: Anton Koberger, 1493), fol. 254r. This image can be viewed in high resolution in color, digitized at the Germanisches Nationalmuseum, Nuremberg: http://dlib.gnm.de/item/2Inc266/568/html. On the paradigmatic significance of the Simon of Trent case, see Magda Teter, *Blood Libel: On the Trail of an Antisemitic Myth* (Cambridge, Mass.: Harvard University Press, 2020), 43-151. Wolfgang Treue, *Der Trienter Judenprozess: Voraussetzungen, Abläufe, Auswirkungen (1475-1588)* (Hannover: Hahn, 1996). R. Po-Chia Hsia, *Trent 1475: Stories of a Ritual Murder Trial* (New Haven, CT: Yale University Press, 1992).

[4] F. J. Stopp, "Verbum Domini Manet in Aeternum. The Dissemination of a Reformation Slogan, 1522-1904," in *Essays in German Culture and Society*, eds. Siegbert S. Prawer, R. Hinton Thomas and Leonard Forster (London: Institute of Germanic Studies, 1969), 123-235.

Image 1.1 Christoph Murer, "Allegory of Good Government with Innocence," 1598. Stained glass, Nuremberg. Detail. Museen der Stadt Nürnberg, Kunstsammlungen. Inv.-Nr. 33 (MM 295). Photo: Richard Krauss

fathers.[5] Innocence, the baby under assault, symbolizes the Christ Child, as did the male child victims in representations of Jewish ritual murder[6] (Image 1.1).

In the 1590s, when Nuremberg commissioned this window, large witch-hunts were taking place in surrounding regions, in Bavaria and in the Franconian hinterland and the nearby Catholic Prince-Bishoprics of Würzburg and Bamberg. Nuremberg remained impervious to the witch-hunt just beyond its borders, however. Nuremberg, along with several other free imperial cities, experienced what historian Alison Rowlands calls

---

[5] The crowned figure "looks through his fingers" (*durch die Finger sehen*), a German figure of speech that means to willfully turn a blind eye to wrongdoing. The text in the book that Truth holds reads: *Verbu(m) Dom(ini) manet in aeternum*. A text inset reads: "The innocent heart and the age known for its purity, becomes everywhere the prey of the furies of war, avarice and envy. But you, truth, certainly see everything, even if the prince shuts his eyes." Thea Vignau-Wilberg, "Zur Entstehung zweier Emblemata von Christoph Murer," *Anzeiger des Germanischen Nationalmuseums*, (1977): 85-94. Thea Vignau-Wolberg, *Christoph Murer und die "XL Emblemata Miscella Nova"* (Bern: Benteli Verlag, 1982), 218-221, 271-272.

[6] R. Po-Chia Hsia, *The Myth of Ritual Murder. Jews and Magic in Reformation Germany* (New Haven: Yale University Press, 1988), 55.

a "restrained pattern of witch-hunting."[7] The city executed no one for witchcraft during the most intense phase of the European witch-hunt in the late sixteenth and early seventeenth centuries.[8]

Nuremberg was similarly uninterested in prosecuting Jewish ritual murder. Even as the city's printing presses profited from texts and images that propagated the blood libel, Nuremberg's leading Protestant reformer and theological adviser to the city council Andreas Osiander authored an anonymous treatise defending Jews against the blood libel. Osiander's *Whether it is True and Believable that Jews secretly Kill Christian Children and Use their Blood* (c. 1530), was instrumental in debunking ritual murder charges against Jews. Osiander contributed to a "disenchantment" of the ritual murder discourse, R. Po-Chia Hsia argues: "Osiander's defense of the Jews fundamentally undermined the structure of ritual murder discourse. The faith in a 'true religion' and the exposition of 'the magic and superstitions' of the Roman church were intellectual commonplaces of all reformers." Consequently, for Protestant intellectuals "the charges of magic and murder" related to the blood libel "would gradually fade into a distant echo."[9]

When Nuremberg's councilors commissioned Murer's glass window featuring the murderous assault upon Innocence by a Jew and a witch, they were relatively unconcerned by threats posed by any actual witches or Jews. The figures were tropes, archetypes of evil that Nuremberg's godly government would vanquish. A second window in Murer's cycle drove

---

[7] Allison Rowlands, *Witchcraft Narratives in Germany: Rothenburg, 1561–1652* (Manchester: Manchester University Press, 2003), 1. For the early sixteenth century Laura Stokes observes that "the only general statement which can be made about the Nuremberg council's propensity to punish witchcraft was that it chose not to do so." Laura Stokes, *Demons of Urban Reform: Early European Witch Trials and Criminal Justice, 1430–1530* (New York: Palgrave Macmillan, 2011), 52.

[8] The total number of executions in Nuremberg territory between 1590 and 1622 that had any connection at all to witchcraft was three. In 1590 Nuremberg executed an itinerant executioner's assistant, Friedrich Stigler, for defaming Nuremberg citizens' wives as witches and for superstitious practices. In 1617 and 1622 Nuremberg executed two other men for an accumulation of capital offenses that included magic. Helmut H. Kunstmann, *Zauberwahn und Hexenprozeß in der Reichstadt Nürnberg* (Nuremberg: Stadtarchiv Nürnberg, 1970), 74-78, 92-93. Frantz Schmidt, *The Executioner's Journal: Meister Frantz Schmidt of the Imperial City of Nuremberg*, trans. Joel Harrington (Charlottesville: University of Virginia Press, 2016), 108.

[9] Andreas Osiander, *Ob es war vn[d] glaublich sey, daß die Juden der Christen kinder heymlich erwürgen, vnd jr blut gebrauchen: ein treffenliche schrifft, auff eines yeden vrteyl gestelt.* ([Nuremberg]: [Petreius], ca. 1530). Hsia, *Myth*, 143.

1 INTRODUCTION 5

Image 1.2 Christoph Murer, "Politia," 1597. Stained glass, Nuremberg, Detail. Nuremberg, Museen der Stadt Nürnberg, Kunstsammlungen. Leihgabe des Freistaats Bayern. Inv. Nr. 33 (MM 296). Photo Credits: Kunstsammlungen der Stadt Nürnberg. Photo: Richard Krauss

home this point. The image shows a crowned woman sitting on a throne. In her right hand she cups her bared breast, from which an arc of breast milk jets forth onto the Nuremberg citizenry kneeling in prayer, women and children featuring prominently among them [Image 1.2]. The arc of breast milk was a symbol of mercy, but this was not *Maria Lactans*, the lactating Virgin Mary who appeared in ecstatic visions of Catholic saints as well as in images of judgment, where Mary held her bared breast to inspire mercy toward sinful humanity.[10] This was *Politia* (the state), a more appropriate figure in a Lutheran allegory of good government. The mercy she

[10] Jutta Sperling, "Squeezing, Squirting, Spilling Milk: The Lactation of Saint Bernard and the Flemish Madonna Lactans (ca. 1430-1530)," *Renaissance Quarterly* 17 (2018): 868-918. Susan Marti and Daniela Mondini, ""Ich manen dich der brüsten min, Das du dem sünder wellest milte sin!'": Marienbrüste und Marienmilch im Heilsgeschehen," in *Himmel, Hölle, Fegefeuer. Das Jenseits im Mittelalter,* ed. Peter Jezler (Munich: Wilhelm Fink Verlag, 1994), 79-90.

exercises toward the pious citizenry is balanced by severity toward malefactors. In her left hand she holds a sword and whip over a group of prisoners being led away in chains, including a turbaned Turk, who like the witch and the Jew was another stereotypical evildoer of the early modern age. A text insert made the moral message explicit: "May the good be rewarded. May the evil receive the punishment they deserve. The republic will stand according to these laws, or fall."[11] This axiom was drawn from Romans 13. The same chapter continues: "For he [i.e., governmental authority] is God's minister to you for good. But if you do evil, be afraid; for he does not bear the sword in vain."[12]

Nuremberg implemented this governing philosophy with uncompromising rigor. In the late sixteenth and early seventeenth centuries the city administered criminal justice with unprecedented severity. These policies yielded results the councilmen never imagined, however. The symbolic violence represented in Murer's stained-glass windows became reality, as Nuremberg's city fathers were confronted with a new kind of ritual murder committed by more mundane killers, their own Lutheran subjects.

The city council commissioned these allegories of good government during the tenure of Nuremberg's master executioner Frantz Schmidt. Schmidt kept a diary in which he documented the executions and other bodily punishments he performed on behalf of the city during his thirty-nine years of service, from 1578 to 1617. "Nuremberg's average execution rate of nine per year during Meister Frantz's lifetime (in a city of forty thousand)," Joel Harrington writes, "was the highest per capita of any city in the empire."[13] These years also saw a dramatic increase in the number of women executed in Nuremberg. As the overall number of executions rose, the proportion of women among executed felons rose to a higher

---

[11] Katja Sperling, "Christoph Murers Glasgemälde," 30-34, 50-52.
[12] Romans 13, 4-5, New King James Version.
[13] Joel Harrington's edition of Schmidt's diary opens an invaluable window onto the day-to-day administration of criminal justice in the city during Schmidt's tenure. Schmidt, *Journal*, xxviii. On Schmidt's life and career see also Joel Harrington, *The Faithful Executioner: Life and Death, Honor and Shame in the Turbulent Sixteenth Century* (New York: Farrar, Straus and Giroux, 2013). On the increase in the number of executions in Nuremberg during these years, see Richard van Dülmen, *Theatre of Horror: Crime and Punishment in Early Modern Germany* (Cambridge: Polity Press, 1990), 140, and Friedrich von Hagen and Michael Diefenbacher, *Die Henker von Nürnberg und ihre Opfer: Folter und Hinrichtungen in den Nürnberger Ratsverlässen 1501 bis 1806* (Nuremberg: Stadtarchiv, 2010).

level than ever before.[14] Anna Strölin, beheaded in 1580, and Anna Freyin, beheaded in 1584, were among them.[15]

On November 12, 1580, Anna Strölin, a forty-five-year-old married peasant woman from the village of Walkersbrunn within Nuremberg's territory, home alone with two young sons, murdered the older boy, six years old, by striking him repeatedly on the head and chest with a hatchet. The arresting official reported that she had murdered her son "at the instigation of the evil enemy." Councilmen administering her criminal trial asked: why did she so gruesomely murder her own flesh and blood? Strölin's only explanation was that the idea came to her to quickly kill her child so that she too could die. She requested that authorities "do justice onto her soon."[16] A legal brief on the case explicitly identified "weariness with life" (*taedio vitae*) as the murder motive. Legal advisers considered a finding of insanity, but ultimately found her criminally culpable.[17] The city council pronounced her death sentence on December 3, 1580, just over two weeks after the murder. Her beheading took place three days later, as executioner Meister Frantz recorded in his diary.[18]

Four years later Nuremberg was confronted with a similar case. On the night of October 30, 1584, Anna Freyin, wife of a Nuremberg clothcutter and citizen, appeared at city hall and alerted the sentry on duty that she had just pushed her two-year-old son into a well near the Franciscan church. Freyin was taken to the dungeon, and her son's body retrieved from the well. She told her interrogators that three years earlier she had committed adultery with a journeyman cutler, who absconded when she became pregnant with the boy she had just killed. Her husband believed the baby was his. Recently she had given birth to a second baby, conceived

---

[14] Peter Schuster, *Verbrecher, Opfer, Heilige eine Geschichte des Tötens 1200-1700* (Stuttgart: Klett-Cotta, 2015), 45-46.

[15] Thank you to Joel Harrington for sharing his transcriptions of the Strölin and Freyin cases.

[16] The local Pfleger reported that Strölin had murdered her son "aus verreizung des bösen feindts." StAN, Bestand 60A, Ratsverläße, 1456, fol. 56v, November 12, 1580. Strölin testified that she "hab halt bey Ir gedacht, sie wöll dz kind flu[p] erschlagen damit sie nur auch vom brot komme, und pitt man woll Ir nur baldt Ir Recht thun." Interrogators followed up: "Weil sie dann fürgebe, sie hab darum dz kind erschlagen, damit sie nur auch hinweg komme," then she must have some other misdeed burdening her conscience, which Strölin denied. StAN, 52b-209, fol. 235r-236v.

[17] Rechtsanwalt Bode, "Die Kindestötung und ihre Bestrafung im Nürnberg des Mittelalters," *Archiv für Strafrecht und Strafprozess*, 61 (1914): 445-448. Bode provides excerpts of two legal expert opinions on this case.

[18] Schmidt, *Journal*, 11-12.

with her husband, who died after six weeks. Since then she felt "afflictions." A kind of demonic entity moved about her chamber, urging her to throw her two-year-old son in the water. "And so, the evil enemy seduced her, and she threw her little son into the well," she testified. "She would like to die, if only she knew that she would not go to hell for it."[19] In Freyin's case, too, the court briefly considered a finding of insanity, but followed legal expert opinion instead: "since this woman herself desires to die, if only she knew that she would be saved and not damned, the council should have her beheaded out of mercy, and in the meantime have ministers earnestly comfort her with God's word, so that she has true repentance for her sins and will be prevented from falling into despair."[20] Freyin was beheaded on November 17, 1584.

These two child murders are the earliest instances that I have been able to identify of a new type of crime that became more common in the seventeenth and eighteenth centuries, in Nuremberg as well as in other cities and territories in the Holy Roman Empire, in Lutheran states like Nuremberg and in Catholic cities and territories as well, most notably the Archduchies of Austria and the city of Vienna in particular. Governments soon realized that murders of the kind committed by Strölin and Freyin were part of a recognizable pattern. Around 1700, governments began to develop legislation to curtail the practice, and by the second half of the eighteenth century such murders became a frequent topic in newly formed legal and medical forensic journals. German jurists called this type of homicide "indirect suicide,"[21] or "Murder out of Weariness with Life."[22] I call it suicide by proxy, in order to emphasize the transactional nature of these crimes. Perpetrators of suicide by proxy committed murder with the intention of "earning" their own death, as they offered up their

---

[19] "hab sie stets dacht, es gehe etwas in Irer kammern umb, das zu Ir sagte, sie solt das kind ins wasser werffen, daher hab sie der böse feind als verführt, das sie hab dasselbe Ir söhnle in den prunnen geworffen." "wöll sie gern sterben, wann sie nur wusste, das sie nit in die höll derwegen keme." StAN, 52b-210, Achtbuch, 1581-1588, 146v-147v.

[20] Quoted in Bode, "Kindstötung," 445.

[21] "Mittelbarer Selbstmord." Karl Ferdinand Hommel, *Rhapsodia quaestionum in foro quotidie obvenientium, neque tamen legibus decisarum*, vol. 5 (Bayreuth: Joh. And. Lubeccium, 1779), 1449-1456.

[22] "Mord aus Lebensüberdruß." Anonym, "Die Dorothee Catharina Wilhelmine Krameriinn tödtet ein fremdes Kind aus Ueberdruß des Lebens," *Annalen der Gesetzgebung und Rechtsgelehrsamket*, 9 (1792): 3-19.

child-victim and themselves.[23] They claimed their execution as an entitlement. Their plan was to avoid the eternal damnation that befell direct suicides. Sometimes such suicidal individuals also committed other capital crimes, such as arson, or confessed to crimes they had not committed, or for which there was no corroborating evidence, usually classic infanticide, that is, the murder of a newborn infant by its unwed mother,[24] or bestiality.[25] The most frequent form of suicide by proxy, however, involved murder. Such killers typically chose children as their victims. They believed, as the eighteenth-century jurist Karl Ferdinand Hommel explained, that the "child they murdered, having not yet sinned, would also attain salvation, and be spared the damnation it might have earned at an older age."[26]

Women made up a clear majority of these killers, a pattern Hommel also observed. The perpetrators were "usually weak females of poor education," he wrote.[27] The gender profile of these murderers is one of the central problematics of this book. Suicide by proxy was an effect, I argue, of how the early modern governments exercised domination over their

---

[23] Such child murderers often used the word *verdienen*, which can be rendered in English as "to earn" or "to deserve." Essentially, they were claiming their "just deserts." The suicidal child murderer Agnes Catherina Schickin, for example, said: "Man solle ihr nur thun, was sie verdient habe, wolle alles von Herzen gern leiden." HStAS, A 209/1806, Agnes Catherina Schickin, 1704.

[24] Throughout, I refer to the murder of a newborn infant by its unwed mother as "classic infanticide" in order to clearly distinguish it from child murders associated with suicide by proxy. Article 131 of the Constitutio Criminalis Carolina, the paradigmatic imperial criminal law code issued by Charles V in 1532, defined infanticide as the murder of newborn infants by their unwed mothers, or also by married women or widows who had committed adultery "for the purpose of concealing their sexual immorality." Other kinds of child killings, including those committed by married women against their legitimate offspring, were prosecuted as murder or manslaughter according to Article 137 of the Carolina on "The Punishment of Murderers and Manslaughterers" (*Straff der mörder und todtschleger ...*). Otto Ulbricht, *Kindsmord und Aufklärung in Deutschland* (Munich: R. Oldenbourg Verlag, 1990), 17-18.

[25] For an example of such a sodomy self-accusation, see the case of Hans Unruhe in 1715, discussed in Johann Christian Fritsch, *Seltsame jedoch wahrhafftige Theologische/Juristische/ Medizinische und Physicalische Geschichten*, vol. 3 (Leipzig: Johann Friedrich Brauns sel. Erben, 1733), 351-416. For an example of suicide by proxy through arson, see E. F. Klein, "Ueber die Brandstiftung der Eva Veronika Chillin, nebst einigen in die Gesetzgebung einschlagenden Bemerkungen, 1) über die Verbrechen, welche aus Ueberdruß des Lebens begangen warden ...," *Annalen der Gesetzgebung und Rechtsgelehrsamkeit* 7 (1791): 3-14.

[26] "daß das von ihnen ... ermordete fremde Kind, da es noch keine Sünde gethan, ebenermaßen die Seeligkeit erlange, oder der Verdamnis, die es bei erwachsenen Jahren sich zuziehen könnte, entrissen werde." Hommel, *Rhapsodia*, vol. 5, 1449-1456.

[27] Hommel, *Rhapsodia*, 117-120.

Image 1.3 *Darstellung der Grausamen Mordthat der Maria Anna Mayrinn ledig Stands 23. Jahr alt von Oberhausen.* Munich: [1783]. Engraving. StadtAA, Strafamt Nr. 162

subjects, and how common people experienced and responded to governmental authority. Suicide by proxy held such appeal for women because they bore the brunt of social disciplining initiatives of the early modern state. Women were the targets of morals campaigns and moral panics from the mid-sixteenth through the mid-eighteenth century. The Protestant Reformation and Catholic Counter-Reformation contributed to the transformation from sin to crime of sexual offenses such as fornication and prostitution. Governments began prosecuting infanticide with great severity around 1560, at the same time as the European witch-hunt accelerated. This growing moral rigorism had a particular impact on women. Suicide by proxy was a psychological response, I argue here, to such unrelenting discipline. I develop this point by embedding the practice of suicide by proxy in the more general history of criminal justice in two cities, Lutheran Hamburg and Catholic Vienna, with brief excursions to Lutheran Nuremberg as well. The gender profile of perpetrators was similar across confessions, as were the general contours of the crime.

These crimes unfolded in a stereotypical sequence of events. Often after a series of unsuccessful suicide attempts, perpetrators of suicide by proxy arrived at the decision to commit a murder. Sometimes they killed their own children, as Strölin and Freyin did, but often they murdered children unrelated to them. Some perpetrators selected a specific child as their victim. Others chose a victim quite at random. In 1709, a Nuremberg butcher's daughter, Christina Forgerin, developed "weariness with her life." For three weeks she harbored the intention to kill "the next best child" who crossed her path. She finally carried out her plan by cutting the throat of a nine-year-old girl. Twelve days later she was beheaded after prior severing of her hand.[28]

Typically, such killers presented themselves at the local jail or at the town hall immediately after the deed and alerted startled authorities to their crime [Image 1.3]. Like Freyin before her, Forgerin went straight to city hall after the murder. Their confessions were spontaneous and uncoerced. None of the confessions of Nuremberg' suicidal murderers were extracted by judicial torture, unlike contemporaneous cases of classic infanticide, where Nuremberg authorities routinely applied judicial torture, or contemporaneous cases of witchcraft in Nuremberg's vicinity. The perpetrators made the motive of the killings explicit, and explained why they chose murder over suicide. In the evening of September 26, 1691, Magdalena Wölffin, daughter of a Nuremberg furrier and citizen, presented herself at the dungeon, demanding to be let in. She had just murdered a little girl. She did not know whose child it was. Earlier in the day she had attempted to drown herself in a pond beyond the city walls. "But then, considering that it would cost her salvation, she repented this

---

[28] Forgerin confessed "daß [sie] durch einen ... geschöpften Verdruß ihres Lebens, von dreyen Wochen her, den bösen Vorsaz gefasset, das nechste beste kind anzufallen, und umbs leben zu bringen." She committed the murder March 14, 1709, and was executed on March 26. StAN, Nürnberger Amts- und Standbücher 225, Malefizurtheilsbuch, March 26, 1709, ff. 57r-58r.

intention," and returned to town.²⁹ There she encountered two young beggar girls, who were minding a baby girl. The moment she laid eyes on the little girl, she decided to kill her. She used a ruse to convince the beggar girls to hand over the baby. She carried the girl outside the city walls and strangled her. Three weeks after the murder, on October 15, 1691, Magdalena Wölffin was beheaded after prior amputation of the hand.

Wölffin's statement that suicide would have "cost her salvation" reflected the conviction among common people, Protestants and Catholics alike, that suicides went to the devil. This had been Catholic doctrine since St. Augustine established that the fifth commandment "Thou shalt not kill" applied to suicide as well as murder. Like murder, suicide was a "mortal sin." Unlike "venial" sins that could be expiated in purgatory, the guilt attached to mortal sins could only be absolved through the sacrament of confession. Since this was no longer available to suicides, they were consigned to eternal damnation. Suicides were denied sacraments and sacramentals, such as a funeral mass and burial in consecrated ground, since such "means of grace" were pointless in their case. If suicides were mistakenly buried in consecrated ground, the remains had to be removed and reburied elsewhere. The graveyard had to be reconsecrated.³⁰

Official Lutheran pronouncements were less categorical. Protestants abandoned the concept of mortal sin. Distinguishing between greater and lesser sins made no sense in Lutheran theology since *all sin* was the expression of human nature utterly corrupted by the fall and would result in damnation unless God granted the sinner grace.³¹ The suicide died unrepentantly in the act of sinning, so it was likely that he or she died an unjustified sinner outside of the state of grace. Nonetheless, damnation was not assured. Catholics expected believers to be able to resist diabolical temptations to suicide, but for Lutherans Satan had become a more formidable

---

[29] "doch in Erwegung, Sie dörffte dadurch umb ihre Seeligkeit kommen, ihr solchen Vorsaz habe reuen lassen, dahero sich widerumb in die Statt begeben." "da sie dann, so baldt sie dieses kindt gesehen, bey sich gedacht habe, sie wollte solches, wann sie es hätte, umbbringen." StAN, Amts- und Standbücher 225, Malefizurtheilsbuch, fol. 15v-17r.

[30] Vera Lind, *Selbstmord in der Frühen Neuzeit: Diskurs, Lebenswelt, und kultureller Wandel am Beispiel der Herzogtümer Schleswig und Holstein* (Göttingen: Vandenhoeck & Ruprecht, 1999), 21-22. Jürgen Dieselhorst, "Die Bestrafung der Selbstmörder im Territorium der Reichsstadt Nürnberg," *Mitteilung des Vereins für Geschichte der Stadt Nürnberg* 44 (1953): 67-73. Marzio Barbagli, *Farewell to the World: A History of Suicide* (Cambridge, UK: Polity Press, 2015), 40-45.

[31] Euan Cameron, *The European Reformation* (Oxford: Oxford University Press, 1991), 112-115.

foe. "I do not agree," Luther wrote, "that those who kill themselves are simply damned, for this reason, that they do not do it gladly, but are rather overpowered by the power of the devil, like one who is murdered in the woods by a robber." Luther described suicides more as Satan's victims than willing accomplices, holding out the possibility that God could forgive them and they might yet be saved. God's judgment in these matters was inscrutable.

Luther did not want his lenient views on suicide to become public knowledge, however. "Common people should not be told [that suicides do not necessarily go to hell], so that Satan is not given the chance of causing a blood bath, and I approve of the strict observance of those political ceremonies by which [the body] is dragged through the threshold, etc." Here Luther was endorsing the rites of desecration to which bodies of suicides were traditionally subjected by secular authorities in both Catholic and Protestant territories (hence "political ceremonies"), but he viewed such measures as a means of deterrence rather than as a reflection of the suicide's spiritual status.[32] Lutherans did refuse to bury suicides in graveyards. However, Lutherans regarded funeral ceremonies an aid for the living rather than for the dead, who were beyond human help. Lutherans no longer consecrated cemeteries, a rite they abolished along with all other sacramentals. Therefore, exclusion from the graveyard did not constitute a denial of the "means of grace" as it did for Catholics. Rather, it was a defamatory punishment and measure of church discipline. Of course, it was deeply stigmatizing in an honor-obsessed society.[33]

In both Protestant and Catholic cities and territories the disposal of the suicide's remains was the responsibility of secular authorities, a task they conferred upon the dishonorable professions of executioner and skinner. In Nuremberg it was customary until the early sixteenth century to cart the body on a hurdle, with the head dangling over the back, to the execution site or to a crossroads beyond the city wall and burn it. Nuremberg discontinued burning of suicides in the 1530s, but the executioner's men

---

[32] H.C. Erik Midelfort, "Religious Melancholy and Suicide: On the Reformation Origins of a Sociological Stereotype," *Graven Images* 3 (1996): 42. On Luther's nuanced position on suicides, see also Alexander Kästner, *Tödliche Geschichte(n): Selbsttötungen in Kursachsen im Spannungsfeld von Normen und Praktiken (1547-1815)* (Konstanz: UVK Verlagsgesellschaft, 2012), 106-119.

[33] Dieselhorst, "Bestrafung," 78-79. Craig M. Koslofsky, "Controlling the Body of the Suicide in Saxony," in *From Sin to Insanity: Suicide in Early Modern Europe*, ed. Jeffrey R. Watt (Ithaca, N.Y.: Cornell University Press, 2004), 52.

routinely interred suicides at the foot of the gallows in a shallow grave in a so-called donkey's burial until the late eighteenth century.[34] In Catholic Bavaria the executioner or skinner buried suicides "at a secluded place where neither man nor beast treads." Other options were cremation, disposal in a river, or burial beneath the gallows.[35] In bi-confessional Augsburg suicides were nailed into a barrel and cast in the river Lech.[36] In Lutheran Wurttemberg the executioner or skinner buried the suicide either in a desolate location or, if the suicide had a particularly bad reputation in life, underneath the gallows.[37] In Lutheran Schleswig and Holstein the executioner buried suicides in a field or with animal carrion. In the Catholic Austrian Archduchies, the executioner disposed of suicide corpses like the remains of "unreasoning animals" in carrion pits.[38] The transport of the body to the burial site sometimes involved additional apotropaic measures designed to prevent the suicide's return as a malicious revenant. To prevent the suicide from finding his or her way home, the body was removed through a hole dug underneath the threshold rather than through the door, a procedure ecclesiastical and secular authorities tolerated though they did not officially authorize it.[39] In Nuremberg the bodies of suicides were lowered out of windows to avoid carrying the body across the

---

[34] Dieselhorst, "Bestrafung," 63, 96, 161. Mary Lindemann, "Armen- und Eselbegräbnis in der europäischen Frühneuzeit," in *Studien zur Thematik des Todes im 16. Jahrhundert*, ed. Paul Richard Blum (Wolfenbüttel: Herzog August Bibliothek, 1983), 125-140.

[35] David Lederer, *Madness, Religion and the State in Early Modern Europe: A Bavarian Beacon* (New York: Cambridge University Press, 2006), 261.

[36] SuStBA, 2° Cod Aug 247, Bürgermeister Amtsinstruktion, II, 1653, fo. 58. David Lederer, "Wieder ein Faß aus Augsburg…" Suizid in der frühneuzeitlichen Lechmetropole," *Mitteilungen. Institut für Kulturgeschichte der Universität Augsburg* (2005), 47-72.

[37] Karin Schmidt-Kohberg, "'und hat sich selbesten an einen Strickhalfter hingehenckt …' Selbstmord im Herzogtum Württemberg im 17. und 18. Jahrhundert," in *Zauberer—Selbstmörder—Schatzsucher: Magische Kultur und behördliche Kontrolle im frühneuzeitlichen Württemberg*, ed. Johannes Dillinger (Trier: Kliomedia, 2003), 142.

[38] Evelyne Luef, "A Matter of Life and Death: Suicide in Early Modern Austria and Sweden (ca. 1650–1750)," (Doctoral Thesis, University of Vienna, 2016), 116.

[39] Lind, *Selbstmord*, 33-34.

threshold.⁴⁰ Similar precautions and rites of desecration were common throughout Europe.⁴¹

Not all suicides were subjected to these penalties by church and state. These measures applied only to "willful," "intentional" suicides, not to the "melancholy" and mentally ill. Canon Law exempted suicides who were mentally disturbed from church penalties in the late twelfth century, a policy the Lutheran Church continued.⁴² Secular authorities generally followed suit. Catholic Bavaria, Lutheran Wurttemberg, Lutheran Electoral Saxony, the Catholic Archduchies of Austria, the Lutheran free imperial city of Nuremberg and Hamburg and bi-confessional Augsburg all followed an essentially identical policy. The authorities conducted an investigation into the suicide's prior circumstances and motives, interviewing his or her priest or pastor, family, neighbors, and witnesses. If they concluded that the suicide was mentally infirm at the time of the deed, he or she received a Christian burial within the graveyard, although usually in the form of a "quiet" burial at night without funeral procession or tolling of bells.⁴³

Granting melancholy suicides a Christian burial posed significant practical problems for authorities and for the community, however. Governments investigated prior conduct of the suicide, and the act itself, in order to determine whether the suicide was criminally culpable or a victim of melancholy. These inquiries could take weeks. During this time the body often remained where it was found. Decomposition and stench

---

⁴⁰ Dieselhorst, "Bestrafung," 63.

⁴¹ Michael MacDonald and Terence Murphy, *Sleepless Souls: Suicide in Early Modern England* (Oxford: Oxford University Press, 1990), 44-49. R. A. Houston, *Punishing the Dead? Suicide, Lordship, and Community in Britain, 1500-1530* (Oxford: Oxford University Press, 2010), 189-225. Riikka Miettinen, *Suicide, Law, and Community in Early Modern Sweden* (Cham, Switzerland: Palgrave Macmillan, 2019), 47, 284-288. On fear of haunting, 63-65. Barbagli, *Farewell*, 36-40. Lieven Vandekerckhove, *On Punishment: The Confrontation of Suicide in Old Europe* (Leuven: Universitaire Pers, 2000), 43-68.

⁴² Schmidt-Kohberg, "Selbstmord," 138.

⁴³ For Bavaria, Lederer, *Madness*, 242-258. For Wurttemberg, Schmidt-Kohberg, "Selbstmord," 142-143. For Electoral Saxony, Kästner, *Tödliche Geschichte(n)*, 192-204. For the Austrian Archduchies, Luef, "Matter of Life and Death," 39. For Nuremberg, Dieselhorst, "Bestrafung," 125. For Hamburg, see Chap. 3. For Augsburg, Kathy Stuart, *Defiled Trades and Social Outcasts: Honor and Ritual Pollution in Early Modern Germany* (Cambridge: Cambridge University Press, 1999), 197-198.

posed threats to hygiene and inconvenienced neighbors.[44] If authorities made the determination that a suicide was melancholic and therefore eligible for a Christian burial, other problems arose. First, there was the question of transport. The removal of a malicious suicide was the responsibility of the executioner and his men, but melancholic suicides were spared the executioner's dishonoring touch. The body of a suicide, whether malicious or melancholic, was a source of contagious dishonor, however, so finding people willing to handle the removal was an intractable problem. In Augsburg people who carried the bodies of melancholic suicides wore masks to conceal their identities, but even so authorities trying to organize the burial of a melancholy suicide in 1761 had such a difficult time finding honorable people willing to do this work that by the time they finally managed to arrange transport "the body smelled foul and was practically flowing apart."[45]

Questions of disgust and dishonor aside, the bodies of suicides posed supernatural danger. This might be expected for the bodies of "intentional" suicides who were presumably damned, but it applied to the bodies of melancholy suicides as well. In Nuremberg the bodies of suicides granted a Christian burial were lifted over the cemetery wall, rather than carried through the gate, yet another apotropaic measure against malicious revenants.[46] The problems did not end once the body was in the cemetery. By granting a Christian burial to melancholy suicides, secular authorities sometimes provoked popular uprisings in which common people took up arms to prevent the burial of the suicide in the local graveyard. Such graveyard revolts occurred in Catholic and Lutheran areas in the seventeenth and eighteenth centuries. Riots occurred in Catholic Bavaria and Upper Austria, in Lutheran Wurttemberg and the Reformed Principality of Lippe, posing a significant challenge, as David Lederer observes, to "the authority of the state both judicially and in terms of the sovereign monopoly of violence."[47] The distinction between melancholy

[44] Luef, "Matter," 103-108. Similarly, in late seventeenth-century Sweden the bodies of suicides were left where they were found for months, or years (!), until the sanity or insanity of the suicide was adjudicated. In an extreme example adjudicated in 1683, a woman was left hanging in her sauna for six years. Evelyn Luef and Riikka Miettinen, "Fear and Loating? Suicide and the Treatment o the Corpse in Early Modern Austria and Sweden," *Frühneuzeit-Info*, 23 (2012): 109. Miettinen, *Suicide*, 45-46.
[45] Stuart, *Defiled Trades*, 243.
[46] Dieselhorst, "Bestrafung," 63-64.
[47] Lederer, *Madness*, 249.

and willful suicide that determined how church and state dealt with the body was irrelevant to common people, who feared that the presence of *any* suicide in the churchyard would bring disaster to their community in the form of hail storms and the destruction of crops.[48] The fact that Protestant cemeteries were no longer consecrated did not lessen the cosmological danger posed by the burial of suicides from the point of view of Protestant common folk.

It is impossible to disentangle secular concerns of social stigma and dishonor, from religious concerns about salvation and damnation, from cosmological dangers posed by the quintessential bad death of suicide. They reinforced one another and together contributed to a prohibition of suicide so powerful, that suicide became literally unthinkable for many desperate individuals who wanted to put an end to their lives. This remained so, long after defaming punishments for suicides had fallen into disuse and suicide had been effectively decriminalized. In 1808 Burckhardt Schulz, a locksmith from Trarbach near Koblenz, beat his two-year-old granddaughter to death with an axe as she lay in her crib. He did it, Schulz explained, "for no other reason than because he did not know any other way to leave the world."[49]

If suicide was taboo, why was murder a better strategic choice to end one's life while also achieving salvation? In his *Praxis Rerum Criminalium* (1554), a handbook on criminal law, Joos de Damhouder, a Flemish Catholic jurist observed: "He who kills himself sins far more than he who kills another; for in the latter case he only kills his neighbor's body, but cannot harm his soul. But he who kills himself indisputably loses both body and soul."[50] The renowned Lutheran Saxon jurist Benedict Carpzov made this same point in his *Practica Nova Imperialis Saxonica Rerum Criminalium,* perhaps the most influential legal text in early modern

---

[48] For Bavaria, see David Lederer, "Aufruhr auf dem Friedhof. Pfarrer, Gemeinde, und Selbstmord im frühneuzeitlichen Bayern," in *Trauer, Verzweiflung, Anfechtung. Selbstmord und Selbsmordversuche in mittelalterlichen und frühneuzeitlichen Gesellschaften,* ed. Gabriela Signori (Tübingen: edition diskord, 1994), 189-209. For Upper Austria, see Luef, "Matter," 124. For Wurttemberg, Schmidt-Kohberg, Selbstmord," 144-159. For Lippe, Michael Frank, "Die fehlende Geduld Hiobs. Suizid und Gesellschaft in der Grafschaft Lippe (1600-1800)," in *Trauer,* ed. Signori, 152-188.

[49] Anon., "Mord aus Melancholie," *Annalen der Gesetzgebung Napoleons,* ed. Franz Georg Joseph von Lassaulx (Koblenz: Pauli und Compagnie, 1808), vol. 2, 261-263, p. 262.

[50] The quote is from the German translation. Joost de Damhouder, *Praxis Rerum Criminalium. Gründliche und rechte Underweysung ... in Rechtfertigung Peinlicher Sachen* (Frankfurt am Main: Basseus, 1575), 580.

German criminal jurisprudence, first published in 1635.[51] Then the Catholic jurist Damhouder's dictum was reprinted verbatim and without comment the 1743 article on suicide published in *Zedlers Universal-Lexikon*, produced in the Protestant publishing house of August Hermann Franke's *Hallische Stiftungen*.[52] Despite the reluctance of Lutheran theologians to make definitive pronouncements about the spiritual status of suicides, educated Catholics and Protestants assumed that suicides went to hell, a belief that was unquestioned among common people. Murder was the lesser evil. It was not outlandish, then, for suicidal individuals to believe that they might achieve death *and* avoid the eternal damnation that followed from suicide by committing murder.

The logic of the crime was based upon the role that the ritual of public execution played in popular imagination and in judicial practice. Catholic and Protestant governments were enormously invested in ensuring that the felons they dispatched might die in a state of grace. Condemned criminals were known as "poor sinners." After their sentencing, they were intensely ministered to by clergymen, who heard the poor sinner's confession, granted absolution, and offered the Eucharist. This procedure did not vary significantly among denominations. Though officially shorn of sacramental status in Lutheran theology, participating in the ritual of confession and absolution remained a prerequisite to partaking of the Eucharist,[53] and Lutheran parishioners continued to experience absolution as an *opus operatum*,[54] theological objections notwithstanding. Confession and absolution remained central to the dramaturgy of executions and Protestant and Catholic lands.

Catholic and Lutheran clergymen encouraged poor sinners to believe that if their repentance was genuine and heartfelt, Christ's grace would not be denied to them. No matter how heinous the crime, repentance

---

[51] "Qui seipsum occidit & animam suam & corpus nefandè perdit, adeoque magis peccat, quam si alium occidat." Benedict Carpzov, *Practica Nova Imperialis Saxonica Rerum Criminalium* (Leipzig: Christian Kirchner, 1669), Pars I, Quest II, 4.

[52] "Selbst-Mordt," in Johann Heinrich Zedler, *Grosses Universal-Lexikon aller Wissenschaften und Künste*, vol. 36 (Halle and Leipzig: Johann Heinrich Zedler, 1743), 1604. Zedlers Universal-Lexikon is available online at http://mdz10.bib-bvb.de/~zedler/zedler2007/index.html.

[53] Susan Karant-Nunn, *The Reformation of Ritual: An Interpretation of Early Modern Germany* (London: Routledge, 1997), 96-99.

[54] Hans-Christoph Rublack, "Lutherische Beichte und Sozialdisziplinierung," *Archiv für Reformationsgeschichte* 84 (1993): 147.

brought absolution. This religious framing of the execution ritual meant that the poor sinner's death was a good death, even a blessed death in Christian eschatology. The poor sinner entered eternity cleansed of sin, unlike regular Christians who had to fear a hasty and untimely death. This cultural context explains how murder could become an instrument of salvation for suicidal individuals.[55]

Despite the social logic of the crime, it was shocking to early modern contemporaries, as it is to modern sensibility, that perpetrators of suicide by proxy sought to avoid eternal damnation that would follow from suicide by committing the mortal sin of murder—and not just any murder, but the murder of a child, a particularly innocent and helpless victim. As shown in the Nuremberg allegory of good government, child murder was a crime often attributed to the worst enemies of Christendom, Jews, and witches.[56] The juxtaposition between the horror crime that suicidal perpetrators chose to commit and the salvation they sought is a quintessential characteristic of suicide by proxy. And yet, as we shall see, perpetrators committed a crime that many contemporaries understood as "reasonable,"[57] even "natural."[58] One task of this book will be to explain why suicidal child murderers' confessions frequently evoked public sympathy, understanding, even admiration—and why they inspired imitators.

Suicide by proxy was not a marginal phenomenon. I have documented ninety-five cases in Catholic Vienna between 1668 and 1783. In Vienna suicide by proxy took two forms, suicidal child murder and, in a

---

[55] On the religious framing of the execution ritual see Richard J. Evans, *Rituals of Retribution: Capital Punishment in Germany, 1600-1987* (Oxford and New York: Oxford University Press, 1996), 65-108; Stuart, *Defiled Trades*, 149-185; Jürgen Martschukat, *Inszeniertes Töten: Eine Geschichte der Todesstrafe vom 17. bis zum 19. Jahrhundert* (Cologne: Böhlau, 2000), 12-53. Gerhard Ammerer and Christoph Brandhuber, *Schwert und Galgen. Geschichte der Todesstrafe in Salzburg* (Salzburg: Verlag Anton Pustet, 2018), 84-86. Schuster, *Verbrecher*, 55-111. For a similar dynamic in Counter-Reformation Italy, see Adriano Prosperi, *Infanticide, Secular Justice, and Religious Debate in Early Modern Europe* (Turnhout: Brepols, 2016), Chapters 18 and 19.

[56] Otto Ulbricht, *Kindsmord und Aufklärung*, 22; Hsia, *Myth*; Charles Zika, "Cannibalism and Witchcraft in Early Modern Europe: Reading the Visual Images," *History Workshop Journal* 11 (1997): 77-105.

[57] Johann Hieronymus Hermann, *Sammlung allerhand auserlesener Responsorum*, vol. 1 (Jena: Joh. Volckm. Marggrafen, 1730), Responsum CXXV, 478.

[58] Klein, "Brandstiftung," 11.

specifically Catholic variant, suicidal iconoclasm, the destruction of crucifixes or host desecration, which were capital offenses.[59] The Lutheran city of Hamburg prosecuted at least ninety-eight people for suicidal child murder or attempted murder between 1662 and 1809. In some years, executions in Hamburg for suicide by proxy outnumbered executions for all other offenses. Even though cases of classic infanticide, understood as the murder of newborns by their unwed mothers, outnumbered suicidal child murders in the city by a substantial margin, executions for suicide by proxy significantly outnumbered executions for infanticide, because of a high rate of unsolved neonaticide cases.[60] Nuremberg prosecuted twelve cases of suicide by proxy between 1691 and 1745, in addition to the two early killings in 1580 and 1584.[61] In Augsburg, a bi-confessional city, five suicidal murders[62] and one attempted murder[63] took place between 1740 and

---

[59] See Chaps. 5–7. Susanne Hehenberger, "'Die beleidigte Ehre GOttes auf das empfindlichste zu rächen, in allweg gesonnen.' Blasphemie und Sakrileg im 18. Jahrhundert," in *Wien und seine WiennerInnen. Ein historischer Streifzug durch Wien über die Jahrhunderte. Festschrift für Karl Vocelka zum 60. Geburtstag*, eds. Martin Scheutz and Vlasta Valeš (Vienna: Böhlau Verlag, 2008), 179-201.

[60] See Chaps. 3–4.

[61] The cases of Anna Strölin (1580), Anna Freyin (1584), Maria Magdalena Wölffin (1691) and Christina Forgerin (1709) are discussed above. Further cases were Maria Helena Längin (1691), StAN, Amts- und Standbücher 225, Malefizurtheilsbuch, ff. 12r-13v; Agnes Maria Fellnerin (1693), Rare Book & Manuscript Library University of Pennsylvania Ms. Codex 1199, May 12, 1693, f. 49r. Anna Margaretha Stöblin (1700), UBA, OWB, Handschriften, III. 3. Fol. 24, ff. 443r-445r. Susanna Wernerin (1701), StAN, Amts- und Standbücher 225, Malefizurtheilsbuch, ff. 41v-42r. Ambrosi Christoph Dörr (1702), Ibid., ff. 45r-45v. Magdalena Wilhelmin (1703), Ibid., ff. 46r-46v. Margaretha Heßmännin (1710), Ibid., f. 58v. Maria Eleonora Schönin (1716), UBA, OWB, III. 3. F. 24, 517-525. Regina Wegfrizen (1744), StadtAN, B 14/IV Nr. 533. Bluturtheil. Susanna Brennerin (1745), GNM, Handschriften, R. 3108: August 5, 1745, unpaginated. The same case also in StadtBN, Amb 307 2°, Malefizbuch, 5. Aug. 1745, unpaginated.

[62] StadtAA, Strafamt 162, Johann Bausch, "Vezeichnis der Maleficanten," May 31, 1740, Jeremias Bertz; March 20, 1742, Elisabeth Beckensteinerin; March 10, 1750, Catherina Wenzerin. SuStBA, 4 S 567-17, *Peinliches Urtheil ... über Maria Anna Lauterin, ... wegen der an Aloysius Pankratius Reich ... verübter Mordthat, den 17. October 1772, ergangen ...* (n.p, n.d); SuStBA, 4 S 567-22: *Peinliches Urtheil ... über Maria Anna Mayrinn ... wegen einer and einem dreijährigen Mädchen vorsäzlich verübten Mordthat den 8 Febr. 1783. ergangen ...* (n.p, n.d).

[63] StadtAA, Strafamt 167, Verbrecherbuch 1700-1806, p. 310, November 20, 1773, Gruberin.

1783. There were four additional likely cases,[64] and in a related phenomenon, two people accused themselves of child murder, but the authorities were not persuaded by their confessions.[65] In Berlin (mostly Lutheran), contemporary publications tell of forty-three suicidal murders that took place between 1706 and 1799.[66]

The phenomenon of suicide by proxy was not limited to cities or towns, but occurred in the countryside as well. Thirty-seven cases have been documented in the mostly rural Lutheran territories of Schleswig and Holstein between 1600 and 1820.[67] Wurttemberg peasants committed at least seven such murders between 1612 and 1723.[68] Cases of suicide by proxy occurred in villages in Brandenburg (Lutheran),[69] Silesia (confessionally

[64] Killings of children that were not classic infanticide, and were not accidental, but where the sources do not record the killers' motive. StadtAA, Strafamt 167, Verbrecherbuch, 1700-1806, p. 265, September 14, 1745, Oriana Magdalena Schiedlin, and p. 307, February 29, 1772, Maria Johanna Christiana Hörmännin; StStBA, Graphic 29/126, *Wahrhaffter Entwurff einer ... Mordthat, so ein ... Handelsman mit Namen Bogner den 21. Mart. Anno 1747 vrybet, in deme er sein eigenes halbjähriges Kindt, ... mit einem Messer, und also aller väterlichen Liebe vergessen ermordet*. (n.p, n.d); Samuel Valentin, *Ein ... Rath der ... Stadt Augsburg hat hiemit zu Urthel und Recht erkannt, daß Samstag den 11. January 1772, Leonhard Fels ... wegen begangener Mord-That an seinem leiblichen Sohn ... mit dem Schwerdt und blutiger Hand vom Leben zum Tod gebracht werden solle* (Augsburg: Brinhaußer, n.d).

[65] StadtAA, Strafamt 167, Verbrecherbuch, 1700-1806, p. 304, April 9, 1771, Rosina Sternin, and p. 367, September 27, 1791, Peter Wechsler.

[66] For example, the case of Anne Rosine Dunkel, 1794, reported in E.F. Klein, "Selbstmord durch Tödtung anderer; dargestellet in der Unsterssuchungssache wider die Anne Rosine Dunkel," *Annalen der Gesetzgebung und Rechtsgelehrsamkeit*, 14 (1796): 220-248. See also Chap. 8.

[67] Vera Lind documented twenty-three cases. Lind, *Selbstmord*, 191. Tyge Krogh identified an additional fourteen cases. Krogh, *Lutheran Plague*, 19.

[68] HStAS, A 209/576, Barbara Seegräberin, 1612; A 209 /166, Hans Bützer, 1678; A 209/1179, Margaretha Mayrin, 1703; A 209/1806, Agnes Catherina Schickin, 1704; A 209/1576, Hans Jacob Reylen, 1710; A 209/1773, Ursula Waser, 1723, and Anna Catherina Fischlerin, prior to 1723.

[69] Anon., "Maria Dorothea Bulsinn, eine unglückliche Versmacherinn," *Annalen der Gesetzgebung und Rechtsgelehrsamkeit* 2 (1788): 170-196.

mixed),⁷⁰ Saxony (Lutheran),⁷¹ Swabia (confessionally mixed),⁷² Bavaria (Catholic),⁷³ in Upper and Lower Austria (Catholic),⁷⁴ and many other regions within the Holy Roman Empire. Such murders are also documented in Hungary in the eighteenth century,⁷⁵ in Poland in the eighteenth century,⁷⁶ in England in the eighteenth century,⁷⁷ and in France in the early nineteenth century.⁷⁸ Suicide by proxy cases were widespread in Scandinavia. Arne Janson has found sixty-two suicidal murders in Stockholm between 1620 and 1719.⁷⁹ Jonas Liliequist has documented

---

⁷⁰ D. Glawnig, "Fünftes Gutachten ueber den Zustand eines Kindermörders," in *Aufsätze und Beobachtungen aus der gerichtlichen Arzneywissenschaft*, vol. 8, ed. Johann Theodor Pyl (Berlin: Mylius, 1793), 263-268.

⁷¹ HStAD, 10024 Geheimer Rat/ Loc 9703/7, Martha Padigen, 1738. Loc 10118/8, Annen Marien Rößlerin, 1730. Loc 9723/7, Johann Georg Dinnebieren, 1779. Loc 12333, Johann Gottfried Gittlern, 1790. StadtAL, Richterstube Strafakten Nr. 719, Johannen Reginen Reißmannin. 1752.

⁷² FÖWAH, Criminalsachen Zusum, VI. 115. 11, Katherina Häuslerin, 1786.

⁷³ Felix Anton von Weittenau, *Centuria Consiliorum Criminalium* (Augsburg: Mathias Rieger, 1763), 399-406, case of "S.A.," 1745.

⁷⁴ OÖLA, HA Puchheim, Schachtel 43, Nr. 32, Eva Lizlfellnerin, 1762; HA Oberwallsee, Schachtel 24, II, 2/i. Gerichtswesen, Kindesmord 1711-1770, Joseph Vogler, 1770. StiftAK, GA Gerichtsakten (Kriminal) 1721-1729, Georg Edlauer 1729. StiftAK, GA Gerichtsakten (Kriminal) 1741-1750, 1750 Sebastian Schachermayr 1750. StiftAK, GA Gerichtsakten (Kriminal) 1751-1760, Maria Anna Quittnerin 1756. StiftAK, XVII/5 Gerichtsakten, 18. Jhdt. Johann Zwirnsberger, 1758. Griesebner, *Konkurrierende Wahrheiten*, 218-222. AMP, Kriminalakten 90/2, 1719 Maria Anna Umgeherin, 1719.

⁷⁵ A woman in Temeswar murdered her three-year-old child and turned herself in to authorities. *Augsburgische Ordinari Postzeitung*, February 21, 1781.

⁷⁶ On September 14, 1754 a gardener in Warsaw cut the throat of his baby, and turned himself in at city hall. He was weary of his life because of debt. Reported in *Staats-Relation Derer neuesten Europäischen Nachrichten*, Nr. CXVI, 463-464.

⁷⁷ Craig Koslofsky and Dana Rabin, "The Limits of the State: Suicide, Assassination, and Execution in Early Modern Europe," *Selbsttötung als kulturelle Praxis. Ansätze eines interkulturellen historischen Vergleichs*, eds. Andreas Bähr and Hans Medick (Cologne: Böhlau Verlag, 2005), 45-63. Amy Milka, "'Preferring Death': Suicidal Criminals in Eighteenth-Century England," *Eighteenth-Century Studies*, 53 (2020): 685-705.

⁷⁸ C. A. Diez, *Der Selbstmord. Seine Ursachen und Arten vom Standpunkte der Psychologie dargestellt* (Tübingen: H. Laupp'schen Buchhandlung, 1838). Diez cites cases from the *Gazette des Tribunaux* (No. 968, Sept 14, 1828) and the works of the French alienist Jean Etienne Georget (1795-1828).

⁷⁹ Arne Jansson, "Suicidal Murders in Stockholm," in Jeffrey R. Watt, *From Sin to Insanity: Suicide in Early Modern Europe* (Ithaca, N.Y.: Cornell University Press), 84. Arne Jansson, *From Swords to Sorrow: Homicide and Suicide in Early Modern Stockholm* (Stockholm: Almqvist & Wiksell International, 1998), 18-21.

200 cases in Sweden between 1635 and 1780.⁸⁰ Lauri Moilanen has discovered thirty-four cases in Finland between 1693 and 1818.⁸¹ The incidence was particularly high in Copenhagen, where Tyge Krogh has found 144 cases between 1697 and 1789.⁸²

What about suicide by proxy in Calvinist or Reformed contexts? The tactic was also known in Reformed Amsterdam. Pieter Spierenburg describes two cases of indirect suicide in 1653 and 1665, when two men accused themselves of murders they had not committed.⁸³ Andreas Berger has documented cases in Reformed Basel in the seventeenth and eighteenth centuries. Two women accused themselves of infanticide in 1634 and 1665, successfully bringing about their executions. Another woman's attempted suicide by proxy in 1774 only failed, because the child she attempted to murder survived.⁸⁴

In Reformed Zürich suicide by proxy emerged in a different form, an illustration of its malleability. Suicide by proxy was a fluid practice that allowed people to adapt to their local cultural and confessional context. In Catholic Vienna desperate people committed suicidal iconoclasm as an alternative to suicidal child murder. In Zürich suicidal people preferred another variant. Zürich prosecuted sodomy, a delict encompassing both homosexual sodomy and bestiality, with great severity. After murder and theft, sodomy was the third most frequent offense punished by execution in the city. Of 1424 documented executions in Zürich between 1400 and

---

⁸⁰ Jonas Liliequist's emeritus project on suicidal child murders in Sweden is ongoing: *From weariness of living to partial insanity: theological, judicial, medical, and popular notions of melancholy and child murder in Sweden 1650-1800*. Case numbers: personal communication.

⁸¹ Lauri Moilanen is conducting doctoral research on *Suicidal murder as a criminal phenomenon in early modern (1690-1818) Finland*. Case numbers: personal communication.

⁸² There were eighty-three murders, forty-six attempted murders, and fifteen cases of "invented murders," people accusing themselves of murders they did not commit in Krogh's sample. Tyge Krogh, A *Lutheran Plague: Murdering to Die in eht Eighteenth Century* (Leiden: Brill, 2012), 21, 19. Krogh found an additional seventeen cases in the rural province of Zealand between 1719 and 1756. (p. 16).

⁸³ Pieter Spierenburg, *The Spectacle of Suffering: Executions and the Evolution of Repression: From a Preindustrial Metropolis to the European Experience* (Cambridge: Cambridge University Press, 1984), 95.

⁸⁴ Andreas Berger, "Bodies in Pain: Early Modern Suicide by Proxy." *German History* 42 (2024). Berger is embarking on a research project on suicide by proxy in early modern Switzerland.

1789, 179, almost 13%, were for sodomy.[85] The bulk of these prosecutions took place in the second half of the seventeenth and the early eighteenth centuries.[86] Accordingly, it made strategic sense for suicidal people to accuse themselves of bestiality or sodomy to extort their execution.

This version of suicide by proxy was not limited to Zürich. In German territories, too, self-confessed sodomites clamored for their executions.[87] In Sweden, self-accusations of bestiality as well as of infanticide were frequent enough to inspire a new idiomatic expression: "lying oneself out of life." Swedish authorities responded to such unprompted confessions with increasing skepticism, and with legislation. In the Code of 1734 the statutory penalty for false confessions with suicidal intent was imprisonment and/or flogging, the same penalty set for attempted suicides.[88] The same development happened in Zürich. Beginning in the middle of the seventeenth century people turned themselves in to the authorities confessing to sodomy, demanding death. The court increasingly declined to prosecute such self-accusers, however, placing them instead in the city hospital to be treated for melancholy.[89] Some people who ultimately did commit suicide had previously accused themselves of capital offenses, demanding their execution. When this failed, their preferred method of suicide was to cut their throat, a "do it yourself" version of the beheading they had hoped to suffer.[90]

Nuremberg was the first city to enact specific legislation to combat suicide by proxy.

In an edict from 1702 the city government first lamented the rising number of cases of classic infanticide and threatened infanticidal mothers with execution by drowning or even being impaled alive. Then it addressed

---

[85] Richard van Dülmen, *Kultur und Alltag in der Frühen Neuzeit*, vol. 2, *Dorf und Stadt. 16.-18. Jahrhundert* (Munich: C. H. Beck, 1992), 268.

[86] Thomas Lau, "Müßigkeit is aller Laster Anfang? Sodomitenverfolgung im Zürich des 17. Jahrhunderts," *Frühneuzeit-Info* 21 (2010): 58-66.

[87] One example is the 1673 sodomy self-accusation of Hans Bützer in Wuerttemberg. HStAS, A 209 /166.

[88] Jansson, "Suicidal Murders," 97. Miettinen, *Suicide*, 56. Jonas Liliequist, "Reverence, Shame and Guilt in Early Modern European Cultures," in: *The Routledge Companion to Cultural History in the Western World*, eds. Alessandro Arcangeli, Jörg Rogge and Hannu Salmi (London: Routledge, 2020), 249-251.

[89] Markus Schär, *Seelennöte der Untertanen. Selbstmord, Melancholie und Religion im alten Zürich* (Zurich: Chronos Verlag, 1985), 112.

[90] Schär, *Seelennöte*, 251.

others who out of an imagined weariness with life and in the Godless opinion, that if only they do [not] rob themselves of life, but instead forfeit life and limb for killing other innocent persons and are executed, then, after coerced and /God knows/ if righteous contrition and penitence, Heaven's gate must stand open to them, and therefore they dare to kidnap other people's innocent children and kill them, and even do not hesitate or have scruples to carry out such evil deeds upon adults.

Such murderers would not suffer a quick death by beheading. Instead the death sentence would be sharpened in such a way, that it would be "far more painful and shameful for them than death itself."[91]

Four years later, in 1706, the Archduchy of Lower Austria was the second state to legislate. Responding to a rash of child murders in Vienna, the edict addressed suicide by proxy specifically:[92]

"[F]or some years ... child murders, not only by birth mothers, but also by strangers and unrelated people, acting out of extreme malice or also weariness with life, are being committed so often and are becoming so rampant, that it almost appears as if such malicious people hold the penalty of the sword set in the criminal code in contempt, ... and the crime of child murder continues to be committed brazenly again and again."[93]

Like the Nuremberg statute, the Austrian edict imposed new, harsher penalties for such killings.[94] The city of Vienna and the Austrian government legislated repeatedly on suicide by proxy over the course of the eighteenth century, including in the "Secret Instruction" to the *Theresiana*, the criminal code issued by Empress Maria Theresia in 1769. Other cities and states to legislate on suicide by proxy were Hamburg (1724, 1756, and 1777),[95] Lübeck (1746),[96] Schleswig and Holstein (1767),[97] and

---

[91] The decree from August 12, 1702, is quoted in Bode, "Kindestötung," 455-456.

[92] "Wie es mit Bestrafung des Kinder-Mords zu halten," March 22, 1706, *Codicis Austriaci* III, 511-512.

[93] March 22, 1706, *Codicis Austriaci* III, 511.

[94] On the calculus of honor and infamy in criminal justice see Stuart, *Defiled Trades*, 121-148.

[95] See Chap. 4.

[96] StadtAL, 8_1_725, fol. 229r. "Warnung an die ruchlose Weibspersonen, welche mit den Gedanken umgehen, unschuldige Kinder zu ermorden," 19. Juli, 1747.

[97] Lind, *Selbstmord*, 62-63.

Prussia (1794).[98] The edict issued in Schleswig and Holstein, then under Danish rule, was identical to a contemporaneous edict issued in the Kingdom of Denmark.[99]

Unlike the mythical child killings associated with Jewish ritual murder,[100] and unlike the familiar subject of classic infanticide,[101] until relatively recently the child murders associated with suicide by proxy have gone largely unnoticed by historians.[102] The first recent work on this subject focuses not on Germany but on Sweden. In *From Swords to Sorrow*, a study of homicide and suicide in early modern Stockholm, Arne Jansson finds that "suicidal murders" became frequent after 1670, at the same time as "direct suicide" rates increased dramatically, while manslaughter and other forms of interpersonal violence underwent a significant decline.[103] Jansson presents a classic Durkheimian argument[104] that modernization (urbaniza-

---

[98] *Allgemeines Landrecht für die Preußischen Staaten von 1794. Textausgabe* (Frankfurt a. M.: Alfred Metzner Verlag, 1970), §. 831 and §. 832, p. 699.

[99] Krogh, *Lutheran Plague*, 137-155.

[100] Most recently Teter, *Blood Libel*. See the comprehensive survey of the historiography there.

[101] Ulbricht, *Kindsmord und Aufklärung* remains the classic work on the subject for Germany. See also Otto Ulbricht, "Kindmörderinnen vor Gericht. Verteidigungsstrategien von Frauen in Norddeutschland 1680-1810," in *Mit den Waffen der Justiz. Zur Kriminalitätsgeschichte des späten Mittelalters und der frühen Neuzeit*, eds. Andreas Blauert, Gerd Schwerhoff (Frankfurt a. M.: Fischer Taschenbuch Verlag, 1993), 54-85; Alison Rowlands, "In Great Secrecy: the Crime of Infanticide in Rothenburg ob der Tauber, 1501-1618," *German History* 15 (1997): 179-199; Ulinka Rublack, *The Crimes of Women in Early Modern Germany* (New York: Oxford University Press, 1999), 163-196; Kerstin Michalik, *Kindsmord. Sozial und Rechtsgeschichte der Kindstötung im 18. und beginnenden 19. Jahrhundert am Beispiel Preußen* (Pfaffenweiler: Centaurus Verlag, 1997). Joel Harrington, *The Unwanted Child: The Fate of Foundlings, Orphans and Juvenile Criminals in Early Modern Germany* (Chicago: University of Chicago Press, 2009), 21-71. Margaret Brennan Lewis, *Infanticide and Abortion in Early Modern Germany* (New York: Routledge, 2016).

[102] To my knowledge, the only secondary literature on this phenomenon prior to 1998 are Dr. Pet. Kaatzer, *Über den indirekten Selbstmord. Psychiatrisch-forensische Abhandlung* (diss., Marburg: no publisher, 1872), a medical dissertation mainly useful for its appendix listing approximately 30 cases, and H. von Weber, "Selbstmord als Mordmotiv," *Monatsschrift für Kriminalbiologie und Strafrechtsreform* 28, no. 4 (1937): 161-181. Weber identifies cases cited in eighteenth-century German legal scholarship, mostly from northern and central Germany.

[103] Jansson, *Swords to Sorrow*. For a summary, see his "Suicidal Murders in Stockholm," 81-98.

[104] Emile Durkheim, *On Suicide* (London: Penguin Classics, 2007). Durkheim's classic *Le Suicide* was first published 1897.

tion, declining integration within the family and occupational groups, increased literacy—and Protestantism) led to increased "individuation" and social isolation, which in turn contributed to a rise in suicidal acts of all kinds. Suicide and homicide were inversely related. "As a general rule," Durkheim wrote, "where homicide is very common it confers a sort of immunity against suicide," and vice versa.[105] Within the cultural climate of orthodox Lutheranism and Pietism, these "suicidal murders" in early modern Sweden constituted a "transitional phenomenon," Jansson argues, in a long-term process in which people increasingly focused aggression and violence on the self rather than on others.[106]

Within German territories, Vera Lind discusses such killings in her magisterial study of suicide in early modern Schleswig and Holstein. She calls these killings "concealed suicides" and interprets them as a form of religious sacrifice,[107] an idea this book will expand upon. Jürgen Martschukat has documented several cases in late eighteenth-century Hamburg and shows that these killings featured prominently in enlightened debates about criminal justice reforms and led to concrete changes in the procedure of public execution in the city.[108] Isabelle Zeder has explored self-accusations of witchcraft in seventeenth-century Catholic Ellwangen and Lutheran Reutlingen as a form of suicide by proxy.[109]

Tyge Krogh tackles the question of the role of religious confession. In *A Lutheran Plague. Murdering to Die in the Eighteenth Century*, Krogh argues, as the title indicates, that "elements of faith specific to the Lutheran confession" underpin that practice of suicide by proxy. Lutheran soteriology allowed Lutheran clergy to offer condemned criminals a more

---

[105] Quoted in Jeffrey R. Watt, *Choosing Death. Suicide and Calvinism in Early Modern Geneva* (Kirksville, Mont.: Truman State University Press, 2001), 53.

[106] Jansson, *Swords to Sorrow*, 69.

[107] Lind, *Selbstmord*, 61-62, 175-177, 180-181. Vera Lind, "The Suicidal Mind and Body," *From Sin to Insanity: Suicide in Early Modern Europe*, ed. Jeffrey R. Watt (Ithaca: Cornell University Press, 2004), 64-80, 77-78.

[108] Jürgen Martschukat, "Ein Freitod durch die Hand des Henkers. Erörterungen zur Komplementarität von Diskursen und Praktiken am Beispiel von 'Mord aus Lebens-Überdruß' und Todesstrafe im 18. Jahrhundert," *Zeitschrift für historische Forschung* 27 (2000): 53-74. Martschukat, *Inszeniertes Töten*, 85-90.

[109] Isabelle D. Zeder, "'mit flehenlich bitten man soll ir einen tod anthüen': Selbstbezichtigungen während der frühneuzeitlichen Hexenverfolgung als 'suicide by trial'." (Master's thesis, Universität Basel, Philosophisch-Historische Fakultät, 2018). Isabelle Zeder, "Selbstbezichtigunge während der Hexenverfolgung als 'suicide by trial.' Eine Fallstudie aus Reutlingen," *Reutlinger Geschichtsblätter* 60 (2021): 77-115.

optimistic assessment of their prospects for salvation than their Catholic or Calvinist counterparts could, Krogh argues. Like Arne Janssen, he sees Pietism as a contributing factor. Krogh presents an archival study of cases in Copenhagen and the rural province of Zealand, where, as indicated above, he found an extraordinarily high number of cases.[110] Drawing on a list of executions in Hamburg compiled by the criminal historian Richard Wosnik, Krogh also finds numerous cases of suicidal child murder there, leading him to conclude that suicide by proxy constituted "one of the dominant criminal problems," eclipsing other crimes, in Stockholm, Copenhagen, and Hamburg from the late seventeenth through the late eighteenth centuries.[111]

Church historian Tine Reeh and psychiatrist Ralf Hemmingsen take on Tyge Krogh's argument that suicidal intent and Lutheran fears about the afterlife were the primary causes of frequent child murders in eighteenth-century Denmark. Drawing on the same trial records that formed the basis of Krogh's study, Reeh and Hemmingsen argue instead that societal stressors and mental illness explain the proliferation of child murders in Denmark. They develop a "retrospective clinical hypothesis," to apply diagnoses such as "acute stress disorder" or "personality disorder" to eighteenth-century child murderers.[112] Some child murderers undoubtedly did suffer from mental illness, as contemporary prosecutors were well aware.[113] However, Reeh's and Hemmingsen's argument begs the question why the murderers' psychiatric disorders manifested in this particular way. Mental illness varies according to its specific historical and cultural context, including prevailing religious ideas—which is why most historians are loathe to apply medical diagnoses to historical actors.[114] In order to grasp the meaning of these murders it is necessary to contextualize trial records in as much detail as possible, drawing on other contemporary

---

[110] Krogh, *Lutheran Plague*, 5, on Pietism, 66-78.

[111] Krogh, *Lutheran Plague*, 17-18, 22.

[112] Tine Reeh and Ralf Hemmingsen, "Common Sense, No Magic: A Case Study of Female Child Murderers in the Eighteenth Century," *1700-tal: Nordic Yearbook for Eighteenth-Century Studies*, 15 (2018): 110-134.

[113] Kathy Stuart, "Melancholy Murderers: Suicide by Proxy and the Insanity Defense," in *Ideas and Cultural Margins in Early Modern Germany: Essays in Honor of H.C. Erik Midelfort*, eds. Robin Barnes and Marjorie Plummer (Aldershot, Hambleton: Ashgate, 2009), 63-77.

[114] Ann Goldberg, *Sex, Religion, and the Making of Modern Madness: The Eberbach Asylum and German Society, 1815-1849* (Oxford: Oxford University Press, 1999), 8-10.

sources, such as sermons, ballads, and clerical commentary, as Krogh emphasizes in his response to Reeh and Hemmingsen.[115] In combination, these sources show that religious beliefs shaped these murders, as this current study will also demonstrate. This is certainly how contemporary authorities explained these crimes, as their legislative response makes clear.

Craig Koslofsky and Dana Rabin extend the geographic boundaries of suicide by proxy beyond continental Europe, identifying a number of cases from eighteenth-century England, where historians had previously not observed this phenomenon, viewing them alongside Swedish and German cases identified by Jansson and Lind. In all of these regions, Koslofsky and Rabin argue, "capital punishment suicide" confronted the early modern state with the "fundamental limits" of its power over its subjects.[116] Expanding upon Koslofsky and Rabin, Amy Milka discusses several eighteenth-century cases of what she terms "judicial suicides" in England. Milka emphasizes the ideological challenge such cases posed: "they manipulated the criminal justice system, exposing legal, moral and spiritual loopholes within England's bloody code."[117] Like their counterparts on the continent, perpetrators attempting judicial suicide in England explicitly articulated their suicidal intent and expressed their desire to be killed by the state rather than to die by their own hand.

---

[115] Tyge Krogh, "Commentary on an article by Tine Reeh and Ralf Hemmingsen in Sjuttonhundratal 2018: 'Common Sense, No Magic: A case Study of Female Child Murderers in the Eighteenth Century'," *1700-tal: Nordic Journal for Eighteenth-Century Studies* 17(2020): 229-232.

[116] Koslofsky and Rabin, "Limits of the State," Additional cases are discussed in Silke Göttsch, "Mörderin an ihrem unschuldigem Kinde aus Überdruß des Lebens," *Bayerisches Jahrbuch für Volkskunde* (1996): 43-49; Andrea Griesebner, *Konkurrierende Wahrheiten. Malefizprozesse vor dem Landgericht Perchtoldsdorf im 18. Jahrhundert* (Vienna: Böhlau Verlag, 2000), 218-222; Maren Lorenz, *Kriminelle Körper—Gestörte Gemüter. Die Normierung des Individuums in Gerichtsmedizin und Psychiatrie der Aufklärung* (Hamburg: Hamburger Edition, 1999), 269-276; Karl Wegert, *Popular Culture, Crime, and Social Control in 18th-Century Württemberg* (Stuttgart: Franz Steiner Verlag, 1994), 183-184. Andreas Hellerstedt, "Ett stort bevis av Evangelii kraft och sanning. Suicidalmord, avrättningar och herrnhutisk teologi," *Historisk tidskrift*, 131, (2011), 491–510 (English summary: http://www.historisktidskrift.se/fulltext/2011-3/2011_3_491-510.htm). Jonathan Strom, *German Pietism and the Problem of Conversion* (University Park, USA: Penn State University Press, 2018), 139-143. For a rare case of an aristocrat committing suicide by proxy, see Florian Kühnel, *Kranke Ehre? Adlige Selbsttötung im Übergang zur Moderne* (Munich: Oldenbourg, 2013), 205-235.

[117] Milka, "Preferring Death," 685-686.

There are some notable differences, however, between the English cases Milka describes and cases in Germany and Scandinavia. People attempting suicide by proxy in Germany and Scandinavia committed or accused themselves of crimes that "cry out to heaven," such as child murder, blasphemy, and bestiality, evoking the specter of divine retribution. In England, some suicidal perpetrators committed murder, but many others committed property crimes or forgery. This would have been an option on the continent as well, since thefts above a certain value were capital offenses, but I have found no equivalent cases. The fact that many English suicidal perpetrators chose to commit less heinous crimes than their counterparts in Germany and Scandinavia may explain another difference. Few people who attempted judicial suicide in England succeeded in bringing about their executions. Many were found *non compos mentis*, sentenced to lesser penalties or transported. The English judiciary seems to have been more adept at fending off such cases than criminal courts in Germany or Scandinavia. Possibly this explains why the tactic of suicide by proxy did not "take off" in England. "Cases of judicial suicide were few" compared to Scandinavia and Germany, Milka notes.[118] In England judicial suicides did not inspire widespread imitation and did not elicit a concerted governmental response. Did the British trial by jury limit the spread of judicial suicides? Was the British public less entranced by the ritual of public execution than German or Scandinavian publics? Did the earlier impact of the Enlightenment in England play a role? Hopefully, future comparative studies will shed light on variations in suicide by proxy in different political, religious, and national contexts. For the purposes of this study, it illustrates the need to embed the practice of suicide by proxy deeply in its local environment to discern what conditions promoted or discouraged the tactic.

Was Lutheranism really the primary cause of the emergence of suicide by proxy, as Tyge Krogh contends? Given the significance of religious confession in German history this is a crucial question. The persuasiveness of the tactic to suicidal Anglicans calls Krogh's argument into question. The high number of cases in Baroque Vienna as well as cases in the Austrian countryside also contradicts his thesis. On the other hand, it is undeniable that more suicidal child murders are documented in Lutheran Berlin and in Brandenburg-Prussia, for example, than in Catholic Munich or Bavaria. But then there is the Lutheran free imperial city of Frankfurt, another

[118] Milka, "'Preferring Death'," 694.

center of Pietism, where despite well-preserved early modern judicial records I have only been able to identify two cases of suicide by proxy.[119] Both defendants were Catholic. In 1715 the sixty-six-year-old Catholic vagrant Niklas Scheffer arrived in Frankfurt and turned himself in at the city gate, claiming to have murdered his wife and young son in a forest near Dessau, more than 200 miles away. Tormented by his conscience, he desired to receive his punishment here. Suspecting that they were dealing with a melancholic making a false confession, Frankfurt nonetheless exercised due diligence, inquiring with Dessau whether anything was known about these murders. Dessau answered that no bodies had been found, nor had anyone seen this beggar and his family around Dessau.[120] In 1732 Johannes Heinrich Schwach, a Catholic journeyman printer from Westphalia, turned himself in at the main constabulary to confess that he had cut the throat of his six-year-old son. This is the only actual suicidal murder I have been able to locate in Frankfurt. Before the murder, Schwach had twice attempted to drown himself. When Schwach appeared at the constabulary, the duty officer tried to turn him away, telling him that "he must be making it up."[121] The officer's incredulous response is an indication that in 1732 authorities in Frankfurt, unlike their counterparts in Hamburg or Vienna, were not familiar with this type of murder.

Explaining why suicide by proxy became a well-known problem in some cities and territories, while others appear to have remained unscathed, poses a problem similar to that of explaining the variations in the intensity of the European witch-hunt in different German states. For example, what accounts for the very different witch-hunting patterns in Rothenburg ob der Tauber and Nördlingen, two mid-sized Lutheran free imperial cities? In Rothenburg ob der Tauber there was only one execution for witchcraft between 1561 and 1652, whereas Nördlingen experienced major

---

[119] On pietism in Frankfurt see Johannes van den Berg and Martin Brecht, *Der Pietismus vom siebzehnten bis zum frühen achtzehnten Jahrhundert* (Göttingen: Vandenhoeck & Ruprecht, 1993), 281-329. Johannes Wallman, *Pietismus Studien. Gesammelte Aufsätze*, vol. 2, (Tübingen: Mohr Siebeck, 2008), 342-361.

[120] ISG, Criminalia Akten 2812, Niklas Scheffer 1715.

[121] Schwach was a Catholic from Westphalia. When he turned himself in at the Hauptwache, the duty officer told him "daß er gewiß fabeln thäte, er habe ihnen aber geantwortet, daß es in der That so seye." ISG, Criminalia Akten 4085, Johannes Heinrich Schwach, 1732.

witch-panics, executing thirty-five between 1589 and 1594. Religious confession was clearly not the determining variable.[122]

I argue here that the practice of suicide by proxy did not derive from the teachings of a specific denomination. Suicide by proxy was a tactic available to Lutherans, Catholics, and Calvinists. It emerged as a psychological response by desperate individuals to disciplining techniques employed by the early modern state, regardless of confession. This explains why suicide by proxy cases were particularly frequent in houses of correction, as prison administrators in Hamburg and Vienna both experienced at the same time. In Hamburg and Vienna, the disciplinary regimes in these institutions depended heavily on catechizing inmates in the Lutheran or Catholic faith, respectively. In both institutions suicide by proxy cases reached crisis levels around the turn of the eighteenth century.[123]

This book presents a "thick description" as well as a longitudinal study of suicide by proxy, based on a close reading of approximately 400 cases from various regions of the Holy Roman Empire. The goal is to explicate the cultural meaning these acts held for perpetrators as well as for their communities. Throughout, I use the term "suicide by proxy," or the eighteenth-century term "indirect suicide," as umbrella terms. Suicidal child murder, suicidal iconoclasm or blasphemy, suicidal arson, and self-accusations of bestiality, earlier infanticides, or witchcraft with suicidal intent were subspecies, or variants, of suicide by proxy. Terms coined by other researchers such as "suicide murder,"[124] "concealed suicide,"[125] "capital punishment suicide,"[126] or "judicial suicide"[127] refer to the same tactic. The cases are drawn from a wide variety of sources, ranging from criminal trial records, chronicles, execution logs, sermons, legal and medical *consilia*, murder and execution pamphlets, newspaper reports, and legal and medical periodicals. Some sources provide greater detail on the motives and intentionality of the perpetrator than others. The richest sources are criminal trial records for particular cases, which often include

---

[122] Alison Rowlands, *Witchcraft Narratives*, 15. Lyndal Roper, *Witch Craze: Terror and Fantasy in Baroque Germany* (New Haven: Yale University Press, 2004), 19, 36-37.

[123] On suicidal murders in Hamburg's house of correction, see Chap. 4. On suicide by proxy in Vienna's house of correction, see Chaps. 5 and 6.

[124] Krogh, *Lutheran Plague*.

[125] Lind, *Selbstmord*.

[126] Koslofsky and Rabin, "Limits."

[127] Milka, "Preferring Death."

detailed testimony by perpetrators about their suicidal ideation and desire for execution. At the other end of the spectrum are brief entries in chronicles, execution registers, and newspaper accounts that provide little information about the killers' individual circumstances or motives, beyond the formulaic phrase "out of despair," shorthand for suicidal intent. An example would be a newspaper report that a woman cut the throat of an unrelated child and then turned herself in. Circumstances, context, clustering of cases, murder method, and contemporary legislation addressing suicide by proxy lead me to categorize such a case as a likely suicide by proxy. Regardless whether cases resulted in criminal convictions and executions, or in findings of insanity, typically imposed against defendants' will, early modern courts understood the crimes as indirect suicides.[128]

Chapter 2 presents an analysis of suicidal child murder as ritual. The most characteristic feature of these killings was the preferred method of murder, the cutting of the child-victim's throat. This chapter contrasts these murders with other kinds of violence against children, both mythical and real. It seems counterintuitive to argue that the emergence of a crime motivated by profound religious concerns about salvation and damnation should depend upon secularization in certain societal contexts. However, suicidal child murders and other forms of suicide by proxy generally emerged only after governments ceased judicial prosecution for the blood libel, and after witch-hunting was in decline. When courts were no longer occupied with mythical crimes, their dockets filled with these new Christian ritual murders. Narratives of mythical murders provided a cultural template for suicidal child killers. Suicide by proxy emerged in tandem with increased prosecution of classic infanticide. The harsh prosecution of unwed mothers led to a dramatic increase in the number of women executed, and shaped public discourse about the nature of women. Both of these developments encouraged women, in particular, to commit suicidal child murders. Many female killers acted with premeditation and planning, leading courts to condemn the extraordinary malice and treachery of women murderers.

What were the societal and cultural conditions that allowed suicide by proxy to emerge and proliferate within a community? To address this question, in Chaps. 3 through 7, I trace the trajectory in two cities, Lutheran Hamburg and Catholic Vienna, where case numbers were so high that authorities experienced the practice as a challenge to

[128] Stuart, "Melancholy Murderers."

governmental authority and threat to public safety. Lutheranism legitimated the authority of the state in Hamburg, as Catholicism did in Vienna. Despite such distinct confessional cultures, however, both cities shared an ideology of governance. Proclaiming the duty of godly government to punish evildoers in a similar vein as the Nuremberg allegories of good government described above, both cities implemented similar policies that produced similar results.

Chapters 3 and 4 reconstruct this dynamic in Hamburg. Chapter 3 sketches the development of criminal justice in Hamburg through the 1660s, in particular the sacralization of capital punishment that followed the introduction of the Protestant Reformation in the city, and charts early cases of suicide by proxy beginning in the 1620s. A distinctive feature of criminal justice in Hamburg involved the ritual display and confrontation of the dead body of the murder victim with the murderer in the public street, as the executioner unsheathed his sword and addressed a ritual hue and cry to the accused murderer. These dramatic and highly emotional performances enthralled the public, and inspired in some the desire to participate in this ritual in the starring role of accused murderer. Chapter 4 follows the dramatic increase in the number of suicidal child murders in the late seventeenth century through their ultimate decline in the early nineteenth century. Some of these murders appear to have been "copycat killings."[129] Hamburg, and also Vienna, experienced cases in clusters, sometimes within days of each other, resembling the phenomenon of "suicide contagion" within communities and close-knit social groups observed by present-day mental health professionals.[130] The city government's efforts to curtail the murders were largely unsuccessful. The killings only stopped when a sharp decrease in the number of executions in the early nineteenth century rendered the tactic of suicide by proxy ineffective.

Chapters 5 through 7 follow the development of suicide by proxy in Baroque Vienna. In Vienna, the pomp and circumstance surrounding public executions was unmatched. The most distinctive feature of the execution ritual here was the prominent role of the imperially chartered lay Confraternity of the Dead, whose high aristocratic members included members of the Habsburg dynasty. The lay brothers accompanied

---

[129] S. Towers et al., "Contagion in Mass Killings and School Shootings," *PLOS ONE* 10 (2015): e0117259.

[130] Muhammed Yildiz et al., "Suicide Contagion, Gender, and Suicide Attempts among Adolescents," *Death Studies* 43 (2019): 365-371.

condemned criminals to the scaffold and buried them afterward. The confraternity was a specifically Catholic institution imported from Counter-Reformation Italy. Religious orders competed for the privilege of ministering to condemned criminals, and authorities spared no effort to enable the felons they dispatched to enter eternity in a state of grace. Chapters 5 and 6 follow the development of the distinctive form of suicide by proxy in Vienna, the destruction of crucifixes and desecration of the host. Chapter 5 explores the cultural meaning of such suicidal iconoclasm. Eucharistic theology and the cult of images was at the heart of Catholic piety during Counter-Reformation, and was central to the political ideology of the Habsburg dynasty. Such blasphemous deeds, normally associated with Jews, witches, and Turks, constituted intolerable provocations. Chapter 6 reconstructs the specific contexts in which these desecrations occurred. Authorities and suicidal people engaged in a kind of cat and mouse game, as governments took punitive measures to quash suicidal iconoclasm, and common people adapted by changing their tactics. When authorities finally stopped executing suicidal individuals for such blasphemous deeds, perpetrators adapted by choosing to murder children instead. These child murders are the subject of Chap. 7, where suicide by proxy is embedded within the history of Viennese criminal justice. This includes a consideration of pastoral care for condemned felons, burial practices and the physical infrastructure of criminal justice that at times merged with the sacred landscape of Baroque Catholicism.

The Conclusion discusses late cases of suicide by proxy and the ultimate decline of the practice in the early nineteenth century, and reflects on the relationship between history and memory. I explore why suicide by proxy quickly faded from public awareness and historical memory, as compared to witch-hunts and classic infanticide, and how this forgetting made the practice largely invisible to historians as well. The agency and premeditation of female child murderers, in particular, could not be reconciled with emerging bourgeois notions of womanhood, and the impotency of the early modern state to curtail these crimes was offensive to the nineteenth-century public. This book corrects this historical repression.

CHAPTER 2

Liturgies of Suicide by Proxy

The chapter sketches the contours and typical features of the practice of suicide by proxy. Early forms of suicide by proxy included self-accusations of witchcraft and bestiality. These non-violent variants of suicide by proxy were largely supplanted by suicidal child murder in the late seventeenth century. Though some desperate individuals continued to make self-accusations, rising judicial skepticism and stricter evidentiary requirements meant that they were less likely to lead to conviction. When self-accusations without material evidence no longer worked, suicidal people turned to child murder instead. Suicidal child murders were characterized by extreme violence. Despite the violence, or rather, *because* of the violence, suicidal child murder had broad-based, cross-confessional persuasiveness and emotional appeal. This chapter seeks to explain why this was so, by situating these murders within the context of a more general societal attraction to the motifs of child slaughter and sacrifice. Catholic and Lutheran perpetrators drew from this same cultural repertoire. However, they also availed themselves of religious resources specific to their confession. Differences in doctrine meant that Catholic and Lutheran clergy played different ritual roles, both during criminal trials and while providing pastoral care to convicted perpetrators before and during their executions. Finally, this chapter shows how suicidal killers, predominantly women, performed child murder as a ritual, a foreshadowing of the beheading they longed for.

© The Author(s), under exclusive license to Springer Nature Switzerland AG 2023
K. Stuart, *Suicide by Proxy in Early Modern Germany*, World Histories of Crime, Culture and Violence,
https://doi.org/10.1007/978-3-031-25244-0_2

"I beg your Grace, by God's mercy, to believe, it is true regarding the cow."

What would have happened if Anna Strölin's hatchet-murder of her six-year-old son in 1580, and Anna Freyin's drowning of her two-year-old son in 1584, discussed in the Introduction, had not taken place in witch-hunting-averse Nuremberg, but instead in a neighboring Catholic prince-bishopric where witch trials were currently ongoing? Anna Srölin testified that she killed her son "at the instigation of the evil enemy." This alone would likely not have attracted witch-hunters' attention, even though child murder in its various forms was a major theme in witch trials. Demonic instigation featured in official accounts of all sorts of crimes well into the eighteenth century, and in the subjective experience of perpetrators for much longer.[1] Anna Freyin's case, however, might have piqued their interest. The devil featured more prominently in her account. A demonic entity was physically present in the room, prodding her, when Freyin formed her intent to murder her son. "And so, the evil enemy seduced her, and she threw her little son into the well," she confessed.[2]

It is likely that these earliest cases of suicide by proxy by means of child murder happened in Nuremberg *because* the city largely avoided witch-hunting. With some exceptions, for example, Hamburg, where witch-hunts ended early, suicidal child murders emerged in German territories after the mid-seventeenth century and became a recognized pattern around 1700. Why not earlier? The religious ritual surrounding capital punishment that encouraged Christians to imagine execution as an entry into paradise was in place since the mid-sixteenth century, when confessionalization and social disciplining campaigns gained traction. The popular theology took shape even earlier, as shown in the stark pen and ink drawing "The Execution" (1512) by the Swiss mercenary soldier and artist Urs Graf. [Image 2.1] The condemned man kneels, as the executioner, standing beside him, readies his sword for the imminent beheading. Before them, the corpses of executed criminals in various stages of decomposition are displayed on gallows and wheels. An eschatological drama unfolds. To the right, a baby bathed in light, representing the soul of the criminal on the wheel, rises into the waiting arms of an angel. To the left, a bawling

---

[1] The devil still featured prominently in the testimony of criminal offenders in early nineteenth-century England, for example. Owen Davies, "Talk of the Devil: Crime and Satanic Inspiration in Eighteenth-Century England," Unpublished manuscript, 2007.

[2] See the discussion of Strölin's and Freyin's trials in Chap. 1.

2 LITURGIES OF SUICIDE BY PROXY 39

Image 2.1 Urs Graf d. Ä. *Richtstätte*. Pen and ink drawing. 1512. The ALBERTINA Museum, Vienna. Inv. Nr. 3050

baby, the soul of a damned criminal, is being snatched away by a demon. The viewer is left to wonder: Which of these fates awaits the kneeling poor sinner?

The history of suicide by proxy and the history of the European witch-hunt intersect. If Anna Freyin had lived in Ellwangen, an ecclesiastical territory about sixty miles southeast of Nuremberg, for example, she might have brought about her execution by accusing herself of witchcraft instead of by murdering her son. The Catholic provosts of Ellwangen were enthusiastic witch-hunters. They conducted major hunts in 1588, and again between 1611 and 1618. The hunt in 1588 led to at least seventeen executions. The extended hunt between 1611 and 1618 claimed approximately 430 victims. This hunt was most intense in 1611 and 1612, when almost 300 people were executed.³ Two-thirds of the victims came from the town of Ellwangen, which had about 1500 inhabitants. The rest came from surrounding villages. In 1612 Jesuit priests prepared 167 condemned witches for their executions. The following year the Jesuit Johann Finck reported on a particularly moving case. In a letter dated September 13, 1613, he wrote:

> If at least the souls were saved after the burning of the bodies! I am willing to give all of my strength, and my life to save these unfortunates. God gave us great comfort through a sixteen-year-old girl, who was executed last month with six others. She could no longer endure the stalking devil, and voluntarily asked to be arrested. With tears streaming, she declared that she would rather suffer death and burning at the stake than to endure the tyranny of the devil any longer. Standing, she received the killing blow [of the sword].⁴

The sixteen-year-old-girl that Finck was so moved by was Maria Ostertag. On July 11, 1613, Maria turned up at the prison and "of her own free will" accused herself of witchcraft, even pointing out a devil's mark in her right armpit. The devil had seduced her when she was nine years old, she told interrogators. She confessed to flying to the witches' sabbath, committing host desecration, cannibalism, performing weather magic, and cooking up salve from child corpses, which she used to murder a little girl. She was condemned to burning at the stake, but pardoned to beheading. After her execution on August 21, her fulsome confession earned her a burial in consecrated ground, a grace rarely granted to executed witches.⁵

Isabelle Zeder's microhistorical research on this and similar cases documents the suicidal ideation of these self-accusers. When Maria Ostertag turned herself in at the prison, she knew that her self-accusation would

---

³Wolfgang Mährle, "Ellwangen – Hexenverfolgungen," in *Lexikon zur Geschichte der Hexenverfolgung*, eds. Gudrun Gersmann, Katrin Moeller and Jürgen-Michael Schmidt, in: historicum.net, URL: https://www.historicum.net/purl/jfzqr/

⁴Quoted in Bernhard Duhr, S.J., *Geschichte der Jesuiten in den Ländern deutscher Zunge in der ersten Hälfte des XVII Jahrhunderts*, vol 2, II (Freiburg in Bresigau: Herderische Verlagshandlung, 1913), 489.

⁵Johannes Dillinger, *Kinder im Hexenprozess. Magie und Kindheit in der Frühen Neuzeit* (Stuttgart: Franz Steiner Verlag, 2013), 125, 134. Isabelle D. Zeder, "'mit flehenlich bitten man soll ir einen tod anthüen': Selbstbezichtigungen während der frühneuzeitlichen Hexenverfolgung als 'suicide by trial'." (Master's thesis, Universität Basel, Philosophisch-Historische Fakultät, 2018), 77.

lead to her death. In all of the witch trials that had gone before, there had not been a single acquittal.⁶ Maria's death wish was obvious. "She pleads that one should do death unto her," the court scribe noted. She begged authorities to expedite her execution because "she did not want to stay many more hours."⁷

Lutheran jurisdictions also were confronted with witchcraft self-accusers. Zeder reconstructs two cases in the free imperial city of Reutlingen.⁸ A town of around 5000 inhabitants, Reutlingen conducted several series of witch trials between the 1550s and 1660s, leading to a total of 53 death sentences.⁹ In 1637 Margaretha Schirm, fourteen, informed authorities that she belonged to the devil. She pleaded with her judges for death: She "begs my gracious lords for mercy, that they would make an end of it, for she can find no rest day or night." In this case, Reutlingen's city councilors did not accede to the desires of the suicidal girl. Her self-confession focused largely on spiritual offenses, so there was no corroborating circumstantial evidence of harmful magic. Her evident death wish led jurists at the law faculty of the University of Tübingen, who provided an expert opinion on this case, to recommend against conviction. She was likely one of those people *quae ex vitae taedio mori et perire festinant* (who out of weariness with life hasten to die and perish). Such people should be helped, not condemned. Margaretha was placed in solitary confinement in a city hospice. Her despair did not abate. "All she desires is to leave the world," a member of the staff reported. Margaretha died the following year.¹⁰

Seven years later another self-accuser in Reutlingen did succeed in bringing about her execution. On July 17, 1644, Catharina Schmid, a maidservant, asked to be taken into custody. Evil entities forced her to harm people around her, she claimed. Conflating religious and legal language, she pleaded for death, begging authorities to expedite her execution: "she counts the hours, until the end will come for her." "One should

---

⁶ Dillinger, *Kinder*, 131.
⁷ Zeder, "Selbstbezichtigungen," 37-38.
⁸ On the Reutlingen cases, see also Isabelle Zeder, "Selbstbezichtigunge während der Hexenverfolgung als 'suicide by trial.' Eine Fallstudie aus Reutlingen," *Reutlinger Geschichtsblätter*, 60 (2021): 77-115.
⁹ Thomas Fritz, "Reutlingen - Hexenverfolgungen." In: *Lexikon zur Geschichte der Hexenverfolgung*, eds., Gudrun Gersmann, Katrin Moeller and Jürgen-Michael Schmidt, in: historicum.net, URL: https://www.historicum.net/purl/jdzr9/
¹⁰ Zeder, "Selbstbezichtigungen," 39, 54.

save her soul," she requested.¹¹ Her execution was her gateway to salvation. She prodded city councilors to do their duty as sovereign authorities. "She knows that her soul will be saved, she will gladly suffer what she owes for her crimes, that my lords will pronounce, the sooner the better. She only asks that one should remove her from the world.... She asks an entire honorable council, for the sake of their office, to sentence her according to imperial law." Schmid's suicide by proxy succeeded because she accused herself of harmful magic in addition to spiritual offenses, prompting people to reinterpret recent deaths as homicides. This provided circumstantial evidence that confirmed her confession and secured her conviction. Catharina Schmid was beheaded on August 21, 1644, thirty-six days after she presented herself at the city jail. Her body was burned.¹²

Loose talk of the devil could precipitate a witch trial, even when an offender turned herself in to authorities for a different crime. In 1686 Appollonia Mayrin, a Catholic woman, accused herself of infanticide in the bi-confessional free imperial city of Augsburg. Whether the infanticide really happened or even if she had ever been pregnant remained unclear. When she testified, however, that Satan had tempted her to commit suicide and had compelled her to kill her child, authorities zeroed in on these diabolical themes. Mayrin ultimately confessed to the standard catalog of offenses associated with the cumulative concept of witchcraft: Signing the devil's pact, diabolical sex, attending witches' sabbaths, committing host desecration, and harming humans and livestock. She was beheaded, and her body burned. In her death sentence the alleged infanticide, with which the case began, was secondary to her witchcraft confession.¹³

Self-accusations of witchcraft with suicidal intent also happened in France. Robin Briggs has called attention to voluntary confessions in Catholic Lorraine that lacked "even the implicit threat of torture."¹⁴ In 1599, Claudon Wannier, an elderly widow, publicly accused herself of witchcraft and turned herself in at the court, claiming to have poisoned two people. The lack of corroborating evidence led interrogators to suspect suicidal intent: "tired of life and seeing herself become old and crippled ... she was trying to achieve the aim of her own death, by ... declaring

---

¹¹ Zeder, "Selbstbezichtigungen," 23-24, 76.
¹² Zeder, "Selbstbezichtigungen," 39, 77.
¹³ StadtAA, Strafamt 107, pp. 563-565. Strafamt 162, pp 243-246. Urgicht 1686 b, II, 22, V, 25.
¹⁴ Robin Briggs, *Witches and Neighbors: The Social and Cultural Context of European Witchcraft* (New York: Viking, 1996), 57.

herself to be a witch," they opined. Nonetheless, Claudon persisted in her self-accusation.[15] Briggs interprets this and similar cases as examples "of the tendency for the disadvantaged to put themselves in positions where they are liable to be destroyed."[16]

Cases of suicide by proxy involving men who turned themselves in to authorities and confessed to bestiality were in many ways comparable to witchcraft self-accusations. Described as an "atrocious," "gruesome crime that cried out to heaven,"[17] the sex act itself evoked associations with diabolical congress, the sexual intercourse with Satan that was required to consummate the devil's pact.[18] Indeed, the two forms of sexual transgression could become indistinguishable. In late seventeenth-century Swedish witch trials, witches confessed to having sex with the devil in the form of a black dog.[19] Authorities classified bestiality as a subspecies of sodomy, adding descriptors such as "*sodomia cum brutis*" (sodomy with a brute animal) or "*sodomia seu bestialitatis*" (sodomy, or bestiality)" to distinguish it from "*sodomia cum hominibus*" (sodomy with men). All forms of sodomy were punishable by death by burning.[20] Governments of all confessions imposed these harsh penalties to forestall the wrath of God. Courts did not hesitate to execute teenage offenders. The most mercy convicted sodomites could hope for was to be beheaded and their body subsequently burned, instead of being burned alive.[21]

Bestiality had in common with witchcraft that it was an occult crime. "This atrocious offense is for the most part committed in darkness and

---

[15] Briggs, *Witches*, 157.

[16] Briggs, *Witches*, 46. Further examples, 57, 157.

[17] Ferdinand Christoph Harpprecht, *Responsorum Criminalium et Civilium*, vol. 4 (Tübingen: August Metzler, 1706), 820.

[18] Walter Stephens, *Demon Lovers: Witchcraft, Sex, and the Crisis of Belief* (Chicago: University of Chicago Press, 2003).

[19] Jonas Liliequist, "Peasants against Nature: Crossing the Boundaries between Man and Animal in Seventeenth- and Eighteenth-Century Sweden," *Journal of the History of Sexuality* 1 (1991): 393-423, 399.

[20] Helmut Puff, *Sodomy in Reformation German and Switzerland* (Chicago: University of Chicago Press, 2003), 29.

[21] In Lutheran Württemberg, the only justification for not executing men for bestiality was to establish that the offender had not ejaculated *into* the animal. Helga Schnabel-Schüle, *Überwachen und Strafen im Territorialstaat. Bedingungen und Auswirkungen des Systems strafrechtlicher Sanktionen im frühneuzeitlichen Württemberg* (Cologne: Böhlau, 1997), 314-317. Prosecutions in Catholic Austria were equally harsh. Susanne Hehenberger, *Unkeusch wider die Natur. Sodomieprozesse im frühneuzeitlichen Österreich* (Vienna: Löcker, 2006), 103-156, 214-217.

secret, and does not leave traces after commission," jurists at the Nuremberg University of Altdorf wrote in a *consilium* published in 1738.[22] Bestiality was far more difficult to prove than homosexual sodomy, where the *corpus delicti* could be established by overlapping confessions by both parties, elicited by torture if necessary.[23] This led some prosecutors to argue that bestiality should be treated as a *crimen exceptum*, an "exceptional crime" like witchcraft, where normal evidentiary requirements were suspended. The Altdorf *consilium* concerned a journeyman weaver, pseudonymously named "Mevius." "Driven by his own bad fearful conscience," Mevius turned himself in to the authorities and confessed to committing sodomy with a cow, a calf, and, "almost unheard of," attempting sodomy with a chicken fourteen years earlier. He had also committed adultery and fornication with various women and attempted incest with his sister.[24] The *consilium* first addressed the question of *corpus delicti*. The prosecution depended solely on the voluntary confession of the accused. No one had observed any suspicious circumstances. Despite the fact that in the inquisitorial procedure confession was considered the "queen of proof," that is, there could be no conviction without confession, or alternatively testimony by two eye-witnesses,[25] a confession standing alone was normally not sufficient for conviction. In Mevius' case, the *corpus delicti* was further called into question, because the investigators observed that the defendant suffered from "extraordinary fear and anxiety" as well as suicidal thoughts, so the court ordered a physician and two clergymen to examine him, to determine whether "the defendant, out of weariness with life or out of melancholy, accused himself of something that he did not even commit."[26]

The Altdorf jurists did ultimately find Mevius guilty, however. The standard of proof was lower in "concealed crimes" such as bestiality. The *consilium* cited Benedict Carpzov, the most influential jurist in early modern German criminal jurisprudence. Carpzov argued "that in concealed crimes that are difficult to prove, presumptions and conjectures are

---

[22] Georg Heinrich Linck, *Consiliorum sive Responsorum* (Nuremberg: Johannis Georg Lochner, 1738), 226-233.

[23] For an example of the use of torture in prosecuting a case of homosexual sodomy, see Linck, *Consiliorum*, 585-589.

[24] Linck, *Consiliorum*, 226-233.

[25] John H. Langbein, *Torture and the Law of Proof: Europe and England in the Ancien Regime* (Chicago: University of Chicago Press, 1977), 3-4.

[26] Linck, *Consiliorum*, 228.

accepted as full and conclusive proof."²⁷ This, of course, was the argument that justified the status of witchcraft as a *crimen exceptum*.²⁸ Early modern jurists drew this connection between witchcraft and bestiality explicitly. A *consilium* published in 1722 on Hans Schachtner, an Austrian peasant who accused himself of committing sodomy with his cow fifteen years earlier, conceded that normally the death penalty should not be applied unless the *corpus delicti* had been established by some other evidence than confession alone. "Especially because there are examples, that someone, from weariness with life..., confesses to a crime, that he never committed." But this caution should be set aside in concealed crimes, where circumstantial evidence should suffice, "for otherwise an infinite number of atrocious crimes would remain unpunished." Drawing on a demonological treatise on how to properly recognize and punish witches, the *consilium* concluded: "To determine the certainty of a confession, nothing else is required than what it is possible to have."²⁹

By the turn of the eighteenth century, however, legal arguments justifying prosecuting occult crime as a *crimen exceptum* became less persuasive. Lutheran and Catholic governments became increasingly wary of convicting on the basis of confession in the absence of other evidence, in cases of both witchcraft and bestiality. At the height of the witch-hunt self-accusations were welcomed as the "surest proof of correctness of the fully developed theory of witchcraft," writes historian Wolfgang Behringer.³⁰ For witch-hunters in Ellwangen, Maria Ostertag's confession in 1613 confirmed the legitimacy of all the trials that had gone before and inspired new ones.³¹ In the waning years of the witch-hunt, however,

---

²⁷ Quoted in Linck, *Consiliorum*, 228

²⁸ Brian Levack, *The Witch-hunt in Early Modern Europe* (London, 1995), 79-80.

²⁹ Vitus Guggenberger, *Processe und vortreffliche Gutachten in Criminalibus* (Augsburg: Daniel Walder Buchhändler, 1722), 253. The demonology that Guggenberger cited was Johann Georg Gödelmann, *Tractatus de magis: veneficis et lamiis, edque his recte cognosendis et puniendis...* (Nuremberg: Tauberus, 1676).

³⁰ Wolfgang Behringer, *Witchcraft Persecutions in Bavaria: Popular Magic, Religious Zealotry and Reason of State in Early Modern Europe* (Cambridge: Cambridge University Press, 1997), 164.

³¹ Dillinger, *Kinder*, 133. H. C. Erik Midelfort, *Witch Hunting in Southwestern Germany, 1562-1684: The Social and Intellectual Foundations* (Stanford, CA: Stanford University Press, 1972), 108.

self-accusations prompted judicial skepticism.³² A legal opinion from 1711 by the Tübingen law faculty in Lutheran Württemberg shows how this played out in practice. Anna Elisabeth R. accused herself of flying to a neighboring town on an oven-fork, where she stole a child and replaced it with a changeling. She also confessed to infanticide, abortion, and attempted suicide. The jurists urged caution. The first duty of the judge was to determine whether any of these offenses had truly been committed. Her confession alone did not provide sufficient justification to proceed to judicial torture, let alone execution. She obviously suffered from melancholy and frequently wished for her own death. Since it was impossible to determine the truth of the matter, the jurists recommended leaving it to "the omniscient God and his just judgment." Ideally, the woman should be cared for in a hospital and receive religious instruction to free her from Satan's snares. Alternatively, she could be banished from the territory as punishment for her disorderly life.³³

Similarly, self-accusations of bestiality were now less likely to lead to conviction. In 1711 the city court of Freistadt in Upper Austria, a Catholic jurisdiction, declined to convict Adam Prandsteter for bestiality, since the only available evidence was his confession. The court acknowledged that the nature of the offense meant that it was impossible to establish the *corpus delicti*. Instead of advocating that the court treat Prandsteter's self-confessed sodomy as a *crimen exceptum*, they reached the opposite conclusion. Citing past cases where people accused themselves of bestiality out of weariness with life, though they were innocent, the court sentenced Prandsteter to flogging and banishment.³⁴

In 1713 Hans Unruhe, a thirty-seven-year-old day laborer from Zweiffelsberg in Lutheran Saxony, turned himself in for committing sodomy with a cow, a horse, and a goat twenty years earlier. He also confessed to various thefts and to committing incest with his mother-in-law.³⁵

---

³² On the role of judicial skepticism in the decline of the witch-hunt, see Brian P. Levack, "The Decline and End of Witch-hunt prosecutions," in *Witchcraft and Magic in Europe: The Eighteenth and Nineteenth Centuries*, eds. Bengt Ankarloo and Stuart Clark (London: Athlone Press, 1999), 1-93.

³³ Michael Grass, *Collectionis novae consiliorum juridicorum Tubingensium*, vol. 5 (Tübingen: J. G. Cotta, 1733), 760-763.

³⁴ Hehenberger, *Unkeusch*, 201-202.

³⁵ Johann Christian Fritsch, *Seltsame jedoch wahrhafftige Theologische/Juristische/Medizinische und Physikalische Geschichten*, vol. 3 (Leipzig: Johann Friedrich Brauns sel. Erben, 1733), 351-416.

Despite their best efforts, authorities were not able to confirm that the alleged bestiality had occurred. They tracked down the owners of the horse, cow, and goat respectively, but the animals were long dead. Asked whether Unruhe had committed "fleshly fornication with [his] horse, and let his semen run into the horse?" the owner was non-committal: "He leaves it open whether it happened or not. It could be, or maybe not."[36] No one had ever seen or suspected anything. A medical report concluded that Unruhe was a melancholic. His self-accusation resulted from "weariness with life." The Saxon Electoral Court in Leipzig convicted him of incest, but found that the *corpus delicti* for sodomy had not been sufficiently established. He was sentenced to whipping and perpetual banishment, a sentence that was reduced to six to eight years in a house of correction, because of his "insanity."[37]

Women who accused themselves of past infanticides now also usually failed to convince authorities to prosecute. Echoes of witchcraft reverberated in the infanticide and arson trial of Margaretha Öttlin, twenty, in 1720–1721. A subject of the Benedictine monastery of Lambach in Upper Austria, Öttlin threatened to stab to death her sister's young son and accused herself of multiple infanticides. She had conceived one of these babies with a journeyman butcher, who turned out to be Satan in disguise. She had disposed of the evidence by summoning three black hell hounds that devoured the dead infant. She also accused herself of setting multiple fires to exact revenge upon relatives who had wronged her and threatened to set further fires if she were released. Local officials wanted to convict and execute her to eliminate a threat to public safety. Officials of the central government in Vienna, however, who reviewed the case, issued a scathing judicial rebuke to local authorities for attempting to convict in the absence of a *corpus delicti*. There was no evidence that she had ever even been pregnant. The fires she allegedly set had been accidental. Her "weariness with life" was obvious, as was her "palpable desire" to secure her own execution.[38] Neither local authorities nor Viennese officials engaged with the diabolical themes of her confession, even though witch-hunting in Austria had not entirely ended in 1721. The central

[36] Fritsch, *Geschichten*, 370.
[37] Fritsch, *Geschichten*, 380-381.
[38] "aus der überall hervorleuchtender Begierdte..." StiftAL, Criminalia 388, Margaretha Öttlin 1722, correspondence from 22 November 1721.

government ordered her placement in a house of correction in Linz, until such time as she showed improvement.[39]

Even without diabolical embellishments likely to prompt skepticism in eighteenth-century prosecutors, self-accusations of infanticide in the absence of an infant corpse typically failed. When Anna Maria Martinin, a single woman briefly imprisoned in a house of correction for theft, turned herself in to authorities in Dippoldiswalde in Lutheran Saxony in 1724, accusing herself of a recent infanticide, authorities questioned her sanity. Unable to find any corroborating evidence, they sentenced her to flogging and banishment.[40]

By the early eighteenth century, at the latest, self-accusations of bestiality, witchcraft, or infanticide were no longer a reliable method of bringing about one's own execution. Suicidal people pining for their execution came to understand that they needed to present authorities with material evidence of the crimes they confessed to, whether that be the corpse of a murdered child or, in Vienna, a mutilated crucifix or desecrated host. In a transitional case, the Lutheran peasant Hans Bützer accused himself of bestiality *and* committed child murder. On the evening of August 19, 1673, Bützer, a sixty-year-old blacksmith from Thaylfingen in Württemberg, turned himself in to the court for stabbing to death his neighbor's eighteen-month-old child.[41] He confessed that he had "acted outside Christianity ... with a one-year-old calf" a few years earlier. Since then he suffered a variety of physical and spiritual afflictions. He could not pray. He could not attend church. He was compelled to bang his head against the wall and to blaspheme. He was constantly fighting off the impulse to stab himself or someone else. He had attempted to drown himself in the river Neckar. Realizing that suicide would mean throwing away his salvation, he stabbed his neighbor's six-month-old son in the heart instead. Authorities initiated a sodomy investigation. He was clearly suffering from melancholy and a fearful conscience, Tübingen jurists wrote in

---

[39] In a tragic outcome to this case, Öttlin was about to be released from the workhouse in Linz for good behavior, when she made her last desperate attempt to coerce her execution. She threw the young child of a fellow inmate into a latrine. Moments later she regretted her deed and alerted the guards. The child was retrieved from the latrine alive. To protect public safety, authorities ordered Öttlin's lifetime confinement in the Benedictine Abbey of Lambach. StiftAL, Criminalia 388, Margaretha Öttlin 1722.

[40] D. Christian Gottlieb Troppanneger, *Decisiones Medico-Forensis* (Dresden: Gottlieb Christian Hilschern, 1733), 44-46.

[41] HStAS, A 209/166, Hans Bützer, 1673.

their opinion on the case, but "whether this resulted from crimes he truly committed, or ones he imagined, is known to an omniscient God." In any case, he was lucid enough when he stabbed the baby to know the difference between good and evil. He was sentenced to beheading for child murder. As far as the sodomy was concerned, there was no evidence other than Bützer's confession, so he was not sentenced as a sodomite. Bützer vigorously protested this outcome, petitioning the duke in his own hand. [Image 2.2]

> I thank your Grace for your sentence, but I did two misdeeds .... I beg your Grace by God's mercy to believe, it is true regarding the cattle. I desire my punishment, particularly the fire, as God himself has proclaimed .... If I must die for the child, but I am spared the greatest penalty, then God is not satisfied with me, or with the judge. Two good deeds deserve to be thanked twice, and so two sins deserve two punishments. According to divine and imperial law, I deserve it.

Bützer received no response. He was beheaded as a child murderer. The calf in question was sold outside the territory, "to avoid scandal."[42]

Even as the witch-hunt waned, themes of diabolical compulsion continued in eighteenth-century suicidal child murder trials. In 1723 Ursula Waserin, a Lutheran peasant woman in Württemberg, murdered the three-year-old daughter of a local schoolmaster by repeatedly striking her in the neck with a "rather blunt axe." She wandered into the schoolmaster's house off the street to find the little girl alone asleep in a day bed, while her parents were working in a nearby field. When the schoolmaster came home, he found Waserin waiting next to his daughter's bloodied body. "One should now take her to Rosenfeld," the seat of the local blood court, she requested, "and do justice onto her, so that she can leave this world."[43] Her intention to murder a child formed about three weeks earlier, because "the Evil One /: God preserve us :/ left her no peace." The devil appeared to her around midnight as she lay in bed. He ordered her to go kill a child. He appeared every night, sometimes hitting her and continuously exhorting her to kill a child. His frightening face and green clothing made her realize she was dealing with the Evil One. He spoke to her in "half-foreign

---

[42] HStAS, A 209/166, Hans Bützer, 1673.
[43] "...man solle sie nur nach Rosenfeld führen und ihr Recht anthun, damit sie ab der Welt komme." HStAS, A 209, Bü 1773. Ursula Waser, August 25, 1723.

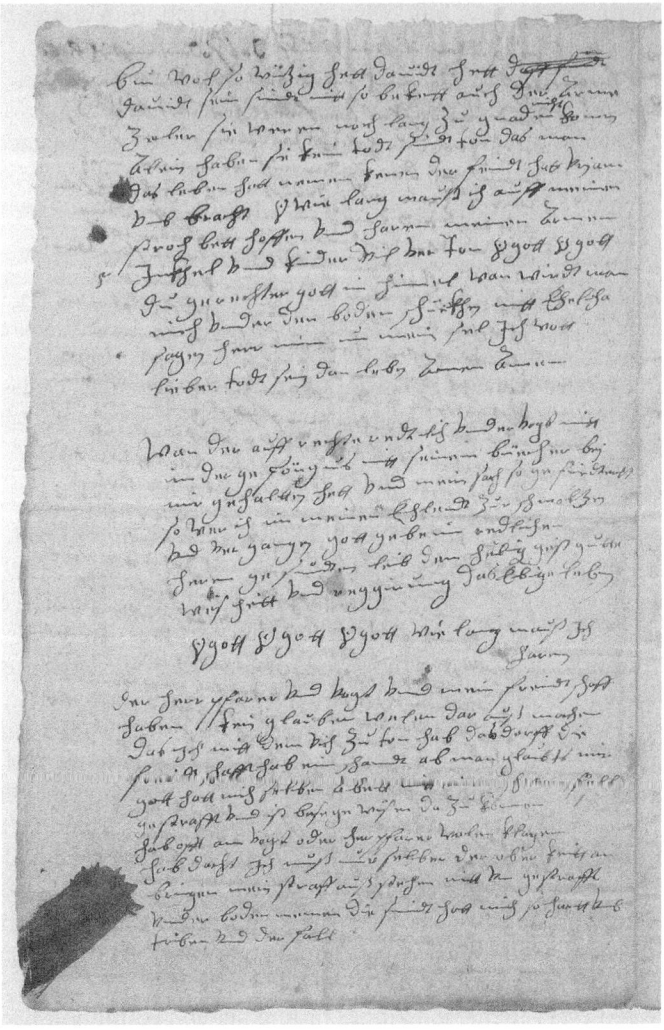

Image 2.2 Hans Bützer's petition to the Duke of Württemberg. Hauptstaatsarchiv Stuttgart, A 209 Bü 166

and rough language."⁴⁴ He did not lay down in bed with her and never stayed more than a quarter of an hour. He had hairy feet.

Waserin's description of Satan was entirely conventional. During witch trials, accused witches usually provided a physical description of Satan as he appeared to them. He mostly dressed in black, but sometimes also wore green. Witches commonly described cloven hooves or other animalistic features.⁴⁵ When Waserin murdered the schoolmaster's daughter, Satan was physically present in the room with her, exhorting her to keep striking the girl until she was dead. He wore the same green coat as during his nightly visits. He had a black hairy face and feet. Unsurprisingly, Waserin's vivid descriptions of Satan prompted the *Vogt*, the local judicial official, to ask if she practiced witchcraft. Waserin denied it. The Vogt insisted: "Did she not learn it? She has the reputation of knowing witchcraft."⁴⁶ Waserin persisted in her denials, though the investigation later revealed that she had accused herself of witchcraft a few years earlier. Perhaps this was her first attempt to commit suicide by proxy? Officials in the central government in Stuttgart were uninterested in pursuing this line of questioning. Waserin was diagnosed as melancholic. Therefore, she was incapable of forming the criminal intent necessary for conviction.⁴⁷ In a grotesque outcome to this case, the court ordered her release because no institution could be found where she could be safely confined.

These cases show that suicidal people attempted and often succeeded in bringing about their executions well before governments became aware of suicidal child murder as a recurring tactic in the late seventeenth and early eighteenth centuries. Suicide by proxy is an unexplored facet in the history of the larger European witch-hunt. At the height of the witch-hunt, self-accusations were an accelerant. When Maria Ostertag accused herself of witchcraft in 1613, she implicated thirty-four people in witchcraft.⁴⁸

---

[44] HStAS, A 209/1773, Ursula Waser, August 25, 1723.
[45] Lyndal Roper, *Witch Craze: Terror and Fantasy in Baroque Germany* (New Haven: Yale University Press, 2004), 87.
[46] HStAS, A 209/ 1773, Ursula Waser, August 25, 1723.
[47] HStAS, A 209/ 1773. Ursula Waser, 1723.
[48] Midelfort, *Witch Hunting*, 108.

Systematic research on self-accusations of witchcraft is likely to reveal further cases of suicide by proxy.[49]

Self-accusations of bestiality were a contemporaneous tactic employed by men. Suicidal men could theoretically have accused themselves of witchcraft as well.[50] Since witchcraft was largely conceptualized as a female crime, however, particularly at the height of the witch-hunt, witchcraft self-accusations were more plausible for women. Self-accusations of bestiality, understood as a male delict, made more sense for men. While witchcraft was an imaginary crime, it is likely that some of the acts of bestiality that men accused themselves of actually happened. Years after their sexual transgression, men felt terror at the damnation they would face if their atrocious sin went unpunished and sought absolution by committing suicide by proxy.[51] Several male self-accusers were older. Hans Bützer was sixty when he committed suicidal child murder and confessed to bestiality. Thomas Hinteregger, a peasant in the Prince-bishopric of Salzburg, was sixty-three or sixty-four in 1734 when he turned himself in to authorities, confessing to dozens of acts of bestiality that he committed between the ages of seven and fifteen.[52] The vagrant Joseph Wachter was sixty-eight or sixty-nine in 1744 when he turned himself in for bestiality in

---

[49] See, for example, Laura Kounine's discussion of a witchcraft self-accusation by Dorothea Rieger in Württemberg in 1678 as a case of suicide by proxy. Laura Kounine, *Imagining the Witch: Emotions, Gender and Selfhood in Early Modern Germany* (Oxford: Oxford University Press, 2018), 163-174. Lyndal Roper discusses the *Witch Craze* trial of Juditha Wagner in Augsburg as a case of suicide by proxy. Roper, *Witch Craze*, 182-196.

[50] In 1665, in a possible case of attempted suicide by proxy, Augustin Gerstecker, a twenty-one-year-old journeyman embroidery-maker in Augsburg, accused himself of a sodomitic *ménage à trois* with Satan and a fellow journeyman, which meant he was confessing to witchcraft and sodomy at once. This is the only self-accusation I have encountered that involved homosexuality instead of bestiality. The fellow journeyman had left the town, so Gerstecker's confession could not be confirmed. Gerstecker was diagnosed as melancholic and released. StadtAA, Strafamt, Urgichten, Augustin Gerstecker, 1665. III, 20, V, 5.

[51] Jonas Liliequist describes a similar dynamic in cases of self-accusations of bestiality in early modern Sweden. Jonas Liliequist, "Reverence, Shame and Guilt in Early Modern European Cultures," in: *The Routledge Companion to Cultural History in the Western World*, eds. Allessandro Arcangeli, Jörg Rogge and Hannu Salmi (London: Routledge, 2020), 240-255, pp. 249-251.

[52] LAS, Pfleggericht Golling, Criminalakt 2. Bund, Nr. 17, Kasten 137 (Criminalia 1731-1735/1).

Schwabmünchen in the Bishopric of Augsburg.[53] As their deaths approached, these old men's dread of hell grew stronger.

It was vexing for authorities to get to the truth of the matter when investigating their subjects' self-accusations of witchcraft, bestiality, or infanticide. Suicidal child murder and suicidal iconoclasm posed a far greater ideological challenge to the legitimacy and smooth functioning of early modern criminal justice, however. It was no surprise to early modern authorities that their subjects might practice witchcraft, or commit bestiality, or infanticide. Confessions by self-accusing witches, sodomites and infanticidal mothers confirmed authorities' pessimistic view of humankind, mired in depravity and sin. This negative anthropology was shared by all governments during the confessional age. It was their duty toward God to contain and punish their subjects' sins. Self-accusations posed the practical problem of determining whether a crime, to which their subjects were generally predisposed, had actually happened in a particular case. As the *consilia* on self-confessed sodomites Mevius and Hans Schachtner discussed above show, governments were aware that some self-accusers confessed to crimes they had not committed "out of weariness with life." Despite this awareness, governments were willing to incur the risk of executing the innocent to avoid letting atrocious sins go unpunished. God would compensate the innocently executed in the afterlife.[54] Or, if the self-accusations were all too implausible, they could be explained as the effect of an imagination corrupted by melancholy. As long as authorities practiced due diligence during investigations and trials, they fulfilled their obligations toward God.

By contrast, when suicidal people murdered a child, or mutilated a crucifix or desecrated a host, and then presented themselves to authorities demanding their execution, authorities were confronted with *proven crimes that would not have occurred, but for their subjects' intent to coerce their executions.* Even though self-accusers of witchcraft, bestiality, and infanticide were acting on the same logic as suicidal child murderers and iconoclasts, their suicides by proxy remained largely "concealed," if not from authorities, then definitely from the broader public. Suicidal child murder and suicidal iconoclasm were publicly visible, and publicly

---

[53] He expired shortly after his arrest. "He was buried as a Christian Catholic." StAA, Hochstift Augsburg NA, Akten 806. 1744-1745 Joseph Wachter.

[54] Catholic clergy made this argument to convince convicted criminals to willingly submit to their death sentence, even if they were innocent of the charges. See Chap. 7.

understood tactics, that others could and did imitate. The outrage and frustration that authorities felt at the brazenness of perpetrators of this novel form of suicide by proxy is palpable in the Austrian edict of 1706 on "How to Punish Child Murders": The killings "are being committed so often and are becoming so rampant, that it almost appears as if such malicious people hold the penalty of the sword set in the criminal code in contempt."[55]

THE ART OF CHILD SACRIFICE

When suicidal people murdered a child, their choice of crime was not merely tactical. They were committing a crime with deep and varied cultural meanings. The motif of child slaughter and child sacrifice captivated the imagination of early modern people, across classes and across confessions. The killing of children in myriad forms inspired at once horror and fascination, revulsion and attraction. One of the best-known biblical motifs involving child sacrifice is the story of Abraham and Isaac, in which Abraham demonstrates his obedience to God by his willingness to sacrifice his son, though his hand was stayed by the angel at the last minute (Gen. 22).[56] Perhaps because Isaac ultimately was not sacrificed, his story had less impact on popular culture than the story of the Massacre of the Holy Innocents, which gained enormous popularity in art and literature in both Catholic and Protestant regions. From the Middle Ages through the eighteenth century, the Gospel story of how King Herod ordered the slaying of all boys two years old and younger in Bethlehem (Matthew 2) was retold, portrayed, and performed in poetry, painting, music, drama, folk art, and folklore. The Cult of the Holy Innocents honored the slaughtered boys as the first Christian martyrs. The fact that these slain boys were Jewish and therefore unbaptized did not pose an obstacle to their cult. According to Catholic doctrine, the boys' close association with the Christ Child temporally and geographically, and their sacrifice in Christ's stead, constituted a baptism "in their own sacrificial blood."[57]

---

[55] "Wie es mit Bestrafung des Kinder-Mords zu halten," 22 March 1706, *Codicis Austriaci* III, 511-512. See the discussion of this edict in Chap. 1.

[56] Erhard Blum and Maren Niehoff, "Isaac", in: *Religion Past and Present*. Consulted online on 12 September 2022 http://dx.doi.org/10.1163/1877-5888_rpp_COM_10564

[57] Diane Peters Auslander, "Victims or Martyrs: Children, Anti-Semitism, and the Stress of Change in Medieval England," in *Childhood in the Middle Ages and the Renaissance: The Results of a Paradigm Shift in the History of Mentality*, ed. Albrecht Classen (Berlin: Walter de Gruyter, 2005), 121-122.

The Feast of the Holy Innocents was celebrated on December 28. Their relics were venerated throughout Europe. Frederick the Wise of Saxony, Martin Luther's territorial lord, had a complete body of one of the Holy Innocents in his relic collection.[58] Medieval plays showing the "slaughter of innocents" included stage instructions that actors playing the victims wear white stoles, symbolizing their sinlessness and spotless purity.[59] The Cult of the Holy Innocents intersected with the blood libel. Before Simon of Trent was beatified in 1588 and received his own feast day, March 24, he was venerated on December 28, along with the Holy Innocents. The pontifical proceedings leading to the beatification of Simon cited the veneration of the Holy Innocents as precedent.[60]

In the sixteenth century the Massacre of the Innocents was a potent motif in confessional polemics. In the Netherlands around 1550, frequent executions of Protestants by Spanish authorities gave the story meaning as a general condemnation of violence against innocents.[61] It never lost its cross-confessional appeal, however. In 1715 the Lutheran writer Barthold Heinrich Brockes, a Hamburg patrician, published his German translation of *The Bethlehemite Massacre of the Innocents* by the Italian poet Giambattista Marino. He dedicated his work to Habsburg emperor Charles VI.[62] The work included an engraving of the slaughter, and, like Marino, Brockes lingered on the various forms of killing, blending sensual descriptions of violence with effusive piety. Brockes' work was a bestseller. It appeared in six editions between 1715 and 1763.[63] In his professional life, Brockes had personal experience with child murder. In 1720 Brockes was elected to the

---

[58] Patricia Healy Wasyliw, *Martyrdom, Murder, and Magic: Child Saints and their Cults in Medieval Europe* (New York: P. Lang, 2008), 30. Treue, *Trienter Judenprozess*, 281.

[59] Jean E. Jost, "Loving parents in Middle English Literature." in *Childhood in the Middle Ages and the Renaissance: The Results of a Paradigm Shift in the History of Mentality*, ed. Albrecht Classen (Berlin: Walter de Gruyter, 2005), 312.

[60] Treue, *Trienter Judenprozess*, 270, fn. 49, 487-490.

[61] Elena Nendza, "'Zerhaut, zerreißt, zerschmettert!' Der Bethlehemitische Kindermord – *ein interkonfessionelles Bindeglied in den europäischen Künsten*," *Daphnis* 45 (2017) 250-273. Elena Nendza, *Der Bethlehemitische Kindermord in den Künsten der Frühen Neuzeit. Studien zu Intermedialen und Interkonfessionellen Popularisierungen und Austauschprozessen* (Berlin: Walter de Gruyter, 2020).

[62] Giambattista Marino, *La strage degl'innocenti : poema* (Naples: Ottavio Beltrano, 1632). Barthold Heinrich Brockes, *Herrn Barthold Henrich Brockes J.U.L. Verteutschter Bethlehemitischer Kinder-Mord des Ritters Marino: Nebst etlichen von des Herrn Ubersetzers Eigenen Gedichten* (Cologne: Benjamin Schillers Wittwe, 1715).

[63] Hans-Dieter Loose, *Barthold Heinrich Brockes (1680-1747); Dichter und Ratsherr in Hamburg ; neue Forschungen zu Persönlichkeit und Wirkung* (Hamburg: Hans Christians Verlag, 1980), 198.

Hamburg Senate, which meant that he served as a juror in murder trials that came before the Superior Court. Later he served as city judge and as administrator in Hamburg's territory.[64] The sources do not illuminate whether the frequent child murders taking place in Hamburg at that time contributed to the emotive appeal of Brockes' poetry or whether his literary imagination shaped his responses to the child murders he was called on to investigate and judge.

Further down the social scale, Catholic peasants in Austria and the Tyrol commemorated the Holy Innocents by portraying their massacre in miniature nativity scenes. Jesuits introduced nativity scenes north of the Alps after 1560, as part of their missionary outreach to common people. By the seventeenth and eighteenth centuries, locals incorporated them into popular culture and folklore. A number of these installations from the eighteenth century have survived. They included hundreds of intricately hand-carved figurines of slaughtered and dismembered infants and their

Image 2.3 Roman soldier stabbing an Infant. Figurine in "Rinner Krippe: Bethlehemitischer Kindermord." Rinn in Tirol, c. 1760. Volkskunde Museum Wien, Vienna. Photo: Birgit & Peter Kainz, facsimile digital. ÖMV/35.899

[64] Loose, *Brockes,* 20-40.

killers.⁶⁵ [Image 2.3] These small-scale artworks were displayed in people's homes, evidence of their emotional engagement with the child massacre.

Contemporaneously, the adoration of the Baby Jesus expanded during the Catholic Baroque. Austrian folklorists have documented twenty miracle-working icons of the Infant Jesus venerated in regular pilgrimages to their shrines in the seventeenth and eighteenth centuries. Nine of these were located in Vienna itself. Pilgrims and parishioners purchased devotional images of the icons. They showed the Baby Jesus sleeping on the cross, or Christ as a young boy carrying the cross, or the Christ Child with the lamb of God, the cross and other instruments of the passion, foreshadowing his coming sacrifice.⁶⁶

Far removed from such officially promoted religious devotions to the Holy Innocents and the Christ Child, Catholic and Protestant governments were confronted with another horror crime that emerged in the second half of the sixteenth century, just as the European witch-hunt accelerated. Governments prosecuted criminal gangs for a particularly gruesome form of child sacrifice. The purpose of the crime was to procure "thieves' candles." During the same years that Master Frantz Schmidt, executioner of Nuremberg, beheaded the city's first documented suicidal child murderers Anna Strölin and Anna Freyin in 1580 and 1584, he recorded three such crimes in his diary. In 1577 Schmidt executed Niklaus Stüller, a highwayman, who confessed to murdering three pregnant women, among other killings. Stüller "cut open a live pregnant woman, in whom was a dead child." Next, he "cut open a pregnant woman who had a girl in her." Finally, on the third try, Stüller found what he was looking for. He "cut open a pregnant woman in whom were two live boys."⁶⁷ Stüller's purpose becomes clear in Schmidt's later entries. In 1588 Schmidt executed two highwaymen, Georg Hörnlein and Jobst Knau, who murdered two newborn baby boys just after their consorts had given birth and

---

⁶⁵ Folklorists have studied these intricate artifacts as a window into the history of daily life among Catholic Austrian peasants in the eighteenth and nineteenth centuries. Franz Grieshofer and Nora Witzmann. *Weihnachtskrippen. Spiegelbilder Vergangener Lebenswelten* (Vienna: Österreichisches Museum für Volkskunde, 2008).

⁶⁶ On the Viennese miracle-working icons of the Christ Child, see Nora Witzmann, *Gnadenreiches Jesulein. Jesukindverehrung in der Andachtsgraphik* (Vienna: Österreichisches Museum für Volkskunde, 1998), 61-66.

⁶⁷ Frantz Schmidt, *The Executioner's Journal: Meister Frantz Schmidt of the Imperial City of Nuremberg*, trans. Joel Harrington (Charlottesville: University of Virginia Press, 2016), 5.

cut off their right hands.⁶⁸ Schmidt explained the motive of these killings in his entry on Bastian Grüble, a highwayman he executed in 1601. Grüble confessed to murdering twenty people, among whom were five pregnant women. He "cut them open and cut off the little hands of the infants to make burglary candles out of them."⁶⁹

Widely documented in criminal trial records, legal compendia, literary sources, grimoires, and folklore collections from the sixteenth through nineteenth centuries, "thieves' candle" were a tool of the trade for criminal gangs and burglars.⁷⁰ As Stüller's repeated attempts illustrate, it was preferable to harvest the right hand from a male fetus. Similarly, the stereotypical victim in blood libel legends was a male child. After drying the infant hand and dipping it in wax, thieves lit the hand to determine whether the occupants of a house were asleep. If all five fingers burned, the coast was clear. Alternatively, lighting the fingers enabled the burglar to place the residents in a preternatural sleep, so he could rob the home undisturbed. Some robbers confessed to harvesting the fetus' heart, in addition to the right hand. Eating the fresh infant heart or drinking blood from it would render the murder invulnerable to stabbing.⁷¹ Or, it would also enable him to withstand judicial torture.⁷²

These crimes were a masculine variant of the stereotypical malevolent magic that female witches confessed to, for example, the magical murder of babies, or digging up infant corpses from cemeteries, to process them into magical salve used for flying or magical poisons, or to consume them at cannibalistic orgies at witches' sabbaths.⁷³ Like the confessions of witches, the confessions of many highwaymen convicted of murdering pregnant women to harvest their fetuses were extracted under torture.

---

⁶⁸ Schmidt, *Journal*, 32.

⁶⁹ Schmidt, *Journal*, 76. Harrington, *Faithful Executioner*, 71, 186-187.

⁷⁰ Christa Agnes Tuczay, "Herzesser und andere Schurken. Medialer Transfer kriminellen Aberglaubens," *Medienimpulse* 59 (2021): 1-28.

⁷¹ B. Ann Tlusty, "Bravado, Martial Magic, and Masculine Performance in Early Modern Germany," in: *Rethinking Europe: War and Peace in the Early Modern German Lands*, eds. Gerhild Scholz Williams, Sigrun Haude, and Christian Schneider (Leiden: Brill, 2019), 9-13, p. 21.

⁷² Franz Wilflingseder, "Gestalten des heimischen Aberglaubens. Aus Kriminalakten der Herrschaft Spital am Pyhrn vom 16. Bis zum 18. Jahrhundert," *Jahrbuch der oberösterreichischen Musealvereines* 112 (1967): 129.

⁷³ B. Ann Tlusty, "Invincible Blades and Invulnerable Bodies: Weapons Magic in Early Modern Germany," *European Review of History* 22 (215): 669. Roper, *Witch Craze*, 69-81.

This was definitely the case, as Michael Kunze has shown, during the trial of the Pappenheimers, a vagrant family tried for witchcraft in Munich in 1600. Male members of the family confessed to murdering several pregnant women and harvesting their fetuses. The men offered widely varying accounts, however, of where, when, and for what purpose they harvested the fetuses.[74] Their confessions resemble those of the Jews of Trent. Under torture, the accused Jews kept offering different reasons for why they needed the blood of Christian children, desperate to hit upon the answer that would satisfy their interrogators.[75] The obvious effect of torture in the Pappenheimer confessions leads Kunze to suggest that the murder of pregnant women to harvest their fetuses was another fantastical crime that sprang from interrogators' demonological imagination.[76]

Not all such confessions were the result of torture, however. Ann Tlusty has found that some confessions originated "with the defendant rather than with the interrogators."[77] Some male defendants volunteered these stories, without leading questions. The context was quite different than in cases of women's witchcraft self-accusations discussed above. These men did not spontaneously show up at the courthouse, accusing themselves of harvesting fetuses. They were already in custody on trial for other capital offenses such as highway robbery and murder. Their death sentences were a foregone conclusion. In this situation, some defendants made a fulsome confession to every offense they had ever committed. Resembling a Catholic general confession, such comprehensive criminal confessions allowed felons to go to their deaths with no unconfessed sins on their conscience.[78] Unlike perpetrators of suicide by proxy, such defendants were not seeking death, but once they found themselves in a situation where their executions were inevitable, they acted upon the same logic.

In contrast to mythical murders of children by Jews, or witches' banquets of infant flesh at sabbaths, it is not implausible that violent criminals actually did murder pregnant women to harvest their fetuses. Since perpetrators of suicide by proxy were willing to murder children to facilitate

---

[74] Michael Kunze, *Highroad to the Stake: A Tale of Witchcraft* (Chicago: University of Chicago Press, 1987), 181-186.

[75] R. Po-Chia Hsia, *Trent 1475: Stories of a Ritual Murder Trial* (New Haven: Yale University Press, 1992), 34-50.

[76] Kunze, *Highroad*, 181-186.

[77] Tlusty, "Invincible Blades," 669.

[78] Moshe Sluhovsky, *Becoming a New Self: Practices of Belief in Early Modern Catholicism* (Chicago: University of Chicago Press, 2017), 96-120.

their own salvation, it is credible that others would kill pregnant women and their fetuses for more nefarious this-worldly ends. Similar crimes occur in present-day Africa, when albino children are ritualistically murdered to harvest body parts for magical purposes.[79] Within the early modern German criminal underworld, it made sense for violent criminals to exploit the potency of child sacrifice for personal power and profit.

In addition to cutting open five pregnant women and harvesting their fetuses, Bastian Grüble and his associates "also stole children and offered them for sale to the Jews," Nuremberg executioner Frantz Schmidt wrote in his journal in 1601.[80] Official prosecutions for Jewish ritual murder mostly ended after the mid-sixteenth century. Popular belief in the blood libel was undiminished, however, and in fact grew stronger in the seventeenth and eighteenth centuries. Blood libel cults underwent a revival during the Catholic Counter-Reformation. The expansion of the cult of Anderl ("Little Andy") of Rinn in Tyrol, a three-year-old boy "martyred" by Jews in 1462, is a clear example. There is no evidence that a historical Anderl of Rinn ever existed. His martyrdom was invented by the Tyrolian physician and polymath Hippolyt Guarinoni in 1621. The seeding of this legend was wildly successful. In 1678 a pilgrimage church was built, where Anderl's alleged relics were exhibited. A lively cult and pilgrimage developed. Beatified in 1752, Anderl was recognized as a blessed martyr equal to Simon of Trent.[81] Catholic martyrologies gave cloying accounts of his death.

Anderl was an exceptionally beautiful child, we are told. He was sweet, lovely, and fair. "Our sweet little Andy must have been of especially lovely appearance, since it is well known, ... that Jews particularly desire those boys, who are without blemish, and beautiful," Ignatius Zach, a cathedral canon in Wilten, wrote in his sumptuously illustrated hagiography of Anderl, published in Augsburg in 1724.[82] [Image 2.4] The Jesuit priest

---

[79] https://www.amnesty.org.uk/ritual-murders-people-albinism-malawi
[80] Schmidt, *Journal*, 76.
[81] Georg R. Schroubek, "Andreas von Rinn. Der Kult eines 'heiligen Ritualmordopfers' im historischen Wandel," *Österreichische Zeitschrift für Volkskunde* XLIX/98 (1995): 371-396. Teter, *Blood Libel*, 311-314. Treue, *Trienter JudenprozessC*, 282-283, 512-515. R. Po-Chia Hsia, *The Myth of Ritual Murder: Jews and Magic in Reformation Germany* (New Haven: Yale University Press, 1988), 217-222.
[82] Ignatius Zach, *Ausführliche Beschreibung der Marter eines heiligen und unschuldigen Kinds Andreae von Rinn in Tyrol....* (Augsburg: Matthias Wolff, 1724), 21-22. Jews preferred beautiful boys because of the Old Testament requirements that sacrificial lambs be without blemish, Zach explained.

2 LITURGIES OF SUICIDE BY PROXY   61

Image 2.4 Anderl von Rinn. Engraving, 1724. Volkskunde Museum Wien, Vienna. ÖMV/34.467

Jacob Schmid, court preacher in Munich, made the same observation in his hagiography published in 1732. "The beautiful appearance of the sweet child" attracted the Jews, Schmid wrote.[83] The Jews abducted the "little angel" and brought him to a boulder in the forest, a kind of natural

---

[83] Jacob Schmid, *Heiliger Ehren-Glantz Der Gefürsteten Graffschafft Tyrol/... Gezieret Haben*, vol. 2 (Augspurg: Matthias Wolff, 1732), 168-190.

altar, "suitable for slaughtering the sweet victim."[84] They proceeded to cut the "sweet little boy" all over his body, collecting his blood. Finally, the rabbi stabbed Anderl in the neck, ending the life of the "little martyr," the "tender little lamb." Venerated as the patron saint of small children, Anderl performed numerous miracles that testified, Schmid wrote, to "the glory of our holy little boy and martyr."[85] *Ex voto* images from the eighteenth century tell of Anderl's miraculous cures and rescues.[86]

Jewish blood libel and host desecration narratives often featured a "bad Christian," a Christian accomplice, paid by Jews to abet their nefarious schemes. Often, though not always, these "bad Christians" were women. In the Anderl von Rinn legend, however, it was his godfather who sold the boy to the Jews.[87] Unlike the core accusation of the blood libel, side plots involving secondary villains likely reflected a social reality. Beginning in the 1560s, after governments largely discontinued prosecuting Jews for ritual murder, authorities prosecuted Christians for abducting children and attempting to sell them to Jews. So firmly did common people believe the blood libel that the imaginary crime inspired real crime.

The bi-confessional city of Augsburg dealt with two such cases after the mid-sixteenth century. In 1560 Augsburg authorities whipped and banished Anna Peurin, a maidservant, for attempting to sell a four-year-old boy to Jews residing in Oberhausen, a village just beyond Augsburg's borders. In 1572, Susanna Schönin, a twelve-year-old girl, persuaded a little boy to come away with her to Oberhausen. When she offered the boy to a Jew, he alerted the bailiff. Like Peurin, Susanna was whipped and banished. Both the maidservant and the twelve year old girl said they learned from other women that Jews paid money for children, though they both denied knowing why Jews wanted them.[88]

Cases like these continued through the late eighteenth century. Several happened in Protestant territories. Pilgrimages and other

---

[84] Schmid, *Heiliger Ehren-Glantz*, 157.

[85] Schmid, *Heiliger Ehren-Glantz*, 166.

[86] Treue, *Trienter Judenprozess*, 512-515. A votive image from 1739 is reproduced in Wilhelm Theopold, *Das Kind in der Votivmalerei* (Munich: K. Thiemig, 1981) 51.

[87] Schmid, *Heiliger Ehren-Glantz*, 155-156. On Christian accomplices, particularly women, in host desecration narratives, see Miri Rubin, *Gentile Tales: The Narrative Assault on Late Medieval Jews* (Philadelphia: University of Pennsylvania Press, 1999), 73-75.

[88] StadtAA, Strafamt, Urgicht Anna Peurin, 1560, July 23. Strafbuch 98, f. 19r., Anna Peurin. Urgicht Susanna Schönin, 1572, January 14-16. Margaret Brannan Lewis, *Infanticide and Abortion in Early Modern Germany* (London: Routledge, 2016), 107.

devotions dedicated to Simon of Trent, Anderl von Rinn and other child "martyrs" were, of course, limited to Catholic territories, but the Reformation did not extinguish the commonsense knowledge of Jewish ritual murder among Protestants. In a remarkable case in the Duchy of Magdeburg, a Lutheran territory, two Jewish women organized a sting operation to ensure the arrest of a Christian kidnapper. Hans Bertzel, a shepherd, approached the Jewish women and offered them a Christian boy for sale. The women invited the man and the boy into their home, secretly summoning the bailiff. When the bailiff arrived, the women asked him to enter incognito, so he could witness the man's attempt to sell the boy. Removing his sword, the bailiff joined the negotiations. Bertzel offered to sell the boy for 100 *Reichsthaler*. The Jewish women made a counteroffer of fifty *Reichsthaler*, which the kidnapper rejected. At this point the bailiff arrested Bertzel. He was tried for child abduction and attempting to sell a child to Jews. By rights, Bertzel should be beheaded for this crime, the court proclaimed. However, because the attempt had not succeeded and no harm had come to the boy, Bertzel was flogged and banished from the territory.[89]

In all of these cases, governments prosecuted the Christian kidnappers, not the Jews. Jewish communities now expected, and received, governmental protection against accusations that might arise from these incidents. The early Enlightenment philosopher and jurist Christian Thomasius wrote about such a case in Helfta, a village in Lutheran Saxony, in 1694, as an example of how common people still believed in the "old myths" that Jews buy and murder children. Andreas Meinart, a sixty-eight-year-old beggar, attempted to sell a boy to local Jews. He was sentenced to a "light" flogging, due to his advanced age, and banished.[90]

In 1732 the Jews of the Country of Baden in the Swiss Confederacy requested and received an official declaration of innocence by the county government, after a twelve-year-old vagrant girl, originally from Zurich, kidnapped a younger child with the intention of selling it to Jews. Upon her arrest, the girl testified that a Jew in Endingen had hired her to procure a child for him. Endingen was the site of a blood libel persecution in

---

[89] This case was discussed in two separate *consilia*. Johann Christian Fritsch, *Seltsame jedoch wahrhafftige theologische, juristische, medicinische und physicalische Geschichte*, vol. 1 (Leipzig: Johann Friedrich Braun, 1730), 180-182. Johann Hieronymus Hermann, *Sammlung allerhand Auserlesener Responsorum*, vol. 2 (Jena: Johann Volckmar Marggraf, 1731), 677.

[90] Christian Thomasius, *Ernsthaffte, aber doch Muntere und Vernünftige Thomasische Gedanken....*, vol. 1, 2nd edition (Halle: Rengerische Buchhandlung, 1723), 223-225.

1470. Since then the townsfolk had venerated their "Innocent Children of Endingen" in yearly processions, bearing the relics of the supposed child martyrs. These processions were only suppressed by Emperor Joseph II in the late eighteenth century.[91] Upon further questioning, the girl admitted that a group of vagrants had advised her to blame the Jews of Endingen.[92] As late as 1780 a vagrant woman in the Archbishopric of Salzburg abducted a nine-year-old boy there and brought him to Regensburg, where she attempted to sell him to a local Jew. The Jew alerted authorities. The vagrant woman was flogged and banished from the territory.[93]

This discussion of real or imagined sacrificial violence against children has shown how deeply embedded the idea of child sacrifice was in early modern culture. It had broad currency in the most varied social settings. In the religious realm, officially sponsored devotions commemorating biblical or mythical child sacrifice allowed believers to tap into its salvific potency. In the arts, child sacrifice evoked horror, empathy, and aesthetic pleasure. In the illicit world of magic and crime, marginalized women and girls, beggars, vagrants, and highwaymen attempted to exploit child sacrifice as a source of power and profit. This cultural context informed how suicidal people performed child murder, and how their communities responded to their crime.

---

[91] On the Endingen blood libel, see Hsia, *Myth* (New Haven: Yale University Press, 1988), 14-41.

[92] The declaration of innocence was issued by the Landvogtei Baden. Johann Caspar Ulrich, *Johann Caspar Ulrichs, Pfarrers zum Frauen-Münster in Zürich, Sammlung Jüdischer Geschichten*.... (Basel: [Nicolaus Kölner?] 1768), 289-290.

[93] Christian Gottlieb Gumpelzhaimer, *Regensburg's Geschichte, Sagen und Merkwurdigkeiten*..., vol. 3 (Regensburg: Friedrich Pustet, 1838), 1699. There were two further cases in Lutheran Frankfurt in 1705 and in 1729, when two women were investigated for attempting to sell a child to Jews residing in the city's Jewish ghetto. ISG, Criminalia Akten 2453, Anna Maria Drechslerin, 1705, and Criminalia Akten 3822, Anna Elisabetha Seibelin, 1729. Augsburg prosecuted two women for attempting to sell a baby girl to Jews in 1742-1743. Anna Maria Käprffin, a Catholic vagrant, was executed for arson and child abduction. StadtAA, Strafamt 167, Verbrecherbuch, f. 255r., 14 February 1743, Anna Catharina Obermüllerin; f. 256r., 20 July 1743, Marianna Kärpffin. Samuel Valentin, *End-Urthel und Verruf... derjenigen Manns- und Weibs-Persohnen so von... Einem...Hochweisen Rath des H.R. Reichs Freyen Stadt Augspurg von... 1649 bis... 1759....zum Tod condemniret* (Augsburg: Brinhaußer, 1759), 46-47.

Catholics and Protestants

Lutheran pastors frequently published sermons they held on the ravenstone after an execution had taken place. Such sermons typically provided a brief account of malefactors' background and crimes, and identified the moral failings and character flaws that had brought them to this sad end. Most pages, however, were dedicated to the pastors' work with the malefactors in the months before their executions, and their successful efforts to bring about a profound transformation in the defendants, from hardened, rageful, even bestial criminals to docile lambs, who went willingly, even joyfully, to their deaths. The pastors described these encounters as heroic struggles with Satan, who did not want to relinquish souls he had long held in his sway. The goal was to effect the criminals' "conversion." In this context, conversion did not mean moving from one Christian confession to another, or converting to Christianity, but rather an "intensification" of faith within one's own denomination.[94] The ministers' diligent, tireless pastoral care enabled poor sinners to fully understand the extent of their sinful depravity and to free themselves from Satan's snares. They achieved genuine, heartfelt repentance. Therefore, God's grace would not be denied to them. Assuredly, they would enter the kingdom of heaven, the ministers wrote.[95]

A prominent example of this genre is the collection of conversion narratives of executed criminals compiled by Württemberg jurist and pietist Johann Jacob Moser. Moser's *Blessed Final Hours of Several Miscreants*

---

[94] Jonathan Strom, "Pietist Conversion Narratives and Confessional Identity, in: *Conversion and the Politics of Religion in Early Modern Germany*, eds. David M. Luebke, Jared Poley, Daniel C. Ryan and David Warren Sabean (New York: Berghahn Books, 2012): 135.

[95] Funeral sermons for the murdered children are a related genre. See, for example, the funeral sermon for three-year-old Daniel Zeibig, whose father, Master Daniel Zeibig, a blacksmith in Jonasbach in Saxony, cut his throat as he slept in his crib on June 26, 1699. Nicolaus Bahn, pastor in Jonasbach, held a funeral sermon for the murdered boy at the father's request six days later. The sermon described Master Zeibig as a respected and pious member of the community and a loving father who held his son's hand as they went to church. Beset by financial worries, Master Zeibig despaired of God's providence and murdered his son. Master Zeibig would be executed for this heinous murder, but his heartfelt repentance ensured that Christ's precious blood would cleanse him of his sins. M. Nicolaus Bahn, *Das unschuldig vergoßne Blut... Bey Christlicher Beerdigung eines kleinen Kindes von 3. Jahren/ Nehmlich Daniel Zeibigs/ So von seinem leiblichen Vater/ Meister Daniel Zeibigen.../ mit einem Scheer-Messer jämmerlich ermordet.../ vorgestellet* (Pirna: Georg Balthasar Ludewig, 1699).

Sentenced to Death, first published in 1740, was a hit. It appeared in five further expanded editions by 1767.[96] *The Thief on the Cross*, compiled by Ernst Gottlieb Woltersdorff, a pietist pastor in Bunzlau in Silesia, was a similarly successful collection, appearing in several editions between 1753 and 1777.[97] Both Moser's and Woltersdorff's collections included the execution sermon that Adam Struensee, a pastor in Halle, held for suicidal child murderer Catharina Uhlin, twenty-two, beheaded in Halle in 1736. Struensee had ministered to Uhlin for ten weeks prior to her execution.[98] Uhlin had gotten involved with a soldier and incited him to desert. For this, she was publicly flogged and sentenced to the house of correction.[99] To free herself from the workhouse, out of "desperation," she cut the throat of the nine-year-old daughter of another female inmate with a blunt knife. When Struensee first visited Uhlin during her trial, he saw in her "a truly diabolical malevolent will." Her principal affect was rage and vengefulness.[100] Struensee went to work. The blood of the murdered child cried out to heaven against her; he chastised her. He made her understand that through her deed she had become a self-murderer. Struensee's admonishments caused Uhlin to feel profound sorrow. She shed copious tears. This was precisely the effect Struensee hoped to have. Such Christian sorrow over one's sins was not to be confused with pathological melancholy, Struensee emphasized. Her godly sorrow and genuine repentance both for the child murder and for her own suicide opened the door to divine grace. As Uhlin's execution approached, through Struensee's unrelenting efforts, "God transformed a pig and tiger into a pure and quiet lamb."[101] The day before her beheading, Struensee provided her with the Eucharist,

---

[96] On Moser's collection and its publication history, see Strom, "Pietist Conversion Narratives," 136, 146, n. 10, 147, n. 11.

[97] Ernst Gottlieb Woltersdorff, ed., *Der Schächer Am Kreutz : Das Ist Vollständige Nachrichten Von Der Bekehrung Und Seligem Ende Hingerichteter Missethäter*, vol 1 (Budißin: Deinzer, 1753).

[98] Johann Jacob Moser, *Seelige Letzte Stunden Einiger dem zeitlichen Tode übergebener Missethäter* (Stuttgart: Erhardt, 1767), 161-189. Struensee published his account shortly after Uhlin's execution. Adam Struensee, *Die Zarte Liebe Jesu zu den Elenden, ...Bey Gelegenheit einer...Enthauptung einer Kinder-Mörderin* (Halle: Waysenhaus, 1736).

[99] On Uhlin's circumstances prior to her arrest, see Johann Christoph von Dreyhaupt, *Pagus neletici et nudzici, oder ausführliche diplomatisch-historische Beschreibung des zum... Herzogthum Magdeburg gehörigen Saal-Kreyses*, vol. 2 (Halle: Verlag des Waysenhauses, 1755), 522.

[100] Woltersdorff, ed., *Schächer*, 629-631.

[101] Woltersdroff, ed., *Schächer*, 654.

which she received with ardor and profound gratitude. She walked in her execution procession with serenity. At the ravenstone, Struensee blessed her one last time. Her eyes were bound. As she cried out "Now Jesus! Jesus! Jesus!" she received the strike of the sword. "Her soul went to GOD," Struensee wrote, "where one day I hope to meet her again among the blessed."[102]

There are no Catholic equivalents to this kind of execution narrative. The paucity of published Catholic execution sermons leads Tyge Krogh to argue that Catholics were less interested in pastoral care for condemned criminals than Lutherans, because Catholic soteriology offered a more pessimistic assessment of executed criminals' prospects for salvation. Krogh suggests that the importance of purgatory in the Catholic model of the afterlife meant that criminals guilty of heinous crimes would have to fear a particularly long stay in purgatory, compared to regular Catholics who had less to atone for.[103] This is a misreading of Catholic soteriology. In fact, the Catholic doctrine of purgatory allowed priests to offer condemned malefactors hope for accelerated entry into paradise. If they

---

[102] Woltersdorff, ed., *Schächer*, 658. Further examples of Lutheran execution sermons for women who committed suicidal child murderers: 1734, Margaretha Ursula Huberin, a twenty-six-year-old woman from Regensburg, who drowned a five-year-old girl in the Danube. Johann Melchior Grimm, *Als Margaretha Ursula Huberin Burgerliche Balln-Binderin allhier in Regenspurg Wegen begangenen Kinder-Mords Nach Urtheil und Recht zum Tode verdammet/ Und darauf Den 21. Octobr. 1734. Durch das Schwerdt Vom Leben zum Todt hingerichtet worden* (Regensburg: Johann Caspar Memmel, 1734). 1744, Gertrude Magdalena Bremmel, twenty, a maidservant in Wernigeroda, who cut the throat of her employer's four-year-old daughter. Her execution sermon was published in at least two editions. Anon., *Die Hirten-Treue Christi, welche er an einem seiner verlornen Schafe, nemlich an Gertrude Magdalene Bremmelin, einer vorsetzlichen Kindermörderin, erwiesen*, 2nd edition ([Werningerode]: Waysenhaus, 1745). It was later included in both Moser's and Woltersdorff's collections. Moser, *Letzte Stunden*, 269-326, and in Woltersdorff, ed., *Schächer*, vol. 1, 2nd edition (Budißin: Deinzer, 1761), 407-471. 1746, Johanna Maria Elisabeth Martauschin, twenty-three, an inmate at the Spandau house of correction in Berlin, who bludgeoned to death the small child of a fellow woman inmate. Woltersdorff, ed., *Schächer*, 2nd edition (1761), 933-957. 1753, Sophia Charlotta Krügerin, an eighteen-year-old maidservant falsely accused of theft, cut the throat of a nine-year-old neighbor boy. Wolftersdorff, ed., *Schächer*, vol. 2, 2nd edition (Budißin: Jacob Deinzer, 1762), 191-232. 1773, Anna Magdelena Schießlin, a nineteen-year-old maidservant and orphan from Regensburg, who drowned a six-year-old boy in the Danube. Johann Christian Breuning, *Rede Bei Der Zu Regensburg Durchs Schwerd Vollzognen Hinrichtung Der Anna Magdalena Schießlin: Auf Öffentlicher Richtsstatt Den 19. Mai 1774 Gehalten* (Regensburg: Keyser, 1774).

[103] Tyge Krogh, *A Lutheran Plague: Murdering to Die in the Eighteenth Century* (Leiden: Brill, 2012), 116-120.

achieved genuine repentance and, crucially, if they *expiated* their sins through *pain* on the scaffold, it was possible for a Catholic executed criminal to enter heaven immediately, like Dismas, the apocryphally named good thief, who entered paradise together with Christ on the day of his crucifixion.[104] This was a grace denied to even the most devout Catholics who led blameless lives, who nonetheless had to expect to spend some time in purgatory. Myriad Catholic devotions aimed to make that time as brief as possible. Catholic criminals, by contrast, if they practiced virtuoso repentance, and if they *suffered enough* on the scaffold,[105] would be with Christ on the day of their death, like apostles, saints, martyrs, and baptized children who died before they reached the age of reason. While few criminals would achieve this exalted level of repentance and expiation, Catholic authorities and clergy went to extraordinary lengths to ensure that condemned criminals died a blessed death and endeavored to reduce their time in purgatory.[106]

Catholic priests did not narrate their interactions with the condemned criminals they attended to, however. To do so would have incurred the risk of "irregularity," and it would have violated the seal of confession. Irregularity was a canonical impediment that made one ineligible to receive Holy Orders or that prevented a cleric who had already received them from exercising his office, that is, an ordained priest who became irregular would no longer be able to celebrate a mass or perform any other sacrament. Various acts or characteristics conferred irregularity, such as physical disability, illegitimate birth, or criminal or infamous acts. What concerns us here is irregularity that resulted from *defectus lenitatis* or defect of mildheartedness. Anyone who was even peripherally involved in a criminal trial

---

[104] The good thief had cross-confessional appeal. Woltersdorff's entire collection of Lutheran execution sermons was entitled *The Thief on the Cross*. Pastor Struensee comforted Uhlin, for example, by emphasizing that the good thief was the very first Christian to be saved by Christ's sacrifice. Woltersdorff, ed., *Schächer*, vol. 1, 650. On Dismas as a model of repentance for Catholics in general and condemned criminals in particular, see the handbook on pastoral care for condemned criminals by Gilbert Bauer, cathedral canon of the Premonstratensian abbey of Marchtal. Gilbert Baur, P. *Gilbert Baur Des Heil. Prämonstratenser-Ordens Chorherrn ... Viertägige Zubereitung Eines Zum Tode Verurtheilten Malefikanten* (Augsburg: Rieger, 1785), and further examples in Chap. 7.

[105] On the salvific effect of torture and pain suffered during execution for Catholics, see the description of the executions of three Austrian soldiers executed for host desecration in Chap. 5.

[106] See the discussion of Catholic soteriology and pastoral care for condemned criminals in Chap. 7.

that resulted in capital punishment, or in bloody punishments to the body involving mutilation, contracted irregularity from defect of mildness. This included judges, witnesses, accusers, court scribes, and of course, the executioner and his men.[107] It derived from the principle *Ecclesia non sitit sanguinem* (The church does not shed [human] blood). This did not mean that officeholders involved in such criminal trials acted immorally or sinfully. Rather, it meant that a person who performed such tasks demonstrated a lack of peacefulness, mildness, and tenderness that were required of members of the clergy.[108]

Irregularity had far-reaching and long-lasting practical consequences for how Catholic clergy interacted with secular officials in the context of criminal justice. Catholic priests who performed prison ministry took care to insulate their sacerdotal functions from the criminal trial. In 1689 the celebrated Capuchin friar Martin von Cochem (1630–1712), for example, warned priests tending to criminal defendants to wait to take the criminal's confession until the trial was over, so that judicial confession and the sacrament of confession remained distinct. Furthermore, if the prisoner recanted his or her judicial confession during sacramental confession to the priest, the cleric should not tell the judge, so as not to break the seal of confession.[109]

Lutheran clergy made no such efforts to separate judicial and pastoral processes. Unencumbered by concern about irregularity, or the seal of confession, Protestant clergy willingly assisted government prosecutors. They did not hesitate to pressure defendants to make a criminal confession, even if such a confession would ensure their death sentence. The infanticide prosecution of Anna Emblin in Nuremberg in 1644 illustrates how this played out in practice. Emblin, twenty-four, was on trial for throwing her newborn infant into the privy. She was treated in the city hospital for complications after the birth and subsequently transferred to the dungeon. During her interrogation, Emblin said that she was unsure if the child had been born dead or alive. Confirming a live birth was necessary to justify a death sentence. Normally prosecutors would now have

---

[107] William Fanning, "Irregularity." *The Catholic Encyclopedia.* Vol. 8. New York: Robert Appleton Company, 1910. 29 Aug. 2022 <http://www.newadvent.org/cathen/08170a.htm>.

[108] Paul Hinschius Paul, *Das Kirchenrecht der Katholiken und Protestanten in Deutschland*, vol. 1 (Berlin: I. Guttentag, 1869), 26-29.

[109] Martin von Cochem, *Das Grössere Krancken-Buch, Sampt vorhergehender Fürbereitung zu einem Seeligen End* (Frankfurt a.M.: Johann Melchior Bencard, 1689), 421-424.

ordered judicial torture to procure the confession necessary for conviction. In this case, however, torture was not an option because of Emblin's fragile physical condition. So the city government enlisted Lutheran ministers to apply a different kind of torture. Prosecutors tasked two clergymen responsible for prison ministry to move Emblin's heart and conscience by telling her, falsely, that the council had already imposed her death sentence. The clergymen promised Emblin that if she made a full confession now, the court would spare her the infamy of putting her head on a spike by the ravenstone. The clergymen saw no conflict between the prosecutor's goals and their pastoral mission. By lying to Emblin they were saving her soul. After they secured Emblin's criminal confession, they prepared her spiritually for death. During her execution procession she commended her soul to her creator, her pastor reported. "Without doubt," he opined, she would be "a child and heir of eternal life."[110]

This type of cooperation with the magistrate during a criminal trial would have been unthinkable for a Catholic cleric. Catholic precautions against irregularity went beyond mere non-participation in judicial processes, however. In a decree from 1765, Maria Theresia expressed her displeasure that Catholic clergy obstructed criminal justice, to the detriment of public good, because of an unjustified fear of irregularity. Catholic clergy refused to allow the exhumation of bodies from graveyards in order to establish the cause of death. This prevented prosecutors from establishing the *corpus delicti* in homicide cases. Thus, the claim of irregularity became a shield for murderers, allowing the most serious criminals to go

---

[110] Hartmut H. Frommer, "Jämmerliche Mordgeschichten. Vom Umgang des Rats 'mit gottlosen Raaben-Müttern welches ihre in Unehren erloffenen Kinder umzubringen sich unterstanden'," *Mittheilung des Vereins für die Geschichte der Stadt Nürnberg*, 99 (2012): 103-104. Emblin's pastor was Johann Hagendorn, whose diary of the prison ministry he provided has now been published. Peter Schuster and Andrea Bendlage, eds., *Die Letzten Tage der Zum Tode Verurteilten. Das Tagebuch des Nürnberger Gefangenenseelsorgers Johann Hagendorn 1605-1620* (Münster: Verlag für Regionalgeschichte, 2022). Thomas Robisheaux describes similar active assistance by Lutheran clergy during the criminal trial of accused witch Anna Schmieg in 1672. The preacher responsible for Schmieg's pastoral care personally attended criminal interrogations conducted by the magistrate and participated in her questioning. Thomas Robisheaux, *The Last Witch of Langenburg Murder in a German Village* (New York: W.W. Norton, 2009), 290. This type of cooperation would have been unthinkable for a Catholic cleric.

free and go on to commit further crimes.[111] Offering asylum to fugitives from the law was a traditional prerogative of the Catholic church,[112] but Catholic clergy often went further, actively assisting fugitives accused of capital offenses to escape.[113]

Writing in 1812, the criminologist Ludwig Pfister observed that Catholic clergy at the scaffold would keep praying with the condemned criminal indefinitely, because their "estate" as ordained priests would not allow them to stop praying on their own accord, because this would have the effect of shortening the life of the poor sinner, putting them at risk of irregularity. Therefore, the executioner should interrupt the prayer and seize the poor sinner from the priest, so that the execution could proceed, Pfister recommended.[114]

Before a criminal was apprehended, and during the criminal trial, Catholic priests played a different ritual role than Protestant pastors. Protestant ministers actively assisted in criminal trials, while Catholic clerics insulated themselves from, and at times even obstructed, judicial processes. This did not mean, however, that the early modern Catholic church questioned the legitimacy or necessity of criminal justice, or of capital punishment. Once a secular court had imposed a death sentence on a malefactor in its custody, Catholic clergy went to work to bring about the criminal's "conversion" with as much zeal as their Lutheran counterparts.

Suicide by proxy posed a significant challenge to both Catholic and Protestant clergies. Lutheran execution sermons engaged with the problematic of suicide by proxy directly. In the execution sermon of Catharina Uhlin discussed above, Pastor Struensee pointed out to her that she was in fact guilty of suicide. The pastor of Johanna Martauschin, twenty-three, an inmate in the Spandau house of correction in Berlin, who faced

---

[111] *Sammlung der älteren Kaiserlich-Königlichen Landesfürstlichen Gesetze und Verordnungen in Publico-Ecclesiasticis:...vom Jahre 1518 bis 1740*, vol. 1, II (Vienna: Johann Thomas Edlen von Trattnern, 1785), 248-253.

[112] Karl Härter, "Asyl für die Rechtsgeschichte," *Rechtsgeschichte Rg* 5 (2004): 235-243.

[113] Maria Theresia's government reprimanded Franciscans outside Prague for helping a self-confessed murderer escape to the Palatinate in 1750. *Sammlung... in Publico-Ecclesiasticis*, 133-134. This was not an isolated incident. See the discussion of the 1783 murder trial of Adelheid Zieglerin in Chap. 7, pp.

[114] Ludwig Pfister, *Aktenmäßige Geschichte der Räuberbanden an den beiden Ufern des Mains* (Heidelberg: Gottlieb Braun, 1812), 312.

execution in 1746 for bludgeoning a small child to death, did the same. "She committed the murder due to weariness with life, she murdered a child and not herself, because she believed that the child would now surely be saved, whereas she as a suicide would have gone to the devil, but now she could still be converted," Martauschin told him. He admonished her that "she had wantonly abused God's grace, and that she was indeed a self-murderer."[115] Their suicides by proxy did not preclude Uhlin's or Martauschin's salvation, of course, because like people who had attempted suicide, or suicides who did not die immediately, they both could still repent and be forgiven. Indeed, both pastors assured their readers that the women had died in a state of grace.

Another fundamental theological error, from the point of view of Lutheran pastors, was that perpetrators of suicide by proxy believed that they could expiate their sins on the scaffold. They spoke a language of payment and exchange that contradicted official Lutheran doctrine that the believer was a passive vessel of grace. Awaiting her execution for cutting the throat of a four-year-old girl Wernigeroda in 1745, Gertrude Magdalena Bremmelin exclaimed: "Let me do good penance here, let me pay with my blood, let me make up for everything with my death!" It was an error, her pastor instructed her, that one could do penance for one's sins through works or suffering.[116] More than two centuries after Luther, pastors were still struggling to inculcate the doctrine of salvation by grace alone.

Catholic clergy who ministered to condemned criminals presumably could and did admonish suicidal child murderers and iconoclasts for their suicidal intent, but they could not argue with the logic of expiating one's sins on the scaffold. Catholic theologians believed, after all, that all Christians were obligated to do penance for their sins, in this life or in purgatory. Catholic handbooks on pastoral care for condemned criminals explicitly taught that poor sinners could expiate all or some of their sins by willingly enduring the pain and suffering of their executions,[117] though for sinners to orchestrate their own executions was not what they had in mind. The one Catholic execution sermon for a perpetrator of suicide by proxy

---

[115] Woltersdorff, ed., *Schächer*, vol. 1 (1761), 940.

[116] Anon., "Die Hirten-Treue Christi, welche er … an Gertrude Magdalene Bremmelin, einer vorsetzlichen Kindermörderin, erwiesen: … nebst einer auf dem Rabenstein gehaltenen Rede, in: Woltersdorff, ed., *Schächer*, vol. 1 (1761), 414.

[117] For example, Cochem, *Krancken-Buch*, 419-454. See discussion in Chap. 7.

that I have found avoided addressing the underlying logic of the crime entirely. Instead, the execution sermon for Maria Anna Mayrin, who had cut the throat of a three-year-old girl in Augsburg in 1783, warned against the dangers of romantic love and the inordinate passions it inspired which had led her astray in the first place.[118] The silence of Catholic clergy on suicide by proxy may reflect a more general Catholic reticence to talk about all forms of suicide.

The question of religious confession bedevils the study of suicide in general. Long before Emile Durkheim formulated the so-called first law of sociology that Protestants commit suicide more often than Catholics, the question of suicide rates became a subject of confessional polemics and remains a matter of controversy among historians today.[119] Erik Midelfort has shown that educated Germans, both Protestants and Catholics, were convinced as early as the sixteenth century that suicide was more common among Protestants. Martin Luther saw "despair" as a necessary step in the process of salvation—believers had to face their own utter inadequacy in the face of God's law before they could become recipients of grace. In this hazardous stage believers were particularly vulnerable to demonic temptation and might fall victim to religious melancholy. This understanding of the salvation process led Lutheran theologians to expect and to be more understanding of suicidal tribulations among their flock. Catholics, conversely, saw the supposed high incidence of suicide among Protestants as confirmation of the impoverishment and error of the Lutheran religion, gleefully declaring that when Lutheran reformers jettisoned the sacraments and traditional religious practices, they left their believers defenseless in the face of the devil. "The apparent rise of Protestant suicide rates," Midelfort concludes, "has largely been an artifact of prior social and religious attitudes," rather than a reflection of an underlying social reality.[120]

---

[118] [P. Bonaventurea Lueger], *Heilsame Ermahnung über die ausschweifende Liebe junger Leute in einer Sittenrede...., als Maria Anna Mayrinn...den 8. Hornung des 1783 Jahrs durch das Schwert vom Leben zum Tod hingerichtet... wurde* ([Augsburg]: Johann Bernhard Stadelberer, [1783]). StStBA, Aug 1477.

[119] David Lederer, "Selbstmord im frühneuzeitlichen Deutschland: Klischee und Gechichte," *Psychotherapie* 4 (1999): 206-212.

[120] H.C.Erik Midelfort, "Religious Melancholy," p. 51. See also David Lederer, "Verzweiflung im alten Reich. Selbstmord während der 'Kleinen Eiszeit'," in *Kulturelle Konsequenzen der 'Kleinen Eiszeit'*, eds. Wolfgang Behringer, Hartmut Lehmann and Christian Pfister (Göttingen: Vandenhoeck & Ruprecht, 2005), 255-280.

Some Catholic trial records reflect an unwillingness on a communal level to explicitly talk about suicide or suicidal ideation. This is particularly clear in the murder trial of Eva Lizfellnerin. In November 1761, Lizfellnerin, a young peasant woman from upper Austria, threw a two-year-old boy into the rapids of the Traun River and then turned herself in to authorities requesting her execution. The investigation revealed that months before the murder she told her family about her distress. "If only she weren't alive," she told her husband, "if only she were gone from the world."[121] She repeated these laments to him, her stepbrother, her sister-in-law, and her mother on several occasions. And yet, her relatives all testified that they had observed no signs of depression in her prior to the murder. Their response is an example of what Lyndal Roper has described as "a strong cultural hostility to feelings of depression."[122] It may be that this cultural hostility was most pronounced among Catholics. The association of depression, suicide, and the devil may have prompted a reaction of denial among family members of a suicidal person. In Lizlfellnerin's case it appears that cultural prohibitions against suicide were so strong that the people around her were simply unwilling or unable to register her despondent utterances as threats of suicide. They advised her to work and pray.

Lizfellnerin's interrogator, by contrast, did not avoid the topic of suicide. He elicited from her an explicit explanation of her motive. "Did she intend to get rid of her own life by means of the child's death?" Her answer revealed her contractual thinking: "She simply thought, if the child dies, it will cost my life too, that cannot be avoided."[123] (Here the scribe switched from the third person, the standard in interrogation protocols, to the first person and underlined the text to indicate that these were Lizfellnerin's exact words.) Other Upper Austrian criminal trials, however, suggest a reluctance to explicitly name suicidal intent as the murder motive. In May 1729 Georg Edlauer, thirty-six, an upper Austrian peasant, subject of the Benedictine Abbey of Kremsmünster, drowned his nine-year-old cousin Georg, who had been in his care for the past four years. Edlauer's neighbors described him as devout, upright, and honorable, but prone to mental disturbance and fits of violence. He was a regu-

---

[121] Her husband testified that Lizlfellnerin told him "wanns nur gleich nicht leben dörffte, ...wanns nur von der Welt weg wäre." OÖLA, HA Puchheim, Schachtel 43, Nr. 32, Eva Lizlfellnerin, 1762.

[122] Roper, *Witch Craze*, 93.

[123] "Wann das Kind sterben mues, so gilts mein Leben auch, es ist hernach wie der wöll." OÖLA, HA Puchheim, Schachtel 43, Nr. 32, Eva Lizlfellnerin, 1762.

lar churchgoer who liked to pray and went to confession often. He loved the murdered boy dearly. In the days before the murder he suffered afflictions. He had a vivid dream where a monstrance bathed in light appeared to him. He awoke and went to pray before the crucifix and figurine of the Virgin Mary in his living room. Finding no relief, he left home at midnight to walk to church, where he arrived at two in the morning. He wanted to give confession, but the priest turned him away. The next day he walked back to church with the young boy, whom he ordered to carry a crucifix as if in a procession, and gave confession. The following night, he got up and drowned the boy. Asked why he murdered the boy, he said: "he had no peace, the idea came to him to murder the boy."[124] The religious framing of the murder makes it likely that Georg Edlauer was attempting suicide by proxy, yet he was unable to articulate his suicidal intent, nor did his interrogator press him to do so.

A Crime of Women

Contemporaries perceived suicide by proxy as predominantly a female crime. Almost thirty years before the jurist Karl Hommel identified the typical perpetrators as "weak females of poor education" in 1779,[125] the city of Lübeck described suicidal child murder as specifically a crime of women. An edict issued in 1747 decried numerous examples over the past several years "of Godless, *wicked women*, who for various malicious and trivial reasons, such as: they felt offended by other people, or their imagined marriage plans went awry, or they felt deprived of the means of subsistence…, out of highly sinful weariness of life, they maliciously attack and gruesomely murder innocent children."[126]

These contemporary observations that suicide by proxy was largely a crime of women reflected social reality. The case studies of Hamburg and Frankfurt in subsequent chapters, where I reconstruct gender patterns over time, confirm that the majority of perpetrators were women, overwhelmingly so in the late seventeenth and early eighteenth centuries.[127] The predominance of women among perpetrators of suicide by proxy is

---

[124] "Er habe…keine Ruhe gehabt, es seye ihm in Sinn gekhomben dz er dz Buebl umbbringen solle." StiftAK, Gerichts Akten (Kriminal) 1721-1729, Georg Edlauer 1729.
[125] Hommel, *Rhapsodia*, 117-120.
[126] StadtAL, 8_1_725_229_r. Emphasis mine.
[127] See Chap. 4, Chap. 6, and Chap. 7.

remarkable, given that men generally outnumber women among recorded cases of direct suicide by a significant ratio, both historically and in the present day. Two-thirds of recorded suicides in Schleswig and Holstein in the seventeenth and eighteenth centuries were male.[128] In early modern Zurich, 75% of recorded suicides were male.[129] In Geneva men outnumbered women among recorded suicides by two to one during the whole of the early modern period, though the gender gap became most pronounced for the period after 1750.[130] Two-thirds of recorded suicides in seventeenth-century Sweden were men.[131] Men made up two-thirds of recorded suicides in early modern England.[132] Seventy-seven percent of recorded suicides in eighteenth-century Paris were men.[133] Intriguingly, these sex ratios have not changed much from the late Middle Ages to the present. According to Vera Lind, the female suicide rate "of approximately one third constitutes a stable phenomenon over centuries," in Schleswig-Holstein, Germany, Europe, and the United States.[134]

Suicide statistics in general are inherently problematic. Vexed questions such as whether the number of suicides actually increased over the course of the early modern era, whether Protestants really did commit suicide more than Catholics, or whether men really did commit suicide more often than women are ultimately unanswerable. Rising rates of recorded suicides might result from more efficient governmental surveillance and prosecutorial zeal.[135] They might reflect changing methods of suicide. Suicide by gunshot allowed for a more conclusive finding than suicide by drowning, for example. Such greater conclusiveness would also impact recorded rates of suicide for men and women, since suicide by gun was gendered male, whereas suicide by drowning was gendered female. Higher numbers could also be an effect of better forensics, in cases of poisoning.

---

[128] Vera Lind, *Selbstmord in der Frühen Neuzeit. Diskurs, Lebenswelt, und kultureller Wandel am Beispiel derr Herzogtümer Schleswig und Holstein* (Göttingen: Vandenhoeck & Ruprecht, 1999), 191-193.

[129] Lind, *Selbstmord*, 192. Lind calculated this percentage on the basis of Schär's data.

[130] Watt, *Choosing Death*, 33-35.

[131] Riikka Miettinen, *Suicide, Law, and Community in Early Modern Sweden* (Cham, Switzerland: Palgrave Macmillan, 2019), 260.

[132] Michael MacDonald and Terence Murphy, *Sleepless Souls: Suicide in Early Modern England* (Oxford: Oxford University Press, 1990), 247.

[133] Jeffrey Merrick, "Patterns and Prosecution of Suicide in Eighteenth-Century Paris," *Historical Reflections* 16 (1989): 1-53.

[134] Lind, *Selbstmord*, 202.

[135] Miettinen, *Suicide*, 135-139.

Rising rates most likely also reflect a greater willingness to recognize and acknowledge suicides—which is in itself an important historical change. The difference between suicide by proxy and direct suicide, of course, is that there is no dark figure for suicide by proxy. Suicide by proxy only worked if the perpetrators revealed themselves to authorities. That was the point of the crime.

The predominance of women among suicidal child murderers runs counter to a commonplace in the historiography on crime: That female criminality was less serious than that of men and that women rarely used physical force or committed acts of violence.[136] The violence associated with suicide by proxy contrasts with the relatively non-violent methods infanticidal mothers typically chose to kill their newborns or that suicidal women chose to kill themselves. In Vienna the most frequent method of infanticide consisted of giving birth into the privy, in which case the infanticidal mother would never touch her infant.[137] Other common methods were neglect and suffocation. Classic infanticide almost never involved the shedding of blood. "What characterized these methods of killing from the perspective of the women," according to Otto Ulbricht, "was the avoidance of violence. These women understood violence as the application of force, the use of instruments or other objects, or in their words: to actively lay a hand on [the child] (*Handanlegen*)."[138]

Female suicides were similarly unbloody. Female suicides in Schleswig and Holstein almost never used weapons. Whereas 15% of men committed suicide by cutting their own throat, women rarely did so. [Image 2.5] Half of all female suicides chose drowning, a passive form of death that left the body physically intact.[139] By contrast, suicides by proxy were often characterized by extreme violence, literally overkill. The most frequent murder method was cutting the victim's throat. The autopsy of a nine-year-old girl murdered by a maidservant in Nuremberg in 1709 gives an idea of the extraordinary violence employed in these killings. The inspection showed that the girl's throat had been slashed, "severing the wind-

---

[136] Otto Ulbricht, "Einleitung," in *Von Huren und Rabenmüttern. Weibliche Kriminalität in der Frühen Neuzeit*, ed. Otto Ulbricht (Cologne: Böhlau, 1995), 1-37.

[137] For example, Eva. N, *WD*, Nr. 501, 22 May 1708. Appollonia N., *WD*, Nr. 584, 6 March 1709. Anna Maria N, *WD*, Nr. 612, 14 June 1709. Maria Magdalene N., *WD*, Nr. 703, 29 April 1709. Catharina P., *WD*, Nr. 2, 5 January 1726. Anna Maria E., *WD*, Nr. 46, 7 June 1727.

[138] Ulbricht, "Kindmörderinnen vor Gericht," 75.

[139] Lind, *Selbstmord*, 325-331.

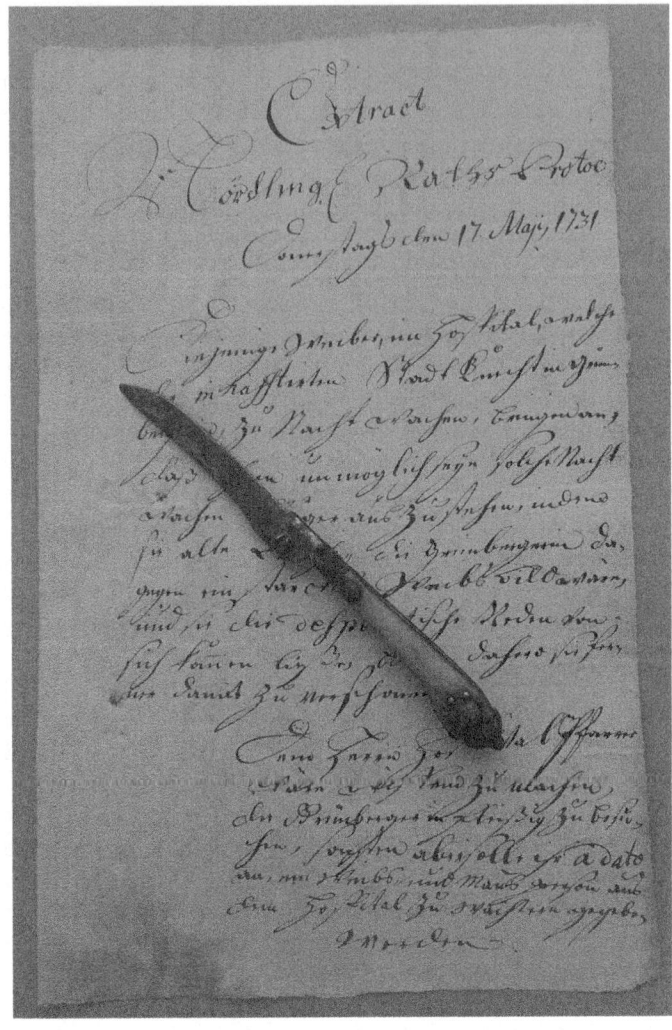

Image 2.5 Knife. 1731. Stadtarchiv Nördlingen. R 39 F2 Fasc 9 Selbstmord, Ao 1731

pipe and all blood vessels right down to the vertebrae, with a knife repeatedly drawn back and forth."[140] In 1723 Ursula Waser, the Wuerttemberg peasant discussed above, killed her three-year-old victim with six blows to the neck with an axe. Blood at the scene spattered five feet (*"fünf Schu"*) high.[141] In 1778 "C.E.N.", a servant woman from Königsberg, managed to decapitate a four-year-old girl with one stroke of the knife.[142]

RATIONALITY, INSTRUMENTALITY, RITUAL, AND SACRIFICE

This level of violence might lead one to conclude that these murders occurred as acts of rage, as impulse crimes, in a "paroxysm of melancholy" as one *consilium* put it.[143] But that was not the case. These killings were characterized by a high level of premeditation and preparation. Women who committed such murders often planned for days or weeks, scoping out suitable victims. They used ruse to gain access to their victims. In 1749, Dorothea Hermlohrin, twenty-one, was on the look-out for a suitable child victim in Vienna. She encountered two little boys. The younger boy was five years old. She gave the older boy money to go buy pastries. Then she lured the five-year-old out into the fields to pick flowers for the Corpus Christi procession the next day. After picking flowers, she took the boy on her lap as if to delouse him and cut his throat.[144] In 1783 Margaretha N., a prostitute from Munich, befriended a mother of two children, invited her for beer, and chatted with her and her small daughter, until she convinced the mother to let her take the girl along on some errands. Out of the mother's sight, she took the girl to the Isar River and drowned her.[145]

---

[140] StAN, Nürnberger Amts- und Standbücher 225, fo. 57r-58v, Christina Forgerin, March 26, 1709.

[141] HStAS, A 209/1773, Ursula Waser, August 27, 1723.

[142] Johann Daniel Metzger, *Gerichtlich-medicininsche Beobachtungen* (Königsberg: Johann Jacob Kantner, 1780), 69.

[143] HstAS, A 209/1179, Margaretha Mayrin, 1703. A consilium from the legal faculty at the University of Tübingen recommended that Margaretha Mayrin be spared the death penalty for the murder of a small girl, since the killing happened during "a paroxysm of melancholy in the second degree."

[144] Anon., *Wohl-verdientes Todtes-Urtheil, so..den 29 Juli...1749 an einer ledigen Weibs-Persohn, Nahmens Dorothea H. ... vollzogen wird* (Vienna: Maria Eva Schilgin, [1749]). ÖNB, Cod. 8363, N. 124, p. 15, 29 July 1749.

[145] *Wohlverdientes Todesurtheil nebst einer Moralrede der Margaretha N. vulgo Schilicheten Grödl* ([Munich]: [1783]).

Perpetrators of suicide by proxy frequently resorted to this kind of deception, which led jurists to condemn them as particularly cold-blooded and treacherous. In Leipzig in 1774 a woman identified only as "Schröterin" suffered the exacerbated penalty of having her body exposed on the wheel after her beheading, a rare penalty for women, because her judges considered her killing of a four-year-old girl to be a *Meuchelmord*, a particularly cowardly and treacherous type of murder. In order to gain access to her victim, she gave the girl's mother some money to go buy pears for the girl. In the mother's absence, she cut the girl's throat.[146]

Where can we situate suicide by proxy in the history of homicide? In his analysis of homicidal violence in Amsterdam from the fifteenth through the nineteenth centuries, Pieter Spierenburg categorizes killings along two axes: The first to distinguish impulsive violence from planned or "rational" violence, and the second to distinguish ritualistic, expressive violence from instrumental violence. According to Spierenburg, late medieval homicides tended to be at once more impulsive and ritualistic, while over time rational violence superseded impulsive violence, and instrumental killings came to predominate over ritualistic ones.[147] Categorizing suicide by proxy along these two axes, one finds that the violence was clearly planned and "rational" rather than impulsive. The instrumental aspect of the killings is quite clear. In a majority of cases the killers achieved their stated goal of orchestrating their own execution. But these killings were as expressive and ritualistic as they were instrumental.

Just like the mythical killings of the blood libel, the killings associated with suicide by proxy unfolded according to a particular liturgy of violence. In the blood libel, groups of Jewish men were believed to murder male Christian children as a form of religious sacrifice. Women were only involved on the periphery. In suicides by proxy, individual Christians acting alone, predominantly women, murdered Christian children of both sexes. They sometimes also killed adults, often in institutional settings—houses of correction, hospitals—where they might have been constrained in their choice of victims. But even here they preferred victims whom they perceived as somehow childlike—the deaf, dumb, and simple-minded. In 1691 Maria Helena Längin, an inmate in the house of correction in

---

[146] Hommel, *Rhapsodia*, vol. 5, 1449-1456.

[147] Pieter Spierenburg, "Faces of Violence: Homicide Trends and Cultural Meanings, Amsterdam, 1431-1816," *Journal of Social History* 27 (1994): 701-716.

Nuremberg, chose a deaf woman as her victim.[148] In 1720 Anna Dorothee Voßin, a prisoner in the workhouse in Helmstädt murdered an eighteen-year-old deaf and dumb girl. She lured the girl, who presumably was being cared for in the institution, into her cell and cut her throat.[149]

Perpetrators of suicide by proxy understood their child murder as a religious offering. As in the child killings associated with Massacre of the Holy Innocents or the blood libel, the child victims of suicide by proxy were constructed as martyrs. A closer look at the interactions between victim and killer will illustrate the ritualistic and sacrificial nature of these murders. Stereotypical elements of the crime emerge clearly in Agnes Catharina Schickin's trial for the murder of seven-year-old Hans Michael Furch in Lutheran Wuerttemberg in May 1704. Schickin, thirty-one, a servant woman, wandered into Hans Michael's village in the morning. She saw four, in her words, "beautiful little boys"[150] playing together by the roadside. She approached them and asked for directions to a nearby town. One of the boys, Hans Michael, son of the local cow-herder, said he knew the way. She offered him a gift and asked him to walk with her. The three other boys wanted to come too, but she turned them away. Agnes and the seven-year-old walked off into the forest alone.

Over the course of the day, Schickin took the boy deep into the forest. They encountered several passersby, who later testified that they saw them walking, talking, and sitting down together. In the afternoon, a passing messenger saw the boy sitting down while she knelt before him, delousing him. Such tenderness ended abruptly. When Hans Michael wanted to return home in the evening, she threw him violently to the ground. Begging for mercy, the boy recited his prayers, the "Our Father," and the creed among them. This was repeated three times. Twice his prayers moved her. She even helped the trembling boy to his feet, but the third time she felt "embittered." Throwing the boy to the ground again, she drew her knife, and cut his throat so deeply that, as she later described, she could "look down into his neck." As his "bright blood" flowed, she said to him: "May God protect you, you sweet angel, you are an angel before God." She announced the murder in the next town and was taken into custody. The child was now "saved," she told interrogators. She had only

---

[148] StAN, Nürnberger Amts- und Standbücher, 225, fo. 12r-13v.
[149] Augustin von Leyser, *Meditationes ad Pandectas* (Leipzig: Meisnerus, 1741-1776), 491-492.
[150] "...gar schöne Büblein..." HStAS, A 209/1806, Agnes Catherina Schickin, 1704.

done it so that she herself could "leave the world" as well; "now the hangman would surely dispatch her."¹⁵¹

Affectionate intimacy, as when Schickin deloused Hans Michael, was a recurring motif in these murders. Margaretha Mayrin's murder of her neighbors' two-year-old daughter in Württemberg in 1703 is a case in point. She dropped by her neighbor, a shoemaker, to borrow some wire to repair her shoes. As she was waiting for the wire, she picked up the toddler, kissed and hugged her, and then took the girl home with her for a visit. After a while, the girl's mother came by to give Mayrin a gift of some milk and to pick up her daughter. Mayrin, in turn, gave the mother some bread and persuaded her to let the girl stay longer. Subsequent to this exchange of gifts, alone with the child again, Mayrin smashed the girl's head against a wall, shattering her skull.¹⁵² Such gifts of food are a common theme, though typically the murderers gave or shared food with their child victim. After she had plied the mother with beer and had gained access to her victim, the prostitute Margaretha N. fed the little girl a bowl of oatmeal just before she drowned her in the Isar.¹⁵³ In 1753 the soldier Daniel Völkner from Mecklenburg shared his evening meal with the little girl who was his intended victim, just before he cut her throat.¹⁵⁴ Sometimes gifts of food were instrumental, a means to draw in their child victim, but they also had ritual meaning. These gifts of food or shared meal are evocative of the "last meal" (*Henkersmahlzeit*) served to condemned criminals before their execution and served the same symbolic purpose. In the days leading up to their execution, "poor sinners" were provided with whatever foods they desired, and in some regions, the condemned shared a meal with judges and executioner. By accepting special food, the condemned expressed that they were at peace with the judges and agreed to play their scripted role during their upcoming execution.¹⁵⁵ Similarly, when perpetrators of suicide by proxy offered food to their victims, such gifts were designed to elicit and express their victims' consent.

---

¹⁵¹ "...das Kindt seye einweg seelig, sie habe es nur gethan, damit sie von der Welt komme, der Henkher werde sie anietzo schon hinweg thun...." HStAS, A 209/1806, Agnes Catherina Schickin, 1704.

¹⁵² HStAS, A 209/1179, Margaretha Mayrin, 1703.

¹⁵³ *Todesurtheil...der Margaretha N. Schilicheten Grödl.*

¹⁵⁴ Anon., "Geschichte des Inquisiten Daniel Völkners, aus den Kriminalakten gezogen," in: *Magazin zur Erfahrungsseelenkunde,* vol. 1, (1783), 97-102.

¹⁵⁵ Stuart, *Defiled Trades,* 175. Hans von Hentig, *Vom Ursprung der Henkersmahlzeit* (Tübingen: J.C.B. Mohr (Paul Siebeck), 1958).

The consent of the murdered child was a recurring theme in the killers' confessions. In his analysis of early modern English murder cases, Malcolm Gaskill has shown that witnesses in murder trials often testified to implausible if not impossible events, such as cruentation, the bleeding of a victim's body in the presence of the murderer. Gaskill sees this as an example of "fiction in the archives" of the sort that Natalie Zemon Davis has discussed.[156] Davis argued that early modern pardon seekers "fictionalized" their account of events, not as a deliberate falsehood, but to craft their "narrative" to give moral meaning to their petition. The testimony of murder witnesses served a similar function, Gaskill suggests.[157] Philippe Aries has described early modern death as "a ritual organized by the dying person himself who presided over it and knew its protocol."[158] In murder cases, Gaskill argues, such ritual orchestration was performed by witnesses on the victim's behalf. Witnesses testified that murder victims had behaved well in their last moments, that they had died a good death.[159] In contrast to much of the homicidal violence in early modern Europe, which took the form of ritualized conflicts among men in public, in the streets, in taverns, and in the market place,[160] suicide by proxy typically had in common with infanticide that victim and murderer were alone. In cases of suicide by proxy, there were no witnesses present who might testify to the victim's good death. Accordingly, it was the murderers themselves who testified to their victims' demeanor at the moment of death, structuring their narrative to emphasize their victims' consent and sanctification.

In 1783 Maria Anna Mayrin from Augsburg described her murder of a three-year-old girl. As she was preparing to cut the girl's throat, she removed the girl's hood and scarf and asked her if she wanted to die. The child answered yes.[161] In 1786 Katherine Häuslerin, subject of the Holy Cross Benedictine Abbey in Donauwörth, testified that just before she drowned her seven-year-old daughter and eleven-month-old son in the Danube, she had the girl kneel and pray for a good death. Häuslerin asked her daughter to plead for her when she came before God, so that she could

---

[156] Natalie Zemon Davis, *Fiction in the Archives: Pardon Tales and Their Tellers in Sixteenth-Century France* (Cambridge: Polity, 1988).

[157] Malcolm Gaskill, "Reporting Murder: Fiction in the Archives in early modern England," *Social History* 23 (1998): 3-5.

[158] Quoted in Gaskill, "Reporting Murder," 25.

[159] Gaskill, "Reporting Murder," 25.

[160] Joachim Eibach, "Städtische Gewaltkriminalität im Ancien Regime. Frankfurt am Main im Europäischen Kontext," *Zeitschrift für Historische Forschung* 25 (1998): 359-382.

[161] *Peinliches Urtheil...über Maria Anna Mayrin*.

join them there soon. Häuslerin herself prayed: "I give into your hands my two children. Please give me the mercy, that I can confess my sins, and give my life for them."[162] Moments before their mother threw them in the river, the little girl kissed her brother and said, "little brother, now we must die."[163]

Häuslerin's testimony, just like Schickin's testimony that her seven-year-old victim recited three sets of prayers three times as she violently assaulted him, attested to their victims' good death. It also established a parallel between the liturgy of the murders and the liturgy of public execution they themselves wished to undergo. No execution pamphlet was complete without describing the condemned criminal's prayers and pious last utterances on the scaffold.[164] The execution of Gertrude Magdalena Bremmelin for cutting the throat of a four-year-old girl Wernigeroda in 1745 is typical. She exclaimed, "Oh Lord Jesus, Mercy! Mercy! Mercy!" as she received the stroke of the sword.[165]

Execution pamphlets echoed the killers' sanctification of their victims, in both text and image, explicitly portraying the children as martyrs, but also established parallels between their murders and the execution of their killers. When Jeremias Bertz, an Augsburg bag-maker, cut the throat of his eighteen-week-old-baby daughter Maria Magdalena in 1740, his deed inspired no fewer than four publications, including several engravings of the dead child and numerous murder ballads circulating in manuscripts, replete with the folksong melodies they were set to. One of the printed ballads publicized his motive:

> *Und weil ich vor Verdruß recht müd war dises Lebens*
> *So kam mir in den Sinn, begehe einen Mord.*
> *Seht was der Satan kan, es war auch nicht vergebens,*
> *Ich folgte ihm so gleich, und thate also fort*
> *Was ich mit Weh und Ach anjetzo stets bereue,*
> *Mit Bitte, daß mir GOTT die grosse Sünd verzeyhe.*[166]

---

[162] Häuslerin prayed: "Himlischer Vater, ich schenke dir in deine hand meine 2 kind, und gib mir die Gnad, daß ich meine Sünden möge beichten und mein Leben für sie geben, weil ich sie ums Leben gebracht." The little girl said: "Komm liber brüdel, jetzt müßen wir sterben." FÖWAH, Criminalsachen Zusum, VI. 115. 11, Katherina Häuslerin, 1786.

[163] Anon., "Katherine Häuslerin," *Magazin zur Erfahrungsseelenkunde*, vol. 6, (1788), 212-214.

[164] Evans, *Rituals of Retribution*, 73-86.

[165] Anon., "Hirten-Treue Christi," 471.

[166] Wuerttembergische Landesbibliothek, Crim.R.qt.K.46-3: *Der in den Todt gehende,... bussfertige Vatter, oder Arme Sünder Jeremias Bertz,... Als derselbe den 31. May 1740 in Augsburg mit dem Schwerdt vom Leben zum Todt gebracht worden* (Augsburg: J. J. Baumgartner, 1740).

And because I was weary of this life,
It entered my mind, commit a murder.
See what Satan can do, and it was not in vain,
I obeyed him immediately, and did right away
What I now lament and repent,
With the plea, that GOD may forgive my grave sin.

Another ballad, entitled "The merely 18-week-old Martyr Maria Magdalena Speaking from the Grave," enacts a conversation between the father and his murdered child. The child, an innocent "lamb" now singing with a choir of angels, laments her father's deed but also exhorts him to repent so she might be reunited with him in heaven.[167] Maria Magdalena was a Protestant child, but the images of her dead body resemble "the corporeal sensuality of pious suffering" that R. Po Hsia has described in the seventeenth-century engravings of several alleged victims of Jewish ritual murder, images "that brings to mind Rubenesque cherubs, redemptive flesh in the sensuous iconography of baroque Catholicism."[168] [Image 2.6] Simon of Trent was often portrayed with the instruments of his martyrdom—evoking the *Arma Christi*, "the weapons of Christ," that is, the instruments of the passion (cross, nails, lance, crown of thorns).[169] Similarly the murder weapon, the knife, figures prominently beneath another portrayal of Maria Magdalena. In "the anatomical-surgical rendering"[170] of the image the viewer can look into the wound it inflicted [Image 2.7].

When Maria Elisabetha Beckensteinerin, an Augsburg cardmaker's wife imprisoned for theft, strangled her six-month-old baby boy in her prison cell two years later, so that she might "earn [her death] by means of her child's death," this murder prompted a similar outpouring. No fewer than

---

[167] StadtAA, Strafamt 162, Bausch, May 31, 1740, Jeremias Bertz.

[168] Hsia, *Myth*, 218.

[169] On the iconography of Simon of Trent, see Treue, *Trienter Judenprozess*, 350-379. On the *Arma Christi*, see Mitchell B. Merback, *The Thief, the Cross, and the Wheel: Pain and the Spectacle of Punishment in Medieval and Renaissance Europe*. (Chicago: University of Chicago Press, 1999), 97-98.

[170] Merback, *Thief*, 114. Merback discusses graphic images of the Passion of Christ that depict Christ's physical wounds with gruesome precision.

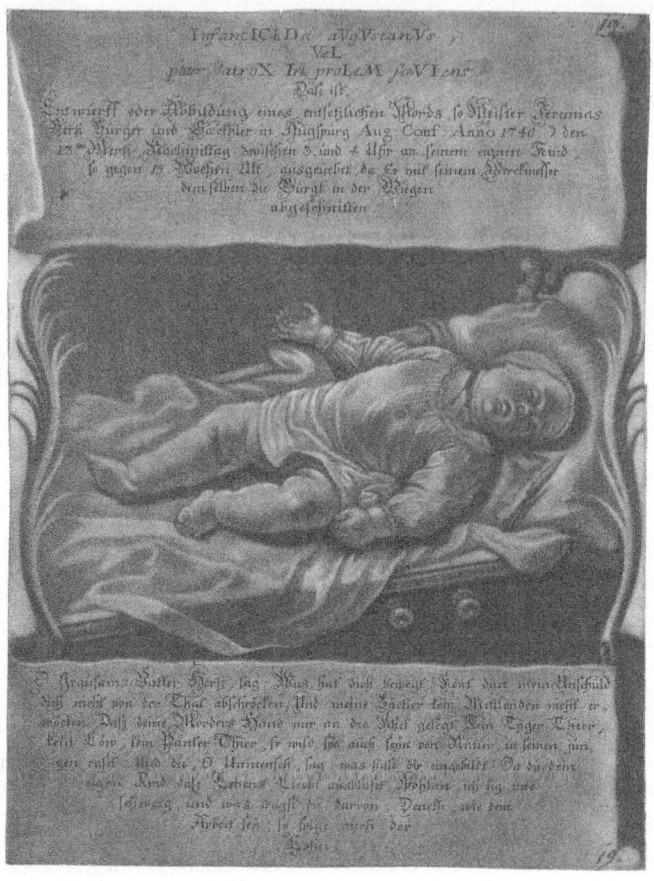

Image 2.6 *InfantICIDa aVgVstUs*, Kunstsammlungen und Museen Augsburg. Inv. Nr. G9740

three engravings portraying the murder were published, and the deed inspired several ballads. One of the images directs the viewer's gaze to the murder weapon in an inset showing the stocking ribbon (*Strumpf-bändel*) with which she strangled him, with the caption "Length and Breadth of the Murder Band." A ballad commemorated the "27-week-old martyr." Another pamphlet [Image 2.8] juxtaposes two images, the moment of the murder as the baby's naked soul leaves his body ascending upward into the

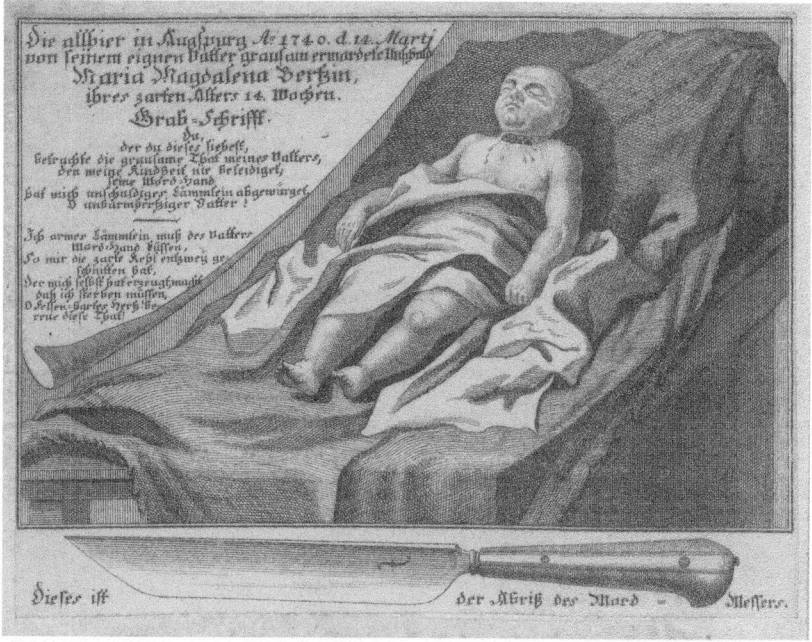

Image 2.7 *Die allhier in Augsburg Ao. 1740 d. 14. Martii von seinem eignen Vatter grausam ermordete Unschuld Maria Magdalen Bertzin....* Engraving. 1740. Staats- und Stadtbibliothek Augsburg: Graph 29/120

waiting arms of an angel and the moment of the mother's execution. The child's salvation has already happened. The salvation of the mother will follow momentarily. A cautionary verse beneath the image warns that repentance often comes too late, but the clergymen who accompanied her to her execution stand with her on the scaffold gesturing toward heaven. Several ballads attested to her heartfelt repentance.

Another parallel between suicides by proxy and public execution was of course the forms of death of victims and perpetrators and the blood symbolism they shared. As we have seen, most victims had their throat cut, and almost all perpetrators who were executed died by beheading.[171] The "blood thirsty murderer" who "washed her hands in the innocent blood

---

[171] In rare cases, suicidal child murderers were executed by breaking by the wheel. Examples in Chaps. 4 and 7.

Image 2.8 *Hinrichtung der Maria Elisabetha Beckensteinerin.... 20 Martii 1742....* Engraving. 1740. Staats- und Stadtbibliothek Augsburg: Graph 29/123

of the child,"[172] victims found lying in a pool of blood, and the blood of the innocent which cried out to God for vengeance[173] are recurrent themes in the pamphlet literature commemorating these crimes. Authorities evoked the Old Testament maxim of blood for blood,[174] and perpetrators offered up their blood in "payment" for their sins. Ultimately, of course,

---

[172] According to her execution sermon, Catherina Uhlin cut a nine-year-old girl's throat, "...und ihre Hände in dessen unschuldigen Blut gewaschen hat." Woltersdroff, ed., *Schächer*, 635

[173] Woltersdorff, ed., *Schächer*, vol. 1 (1761), 436.

[174] During her interrogation Agnes Catharina Schickin was asked: "Ob sie nicht gewußt das eine solche Mordthat eine erschröckliche Sündt seye, und in Gottes Wort befohlen, wer Menschenbluth verguesst, dessen Bluth solle wider vergossen werdten?" She answered: "Freylich, es stehe ja in den Gebotten Gottes, du sollst nicht tödten, sie wolle gern sterben, man solle sie nur baldt von der Welt hinweg thuen." HStAS, A 209/1806, Agnes Catharina Schickin, 1704.

it was the blood of Christ that would wash away the killers' sin.[175] The promise of redemption on the scaffold exercised a powerful hold on the imagination of perpetrators of suicide by proxy. Several of them formed the intent to commit murder after witnessing a public execution.[176] In a remarkable analogy, the defense advocate of Elisabeth Schmied, who had cut the throat of a six-year-old girl in Leipzig in 1714, claimed that a criminal's recent "beheading and salvation" (sic!) had made such an "impression" on her that "as if captured by the furor of love, she did not know right from wrong."[177]

Governmental authorities were appalled that the punitive rituals they orchestrated to inspire maximum deterrence instead attracted many of their subjects, like moths to the flame. This chapter set out to explain why suicidal child murder made sense to desperate individuals and why they performed the killings in the manner that they did. The next two chapters turn from individual killings to the societal setting in which they occurred and the confounding challenge that desperate subjects' rush to self-destruction posed for their rulers. The government of Hamburg struggled for two centuries to quash the ritual violence that claimed numerous child victims in the city.

---

[175] The execution sermon of Catherina Uhlin recorded her prayers: "das Blut des von mir ermordteten Kindes schreyet zwar Ach und Wehe über mich: aber das Blut meines Jesu redet besser, und rufet zu Gott, Gnade und Vergebung der Sündten." Woltersdorff, ed., *Schächer*, vol. 1 (1761), 654.

[176] On trial for cutting a little girl's throat in 1745, Gertrude Magdalena Bremmelin, "da sie ehemals eine Execution mit angesehen, und sich darbey vorgestellet, daß, wer also stürbe, nicht anders als selig werden müsse." Woltersdorff, ed., *Schächer*, vol 1 (1761), 416.

[177] Anon., *Casus Philantropophonias et Homicidii Benevolenti, in rechtlicher Defension einer jungen, und wegen verübten Mords an einem kleinen Waysen-Mädgen verurtheilten Weibs-Person* (s.l: 1719), 6.

CHAPTER 3

"Fear God and the Court, while there is still Time." Crime and Zealous Prosecution in Early Modern Hamburg

"Child murder, Alas!, has been rampant in Hamburg for some time," the *Augspurgische Ordinari Postzeitung*, a south German daily paper, reported on December 5, 1777.[1] Although suicide by proxy was a well-known phenomenon throughout Germany by the late eighteenth century, Hamburg acquired a particular notoriety far beyond its borders for the sheer number of child murders within its walls. The Augsburg paper had just reported on the latest killing in Hamburg six weeks earlier. In its October 16 edition, the paper reported on the murder of a young child that had taken place on October 7. With the parents' permission, a young maidservant had taken her employers' three-year-old daughter for a walk on the ramparts. There she cut the little girl's throat with a bread knife. Then she went straight to the next constabulary and turned herself in. "Presumably she had been driven to extremes by despair or melancholy," the correspondent in Hamburg surmised.[2] Trial records show that this maidservant was Catharina Hölsen, alias Kuhls.[3] Over the next weeks, various papers covered Hölsen's trial, and ultimately her execution on December 15, nine weeks after the murder. They also reported on Hamburg's latest

---

[1] "Weil seit einiger Zeit der Kinder-Mord in Hamburg leider! überhand genommen...." *Augspurgische Ordinari Postzeitung*, Nr. 291, 5 December 1777.
[2] *Augspurgisches Extra-Blatt*, Nr. 248, 16 October 1777.
[3] StAH, 111–1, Senat, Cl.VII, Lit.M6, Nr.3, Vol.5.

© The Author(s), under exclusive license to Springer Nature Switzerland AG 2023
K. Stuart, *Suicide by Proxy in Early Modern Germany*, World Histories of Crime, Culture and Violence,
https://doi.org/10.1007/978-3-031-25244-0_3

legislative attempt to quash child murders of this kind, enacted October 29, 1777, while Hölsen's trial was ongoing.[4]

Suicide by proxy first emerged in Hamburg in the 1620s and 1630s, contemporaneous with the last witch trials in the city. In Hamburg as elsewhere in the Holy Roman Empire, suicidal child murders did not become common until witch-hunting had subsided. Cases accelerated from the late 1660s, both in the city at large and within Hamburg's prisons, where cases reached crisis levels in the 1690s and early eighteenth century. Child murders continued at a rapid pace in the eighteenth century, leading a prosecutor in 1786 to lament "the unbelievably frequent examples of such murders committed solely out of weariness with life."[5] Hamburg prosecuted at least ninety-eight suicidal child murders or attempted murders between 1662 and 1810, though the real number of cases was likely higher. A disastrous fire in 1842 destroyed the bulk of Hamburg's criminal trial records. The numbers here are gleaned from incomplete execution lists, chronicles, newspaper reporting, and the fragmentary individual trial records that have survived. The city government responded with consternation to these child killings and made various, unsuccessful, attempts to stop the practice over the course of the eighteenth century. The new law of 1777 was the city's third such legislative initiative since 1724.

In Hamburg, as elsewhere, suicide by proxy would never have developed without the sacralization of public execution. Hamburg was a staunchly Lutheran city, renowned as "the orthodox Zion of the north."[6] As was common during the confessional age throughout Germany, religion in Hamburg functioned as an ideology of state, permeating all aspects of government and public life. Public executions, too, were shaped by Lutheran confessional culture. However, Lutheranism was not the primary cause of Hamburg's frequent child murders. Other Lutheran cities experienced few cases. In staunchly Lutheran Frankfurt, for example, I

---

[4] *Augspurgische Ordinari Postzeitung*, Nr. 254, 23 October 1777 and Nr. 310, 27 December 1777; *Bayreuther Zeitung*, Nr. 127, 23 October 1777; *Neue Europäische Zeitung*, 176tes Stück, 8 November 1777. The decree is reprinted in Christian Daniel Anderson, *Sammlung hamburgischer Verordnungen...* (Hamburg: Carl Wilhelm Meyn, 1783), 245–246.

[5] "...die in neueren Zeiten unglaublich häufigen Beispiele solcher Mordthaten..., die aus bloßem Überdruß des Lebens vollbracht worden...." StAH, Cl.VII, Lit. Me, Nr.8, Vol. 2b, 15. September 1786.

[6] Mary Lindemann, *The Merchant Republics Amsterdam, Antwerp, and Hamburg, 1648–1790* (Cambridge: Cambridge University Press, 2017), 9.

have only located two cases. Both defendants were Catholics.[7] Instead, it was a particular blend of political ideology and performances of state power, harsh criminal justice marked by distinctive ritualization, in combination with elaborate pastoral care and discipline deployed by the Lutheran state church that account for the many suicidal child murders here. This dynamic was not specific to Lutheranism. In arch-Catholic baroque Vienna, the disciplinary regimes of state and church intersected in similarly fateful ways to induce many suicidal individuals to commit suicide by proxy, as will be shown in subsequent chapters.[8]

This chapter and the next recount in the most granular detail that the sources allow the sequence of child murders as they unfolded in Hamburg. Placing these killings in their local context makes it possible to discern what factors contributed to the emergence of suicidal child murders and how they coalesced into a cultural practice that proved remarkably resistant to all government efforts to suppress it. This chapter shows what set of circumstances needed to be in place for the practice of suicide by proxy to emerge in the city beginning in the 1620s and to accelerate in the second half of the seventeenth century. In the late sixteenth and seventeenth centuries, the city government embarked on a comprehensive campaign of morals policing that had the unintended consequence of promoting suicidal child murders. As one facet of this campaign, authorities engaged in more aggressive, public desecrations of the bodies of direct suicides, compounding the damnation that was believed to follow suicide with heightened worldly infamy. At the same time, the criminalization of sexual offenses and zealous prosecution of "female" crimes such as witchcraft and infanticide led to greater visibility of women in criminal justice generally and to significantly higher execution rates for women. The ultimate desire of perpetrators of suicide by proxy was to die by public execution, so their deeds must be understood within the general history of capital punishment. Changing patterns of criminality and changing targets and priorities of criminal prosecution influenced when suicidal child murders became frequent in Hamburg and who committed them. When a young woman attended a public execution and saw another woman dying on the scaffold, this experience contributed to her eventual decision to murder a young child. In Hamburg, as in Germany in general, women made up the majority of suicidal child killers. As more women died on the scaffold,

---

[7] See Chap. 1.
[8] See Chaps. 4, 5, and 6.

women spectators envisioned themselves dying at the executioner's hand as well. The overarching religious understanding of government in general and criminal justice in particular was indispensable to this dynamic.

Secular ritual, too, played an important role. The city's practice of criminal justice took place within a ritual edifice that accumulated and expanded over centuries. Some judicial rituals that originated in the Middle Ages remained unchanged until the mid-1780s. Others persisted into the Napoleonic era. Various practices incorporated archaic and magical elements. Most prominent among these was the so-called Justice of the Street, a dramatic public confrontation of the accused murderer with the corpse of his or her victim in the street, a ceremony by which Hamburg initiated felony murder trials. This high level of ritualization, both religious and secular, contributed to the appeal and persuasiveness of suicide by proxy in Hamburg. Suicidal child killers were enthralled by their encounters and experiences with criminal justice in the public life of the city.

The City

The worldview and mentality of Hamburg's city fathers, their performances of governmental sovereignty, and the experiences and responses of common people subjected to governmental authority created a moral environment in which child murder became an attractive, even irresistible option for suicidal individuals. Hamburg was a self-governing Lutheran republic.[9] Johannes Bugenhagen, a close friend and confessor to Martin Luther, known as "the second apostle of the north" for his role in implementing the Lutheran Reformation in several north German cities and territories and in Denmark, formally introduced the Reformation in Hamburg in 1529.[10] Bugenhagen authored the city's church ordinance, a constitutional document that made Lutheranism an organizing principle of civic identity. It remained in effect throughout the early modern peri-

---

[9] Hamburg officially acquired the status of a free imperial city in a decision by the imperial chamber court in 1618. De facto Hamburg had been treated as a free imperial city since the fifteenth century, but this status remained precarious because of claims of lordship over the city by Denmark. Denmark finally officially relinquished any claims of sovereignty over the city in 1768. Rainer Postel, "Reformation und Gegenreformation, 1517–1618," in *Hamburg*, eds. Jochmann and Loose, 200, 246–7.

[10] Carl P. E. Springer, *Cicero in Heaven: The Roman Rhetor and Luther's Reformation* (Leiden: Brill, 2017), 147.

od.[11] Only Lutherans could be citizens, participate in politics or hold any public office. This was enshrined in Hamburg's civic code of 1603 and reconfirmed in the "principal recess," the city's revised constitution of 1712. [12]

When Hamburg introduced the Reformation, the city government acquired a certain "transcendental quality," to use Rainer Postel's phrase. The idea that the sovereign authority of the city government derived from God predated the Reformation, but it received significant ideological support from the Lutheran clergy. In line with Luther's teaching on the authority of worldly government, Protestant reformers drew on Romans 13 to teach that government was established by God and so it was necessary for Christians to obey government, just as one obeyed God himself. The senate, as the city council in Hamburg was called, saw itself as Christian government. Citizens owed obedience and submission to its divinely established sovereign authority. This vision was shared beyond government circles. Chronicles portrayed obedience to government not only "loyal" or "righteous," but also "devout" (*fromm*). In a development common to Catholic and Protestant states, government took on the duty to combat blasphemy, immorality, and fornication, expanding its authority into areas previously under the purview of ecclesiastical courts.[13] Lutheran political theory held that secular government exercised sovereign authority over the Lutheran state church. By the end of the sixteenth century the

---

[11] Susan C. Karant-Nunn, "The Reformation of Liturgy," in *The Oxford Handbook of the Protestant Reformations*, ed. Ulinka Rublack (Oxford: Oxford University Press, 2017), 415. Postel, "Reformation," 181–258.

[12] Several religious minorities resided in the city, including Dutch Calvinists and Sephardic Jews from Portugal. There were also small communities of Catholics and German Ashkenazi Jews. To the chagrin of the large and influential body of Lutheran clergy, the city government adopted a relatively pragmatic policy toward religious minorities, allowing them to live and work in the city, but prohibiting public exercise of their faiths. Religious minorities could take the short walk to neighboring Altona and attend public services there. Altona's overlords, the Counts of Schaumburg and, after 1640, the Kings of Denmark, granted religious toleration to Jews, Catholics, Calvinists, and Mennonites, in an ultimately unsuccessful mercantilist effort to compete economically with Hamburg. The presence of religious minorities in Hamburg never called into question city's fundamentally Lutheran identity, however. Joachim Whaley, *Religious Toleration and Social Change in Hamburg, 1529–1819* (Cambridge: Cambridge University Press, 1985), 23, 35–36.

[13] Rainer Postel, "Obrigkeitsdenken und Reformation in Hamburg," *Archiv für Reformationsgeschichte* 70 (1979): 169, 173–174, 184–185, 193–194.

Hamburg senate constituted the highest authority in all matters of religion.[14]

Meanwhile the city prospered. Celebrated in the sixteenth century as the "most flourishing market of all of Germany" (*florentissimum Emporium totius Germaniae*), Hamburg's population grew from 14,000 in 1500 in to just under 40,000 by 1600. The city was an economic juggernaut through the early modern period, becoming "a commercial nerve center for half the continent" by the eighteenth century, Mary Lindemann writes.[15] The city's rapid population growth continued through the seventeenth century. By 1710, Hamburg had 75,000 inhabitants.

A series of constitutional conflicts over the nature of governance within the city dominated political life in Hamburg during the seventeenth century. Unlike most other self-governing cities, Hamburg had no legally defined patriciate. Most free imperial cities had a closed patriciate that monopolized government office and blocked access to political power by rising merchant families. In Hamburg, the governing class remained fluid, so that newcomers gained seats on the senate. Despite this openness, a conflict between the senate and the politically enfranchised citizenry over the source of governmental authority in the city festered for most of the century, at times erupting into violence. The question at issue was whether the relationship between senate and citizenry was one of sovereign and subjects, or whether the senators governed as representatives of a sovereign citizenry.

In 1686, the government executed two leaders of the citizen opposition, Cord Jastram and Hieronymus Snitger, for treason. In the aftermath, the senate proclaimed that because every government was instituted by God and would be judged by him, subjects did not have the right to resist governmental authority, for this would preempt God's judgment. Jastram's and Snitger's executions were divine retribution for their contempt of government, the senate declared. Like a divine right monarch, in other words, the senate was accountable to God alone. This argument, unsurprisingly, failed to persuade the opposition, who argued that sovereignty resided with the enfranchised citizenry, but it gives insight into the political philosophy of senators, a worldview they shared with patrician city councilors in cities with a less fluid ruling class than Hamburg. Ultimately,

---

[14] Whaley, *Religious Toleration*, 25.

[15] Mary Lindemann, *Patriots and Paupers: Hamburg, 1712–1830* (New York: Oxford University Press, 1990), 3.

this constitutional conflict was resolved through the intervention of an imperial commission that helped facilitate a power-sharing agreement. The outcome was Hamburg's new "fundamental law," the "principal recess" of 1712. It established that sovereignty resided "inseparably conjoined" in both the senate and the politically enfranchised citizenry.[16]

Contemporary political theorists praised the new constitution for combining aristocratic and democratic elements in republican government in a way uniquely conducive to social harmony. The political settlement coincided with an era of unparalleled growth and prosperity. The city's population grew to 90,000 by 1750 and reached 130,000 by the end of the eighteenth century. The openness of Hamburg' government and its dynamic economy contrasted with the ossification and retrenchment that took hold in many other German cities during the seventeenth and eighteenth centuries, making Hamburg "a special case in German history," Hamburg historian Percy Ernst Schramm has famously argued.[17] In a similar vein, Franklin Kopitzsch described Hamburg's governing class in the eighteenth century as "a politically autonomous, economically self-confident and culturally independent bourgeoisie, rarely found in the era of absolutism."[18] Hamburg's political class was also notable for its early and enthusiastic embrace of the Enlightenment. Hamburg was home to the "moral weekly" *Der Patriot*, published in 1724–1726, one of Germany's most influential early enlightenment periodicals. Several government officeholders were among its editors.[19]

Nonetheless, the vast majority of Hamburg's inhabitants had no voice in government. Citizens made up a minority of the population. Non-guild artisans, manual laborers, domestic servants, sailors, and others employed in "petty occupations" typically could not pay the full citizenship fee, and instead paid a small annual fee for *Schutzverwandschaft*, the status of "protected denizen," that allowed them to take up permanent residence in

---

[16] Hans-Dieter Loose, "Das Zeitalter der Bürgerunruhen und der großen europäischen Kriege, 1618–1712," in *Hamburg*, eds. Jochmann and Loose, 269, 286.

[17] Percy Ernst Schramm, *Hamburg, ein Sonderfall in der Geschichte Deutschlands* (Hamburg: H. Christians Verlag, 1964).

[18] Franklin Kopitzsch, "Zwichen Hauptrezeß und Franzosenzeit, 1712–1806," in *Hamburg*, eds. Jochmann and Loose, 352.

[19] Kopitzsch, "Zwichen Hauptrezeß und Franzosenzeit," 377–390.

Hamburg.[20] Even among the citizens, only a minority were fully enfranchised. A substantial property requirement blocked most citizens from membership in the citizen-assembly. Only freeholders (*Erbgesessene*) who owned unmortgaged property within the city worth 1000 *Thaler* were eligible. This meant that around 1800, when the population in the city had grown to around 130,000, only between 3000 and 4000 men were fully politically enfranchised. Of these, only around 300 held government office.[21] For the bulk of the population, then, Hamburg's much-lauded constitutional order had little impact on how they experienced governmental authority. For them, the city government constituted *Obrigkeit*, sovereign authority that ruled over them as subjects. As Jürgen Martschukat suggests, in the context of criminal justice, especially, Hamburg was not a "special case in German history." Instead, the merchants and jurists who made up Hamburg's ruling class constituted a "senatorial aristocracy" that ruled over its subjects, in much the same way as patrician, aristocratic, or monarchical governments did.[22] Perpetrators of suicide by proxy perceived and experienced governmental authority as divinely instituted dominium. Attracted by the "transcendental" quality of government, they desired to find relief from their suffering in their ultimate submission to its authority on the scaffold.

CRIME AND PUNISHMENT IN HAMBURG

A striking feature of criminal justice in Hamburg is the continuity of medieval judicial practices into the late eighteenth century and beyond. The antiquity of judicial rituals was a source of their power and legitimacy. Most cases of suicide by proxy in Hamburg happened in the eighteenth century, yet trials of suicidal child murderers began with the same judicial

[20] Mary Lindemann, "Fundamental Values: Political Culture in Eighteenth-Century Hamburg," in *Patriotism, Cosmopolitanism and National Culture: Public Culture in Hamburg, 1700–1933*, ed. Peter Uwe Hohendahl (Amsterdam: Rodopi, 2003), 17–32, pp. 20–21.
[21] Lindemann, *Merchant Republics*, 53.
[22] Martschukat writes: "Zudem ist mittlerweile deutlich geworden, dass der angebliche 'Sonderfall' Hamburg weniger absonderlich ist, als es lange den Anschein hatte. Es lässt sich vielmehr das Bild einer aus Kaufleuten und Juristen konstituierten 'Senatorenaristokratie' zeichnen, und es ist folglich auch im Hamburger Kontext angebracht von 'Herrschaftsträgern,' von einem 'Souverän,' von 'Obrigkeiten' oder von einer 'Ordnung der Unterordnung' zu schreiben." Jürgen Martschukat, *Inszeniertes Töten. Eine Geschichte der Todesstrafe vom 17. bis zum 19. Jahrhundert* (Cologne: Böhlau Verlag, 2000), 9.

ceremony that initiated murder trials in the Middle Ages. This ritual is vividly portrayed in Hamburg's municipal code of 1497. A miniature illumination introduces each section of the code. These images provide insight into the legislators' mentality and ideals of justice. The chapter on criminal law is entitled "On Felonies, pertaining to the Highest [Penalties]," that is, capital crimes. The illumination introducing this chapter provides a synoptic view of all the essential features that would shape criminal prosecution in the city through the early modern era.[23] At the top of the image, a textual banner proclaims a judicial philosophy of deterrence: "Punish sinners in the presence of all, so that others may be afraid (Image 3.1)." The busyness of the scene shows how authorities put this precept into practice, as the public participates and engages with judicial rituals. The action plays out to the right and left of a center axis that divides the image into two halves. The main scene to the left shows a malefactor tied to a pillory, bare-chested, crying out in anguish as a bailiff flogs him, wielding a bundle of birch-rods in each hand, and onlookers watch. At the top of the pillory is a cage. Here a man and a woman, presumably adulterers, are both chained to the column by the neck and exposed to public view. The code established exposure at the pillory as the statutory penalty for adultery. To the far left, undistracted by the action outside their open window, officials hold a hearing in Hamburg's Lower Court. This is the court that conducted criminal trials in Hamburg from the Middle Ages until the Napoleonic era.[24]

Center left, just below the cage topping the pillory, behind the men watching the flogging, we can peer into an alcove where a witch brews a potion, as she fashions a pentagram out of string. A bat-like demon sits on her shoulder looking on. The main scene to the right of the axis, parallel to the flogging on the left, centers on a coffin holding a murder victim, surrounded by officials and spectators. This scene depicts a "Justice of the Street" (*Gassenrecht* or *Straßenrecht*), the ceremony that formally initiated murder trials in Hamburg. Prosecutors carried out this ritual, one of the most distinctive and dramatic features of criminal justice in the city, from

---

[23] The image is entitled, in low German, *Van pynliken saken dat hogeste belangende*. The Latin banner at the top reads: *Peccantes coram omnibus argue, ut ceteri timorem habeant*. The Latin banner at the bottom reads: *Maleficos ne pacieris viuere super terram*, from Exodus 22:18. For analysis of the image, see Beate Binder, *Illustriertes Recht. Die Miniaturen des Hamburger Stadtrechts von 1497* (Hamburg: Verlag Verein für Hamburgische Geschichte, 1988), 125.
[24] Binder, *Illustriertes Recht*, 66–74.

Image 3.1 "Van pynlikē sakē dat hogeste belangende." Miniature. Hamburg *Stadtrecht*, 1497. Hamburg Staatsarchiv, 111-1 Senat Cl. VII Lit. La Nr. 2 Vol. 1c, f. 250v

the Middle Ages until 1784, when the senate abolished the ceremony. Until then, frequent performance of this ritual contributed to a moral atmosphere that encouraged the practice of suicide by proxy.[25]

---

[25] We return to a more detailed discussion of this judicial ritual below.

Just behind the men surrounding the coffin is a prison where felons await trial. Top right, beyond the city wall, we see "the highest" penalties being imposed. The executioner has just beheaded a malefactor. He resheathes his sword. Behind him, a body hangs from the gallows. Wheels atop posts expose to the elements the bodies of malefactors who have been broken by the wheel. In the background, to the left of the gallows and the wheels, we see a man and a woman galloping away on horseback. This most likely depicts the crime of abducting a virgin, an offense punishable by death. Finally, at the bottom of the image a textual banner commands: "Do not suffer the witch to live on earth," from Exodus 22:18.

The illumination thematized witchcraft twice. Within the text of the code, however, witchcraft receives only brief mention: "When a Christian man or woman, who is an unbeliever and practices sorcery or poisoning, is caught in the act, he [or she] should be burned at the stake."[26] The association of sorcery and poisoning in the article, and its placement in the code alongside crimes against life and limb, shows that at this time authorities in Hamburg prosecuted sorcery as tangible harmful magic. The *Malleus Maleficarum*, the famous witch-hunting manual by the Dominican inquisitors Johann Sprenger and Heinrich Institutoris, had just been published in 1487, ten years before Hamburg promulgated its new municipal code. The two inquisitors promoted a new witchcraft doctrine, the cumulative concept of witchcraft, in which the demonic pact became the essential element of the crime.[27] This new doctrine did not influence sorcery prosecutions in Hamburg for several decades, however. Hamburg occasionally executed both men and women for sorcery in the late Middle Ages and early decades of the sixteenth century, but the conflation of poisoning and sorcery makes it unclear how many of these cases were murder trials. Diabolism did not feature in Hamburg witchcraft trials

[26] Section O, Article XIX of the 1497 *Hamburger Stadtrecht*: "Welck crysten man este wyf de vnghelouych ys, edder myt touerye vmmegheyt edder vorghiftnysse, vnde myt der verschen daet begrepen wert, der schalmen vuppe de hoert bernen..." Johann Martin Lappenberg, *Hamburgische Rechtsalterthümer*, vol. 1. *Die ältesten Stadt- Schiff- und Landrechte Hamburgs* (Hamburg: Johann August Meissner, 1845), 305. See also the discussion of the article in Roswitha Rogge, "Hexenverfolgung in Hamburg? Schadenzauber im Alltag und in der Justiz," *Geschichte in Wissenschaft und Unterricht* 46 (1995): 385–386. Carl Trummer, *Vorträge über Tortur, Hexenverfolgungen, Vehmgerichte, und andere merkwürdige Erscheinungen in der Hamburgischen Rechtsgeschichte*, vol. 1 (Hamburg: Johann August Meißner, 1844), 106–107.
[27] Brian Levack, *The Witch-Hunt in Early Modern Europe* (Harlow, England: Pearson Longman, 2005), 33–40.

before the middle of the sixteenth century. The city conducted its largest witch-hunts in the 1540s and 1550s, at the beginning of the wider European witch-hunt.[28]

By the second half of the eighteenth century, women made up fully 50% of executed felons in Hamburg. In 1497, however, when the illumination of the municipal code showcased two female felons, the adulteress and the witch, women made up only a small fraction of executed criminals. From the late Middle Ages through the early sixteenth century, the suppression of piracy was the government's most pressing concern.[29] Records of executions are fragmentary, so the following figures inevitably are an undercount of the number of people executed in Hamburg. Nonetheless, they illustrate trends, changing governmental priorities and, significantly, the increasing rate at which women were executed over time. Between 1390 and 1499, Hamburg executed 212 men. In the same years, Hamburg executed five women, one for adultery and murder, three for harmful magic, and one for host desecration. The execution rate for women was 2.3%. The city executed men for murder, robbery, theft, and sedition, but a large majority of the men were pirates. On several occasions, the city beheaded pirates *en masse*, in groups as large as seventy-four at a time, and impaled their heads on posts. Such mass executions became the stuff of legend. Chroniclers marveled at the executioner's virtuosity in dispatching so many men at once. Centuries later, the city still celebrated these spectacles. In 1701 a commemorative broadside marked the anniversary of the executions of two famous pirates and their crews 300 years earlier. An engraving showed the beheadings and the display of the pirates' impaled heads afterward.[30] Group executions like these and their embellishment in local lore and media established Hamburg's reputation and self-image as a city that dispensed swift and rigorous justice. Journeymen

---

[28] Elsa Hennings, *Das Hamburgische Strafrecht im 15. und 16. Jahrhundert und seine Verwirklichung* (Hamburg: Hansicher Gildenverlag, 1940), 91–94.

[29] In 1359, Emperor Charles IV empowered Hamburg to drive pirates out of the River Elbe. Hamburg waged a relentless campaign against piracy until the 1570s, earning the city the moniker "*dominatrix piratorum*" (conqueror of pirates). Matthias Blazek, *Seeräuberei, Mord und Sühne. Eine 700-jährige Geschichte der Todesstrafe in Hamburg, 1292–1945* (Stuttgart: Ibidem Verlag, 2012), 32.

[30] "Die hingerichtete See-Räuber Störtebeck und Gödeke Micheel." (Hamburg, 1701). In: Deutsches Textarchiv <http://www.deutschestextarchiv.de/nn_stoertebeck_1701>, abgerufen am 09.12.2020.

executioners traveled to Hamburg from far and wide to learn the tricks of the trade from the city's master executioner.[31]

The inclusion of the adulteress and the witch in the 1497 illumination of the municipal code clearly was not a reflection of judicial practice at that time, since men made up the overwhelming majority of criminals executed in Hamburg before 1500. It does show the importance of female malefactors in the moral imagination, however. It was also a harbinger of things to come. It illustrates a disciplinary vision that authorities would act upon after the implementation of the Protestant Reformation, beginning in the late sixteenth century. When the government engaged in more aggressive policing of morals during the confessional age, and when they turned their attention to sexual offenses in particular, more women became targets of prosecution.

For the first half of the sixteenth century, however, as the population grew from 15,000 to 20,000, Hamburg continued to execute mostly men. Between 1500 and 1549, Hamburg executed 163 men and 13 women. The execution rate for women rose to 7.4%. Prosecutions of men continued to focus on crimes of violence. Again, there were mass executions of pirates. Hamburg also executed men for robbery, murder, and, in one instance, blasphemy. Eleven of the women were executed for sorcery, poisoning, or witchcraft. One witch was burned in 1529 and another in 1533. The pace of witchcraft prosecutions picked up after 1540. That year, the city arrested several women for witchcraft but ultimately set them free. In 1544, two women were executed as poisoners (*veneficae*), and six sorceresses were burned the following year. Hamburg executed two women for non-magical violent crimes. One murdered her husband in 1542, and the second stabbed her child to death in 1543. This was the first documented execution for child murder in Hamburg.[32]

The authorities showcased the ideology and values that shaped their administration of criminal justice in the physical structures in which they judged and punished the malefactors who came before them. In 1559, the city completed the construction of a new courthouse. The new seat of the Lower Court was a two-story building. It was immediately adjacent and

---

[31] Otto Beneke, *Von unehrlichen Leuten. Cultur-Historische Studien und Geschichten* (Hamburg: Perthes, Besser und Mauke, 1863), 165.

[32] Anon., *Ausführlicher Bericht über die hingerichteten Missethäter in Hamburg....*Neue Auflage. (Hamburg: Heyde's Officin [1858?]), 4. There were mass executions of pirates, seventy-five men in 1515 and seventy-one men in 1525.

attached to the larger city hall. On the façade of the new courthouse, at the level of the second floor, was a plaque. It displayed a poem in golden letters easily read from the street below. The poem made known the judicial philosophy that shaped criminal justice in Hamburg in 1559. It put criminals on notice and warned passersby to keep God before their eyes[33]:

> *Alle de da morden, brennen, roven und stehlen,*
> *Tövern, verraden, horen und spehlen,*
> *Vele borgen, dregen und wenig gelden,*
> *De bestahn im Rechte gar selden.*
> *Drum fürchte Gott und dat Richt,*
> *De Tydt kumpt, idt reuet di nicht.*

> All those who murder, burn, rob and steal,
> Practice magic, treason, whoring and gambling,
> Who borrow much, do fraud, pay little,
> Rarely prevail in law.
> Therefore, fear God and the court,
> While there is still time. You will not regret it.

Anyone who entered the courtroom was surrounded on all sides by rich religious imagery that communicated the awesome responsibility of officials who meted out justice here. Judges and jurors were bound by the religious instruction imparted in the elaborate iconographic program presented here. The message was not subtle. Accountable to God, judges had the duty to punish crime in conformity with divine law. Paintings covered the walls. There was a painting of the savior. There were the theological virtues: Faith, Hope and Love, and finally, Patience. On the chimney, a plaque with Bible verses, placed in 1626, warned judges to mete out impartial justice, or God would hold them accountable: "Take heed what ye do: for ye judge not for man, but for the LORD, who *is* with you in the judgment" (2 Chronicles, 19, 6–7).[34]

Here the lower court pronounced sentence on Wednesdays. Two days later, on Fridays, cases moved to city hall, next door. There the superior

---

[33] For a detailed description of the exterior and interior of the courthouse, see Daniel Heinrich Jacobi, *Geschichte des Hamburger Niedergerichts* (Hamburg: Gustav Edouard Nolte, 1866), 22, 121–124. Jacobi reproduces a 1716 lithograph that shows the location of the plaque on the façade of the building.

[34] Jacobi, *Niedergericht*, 122–123.

court, made up of the entire senate, reviewed lower court verdicts. The lower court had no discretion to deviate from the letter of the law, but the superior court had the power to pardon or mitigate a sentence or, alternatively, to impose a harsher one. When the superior court handed down the final sentence, the senators assembled in a vaulted great hall, large enough to accommodate members of the public admitted to city hall to hear the sentencing.[35] Here too artwork reminded the senators of their accountability to God. It had been customary in Hamburg since the fourteenth century to display an image of the Last Judgment behind the seats of the Burgomasters. In 1703 the Hamburg senator and jurist Matthäus Schlüter, who by virtue of his office acted as juror in capital cases, described the display he saw in Hamburg's great hall on these occasions: "High on the wall where the four Burgomasters sit, the Last Judgment has been painted very artfully." Schlüter explained that medieval Saxon customary law required city governments to display the Last Judgment in their town halls.[36] The law stated that the display of the Last Judgment would remind officials "that when the judge pronounces a sentence, in that same place, and at that same hour, God sits in divine judgment of the judge and the jurors."[37] The iconographic program did not end there. Beneath the fresco of the Last Judgment, Schlüter continued, hung a painting of "our LORD Christ and the twelve apostles. Further down, directly behind the seat of the Burgomasters is another painting of Christ holding an open book." The pages displayed the same Bible verses shown on the plaque on the chimney in the lower court building.[38] Here the councilors sat as they imposed sentence on the criminal defendants who appeared before them.

These religious displays at the heart of Hamburg's secular government, in the courthouse and in the town hall, were not unique to Hamburg. It had been common practice since the fourteenth century throughout

---

[35] Jonas Ludwig von Hess, *Hamburg topographisch, politisch und historisch beschrieben*. 2nd ed., vol. 2, (Hamburg: Selbstverlag, 1811), 333–334.

[36] Matthäus Schlüter, *Historisch- und Rechtsbegründeter Tractat von dem Verlassungs-Recht*, (Hamburg: Zacharias Hertel, 1703), 37–39.

[37] Quoted in Georg Troescher, "Weltgerichtsbilder in Rathäusern und Gerichtsstätten," *Westdeutsches Jahrbuch für Kunstgeschichte: Wallraf-Richartz Jahrbuch* 11 (1939): 148.

[38] Schlüter's 1703 description explained that the text in Christ's open book was derived from Psalm 82, v. 3 and 2 Chronicles, Chap. 19, v. 6, 7. Troescher, "Weltgerichtsbilder," 150, 173–174.

Central Europe to display Last Judgment scenes in town halls and courthouses. Municipalities regularly commissioned religious frescoes and paintings until the end of the seventeenth century and continued to restore them in the eighteenth century. Only after 1750, during the Enlightenment, did city governments lose interest in maintaining this religious iconography in secular government buildings. This reflects an incremental secularization among government officials that finally freed them of the constraints of divine law, allowing criminal courts to develop more flexible responses to the criminal cases they judged.[39]

In 1559, when the poem threatening witches and felons was placed on the façade of the new courthouse, Hamburg had been aggressively hunting witches for about two decades. After Hamburg executed eight witches in 1544, prosecutions continued in the 1550s. The city executed one woman as a poisoner in 1553. Hamburg's largest early modern witch-hunt took place two years later. In 1555 two women were tortured to death in prison. Nine others were burned at the stake. Witch-hunting caused the proportion of women among executed felons to rise in the second half of the sixteenth century, though men still made up a substantial majority, and men, too, were executed for witchcraft. From 1550 to 1599, Hamburg executed 173 men and 33 women, along with 10 other people whose gender was not recorded.[40] Women now made up 16% of the executed felons whose gender is known. Piracy still remained a major concern. Fifty-nine of the executed men were pirates. The city also executed men for murder, manslaughter, arson, burglary, and theft. Five men were executed for witchcraft. The majority of women were executed for witchcraft. In addition to the witches executed in the 1550s, the city burned six witches in 1581, and there were several other executions of individual witches in the 1580s and 1590s. It is impossible to know what role the cumulative concept of witchcraft played in the group trials of the 1540s and 1550s, since no trial records have survived. By the 1580s at the latest, however, prosecutions focused on full-fledged diabolical witchcraft, including apostasy, demonic pact, and sex with the devil, rather than simply on tangible harmful magic and poisoning. In 1583, in the only trial for which records have survived, Abelke Bleken confessed to satanic pact and sex with Satan, as well as poisoning people and livestock. In 1594 Lemken

---

[39] See Chap. 4.
[40] For ten executions, the gender was not recorded.

Meyers was convicted of satanic pact and poisoning pastures with the help of "her lover Satan."[41]

As a matter of course, the bodies of suspected witches who died in prison, presumably from the effects of torture, were dragged to the execution site and burned, as happened with the body of Gretje Wippers, who died in prison on 1594.[42] In the late sixteenth century, Hamburg began performing post-mortem punishment on the bodies of other felons as well. The punishment of dead bodies was not unique to Hamburg, but the city stands out for the frequency, rigor, and elaborate ritualization with which it imposed these penalties.[43] The zealous prosecution even of the dead impressed upon the city's residents how conscientiously the senate fulfilled its obligation as Christian government to let no crime go unpunished. The city began orchestrating posthumous executions in the 1570s. This practice was distinct from the routine desecration inflicted on the dead bodies of criminals after their execution, most commonly the indefinite exposure of their bodies on the gallows or wheel, or, in the case of particularly notorious criminals, the display of their dismembered body parts at strategic locations around this city. Instead, these were theatrical punishments imposed upon the dead bodies of malefactors who died before they were arrested or of criminal defendants who died in prison before sentencing. These performances sometimes involved mock trials and mock execution processions. In 1573, the pirate captain Rode Clauß jumped overboard to escape capture when Hamburg forces seized his ship. Rode drowned, but authorities made a point of retrieving his body. Rode's men had already been decapitated and their heads impaled, the standard penalty for piracy, when Rode's body was taken before the court and sentenced to beheading too. After his decapitation, his head was impaled and displayed along with the heads of his crew.[44] In 1578, when the criminal defendant Cord Besche died in prison before sentencing, the

---

[41] Roswitha Rogge, "Schadenszauber, Hexerei und die Waffen der Justiz im frühneuzeitlichen Hamburg," in *Hexerei, Magie und Volksmedizin. Beiträge aus dem Hexenarchiv des Museums für Völkerkunde Hamburg*, ed. Bernd Schmelz (Bonn: Holos Verlag, 1997), 155–160. Claus Brahmst, *Das Hamburgische Strafrecht im 17. Jahrhundert. Der Übergang vom städtischen zum gemeinen Strafrecht* (Hamburg: Ludwig Appel Verlag, 1958), 102–105.

[42] Trummer, *Vorträge*, 449.

[43] Floris Tomasini, *Remembering and Dismembering the Dead: Posthumous Punishment, Harm and Redemption over Time* (London: Palgrave Macmillan, 2017).

[44] Trummer, *Vorträge*, 447.

judges ordered his body in its coffin to be brought before the court. The court imposed a sentence of hanging, an indication that Besche had been a thief. Then the executioner's assistant transported his body to the execution site and hung it on the gallows.[45]

Authorities made every effort to approximate the normal execution ritual as closely as possible. As we have seen, the Superior Court customarily imposed death sentences on Fridays. After the customary three days granted to condemned criminals to prepare spiritually for death, the execution procession set off precisely at noon the following Monday. Authorities followed this same schedule during the posthumous execution of Jochim Schutte, a coin clipper, in 1585. Schutte died at home before being arrested. On November 12, 1585, a Friday, bailiffs took Schutte's body from his house and dragged it to the courthouse. There the lower court sentenced his body to be burned, the statutory penalty for coin clippers. Then bailiffs transported his body to city hall, to the vaulted great hall where the full senate, acting as the Superior Court, was in session. The Superior Court confirmed the sentence of burning. Since Schutte was already dead, he could no longer reap any spiritual benefit from the three-day grace period granted to living criminals to prepare for death. Nonetheless, authorities observed the customary schedule and waited until Monday to carry out the mock execution. On Monday at noon, his body was transported to the execution site and burned.[46]

Even deceased felons who were already buried could not escape the government's punitive zeal. In 1589 Wilcken Wetten, a magician, was sentenced to be burned. During his trial, it came to light that his late wife had been his accomplice, so her body was exhumed and thrown onto the pyre with her husband.[47] Hamburg continued to carry out post-mortem executions until the end of the seventeenth century. Ranging from the mundane to the spectacular depending on the culprit's crime, these

---

[45] Richard Wosnik, *Beiträge zur Hamburgischen Kriminalgeschichte* (Hamburg: Selbstverlag, 1926), 27.
[46] Trummer, *Vorträge*, 447–448.
[47] Trummer, *Vorträge*, 447–448.

spectacles instructed the public that even physical death did not place offenders beyond the reach of Godfearing, avenging government.[48]

The government's morals offensive intensified in the seventeenth century. Hamburg promulgated a new municipal code in 1603 that reflected the heightened moral rigor of the age. The primary purpose of the new code was to incorporate and adapt to Roman law. The previous code of 1497 had not included any elements of the "common law," as Roman law became known. As Roman law increasingly influenced imperial law, Hamburg's accommodation to the "common law" became a practical necessity. The new code remained in effect for the next 250 years. Criminal law remained mostly unchanged, but some innovations show government's changing priorities. The code made clear in the very first lines of the text that divine law formed the foundation of jurisprudence in Hamburg: "In the name of the Holy Trinity. We mayors and councilmen of the city of Hamburg make known to every and all citizens of this town, and to residents and subjects, that all human legislation, Justice and Courts, instituted to protect the pious and punish the evil, derive from God."[49] The section of the code on criminal law classified felonies according to the Decalogue, beginning with crimes against God. Article One of the section on criminal law dealt with blasphemy. Blasphemy had not featured at all in previous municipal codes, although on at least one occasion Hamburg did execute a blasphemer.[50] The classification of blasphemy as first among felonies in the new code demonstrates the increased influence

---

[48] The most extravagant posthumous execution on record was that of Daniel Holst in 1589. A treasonous chancellery scribe, he died in prison before trial. His body was brought before the court, where judges pronounced sentence over it. His hand was amputated at the pillory and attached there. After decapitation at the ravenstone, he was disemboweled and his entrails burned. He was quartered, and his head and body parts affixed in prominent locations at city gates. Disemboweling and quartering was the standard penalty for high treason, a penalty the city continued to impose through the end of the seventeenth century, as will be shown below. Trummer, *Vorträge*, 448–449. One of the last posthumous executions on record happened in1687. A gardener cut the throats of his two young sons and then killed himself. His body was dragged out to the ravenstone and broken by the wheel from the bottom up, and then braided upon the wheel. Adam Olearius, *Continuirte Fortsetzung der hollsteinischen Chronica von Anno 1662 bis 1702* (Frankfurt: Georg Heinrich Öhrling, 1703), 65.

[49] *Der Stadt Hamburgk Gerichtsordnung und Statuta* (Hamburg: Frobenius, 1605), ii r–ii v.

[50] "Articulus I. Straffe der Gotteslesterer," *Hamburgk Gerichtsordnung*, 350–351. Trummer, *Vorträge*, 106. Brahmst, *Hamburgische Strafrecht*, 99.

of Biblicism in post-Reformation jurisprudence. Hamburg's classification was typical of early modern criminal law. All new criminal codes promulgated in the Holy Roman Empire during the confessional age, in Catholic and Protestant states, placed blasphemy at the top of the list of felonies.[51]

Next, Article Two of the revised code dealt with "Sorcerers and Sorceresses." The placement of sorcery in second place right after blasphemy in the list of felonies shows that legislators now classified it as a crime against God, as much as a crime against people. Hamburg had been prosecuting diabolical witchcraft since the 1580s, as we have seen, and now the 1603 code caught up with judicial practice by incorporating the new witchcraft doctrine. The article dealt with traditional harmful magic ("using forbidden means to harm people or animals in life or limb"), but now it also addressed diabolical witchcraft. People who "maliciously turn against God and his holy word and form special egregious alliances with the evil enemy" now faced the same penalty as traditional sorcerers, execution by fire or sword.[52]

The new witchcraft law did not result in an expansion of witch-hunting, however. In fact, by the time that Hamburg legislators officially codified diabolical witchcraft as a crime, authorities were losing interest in witch-hunting. Hamburg's most intense witch-hunts lay in the past. There were no executions of multiple defendants in any one year in the seventeenth century, as there had been in the 1540s and 1550s. There were only individual trials with no more than one defendant. Hamburg executed six women for witchcraft in the seventeenth century. In 1642 Cissie Hempels was the last woman executed as a witch in Hamburg. She was convicted of an accumulation of offenses, however, rather than witchcraft alone. She had murdered her husband, in addition to practicing sorcery. She was broken by the wheel as a murderess, and then her body was burned, a cumulative penalty reflecting two crimes.[53] A trial in 1653 of a woman accused of poisoning shows that by this time Hamburg authorities no longer understood poisoning as a magical crime. Anna Wessels was broken by the wheel after her flesh was torn with red-hot pincers for poisoning several people. The execution method shows that authorities prosecuted

[51] Helga Schnabel-Schüle, *Überwachen und Strafen im Territorialstaat: Bedingungen und Auswirkungen des Systems strafrechtlicher Sanktionen im frühneuzeitlichen Württemberg* (Cologne: Böhlau, 1997), 201–204. On the placement of blasphemy in seventeenth- and eighteenth-century criminal codes in Catholic Austrian Archduchies, see Chaps. 5 and 6.

[52] *Hamburgk Gerichtsordnung*, 351.

[53] Brahmst, *Hamburgische Strafrecht*, 104–105.

her for the secular crime of homicide, rather than for sorcery.[54] A few years later, in 1659, authorities chose to prosecute sorcery as fraud rather than diabolical witchcraft. Giesel Dovings, a procuress, was whipped, branded, and banished along with female accomplice Gesche Huttmanns for conjuring ghosts.[55]

In 1609, six years after the publication of the new municipal code, the city erected a ravenstone. It was located outside the city walls northeast of the city in the fields outside Stone Gate near the suburb of St. Georg. Wooden gallows had stood at this location since 1554. When the wooden gallows became dilapidated in 1565, Hamburg replaced it with a permanent stone structure. The new gallows consisted of three stone columns on a stone foundation connected by crossbeams. It is visible in Braun and Hogenberg's 1588 map of Hamburg. A lone post topped by a wheel stands next to the gallows. The city also carried out beheadings at this location on a raised grassy mound dubbed *Köppelberg* or *Köpfelberg* (beheading hill) by the locals (Image 3.2).[56]

The new ravenstone erected in 1609 was a more monumental structure. The British traveler John Taylor attended an execution here in 1616. He described the spectacle in his travel journal. The condemned man was a murderer sentenced to breaking by the wheel. On Monday, August 19, at noon, the execution procession departed from the prison: "the people of the town in great multitudes flocked to the place of execution; which is half a mile English without the gates built more like a sconce than a gallows, for it is walled and ditched about with a drawbridge and the prisoner came on foot with a Divine with him, all the way exhorting him to repentance." The structure was sufficiently elevated so that spectators could watch the execution from a distance of a quarter mile. The Hamburg executioner, assisted by two colleagues from neighboring towns, broke the man by the wheel. Finally, the executioner "took the broken mangled corpse and spread it on the wheel and thrust a great post or pile into the nave or hole of the wheel and then fixed the post into the earth some six foot deep being in height above the ground some ten or twelve foot and there the carcass must lie till it be consumed by all consuming time or

---

[54] *Ausführlicher Bericht*, 6 September 1653, 9.
[55] Trummer, *Vorträge*, 140.
[56] Kristiane Lutz, "Der Stadtteil St. Georg im Wandel. Veränderungen im Wohnquartier aus der Sicht zweier Stadtteil-Vereine" (Master's Thesis, University of Hamburg, 2004), https://www.grin.com/document/47712.

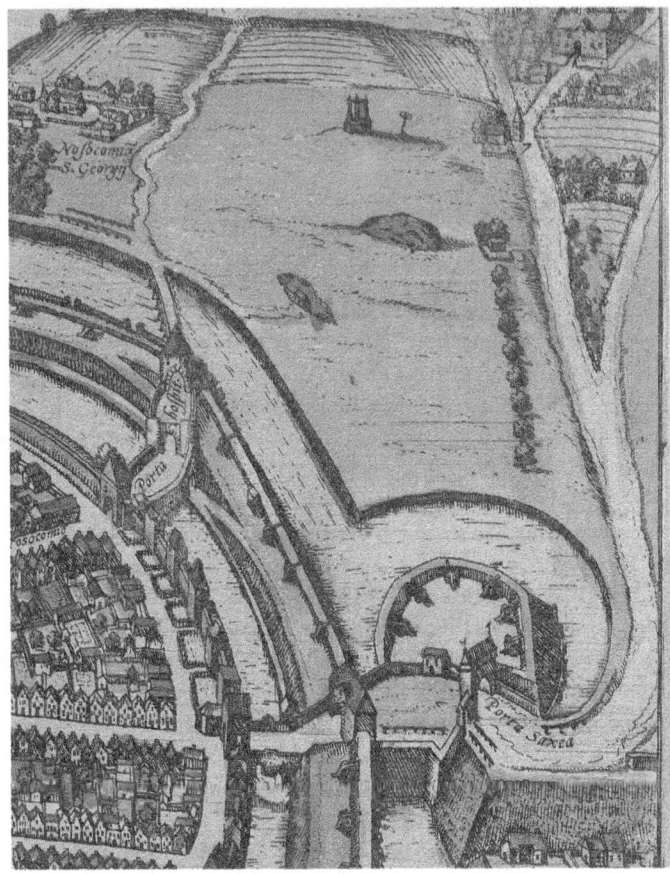

Image 3.2 "Hamburgum," Map (Detail), in Georg Braun and Franz Hogenberg, *Civitates Orbis Terrarum*, vol. 4. Cologne: 1588. Staats- und Universitätsbibliothek Hamburg, Signatur Kt H 202

ravening fowls." Taylor saw twenty such posts with wheels surrounding the ravenstone, "with the heads of men nailed on the top of the posts, with a great spike driven through the skull."[57]

Hamburg carried out executions here until the early nineteenth century. In 1789, the topographer Jonas Ludwig von Heß described the ravenstone as a shortened cone, with a chamber in its interior. Surrounded by a moat filled with water, the only way to access it was to pass over a drawbridge. Once the executioner and his men, the poor sinner, and the clergymen ministering to him or her had crossed onto the ravenstone, the executioner's men raised the drawbridge to prevent spectators from pushing their way onto the platform.[58] On several occasions when the executioner bungled a beheading, taking two or more sword strikes to dispatch the poor sinner, he took refuge from the angry crowd in the interior chamber, until the military could escort him to safety. An engraving of the execution of the Cord Jastram and Hieronymus Snitger, the two leaders of the citizen opposition executed in 1686, shows this imposing edifice. When Hamburg completed its new ravenstone in 1609, this was part of construction boom in the architecture of capital punishment taking place throughout the empire at this time, as cities and territories replaced modest medieval execution sites with more substantial structures, making stone gallows and ravenstones iconic features of the early modern landscape (Image 3.3).[59] Hamburg's ravenstone, complete with moat and drawbridge, was more monumental than most.

In Taylor's account of the execution he witnessed in 1616, he drew attention to the zealous efforts of the clergyman who walked with the condemned man to the ravenstone, "all the way exhorting him to repentance." The pastor's efforts were indispensable to bringing about the desired result that the poor sinner "die resolutely" and to avoid the dreaded outcome that he would die "desperately," for then he would suffer eternal damnation.[60] The participation of the clergy in the execution procession and on the scaffold was the most visible aspect of the sacralization of capital punishment, and of criminal justice more generally, in the

---

[57] Quoted in Richard J. Evans, *Rituals of Retribution: Capital Punishment in Germany, 1600–1987* (Oxford: Oxford University Press, 1996), 27–28.

[58] Jonas Ludwig von Heß, *Hamburg topographisch, politisch und historisch beschrieben*, vol. 2 (Hamburg: Selbstverlag, 1789), 9.

[59] On archaeological research on historical execution sites, see Jost Auler, ed., *Richtstättenarchäologie*, 3 vols., (Dormagen: Archaeotopos-Buchverlag, 2008–2012).

[60] Evans, *Rituals*, 27–28.

Image 3.3 Execution of Cord Jastram and Hieronimus Schnitger, 1687. Engraving (Detail). "Außführung Cord Jastrams und Hieronymi Schnitgers." Hamburg Staatsarchiv, A 320/22

early modern period. The proliferation of religious ritual around executions was a necessary precondition for the development of the practice of suicide by proxy. Numerous engravings of execution scenes from all over the empire show the close involvement of clergy in early modern executions. The engraving showing the executions of Jastram and Snitger is typical in this regard. On the right, marked number 1, Snitger's decapitation is imminent. Snitger kneels as an executioner's man grabs the hair from the top of his head to force him to extend his neck. The executioner stands ready to swing his sword. Just out of reach of the executioner's sword, two clergymen stand close by, recognizable by their long black robes and clerical collars. A short while earlier these same clergymen had walked alongside Snitger in his execution procession, as shown in a companion piece to this engraving. On the left, Jastram's headless body is displayed, labeled number 2. Two of the executioner's men disembowel and quarter his corpse, the traditional penalty for high treason. The two clergymen who had walked with Jastram to the scaffold, and had stood by as close as safely possible during his beheading moments before, look on, their duty not yet done. Subsequent to the action shown here, the bodies of the two men would be interred by the ravenstone, and their heads impaled on posts above two major city gates.[61]

The executions of Jastram and Snitger were more extravagant than most, a reflection of the politically explosive nature of this case. However, most elements shown in this engraving and in its companion piece figured in more mundane executions of regular felons as well. The execution procession and the fervent engagement of the crowd were constant features. Crucially, the close and intensely public involvement of the clergy during the procession and during the execution itself continued until the late eighteenth century. In 1784, the senate ended the participation of clergy in public executions, a dramatic and controversial change to the traditional execution ritual. The senate deliberately secularized executions for the explicit purpose of gaining control of the frequent suicidal child murders in the city.[62]

The sacralization of executions, which the senate set out to undo in 1784, was an early modern, not a medieval, phenomenon. In the Holy Roman Empire, the insertion of religious ritual in executions began, haltingly, in the fifteenth century. The medieval church had been hostile to capital punishment and forbade clergy to be involved. In the fourteenth and fifteenth centuries, however, church authorities began to express concern for the spiritual welfare of condemned criminals. Church synods pressured secular authorities to allow condemned criminals to receive the sacraments, something that had traditionally been denied to them. Secular authorities responded slowly. Beginning in the fifteenth century some German free imperial cities allowed condemned criminals to receive the Eucharist.[63]

Hamburg was not among them. Here condemned criminals did not receive the Eucharist until 1529. Pastoral care to condemned criminals

---

[61] Kai Lohsträter, "Hinter den Kulissen eines Schreckenstheaters: Der Fall Jastram und Snitger in der Theatrum-Literatur des 17. Jahrhunderts," in *Theatralität von Wissen in der Frühen Neuzeit*, eds. Nikola Roßbach and Constanze Baum, 2013, http://diglib.hab.de/ebooks/ed000156/id/ebooks_ed000156_article09/start.htm.

[62] This will be developed in Chap. 4.

[63] Peter Schuster, *Verbrecher, Opfer, Heilige. Eine Geschichte des Tötens 1200–1700* (Stuttgart: Klett-Cotta, 2015), 34, 56–57.

was first introduced in Hamburg in limited form with a pious donation in 1424. A private donor established a charitable endowment to pay a priest to display the sacrament in a monstrance from a window of the cathedral to condemned criminals as they passed by on the way to their execution and to pray the credo over them and grant them an indulgence.[64] Even though condemned criminals did not receive the Eucharist, the pious donation provided them with the opportunity to perform the "salvific gaze," the act of simply looking upon the Eucharist that also conveyed spiritual benefit.[65] Then the execution procession continued on along Steinstraße toward the city gate, where it passed a beguine convent. Here the youngest sister would offer the poor sinner a draft of wine.[66] This was the extent of pastoral care provided to condemned criminals in Hamburg prior to the Reformation.

More elaborate pastoral care for felons awaiting execution began with the Protestant Reformation. The prominent role that the clergy would play in early modern executions grew out of instructions in Johann Bugenhagen's church constitution of 1529. Article XXVI of the church ordinance mandated that condemned criminals be given the opportunity to confess their sins and receive the Eucharist: "Priests should be able to attend to malefactors, not only when they are led out [to the ravenstone], but more often, to teach them and talk to them, so they can come to know the gospel of Christ. This is a work of mercy that Christ will recognize at the Last Judgment. If God grants them the grace that they earnestly confess their faith, and they request the sacrament, then it should not be denied to them, as happens in many places."[67]

Such ritual innovations were not specific to Protestantism, however. As we have seen, these changes predated the Reformation in some areas. In

[64] Nicolaus Staphorst, *Historia ecclesiæ Hamburgensis diplomatica, das ist: Hamburgische Kirchengeschichte...*, vol. 1, 2. (Hamburg: Theodor Christoph Felginern, 1725), 254–256. Johannes Klefeker, *Sammlung der Hamburgischen Gesetze und Verfassungen...*, vol. 8 (Hamburg: J. C. Piscator, 1770), 131, footnote *.

[65] Anton Mayer-Pfannholz, *Die heilbringende Schau in Sitte und Kult* (Münster: Aschendorff, 1938).

[66] Beneke, *Von unehrlichen Leuten*, 106.

[67] Bugenhagen's church ordinance in low German is included in Klefeker, *Sammlung*, vol. 8. The article in question is "Articulus XXVI: Von den Mißdedern tho besokende," 130–131. Johann Melchior Goeze provides a transcription of the article into high German. Johann Melchior Goeze, *Gewissenhafte Erinnerungen zu der Schrift: Ueber die Gewohnheit, Missethäter durch Prediger zur Hinrichtung begleiten zu lassen.* (Hamburg: Dieterich Anton Harmsen, 1784), 9.

1532, just three years after the publication of Bugenhagen's church ordinance, the *Carolina*, the imperial criminal code promulgated by Emperor Charles V, directed local authorities to allow condemned criminals to confess their sins and to have clergy accompany them during their execution procession.[68] Catholic and Protestant territories throughout the empire introduced similar routines of pastoral care. Early modern pastoral care to criminals grew out of the increasing accommodation of both Catholic and Protestant churches to criminal justice administered by the early modern state and did not depend on the specific doctrine of any one confession. Baroque Vienna, as will be shown in Chap. 6, was second to none when it came to elaborate religious ceremonial during public executions.

In the early seventeenth century public desecration of suicides began to play a more prominent and public role in criminal justice, an amplification of the religious discourse on the damnability of suicide. Hamburg's municipal codes of 1497 and 1603 did not legislate on suicide. Nonetheless, the denial of a Christian burial had long been traditional practice.[69] The dishonorable burial of suicides' corpses in Hamburg dated back to the late Middle Ages, if not earlier.[70] It was only in the early seventeenth century, however, that chronicles and execution lists began to record these events, a sign of the rigor with which authorities now enforced the dishonorable burial of suicides.[71] In 1629 Hinrich Dreckmann hung himself in his home. Initially he was interred in the cemetery in a quiet nighttime burial, but apparently his family acted without official permission. The next morning, he was dug up and disposed of in the carrion pit.[72] In 1641 a military trumpeter stabbed his lieutenant to death in a tavern. Taken to prison, he hung himself in his cell. Prison guards covered his body with a tarp and carted it out to the carrion pit. But again, the disposal of the body had apparently not been officially approved. Guards retrieved the body from the pit, transported it back to the city uncovered, carting it through the city in broad daylight for all to see. This infamous exposure replaced what would have been the trumpeter's execution procession. Finally,

---

[68] Josef Kohler and Willy Scheel, eds., *Die peinliche Gerichtsordnung Kaiser Karls V. Consitutio Criminalis Carolina* (Halle a. S.: Verlag Buchhandlung des Waisenhauses, 1900), Article 102, p. 47.
[69] Brahmst, *Hamburgische Strafrecht*, 96.
[70] Beneke, *Von unehrlichen Leuten*, 241–243.
[71] Beneke, *Von unehrlichen Leuten*, 241–243.
[72] Trummer, *Vorträge*, 455.

guards disposed of his body in the carrion pit for a second time.[73] In 1654, when a woman arrested for fraud stabbed herself to death in her cell, authorities dispensed with such a procession, however, and simply disposed of her body in the carrion pit.[74]

By the early seventeenth century the legal framework, physical infrastructure, iconography, and ritual practices that shaped criminal justice in Hamburg until the late eighteenth century were in place. By now Hamburg had vanquished piracy in its waters. The last mass execution of pirates happened in 1578, when the city beheaded twenty-one pirates.[75] According to execution lists, from 1600 to 1649 Hamburg executed sixty-one people, forty-five men and nine women, a significant decline in the number of executions compared to the previous fifty years.[76] To the extent that these numbers represent a real decline and not underreporting, the successful suppression of piracy and the disruptions of the Thirty Years' War likely contributed to falling execution rates. While the total number of recorded executions fell, the proportion of women among executed felons remained at 16%. Most executions of men continued to be for murder, robbery, and theft, though there were also executions for treason, desertions, and for the first time, in 1647, rape, a preview of a more aggressive prosecution of sexual offenses during the second half of the seventeenth century. Two women were executed for infanticide, in 1631 and 1632. As we have seen, Hamburg executed six women for witchcraft between 1600 and 1642. The earliest documented cases of suicide by proxy coincided with these last witch trials.

A New Rationale for Murder: Precursors

The first documented case of suicide by proxy in Hamburg happened in 1624. A young man identified only as "a hunter's son" was flogged at the pillory and then sentenced to ten years "at the cart" for some unspecified "knavery." Cart-pulling was a form of forced labor introduced in Hamburg in 1609 as an alternative to the death penalty. Teams of prisoners swept

---

[73] Trummer, *Vorträge*, 455.
[74] Trummer, *Vorträge*, 455.
[75] Ralf Wiechmann, Eilin Einfeldt and Klaus Püschel, "'...Man soll ihnen ihre Köpfe abschlagen und sie auf einen Stock nageln.' Die Piratenschädel von Grasbrook," in Ralf Wiechmann, Günter Bräuer and Klaus Püschel, eds., in *Klaus Störtebeker. Ein Mythos wird Entschlüsselt*, eds. Ralf Wiechmann, Günter Bräuer and Klaus Püschel (Munich: Wilhelm Fink Verlag, 2003), table 1, p. 94.
[76] For seven executions, no gender is given.

the streets while chained to large two-wheeled carts that they pulled along to transport refuse. Cart-prisoners wore an iron rod fastened to their clothing with bells hanging from it. The number of bells symbolized the length of the prisoner's sentence. Whenever a prisoner had served a year of his sentence, one bell was removed. The hunter's son, a chronicle reports, "finally became weary of such a miserable life."

Somehow, he got his hands on a knife and stabbed a man, apparently a target of opportunity. The man "died on the spot."[77] The cart-prisoner was beheaded. His execution did not go smoothly. Moved by the cart-prisoner's tragic fate, Hamburg executioner Valentin Matz botched the beheading so badly that spectators became incensed. Matz only narrowly escaped the crowd. After this incident, Hamburg abolished cart-pulling as a criminal penalty. By this time, Hamburg's house of correction, founded in 1614 and operational by the early 1620s, provided an alternative.[78]

It was within the walls of this new institution that the next documented case of suicide by proxy took place in 1635. This was the first of a series of murders and attempted murders that by the end of the century escalated into what nineteenth-century prison director Adolf Streng called a "murder epidemic" in Hamburg's carceral institutions.[79] This first attempt, however, was unsuccessful, though not for lack of preparation. Inmate Valentin Kohl decided to escape the house of correction by beating to death a fellow prisoner. After the attack, Kohl told interrogators that his intent had been to be placed into the hands of the judges to stand trial for the murder and thus escape the workhouse. He acted strategically and

---

[77] Chronicler Wolfgang Heinrich Adelung reports that the hunter's son received this sentence *"seiner Büberey halber"* ("because of his knavery"). Wolfgang Heinrich Adelung, *Kurtze Historische Beschreibung der Uhr-Alten Kayserlichen und des Heil. Römischen Reichs Freyen An- See- Kauff- und Handels-Stadt Hamburg* (Hamburg: Conrad Neumann, 1696), 105–106. An execution chronicle gives the date of his execution as April 29, 1624. *Ausführlicher Bericht*, 7.

[78] Johann Gustav Gallois, *Hamburgische Chronik von den ältesten Zeiten bis auf die Jetztzeit*, vol 2 (Hamburg: s.n., 1862), 36. *Ausführlicher Bericht*, 7, for April 29, 1624. Beneke, *Von unehrlichen Leuten*, 150. On the penalty cart-pulling (*Karrenstrafe*) in Hamburg, see Dirk Brietzke, *Arbeitsdisziplin und Armut in der Frühen Neuzeit. Die Zucht- und Arbeitshäuser in den Hansestädten Bremen, Hamburg und Lübeck und die Durchsetzung bürgerlicher Arbeitsmoral im 17. und 18. Jahrhundert* (Hamburg: Verein für Hamburgische Geschichte, 2000), 521–523.

[79] Adolf Streng, *Geschichte der Gefängnissverwaltung in Hamburg von 1622–1872* (Hamburg: Verlagnsanstalt und Druckerei Aktien-Gesellschaft, 1890), 57–58. I discuss the specific institutional culture that encouraged such killings in the next chapter.

with premeditation. Prior to the assault, Kohl went so far as to inquire with the schoolmaster employed in the workhouse whether any inmate who killed someone would be transferred out of the house of correction into the custody of the criminal court to face prosecution. The schoolmaster answered affirmatively—apparently without becoming suspicious—and Kohl carried out his attack. His plan only failed because his victim survived.[80]

Four years later a dramatic murder trial and execution captivated public attention. In 1639 Johann Körner, a journeyman shoemaker, went to the home of executioner Valentin Matz and demanded to be arrested and tried for a murder he had committed in Hamburg seven years earlier. This was not a case of suicide by proxy, but it illustrates how people conceived of public execution as an instrument of salvation. Körner had stabbed his brother-in-law to death over an inheritance dispute in 1632. Though Körner fled town right after the murder, suspicion did not fall on him at the time. He earned his living as a traveling journeyman. The murder remained unsolved and was all but forgotten when Körner turned up at the executioner's home seven years later. The executioner lived within the city prison, so Körner asked Matz to lock him up then and there and to inform the city council, so that he would finally "receive his just deserts." Believing Körner was out of his senses, Matz chased him off. Körner returned the next day, in tears, imploring the executioner to lock him up. He had recently attended a church service, Körner explained, in which the pastor delivered a sermon on the words God had spoken to Cain: "The voice of thy brother's blood crieth unto Me from the ground" (Genesis 4:10). Since then, Körner said, his conscience left him no peace. He pleaded for the death he so richly deserved. Matz now reported the matter to his superiors. Finally, the city council ordered Körner's arrest and trial. The criminal court convicted Körner and sentenced him to death by beheading. At the sentencing, Körner thanked his judges, shaking their hands. A stone had been lifted from his heart, he told them.

He cut a striking figure during his execution procession, wearing a long black coat and a mourning band on his arm. On the scaffold, he showed exemplary penitence. He prayed loudly and bade farewell to the crowd. Then he threw his arms around the executioner's neck and thanked him. Startled, Matz brusquely pushed him away but could barely contain his tears. Emotionally distraught, the executioner needed three strikes to

[80] Brietzke, *Arbeitsdisziplin*, 477, footnote 1330.

complete the beheading. Enraged, the crowd began stoning the executioner and tried to storm the scaffold. Matz took refuge in the interior chamber of the ravenstone. It took a hundred militiamen to escort him to safety. City chronicles reported this story with relish, lingering on the pathos and drama of the case. Whether or not all details of the account were true, the morally instructive story illustrated how the prick of conscience would become excruciating over time. Körner's repentance made him the hero of the story, despite, or perhaps because of, his gruesome death. His botched execution did not dissuade others from seeking death at the executioner's hands.[81]

These three cases, Körner's murder trial and execution, the cart-prisoner's suicidal murder in 1624, and Valentin Kohl's murder attempt in 1635, all illustrate the attraction that public execution held in Hamburg in the early seventeenth century. Körner believed he could expiate his sin on the scaffold. The cart-prisoner and Kohl clearly instrumentalized murder so that they might die by the executioner's sword. However, these two early cases of suicide by proxy do not yet exhibit all the characteristic features the practice would develop later in the century. The cart-prisoner and Kohl each attacked an adult man instead of a child. The cart-prisoner presumably had little choice. Chained to the cart, he had to avail himself of whatever victim was within reach. Kohl, however, could easily have chosen a child as his victim, if this had been important to him. There was always a large number of children in custody in the house of correction, as will be shown in the next chapter. Kohl attacked a man rather than a child, however.

These early cases show that in Hamburg in the 1620s and 1630s the logic and liturgy of suicide by proxy was not yet fully developed. Over the coming decades, however, suicide by proxy in Hamburg underwent a "consolidation of a discourse." This is how historian R. Po-Chia Hsia describes the standardization of blood libel cases from the Middle Ages

---

[81] An execution chronicle gives the date of his execution as February 4, 1639. *Ausführlicher Bericht*, 8. Executioner Valentin Matz lost his position after this execution and settled in the city as a medical practitioner. Adelung, *Historische Beschreibung*, 111. Jacob Daniel Ernst, *Die neu-auffgerichtete Schatz-Cammer vieler hundert... Erzehlungen* (Altenburg: Gottfried Richters seel. Erben, 1696), 770–773. The most detailed account of the case is in Michael Gottlieb Stelzner, *Versuch einer zuverlässigen Nachricht von dem kirchlichen und politischen Zustande der Stadt Hamburg*, vol. 3 (s.l., 1733), 355–358. Otto Beneke, *Hamburgische Geschichten und Sagen*, 2nd edition (Hamburg: Perthes, Besser & Mauke, 1854), 301–307. Beneke, *Von unehrlichen Leuten*, 150–151.

through the 1470s. In early Jewish ritual murder accusations, Hsia shows, the victimology varied more than in later cases, as did the alleged murder method. Twelfth-century ritual murder legends involved mock crucifixions rather than the stereotypical draining of blood of later cases. Early blood libel cases featured mostly male victims, as would later cases, but there were also girls, a woman, even an entire family. Male victims in early cases ranged in age from infancy to adolescence. After the paradigmatic case of Simon of Trent in 1475, however, accusations crystalized to focus "on boys between infancy and age seven, the age of childhood." With this standardization of the victimology, Hsia argues, "representations of boy victims and the Child Jesus became fused."[82] In contrast to the imagined Jewish killers of ritual murder legends, actual perpetrators of suicidal murders killed victims of both sexes. As the practice of suicide by proxy became established, however, suicidal murderers overwhelmingly chose to murder young children, as two concepts merged: The desire to die a blessed death as a penitent poor sinner on the scaffold and the idea of child sacrifice.

INVOKING DIVINE INTERVENTION: THE "ORDEAL OF THE BIER" AND THE "JUSTICE OF THE STREET"

Beginning in the 1640s Hamburg authorities had to deal with a growing number of child murders, both fabricated and real. In 1642, the same year that the last execution for witchcraft in Hamburg took place, prosecutors investigated the case of Maria Behont, who accused herself of infanticide. Unable to discover any corroborating evidence, they concluded that

---

[82] R. Po-Chia Hsia, *The Myth of Ritual Murder: Jews and Magic in Reformation Germany* (New Haven: Yale University Press, 1988), 54–55. On the diversity of victims and methods in early blood libel legends, see also Wolfgang Treue, *Der Trienter Judenprozess: Voraussetzungen, Abläufe, Auswirkungen (1475–1588)* (Hannover: Verlag Hahnsche Buchhandlung, 1996), 33–38. Female victims in blood libel cases were a seven-year-old girl, Margaretha of Pforzheim, variously dated between 1260 and 1271, and the three- or four-year-old girl Ursula Pöck, also known as Ursula von Lienz, in 1443. On Margaretha, see Herbert Ruff, "Die Margaretha von Pforzheim—Geschichte, Legende, Tradition," in *Ängste und Auswege. Bilder aus Umbruchszeiten in Pforzheim*, vol. 1, ed. Gerhard Brändle (Ubstadt-Weiher: Verlag Regionalkultur 2001), 139–170. On Ursula Pöck, see Meinrad Pizzini, "Ursula Pöck—eine mittelalterliche Ritualmordlegende aus Lienz," *Veröffentlichungen des Tiroler Landesmuseums Ferdinandeum* 70 (1990): 219–234.

Behont had accused herself out of "weariness with life." The court absolved her of all charges.[83]

After 1650 the number of recorded executions rose again, though they never came close to sixteenth-century levels. Hamburg executed 108 people from 1650 to 1699, eighty men and twenty-eight women. Women now made up 24% of executed felons. Murder, robbery, and theft continued to account for most executions of men. There were also executions for sedition, arson, and coin clipping. However, in a change from the past, rape, sodomy, bigamy, incest, and adultery now also featured among the offenses of men executed in Hamburg, another sign of the increasing severity with which prosecutors in the second half of the seventeenth century handled sexual offenses. Women were executed for poisoning, murder, robbery, and theft. Several women were executed for infanticide and abortion. Beginning in the 1660s, several women committed suicide by proxy.

In 1665, an execution chronicle reported, a woman named Berte Petersen was beheaded, and her head was impaled on a post for cutting her own child's throat.[84] This woman's motives are unknown, but this does not appear to have been a classic case of infanticide. Typically, when an unwed mother killed her newborn infant, the chronicle referred to the woman as "a whore."[85] When Petersen cut her child's throat, she chose the murder method employed by almost all suicidal child murderers over the next 150 years. By contrast, in classic infanticide cases unwed mothers typically chose a less violent, more passive method.[86]

The first fully documented case of suicidal child murder happened in 1668. Here the killer clearly articulated her suicidal intent. On February 4, 1668, Adelgunda Walters cut the throat of her seven-year-old sister. She then immediately approached the judge to announce her deed. Six weeks later, on March 16, she was beheaded and her head impaled on a post. The

---

[83] The legal decision from March 28, 1642, is mentioned in the footnotes to Article 23, "Punishment of those who murder their parents, children, sisters, brothers, or other close relations," of Hamburg's revised civic code of 1603. Verein für Hamburgische Geschichte, ed., *Der Stadt Hamburg Gerichts-Ordnung und Statuta* (Hamburg: Perthes, Besser & Mauke, 1842), 534. It is unclear what if any consequences Maria Behont faced for what authorities believed was her false self-accusation.

[84] *Ausführlicher Bericht*, 11, for 4 December, 1665.

[85] As, for example, in this case: "1632, den 20 Januar, ist eine Hure enthauptet; weil sie ihr Kind ermordet." *Ausführlicher Bericht*, 8.

[86] See Chap. 2.

executioner threw her body in a ditch, beneath the wheel that would have broken her body, had she received the statutory penalty set for her crime.[87] Hamburg's criminal law code of 1603 followed the cue of the *Carolina*, the imperial criminal code, in punishing the murder of blood relatives more severely than other homicides. Article Twenty-three of the Hamburg code, "On those who murder their parents, children, sisters, brothers or other close relatives," set the normative penalty. Children who murdered their parents, or parents who murdered their children "out of evil devilish intent," would have their flesh torn with red-hot tongs prior to being broken "alive" by the wheel. This meant that the executioner would administer the blows of the wheel "from the bottom up," that is from the feet, working his way up to the final fatal blow at the neck, in order to prolong the agony of the condemned. Those who murdered siblings or other relatives would also be broken by the wheel, but the article did not specify that these murderers would be broken "alive," so we can assume they were to be broken "from the top down," that is, the executioner would break their neck first before breaking the rest of the body.[88] Adelgunda Walters did not die by the wheel, however. She was "a young woman." Perhaps her youth influenced the judges. More important, however, was her motive: "she was affected by despair, and confessed that she did it because she was weary of her life." Her state of mind justified the reduced sentence.

Adelgunda "endured her punishment with a joyous heart," a news digest published the following year reports.[89] The digest described the circumstances surrounding the murder. It happened during Carnival. The seven-year-old girl asked her sister for a cookie commonly given to children during this festive season. "Come, let me bind your eyes, we will play Carnival," Adelgunda answered, "I will give you a cookie." She led her

---

[87] [Johann Christoph Beer] *Historischer Rosen-Garten, bestehend in drey Hundert...Historien....* (Frankfurt/Leipzig, Michael Schmatz, 1710), 1005–1006. Beer does not identify Adelgunda Walters by name, but the execution register records her execution for cutting her sister's throat six weeks after the murder. *Ausführlicher Bericht*, 11. The rationale for the sentencing is explained in Christian van Nettelbladt, *Thesaurus Iuris Provincialis Et Statutarii Illustrati Germaniae....* (Giessen: Johann Christoph Schroeder, 1756), 1028.

[88] *Hamburgk Gerichtsordnung*, Artic. 23, p. 364.

[89] "...stund ihre Strafe mit freudigem Hertzen aus." Johannes Praetorius, *M. DC. LXVIII. Zodiacus Mercurialis eXpLICanDIssIMVs. Das ist: Jährige Europaeische Welt-Chronick....* (Jena: Johannes Nisius, 1669), 9–10.

sister into the attic and bound her eyes. Then she slashed the girl's throat. In contrast to court records, the digest does not mention Adelgunda's suicidal intent as a murder motive. Instead, it explains the murder as a revenge killing. We learn that the little girl had tattled on her sister for some unspecified misbehavior. This element conforms to a recurring pattern in the confessions of many perpetrators of suicide by proxy. The exposure of some minor, even trivial infraction led to a loss of face so profound that it sparked suicidal despair.[90] This may have been Adelgunda's emotional state when she resolved to bring about her own death by murdering her sister, though a desire for revenge may well have played a role. Immediately after the murder Adelgunda ran "out of the house to the judge covered in blood" to report her crime. Despite the blood, officials initially believed that she was out of her senses, an indication that in 1668 suicidal child murders had not yet become so common in Hamburg that authorities immediately recognized the type of crime they were dealing with. Their doubts were dispelled when they found the body.

Official proceedings began the next day. In a dramatic public ceremony, authorities confronted Adelgunda with the body of her sister. "By means of the known blood signs the murdered child attributed the murder to the murderess as she was judicially led up [to the body]," the digest reports.[91] Seventeenth-century readers would have understood what these "known blood signs" were. This was cruentation, also known as ordeal of the bier. Cruentation (from the Latin *cruentare*, to make bloody) was a medieval and early modern judicial ordeal used to identify a murderer. Murder suspects had to approach the body, sometimes in the nude or dressed only in a new white shift. Then they touched the body or stroked its wounds while swearing an oath to their innocence, an act they had to repeat three times. If the body bled, this proved their guilt.[92]

---

[90] See Chap. 8.

[91] "…und wies auch des andern Tages das ermordete Kind durch bekannte Blutzeichen/ der rechtlich hinzugeführten Mörderin ihre Mordthat aus/…" Beer, *Historischer Rosengarten*, 1006.

[92] A famous visual representation of the ritual of cruentation is contained in the 1513 Chronicle of Lucerne by Diebold Schilling. It shows the naked accused wife murderer Hans Spiess stroking his wife's body in her coffin in 1503. The body bleeds profusely at his touch. Spiess then confessed. The next image shows Spiess being broken by the wheel for his crime. Alfred A. Schmid, ed., *Die Schweizer Bilderchronik des Diebold Schilling*. (Faksimile-Verlag: Luzern, 1981), 319–320. The image can be viewed online here: https://de.wikipedia.org/wiki/Hans_Spiess#/media/Datei:Bahrprobe_und_R%C3%A4dern_(Hans_Spiess).jpg

Contemporaries offered a variety of explanations for such wondrous post-mortem bleeding. Folk beliefs centered on the idea of the "living corpse." Some residue of life or of the soul remained in the body and continued to animate the blood after death. When the murderer approached, the victim's blood reacted with violent antipathy. Opinions differed whether this was a natural or supernatural effect. The predominant explanation, however, was the Christian idea that the blood of the victim cried out to God for vengeance. God caused the body to bleed as a divine sign, by which he made hidden sin manifest.[93] The use of cruentation was controversial. In 1215, the Fourth Lateran Council outlawed the participation of clergy in other medieval judicial ordeals, such as ordeals by fire, water, or combat. By the late Middle Ages, as the inquisitorial procedure became established, ordeals in general were increasingly marginalized and condemned as superstitious. Nonetheless, courts continued to use cruentation.[94] As late as 1511 Hamburg authorities officially used the ordeal of the bier in a murder case, confronting a man with the body of a smith he was suspected of killing. In this case, the corpse gave no sign. The court did not accept this lack of bleeding as sufficient proof of innocence, however. Officials proceeded to question the suspected murderer under torture and extracted a confession. The court convicted him and sentenced him to beheading.[95]

In the sixteenth and seventeenth centuries, jurists educated in Roman law attempted to suppress the use of "irrational proofs" in criminal law. Benedikt Carpzow (1595–1666), perhaps the most cited jurist in early modern criminal jurisprudence and enormously influential in Hamburg, was among them.[96] Despite their efforts, there were examples through the late eighteenth century when courts resorted, officially or unofficially, to the ordeal of the bier. Popular belief in the efficacy of cruentation persisted

---

[93] Werner Ogris, "Bahrprobe," in: *Lexikon zur Geschichte der Hexenverfolgung*, eds. Gudrun Gersmann, Katrin Moeller und Jürgen-Michael Schmidt, in: historicum.net, URL: https://www.historicum.net/purl/jfzna/ (2.23.2020); Robert P. Brittain, "Cruentation in Legal Medicine and in Literature," *Medical History* 9 (1965): 82–88.
[94] A. Erler, "Gottesurteil," *HRG* 1, (Berlin: Erich Schmidt Verlag, 1971), 1769–1773.
[95] Frank Eichler, ed., *Die Langenbeck'sche Glosse zum Hamburger Stadtrecht von 1497* (Hamburg: Mauke Schweitzer Gruppe, 2008), 397.
[96] Gerd Kleinheyer and Jan Schröder, eds., *Deutsche und Europäische Juristen aus neun Jahrhunderten. Eine biographische Einführung in die Geschichte der Rechtswissenschaft* (Tübingen: Mohr Siebeck, 2017), 94.

well into the nineteenth century.[97] Writing in the 1780s, the Hamburg historian Leonhard Wächter commented on the practice of cruentation in Hamburg in his own time. Prosecutors in Hamburg still performed the Ordeal of the Bier, he wrote, not because they expected the corpse to produce a wondrous sign, but in order to apply psychological pressure to murder suspects and induce a confession.[98]

We do not know whether cruentation played any official role in the criminal trial of Adelgunda Walters, as the news digest claimed. In any event, proof by cruentation would not have been necessary in this case, since Adelgunda freely confessed to the murder and told authorities where to find her sister's body. The news digest was accurate, however, in reporting Adelgunda Walters' confrontation with the body of her victim. This dramatic judicial ritual bore a striking resemblance to the ordeal of the bier. During the Middle Ages and the early modern period, Hamburg authorities performed a ritual "hue and cry" over the corpses of all murder victims, as an indictment of the murderers, whether known or unknown, whether present or absent. This marked the formal beginning of any felony murder trial. This solemn ceremony happened as soon as possible after the discovery of the body. It was called the "Justice of the Street" (*Strassen Recht*, or *ius viarum* in Latin), and as the name indicates, it took place in the public street, usually at or as close as possible to the place where the murder had occurred. The "Justice of the Street" was not unique to Hamburg. The *Carolina* left it to the discretion of local governments whether to perform the ceremony.[99] Most jurisdictions no longer performed this ritual in the early modern period, but Hamburg and

---

[97] Owen Davies and Francesca Matteoni, *Executing Magic in the Modern Era: Criminal Bodies and the Gallows in Popular Medicine* (Basingstoke: Palgrave Macmillan, 2017), 21–24.

[98] Wächter equated the "Justice of the Street" with cruentation. Veit Weber [Leonhard Wächter], *Sagen der Vorzeit*, vol. 1 (Berlin: Friedrich Maurer, 1787), 143, fn. a. Wächter published under the pseudonym Veit Weber.

[99] Heinrich Zoepfl, ed., *Die Peinliche Gerichtsordnung Kaiser Karl's V nebst der Bamberger und der Brandenburger Halsgerichtsordnung...* (Leipzig: C.F. Winter, 1883), 231, Artikel LXXXVII. "Von beschreien des beklagten: Item mit dem beschreien der übelthetter soll es imm selbigen stuck auf gegenwertigkeit vnd beger des anklegers nach jedes gerichts gutter gewonheyt gehalten werden...."

neighboring Lübeck did.[100] The eighteenth-century Hamburg jurist Johann Klefeker explained the purpose of the ceremony: "The display of the body justified the felony accusation, and the hue and cry initiated it .... Before the formal beginning of trial the body in the coffin is carried into the circle .... The purpose was to assemble the people, in whose presence the casket is opened, the body displayed and the death publicly proven, establishing the *corpus delicti*."[101]

The main actors in the ritual were the warden (*Vogt*), the chief court officer who presided over criminal trials, the prosecutor, the executioner, and the accused murderer, if he or she was in custody. All gathered around the open casket in which the murder victim lay. The warden initiated a formulaic exchange, following a script that did not vary over the centuries. The prosecutor spoke on behalf of the murder victim. Indeed, the original medieval ritual conceived of the dead person as a participant in the ceremony who spoke through the prosecutor.[102] Then the executioner summoned the accused to appear, ritualistically repeating the formulaic summons three times. If the accused murderer was present, the prosecutor then asked for a confession. The accused pled guilty or not guilty. Then followed the most dramatic moment: The executioner unsheathed his sword, raised it above his head, and cried out loudly over the dead body, and over the murderer, if present. He cried out what was known as the *Zetergeschrei* in German, or *clamor violentia* in Latin: "Hue and cry over this murderer ... who did the murder in this honorable city of Hamburg."[103] Like the original summons, the executioner repeated this ritual cry three

---

[100] In some other jurisdictions, notably in Saxony, a pared-down version of the ritual was still performed, where the ritual hue and cry was combined with the proclamation of the verdict at the conclusion of the criminal trial. In this variant of the ritual there was no confrontation between the accused murderer and his or her victim, since the murder victim was long buried. According to Zedler's Universal-Lexikon "ist solche Proclamation nach der Zeit abkommen, und bis auf die letzte Session des Blut-Gerichts verschoben worden." The ritual immediately preceded sentencing and execution. "Zetter-Geschrey," *Universal-Lexikon*, vol. 61 (1749), 1813–1814. For Saxony, see Benedict Carpzov, *Peinlicher sächsischer Inquisition- und Achts-Proceß* (Leipzig: Johann Christoph Tarnov, 1673), 170–174.

[101] Klefeker, *Sammlung*, vol. 5 (Hamburg: J. C. Piscator, 1768), 572–573.

[102] D. Werkmüller, "Klage mit dem toten Mann," *HRG* 2 (1978), 849–851.

[103] "Zetter uber diesen Mörder.../so diesen Mord... in...dieser Ehrenreichen Stadt Hamburg...gethan hat." Jacob Daniel Horb, *Disputatio inauguralis de jure viarum circa clamorem violentiæ, vulgo Strassen Recht das Mordgeschrey betreffend* (Franeker: Johannes Gyzelaar, 1699),13–14. Peter Mascov, *Dissertatio iuridica de clamore violentia, vulgo Vom Zetter-Geschrey* (Greifswald: Matthaeus Doischerus, 1746).

times. An eighteenth-century English dictionary explained to contemporary English readers what was happening here. The executioner's cry was "an act of justice, like that in England of the Coroner and Jury of twelve men's sitting upon the body of such as have been found dead; they beshrew, cry out upon, accuse and threaten the murtherer where-soever he be, to summon and call upon him to appear before the justice and receive his deserved punishment."[104] After the conclusion of the executioner's hue and cry, the warden ended the ceremony by ordering the burial of the murder victim, "since it is not possible that the dead body can remain among the living." If the suspect was in custody, the executioner then escorted him or her to prison, which was also the executioner's residence. There the accused remained for the duration of the felony murder trial that followed.[105]

The illumination from Hamburg's law code of 1497 gives an idea of what the "Justice of the Street" looked like as it played out in the public square. At the center right of the image we see the open casket with the murder victim in his shroud, his bloody head wounds prominent (Image 3.1). Onlookers mill about. At the head of the coffin, the executioner has unsheathed his sword. This was the climactic moment when he would cry out over the murderer. The accused stands to the right of the executioner, his hands bound in front of him. The executioner holds his sword over the man's head.[106]

The "Justice of the Street" bore an unmistakable resemblance to the ordeal of cruentation. Both ceremonies involved a ritualistic repetition of a set verbal formula. In cruentation, the accused swore an oath of innocence three times while touching the body. In the "Justice of the Street," the executioner uttered his hue and cry over the murderer three times. Most importantly, if the accused murderer was in custody, both rites featured a dramatic confrontation between the murderer and the dead body of his or her victim. Given these similarities, it is not surprising that the 1669 news digest described Adelgunda Walter's confrontation with her sister's body as an ordeal of cruentation. Even though the ordeal of the bier was disappearing in official jurisprudence by the seventeenth century,

---

[104] "Beschreien," in Christian Ludwig, *Teutsch-Englisches Lexicon*... (Leipzig: Johann Friedrich Gleditschens, 1789), 249.

[105] The words that the court officers had to speak over the dead body are reproduced in Klefeker, *Sammlung*, vol 5. 5 (Hamburg: J. E. Piscator, 1768), 559–568. The ritual unfolded similarly, whether the accused was present or not.

[106] Binder, *Illustriertes Recht*, 69–70.

many contemporaries believed that such post-mortem bleeding was a wondrous sign of God's providence that made hidden sin manifest.[107] Jurists and theologians cited the same Old Testament verse to justify and explain the ritual that had moved fugitive murderer Johann Körner to surrender to authorities in 1639. God cursed Cain after he murdered Abel: "the voice of thy brother's blood crieth unto me from the ground" (Genesis, 4:10–11).[108] In his 1699 doctoral dissertation, the Hamburg jurist Johannes Horb drew on this same verse to explain the origin of Hamburg's "Justice of the Street," another indication of the similarity between the two rituals.[109]

Hamburg authorities performed the "Justice of the Street" continuously from the Middle Ages until the late eighteenth century. In her study of the cultural history of death, Irmgard Wilhelm-Schaffer emphasizes the continuity and immutability over centuries of ritual surrounding death. One striking example of such continuity is mortuary ritual in the region around Trier in the 1950s that included songs and prayers that has been in use for more than 1100 years. Such persistence and inertia in death ritual meant that change only happened, Wilhelm-Schaffer argues, in response to significant transformations in culture and mentality. The same is true of judicial ritual. The "Justice of the Street" was at once judicial ritual and death ritual. Hamburg authorities finally abolished the ceremony in 1784, one month after they ended the participation of clergy in executions. The city council's decision to end a centuries-long practice was an expression of profound cultural change that ultimately contributed to the decline in the practice of suicide by proxy.[110] Until then, members of the public who attended these spectacles experienced them as hallowed by law and custom and mandated by divine authority. As late as 1777 Johann Melchior Goeze, one Hamburg's most prominent pastors and pugnacious represen-

[107] Beer explained how cruentation worked here: "es geschehe solches durch extraordinary Mitwürkung GOttes/ die Abscheulichkeit solches Lasters dardurch verstehen zu geben." Johann Christoph Beer, *Historisches Spatzier- und Conversation ... Büchlein, von 300. auserlesenen theils lust- und lehrreichen, theils schrecken-vollen Trauer-Geschichten ... In dreyen absonderlichen Theilen ... aus bewährten Autoren vorgestellet* (Nuremberg: Wolffgang Michahelles and Johann Adolph, 1701), 66.

[108] See above.

[109] Jacob Daniel Horb and Jacobus Rhenferd, *Disputatio inauguralis de jure viarum circa clamorem violentiæ, vulgo Strassen Recht das mordgeschrey betreffend* (Franeker: Johannes Gyzelaar, 1699), 7.

[110] Late eighteenth-century criminal justice reforms and their impact on suicide by proxy in Hamburg will be discussed in the next chapter.

tative of Lutheran orthodoxy, argued that the hue and cry over the dead body, "as is still customary among us," originated in biblical command. "Which sad spectacle, alas! we have to see so often," he lamented.[111] These were emotionally fraught, charged occasions where onlookers were primed to witness the uncanny, some kind of supernatural sign. Every time a suicidal child murderer, infanticidal mother, or any murderer was confronted with the body of his or her victim in the public street, spectators undoubtedly watched the corpse carefully, even as they scrutinized the demeanor of the accused.[112]

Forty-two years after Adelgunda Walter's execution, the Lutheran theologian Johann Christoph Beer (1638–1712) included her case his *Historical Rose Garden*, a compilation of edifying stories published in 1710.[113] Beer lived in Nuremberg, another center of Lutheran orthodoxy. He worked as a proofreader in Nuremberg printing houses.[114] This may be where he came across Adelgunda Walter's case. Collecting and compiling crime stories was a lucrative business. Protestant pastors and theologians were the most productive collectors and publishers of crime stories because they saw it as part of a larger moral enterprise. True crime reporting illustrated human moral depravity and vulnerability to instigation by the devil, a central tenet of Lutheran teaching.[115] Recycling the 1669 news digest on Adelgunda Walter more or less verbatim, Beer warned that Satan could ensnare even the most young and innocent soul, a reference to Adelgunda's youth. The "known blood signs" by which the murdered child identified Adelgunda as her killer, as the 1669 report described, was most likely what drew Beer's attention this case. Beer was an enthusiastic believer in the efficacy of cruentation, and the ordeal of the bier featured in a number of

[111] Goeze suggests that the ceremony was based on 5 Moses 21, 1–9 (Deuteronomy 21; 1–9). Johann Melchior Goeze, *Johan Melchior Goezens, Pastoris zu St. Cathar. in Hamburg, Auszüge aus seinen Sontags-, Fest- und verschiedenen Wochen-Predigten des 1777 Jahres* (Hamburg: Dietrich Anton Harmsen, 1777), 275.

[112] For additional accounts of the "Right of the Street," see Wolfgang Jacob Geiger, *Theatri Europaei. Das ist: Glaubwürdige Beschreibung Denckwürdiger Geschichten ...*, vol. 10 (Frankfurt a.M: Johann Görlin, 1703), 178.

[113] [Beer], *Historischer Rosen-Garten*, 1005–1006.

[114] G. C. A. M van Gemert, "Beer, Johann Christoph (1638–1712),"in *Killy Literaturlexikon. Autoren und Werke des deutschsprachigen Kulturraums*, vol 1, 2nd edition (Berlin/New York: De Gruyter, 2008), 312.

[115] On the prominence of Protestant clergy among authors and collectors of crime stories, see Joy Wiltenburg, *Crime and Culture in Early Modern Germany* (Charlottesville: University of Virginia Press, 2012), 88–110.

his stories. Among them was a ritual murder legend about the murder of a young orphan girl in Pforzheim by Jews in 1271. The body of the martyred girl bled miraculously to expose her Jewish killers, whose execution followed promptly.[116] Cruentation was a recurring feature of blood libel legends. The stories featured child martyrs who revealed the guilt of the Jews by miraculous post-mortem bleeding in the presence of their killers.[117] The portrayal of the "Justice of the Street" held over Adelgunda Walter's slain sister as an ordeal of the bier in the 1669 news digest, and in Beer's retelling in 1710, made the echoes of the blood libel more prominent.

In the 106 years that elapsed between Adelgunda Walter's trial in 1668 and 1784, the year that Hamburg finally discontinued the ritual hue and cry over the corpses of murder victims and their killers, inhabitants of Hamburg had witnessed a "Justice of the Street" over the body of a slain child and his or her murderer at least sixty-four times. In addition to the victims of suicidal child murder, Hamburg also performed the "hue and cry" over the corpses of newborn infants discovered within the city. Cases of infanticide increased in the seventeenth century, though it is impossible to offer precise numbers.

The prevalence of infanticide is an important aspect of the societal context of suicide by proxy, although unwed mothers who killed their newborns had a very different murder motive than did the suicidal child killers we are discussing here. Like witch-hunting, prosecutions of infanticidal mothers increased the number of women subjected to capital punishment. Women in the crowd of spectators were more likely to identify with a young woman dying on the ravenstone, and the public discourse about women's murderous nature that these prosecutions entailed also influenced women's choice to commit suicide by proxy. Perhaps most

[116] Beer, *Spatzier- und Conversation … Büchlein*, 68–69. Beer does not provide the name of the young Christian girl, but this story refers to the blood libel case of Margaretha of Pforzheim, variously dated as 1260 or 1267. Incidentally, Margarethe was allegedly seven years old at the time of her martyrdom, the same age as Adelgunda Walter's sister. However, Beer does not give her age in his story. On the role of cruentation in the Margaretha von Pforzheim case, see Irven M. Resnick, "Cruentation, Medieval Anti-Jewish Polemic, and Ritual Murder," *Antisemitism Studies* 3 (2019): 95–131.

[117] For example, Heinrich Menger, 1260 in Weissenbrunn. Resnick, "Cruentation," 99, 114. A boy in Überlingen, 1331. Johannes Vitoduranus, "Die Chronik des Minderbruders Johannes von Winthertur III," *Neujahrs-Blatt der Bürgerbibliothek in Winterthur* 22 (1861): 145–147. Simon of Trent, 1475. R. Po-Chia Hsia, *Trent 1475: Stories of a Ritual Murder* (New Haven: Yale University Press, 1992), 3.

importantly, in Hamburg the recurring spectacles of infant corpses ritually displayed during the "Justice of the Street" contributed to the fraught moral atmosphere that encouraged suicidal child murders.

The number of infanticides in Hamburg was far greater than the number of infanticidal mothers listed in execution chronicles. Some infanticidal mothers were spared execution due to mitigating circumstances, and the number of unsolved cases was high. In 1607, an infanticidal mother was whipped at the pillory and banished for life. The woman's mother was prosecuted as an accomplice and banished for life as well.[118] In 1608 Gretkin Siners was whipped at the pillory and banished for life. She had given birth in secret. Her infant's body was found in a drawer. The midwife's testimony that the baby was most likely stillborn, along with Siner's youth and simplemindedness spared her the death penalty.[119] The trial of Engelen Eilers in 1609 had a different outcome. She "acted counter to natural love and the 5th commandment of God and with malicious intent gruesomely murdered her own child born of her body right after birth." She had broken her infant's neck. She had been surprised by the birth, her defense advocate argued. Suffering severe pain during labor, she had succumbed to the instigation of the evil spirit, unaware of what she was doing. The defense advocate's plea for a merciful sentence failed. Engelen's act of breaking her child's neck, as opposed to the more passive means chosen by most infanticidal mothers, all but assured her death sentence. Eilers had acted in complete disregard of natural love, worse than a brute animal, the prosecutor argued. The court sentenced her to beheading.[120] Hamburg beheaded two women, each labeled a "whore," for infanticide in 1631 and 1632.[121] In 1635, the Lower Court sentenced Anneken Cordes to death by beheading for infanticide, but the Superior Court changed the sentence to whipping at the pillory and banishment for life. Even under torture, she insisted that she had no memory of giving birth or hiding her infant behind the bed. Her defense advocate argued that she was afflicted by puerperal madness.[122] There were further beheadings of infanticidal mothers in 1653, in 1658, and in 1663.[123]

[118] Brahmst, *Hamburgische Strafrecht*, 44.
[119] Trummer, *Vorträge*, 440.
[120] Jacobi, *Niedergericht*, 260–261.
[121] *Ausführlicher Bericht*, 9–10.
[122] "...furorum mentis in partu." *Der Stadt Hamburg Gerichtsordnung und Statuta* (Hamburg: Perthes-Besser & Mauke, 1842), 534–535. Trummer, *Vorträge*, 440.
[123] *Ausführlicher Bericht*, 9–10; StAH, 111-1, Senat, CI.VII, Lit. Mb, No.3, Vol.1, 363.

Many infanticide cases in Hamburg, indeed perhaps most, were never solved. How high was the "dark figure" for infanticide? The question of how many neonaticides actually occurred, as opposed to how many cases led to prosecution or conviction, is usually impossible for historians to answer. Exceptionally, a bureaucratic dispute in 1696 sheds some light on this question. In that year *Stadtphysicus* Dr. Johann Garmers, the appointed city physician, became embroiled in a conflict with the newly appointed senior prosecutor about the proper procedure to follow when an infant corpse was discovered in the city. The prosecutor wanted to require Garmers or his assistant, the junior city physician, *Subphysicus* Dr. Biester, to perform their examinations of any recently discovered infant corpse at nine in the morning and provide him with their written report by ten, so he would have it in hand to present to the city council meeting later in the day.

Dr. Garmers had entered city service a junior physician in 1659 and advanced to the senior position in 1672. He now drew on his decades of experience to argue that the prosecutor's new directive was burdensome and counterproductive. The last time any prosecutor had made a similar request was thirty-six years ago, in 1660, Garmers claimed. In that year infanticides had been so rampant that in the month of July alone twelve dead infants had been found in the city. In every case, the cause of death had been a torn umbilical cord. It had been customary in 1660 to complete medical reports on the cause of death for each case, but Garmers' superior, *Stadtphysicus* Dr. Huswedel, had raised the concern with the presiding mayor that the medical reports might actually encourage infanticides by publicizing the most efficient method of killing newborns.

The mayor directed that henceforth such clinical details should be kept secret. People who delivered infant corpses (to the *Stadtphysicus*' personal residence!) should be instructed that "a hue and cry must be held over the child, since it died a violent death."[124] In other words, the public-facing response to infanticide was the "Justice of the Street," though city physicians continued to perform medical inspections and record them in their

---

[124] "Das Kind müsse beschrien werden, weilen es gewaltsamen Todes gestorben." Herman Gustav Gernet, *Mittheilungen aus der älteren Medicinalgeschichte Hamburgs. Kulturhistorische Skizze auf urkundlichem und geschichtlichen Grunde* (Hamburg: W. Mauke Söhne, 1869), 219.

protocol book. The new prosecutor's insistence that he needed timely autopsy reports as evidence in criminal trials was specious, Garmers argued. In his thirty-six years of service to the city, no infanticidal mother had ever been identified. In the unlikely event that the discovery of a dead newborn did result in criminal prosecution, he argued, the cause of death could be copied from the physicians' protocol book. Garmers' claim that no case of neonaticide had been solved in thirty-six years is remarkable. Execution lists seem to support his claim, however. In 1660, the year that twelve infant corpses were found in the month of July, execution lists do not record a single execution for infanticide. From 1660 to 1696, there were thirteen recorded executions for child murder. None of them involved a clearcut case of neonaticide. The victimology and murder method employed in eleven of them suggest that these were cases of suicide by proxy.

Regardless of whether a neonaticide resulted in a trial and execution of the infanticidal mother, or whether the murder went unsolved, the regular discovery of dead infants in the city contributed to an atmosphere of moral crisis. Every infant corpse found in the streets prompted the city to hold the dramatic public ceremony of the "Justice of the Street." In contrast to the ceremonies occasioned by cases of suicide by proxy, in infanticide cases the perpetrator often had not been identified and was therefore not present to hear the executioner's cry. A description of one such ceremony in 1701 gives an idea of what the public saw and heard on these occasions. The "Justice of the Street" took place in the market place on February 3, after a dead newborn infant had been discovered buried in a cabbage patch two days earlier. The prosecutor loudly proclaimed that killing was forbidden in divine and imperial law, and was punishable by death. "But, alas!" he continued, "it was discovered day before yesterday that a more than unchristian mother ... buried her newborn child in the earth and suffocated it. It lies here, pale and dead before our eyes. This horrific murder of an innocent child goes against nature. It cannot remain unpunished by worldly authority." The prosecutor requested a sentence of beheading for the infanticidal mother, once she was apprehended, and finally, he asked for permission to bury the infant at the conclusion of the ceremony, "because this pale little body cannot remain unburied above ground." Then the executioner three times ritually summoned the unknown child murderess to appear. When she failed to present herself, he thrice uttered the hue and cry, holding his unsheathed sword overhead.[125]

Every time a prosecutor denounced such "a more than unchristian mother" in these public ceremonies, it reinforced the notion in the minds of spectators that child murder is something that lay in women's nature. It encouraged the women in attendance to consider that the potential to commit child murder lay in their nature, too. Every such display of a murdered child in the street, whether this was a victim of infanticide or of suicide by proxy, offered members of the public the opportunity to engage emotionally with the case and to mourn the innocent child victim.

Conclusion: The Stage Is Set

Hamburg's government communicated its moral vision and its desire to discipline its subjects in the law book of 1497, particularly in the illumination that introduced the section on felonies. After the city vanquished pirates in its waters in the late sixteenth century, the government was finally in a position to implement this vision. For both the senate and the public the rigorous prosecution of crime constituted part of government's divine mission. Authorities communicated and reinforced this ideology in the religious iconography on display at the seat of government, in the courthouse and in city hall. By the late sixteenth century, the government's program of social discipline included a more public, aggressive prosecution of direct suicides. Spectacles of desecration reinforced the popular taboo against suicide. In addition to the bodies of suicides, authorities also punished the corpses of other malefactors who died before criminal sentences could be imposed or carried out. By imposing such post-mortem punishments, the government demonstrated its power and commitment to fulfilling its responsibility toward God to let no crime go unpunished. The new civic code of 1603 set the legal and ideological

---

[125] "So hat sich doch leider! vorgestriges Tages gefunden, daß eine mehr denn unchristliche Mutter ihr neugeborenes allhier vor Augen erblaßet liegendes todtes Kind ...in die Erde verscharret und solcher Gestalt ersticket... Wann denn nun diese abscheuliche und wieder die Natur laufende, an einem unschuldigen Kinde begangene Mordthat auch von der Weltlichen Obrigkeit nicht ungeahndet gelaßen weden kann. ... Und weilen dieses erblaßte Cörperlein unbegraben nicht über der Erden bleiben kann, ...daß Selbiges der Erden einverleibet werden möge." Chr. Petersen, "Zioter (Zeter) oder Tiodute (Jodute), der Gott des Kriegs und des Rechts bei den Deutschen. Eine rechtsgeschichtliche und mythologische Untersuchung," *Forschungen zur deutschen Geschichte* 6 (1866): 274–275.

framework in which felonies were adjudicated for the next two centuries. With the construction of the new ravenstone in 1609 the stage was set, literally, for the frequent performances of retributive justice that now took place. The sacralization of capital punishment, introduced in Hamburg with Bugenhagen's church ordinance of 1529, was on full display.

The idea to commit murder in order to instrumentalize criminal justice to bring an end to one's own life first emerged in Hamburg in the 1620s and 1630s, just as witch-hunting in the city was waning. After the last execution for witchcraft in 1642, authorities focused their prosecutorial zeal on other offenses. Witch trials had contributed to rising execution rates for women. As authorities turned their attention to other moral offenses and sex crimes in particular, this trend continued. The number of women caught up in criminal justice increased, as did the proportion of female felons who died on the scaffold. Infanticides in the city were frequent and often went unsolved. The discovery of infant corpses, as well as the bodies of other murder victims, led to frequent performances of the "Justice of the Street," the most dramatic and distinctive feature of criminal justice in Hamburg short of the execution ritual itself. These ceremonies contributed to a public culture where supernatural manifestations might occur at any moment and where suicide by proxy made sense. The "transcendental quality" that government acquired after the Protestant Reformation made distressed subjects seek resolution of their deepest existential crises by placing themselves in the hands of the authorities. By the 1660s the desire to die a penitent sinner on the ravenstone combined with an attraction to child sacrifice. The liturgy of suicide by proxy was fully formed. The conditions were in place that facilitated the increasing incidence of suicidal child murders over the coming decades.

CHAPTER 4

"The Unbelievably Frequent Examples of such Murders Committed solely out of Weariness with Life." Hamburg, 1668–1810

The last chapter laid out the conditions that made Hamburg fertile ground for the practice of suicide by proxy to emerge in the seventeenth century. Some of these conditions, such as the elaborate ritualization of criminal justice in the "Justice of the Street" and the frequent theatrical post-mortem trials and executions for criminals who eluded justice during life, were distinctive to Hamburg.[1] Others, such as the intensification of morals policing after the Reformation and Counter-Reformation and rulers' accountability

---

The quotation in the title is from the prosecutor's brief in the 1786 trial of Anton Lorenz Ammon for suicidal murder. "die in neueren Zeiten unglaublich häufigen Beispiele solcher Mordthaten..., die aus bloßem Überdruß des Lebens vollbracht worden." StAH, Cl.VII, Lit. Me, Nr.8, Vol. 2b, 15 September 1786.

[1] The ritualization was *distinctive* but not *unique* to Hamburg. The "Justice of the Street" was performed in the same manner in Lübeck. Leipzig incorporated elements of this ritual in their execution ceremonial, such as the executioner's hue and cry, but this no longer happened at the beginning of the felony murder trial in the presence of the victim's corpse, but at the end, absent the victim's body, imminently before the execution. As shown in the last chapter, the *Carolina* gave localities discretion to perform the ritual or not. Most territories discontinued it. Internal deliberations by Hamburg's senate in 1784 explain the history and contemporary practice of the ceremony, as will be developed below.

© The Author(s), under exclusive license to Springer Nature Switzerland AG 2023
K. Stuart, *Suicide by Proxy in Early Modern Germany*, World Histories of Crime, Culture and Violence,
https://doi.org/10.1007/978-3-031-25244-0_4

to God for their administration of criminal justice, characterized the stance of governments generally during the confessional age, in Catholic and Protestant territories. This chapter reconstructs the sequence and momentum of suicidal child murders in Hamburg in the later seventeenth and eighteenth centuries, as one case seeded another and the practice of suicide by proxy became endemic in the city. The focus is on suicide by proxy as a problem of governance. The interactions between authorities, the plebian perpetrators of suicide by proxy, and the general public shaped the practice of suicide by proxy. For more than a century, authorities attempted to quash suicidal child murders in the city, but, again and again, authorities made the experience that this type of perpetrator was impervious to escalating punishments, traditional deterrence, and discipline. Indeed, punishments encouraged the very crimes they were intended to suppress.

Nowhere was this dynamic more evident than in Hamburg's prisons, the house of correction, founded in 1614, and the Spinnhouse, a penitentiary for serious felons, founded in 1666. In these two carceral institutions Hamburg's city fathers could implement their disciplinary vision in its purest and most distilled form. However, in spite of, or rather because of, the comprehensive discipline imposed here, these institutions became incubators of sorts for suicide by proxy. In the late seventeenth and early eighteenth centuries the house of correction and Spinnhouse experienced a "murder epidemic," as nineteenth-century prison director Adolf Streng described it.[2] The notoriety of child murders in the prisons and the spectacular executions they entailed publicized the logic of suicide by proxy and inspired copycat killers within the city at large.

In the late seventeenth and early eighteenth centuries, there was considerable overlap between the mental worlds of Hamburg's magistrates and their subjects. Lutheran orthodoxy and traditional "rituals of retribution" in criminal justice shaped public policy.[3] With few exceptions, desecrations of the bodies of direct suicides remained standard practice. Around 1740, however, under the influence of the Enlightenment, the world views and sensibilities of Hamburg's ruling class and common inhabitants began to diverge. Among government officials there was new ambivalence toward the customary theater of criminal justice, and senators

---

[2] Adolf Streng, *Geschichte der Gefängnissverwaltung in Hamburg von 1622–1872* (Hamburg: Verlagsanstalt und Druckerei Aktien-Gesellschaft, 1890), 57–58.

[3] The phrase is from Richard J. Evans, *Rituals of Retribution: Capital Punishment in Germany, 1600–1987* (Oxford: Oxford University Press, 1996).

sought to distance themselves personally and bureaucratically from long-established ritual. Nonetheless, punishment practices for the most part did not change before the late eighteenth century. Official policy toward direct suicide changed earlier, however. After tentative, first steps toward the medicalization of suicide in the late seventeenth century in select cases, by the middle of the eighteenth century, magistrates generally dispensed with traditional desecrations and granted most suicides a Christian burial. Only those who killed themselves in order to escape a criminal penalty were still subjected to the traditional ritual. This changed stance by government had little impact on common people, however, whose continued fear of the ritual pollution associated with suicide posed ongoing practical problems for government.

The year 1784 was pivotal in the administration of criminal justice in Hamburg. In that year, twenty years after the publication of Cesare Beccaria's *On Crimes and Punishments* in 1764, the senate took dramatic and controversial steps to desacralize executions and pare down the ritualization of criminal justice generally, with the specific goal of making the idea of death on the scaffold less appealing to their suicidal subjects. The clash between traditional attitudes and new Enlightenment-inspired public policy came to a head in a polemical exchange between two Lutheran clergymen, Johann Melchior Goeze, chief pastor at St. Catherine's, a fierce combatant for Lutheran orthodoxy, who opposed the reforms, and his younger colleague Christoph Christian Sturm, chief pastor at St. Peter's Church, a proponent of the Protestant Enlightenment, whose reform proposals won the day.

And yet, even these reforms did not end suicidal child murders in Hamburg. In the late eighteenth and early nineteenth centuries, suicidal individuals continued to resort to child murder, even as religious prohibitions against direct suicide finally weakened among common people. Child murder had become a suicidal reflex that the perpetrators themselves could no longer fully explain. In the last years of the eighteenth century the gender profile of suicidal child murders changed. What began as a mostly female practice in the seventeenth and early eighteenth centuries now attracted mostly men. This was a direct response to the significant decline of executions of women for all crimes in the late eighteenth century. Ultimately, however, only the drastic decline in the overall number of executions for both sexes in the early nineteenth century rendered suicide by proxy ineffective as a means of exiting this world for both men and women.

Direct Suicide: Ongoing Desecrations and an Emerging Insanity Defense in Select Cases

In the second half of the seventeenth century Hamburg continued to treat direct suicides with exemplary severity in most cases. A particularly dramatic example of the traditional spectacle of desecration took place in 1662. As in the post-mortem trials of dead malefactors, the authorities' handling of this case demonstrated their commitment to allow no malefactor to escape justice. A journeyman stonemason stabbed himself to death at his parents' house on January 6. His mother raised alarm, claiming that brigands had chased her son home and stabbed him to death at their doorstep. Authorities believed her story and performed the customary "Justice of the street" as they would for any murder victim, although they had not identified any suspects. As customary, at the climactic moment of the ritual hue and cry, the executioner held his sword overhead and three times summoned the unknown murderers to appear. At the conclusion of the ceremony, the young man's funeral service took place at the cathedral with a large funeral party. After the burial, the mother got drunk and told confidantes about her son's suicide. Rumors began to circulate, prompting the city government to investigate. On January 28, after the young man had been buried for more than two weeks, the court ordered his body to be exhumed. The skinner carted his corpse to the gallows field by the ravenstone and buried it in a shallow grave. His parents were punished for their deception.[4]

The first documented cases of an insanity defense in cases of direct suicide happened just a few years after the young man's infamous disinterment, however. Beginning in the late 1660s, chronicles recorded a few instances where authorities granted suicides a quiet Christian burial instead of infamous disposal in the carrion pit. In one case in 1668, Ernst Koch, a brandy-maker, allegedly left his house at midnight and drowned himself "out of desperation." Rumors circulated that he had actually hanged himself at home but family members had thrown his body in the water, presumably to make his death appear like an accident. His body was recovered three days later. Authorities granted him a Christian burial. In his funeral

---

[4] Michael Gottlieb Steltzner, *Versuch einer zuverlässigen Nachricht von dem kirchlichen und politischen Zustande der Stadt Hamburg*, vol. 3 (s. l., 1733), 808–809. Otto Beneke, *Hamburgische Geschichten und Sagen*, 2nd ed. (Hamburg: Perthes, Besser & Mauke, 1854), 322–324.

sermon, the pastor of St. Catherine's suggested that Koch died in a state of grace, despite his self-inflicted death. Koch had been a man of means, the pastor told the congregation. Nonetheless, he imagined that he would not be able to make ends meet, prompting him to fall into despair. By emphasizing that Koch's economic problems were imaginary, not real, the pastor was suggesting that he was a victim of melancholy, not a willful intentional suicide. An overwrought, corrupted imagination was one of the primary symptoms of melancholy.

A few other well-to-do or well-connected men who committed suicide received similar leniency in the late 1660s and early 1670s.[5] The tentative application of the insanity defense in Hamburg in the later seventeenth century runs parallel to similar developments in other territories in the Empire, both Catholic and Protestant.[6] The surviving sources in Hamburg are too laconic to reveal according to what criteria authorities classified

[5] On the same night that Koch committed suicide, January 12, 1668, a tavern-keeper drowned himself. Initially authorities refused to grant him a Christian burial, because he had intentionally drowned himself. But his family members cited the case of Ernst Koch as precedent, so they too received permission to perform a quiet Christian burial. Steltzner, *Versuch*, vol. 3, 952–953. In one well-publicized case, Johann Blume, librarian at the famed Johanneum, the Latin school founded by the reformer Johannes Bugenhagen in 1529, hanged himself in the library in 1672. A reclusive scholar with a reputation for melancholy, Blume attempted to provide a Christian frame of his suicide. He wrote a note making a charitable bequest to the city orphanage and commending his soul to Jesus: "May the Lord Jesus, who has saved me, have mercy on me and my poor soul." His medical doctor attested that Blume's suicide was the result of melancholy. Diseased abdominal organs had corrupted his mind. The city council ordered his body to be taken down by a bailiff, rather than by the executioner. He received a quiet Christian burial by night. "Der Herr Jesus, der mich erlöset hat, wolle mir und meiner armen Seele gnädig seyn." Steltzner, *Versuch*, vol. 3, 987–988. Beneke, *Hamburgische Geschichten*, 225–229. Also in 1672, a Danish postal official from a good family stabbed himself to death with his rapier. Out of consideration for his family, authorities spared him the infamous removal by the executioner and allowed family retainers to transport his body to Danish territory. Carl Trummer, *Vorträge über Tortur, Hexenverfolgungen, Vehmgerichte, und andere merkwürdige Erscheinungen in der Hamburgischen Rechtsgeschichte*, vol. 1 (Hamburg: Meißner, 1844), 456.

[6] Catholic Bavaria began implementing more lenient burial practices toward direct suicides two decades earlier, in the 1640s, as authorities judged more suicides to be victims of madness rather than intentional actors guilty of religious despair. *David Lederer, Madness, Religion and the State in Early Modern Europe: A Bavarian Beacon* (New York: Cambridge University Press, 2006), 255.

some direct suicides as victims of melancholy and others as intentional actors guilty of damnable despair. Social status clearly played a role.[7]

Hamburg authorities continued to deal harshly with suicides of humbler status or questionable reputation. In 1674, for example, a maidservant hid her newborn infant in a closet where it suffocated and then poisoned herself. Her body was disposed of in the carrion ditch, as was the body of a journeyman barber-surgeon who hanged himself in the house of correction in 1677.[8] Another suicide in the house of correction a few years later gives an idea of how government officials approached such cases. During the night on the eve of the feast day of St. John the Baptist, June 24, 1685, Marten Behnke, an inmate in the house of correction, hanged himself in his cell. Behnke, a day laborer, had been in custody for just one month. No one had observed any sign of melancholy in him, the prison director noted in his log, though on the evening before his suicide Behnke did request that the inmate in the neighboring cell recite evening prayers aloud. The director refused to allow a quiet Christian burial for the day laborer. It was "necessary for the executioner to cut him down, and dispose of him in the carrion ditch, as is customary in such cases, so that other prisoners in the house of correction see this example," the director wrote. A dispute over the executioner's fee delayed the removal of the body, so Behnke was left hanging for two days. Finally, on June 26 the executioner's men cut him down and disposed of him. "May God, whose judgement and ways are unknowable, have mercy on his soul," the director concluded his log entry.[9]

Case Numbers Rise

Such public desecrations of the bodies of suicides reinforced common people's pollution anxieties and encouraged suicidal individuals to commit suicide by proxy instead. Seven years after the execution of Adelgunda

---

[7] Similarly, Swedish suicides of higher social estate were more likely to be found insane than landless suicides. Riikka Miettinen, *Suicide, Law, and Community in Early Modern Sweden* (Cham, Switzerland: Palgrave Macmillan, 2019), 269–284.

[8] The journeyman barber-surgeon was Bonaventura Wullsack. Trummer, *Vorträge*, vol. 1, 457.

[9] "es müßte, wie in solchen Fällen gebräuchlich wäre, der Frohn solchen abschneiden, und weg zu dem Fildgruben führen, damit die andere Gefangene im Zuchthuas ein Exempel daran sähen." "GOTT, dessen Gerichte und Wege unerforschlich sind, sey seiner armen Seelen gnädig." StAH 242-1 I, A14 Bd. 2, pp. 60–64.

Walters in 1668,[10] another woman committed suicide by proxy, although it is unclear whether a murder actually occurred in this case. Margaretha Schmidts, a "foolish, simpleminded person," serving a sentence for theft in Hamburg's Spinnhouse, accused herself of infanticide. She had given birth to a child "years ago" in a marsh along the Elbe River, she claimed, and poisoned it eight weeks later. (This, presumably, was one of the only cases without a "Justice of the Street," since no body was on hand.) Unlike Maria Behont's self-accusation in 1642,[11] the court believed Schmidt's unsolicited confession. Her status as a Spinnhouse inmate may have lent her self-accusation greater credibility. She was beheaded in January 1675. "Out of mercy," the court spared her the statutory penalty of breaking by the wheel.[12]

Child murders became more frequent in the city at large. In May 1678, Judith Wittenberg was beheaded for cutting her own child's throat.[13] In 1683 Anna Fresen was beheaded and her head impaled on a post for cutting her own child's throat.[14] In 1685 Catharina Spirlings was beheaded for cutting the throat of an unrelated child.[15] There were five child murders in 1686. For the first time men were among the child murderers. On April 17, an eighteen-year-old linen weaver cut the throat of a nine-year-old boy outside the city wall. Around the same time, a maidservant cut the throat of her eighteen-month-old half-sister just outside Hamburg's jurisdiction, in Danish territory. The young linen weaver was executed on May 10, less than a month after he killed the boy. On this occasion, Hamburg staged a double execution. Another man, Caspar Neubauer, had also cut a

---

[10] Chapter 3.
[11] Chapter 3.
[12] Christian van Nettelbladt, *Thesaurus Iuris Provincialis Et Statutarii Illustrati Germaniae...* (Giessen: Johann Christoph Schroeder, 1756), 1027–28. *Ausführlicher Bericht*, 11, January 15, 1675. Verein für Hamburgische Geschichte, ed., *Der Stadt Hamburg Gerichts-Ordnung und Statuta* (Hamburg: Besser & Mauke, 1842), 534.
[13] Wittenberg was beheaded on May 15, 1678. Her murder method and the fact that the execution register does not describe her as an unwed mother make this a likely case. *Ausführlicher Bericht*, 12.
[14] Anna Fresen was executed on March 20, 1683. Her murder method and the fact that the execution register does not describe her as an unwed mother make this a likely case. *Ausführlicher Bericht*, 12.
[15] Catharina Spirlings was beheaded on June 6, 1685. *Ausführlicher Bericht*, 13.

child's throat. He and the linen weaver were beheaded together.[16] In June, a Hamburg tailor's wife who lived in strife with her husband cut the throat of an unrelated child in the nearby town of Altona, just outside of Hamburg's jurisdiction. "Rage and lust for revenge" motivated her, a chronicle reported.[17] Many suicidal child murderers described a similar emotional dynamic in their confessions. People who had been wronged in some way were unable to exact revenge upon the person who had harmed them. Impotent rage sparked suicidal despair prompting them to kill a random child.[18] In October, a maidservant was beheaded and her head impaled on a post because she had cut the throat of a beer deliveryman's child.[19]

A case in 1687 was unusual because of the elevated social status of the murderer and because of the legal outcome. Catherina Steinhäuserin, thirty-three, was the wife of Upper-Court Advocate Albert Georg Steinhäuser, who had been sworn into office in 1676. She "gruesomely murdered" her child by cutting its throat. The Lower Court imposed a sentence of breaking by the wheel after her flesh was torn by red-hot tongs. Before sentencing by the Superior Court, however, two medical doctors examined her and diagnosed her with melancholy delirium. Hamburg sent the complete court records to three university law faculties to solicit their expert opinions and sentence recommendations. Soliciting expert opinions before rendering a final judgment was a frequent legal practice in complex cases. The three legal faculties found that her melancholy made her ineligible for the death penalty. There is no way of knowing whether Steinhäuserin welcomed an insanity defense at this point. In any event, her court-appointed defense advocate would have made every effort to secure one on her behalf, regardless of her desires. As in the case of direct suicides, Hamburg sources do not reveal according to what criteria the court found some suicidal child murders criminally liable while categorizing others as melancholics incapable of forming criminal intent. On July 19, 1687, the superior court remitted Catherina Steinhäuserin's

---

[16] *Theatrum novum politico-historicum, das ist eine... Erzehlung... was sich in dem 1686 Jahr...begeben hat...* (Würzburg: Quirinus Heyl, 1687), 244. *Ausführlicher Bericht*, 13, May 10, 1686.

[17] Because the tailor's wife killed the child in Altona, not in Hamburg, she was arrested and prosecuted there. *Theatrum novum*, 359.

[18] For examples of the revenge motif, see the cases of Catharina Koenig, below, and Catharina Jacobin, 1769, and Adelheid Zieglerin, 1783, in Vienna, Chap. 7.

[19] *Ausführlicher Bericht*, 13, October 11, 1686.

death sentence to life imprisonment in the Spinnhouse. She would be housed there at her own expense in a single room separate from other inmates, "so she would not harm herself or others." Authorities did not spare her the infamy of being escorted from the prison to the Spinnhouse by the executioner, however. On April 12, 1707, after almost twenty years in the Spinnhouse, the city government released her into the custody of three citizens, who offered to serve as guarantors. One of her guarantors housed her in his home, promising to supervise her and keep her confined to the house.[20]

The House of Correction

The number of suicidal murders in Hamburg's prisons, the house of correction and the Spinnhouse, increased markedly in the 1690s and the early 1700s. The house of correction, founded in 1614, was modeled on the Amsterdam *Rasphuis*, the first prison-workhouse in continental Europe, founded in 1596. Hamburg's house of correction, one of the first such institutions in the Holy Roman Empire, was part of a wave of such foundations, first in Protestant territories and a few years later in Catholic territories as well.[21] Houses of correction were emblematic of the moral ideals of the age. Fascinated by these novel institutions, jurists, theologians, and government officials throughout Germany could not contain their enthusiasm for the expected salutary effects of workhouses in this world and their contribution to inmates' salvation in the next.[22] Martin Geier, chief court preacher at the Electoral court of Saxony in Dresden, writing in 1670, described the house of correction as a kind of model or microcosm

---

[20] StAH, 111-1, Senat, CI.VII, Lit. Mb, No.3, Vol.1, 363, "Kurtzer Auszug," unpaginated, 8 July, 1687. Catherina Steinhäuserin was sentenced to the Spinnhaus "*ad dies vitae..., ne noceret sibi at aliis.*" Nettelbladt, *Thesaurus Iuris Provincialis*, 1028. Trummer, *Vorträge*, vol. 1, 441–442. Dirk Brietzke, *Arbeitsdisziplin und Armut in der Frühen Neuzeit. Die Zucht- und Arbeitshäuser in den Hansestädten Bremen, Hamburg und Lübeck und die Durchsetzung bürgerlicher Arbeitsmoral im 17. und 18. Jahrhundert* (Hamburg: Verlag Verein für Hamburgische Geschichte, 2000), 429.

[21] Hamburg was the third such institution within the Holy Roman Empire, after Bremen in 1608/1613, and Lübeck in 1613. Joel F. Harrington, "Escape from the Great Confinement: The Genealogy of a German Workhouse," *The Journal of Modern History* 71 (1999): 325, fn. 40.

[22] On the potential of prison-workhouses to save the souls of their inmates, see Pieter Spierenburg, *The Prison Experience: Disciplinary Institutions and their Inmates in Early Modern Europe* (New Brunswick, NJ: Rutgers University Press, 1991), 46–47.

of the world at large: "the entire world is nothing other than God's house of correction, in which he knows how to correct unbridled hardheaded people, with sharp discipline, hunger, humiliation and beatings, so that some still become human by these means, who might otherwise have remained unreasonable beasts."[23] Others described it as a metaphor of the human condition, medical treatment for diseased souls, or a this-worldly purgatory.[24]

The series of murders that took place in Hamburg's prisons is an illustration of how discipline could go awry. Suicide by proxy became entrenched as a tactic of resistance for inmates in Hamburg's house of correction and Spinnhouse. Hamburg's prisons were not unique in this regard. The specific disciplinary regime deployed in these institutions, a combination of brutal coercion and all-pervasive, unrelenting religious indoctrination, practiced in both Catholic and Protestant workhouses, promoted the practice. In the very same years that Hamburg experienced a rise in cases within its prisons, the house of correction in Catholic Vienna had to contend with a large number of suicide by proxy cases as well, as will be shown in subsequent chapters.

Hamburg's house of correction was operational by the early 1620s, approximately six years after its official founding. An ordinance from 1622 describes its Godly mission. "GOD Almighty awoke pious, Christ-loving, wise, goodhearted people, and opened their eyes and heart, so they saw the suffering and misery of the poor."[25] It was a moral imperative to care for the deserving poor. However, there were tares among the wheat.[26] An inscription at the gate of the house of correction announced to all who entered, and to the public beyond its walls, what type of regime operated within: *Labore nutrior, labore plector*. (By work I am nourished, by work I am punished.) While some poor people were unfortunates who became impoverished through no fault of their own, others were "strong, lazy,

---

[23] Quoted in Brietzke, *Arbeitsdisziplin*, 13.

[24] Fridrich Krausold, *Friderici Krausoldi Discursus iuridico-politicus de miraculis et egregiis usibus S. Raspin* (Merseburg: Georg Christian Forberger, 1698), 126–129.

[25] "Ordnung des Zucht-Hauses, vom 8. März 1622," in Johann Klefeker, *Sammlung der Hamburgischen Gesetze und Verfassungen...*, vol. 1 (Hamburg: J.E. Piscator, 1765), 373–407.

[26] Klefeker, *Sammlung*, vol. 1, 373–374.

lustful, Godless, insolent and disobedient" street beggars.[27] Beadles rounded up beggars in the streets and delivered them directly to the house of correction where they performed forced labor.[28]

In addition to the deserving poor and insolent street beggars, there was another group of inmates comprising petty criminals sentenced to the house of correction as "correctional inmates" (*Züchtlinge*). Correctional inmates needed to be "punished" by labor. The house of correction did not accept serious felons, because the workhouse was supposed to be an honorable institution, whose inmates might reenter the labor force upon release. By excluding felons who had become legally infamous by being exposed at the pillory or flogged by the executioner, Hamburg authorities hoped to insulate staff and inmates in the house of correction from their contagious dishonor.[29] The new institution's intended clientele included small-time thieves and women guilty of fornication. The prison did not admit professional prostitutes, whose presence would have dishonored the institution. Even petty criminals required a firm hand, however. For years they had been living "in sin and shame like wild animals." Like mules, their "mouth must be held in with bit and bridle" (Psalm 32). The ordinance concluded ominously: "if they [the correctional inmates] are not helped in time, they might come under the hands of another," that is, if they were not corrected and turned from their dissolute ways promptly, they would end up under the hands of the executioner.[30]

Many children were in custody at the house of correction. Occupancy in the workhouse typically ranged from 400 to 600 from the late seventeenth century through the late eighteenth century. Beggars made up the majority of inmates. In 1756, for example, 316 beggars were in custody compared to 84 correctional inmates. Women typically made up the majority of beggars. In 1788, 66% of beggars in custody were women.

---

[27] In addition to the poor without means, the workhouse was intended to house "starke, faule, geile, gottlose, muthwillige und ungehorsame, versoffene Trunkenbolde und Bierbalge." Jonas Ludwig von Heß, *Hamburg topographisch, politisch und historisch beschrieben*, vol. 2, 2nd ed. (Hamburg: Der Verfasser, 1811), 107.

[28] Friedrich Georg Buek, *Hamburgische Alterthümer: Beitrag zur Geschichte der Stadt und ihrer Sitten* (Hamburg: Perthes-Besser & Mauke, 1859), 133–138.

[29] On dishonor contagion in the context of criminal justice and the often-unsuccessful efforts to contain it, see Kathy Stuart, *Defiled Trades and Social Outcasts: Honor and Ritual Pollution in Early Modern Germany* (Cambridge: Cambridge University Press, 1999), Chap. 5.

[30] Heß, *Hamburg topographisch*, vol. 2, (1811), 108.

Women arrested while begging with young children were imprisoned together with their children. Beadles also delivered children caught begging on their own directly to the workhouse. The city orphanage only accepted children of Hamburg citizens and legal residents of legitimate birth.[31] Orphans who did not meet these requirements ended up in the house of correction. In 1694, administrators complained that there were thirty-six orphans housed there that year. The presence of these young children hindered the smooth operation of the workhouse. "Not only can they not work themselves, others who have to mind them and keep them clean are also prevented from working," the prison director complained.[32] By 1725, of the 500 inmates in custody that year, 190 were children.[33] Clearly, there was no shortage of potential victims for inmates who chose to escape the institution by murdering a child.

"Idleness is the devil's pillow, and the root of all evil," the workhouse ordinance of 1622 warned. Therefore, all inmates spent most of their waking hours working.[34] Labor consisted of carding wool, spinning, weaving, knitting, or processing silk. Male correctional inmates performed more arduous labor, rasping brazilwood for dye in the textile industry. Inmates had to produce a set amount of finished product by the end of the day or face punishment.[35] Prisoners who were not industrious enough received reduced food rations. Overseers administered this penalty with sadistic flourish. "Lazy" inmates had to climb into a large basket that was hoisted up to the rafters of the mess hall. From this basket, they looked down on other inmates being fed below.[36] A contemporary British engraving, "Method of Punishing the Idle at the Poor House at Hamburg," shows this penalty[37] (Image 4.1). If any inmate had ever seen this engraving, it would have added insult to injury. We see the industrious inmates at the

---

[31] The ordinance specified: "Die Kinder, deren unehrliche Geburt bekannt, sollen keineswegs hereingenommen werden." "Ordnung des Zucht-Hauses, vom 8. März 1622," in Klefeker, *Sammlung*, vol. 1, 331.

[32] Brietzke, *Arbeitsdisziplin*, 454.

[33] Brietzke, *Arbeitsdisziplin*, 456.

[34] Klefeker, *Sammlung*, vol. 1, 390.

[35] Brietzke, *Arbeitsdiziplin*, 65.

[36] Brietzke, *Arbeitsdisziplin*, 605–606.

[37] "Method of punishing the idle in the poor house at Hamburgh, by suspending them in a basket over the table where the more industrious are at meals." 1778. Print: engraving, with etching. https://wellcomecollection.org/works/v2fnrne5.

4 "THE UNBELIEVABLY FREQUENT EXAMPLES OF SUCH MURDERS... 151

Image 4.1 "Method of Punishing the Idle at the Poor House at Hamburgh." 1778. Wellcome Collection 43268i

table below enjoying a far more sumptuous repast than ever was served in the Hamburg house of correction. Standard fare at the workhouse consisted of cabbage and legumes, served with "thin beer." Four inmates ate out of a common tin bowl.[38]

If cutting rations failed to produce compliance, overseers administered a variety of physical punishments. Floggings with bundles of birch rods were standard practice in German houses of correction and in German criminal justice generally, as shown in the 1497 illumination of Hamburg's municipal code.[39] Hamburg, a port city, also introduced naval discipline in the workhouse, such as floggings with ship's ropes with knotted ends. The harshest penalty, reserved for male inmates, was riding "the wooden horse," a punishment that many prison-workhouses adopted from military justice.[40] This involved a large wooden horse, adorned with a horse's head and tail, often on wheels, as was the case for Hamburg's model. The horse's back was sharply angled. An engraving from 1726 in a handbook on military justice shows soldiers being disciplined in this way[41] (Image 4.2). This was at once an honor punishment that evoked folkloric humiliations like Charivari and a physical punishment. The agony of soldiers or inmates riding the horse might be increased by attaching cannon balls or other weights to their feet, standard practice in Hamburg's house of correction. Prisoners in Hamburg rode the horse for a minimum of one hour, but more commonly for two to three hours for several days in a row. Inmates pulled the wooden horse around the courtyard while the offender riding the horse was flogged.[42]

Hamburg authorities did not want to exact obedience by coercion and violence alone, however. Prison administrators wanted to produce a spiritual and psychological transformation in their charges. The goal was for inmates to submit willingly. Religious indoctrination was key to this moral project. A 1725 instruction to the prison pastor summed up the pedagogical program: "to provide ignorant and neglected youth with a necessary knowledge of God and their savior JEsus Christ and teach them the foundation of Christian faith, to instruct wild ungoverned old people in

---

[38] Heß, *Hamburg topographisch*, vol. 1, (1787), 352.
[39] See Chap. 3, Image 3.1.
[40] According to the Workhouse ordinance of 1622, inmates rode the wooden horse after the fourth infraction, if food deprivation and floggings did not lead to compliance. Klefeker, *Sammlung*, vol. 1, 401–402.
[41] Hanns Friedrich von Fleming, *Der Vollkommene Teutsche Soldat* (Leipzig: Johann Christian Martini, 1726), between pages 184–185.
[42] Inmates wore weights of fifteen pounds on both feet. Brietzke, *Arbeitsdisziplin*, 607–612.

Image 4.2 Soldiers disciplined by riding "the wooden horse." Engraving. Hanns Friedrich von Fleming, *Der Vollkommene Teutsche Soldat* (Leipzig: Johann Christian Martini, 1726), 184–185. ETH-Bibliothek Zürich, Rar 9315

articles of the faith, and lead recalcitrant correctional inmates to understand their sins, and direct them toward salvation of their souls through true repentance."[43] From its inception, the workhouse sought to produce the proper mindset in its charges with an elaborate daily schedule of devotions, detailed in the ordinance of 1622. Compulsory singing was an important tool of religious instruction. On Sundays and holidays, inmates attended a prayer hour from seven to eight in the morning, reciting Bible verses they were required to learn by heart. At nine, they assembled in

[43] Brietzke, *Arbeitsdisziplin*, 578.

church. These services were open to the community but inmates sat separately behind a wall with windows opening into the nave, so that the public could hear them but not see them, as they sang and prayed. Overseers punished any unauthorized sound or utterance by inmates severely.[44] Services followed a set program. Inmates sang a sequence of hymns with the congregation, beginning with *Te Deum Laudamus*,[45] or alternately with *Veni Sancte Spiritus*,[46] followed by *Gloria in Excelsis Deo*.[47] After the reading of an Epistle, everyone sang the Lutheran hymn "We now Implore the Holy Ghost."[48]

1 Nun bitten wir den heilgen Geist
um den rechten Glauben allermeist,
daß er uns behüte an unserm Ende,
wenn wir heimfahr'n aus diesem Elende.
Kyrieleis!

4 Du höchster Tröster in aller Noth,
hilf, daß wir nicht fürchten Schand noch Tod,
daß in uns die Sinne nicht verzagen,
wenn der Feind wird das Leben verklagen.
Kyrieleis![49]

1 We now implore God the Holy Ghost
For the true faith, which we need the most,
That in our last moments He may befriend us
And, as homeward we journey, attend us.
Lord, have mercy!
…

---

[44] Brietzke, *Arbeitsdisziplin*, 574.
[45] *Lutherisches Gesangbuch* (s.l., 1770), 185.
[46] *Neu-Vollständigers Marggräfl. Brandenburgisches Gesang-Buch* (Bayreuth: 1672), 114–117.
    In English: https://www.lutheranchoralebook.com/texts/come-holy-ghost-god-and-lord/.
[47] *Brandenburgisches Gesang-Buch*, 119.
[48] "*Nun bitten wir den Heiligen Geist*," https://hymnary.org/text/nun_bitten_wir_den_heiligen_geist. In English: http://www.lutheran-hymnal.com/lyrics/tlh231.htm. After singing this hymn, regular Sunday services in the house of correction continued with a sermon or gospel reading, another song and prayer, concluding with a final blessing.
[49] https://hymnary.org/text/nun_bitten_wir_den_heiligen_geist.

4 Thou highest Comfort in ev'ry need,
Grant that neither shame nor death we heed,
That e'en then our courage may never fail us
When the foe shall accuse and assail us.
Lord, have mercy!⁵⁰

After singing this hymn during every Sunday and holiday service, inmates who escaped the institution by committing suicide by proxy would hear it again during their executions. Known as "the Poor Sinner's Song," choirs routinely performed it during executions in Hamburg and most other Lutheran jurisdictions. In a well stage-managed beheading, the singers would intone the last stanza just as poor sinner's head fell.[51] In Hamburg, executioners also attempted to time a breaking of the wheel so that the condemned drew his last breath as the hymn ended.[52]

At one o'clock, inmates gathered for another prayer meeting. After singing a psalm, the pastor or schoolmaster drilled them on their catechism lessons (Image 4.3). Then they sang the *Magnificat*[53] and heard another reading from an Epistle or a section of the Catechism. Finally, after a blessing, the meeting ended with singing a litany.[54] On Thursday afternoon inmates attended a second sermon. Workdays began with morning prayers and recitation or singing of the catechism. On Monday mornings, the pastor or schoolmaster examined inmates individually about the content of Sunday's sermon. Inmates sang and prayed before and during the midday meal and supper. During work hours, overseers patrolled the workshops and led inmates in psalm-singing. A prayer bell rang every day at noon and in the evening. Inmates fell to their knees, prayed "Our Father," and sang a hymn by Martin Luther, "Graciously grant us peace." The lyrics taught a lesson of submission to governmental authority:

---

[50] https://hymnary.org/text/we_now_implore_god_the_holy_ghost.

[51] Jürgen Martschukat, *Inszeniertes Töten. Eine Geschichte der Todesstrafe vom 17. bis zum 19. Jahrhundert* (Cologne: Böhlau Verlag, 2000), 41. Eduard Emil Koch, *Geschichte des Kirchenlieds und Kirchengesangs der Christlichen, insbesondere der deutschen evangelischen Kirche*, vol. 8, 3rd ed. (Stuttgart: Chr. Belser, 1876), 91.

[52] During the 1735 execution of the murderer Jürgen Hinrich Wichers, who was broken by the wheel from the bottom up, Wichers did not seem close to death as the choir was singing the last stanza, so the executioner and his assistants expedited the process by suffocating him. StAH, 111-1, Senat, Cl.VII, Lit. Mb, No.3, Vol.4a, 5 May, 1735.

[53] https://hymnary.org/hymn/ELKG1842/227?highlight=4.6.4.6&media=text.

[54] Brietzke, *Arbeitsdisziplin*, 574–575.

Image 4.3 Frontispiece. Gerhard Hackmann, *Catechismus-Schule: Darinn Die Jugend in den Häuptstücken unserer wahren Christlichen Religion/ ...unterrichtet wird*. Hamburg: Werner, 1641. Forschungbibliothek Gotha, Signatur Theol 8° 00371/09

Gib unserm Land und aller Obrigkeit
Fried' und gut Regiment, daß wir unter
Ihnen ein christlich, ehrbar, geruhig
Leben führen mögen, in aller
Gottseligkeit und Wahrheit.[55]

Grant to our princes and those in authority
peace and good government
so that we under them
may lead a calm and peaceful life
in all godliness and respectability.[56]

All inmates over the age of fifteen or who "had otherwise reached the age of reason" were required to receive the Lord's Supper twice a year at a minimum but only after they had been sufficiently prepared.[57] David Sabean's study of village culture in early modern Lutheran Württemberg gives an idea what this preparation entailed. The requirement to take Communion provided authorities with a powerful instrument of psychological control. Villagers had to take communion regularly within their own parish. However, in order to receive the Eucharist, communicants had to attend confession first. In Württemberg, as in many Lutheran states, confession did not entail individual oral confession, as it did for Catholics. Württemberg villagers attended confession collectively and were expected to confess their sins to God and demonstrate contrition. Pastors could exclude immoral or impenitent parishioners from the sacrament. Access to the sacrament required more than external compliance. Villagers had to cultivate the proper emotional state. If they took Communion with an "agitated heart," in a state of conflict, harboring feelings of hostility, anger, or hatred, they risked their very souls. "Periodically, every member of the community was subjected to the ordeal of examining his heart for resentment. One either had to reconcile oneself to the authorities—to forgive—or face spiritual danger in taking the sacrament. The biblical text ... was clear—anyone who ate and drank

---

[55] "Verleih uns Frieden Gnädiglich," by Martin Luther, 1527. https://hymnary.org/text/verleih_uns_frieden_gnadiglich.
[56] http://www.bach-cantatas.com/Texts/Chorale169-Eng3.htm.
[57] Streng, *Gefängnissverwaltung*, 181, Appendix 1, Ordnung des Zuchthauses, 1622.

'unworthily,' ate and drank 'judgement upon himself.' "[58] In this sense, the sacrament became an ordeal, a poison ritual.[59] Communicants had to reconcile and forgive, or risk damnation. In Hamburg the coercive potential of taking communion was even greater than in Württemberg, because here parishioners did go to confession individually. Klefeker described the practice in Hamburg: "Our confessional does have a certain similarity with Roman-Catholic confession, in that anyone who wants to take the Lord's Supper must step into it individually, and reveal the state of his soul to the father confessor, and seek personal absolution."[60] Within Hamburg prisons, this practice meant that inmates faced massive pressure to submit and surrender themselves with a willing heart to the disciplinary regime of the institution.

THE SPINNHOUSE

Hamburg established a second prison, the Spinnhouse, in 1666. The new institution took its name from the predominant type of labor inmates performed, spinning. Male inmates also rasped hardwood, as they did in the house of correction. In contrast to the house of correction, that only accepted petty criminals and first-time offenders, the Spinnhouse housed serious felons, recidivist offenders, professional prostitutes, and thieves. Many of these had previously been flogged by the executioner or exposed at the pillory and were thus infamous. The stated purpose of the new institution was to provide courts with an alternative penalty to traditional punishments like whippings, brandings, and banishment. Traditional penalties, Hamburg authorities came to believe, were ineffective because banished felons simply snuck back into the city, where many ultimately lost their lives on the ravenstone. Such criminals, the Spinnhouse ordinance of 1669 warned, were in imminent danger of "losing the salvation of their souls, and ultimately falling to the stalking devil, who has ensnared them in his

---

[58] David Warren Sabean, *Power in the Blood: Popular Culture and Village Discourse in Early Modern Germany* (Cambridge: Cambridge University Press, 1992), 41. The scriptural text is 1 Cor. 11.27–30.

[59] David Warren Sabean, "Production of the Self during the Age of Confessionalism," *Central European History* 29 (1996): 3.

[60] Klefeker, *Sammlung*, vol. 8, 793–794. Joachim Whaley, *Religious Toleration and Social Change in Hamburg, 1529–1819* (Cambridge: Cambridge University Press, 1985), 28.

bonds."[61] The founder of the Spinnhouse was Peter Rentzel, a jurist and city councilor who had overseen the administration of criminal justice in the city during his long career. He conceived of "the Christian idea, for God's honor and to save the souls of many evil people, to have a Spinnhouse built at his own expense…, so that such evil people can be brought there, and taught to fear God and to work, so they might be saved from temporal and eternal ruin."[62] The sandstone portal at the entrance of the Spinnhouse bore an inscription that commemorated his bequest and stated the purpose of the new institution: "*in honorem Dei et flagitiosorum emendationem hoc ergastulum sumptibus suis extructum est*" (in honor of God and for the improvement of the profligate, this prison-workhouse was constructed at his expense).[63]

The Spinnhouse was smaller than the workhouse, with occupancy ranging between 50 and 100. Whereas workhouse inmates rarely served more than three years, Spinnhouse inmates received long sentences, often twenty-five years to life.[64] Melancholy Catharina Steinhäuserin, as we have seen, was sentenced to the Spinnhouse for life in 1687, after she cut her child's throat. The court sentenced felons to the Spinnhouse as an alternative to the death penalty.[65] Many female inmates were infanticide suspects, women who had concealed pregnancies and secretly given birth to infants that they claimed were stillborn. If authorities could not prove the infanticide, they sentenced such women to the Spinnhouse.[66] In one such case, Catharina Scharenberg, a maidservant, was arrested on suspicion of infanticide on October 31, 1726, when her dead infant was discovered in her footlocker. During the "Justice of the Street" over this dead infant the accused infanticidal mother would have been present, in contrast to the many unsolved neonaticide cases. Prosecutors could not prove the infanticide during her felony murder trial, however. Physical evidence suggested that the child was likely stillborn. Nonetheless, the court found,

---

[61] "Spinnhaus-Ordung von Anno 1669, 12 May," in Klefeker, *Sammlung*, vol. 1, 422.
[62] Buek, *Hamburgische Alterthümer*, 139.
[63] Buek, *Hamburgische Alterthümer*, 141.
[64] Streng, *Gefängnissverwaltung*, 77.
[65] According to Hamburg syndicus Johann Klefeker, the Spinnhaus was intended for offenders whose crimes fall just short of meriting the death sentence, or whose death sentences had been remitted. They were sentenced to hard prison labor. Klefeker, *Sammlung*, vol. 1, 306–307.
[66] Heß, *Hamburg topographisch*, vol. 1, (1810), 165.

Scharenberg's concealment of her pregnancy and refusal to get help during birth contributed to her child's death and made it likely that she had intended to commit infanticide. "Murders of children conceived in dishonor, especially by servants, who have frequent opportunity to fornicate with one another, have become rampant at this time," the court observed. On April 4, 1727, five months after her arrest, the Superior Court sentenced Scharenberg to public flogging at the pillory and twenty years in the Spinnhouse, "as a deterrent example to other such unchaste women who conceal their pregnancies."[67] The executioner personally delivered such female convicts from the city prison where they were held during their trials to the Spinnhouse, an infamous procession that heightened the visibility of women in non-capital criminal cases, while drawing attention to women's culpability in child deaths, even in cases where intentional homicide was not proven.[68]

Spinnhouse inmates followed the same regimented routine of work and prayer as workhouse inmates did. In the Spinnhouse, too, compulsory psalm-singing was part of the daily program, though not all inmates performed the required religious devotions with the zeal that prison administrators desired. Therefore, an ordinance of 1680 introduced measures to ensure compliance. Overseers chained prisoners who did not perform their morning prayers to a heavy but movable wooden block for three days. The inmates had to carry the block with them from room to room throughout the workday. Those who failed to sing a required psalm in the morning and at noon spent two days chained to the block. Inmates who failed to stand and recite the required prayers before and after meals were chained in a cell for twenty-four hours, and so on.[69] Spinnhouse inmates were required to take communion four times a year, after the customary preparation.[70]

Hamburg authorities established a maternity ward in the Spinnhouse for pregnant vagrants and for pregnant criminal defendants, transferring them from the city prison for the duration of their pregnancy and lying-in

---

[67] Johann Gustav Gallois, *Hamburgische Chronik von den ältesten Zeiten bis auf die Jetztzeit*, vol 3 (Hamburg: s.n., 1862), 54. Klefeker, *Sammlung*, vol. 5, 487–500.

[68] On the infamous escort to the Spinnhouse by the executioner, see Spierenburg, *Prison Experience*, 153.

[69] "Ordnung der Züchtlinge im Spinnhause von Anno 1680, den. 1. Juli," in Klefeker, *Sammlung*, vol. 1, 442–447.

[70] Streng, *Gefängnissverwaltung*, Appendix 3, Spinnhausordnung von Anno 1669, 12. Mai, 206.

period. Within the crowded Spinnhouse, administrators could not keep these women and their newborns separate from regular inmates. Prisoners who wanted to escape the institution by committing suicide by proxy had easy access to suitable victims, killing either their own or an unrelated child.[71] On August 9, 1694, Spinnhouse inmate Margaretha Stubs cut the throat of her three-week-old baby. Guards transferred her to the city prison that same evening. Two days later, authorities performed the "Justice of the Street" over her and her dead child outside the gates of the Spinnhouse. "All prisoners had to watch this spectacle from the windows. They were reprimanded and warned to mirror themselves in this," the Spinnhouse director noted in his daily log. On the day of her execution, August 27, the execution procession stopped at the Spinnhouse. Here the executioner tore her flesh with red-hot tongs. Then the procession continued to the ravenstone, where she was decapitated and her head impaled on a post.[72]

Meanwhile, child murders continued outside the prison. In April 1695, six months after Margarethe Stubs' execution, Hamburg staged a triple beheading of three child murderers. Franz Wolf had cut his son's throat. Two women, Margaretha Trogs and Ilsabe Krohns, had each cut the throat of an unrelated child.[73] Within the house of correction administrators managed to prevent another suicidal murder in November of that year. Two female inmates alerted prison staff that Anna Gertrud Krögers, imprisoned for fornication, was threatening to kill someone, so that she would be tried for murder. The person she planned to kill "would not be large, but small," she said, presumably a child. The prison director requested instructions from the city council, so prison staff "would not be held responsible" for any tragedy that ensued. It was "difficult to keep such a person in the prison," he warned his superiors. The council instructed him to avail himself of the disciplinary tools at his disposal. He

---

[71] Mary Lindemann, "Maternal Politics: The Principles and Practice of Maternity Care in Eighteenth-Century Hamburg," *Journal of Family History* 9 (1984): 44–63. Streng, *Gefängnissverwaltung*, 86.
[72] StAH, 242-1, I, A29, Bd.1, Spinnhaus Verwaltungsprotokoll, p. 131. The execution chronicle gives the date of her execution as October 4, 1694, *Ausführlicher Bericht*, 14, but the Spinnhouse protocol is the more accurate source. See also Streng, *Gefängnissverwaltung*, 86.
[73] *Ausführlicher Bericht*, 14, April 15, 1695.

placed Krögers in a pitch-dark cell in chains on a diet of bread and water for eight days. Later, she slept and worked in solitary confinement.[74]

1697: Female Inmates Form a Murder Plot

Two years later staff in the house of correction were unable to prevent a suicidal child murder. The director described the event in in his logbook.[75] On the afternoon of November 24, 1697, two female inmates cut the throat of a four-year-old girl. They were two young maidservants, Agnes Julia Flor and Trine Henrichs. The two women were very forthcoming in their account of the events leading up to the murder and the deed itself. They had formulated their plan four days earlier. That evening Flor was sitting by herself dejectedly, crying ("without doubt out of malice," the director opined). Henrichs approached her to ask what was wrong. "She is weary of her life and wishes that she could see the end of it," Flor answered. "She also wishes that she could die," Henrichs responded.[76] (In the prison director's narrative, he rendered the women's testimony in the third person, as was standard practice in interrogation protocols.) Flor suggested that they should murder a child, and Henrichs agreed. This was the most effective way to achieve their goal, they decided, because then they too would have to die. After forming this "devilish" plan, as the director described it, the two women chose as their victim a particular child, Elisabeth Margareta Carpents. This little girl had always been sickly, and so, the women believed, they would end the child's suffering along with their own. Over the next four days, Flor befriended the girl and gave her treats. The women planned to commit the murder when other inmates were at lunch, so they would remain undisturbed. On the appointed day, Flor bought some cake and offered it to the child. Now they had to

---

[74] Krögers threatened, "fals sie nicht bald aus dem Zuchthause würde entlassen werden, so wolte sie jemanden im Hause ermorden, damit sie hernachmahls fürs Gericht möchte geführt werden, ...auch solte die Persohn die sie gedachte zu ermorden, nicht groß sondern klein seyn." The director informed the council "daß es schwer wäre eine solche Person so zu bewahren" and requested instructions "damit wir nach diesem außer Verantwortung möchten bleiben." StAH, 242-1, I, A14 Bd. 2, Zuchthaus Verwaltungsprotokoll, 344–346. Brietzke, *Arbeitsdisziplin*, 477–478.

[75] StAH, 242-1, I, A14, Zuchthaus Verwaltungsprotokoll, Bd. 2, 445–450.

[76] Flor said "sie wäre ihres Lebens müde und wünschete daß sie dessen ein Ende sehen mögte, darauf die andere, nemlich Trine Henrichs geantwortet, sie wünschte gleichfals, daß sie sterben könnte." StAH, 242-1, I, A14, Zuchthaus Verwaltungsprotokoll, Bd. 2, 445.

procure a knife. Flor already had a knife, but they wanted a second knife so that each woman could cut the child with her own weapon. Flor sent the child with the cake to her grandmother, also a workhouse inmate, to ask for a knife, ostensibly to cut the cake. When she returned with the knife and the cake, the two women took turns cutting the little girl's throat. Covered in blood, they alerted the prison staff to the murder. The prison director voiced his horror: "Oh God, these hideous beasts and more than cruel tiger hearts."[77] Even as the child cried out, the women testified, they persisted in their assault. Once they started the attack, they had to see it through, Henrichs explained. If they merely wounded the child, they would be exposed at the pillory. This shame she could not endure. She would rather die.

That very evening the director convened a meeting of the prison's board of supervisors. Despite the short notice, six of eight members appeared. After the two women repeated the confession they had just made to the director to the assembled gentlemen, the director had them locked away for the night in solitary confinement. But "the murderous devil had even more in mind," the director warned the board members.[78] Three other female inmates had made similar sinister statements, raising the suspicion that they too were plotting murder. "How could he prevent this?" the director asked. The board could come up with no other solution than to appease the women, offering them hope of freedom in exchange for good behavior. The gentlemen then summoned the three women before them. The women promised to comply, but "their treacherous character was clearly visible on their faces," the director observed. "May the great God have mercy on them for Christ's sake, and banish the murder devil from their hearts. May he grant them a calm and contented mind, forestalling further tragedy out of fatherly grace."[79] The next day guards transferred Flor and Henrichs to the city prison for criminal

---

[77] "Ach Gott, die abscheuliche Bestien und mehr als grausame tiegers hertzen..." StAH, 242-1, I, A14, Zuchthaus Verwaltungsprotokoll, Bd. 2, 447.

[78] "...dz es schine dz der Mordt teufell noch mehr böses im Sinne hette..." StAH, 242-1, I, A14, Zuchthaus Verwaltungsprotokoll, Bd. 2, 447.

[79] "mann siehet aber dennoch ihre tückische Gemüther aus ihren Angesichtern hervor blicken, undt wolle der große Gott umb den Christi willen sich Ihrer erbarmen, den Mord Teufell aus Ihren Hertzen bannen, und sie ein geruhiges und zufriedenes Gemühte geben, und von mehreren Unfall aus Gnaden Väterlich bewahren." StAH, 242-1, I, A14, Zuchthaus Verwaltungsprotokoll, Bd. 2, 447–448.

prosecution. "Justice will be meted out to them, and they will receive what their deeds merit," the director wrote.[80]

The next morning, November 26, the executioner's men escorted the two women back to the house of correction, where authorities performed the "Justice of the Street" over them and the murdered child just outside the prison gate. Soldiers formed a circle. A female inmate carried the child's coffin into the circle and placed it on a bier. After the ceremony, the child was buried in the prison cemetery. Then the director met with the board at the prison to discuss how to prevent further killings. All inmates were in a state of emotional upheaval, he informed the members. Some pitied the murdered child, while those who were friends of Flor and Henrichs felt compassion for them ("of which they were unworthy," the director observed). Others, "out of corrupted evil nature," would not stop making desperate utterances, declaring that they too wanted to kill someone to bring their lives to an end. Under these conditions, it was difficult to administer the prison. "I wish that God would convert these people, and give them other ideas," the director wrote. "With so many desperate people" residing in the house, he did not know how to prevent further tragedy.[81] He had only a limited number of cells available for solitary confinement. Furthermore, it was winter, and these cells could not be heated, so inmates could not survive in them for long. If he locked inmates who made such threats in these cells for short periods, they would only be more embittered when they reentered the general population. At the same time, the court could not simply release these prisoners from the workhouse. Otherwise, every prisoner would simply threaten to commit murder to coerce his or her release. Moreover, such prisoners could not be set loose within the city. If they could not support themselves, they would become even more desperate than they had been in prison and commit suicidal murders in the city at large. He also worried about keeping these prisoners in the general population, because "such treacherous murderers try to conceal their malice" only to strike suddenly when opportunity presented itself.[82] He feared that they would attack fellow inmates in church when they were all sitting close together. His superiors instructed him to

---

[80] StAH, 242-1, I, A14, Zuchthaus Verwaltungsprotokoll, Bd. 2, 448.

[81] StAH, 242-1, I, A14, Zuchthaus Verwaltungsprotokoll, Bd. 2, 449.

[82] "Zumahlen solche Meuchelmörder Ihre Bosheit suchten zu verbergen undt also bey vorfallender Gelegenheit ds ins werck richten könten was mann besorgete." StAH, 242-1, I, A14, Zuchthaus Verwaltungsprotokoll, 450.

string the women along, coaxing them into compliance with the prospect of release in exchange for good behavior. One idea never came up in the discussion: To improve living and working conditions within the prison in order to lessen inmates' suicidal despair.

Later, the director ordered a thorough search of the prison. Guards confiscated over fifty knives from inmates.[83] The execution of the two young maidservants took place just over two months later. Their execution procession made a stop at the house of correction, where the executioner tore their flesh with red-hot tongs. After their decapitation, the executioner impaled their heads on posts and interred their bodies beneath them.[84]

1698–1699: CHILD MURDERS IN PRISON
AND IN THE STREETS

Less than three months later, in late April, a prostitute imprisoned in the Spinnhouse murdered a twenty-month-old toddler by throwing it into the latrine. Perhaps she was unable to get her hands on a knife. Authorities performed the "Justice of the Street" outside the gates of the Spinnhouse. Soldiers and officers of the court formed a circle around open casket with the child's body. As the woman stood at the coffin, the executioner swung his sword three times, uttering the hue and cry over the murder committed "in this honorable city." The prosecutor then handed her over to the executioner, who delivered her to the city prison. Her trial lasted two weeks. On May 16, 1698, her execution procession stopped in front of the Spinnhouse. Prison inmates lined the windows overlooking the street. They intoned the Lutheran hymn "Have Mercy on Me, Oh Lord," drawn from Penitential Psalm 51:

Erbarm' Dich mein o Herre Gott!
nach Deiner groß'n Barmherzigkeit,
wasch' ab mach' rein mein' Missethat,

---

[83] Brietzke, *Arbeitsdisziplin*, 596.

[84] The execution chronicle gives the date of their execution as January 31, 1698. *Ausführlicher Bericht*, 15. The newspaper *Mercurii Relation, oder wochentliche Reichs Ordinari Zeitungen...*, in the issue of 22 February, 1698, gives an execution date of February 10, 1698. The case is also described in Heß, *Hamburg topographisch*, vol. 2, (1810), 140, and W. L. Meeder, *Geschichte von Hamburg, vom Entstehen der Stadt bis auf die neueste Zeit*, vol. 2 (Hamburg: J. J. S. Wörmer, 1839), 287–288.

> *ich kenn' mein' Sünd' und ist mir leid;*
> *allein ich Dir gesündigt hab',*
> *das ist wider mich stetiglich;*
> *das Bös' vor Dir mag nicht bestahn,*
> *Du bleibst gerecht, ob Du urtheilest mich.*
>
> O God, be merciful to me,
> According to Thy great pity;
> Wash off, make clean my iniquity:
> I acknowlege my sin, and it greeveth me
> Against Thee, against Thee only
> Have I sinned, which is before mine eye:
> Though Thou be judged in man's sight,
> Yet are Thy words found true and right.[85]

As the inmates sang, the executioner tore the flesh of the condemned woman's right arm with red-hot tongs. The singing could not drown out her screams. Then the procession continued to the ravenstone. After her decapitation, the executioner braided her body onto a wheel leaving it exposed to the elements.[86] In response to this murder, Spinnhouse administrators began transferring newborns to the city orphanage as soon as possible after birth, though this resulted in high mortality rates for "Spinnhouse children," fed pap instead of breast milk.[87]

Four months later, on September 12, 1698, Hamburg executed another woman for child murder within the city at large. As in the previous cases, the woman, a prostitute, cut a child's throat. She walked to her execution with open flying hair, dressed in sackcloth. The bloody knife hung from her neck. On the way, presumably at or near the site of the murder, the executioner tore the woman's flesh with red-hot tongs. After her beheading, the executioner braided her body onto the wheel.[88] The purpose of the woman's "hideous" attire during her execution procession, as an

---

[85] The hymn is "Erbarm dich meyn o here got" by Erhard Hegenwald, first published 1524. The English and German lyrics can be found here: http://www.bach-cantatas.com/Texts/Chorale305-Eng3.htm. I have modernized the English spelling for readability.

[86] *Der Stadt Hamburg Gerichtsordnung und Statuta*, ed. Verein für Hamburgische Geschichte. (Hamburg: Perthes-Besser & Mauke, 1842), 530. Streng, *Gefängnissverwaltung*, 86. *Ausführlicher Bericht*, 15.

[87] Lindemann, "Maternal Politics," 48.

[88] *Ausführlicher Bericht*, 15, September 12, 1698.

eighteenth-century observer described it, was to instill horror and revulsion in the spectators.[89] The effect of the "infamous" costume was to make onlookers "shudder" and "recoil," wrote the jurist Johann Klefeker, in order to heighten the deterrent effect of the execution.[90] Male child killers, too, would soon be made to walk to their executions in sackcloth, the murder weapon fastened to their chests. But the open, flying hair now became a regular feature of the executions of women. This specifically female shaming ritual intensified the infamy of murderous women by drawing a contrast between them and respectable married women who wore their hair bound. Wild, open hair signaled a woman's sexual licentiousness.[91] The woman executed on this occasion was a prostitute, but many other women executed for suicidal child murder were not accused of any sexual immorality. The symbolism of sexual dishonor served as a generic idiom that communicated female dishonor in other contexts.

The authorities' efforts to deter suicidal child murders by intensifying the infamy of their executions were not successful. They may even have been counterproductive. The infamy imposed on condemned criminals during and after their executions had a different meaning than the rites of desecration performed on the corpses of suicides. When the executioner's men disposed of the corpse of a direct suicide in the carrion pit, this infamy happened in addition to the damnation the suicide presumably faced in the afterlife. It amplified the supernatural danger associated with such bad deaths. The mixing of the suicide's body with animal remains reflected how he or she had died. "To die like a brute beast" was a common expression to describe dying unrepentantly without the comforting rites of the

---

[89] The cameralist Christian Ludewig von Griesheim argued that all condemned criminals should be clothed in shameful clothing during the execution, as Hamburg customarily did with women who murdered children. Grießheim, *Anmerk. u. Zugaben über den Tractat: die Stadt Hamburg nach ihrem politischen, oeconomischen und sittlichen Zustande* (Hamburg: Wilhelm Drese, 1759), 138.

[90] Describing the 1768 death sentence of Elizabeth Wessels, an infanticidal mother, Klefeker writes: "es ward ihr die Todes-Strafe mit einer dazu gefügten, sonst auch wohl bey uns gewöhnlichen Hinausführung, in einem schauder- und schreckhaften Bekleidungs-Aufzuge in judico superiori zuerkannt." Klefeker, *Sammlung*, vol. 5, 503.

[91] On wild, open hair and sexual dishonor, see Lyndal Roper, *Witch Craze: Terror and Fantasy in Baroque Germany* (New Haven: Yale University Press, 2004), 151, 165.

church.⁹² The infamy associated with public executions was of a very different nature. The condemned criminal who performed his or her scripted role correctly during the execution ritual died with the most comprehensive religious support. The "hideous" attire the condemned criminal wore during the execution procession and the dismemberment of his or her body during or after an execution served as a foil, a point of contrast to the glory of salvation that the repentant malefactor and the spectators at the execution hoped for and expected. Even indefinite exposure of the criminal's corpse on the wheel at the ravenstone did not diminish his or her prospect of salvation. In 1699, the year after the prostitute suffered her exacerbated execution for child murder, four women committed suicide by proxy, a clear illustration of the ineffectiveness of infamous refinements of the execution ritual at deterring these kinds of murders.⁹³

THE EARLY EIGHTEENTH CENTURY

The number of recorded executions for all offenses rose in the first half of the eighteenth century, compared to the previous half century. Between 1700 and 1749, Hamburg executed 120 people, 102 men and 18 women. The percentage of women among executed felons dropped to 15%. The increase in the proportion of men among executed felons resulted in large part from a draconian prosecution of theft. Forty-eight men were hanged for theft. Other men were executed for murder, robbery, arson, and coin clipping. There were also executions for bigamy and sodomy. Women were executed for murder, arson, and theft. There was a sensational case of a lesbian crossdresser who was broken by the wheel with her lover for sodomy and murder in 1702.⁹⁴

---

⁹² This type of language was cross-confessional. In Catholic Austria, the corpses of sane suicides were disposed of like "unreasoning animals" (*"unvernünftiges Vieh"*). Evelyne Luef, "A Matter of Life and Death: Suicide in Early Modern Austria and Sweden (ca. 1650–1750)," (Doctoral Thesis, University of Vienna, 2016), 115–116.

⁹³ On January 23, 1699, a woman was beheaded for poisoning a child. On March 27, 1699, a prostitute was executed for cutting a child's throat. On May 1, 1699, a woman was beheaded after her flesh was torn with red-hot tongs for throwing a child into a latrine. On November 13, 1699, a woman was beheaded for cutting her own child's throat *Ausführlicher Bericht*, 15.

⁹⁴ Mary Lindemann, "Gender Tales: The multiple Identities of the Maiden Heinrich, Hamburg 1700," in *Gender in Early Modern German History*, ed. Ulinka Rublack (Cambridge: Cambridge University Press, 2002), 131–151.

At least five women were executed for neonaticide: Three by simple beheading and two suffered exacerbated executions.[95] The number of unsolved neonaticide cases remained high. In the years 1742 and 1743, for example, the corpses of six newborn infant were discovered in the city, but the mothers were never identified. In 1744 authorities found nine dead infants. Seven cases remained unsolved; in two cases the court identified and prosecuted the mothers.[96] In 1748, perhaps in response to the large number of unsolved neonaticides, the court condemned Maria Bruns, who had drowned her newborn, to be broken by the wheel. Wearing sackcloth, she was transported to the ravenstone in wagon because she was too weak to walk. After her execution, her body was exposed upon the wheel.[97] The following year, authorities discovered ten dead infants in the city. Nine were never identified; only one case led to an infanticide prosecution.[98]

In the same fifty years Hamburg prosecuted at least thirty-three cases of suicide by proxy. Preventing child murder in the house of correction remained a challenge. In 1700, the prison director ordered female inmates who uttered murder threats to be chained from their right hand to their

[95] In 1709 Catherina Heitmann was torn with hot pincers and beheaded for murdering her infant and attempting to dispose of its body. The executioner impaled her head on a post and braided her body onto the wheel. *Der Stadt Hamburg Gerichtsordnung und Statuta* (Hamburg: Perthes-Besser & Mauke, 1842), 535. *Ausführlicher Bericht*, 17, February 4, 1709. In 1720 Margarete Starfsche was beheaded for infanticide and attempting to dispose of the baby's body in a drain. *Ausführlicher Bericht*, 20, January 22, 1720. In 1728 Margaretha Ilsabe Becker was beheaded for tearing her infant's umbilical cord and disposing of it in a latrine. *Der Stadt Hamburg Gerichtsordnung*, 535. *Ausführlicher Bericht*, 22, November 29, 1728. In 1747 Anna Hillersch was beheaded for burying her newborn in a barn. *Ausführlicher Bericht*, 26, December 4, 1747.

[96] Rodegra et al. compiled statistics for the years 1742–1757, 1770–1782, and 1785–1800, juxtaposing the number of dead infants never identified with the number of prosecutions for secret pregnancies and/or infanticide.

From 1742 to 1757, of eighty suspicious infant deaths, sixty-three dead infants remained unidentified, while authorities prosecuted seventeen mothers. Between 1770 and 1782 the population approached 100,000. Of fifty-four dead infants, thirty-eight remained unidentified, compared to sixteen prosecutions. Between 1785 and 1800, of sixty-four dead infants, forty-one were not identified, while twenty-three women were prosecuted. The total population was c. 130,000 in 1794. Heinrich Rodegra, Mary Lindemann, and Martin Ehwald, "Kindsmord und verheimlichte Schwangerschaft im 18. Jahrhundert," *Gesnerus* 36 (1978): 278–279.

[97] *Ausführlicher Beircht*, 26, January 22, 1748.
[98] Rodegra et al, "Kindsmord," 278–279.

left foot, in a posture that enabled them to continue working at the spinning wheel while restricting their movements. Three women suspected of planning suicidal child murders were released from the house of correction and banished from the city.[99] Presumably, this outcome was beyond the women's wildest dreams.

In early 1702 another murder plot by female inmates came to light. The conspirators were Barbara Kohnaus, 21, and Barbara Hansen, 23. The director questioned both women. On December 30 the previous year, Hansen had told Kohnaus that she planned to kill someone and asked Kohnaus to participate. Kohnaus agreed. They selected a four-year-old girl as their victim. The liturgical element of suicidal child murder is particularly clear in this case. They chose a symbolic time and place to carry out the murder. They would perform "the sacrifice," as topographer Jonas Ludwig von Heß characterized it in his late eighteenth-century account, at the entrance of the prison church at seven in the evening on the feast day of the Epiphany.[100] The holiday falls on January 6 and celebrates the Adoration of the Christ child by the three Magi. Did the two women choose this date to symbolize some kind of correspondence between their chosen child victim and the Christ child? More likely, any Christian holiday would have been an auspicious time to carry out this kind of ritual murder. At the agreed-upon time, Kohnaus took the child onto her lap, as Hansen stood ready with the knife. They had already removed the little girl's neckerchief, when Kohnaus decided to pray over the child before the killing. She recited "Our Father" and two other Lutheran prayers. Moved by the prayers, the women had a change of heart. They returned the little girl unharmed to her mother, a fellow inmate. During their subsequent interrogation, the two women said that the purpose of the intended murder had been to gain "freedom from the house." Instead, the director transferred them from the house of correction to the Spinnhouse.[101] Seven months later, in July 1702, prison staff got wind of another child murder plot by two inmates. The two "persons" (the director did not give their gender) were held in a pitch-dark cell on a

---

[99] Streng, *Gefängnisverwaltung*, 57–58.

[100] The topographer Jonas Ludwig von Heß describes the little girl as a "sacrificial victim" ("*Schlachtopfer*"), in his *Hamburg topographisch*, vol. 2 (1810), 141.

[101] StAH, 242-1, I, A14, Bd.3, Zuchthaus Verwaltungsprotokoll, 132–134. Brietzke, *Arbeitsdisziplin*, 597. Beneke, *Hamburgische Geschichten*, 340–342.

diet of water and bread for four weeks, flogged, and released to the supervision of their families.[102]

At the same time, child murders continued outside the prison. A journeyman cheesemonger was beheaded in March 1702 for cutting the throat of an eleven-year-old girl. He turned himself in directly after the murder.[103] On May 19, 1703, a widow cut the throat of a six-year-old girl. An event earlier in the day may have encouraged her to commit murder instead of suicide. A journeyman tailor had stabbed himself to death, and the skinner disposed of his body in the carrion field, a reminder of the infamy attached to direct suicide.[104] On September 2, an unmarried woman was beheaded for cutting a child's throat.[105] On October 3, a woman was beheaded for cutting the throat of a soldier's child. On December 15, a woman was decapitated and her head impaled on a post for cutting her own child's throat.[106]

There was yet another murder plot among female inmates in the house of correction in 1707. Two female prisoners, Sophie Schmans and Liesche Kösters, convinced a fellow inmate to entrust them with her twenty-two-week-old baby boy, saying they wanted to play with him. Schmans attempted to cut the boy's throat while Kösters held him, but the knife was blunt. Alerted by the boy's screams, his mother rushed in and saved him. During their subsequent interrogation, Schmans testified that she had approached Kösters two weeks before the attempt to ask her to join in murdering a child. Kösters initially "could not resolve to do it," but ultimately, she agreed. "Did she not think that God would punish her?" the director asked. "The devil had seduced her," Schmans responded. "She wanted to get out of the House." Liesche Kösters also said that she "wanted to be free." "Did she not think that God the Lord would punish her severely for this?" the director asked. "She really wanted to get out of the house," Kösters answered. "The devil had seduced her, but now she

---

[102] StAH, 242-1, I, A14, Bd.3, Zuchthaus Verwaltungsprotokoll, 140. Brietzke, *Arbeitsdisziplin*, 597.

[103] *Ausführlicher Bericht*, 13 March, 1702, 17.

[104] Gallois, *Hamburgische Chronik*, vol. 2, 783.

[105] Gallois, *Hamburgische Chronik*, vol. 2, 783.

[106] This woman was identified only as "die Falskauferische." Richard Wosnik, *Beiträge zur Hamburgischen Kriminalgeschichte* (Hamburg: Selbstverlag, 1926), 39.

regrets it with all her heart and requests a merciful punishment." The women were flogged and transferred to the Spinnhouse.[107]

The child murders continued. Over the next seventeen years, through 1724, there were thirteen further child murders, occurring at a rate of close to one per year. Nine of the killers were women, and four were men. One woman died in prison before the conclusion of her trial. She was interred at the ravenstone.[108] All others were executed. Two women and two men died by simple beheading. The others suffered exacerbated executions, typically their flesh was torn by hot tongs on the way to their beheadings, and their bodies braided on the wheel afterward. Two women and one man were broken by the wheel.[109] Two of the murders happened in the house of correction. One of these was a direct reaction to prison discipline. In 1719 Margaretha Meyer, a twenty-six-year-old prostitute, was flogged with a ship's rope and chained by the leg to a heavy wooden block for eight days for stealing some wool. In response, when she regained her freedom of movement, she threw a five-year-old boy into a forty-feet-deep latrine.[110] In 1720 Hinrich Gößler, a young male prisoner, cut the throat of a thirteen-year-old boy.[111]

Meanwhile, the desecrations of direct suicides continued. On March 18, 1724, a maidservant cut her own throat in St. Nicolai Church. Immediately prior to her suicide she had attended confession, an effort to

---

[107] Interrogation of Sophie Schmans: "Warumb sie eine solche Mordthat hette vorgenohmen? Antw. Sie hette aus dem Hause gewolt.... sie hette es die Köstersche vor 14 Tagen offenbahrt, das sie willens were ein Kind umb zu bringen, die Köstersche hette gesagt sie könte dazu sich noch nicht resolviren, were aber nach der Zeit mit sie einig geworden ein Kindt zu morden. ... Ob sie nicht gedacht das sie Gott würde straffen? Antw. Der Teuffel hette sie verführt." Interrogation of Liesche Kösters: "Ob sie nicht gedacht daß Gott der Herr sie wurde dafür hardt straffen? Antw. Sie hette gern aus dem hause gewollt und der teuffel hette sie verführt, aber nun were es ihr von hertzen leidt und bitte umb genädige strafe." StAH, 242-1, I, A14, Bd. 3, 254–256. Brietzke, *Arbeitsdisziplin*, 597.

[108] She is described as "*eine reformierte junge Frau.*" Gallois, *Hamburgische Chronik*, vol. 2, 820.

[109] October 1707, a young woman. Gallois, *Hamburgische Chronik*, vol. 2, 820. January 17, 1708, Anna Catherina Fosch. January 18, 1712, Maria Bündels and Catherina Stoppelmann. March 17, 1713, Elisabeth Strusi. September 17, 1717, Catharina Margarete Moller. May 2, 1718, Martha Leranish. *Ausführlicher Bericht*, 17–18.

[110] Heß, *Hamburg topographisch* (1810), 140–141. *Der Stadt Hamburg Gerichtsordnung*, 530. *Ausführlicher Bericht*, 19, March 27, 1719.

[111] *Ausführlicher Bericht*, 20, February 5, 1720. Johann Gustav Gallois, *Hamburgische Chronik von den ältesten Zeiten bis auf die Jetztzeit*, vol. 2 (Hamburg: s.n., 1862), 33.

mitigate the sinfulness of her deed. Authorities were unmoved by her pious framing of her suicide. Three days later the executioner's men carted her body, draped in sackcloth with the bloody knife around her neck, to the gallows, and interred it there.[112] Just over a month after the infamous disposal of the maidservant's corpse, on April 24, Friedrich Neujahr, a local orphan and apprentice chimneysweep, cut the throat of a four-year-old girl on a market square. The duty officer in the constabulary when Neujahr was first brought in for questioning that evening was so outraged by the murder that he offered a suggestion to the criminal court: "since horrific child murders are increasing daily ..., this murderer should be attired in his blood-drenched clothes, the bloody knife hanging on his chest, during the hue and cry, so that others will mirror themselves in that."[113] We do not know if Neujahr did indeed attend his "Justice of the Street" in blood-drenched clothes, but on the day of his execution on July 10 he walked to the scaffold dressed in sackcloth, the murder knife dangling from his neck. The executioner tore his flesh with red-hot tongs before breaking him by the wheel and braiding his body into it.[114] Five months later, on December 11, 1724, Anna Ilsabe Dittmers was broken by the wheel after the executioner tore her flesh with red-hot tongs for cutting the throat of her ten-year-old child[115] (Image 4.4).

Legislation Fails to Stop the Killings

The senate finally responded this series of child killings with specific legislation in 1724. The edict, dated October 18, 1724, decried that child murders had "become rampant for some time," despite the most severe penalties. There were two kinds of child killers, the edict explained. First, "some malicious monstrous people driven by a lust for murder do not shy away from murdering unrelated children in the most horrific manner." Secondly, there were cruel parents who acted "counter to all natural emotions" and killed their own children. These were mostly unwed mothers

---

[112] Trummer, *Vorträge*, vol. 1, 457.

[113] "weil aber das abscheuliche Kindermorden leider täglich zunimbt, so wolte woll unvorgreiflich vorschlagen, wen es E. E. Rath mochte gefellig sein, das dieser Mörder bey der Beschreiung möchte mit seinen blutigen Kleidern angetan, und das blutige Messer auff der Brust hangendt habende, zum Schein geführet werden, ob noch einer oder anderer sich daran spiegeln möchte." StAH, 111-1, Senat, Cl.VII, Lit.Me, Nr.8, Vol. 2b, Fasc. 1a, 24 April 1724.

[114] *Ausführlicher Bericht*, 21. Gallois, *Hamburgische Chronik*, 47.

[115] *Ausführlicher Bericht*, 21. Gallois, *Hamburgische Chronik*, 47.

Image 4.4 Title page. *Ausführlicher Bericht/ Derer in Hamburg hingerichteten Missethäters* ([Hamburg], c. 1720). Hamburg Staatsarchiv, 111-1, Senat, CI.VII, Lit, Mb, No.3, Vol. 1

attempting to conceal their shame. The edict offered no explanation of the motive of the "monstrous people" who killed unrelated children, beyond imputing to them a generic "lust for murder." This diffidence contrasts with earlier legislation from Nuremberg (1702) and Vienna (1706), where authorities did explain and condemn the suicidal intent of perpetrators of suicide by proxy.[116] Perhaps Hamburg authorities chose not to publicize the motives of suicidal child murderers for fear of inspiring imitators. Both kinds of child murder loaded bloodguilt upon the city, the edict warned. Moreover, the killers of unrelated children "robbed pious parents of their innocent children, throwing them into the deepest grief." Christian government was duty-bound to prevent such "sins that cry out to heaven" and to punish them, when they occurred. To that end, the edict exhorted employers and midwives, at the risk of their own souls, to alert authorities to women they suspected of concealing their pregnancies or having committed infanticide. The edict offered no specific remedy to suicidal child murder. The earlier edicts in Nuremberg and Vienna had threatened such killers with exacerbated executions, but Hamburg already imposed the harshest penalties.[117]

Unsurprisingly, the edict did nothing to curtail further child murders. Infamous disposals of the bodies of suicides also continued. In July 1725 the executioner's men transported another female suicide to the gallows on the skinner's cart and buried her there.[118] Five months later, on December 12, 1725, almost a year to the day after the execution of Anna Ilsabe Dittmers for killing her ten-year-old child, shopkeeper Daniel Sottmann was beheaded for cutting the throat of his four-year-old stepson. A legal summary described Sottmann as "of sad and depressed temperament," but it provided no further explanation of motive. He succumbed to a sudden irresistible urge to murder the child. After the murder, he turned himself in at the next constabulary, confessing the child murder amid "tears and sighs." The court found that he suffered from melancholy, but not of sufficient degree to spare him the death penalty. The court sentenced him to simple beheading and granted him a Christian burial, instead of interring him at the scaffold, as many other child

---

[116] See Chap. 1.

[117] This was Anna Catherina Nohren, interred July 11, 1725. [Johan Friedrich Blank], *Sammlung der von E. Hochedlen Rathe der Stadt Hamburg so wol zur Handhabung der Gesetze und Verfassungen als bey besonderen Eräugnissen ... ausgegangenen allgemeinen Mandaten*, vol. 2 (Hamburg: J. C. Piscator., 1764), 1124–1127.

[118] Trummer, *Vorträge*, vol. 1, 457.

murderers were.[119] The following June, the cooper Johann Claessen cut the throat of his fourteen-year-old stepdaughter "out of desperation," that is, out of suicidal despair. He went straight to the city prison to turn himself in. One month later, he was broken by the wheel.[120]

In the 1730s, the proportion of male perpetrators rose. Hamburg prosecuted eight cases in that decade, seven murders and one attempted murder, perpetrated by six men and two women. In the attempted murder case, a male inmate at the house of correction tried to strangle an eight-year-old boy in custody there, after trying unsuccessfully for days to get his hands on a knife. Witnesses pulled him away from the boy in time. He was exposed at the pillory and transferred to the Spinnhouse.[121] Five of the seven murderers were executed by beheading or breaking by the wheel.[122] One man died in prison before sentencing. The skinner interred him in shallow grave by the ravenstone.[123] One female killer received an insanity defense. In 1736, Anna Maria G., a married woman, was sentenced to the Spinnhouse for life, after she had murdered a five-year-old boy "out of severe melancholy." Her melancholy made her ineligible for the death penalty, but lifetime confinement was necessary to prevent her from harming herself or others. The court directed prison staff to treat her more leniently than other inmates and to allow regular visitation by her

---

[119] Klefeker, *Sammlung*, vol. 5, 447–448. *Ausführlicher Bericht*, 21. Trummer, *Vorträge*, vol. 1, 442. Mary Lindeman, "Murder, Melancholy and the Insanity Defence in Eighteenth-century Hamburg," in *Medicine, Madness and Social History: Essays in Honour of Roy Porter*, eds. Roberta Bivins and John V. Pickstone (Basingstoke, Palgrave Macmillan, 2007), 164.

[120] "Poena rotae simpliciter ratione querundam circumstantiarum dictate Johann Classen filiae occisiori 1726." *Der Stadt Hamburg Gerichtsordnung*, 535. His last name is spelled alternately as Classen or Claessen. Gallois, *Hamburgische Chronik*, 47. *Ausführlicher Bericht*, 21, July 22, 1726.

[121] January 27, 1737, Johann Jurgen Schult. StAH, 242-1 I, A14, Bd. 6, pp. 274–276. Zuchthausverwaltungsprotokoll.

[122] Ilsabe Stadt'sche, beheaded October 15, 1731, because she had "murdered her seven-year-old daughter with a knife." Jürgen Degler, broken by the wheel, 4 February 1732, for cutting his stepdaughter's throat. Johann Philipp Breyer, beheaded 8 December 1732, for killing his employer's son. Hein Hammann, beheaded 23 April 1736, because he had cut his child's throat "out of desperation." Hermann Götsch, 9 November 1739, for murdering his child. *Ausführlicher Bericht*, 22–25. On Anna Maria G, sentenced 1736, see below.

[123] 20 February, 1737, Hinrich Röhrs. *Ausführlicher Bericht*, 24.

husband, her parents, and a medical doctor hired by her husband.[124] That her husband could afford to pay for regular visits by a medical doctor is an indication that Anna Maria G. was of higher social status than many other child murderers prosecuted in Hamburg. She received similar consideration as the child murderer Catherina Steinhäuserin, wife of Upper-Court Advocate Steinhäuser, whom the court sentenced to life-long confinement in the Spinnhouse in 1687.

1737: Direct Suicide—Official Mercy vs. Popular Taboo

In April 1737, a suicide took place in the house of correction. The government's humane handling of this case reflects a change in mentality among officials around mid-century. In 1685, when the last recorded suicide in the house of correction took place, authorities responded with uncompromising severity, as shown above. In the name of deterrence, the prison director at that time insisted that the body be left hanging until the executioner finally removed it for burial at the gallows two days later. His successor in office acted differently. At 5:30 in the evening on April 13, 1737, the prison director was attending a formal dinner, when the prison scribe and the cook came running. Half an hour earlier an inmate had been found hanging in the prison dormitory, they informed him, where he was hanging still. The director was dismayed that the staff had not cut the man down, for he might yet have been saved.

The director rushed to the dormitory and ordered the body to be cut down. Out of "foolish fantasy," however, as the director wrote in his log, his entire staff refused. They insisted that the director personally lay hands on the body first, before they would consent to touch it.[125] Here the prison staff were taking precisely the same ritual precaution that carpenters and stonemasons took to insulate themselves from dishonor contagion when they made repairs to the gallows or ravenstone. The ritual dishonor of the executioner permeated all physical objects involved in the administration of criminal justice, from instruments of torture, to the wagon wheel the executioner would use to break someone by the wheel, to

---

[124] Anna Maria G. was on trial "wegen der an einem fünfjährigen Knaben aus schwerer Melancholie begangenen Entleibung." Trummer, *Vorträge*, vol. 1, 442–443. Streng, *Gefängnissverwaltung*, 78.

[125] StAH, 242-1 I, A14, Bd. 6, fol. 283–284.

physical structures like the pillory, gallows, or ravenstone. Honorable guildsmen refused to lay hands on such objects before the appropriate steps had been taken to neutralize dishonor. Throughout the Holy Roman Empire, from the fifteenth century through the end of the eighteenth century, governmental authorities and honorable guildsmen cooperated in elaborate ceremonies to make the construction or repair of ravenstones and gallows ritually safe. Guildsmen marched collectively to the construction site in a formal procession headed by high government officials. At the ravenstones or gallows, magistrates declared the site to be honorable and personally touched the structure, often hammering in the first nail. Only then was it safe for guildsmen to touch. The logic underlying such ceremonies was that high magistrates representing sovereign governments were not only personally immune to dishonor pollution, but by virtue of their office they could ritually cleanse objects of dishonor, making them safe for people of lower social estate to touch.[126]

The prison staff demanded this same protection before they would obey the director's order to cut down the body. They believed that the director, a government official, would by his touch neutralize the dishonor that suffused the body of a suicide, if he lay hands on it first, rendering it safe for them to touch in turn. The director had no choice but to appease his staff. Once he laid hands on the body, the staff willingly cut him down. The inmate's body was still warm to the touch. The director was convinced that the man could have been saved if he had been cut down when he was first discovered. Two days later the senate granted permission for the inmate to be buried in a cemetery, based on a medical doctor's report that he had been of unsound mind. On April 16, the director hired some sailors, less touchy about dishonor contagion than artisans, to discreetly remove and bury the body.

Finally, the director summoned his subordinates to appear before the prison's supervisory board. The director and board members reprimanded them for their "delusional belief, that they would become dishonorable and would be doing executioner's work, if they had cut someone down who had hung himself." The officials condemned this "unreasonable opinion" and urged the staff to consider what tragedies they might prevent by acting in a timely manner. They promised to comply.[127] It is likely

---

[126] For a discussion of the symbolic logic underlying this ritual, see Stuart, *Defiled Trades*, 125–128.

[127] StAH, 242-1 I, A14, Bd. 6, fol. 283–284.

that the prison staff's obeisance amounted to little more than lip service. In 1769 the city government was still confronting the refusal of the public to administer first aid to drowning victims. A decree exhorted the public to render aid to drowning victims and condemned the inhumanity of refusing aid due to the "specious delusion" that touching them would leave a taint on a person's honor. The decree implored the public: Far from being dishonorable, rendering such aid was a Christian and meritorious act.[128]

To the extent that the prison director's and the senate's compassionate response to the workhouse inmate's suicide in 1737 reflected a more lenient attitude toward suicide among government officials, this did not weaken the popular taboo associated with suicide, nor did it dissuade desperate individuals from committing suicide by proxy. In 1739, Hermann Götsch received a quiet Christian burial after he was beheaded for murdering his child.[129]

1740: SENATORS' DISCOMFORT WITH A TRADITIONAL RITUAL

In 1740 the government discontinued a traditional annual ceremony in which senators had symbolically performed their duty as city fathers to supervise how the executioner carried out his office. The executioner, as we have seen, resided in the same prison complex as the felons whom he dispatched. He served as the *pater familias* of the institution and of the malefactors imprisoned there. Like any other head of household, it was his responsibility to care for the spiritual welfare of his dependents. This included not only his family and staff, but his prisoners as well. His superiors expected him to make sure that inmates performed their daily devotions. Among his regular duties was the requirement to pray and sing with his prisoners every morning and evening.[130] To modern sensibility it is positively bizarre that the executioner led prisoners in morning and evening prayers, whom he had or would personally torture during interrogations, and whom he would personally flog, maim, brand, behead, break by the wheel, or hang, according to their final sentence. This cultural practice

---

[128] Klefeker, *Sammlung*, vol. 12 (1773), 464, 462–466.

[129] *Ausführlicher Bericht*, 25, November 9, 1739.

[130] Otto Beneke, *Von unehrlichen Leuten. Cultur-Historische Studien und Geschichten* (Hamburg: Perthes, Besser und Mauke, 1863), 175.

brings to mind Robert Darnton's famous methodological observation in *The Great Cat Massacre*: "the best points of entry in an attempt to penetrate an alien culture can be those where it seems to be the most opaque. When you realize you are not getting something—a joke, a proverb, a ceremony ... you can see where to grasp a foreign system of meaning in order to unravel it."[131] To residents of Hamburg, both elite and commoner, however, the executioner's prayer sessions with his charges were just one element in a comprehensive program of pastoral care that was inextricably intertwined with the criminal justice system. Authorities remained heavily invested in caring for the spiritual welfare of the felons they prosecuted, and this priority shaped the day-to-day operation of the city jail run by the executioner, as it did in the house of correction and Spinnhouse. When prisoners prayed with their executioner they demonstrated their consent and submission to the punishment that divinely instituted governmental authority would impose.

The government bestowed the executioner's religious duties upon him in an annual ceremony. Every year on the feast day of Thomas the Apostle (December 21) the executioner appeared before the senators. Following an established script, the officiating mayor addressed him: "Executioner, do you sing and pray with your prisoners, mornings and evenings?" After a lengthy formulaic exchange, the ceremony concluded with the mayor's instruction: "Executioner, an honorable council admonishes you to zealously attend services and hear God's word with your household in the upcoming high Christmas holiday. In general, you must live in sober moderation, and supervise your prisoners and treat them well, and sing and pray with them reverently."

In 1740 the council abolished this yearly ceremony because it no longer fit the sensibility of their time: "Under present circumstances," the decree stated, the ritual had become "useless and downright offensive."[132] The senators did not explain what precisely offended them. Had the executioner's spiritual care of prisoners whom he would personally kill now become distasteful to them? Or was it their own personal participation and engagement with the executioner in a ritual that they now experienced as archaic? In any event, by abolishing their yearly ritual dialogue with the executioner, senators created more bureaucratic distance between

---

[131] Robert Darnton, *The Great Cat Massacre and other Episodes in French Cultural History* (New York: Basic Books, 2009), 78.
[132] Beneke, *Von unehrlichen Leuten*, 175–176.

themselves and the day-to-day operations of a criminal justice system that they authorized and endorsed.[133]

Meanwhile, suicidal child murders continued through the 1740s. In 1740, Anna Rebecca Meyers was beheaded for murdering an unrelated child.[134] In 1741, Gerhardt Kummerfeldt was beheaded for murdering his own child. The court granted him a quiet Christian burial.[135] "Out of desperate temperament," a man attempted to murder his thirteen-year-old son with a knife in 1745, wounding him severely.[136]

1750–1784: CHILD MURDERS CONTINUE, DESPITE OFFICIAL LENIENCY TOWARD DIRECT SUICIDE

After 1750 the overall number of executions fell dramatically, even as Hamburg's population grew from around 90,000 in 1750 to 130,000 in 1800. Hamburg executed 42 people in the second half of the century, down from 120 recorded executions in the previous half century. There were fewer executions for theft, particularly in the late eighteenth century, though they did not end entirely. The last hanging for theft took place in 1806. There were no further executions for moral offenses or sex crimes. With the decline in the total number of executions, women now made up fully half of executed felons. Hamburg executed twenty-one men and twenty-one women from 1750 to 1799. Most men were executed for murder and suicide by proxy. Women were executed for murder, neonaticide, and suicide by proxy.[137]

In the second half of the eighteenth century, authorities responded to cases of direct suicide with greater understanding, often sparing suicides and their families the dishonoring removal and disposal by the executioner. Such leniency resulted in a painful cut in income for the executioner. In addition to his annual salary, the executioner was paid a fee for each particular task he performed. In 1751 his fee for the removal of a suicide and interment in the gallows field was 10 *Thaler*. In 1762 the senate began to indemnify the executioner for lost income in those cases

[133] StAH, Cl.VII, Lit.Mb, Nr.3, Vol. 5, 2 August and 20 August 1760.
[134] *Ausführlicher Bericht*, 25, November 28, 1740.
[135] *Ausführlicher Bericht*, 25, May 8, 1741.
[136] Klefeker, *Sammlung*, vol. 5, 270.
[137] *Ausführlicher Bericht*, 26–31. Matthias Blazek, *Seeräuberei, Mord und Sühne. Eine 700-jährige Geschichte der Todesstrafe in Hamburg, 1292–1945* (Stuttgart: Ibidem Verlag, 2012), 96–101.

when authorities allowed suicides to receive a Christian burial. Now he would be paid the same fee "also for those suicides, by whatever method they killed themselves, who by indulgence of the senate are not disposed of by the executioner, but receive a quiet burial." The decree is an indication that such indulgence by the council toward suicides was becoming more common at this time.[138] Klefeker wrote in 1770 that all suicides who did not kill themselves because they were guilty of a crime, but because they were suffered from weariness with life, or were overcome by depression or melancholy were buried in the churchyard of St. Anne's, a cemetery designated for that purpose.[139]

The senate's more lenient policy toward suicides elicited resistance. The firebrand Lutheran clergyman Johann Melchior Goeze, chief pastor at St. Catherine's, attempted to hold the line. In a polemic against suicide written in 1775, Goeze argued that the essential element of God's highest honor was to be "the highest and sovereign Lord of human life. Therefore, an intentional and premeditated suicide is the most sacrilegious transgression .... Such a suicide dies in the most damnable rebellion against God." Apologists of suicide likewise committed sedition against God. Goeze issued a dire warning: Secular governments who did not punish such rebels would be held to account and receive their sentence from God.[140]

The government encountered defiance from more humble quarters as well. Once officials decided to allow a particular suicide to receive a Christian burial, they had to deal with the practical problem of the removal of the corpse. The pollution anxieties of common people continued to present obstacles. On November 21, 1777, the Hamburg correspondent for the *Bayreuther Zeitung* reported on the suicide of a young woman. Disappointed in love, she drowned herself in the Alster River. The city government tasked a charitable fraternity with carrying her body to the graveyard. The fraternity members were unaware of the circumstances of the young woman's death. Just as they were about to transport the body, a woman in the crowd of onlookers told them that this was the body of a suicide. The men immediately put down the body and left. They could not be persuaded to return and finish the task. It was not until the next day

---

[138] Beneke, *Von unehrlichen Leuten*, 167.

[139] Klefeker, *Sammlung*, vol. 8, 774–775.

[140] Johann Melchior Goeze, *Johan Melchior Goezens, Pastoris zu St. Cathar. in Hamburg, Auszüge aus seinen Sontags-, Fest- und verschiedenen Wochen-Predigten des 1775 Jahres* (Hamburg: Dietrich Anton Harmsen, 1775), 263–264.

that the city officials were able to hire other men willing to transport the body. The newspaper report makes clear that the journalist did not altogether approve of the government's leniency toward suicides. The fraternity members were guilty of prejudice, he conceded, but their prejudice was understandable. "Many a person who has not been educated by modern philosophers, can be deterred from taking his own life by the thought that his body will be dishonored after his death."[141]

The government's greater leniency toward direct suicides did not prevent a rash of new cases of suicide by proxy. The child murders continued unabated in the second half of the eighteenth century. In 1751 Hein Clas Schölermann, who had cut his own child's throat, was beheaded and granted a Christian burial in St. Jürgen's Graveyard.[142] In 1753, Maria Dorothea Heidmanns walked in her execution procession with open flying hair, dressed in sackcloth with the murder knife hanging around her neck, and was beheaded for cutting her own child's throat. Authorities granted her a quiet Christian burial as well.[143] The court was less generous with Cicilia Massaus in 1754. She had murdered her nine-year-old daughter. Like Heidmanns, Massaus walked in her execution procession with open, flying hair dressed in sackcloth. The murder knife hung from her neck. She was broken by the wheel, and her body was woven into it, left exposed to the elements.[144]

A murder trial the following year led to a different outcome. Engel Sellenschloen was a young woman of sterling reputation, known from youth for her God-fearing morally upright life. She became sorrowful after her marriage, however, sighing frequently as she read the word of God. Efforts by her pastor, her husband, her father, and other relatives to raise her spirits were in vain. Asked why she was so sad, she said only "she was of no use to the world anymore." She became convinced "that she had to be removed [from the world] one way or another." She did not want to commit suicide, so that she would not die in a state of sin. She had recently given birth to a baby boy. She had trouble breastfeeding him, but refused to hire a wet nurse. She felt confused and found it difficult to manage the household. Overcome by depression, she felt compelled to kill her son, "as

---

[141] *Bayreuther Zeitung*, Nr. 142, 27 November 1777, 797. https://digipress.digitale-sammlungen.de/view/bsb10505358_00791_u001/5?cq=hamburg.
[142] *Ausführlicher Bericht*, 26, February 1, 1751.
[143] *Ausführlicher Bericht*, 26–27, April 9, 1753.
[144] *Ausführlicher Bericht*, 27, March 11, 1754.

if an evil spirit pulled her with a strong cord." Sending a servant out of the room, she cut her baby's throat. Then she promptly called the servant back in and confessed. She wept profusely and pleaded for mercy from God and from the court. To the present-day reader, Sellenschloen's condition resembles postpartum depression, but this is not how her contemporaries explained her crime. Doctors examined her. She was blood-let. The physicians discerned in her blood "signs of a person suffering from the most severe melancholy." Nonetheless, the prosecutor charged her with child murder and requested the most severe death sentence, that is, the statutory penalty of breaking by the wheel after tearing her flesh with hot pincers. On January 17, 1755, the lower court sentenced her to simple beheading. The death sentence was justified, the lower court found, because her decision to kill the child rather than commit suicide demonstrated that she had criminal intent and had murdered the child with premeditation.

The Superior Court arrived at a different conclusion. Issuing its final sentence on June 6, the Superior Court found that Sellenschloen was ineligible for the death penalty or any other physical punishment, because she had not murdered her child out of malice. Instead, a deep-rooted, overwhelming melancholy rendered her incapable of forming criminal intent. The melancholy corrupted her imagination, compelling her to kill her son. The court sentenced her to confinement, at her husband's expense, in a former plague hospice where mentally ill people were cared for. There she would remain, housed in a secure but comfortable cell, until she showed improvement in her mental state. Sellenschloen, like Catharina Steinhäuserin and Maria Anna G. before her, seems to have come from a family of means, as the presence of a servant, the involvement of medical doctors, and her husband's ability to pay for her confinement indicate. Like them, Sellenschloen received more lenient treatment than many other child killers. The jurist Johann Klefeker, writing in 1768, reported that she received spiritual care in the hospice and recovered sufficiently to recognize her sins and pray to her savior for forgiveness. She died there a few years later, "escaping the chains of her miserable life."[145]

---

[145] Sellenschloen said, "daß sie in der Welt nichts mehr nütze sey," "…daß sie auf eine oder andere Weise herausgeschaffet werden müsse." She experienced the compulsion to murder her son "als mit einem starken Stricke von einem bösen Geist gezogen." "Die Herren Physici funden in dem Blute die Merkmale eines zur äussersten Melancholie gekommenen Menschen." Klefeker, *Sammlung*, vol. 5, 462–465. Trummer, *Vorträge*, vol. 1, 444.

In the second half of the eighteenth century, the senate remained deeply committed to providing intensive pastoral care for prisoners awaiting sentencing or execution. At the government's behest, pastors and theology students regularly attended to prisoners, distributing songbooks and catechisms. In 1760 pastors asked the senate to fund hiring a professional singer to perform at prayer services in the prison.[146] Authorities hired an orphan boy as lead singer.[147] Services at the prison attracted considerable public interest. That same year, the government investigated rumors that the executioner was charging admission from members of the public who wanted to attend the Sunday services on the eve of an execution scheduled for the following day. The senators deemed the executioner's entrepreneurship unseemly.[148]

Child murders continued through the 1760s and 1770s. In November 1765, the city council reissued its 1724 edict on child murder and posted it in public places throughout the city, to little effect.[149] Authorities prosecuted at least eleven cases, nine murders and two attempted murders, in these two decades. The majority of the perpetrators were women: There were three men and eight women.[150] Ilsabe Catharina Hölsen's murder of a three-year-old girl in the fall of 1777 received extensive press coverage.[151] According to a report from the *Augspurgisches Extra-Blatt*, Hölsen

[146] StAH, Cl.VII, Lit.Mb, Nr.3, Vol. 5, 20 August 1760.
[147] Beneke, *Von unehrlichen Leuten*, 175.
[148] StAH, Cl.VII, Lit.Mb, Nr.3, Vol. 5, 2 August and 20 August 1760.
[149] Johann Klefeker, *Sammlung*, vol. 6, 90, November 4, 1765.
[150] 28 April 1760, Susanna Margaretha Rahmlauen, a maidservant, beheaded for cutting the throat of her employer's child. 6 June 1765, Johann Jürgen Günther, beheaded, braided into wheel, for killing unrelated child. 4 December, 1769, Johann Christoper Leck, beheaded, for cutting his own child's throat. 18 May 1772, Anna Catherina Knurschen, beheaded for cutting a neighbor child's throat. *Ausführlicher Bericht*, 28–29. 6 December 1773, Sophia Margaretha Dittmers, beheaded for cutting her son's throat. *Erlanger Real-Zeitung*, Nr. 51, 25 June 1773. *Ausführlicher Bericht*, 29. October 23, 1777, woman inmate in plague hospice attempts to cut child's throat. 24 October 1777, woman cuts her own child's throat. *Reichs Post Reuter*, Nr. 170, 24 October 1777. 15 December 1777, Ilsabe Catharina Hölsen, beheaded for cutting the throat of her employers' three-year-old daughter. *Augspurgische Ordinari Postzeitung*, Nr. 310, 27 December 1777. 17 July 1778, a woman sentenced to life in the Spinnhouse for cutting the throat of her six-month-old son. Trummer, *Vorträge*, vol. 1, 444. 28 June 1778, Johann Scheideler, inmate in the house of correction attempted to cut a boy's throat. StAH, 242-1 I, A14 Bd. 11. 240–241, 28 June 1778. September 1778, a woman murdered an eight-year-old child after her lover abandoned her when she became pregnant. *Reichs Post-Reuter*, Nr. 148, 16 September 1778.
[151] Chapter 3.

was a maidservant, approximately twenty years old, "presumably driven to extremes by desperation or melancholy." On October 3, the young woman asked her employers' permission to take their three-year-old daughter out for a walk along the city wall. There she slashed the girl's throat with a bread knife. She went straight to the next constabulary and turned herself in. The child was still alive when sentries found her. There was hope that she might yet live. The maidservant's demeanor at the constabulary was very calm, the correspondent noted, a sign, he believed, of her despair and melancholy. (Coincidentally, the report continued, a murdered newborn infant had been discovered in front of St. Catherine's Church the day before.)[152]

The next dispatch from Hamburg reported that the little girl did not survive. Authorities held the "Justice of the Street" over the child's corpse on October 10. As usual on these occasions, authorities confronted the maidservant with the body of her victim. The correspondent carefully observed the young woman's demeanor. "During the entire solemn, and indeed horrible, ceremony she remained unmoved. Asked by the warden if she had committed the murder, she answered clearly, yes. She even laughed when the executioner unsheathed his sword." After the executioner's hue and cry, protocol called for the warden to conclude the ritual by ordering the burial to proceed. On this day, however, after the ceremony had already ended and the casket was closed, the maidservant suddenly "requested to see the child, whom she loved more than the parents' other children, one more time. After some consideration, the praetors granted her request. The coffin was opened, and she ... kissed the child and shed copious tears over her." "A circumstance," the correspondent emphasized, "that should be taken into consideration for the forthcoming defense of the murderer." Clearly, he believed that Hölsen deserved an insanity defense.[153]

Less than two weeks after this dramatic scene, Hamburg authorities were confronted with two cases two days in a row, on October 22 and October 23. First, a young woman in custody in the so-called plague hospice, an institution where mentally disturbed people were confined,

---

[152] Her sentence identifies her as Ilsabe Catharina Hölsen, alias Kuhls. StAH, 111-1, Senat, Cl.VII, Lit.Mb, Nr.3, Vol.5, December 12, 1777. *Augspurgisches Extra-Blatt*, Nr. 248, 16 October 1777. https://digipress.digitale-sammlungen.de/view/bsb10505143_00281_u001/1.

[153] *Augspurgisches Extra-Blatt*, Nr. 254, 23 October 1777. https://digipress.digitale-sammlungen.de/view/bsb10505143_00305_u001/3.

attempted to cut the throat of a staff member's child with a blunt pocket-knife. The next morning, in the city, a married woman cut the throat of her six-month-old son and walked into the next constabulary to turn herself in. The day before, her husband had been released from the same plague hospice where the murder attempt happened, where he had been held for dissolute behavior. Presumably, he told his wife about the attempted child murder that had just happened there. On his first evening home, he brutally beat his wife. She decided to cut short her life by killing her infant son.[154]

Five days later, on October 29, 1777, the city government responded to these latest cases with new legislation. Unlike the previous decree first published in 1724 and reissued in 1765, the new edict did not mention neonaticide by unwed mothers. The edict of 1777 addressed suicide by proxy exclusively. In contrast to earlier legislation, the decree directly acknowledged the killers' suicidal intent. The edict lamented the high number of premeditated murders of children that had plagued the city "for some time." People felt weariness with life because their previous dissolute life led them to fall into misery and disgrace. Others responded to some kind of dispute or conflict by "inhumanly" directing their desire for revenge toward some uninvolved third party. "People who develop weariness with life for these or other reasons are induced to murder their own or other people's innocent children in the most horrific and cruel manner." The murderers robbed parents of their children and threatened public safety. Evoking the specter of divine wrath that might strike Hamburg in response to such killings, the decree warned that such ungodly people heaped bloodguilt upon the city. Therefore, such murderous, vengeful spirits should be warned they would face exacerbated death penalties, including tearing the flesh with hot pincers, dragging to the execution site, placing the body on the wheel, or throwing it into a carrion pit.[155] The penalties threatened in this edict were nothing new, of course. Hamburg had been imposing these very penalties for decades. Like the decree of 1724, this new edict offered no new remedies to the type of murder, and it too failed to quash the killings.

[154] *Reichs Post Reuter*, Nr. 170, 24 October 1777. https://books.google.com/books?id=lFBlAAAAcAAJ&pg=RA5-PA17#v=onepage&q=ermordet&f=true.

[155] Christian Daniel Anderson, *Sammlung hamburgischer Verordnungen...* (Hamburg: Carl Wilhelm Meyn, 1783), 245–246.

Meanwhile Ilsabe Catharina Hölsen's trial progressed quickly. Hölsen's emotional display over the body of her three-year-old victim did not convince her judges to allow an insanity defense. Less than two months after her "Justice of the Street," the *Augspurgisches Extra-Blatt* reported on her execution on December 15, 1777, after her death sentence had been pronounced on December 12. Like so many others before her, Hölsen was led out dressed in sackcloth, the murder knife hanging around her neck. After her beheading, the executioner braided her body into the wheel, and her head was nailed to a post "as a deterrent example for others." The senate had instructed the court to expedite the Hölsen's trial, the correspondent reported, "so that it would make more of an impression." Customarily, he noted, such cases proceeded slowly since a human life hung in the balance.[156]

Despite the draconian language in the 1777 child murder decree, Hamburg never again imposed the exacerbated executions threatened therein. In a sign of changing sensibilities, since about 1760 the court dispensed with imposing add-on penalties such as tearing the flesh of condemned criminals with red-hot tongs as they walked to their executions, as had been so common in previous decades. Simple beheading now became the standard form of execution. Murderers did still walk to their execution in infamous attire, however, dressed in sackcloth with the murder knife fastened to their chests. In the 1760s and 1770s women still walked to their executions with open, flying hair.

In the 1780s, there was a marked shift in the gender profile of suicidal child killers. There were five documented cases over the course of the decade. All of the perpetrators were male. Three of the men killed their own children. Two men killed unrelated children. In 1781, Johann Christian Carstens was beheaded for cutting the throat of his youngest child, a boy of five or six. Carstens, 34, a recently widowed father of three, became despondent when an injury left him unable to work. Unable to support his children, beside himself with worry, he wished "to be out of the world." He considered killing himself but managed to suppress the thought. Instead, he killed his son in a sudden impulsive act. The court found that his despair and weariness with life did not free him from criminal responsibility. In fact, his ability to resist the temptation to commit

---

[156] *Augspurgische Ordinari Postzeitung*, Nr. 310, 27 December 1777. https://digipress.digitale-sammlungen.de/view/bsb10505143_00517_u001/1; StAH, 111-1, Senat, Cl. VII, Lit.M6, Nr.3, Vol.5, December 12, 1777.

suicide indicated that he was in his right mind. On the other hand, the impulsiveness of his deed meant that this was not premeditated murder, precluding a sentence of breaking by the wheel. Carstens had lived a moral life previously and was an affectionate father. Imposing additional defaming penalties would dishonor his relatives. The court sentenced Carstens to simple beheading and granted him a Christian burial.[157]

In 1782, David Faltzer cut his own child's throat and turned himself in after the deed. He was beheaded.[158] On May 10, 1784, Hans Jakob Beyn cut the throat of Johann Peter Hügel, a five-year-old neighbor boy. After the murder, Beyn stopped by the home of an adult daughter to hand over the family Bible, before turning himself in at the home of the chief prosecutor. On May 12, authorities performed the "Justice of the Street" over Beyn and the murdered boy. These ceremonies normally took place as close as possible to the murder location, but on this occasion, authorities performed the ritual at some distance from the child's home, out of consideration for the parents. The court published Beyn's death sentence on Friday, November 12, briefly describing his motives. Beyn's declining economic circumstances caused him to become despondent and develop weariness with his life. He murdered the boy "with the sole intention of being removed from the world by the hands of justice." "As a deterrent example to other such inhuman individuals," the court sentenced Beyn "to be led to the scaffold in sackcloth, the bloody knife fastened to his chest" and decapitated.[159] His execution took place three days later, on Monday, November 15.[160]

---

[157] StAH, 111-1, Senat, Cl.VII, Lit.Me, Nr.8, Vol.2b, Fasc. 5. *Ausführlicher Bericht*, 30, 16 July 1781.

[158] *Ausführlicher Bericht*, p. 30, 1782. The execution chronicle does not give a more precise date.

[159] "daß er geständlich an einem fünfjährigen Knaben einen Mord bloß in der Absicht verübet, um bald durch die Hände der Gerechtigkeit wider aus der Welt geschaffet zu werden." The court sentence him "ihm zur wohlverdienten Strafe, und anderen dergleichen unmenschlichen Gemüthern zum Abschreckenden Exempel, in einer harnen Decke, mit einem blutigen Messer auf der Brust, nach dem Gerichts-Platze hinzuführen und daselbst mit dem Schwerte vom Leben zum Tode zubringen." StAH, Cl.VII, Lit.M6, Nr.3, Vol.5, 12 November 1784. StAH, 412-1, 1072, Hans Jakob Beyn, 1784.

[160] StAH, 111-1, Senat, CI.VII, Lit. Mb, No.3, Vol.4a. *Ausführlicher Bericht*, 30.

1784: Desacralization and Deritualization

In response to these latest killings, the city government finally implemented changes in the ritual surrounding criminal justice with the goal of making suicide by proxy less alluring to their most desperate subjects. Within months the senate abolished two rituals that had shaped the way the public had experienced criminal justice for centuries. In July 1784 the senate ended the public participation of the clergy during executions that had first been introduced with Bugenhagen's church constitution of 1529. In September 1784 the senate put a stop to the "Justice of the Street," a ritual that had been performed in Hamburg since the Middle Ages. The senate began debating these changes on May 17, seven days after Beyn's murder of five-year-old Hans Peter Hügel.

Authorities had been aware for some time of the impact that the ritualization of criminal justice had on their emotionally vulnerable subjects. "We know from experience," the cameralist Christian Ludwig von Griesheim observed in 1760, "that the delicate death costume, and many other signs of pity accorded to condemned criminals, make such an impression on both sanguine and melancholy temperaments among the flighty mob, who are ignorant of the true principals of religion, that it has inspired gruesome deeds that shock human nature."[161] And yet it took until 1784 for Hamburg's senators to finally muster the political will to make changes to the traditional ceremonial surrounding capital murder trials and public executions. Now the government embarked upon a comprehensive program of deritualization of criminal justice.

No longer would the public witness the clergy's consolation, the laying on of hands, and the blessings that had featured so prominently in the traditional execution ritual. The reform did not change pastoral care for criminals behind prison walls away from public view, but it did end the malefactor's "triumphal" procession to the ravenstone flanked by clergy. The "common mob," the senators lamented, invariably understood the clergy's ministrations to the poor sinner during the procession and the rites on the ravenstone as a "public guarantee that the soul of the malefactor ascended straight to heaven." The desacralization of the public ritual was indispensable to prevent tragedies like the multiple recent examples of

---

[161] Christian Ludwig von Griesheim, *Verbesserte und vermehrte Auflage des Tractats: die Stadt Hamburg in ihrem politischen, öconomischen und sittlichen Zustande...* (Hamburg: Wilhelm Drese, 1760), 137–138.

"parents killing their children, or of disturbed people, who had nothing to hope for in the world and nothing to lose, killing people they do not know, the first to cross their path on the street, just so they could die in a state of grace, so they said and believed." Such religious "enthusiasm" (*Schwärmerei*) posed an intolerable threat to public safety and needed to be contained.[162] On July 12, 1784, Hamburg carried out the first execution without clerical accompaniment.[163] On November 15, Beyn was the first suicidal child murderer to walk in his execution procession without the consolation of clergymen by his side. Nonetheless, the city did pay for prayer services for Beyn in the city's five main churches and the city orphanage prior to his execution, a standard practice in all capital cases that the 1784 reform did not end. Beyn received a Christian burial.[164]

Ending the participation of the clergy in public executions was controversial. The Lutheran clergy, in particular, anticipated a hostile response from the public. The *Ministerium*, the college of Lutheran pastors, asked the senate to issue a public proclamation, explaining that the purpose of the reform was only to deter people from committing these kinds of murders, but that it would not deny spiritual care for condemned criminals. The public should be assured that ministers would continue to prepare condemned criminals for death behind prison walls. Furthermore, the senate should inform the public that it was secular government, not the ministers, who initiated this ritual change. Concerned about the impact the reform would have on condemned criminals, as well as on the spectators, the ministers insisted: "We do not want to take responsibility for this."[165]

Some ministers advocated for the reform, but others were vehemently opposed. The disunity among the clergy played out in public view in an exchange of pamphlets between two of Hamburg's most prominent ministers. Christoph Christian Sturm (1740–1786), chief pastor at St. Peter's Church, was a proponent of the Protestant Enlightenment. Sturm

---

[162] "ein öffentlich ertheilten Freybrief, wodurch die Seele des Missethäters schnurgerade zum Himmel auffahren müsse." "Die Fälle sind bekannt und erinnerlich, wo Eltern ihre Kinder, und Unmuthsvolle Leute, die auf der Welt nichts zu verlieren oder zu hoffen, unbekannte Personen, den ersten Besten, auf der Strasse umgebracht haben, blos um, wie sie sagten und dachten, selig zu sterben." StAH, 111-1, Bd. 75, Cl.VII Lit Mb No. 3 Vol. 4b, 17 May 1784.

[163] *Ausführlicher Bericht*, 30, July 12, 1784; Blazek, *Seeräuberei*, 99.

[164] StAH, 111-1, Senat, Cl.VII, Lit. Mb, No.3, Vol.4a. *Ausführlicher Bericht*, 30.

[165] "...wir mögten nicht gerne die Verantwortung dafür übernehmen." StAH, 111-1, Bd. 75, Cl.VII Lit Mb No. 3 Vol. 4b, 5 July 1784.

published a pamphlet, *Concerning the Custom of Having Ministers Accompany Malefactors to Their Execution*. Not only did participation of the clergy have no benefit, Sturm argued, it was actively harmful.[166] Sturm's ideas elicited opposition from the orthodox Lutheran clergy. Chief among them was Johann Melchior Goeze (1717–1786), senior pastor at St. Catherine's Church. Goeze had long been one of the most prominent defenders of orthodox Lutheranism in Germany. He had gained notoriety beyond Hamburg for his role in the so-called Fragments Controversy (*Fragmentenstreit*) in the late 1770s, in which Goeze became embroiled in a polemical exchange with Gotthold Ephraim Lessing, perhaps Germany's most preeminent Enlightenment philosopher. After Lessing published selections ("Fragments") of a deistic critique of revealed Christianity by an anonymous Hamburg author, Goeze's attacks on Lessing and other advocates of the Enlightenment earned him the moniker "Hamburg's Guardian of Zion."[167] Goeze saw Sturm's reform proposals as yet another assault on traditional Christianity. He responded with his own pamphlet, *Conscientious Rejoinder*, in which he endeavored to refute Sturm's argument point by point.[168]

Sturm coached his argument in confessional terms. The central role that the clergy played during executions, Sturm argued, was a relic of Catholic superstition that Protestant churches had failed to purge during the Reformation. The practice originated in an effort by the Roman church to demonstrate their spiritual charisma and superiority over secular government, Sturm claimed.[169] Sturm was quite wrong on this point. As we saw in Chap. 3, the elaborate pastoral care that condemned criminals

---

[166] [Christoph Christian Sturm], *Ueber die Gewohnheit, Missethäter durch Prediger zur Hinrichtung begleiten zu lassen* (Hamburg: Gottlieb Friedrich Schniebes, 1784). Artikel "Sturm, Christoph Christian" von Paul Tschackert, *Allgemeine Deutsche Biographie*, ed. Historische Kommission bei der Bayerischen Akademie der Wissenschaften, vol. 37 (1894): 4–5, Digitale Volltext-Ausgabe in Wikisource, URL: https://de.wikisource.org/w/index.php?title=ADB:Sturm,_Christoph_Christian&oldid=- (Version vom 8. Mai 2021, 01:36 Uhr UTC).

[167] Georg Daur, "Goeze, Johann Melchior" in *Neue Deutsche Biographie* 6 (1964): 598–599 [Online-Version]; https://www.deutsche-biographie.de/pnd118540386.html#ndbcontent. Georg Reinhard Röpe, *Johann Melchior Goeze. Eine Rettung* (Hamburg: Gustav Eduard Nolte, 1860), 47.

[168] Johann Melchior Goeze, *Gewissenhafte Erinnerungen zu der Schrift. Ueber die Gewohnheit, Missethäter durch Prediger zur Hinrichtung begleiten zu lassen* (Hamburg: Dietrich Anton Harmsen, 1784).

[169] Sturm, *Gewohnheit*, 3.

received in Hamburg during the early modern period grew out of ritual innovations introduced by Hamburg's Protestant reformer Bugenhagen. Delighted to point out Sturm's historical error, Goeze reviewed Hamburg church history in detail, citing all the relevant sources, in particular Bugenhagen's 1529 church ordinance.[170] (In early modern Europe generally, the clergy of all major denominations played a prominent role in execution ritual, as territorial churches met the institutional requirements of early modern state.) Sturm's historical error notwithstanding, however, his portrayal of clerical preeminence in execution ritual as the church's encroachment on the prerogatives of secular governance undoubtedly appealed to Hamburg's enlightened senators in the late eighteenth century.

Sturm and Goeze had both attended public executions. The two men gave starkly different accounts of their experiences. Sturm had personally ministered to a condemned criminal and walked with him during his execution procession on at least one occasion, an experience that left him shaken and distraught. It had been difficult, Sturm wrote, to maintain his composure during the event. Prisoners who had endured months in isolation and sensory deprivation in prison during their criminal trial could not possibly derive any spiritual benefit from pastoral care during the execution procession, Sturm argued, because they would be overwhelmed by the noise of many thousand spectators as they were led through the streets. Dazed, shaking, weak-limbed, as if under the influence of a large dose of opium, condemned criminals were in such a state of excitation that they would be unable to listen to or even hear the ministrations of the preacher. The crowd, motivated by curiosity and bloodlust, was also not receptive to religious instruction.[171]

Goeze's rejoinder to this point gives an idea of the intense fascination and engagement by the public with criminal trials. Far from being overwhelmed by the thousands of spectators lining the streets during their execution processions, Goeze argued, condemned criminals would have grown quite accustomed to large crowds during their months-long criminal trials. During criminal investigations and trials, bailiffs escorted defendants from the prison to the home of the praetor for questioning at least once a week. On these occasions the crowds lining the streets were almost as large as during execution processions. Nor were defendants deprived of

[170] Goeze, *Gewissenhafte Erinnerungen*, 6–9.
[171] Sturm, *Gewohnheit*, 5–9.

human interaction in prison. Every Thursday one of the four junior pastors led a prayer service and catechism lesson in prison, and every Sunday there was a church service open to the public. The prison chapel was always filled to capacity. The formal sentencing on Fridays happened at city hall in public session before the entire senate. The crowd in attendance inside the great hall, and outside of city hall, was every bit as large as the crowd on the day of execution the following Monday. During their last three days of life, condemned criminals were rarely alone. They received visitors, and on Sunday the pastor who had prepared them for death presided over the church service and provided them with the Lord's Supper, in front of a sizeable crowd of parishioners. Even if some condemned criminals derived no spiritual benefit from clerical accompaniment, Goeze argued, this was not true for all. If the good thief could receive saving grace on the cross, so too could condemned criminals on the way to their executions. Goeze also perceived the crowd very differently than Sturm. Where Sturm saw wild abandon of a frivolous mob, Goeze described a hushed solemnity that came over the crowd as the execution procession passed by. Spectators reverently joined in the hymns sung by the choir walking in the procession. Fellow ministers had never complained that the behavior of the crowd had distracted them from ministering to the offender, Goeze claimed.[172]

Sturm argued that the traditional ritual lulled condemned criminals into a false confidence regarding their salvation. "Preachers and criminals collude to give a certain sensual performance of eagerness for death and a certain triumphant contempt of death, as if this were the only reliable sign of dying in a state of grace."[173] Eagerness for death was no sure sign of grace any more than fearfulness was a sign of damnation, Sturm insisted. This placed excessive value on externalities, while neglecting the essential interior change of heart and abhorrence of sin. Moreover, such performance undermined the very purpose of public executions. When the malefactor was led out in triumph as a martyr suffering for a glorious cause and died in a manner that evoked admiration from the crowd, the execution lost its deterrent effect and made the weak-minded long to die in like manner. "A child murderess, beribboned and dressed entirely in white, hurrying joyfully alongside the preacher as if headed to her spiritual

---

[172] Goeze, *Gewissenhafte Erinnerungen*, 11–16.
[173] Sturm, *Gewohnheit*, 14.

wedding, is a spectacle that endangers the lives of other people."[174] If ending clerical accompaniment during the execution procession meant that condemned criminals experienced greater distress on their walk to the scaffold, this was not a bad outcome. In order for executions to have a deterrent effect, it was necessary that condemned criminals experience their execution as punishment rather than a gift and that the public perceive it that way too. The reform of the execution ritual was the latest measure in the government's ongoing effort to suppress "the spirit of murder that has been so horrifically raging among us for some time."[175]

Goeze's counterargument reflects the cultural distance separating proponents of the Protestant Enlightenment from orthodox Lutherans and also illustrates to what extent public executions remained fraught and perilous affairs even in the late eighteenth century. The purpose of execution was not merely deterrence, Goeze insisted, but also to absolve the blood-guilt that stained the city as a result of murder committed within its jurisdiction. If authorities allowed a murder to go unpunished, they and the entire community would be held accountable by God. This kind of traditional religious language had more or less disappeared from internal government correspondence by the 1760s, nor was it to be found in the writings of Goeze's enlightened colleague Sturm. Furthermore, Goeze continued, deterrence was not necessarily served by denying clerical consolation to condemned criminals on their last walk. The spectacle of an unrepentant criminal in total despair, bound hand and foot, being dragged to the scaffold like a wild animal did not serve the public interest. The public was moved to compassion toward a condemned criminal treated with excessive harshness, as demonstrated by the crowd's violent response when the executioner botched a beheading. Such an outcome was more easily avoided if the prisoner was compliant. The presence of preacher on the ravenstone even offered protection to executioner, since an enraged crowd was less likely to storm the scaffold if they risked harming the preacher along with executioner.

Goeze could take his opposition to the reform only so far, however, since the Hamburg senate exercised sovereign authority over the Lutheran state church.[176] "Government has a completely unlimited right to decide the matter," Goeze acknowledged, prudently presenting his dissent as

---

[174] Sturm, *Gewohnheit*, 15.
[175] Sturm, *Gewohnheit*, 16.
[176] Whaley, *Religious Toleration*, 25.

criticism of Sturm for overreach, rather than as overt resistance to the reform implemented by government.[177] "May God, the lover of life, grant success to our cherished government in all their present and future efforts to quash the murderous spirit that is raging among us lately, and save us from accumulated bloodguilt," Goeze piously concluded.[178]

Two months later the senate abolished the "Justice of the Street." After secularizing the ritual of public execution, authorities pared down the pomp and circumstance surrounding criminal justice even further by discontinuing what had been one of the most distinctive features of criminal justice in Hamburg. The deliberations on the reform contain a legal brief that explained to the senators the origins and history of a ritual they no longer understood. The hue and cry dated back to medieval Saxon law, when criminal trials were conducted rapidly according to the accusatorial procedure. After the adoption of the inquisitorial procedure and the reception of Roman law, the ceremony no longer served any useful purpose, the senate concluded. It had become "merely a show" that was detrimental to the dignity of the court and demeaning to the officers of the court who presided over it, "all the more so because the old formula that are recited there are understood by few, possibly not even by the officials reciting them." It was nothing more than "tragic pomp." Since the *Carolina* left it to the discretion of local authorities whether to perform the ritual or not, the senate could discontinue it on its own authority. Accordingly, on September 17, 1784, the senate decreed "that the Justice of the Street that has been customary heretofore shall be abolished in regular practice, and shall only be performed in special cases with prior approval by the senate."[179] There is no documented case of a "Justice of the Street" being performed in Hamburg after this date.[180]

---

[177] Goeze, *Gewissenhafte Erinnerungen*, 2.
[178] Goeze, *Gewissenhafte Erinnerungen*, 20.
[179] "sonst scheint sie mir ein bloßes Spielwerk und der Würde des Gerichts und der dabey assistierenden Gerichts Personen kaum anständig zu seyn, um so mehr die dabey recitiert werdenden alten Formeln von wenigen, und vielleicht kaum von den Recitenten selbst mehr verstanden werden." 17 September 1784, StAH, 111-1 Bd. 73, Cl.VII Lit Ma No9 Vol. 1b.
[180] Chr. Petersen, "Zioter (Zeter) oder Tiodute (Jodute), der Gott des Kriegs und des Rechts bei den Deutschen. Eine rechtsgeschichtliche und mythologische Untersuchung," in *Forschungen zur deutschen Geschichte*, vol. 6, ed. Königlich Bayerische Akademie der Wissenschaften (Göttingen: Dieterich, 1866), 260.

Late Cases: Child Murder as a Suicidal Reflex

If the senators hoped that the deritualization of criminal justice would finally end the scourge of suicidal murders in the city, they were disappointed. The particularly well-documented trial of Anton Lorenz Ammon, who cut the throat of his eight-day-old daughter in 1786, gives insight into the life story of one such killer and the circumstances that culminated in murder.[181] Anton Lorenz Ammon was twenty-nine years old in June 1786. A native of Hamburg, Ammon was the son of a local schoolmaster. His father died when he was two. His mother never remarried. She raised him until he was nine, when she placed him in the Hamburg orphanage. This was not an abandonment. Many early modern parents availed themselves of a variety of formal or informal systems of child placement, in what historian Joel Harrington describes as the "circulation of children."[182] Ammon maintained a close relationship with his mother until the end of his life. "He was thoroughly educated in Christianity and other necessary knowledge" during his time in the orphanage, Ammon testified.[183] After his confirmation and partaking of the Lord's Supper, he left the orphanage at the age of seventeen to enter service as a shopkeeper's apprentice, later advancing to journeyman. When he lost his position, he did odd jobs as a scribe and military recruiter.

Around Pentecost (May) 1785, he developed a relationship with Anna Maria Mollenberger. She became pregnant, and Ammon wanted to marry her, but his mother objected because she considered Mollenberger a "loose woman," presumably because she had fornicated with her son outside of wedlock. Instead of breaking it off with Mollenberger, as his mother wanted, Ammon lived with her "as husband and wife" in a common law marriage in various Hamburg rooming houses. Without regular employment, he made ends meet by successively pawning off his possessions. When Mollenberger approached her due date, Ammon's mother

---

[181] StAH, 331-2, 1786, Nr. 0002 B, Anton Lorenz Ammon, Krautkrämergeselle: Untersuchung und Strafprozess wegen Mordes an seiner 8 Tage alten Tochter, 1786. Jürgen Martschukat, "Ein Freitod durch die Hand des Henkers. Erörterungen zur Komplementarität von Diskursen und Praktiken am Beispiel von 'Mord aus Lebens-Uberdruß' und Todesstrafe im 18. Jahrhundert," *Zeitschrift für historische Forschung* 27 (2000): 54. See also Martschukat, *Inszeniertes Töten*, 88.

[182] Joel Harrington, *The Unwanted Child: The Fate of Foundlings, Orphans and Juvenile Criminals in Early Modern Germany* (Chicago: University of Chicago Press, 2009), 7.

[183] Ammon's testimony, June 30, 1786. StAH, 331-2, 1786, Nr. 2 B.

finally dropped her opposition to the marriage. The young couple now made speedy preparations to celebrate their wedding before the birth of their child. They publicly announced their engagement in St. Michael's, their local parish church. Mollenberger's mother, a sixty-year-old soldier's widow from nearby Ratzeburg, came to stay with them to help her daughter during the birth and her lying-in. The couple went to confession on Saturday, June 17, in order to take the Lord's Supper on Sunday. The wedding was set for the following Sunday, June 25.

Mollenberger went into labor early that evening, so on Sunday Ammon went to church and took communion alone. Sunday evening, June 18, his bride, as he described her, gave birth to a healthy baby girl. On Monday, the new mother received communion in their rented room. Ammon and his bride delayed the baptism of their baby daughter, hoping to celebrate their wedding as scheduled the following Sunday. After the wedding, they would baptize their baby as a child of legitimate marriage, and her birth would be recorded in parish registers as such. This was a fraught decision for the new parents. Given high rates of infant mortality, they had to weigh the very real risk that their baby might die before baptism against the social disadvantages suffered by children of illegitimate birth. Catholic parents, who believed that unbaptized infants would spend all eternity in the antechamber of hell, most likely would have made a different calculation.[184] In the end, their baby did live to be baptized.

Mollenberger, however, did poorly during her lying-in. She died the following Saturday, June 24, on the eve of her scheduled wedding day. That night Ammon got drunk on brandy. He recovered enough by the next day, Sunday, to have his daughter baptized Anna Maria Sophia Ammon. His deceased bride and his mother were both named Anna Maria. Now Ammon faced the task of making funeral arrangements. His bride's body had lain in the hallway outside his room since Saturday. He did not have enough money to cover burial expenses. He approached his common law mother-in-law, who was still staying with him, and his own mother for help with the costs, but both widows depended on alms themselves and were unable to contribute. His mother advised him to pawn his silver pocket watch, but Ammon knew from prior experience (having

---

[184] On the post-mortem status of unbaptized infants in Catholic and Lutheran doctrine, see Irmgad Wilhelm-Schaffer, *Gottes Beamter und Spielmann des Teufels. Der Tod im Spätmittelalter und Früher Neuzeit* (Cologne: Böhlau, 1999), 132–137.

pawned it once before) that he would not get enough money for it to pay for the funeral.

On Monday, June 26, Ammon walked the streets of Hamburg dejectedly, unable to come up with a solution to his predicament. He ran into some soldiers he was acquainted with and drank several shots of brandy with them. He arrived home on Monday afternoon somewhat drunk, but "in full possession of his senses," as he emphasized during his subsequent interrogation.[185] Waiting for him were his bride's mother and her two adult daughters, who had come from nearby Altona to learn when their sister would be buried. Crying, he paced the hallway where his daughter slept in her crib and her mother's body lay. Her sisters offered to brew some tea, which they would drink together "as friends, and brother and sister."[186] He accepted, and the women went into the room to brew the tea. He sat in the hallway, next to his daughter's crib. His gaze fell on his dead bride's body. Suddenly he became so distraught, he later testified, that he decided to murder the baby in her crib, "just so that he would get out of the world, when he receives his punishment." As quickly as he conceived of the idea, he carried it out, grabbing his dinner knife and cutting his baby's throat.[187] The women brewing tea inside his room saw him attack the baby in the hallway through the open door. His bride's mother rushed out and tore the knife from his hands, shoving him away from her grandchild, but it was too late. The women ran out into the street screaming. Ammon waited until the constables arrived.

The judicial machinery kicked into gear. Over the next several days, officials interviewed all witnesses and interrogated Ammon twice. During Ammon's second questioning on June 30, the interrogator asked: "Did he repent the murder afterwards, and does he still regret it now?" Ammon answered: "Right after the deed he repented the murder, and he still regrets it wholeheartedly. He obediently requests an expedited and

---

[185] "…jedoch völlig bey Verstande gewesen." Ammon's testimony, June 30, 1786. StAH, 331-2, 1786, Nr. 2B.

[186] June 28, 1786. StAH, 331-2, 1786, Nr. 2 B.

[187] "habe er hierbey auf der Diele ganz plötzlich den Entschluß gefasst, das junge Kind in dem Bette umzubringen, damit er auch nur bald aus der Welt kommen mögte, wenn er seine Strafe dieserwegen bekommen würde. Worauf er auch gleich diesen gefassten Entschluß eben so plötzlich würcklich vollführet." Ammon's testimony, June 30, 1786. StAH, 331-2, 1786, Nr. 2 B.

merciful death sentence."[188] Now the prosecutor and defense advocate presented their cases. It was standard procedure in Hamburg criminal trials for the court to appoint a defense counsel to represent the accused, whether the defendant wanted one or not, which presumably in this case he did not. As we saw, Ammon did his best to preempt an insanity defense by insisting that he was "in full possession of his senses" at the time of the murder.[189] Nonetheless, the defense counsel made a valiant effort to save Ammon's life. Dire poverty prompted an outbreak of strong passions in Ammon, he argued. He did not commit the murder out of self-interest, for profit or revenge, but for the sole purpose of realizing his unreasonable idea of becoming a victim of criminal justice and thus get out of the world. This unreasonable purpose was an indication that Ammon was incapable of rational thought at the time of the murder and therefore did not have capacity to form criminal intent. Furthermore, the defense counsel argued, the death penalty should not be imposed on someone who committed a crime with the express purpose of being executed. For such an offender a death sentence would be a gift, not a punishment. Therefore, imprisonment was a more appropriate penalty.[190]

The prosecutor blamed Ammon's sad fate on idleness, a dissolute life, and consorting with "bad people." He was referring to Ammon's bride. Officials concurred with Ammon's mother that she was a "loose woman." Ammon's drunkenness and his dejectedness over his inability to pay for his bride's funeral did not rise to a sufficient level of "delirium" that would justify an insanity defense. To spare him the statutory death penalty for child murder would be to disrespect the law, the prosecutor argued. Here the late eighteenth-century prosecutor used a very different language than prosecutors a generation earlier, who would have cited to the decalogue, the biblical command of "blood for blood." They would have raised the

---

[188] Question 29: "Ob ihm diese Mordthat nachher gereuet, und solche ihm noch jetzt leyd wäre?
Answer 29: "Gleich nach geschehener That hätte ihm diese Mordthat gereuet, und wäre ihm solche noch jetzt von Hertzen leyd. Er bathe hiemit gehorsamst, um eine baldige und gnädige Todessstrafe." Interrogation of Ammon, June 30, 1786. When Ammon requested a "merciful" death sentence, he was not asking for a lenient or painless sentence. Rather, this was a formulaic way that subjects addressed their rulers. StAH, 331-2, 1786, Nr. 2 B.

[189] Ammon's testimony, June 30, 1786. StAH, 331-2, 1786, Nr. 2B.

[190] "einzig und allein hatte er den unvernüftigen Gedanken hiedurch ein Opfer der strafenden Gerechtigkeit zu werden, und bald selbst aus der Welt zu kommen." Defensionales, no date. StAH, 331-2, 1786, Nr. 2 B.

specter of bloodguilt (just as the orthodox Lutheran pastor Goeze had done two years earlier), a stain that could only be erased by the blood of the malefactor according to criminal law derived from divine commandment. By contrast, for Ammon's prosecutor, the authority of the law had replaced God as the foundation of his argument. He did not refer to God or religion anywhere in his brief.

The prosecutor agreed with the defense advocate that executing offenders like Ammon was counterproductive. "Indeed, it is hard to think of anything more inadequate," the prosecutor conceded, than to execute offenders who committed the crime with the specific intent of being put to death. But this was beside the point in the present case, because the court was bound to act within existing law.[191] However, as a matter of policy going forward, "when one thinks of the unbelievably frequent examples of such murders committed solely out of weariness with life," it was the obligation of government to develop an effective strategy to suppress such killings.[192] The recent removal of the clergy from execution processions had been insufficient. Therefore, the prosecutor suggested, government could issue new legislation imposing a sentence of life in prison instead of death for such murders. Alternatively, if public legislation were too politically controversial, the senate could issue an internal memorandum to the courts, instructing them to impose life sentences in such cases, a step that could be justified by the senate's pardon power.

On September 15, Hamburg's senate in its function as Superior Court condemned Ammon to death by beheading. Ammon's misfortune was the result of his own dissolute life, the court found. The court referred only indirectly to Ammon's motive, noting that his punishment should serve as "a deterrent example to similar individuals, who blindly give themselves over to their passions and prejudices." Like so many other suicidal child murderers before him, Ammon walked to his execution dressed in sackcloth, the murder knife pinned to his chest. He received a Christian

---

[191] "In der That kann man sich nicht leicht etwas inadequateres denken, als diejenigen mit dem Tode zu bestrafen, die ihr Verbrechen aus keiner anderen Absicht begangen haben, als um ihn zu verdienen." StAH, 111-1, Senat, Cl.VII, Lit. Me, Nr.8, Vol. 2b, Fasc. 6b, 15. September 1786.

[192] "die in neueren Zeiten unglaublich häufigen Beispiele solcher Mordthaten..., die aus bloßem Überdruß des Lebens vollbracht worden." StAH, 111-1, Senat, Cl.VII, Lit. Me, Nr.8, Vol. 2b, Fasc. 6b, 15. September 1786.

burial.¹⁹³ There is no record whether the senate acted upon the prosecutor's proposal.

In three later cases, the court accepted an insanity defense. In 1789, the council sentenced a man who had murdered a six-year-old boy in a "temporary melancholy delirium." The council found that his mental state made him ineligible for the death sentence requested by the prosecutor and sentenced him to the Spinnhouse for life at moderate labor. He hanged himself in his cell the following year. The council granted him a quiet Christian burial.¹⁹⁴

In 1790, the court tried nineteen-year-old Elisabeth Jentzen for child murder. Again, the council arrived at a finding of insanity. The sentencing recommendation by one of the voting senators shows that the Age of Sensibility now shaped attitudes of the ruling class: "It is the duty of the humanely thinking criminal judge" to seek to mitigate criminal sentences whenever possible, arriving at a just sentence "by means of reason and feeling, which he must never deny." This was not an intentional, premeditated murder, the senator argued. Witnesses described Jentzen as dazed, confused, anxious. "She had no particular reason for murdering this child," she testified. "She did not care which child she murdered. She was very fond of this child. She had no quarrel or resentment against its parents." And crucially: "No weariness with life impelled her to do it." The deed resulted from bodily infirmity that brought on a sudden corruption of her reason, the senator concluded. There was no criminal intent; therefore, she was not criminally liable. The court placed her in custody in the Spinnhouse until there was no danger of further melancholy episodes and she could be safely released.¹⁹⁵

In 1803, the court also arrived at a finding of insanity for Johann Wilhelm Khörse, who had attempted to cut the throat of an eight-year-old boy the year before. On August 10, 1802, Khörse, a fifty-six-year-old unemployed ship's carpenter, attacked the son of his upstairs neighbor, throwing him to the ground and slashing his throat. Hearing the commotion from above, the boy's mother rushed downstairs and shoved him away from her son. "Khörse, what are you doing?!" she screamed. "Are

---

[193] "ihm zur wohlverdienten Strafe, andern dergleichen, ihren Leidenschaften und Vorurtheilen sich blindlichs überlassenen Gemüthern zum abschreckenden Exempel." StAH, 331-2, 1786, Nr. 2 B. *Ausführlicher Bericht*, 30.

[194] Trummer, *Vorträge*, vol. 1, 445.

[195] StAH, 111-1. Senat, Cl.VII, Lit.Me, Nr.8, Vol.2b, Fasc. 6c, 15 March 1790.

you trying to murder my child?!" "He has enough. He will surely die," Khörse answered. He tried to leave to turn himself in at the constabulary, but neighbors detained him until sentries arrived. The boy's father staunched the bleeding. The boy survived, though he never would hold his head upright again, a surgeon reported, due to injuries he sustained to his neck muscles and sinews. During his interrogation, Khörse testified that he had just lost his stipend from the ships' carpenters' union and was about to be evicted for not paying rent. In a state of despair, he assaulted the boy in "a fit of melancholy." Asked with what intention he attacked the boy, Khörse said he did not know. He felt dazed. The idea came to him suddenly as the boy passed him in the hallway. Five days later, Khörse tried to hang himself in prison with his stocking bands, but guards cut him down in time. The court handed down its sentence nine months later, on May 4, 1803. The fact that Khörse had attacked the boy completely without cause demonstrated that he had acted in a fit of madness. Therefore, he could not be held criminally responsible. He was clearly a danger to society, so he would be confined to a hospital until he recovered from his mental illness.[196]

This was a remarkable ruling. As they judged this case, Hamburg jurists could draw on 180 years of experience with suicidal murders. Yet they chose not to categorize Khörse's attack as this type of attempted murder. Historian Jürgen Martschukat discusses this case as an example of the novel medical diagnosis of "hidden madness" (*amentia occulta*), first formulated by the Leipzig physician Ernst Platner in 1797.[197] To the untrained eye, people afflicted by this mental illness were perfectly sane. People suffering from hidden madness tended to erupt in paroxysms of violence without warning. It took a trained Mad-doctor to diagnose the condition. As "hidden madness" became a fashionable diagnosis in the early nineteenth century, it increased the influence of medical doctors in criminal jurisprudence. "There can be no doubt," the medical doctor who examined Khörse argued, that this "hideous deed could only be done by

---

[196] StAH, 331-2, P-K, 1802, Nr.81. Untersuchung und Strafprozess gegen den Schiffszimmermann Johann Wilhelm Köhrse wegen Mordversuch an dem 8jährigen Johann Martin Heinrich Lembcke, (1774) 1802–1803.
[197] Martschukat, *Inszeniertes Töten*, 164, 154–157. Ernst Platner, *Questiones Medicinae forensis et medicinae stadium octo semestribus descriptum* (Leipzig: s.n., 1797).

someone, whose body was in a diseased state causing the forces of his mind to flow in the wrong direction."[198]

Three other child murders in the early years of the nineteenth century did result in executions, however. Carsten Christopher Voß was beheaded in 1808 for cutting his own child's throat.[199] Johann Christian Schröder was beheaded in 1809 for cutting the throat of an unrelated child.[200] On September 18, 1809, Catharina Maria Koenig became the last woman executed for killing a child in Hamburg, whether for suicidal child murder or neonaticide.[201] Koenig had migrated to Hamburg in search of work as a young woman in the late 1780s. She ended up working in a brothel. Here she met her future husband. They married around 1790. Their marriage was peaceable at first, but a series of miscarriages and declining economic circumstances strained their relationship. Witnesses described her as hot-tempered and quarrelsome, prone to jealous rage over real or imagined relationships of her husband with other women. She developed weariness with life. In May 1808, she left her husband and took lodging with a widow. She developed an affectionate relationship with the widow's seven-year-old daughter, whom she often cared for. Her weariness with her life intensified. She wanted to exact revenge. On September 7 at noon, she left the house with the little girl with the intention of cutting her throat. She took a bread knife with her for this purpose. She had formed the idea three days earlier, because she wished to be away from the world, where she could no longer find rest or pleasure. Over the course of the day, she and the girl strolled along the ramparts. In the evening, she fed the girl bread and milk. At nightfall, they lay down together on a bench. She covered the girl with her cloak to keep her warm. While the girl slept, Koenig said prayers from Hamburg's officially approved evangelical songbook. In the early morning hours, she cut the girl's throat.[202]

Her lawyer presented an insanity defense. She suffered temporary madness at the time of the murder, afflicted by profound depression, he

---

[198] "Es ist nicht zu bezweifeln, daß diese mit kalter Überlegung ausgeführte scheussliche That nur von dem vollführt werden kann, der im kranken zustand seines Körpers eine falsche Richtung seiner Seelen Kräfte erlitten hat." StAH, 331-2, P-K, 1802, Nr. 81.

[199] *Ausführlicher Bericht*, 31, May 30, 1808.

[200] *Ausführlicher Bericht*, 31, January 23, 1809.

[201] *Ausführlicher Bericht*, 32. Blazek, *Seeräuberei*, 104.

[202] StAH, 111-1, Senat, Cl.VII, Lit.Me, Nr.8, Vol.16, Relation Urthel etc. in pein. Sachen wider Cath. Maria Koenig geb. Hartung, wegen Ermordung eines Kindes zum Schwerte verurtheilt, 1809.

argued. Previously, she had attempted suicide twice. Once she wanted to jump to her death from the ramparts and desisted only when her husband threatened to kill himself too, if she went through with it. Another time she wanted to drown herself, but a passerby prevented her. The fact that she read prayers all night before the murder showed that she was affected by religious enthusiasm that exacerbated her other afflictions. That she had murdered an innocent child after spending so many hours affectionately caring for her was in itself an indication of madness.

Physicians who examined her found no sign of insanity, however. Instead, she had serious character flaws. She was angry, sharp-tongued, quarrelsome, suspicious, jealous, and vengeful. She expressed repentance but showed little sorrow over the child's death. Ultimately, the prosecutor prevailed. Just because she had recited some prayers before the murder did not mean that she was afflicted by religious enthusiasm. She showed no other signs of particular religiosity, so her prayers were merely a rote mechanical exercise, a habit acquired in youth, not an expression of true interior piety. She murdered the child to exact revenge from her husband and other relatives who had offended her. She knew that her death on the scaffold would dishonor them. She was too cowardly to lay hands on herself or those who had wronged her. Instead, she acted out her rage upon the innocent child. The prosecutor was appalled by Koenig's abrasive, aggressive personality. Her demeanor and affect violated bourgeois notions of virtuous womanhood—in contrast to the weak, dazed nineteen-year-old child killer Elisabeth Jentzen, whom the court found insane in 1790. Undoubtedly, Koenig's violation of gender norms contributed to her death sentence. One year after the murder, on September 18, 1809, the court sentenced her to beheading.

Conclusion

The pace of suicidal child murders in Hamburg accelerated in the 1680s. Murders, attempted murders, and murder threats in the 1690s and early 1700s constituted a "murder epidemic" in Hamburg's prisons, but the phrase also describes the situation in the city at large. There were years when executions for suicide by proxy outnumbered executions for all other offenses, as, for example, in 1698, when the beheadings of four women for suicidal child murder were the only executions in that year. In 1703, Hamburg beheaded three women for suicidal child murder and one man who had murdered his wife. Between 1668 and 1699, nineteen of sixty-four recorded executions were for suicidal child murder. Between 1700 and 1740, of 117 recorded executions, 23 were for suicidal child murders. After 1740, as the total number of executions began to decline, the proportion of suicidal child murders rose. Between 1740 and 1759, suicide by proxy cases accounted for close to a third of all executions, seven of twenty-five executions. In the 1760s, executions for suicide by proxy outnumbered other executions. There were four executions for suicidal child murder and three for other crimes. Two of these were for neonaticide by unwed mothers, that is, six of the seven executions in that decade were for child murder. Between 1770 and 1809, eleven of twenty-nine executions were for suicidal child murder.[203]

In Hamburg, as elsewhere, suicide by proxy was gendered female. Of the ninety-eight people prosecuted for suicidal child murder or attempted murder in Hamburg between 1668 and 1809, there were sixty-three women and thirty-three men. In two cases, the sex is unknown. Gender proportions changed over time, however. In early cases, perpetrators were overwhelmingly female. Of twenty-six defendants between 1668 and 1699, twenty-three were women and three were men. Of nineteen defendants between 1700 and 1719, there were sixteen women, one man, and in two cases, the sex is unknown. Infanticides outnumbered suicidal child murders by a significant margin, but executions of suicidal child murderers were more frequent than executions of infanticidal mothers, because of the high number of unsolved infanticide cases and the diversion of suspected infanticidal mothers to the Spinnhouse, if their homicidal intent could not be proven. The high number of child murders within the city, both suicide by proxy and neonaticide cases, contributed to an atmosphere of moral crisis and encouraged women to imagine themselves as child murderers.

Beginning in the 1720s, men began to catch on to the idea of suicide by proxy. Of eighteen cases between 1720 and 1739, four of the perpetrators were women and fourteen were men. Between 1740 and 1779, Hamburg prosecuted eighteen women and seven men. After 1780, however, gender patterns changed dramatically. Suicide by proxy was now gendered male. Of ten people prosecuted for suicidal child murder between 1780 and 1809, there were eight men and two women. This shift in the gender profile of perpetrators of suicide by proxy also occurred elsewhere in the Holy Roman Empire.

[203] *Ausführlicher Bericht*, 11–31.

The dramatic accounts by directors of the house of correction and Spinnhouse of child murders and attempted murders within their institutions illustrate to what extent the practice of suicide by proxy disrupted the smooth operation of prisons. Committing or threatening to commit suicidal child murder became part of prison culture. Most perpetrators of suicide by proxy in prison were women. A striking feature of these cases is that women formed conspiracies to commit child murder together. When men in prison attacked children, they acted alone. Suicide by proxy offered prisoners a form of resistance, albeit a self-destructive one, to unrelenting prison discipline. These cases demonstrate that brutal discipline, once it went beyond a certain level, offered authorities diminishing returns and actually undermined social control. Within the city at large, authorities also made the experience that cumulative add-on penalties during executions, such as infamous attire during execution processions, tearing the flesh with red-hot tongs prior to execution, impaling heads on posts or braiding bodies into the wheel, or even sentencing child killers to breaking by the wheel instead of beheading, did little to stem the tide of suicidal child murders. The traditional response of early modern criminal justice had always been to increase the severity of punishments in the face of rising case numbers, but this approach failed to deter perpetrators of suicide by proxy.

There was a change in the mentality of government officials beginning around 1740. This was reflected in a more lenient official policy toward suicides and in government attempts to persuade their subjects to come to the aid of people who attempted suicide. Despite such governmental initiatives, common people's fear of ritual pollution by contact with suicides was undiminished. The stigma associated with direct suicide continued to encourage suicidal people to commit suicide by proxy. Authorities also began to develop ambivalence toward some of the traditional ritualization of criminal justice. This was particularly clear in 1740 when the senators discontinued the annual tradition of their ritual dialogue with the executioner on the feast day of Thomas the Apostle because it had become "useless and downright offensive."[204] This ambivalence developed into distaste and incomprehension by the 1780s, culminating in the exclusion of clergy from the execution ritual and the abolition of the "Justice of the Street" in 1784. Authorities decried the prejudices of their subjects and the superficiality of their religious beliefs, devoid of the interiority of true religion.

[204] Beneke, *Von unehrlichen Leuten*, 175–176.

The deritualization of criminal justice did not lead to an end of suicidal child murders, although the incidence declined.

Catharina Maria Koenig's trial in 1809 represents the end of an era. She was the last suicidal child murderer executed in Hamburg. Her repeated suicide attempts, as well as the prosecutor's comment that she was too cowardly to lay hands on herself, show that religious prohibitions of suicide no longer held sway over perpetrators or over prosecutors. Direct suicide had become a conceivable option. As we saw, the man who murdered a six-year-old boy in a "temporary melancholy delirium" in 1789 ultimately committed suicide in prison. In 1802, Johann Wilhelm Khörse tried to hang himself in prison with his stocking bands after his arrest for attempting to cut the throat of an eight-year-old boy.

The religious taboo against direct suicide had clearly weakened. Nonetheless, suicidal individuals still chose to murder children, as if by default. Some perpetrators could no longer offer any reason at all for why they had killed a child. During her murder trial in 1790 nineteen-year-old Elizabeth Jentzen said, "She had no particular reason for murdering this child." Khörse also said he did not know why he attacked the boy. The idea came to him suddenly as the boy passed him in the hallway. Even those killers who did express their desire to die on the scaffold, like Anton Lorenz Ammon in 1786, or Catharina Maria Koenig in 1808, no longer expounded upon why they preferred to die at the hands of the executioner rather than killing themselves. Or perhaps prosecutors, weary of hearing the religious ruminations of the murderers they interrogated, simply no longer asked. Prosecutors may also have kept the motives of such child killers under wraps to avoid inspiring imitators.

God, the devil, sin, or the prospect of damnation no longer featured in the trial records of late eighteenth- and early nineteenth-century suicide by proxy cases. In 1809, during the murder trial of Catharina Maria Koenig the prosecutor described her recitation of prayers during the night before she cut the throat of her seven-year-old victim as a mechanical exercise, born out of habit. The same might be said of the practice of suicide by proxy in the last years of the eighteenth century and early 1800s. Child murder had become an established cultural practice. It became a default solution for people experiencing mental distress or suicidality, even though they no longer cared to, or could, explain the logic of their action. Suicide by proxy finally lost its appeal only after the number of executions declined dramatically in the early nineteenth century.

CHAPTER 5

Mary with the Axe: The Cult of the Injured Icon in Baroque Vienna

A beheading took place in Vienna in October 1713. The scaffold just beyond the Carinthian city gate was normally reserved for military executions, but on this day nineteen-year-old Magdalena N. died there. For three days preceding her execution she had stood on this same scaffold exposed to public view for an hour a day, tethered to a column where she received five lashes during each display. On the day of her execution, moments before her beheading, as the executioner was poised to strike the fatal blow, his assistant struck off her right hand with an axe. Later, her hand was attached to the scaffold for permanent display. Magdalena N. was condemned to death for "breaking and biting" a crucifix.[1] The *Wienerisches Diarium*, Vienna's biweekly newspaper, reported on her brazen and outrageous deed. Regular readers of the paper and the Viennese public at large would have recognized a familiar pattern in Magdalena N.'s blasphemous act. Sacrilegious assaults upon crucifixes and upon transubstantiated hosts occurred with shocking frequency in Vienna at the turn of the eighteenth century. Authorities responded to the rising number of such blasphemous attacks with ever more extravagant displays of punishment. Magdalena N. was one of thirty-three overwhelmingly young offenders

---

[1] "um willen sie an einem Crucifix/ mit Verbrech- und Verbeissung desselben/ sich höchst freventlich vermessen/ und eine Gotteslästerliche That verübet." *WD*, Nr. 1066, October 20, 1713.

© The Author(s), under exclusive license to Springer Nature Switzerland AG 2023
K. Stuart, *Suicide by Proxy in Early Modern Germany*, World Histories of Crime, Culture and Violence,
https://doi.org/10.1007/978-3-031-25244-0_5

condemned to death in Vienna between 1688 and 1731 for the crime of blasphemy. During the first half of the eighteenth century an additional twenty-two blasphemers suffered lesser penalties, such as imprisonment in the house of correction, floggings, banishments, or deportation to Naples to row in the galleys.

When Magdalena N. bit and broke the crucifix, she was committing suicidal iconoclasm. This was a peculiarly Catholic variant of suicide by proxy. Perpetrators of these blasphemous deeds made their suicidal intent explicit, and prosecutors fully understood their motives. Many of these assaults on holy objects were performed by prisoners in Vienna's house of correction. Inmates explained that they committed these sacrileges in order to escape the harsh treatment, stench, and hunger they suffered in the prison. They "choose death, and, by committing a capital crime out of weariness with life, submit to the executioner's sword," Lower Austrian government officials reported to the imperial government in 1712.[2] An imperial edict of 1715 elaborated: "several people commit these godless deeds, claiming that they committed these crimes out of faint-heartedness, and the weariness with life that resulted from it."[3] It is unclear whether suicidal blasphemy first emerged in the prison-workhouse or in the city at large. Once the practice took hold in Vienna in the late seventeenth century, however, cases happened in short succession in the prison and in the city, one case inspiring the next. This was the same dynamic that played out contemporaneously in Lutheran Hamburg, as suicidal child murders proliferated there. In Vienna, at the same time that acts of suicidal iconoclasm multiplied in the city, there were also numerous cases of suicide by proxy in its classic form of child murder. These killings continued long after suicidal iconoclasm in the city subsided after 1730. In the late

---

[2] "daß sie lieber den Tod erwöhlen, und sich durch Begehung eines Criminis Capitalis aus Verdruß des Lebens dem Henckersschwerdt unterwerffen, als länger in simili Squallor carceris verharren wollen." WStLA, Alte Registratur, 1.2.1.A1—Zusammengelegte Akten/ 1700-1759 92 ex 1712, A 1-18. 7. 8ber [October] 1712.

[3] "verschiedene Personen auf dergleichen gottlosen Thaten sich betreten lassen, mit dem Vorgeben, daß sie solche Verbrechen aus einer Kleinmüthigkeit, und hieraus entstehenden taedio vitae, ausgeübet hätten. *Sammlung Oesterreichischer Gesetze und Ordnungen, wie solche vor Zeit zu Zeit ergangen und publiciret worden, So viele deren ueber die in Parte I & II Codicis Austriaci eingedruckten bis auf das Jahr 1720 weiter aufzubringen waren, gesammelt und in diese Ordnung gebracht von S.G.H.* (Leipzig: Zacharias Heinrich Eisfeld, 1748), 801–802, August 30, 1715.

seventeenth and early eighteenth centuries, however, suicidal iconoclasm was the dominant variant of suicide by proxy in Vienna.

Suicidal iconoclasm as a widespread cultural practice seems to have been specific to Vienna. I have found no parallels in any other city or territory. Everywhere else most perpetrators of suicide by proxy, whether Catholic or Protestant, committed child murder. The goal of this chapter is to explain how the specific political, religious, and cultural environment in Vienna nurtured this variant of suicide by proxy. Suicidal people in Vienna who chose to attack crucifixes or commit host desecration were responding to the intensive missionary campaign launched by church and state as part of the Catholic Counter-Reformation. Eucharistic theology and the cult of images were central elements of this Catholic mission. What made imperial Vienna distinctive, compared to other Catholic cities like Munich, was the specific performance of sovereignty by Habsburg rulers, the *pietas austriaca*, the fabled piety of the House of Habsburg. This exemplary piety formed the foundation of the dynasty's reign over its extensive dominions, contemporary political theorists taught. This political ideology made the outrageous acts of blasphemy committed by Vienna's suicidal iconoclasts an intolerable provocation to the Habsburg monarchy.

The majority of Vienna's suicidal iconoclasts were women. Stereotypical blasphemers, by contrast, were men. When suicidal people in Vienna attacked a crucifix or desecrated the host, they were committing a crime normally associated with societal arch-villains and enemies of the true faith. In Austrian history and lore these were typically male Protestants, Turks, witches, and Jews. In Austrian lands the largest witch-hunts happened after 1650. By this time the gender profile of the typical witch was changing. In Austria in this late phase of the European witch-hunt, the number of male witches matched or even exceeded the number of women prosecuted for witchcraft. Stories and legends circulating in Vienna around 1700 about historical or mythical blasphemies, featuring the dramatic, often miraculous exposure and exemplary punishment of the malefactors, and subsequent commemoration of the injured host or icon, informed the public what the crime of blasphemy was all about. Suicidal blasphemers knew what punishment they could expect, and demand, for their sacrilegious assaults.

The Viennese criminal court punished Magdalena N. and other Viennese blasphemers harshly. At first sight, this severity may seem unsurprising. Early modern criminal codes throughout Europe threatened draconian punishments for blasphemy. The Imperial Police Ordinance of 1548 threatened execution or "amputation of various limbs" for blasphemy.[4] In Sweden, the death penalty for blasphemy remained on the books until 1864.[5] Governments portrayed blasphemy as an existential threat. Law codes exhorted authorities to punish blasphemy severely. Otherwise, divine wrath threatened to ravish the land. The Justinian Novella 77 of 578 CE was a model of subsequent secular legislation against blasphemy. It warned that the crime of blasphemy would cause "famine, earthquake and pestilence." It imposed the "punishment of death" on persistent blasphemers. Rulers who treated blasphemy leniently placed their own salvation at risk. Magistrates who failed to prosecute blasphemers "shall be condemned by God," the Novella warned.[6]

In practice, however, governments rarely imposed harsh penalties. In both Catholic and Protestant countries, executions and other severe bodily penalties for blasphemy were exceptional. Fifteenth- and sixteenth-century Italian city states, for example, typically punished blasphemy by fines. Blasphemers who could not pay up were subjected to relatively minor penalties, short prison sentences or corporal punishments that did not permanently mark or disable the offender. More severe punishments to the body, like piercing of the tongue or execution, were theoretically possible but hardly ever imposed.[7]

---

[4] Gerd Schwerhoff, „Gott und die Welt herausfordern. Theologische Konstruktion, rechtliche Bekämpfung und soziale Praxis der Blasphemie vom 13. bis zum Beginn des 17. Jahrhunderts," Habilitationsschrift Bielefeld, 1996, 124.

[5] Soila-Maria Olli, "Blasphemy in Early Modern Sweden—An Untold Story," *Journal of Religious History* 32 (2008), 457–470. This article does not make clear how often the death penalty was imposed for blasphemy in practice.

[6] Novella 77, c. 1. http://droitromain.upmf-grenoble.fr/Anglica/N77_Scott.htm. R. Lieberwirth, "Gotteslästerung," *HRG*, vol. 1 (Berlin: Erich Schmidt Verlag, 1971), 1765–1766.

[7] On Venice, see Andrea Martignoni, "Langue Blasphématoire et Geste Iconoclaste. Blasphèmes et Pouvoirs dans la Terre Ferme Vénitienne à la fin du Moyen Age," *Studi Veneziani* 49 (2005): 105, 98–105. Elizabeth Horodowich, "Civic Identity and the Control of Blasphemy in Sixteenth-Century Venice," *Past & Present* 181 (2003): 11. In Florence the usual penalty was a fine. When one notorious blasphemer, Antonio Rinaldeschi, was hanged in 1501 for throwing dung at a statue of the Virgin Mary, this was truly an exceptional event, precipitated by an atmosphere of political crisis in the city just after the end of the Savonarolan regime. William J. Connell and Giles Constable, *Sacrilege and Redemption in Renaissance Florence: The Case of Antonio Rinaldeschi* (Toronto: Centre for Reformation and Renaissance Studies, 2005), 45–47.

In the Holy Roman Empire serious criminal punishments, and particularly executions, for blasphemy were uncommon throughout the early modern period. During the entire sixteenth century, the city of Cologne (Catholic) executed one person for blasphemy; Nuremberg (Lutheran) executed two.[8] Hamburg executed one man for blasphemy in 1524, prior to the introduction of the Protestant Reformation in the city.[9] The city of Danzig (Lutheran) executed no one for blasphemy between 1558 and 1731. Danzig prosecuted five people for blasphemy during these years; all were whipped and banished.[10] The Protestant free imperial city of Speyer did not execute anyone for blasphemy after the mid-fifteenth century. Most blasphemers faced whipping, banishment, or a combination thereof. In 1718, Speyer banished an egregious blasphemer only because he was unable to pay a fine.[11] The city of Basel (Reformed) executed one blasphemer between 1674 and 1798, beheading a blasphemous cavalry officer in 1725, but blasphemy was only one of his numerous transgressions that included violence, suspicion of poisoning and sorcery.[12] The Catholic Prince-Bishopric of Trier engaged in major witch-hunts during the early modern period, but showed little interest in prosecuting blasphemy. During the entire early modern period, Trier executed only one person for blasphemy in 1698. In Trier, too, the standard penalty was a monetary fine.[13] The Archbishopric of Salzburg carried out large witch-hunts, particularly in the late seventeenth century, but executed no one for blasphemy as the lone offense during the early modern period. The one execution in which blasphemy played any role occurred in 1534, when a woodworker swore by the Passion of Christ after losing a game of dice. Sentenced to lock-up for this verbal blasphemy, he attacked the judge with

---

[8] Gerd Schwerhoff, *Zungen wie Schwerter. Blasphemie in alteuropäischen Gesellschaften 1200–1650* (Konstanz: Universitätsverlag Konstanz, 2005), 171.

[9] Ralf Wiechmann, Eilin Einfeldt and Klaus Püschel, "'Man soll ihnen ihre Köpfe abschlagen und sie auf einen Stock nageln.'—Die Piratenschädel von Grasbrook," in *Klaus Störtebeker. Ein Mythos wird entschlüsselt*, eds. Ralf Wiechmann, Günter Bräuer and Klaus Püschel (Munich: Wilhelm Fink Verlag, 2003), 93, table 1.

[10] Richard van Dülmen, *Kultur und Alltag in der Frühen Neuzeit*. Vol. 2. *Dorf und Stadt* (Munich: C.H. Beck, 1992), 248.

[11] Theordor Harster, *Das Strafrecht der freien Reichsstadt Speier* (Breslau: Verlag von M. & H. Marcus, 1900), 236–238.

[12] Rebekka Schifferle, "Gotteslästerung in der Stadt Basel 1674–1798: ein Werkstattbericht," *Basler Zeitschrift für Geschichte und Altertumskunde* 105 (2005): 138.

[13] Arno Lott, *Die Todesstrafen im Kurfürstentum Trier in der frühen Neuzeit* (Frankfurt a.M.: Peter Lang, 1998), 130–131.

a knife. Salzburg then condemned him to death not for blasphemy but for his attack on the judge, which constituted the crime of "injury to majesty," that is, a transgression against the sovereignty of the ruler.[14] Salzburg typically punished blasphemers with brief imprisonment or banishment, and even these sentences were often reduced.[15]

One city that bucked this trend was Reformed Zurich. Zurich executed eighty-four people for blasphemy between 1501 and 1747. Here as elsewhere, however, most blasphemers who faced execution were condemned for an accumulation of serious offenses rather than for blasphemy alone. Nonetheless, Zurich did execute nineteen blasphemers who had committed no other crime, so the reformed city did punish blasphemy with exceptional severity, though still less frequently than Vienna.[16]

Over the course of the seventeenth century severe bodily punishments became rarer still, though they remained theoretically possible and governments very occasionally imposed them. Fines, whippings, and short prison sentences became the standard penalties for blasphemy.[17] The contrast between the draconian legislation and harsh official pronouncements concerning blasphemy and actual judicial practice leads historian Gerd Schwerhoff to describe public policy toward blasphemy as "ambivalent." Strong condemnations and severe penalties prescribed in law contrasted with lenient, even trivializing, treatment in practice. This ambivalence, Schwerhoff argues, shaped legal practice toward blasphemy in both Catholic and Protestant lands.[18]

There was no such ambivalence in Vienna. Here authorities punished blasphemy with extraordinary zeal, executing offenders at an exceptional rate. Even more unusual than the sheer number of blasphemy executions in Vienna, however, was their timing. All of these executions occurred in the late seventeenth century and first half of the eighteenth century. Even

---

[14] "*Crimen laesae majestatis*," that is, injury to the sovereignty of the ruler. Peter Klammer, *Peinliche Ordnung. Von Giftmördern und anderen malefizigen Personen im Erzstift Salzburg* (Maria Pfarr: Peter Klammerer Verlag, 2010), 153–156.

[15] After banishing a notorious recidivist blasphemer from the territory for life in 1668, authorities pardoned him less than a year later and allowed him to return to the archbishopric Klammer, *Peinliche Ordnung*, 159–168.

[16] Francisca Loetz, *Mit Gott handeln. Von den Zürcher Gotteslästerern der Frühen Neuzeit zu einer Kulturgeschichte des Religiösen* (Göttingen: Vandenhoeck und Ruprecht, 2002), 181.

[17] Schwerhoff, *Zungen*, 171–172.

[18] Schwerhoff, *Zungen*, 54.

in Zurich, the only other German-speaking city that even came close to matching Vienna's severity, executions had all but ceased by this time.[19]

The Viennese cases were also different from most blasphemy prosecutions in early modern Europe because they almost always involved *physical* rather than *verbal* assault upon the divinity. These perpetrators committed a blasphemous *deed* (*gotteslästerliche That* or *blasphemia realis*, i.e., material blasphemy) as opposed to verbal blasphemy (*blasphemia verbalis*). This theological terminology corresponded to the legal distinction that shaped prosecutions for insult (verbal injury or *injuria verbalis*) and violence (material injury or *injuria realis*) between people. Magdalena bit the crucifix in 1713, as did another woman, beheaded in 1720 after amputation of her hand for "biting through a crucifix."[20] Other blasphemers threw the crucifix on the ground, kicked it, or jumped on it. Some attacked the host. In 1697 Maria Anna Rossenberger, nineteen, was beheaded for committing some kind of unnamed blasphemy against the host. In 1702 Anna Rosina had her hand severed and was then beheaded for cutting up "the most Venerable," that is, the host.[21] Yet others attacked both host and crucifix. Maria Francisca Rosenburgerin, nineteen, was beheaded in 1705 for taking the host out of her mouth after communion and piercing it with a needle and kicking a crucifix with her feet.[22] In 1708, Elisabeth Stainin, twenty-three, spat out the host after communion, threw a crucifix to the ground, stepped on it with both feet, and finally jumped on it.[23] In 1712, Rosina Weniger, seventeen, hid the host in her handkerchief after receiving communion and then tore it in half. Then she committed a "blasphemous deed" against a crucifix. People attacked other sacred objects as well. Franz Wunderlich, beheaded in 1688, used a sword in his assault. After "blasphemously sinning gravely against the Holy Trinity and all Saints of God," he attacked a Marian icon and "ran through the Christ Child" with his sword.[24] In 1710, Maria Anna, twenty-eight, "dishonored" in some unspecified way

---

[19] Only two of the nineteen executions for blasphemy in Zurich during the early modern period occurred between 1690 and 1747. Loetz, *Mit Gott Handeln*, 214.

[20] Magdelena N., October 20, 1713, *WD*, Nr. 1066. ÖNB, Cod 8363, p. 9, Nr. 74, "Weibsbildt."

[21] J. E. Schlager, *Wiener Skizzen aus dem Mittelalter* (Neue Folge) (Vienna: Carl Gerold, 1842), vol. 2, 127. The *Stadtprotokoll*, the source cited by Schlager does not give Anna Rosina's last name.

[22] ÖNB, Cod 8363, p. 3, No. 16, 1705, May 13; *WD*, Nr. 186, May 13, 1705.

[23] Schlager, *Wiener Skizzen*, 128; *WD*, Nr. 482, March 16, 1708.

[24] Schlager, *Wiener Skizzen*, 126–127.

a picture of the Passion of Christ that had been cut out of a book or pamphlet, and then threw the picture to the ground.[25]

Some blasphemers committed both physical and verbal blasphemy. In 1715 Adam N., fifteen, destroyed two brass crucifixes, smashing one with a stone and hacking the other into pieces with a knife, simultaneously uttering some unspecified verbal blasphemy.[26] Only two offenders were executed for verbal blasphemy alone. In 1709, Hans Georg Fritsch, forty-seven, was beheaded for cursing and defaming the Holy Trinity and the Mother of God.[27] In 1715, Andreas Frisch, sixteen, had his tongue cut out before being beheaded for committing verbal blasphemy of some kind.[28]

Such physical destruction of crucifixes and Marian images bring to mind the iconoclastic riots of the storm years of the Protestant Reformation. The assaults on the host evoke hoary tales of Jewish host desecration or demonologists' vivid accounts of goings-on at witches' Sabbaths. During peak periods of confessional conflict, Protestants also mocked or attacked the Catholic transubstantiated host, but by 1700 such confrontations had all but ceased. Religious boundaries were set and competing confessions had, for the most part, worked out a *modus vivendi* with one another. So it is surprising to see such a large number of public blasphemous assaults on holy objects in the first half of the eighteenth century.

When sixteenth-century Calvinist iconoclasts attacked Catholic images, it was not their intent to commit blasphemy. Much to the contrary, their goal was to combat blasphemy by putting an end to what they saw as the idolatrous Catholic image worship that had corrupted true religion.[29] Blasphemers, by contrast, did not attack icons merely as symbols. Blasphemers' intent was to injure the holy person—Jesus, Mary, or a saint—represented by the icon, whom they believed to be in fact really present in the image.[30] The seventeenth- and eighteenth-century Viennese

---

[25] *WD*, Nr. 704, May 2, 1710.

[26] *WD*, Nr. 1239, June 18, 1715. Schlager, *Wiener Skizzen*, 131. Schlager, citing a no longer extant source, gives his name as Adam Hirschbeck.

[27] *WD*, Nr. 611, June 11, 1709. ÖNB, Cod 8363, "Verzeichnis," p. 5, Nr. 33, June 11, 1709, Hans Georg Fris. Schlager, *Wiener Skizzen*, p. 128, Joannes Georgius Friss.

[28] *WD*, Nr. 1291, December 13, 1715, Andre N., ÖNB, Cod 8363, "Verzeichnis," p. 8, Nr. 60, Andre Frisch. Schlager, *Wiener Skizzen*, 131, Andreas Fruscht. Schlager gives his age as seventeen.

[29] Carlos M. N. Eire, *War against the Idols. The Reformation of Worship from Erasmus to Calvin* (Cambridge: Cambridge University Press, 1986).

[30] Schwerhoff, *Zungen*, 243.

host desecrators and image-breakers were blasphemers in this sense. They quite consciously and intentionally committed acts of blasphemy, as they themselves insisted. Their actions did not result from confessional conflict, nor did they reflect crypto-Protestant hostility toward sacred images. In fact, all of these iconoclastic acts were performed *by* Catholics *for* a Catholic audience.

Imperial legislation specifically targeted suicidal iconoclasts in Vienna's house of correction,[31] but people beyond the prison walls were familiar this variant of suicide by proxy as well and availed themselves of it. In 1710 Rosina Wagnerin, a supervisor in the city hospital, was arrested for committing physical blasphemy. In contrast to the suicidal blasphemers within the workhouse, Wagnerin did not face criminal prosecution for her sacrilege. She had acted out of "the most severe melancholy and loss of her mind," authorities concluded. The court placed her under suicide watch in the city hospital where she had previously worked: "Wagnerin should never be left alone, so that she cannot escape or do harm to herself." Authorities were perhaps more open to an insanity defense in her case because they were dealing with an upstanding citizen rather than a prison inmate.[32]

This particular form of suicide by proxy was an option for Catholics only. It would not have made sense for a Protestant to attack a crucifix with the intention of bringing about his or her execution for blasphemy. Over the course of the Reformation all Protestant denominations desacralized images and icons. Even in regions where reformed iconoclasts did not destroy images, icons were disempowered. No longer suffused with divine immanence, images were "indifferent things" (*adiaphora*), wrote Martin Luther, "neither here nor there, neither evil nor good." Protestants might choose to keep images in their churches, or they might not. Images might serve useful purposes of commemoration and instruction, but they were no longer a conduit to the divine, as they had been for medieval Christians and remained for early modern Catholics.[33] Therefore, for Protestants, images and icons were not suitable objects for blasphemy. From the Protestant perspective, to destroy a religious image or statue was

---

[31] *Sammlung Oesterreichischer Gesetze*, 801–802, August 30, 1715.
[32] "ex summa melancholia et praecipitio mentis..." WStLA, B6-2, Decretenbuch 1703–1711, fol. 357r-v, October 18, 1710. The governmental decree does not specify Wagnerin's legal status, but her employment as *Stubenmutter im Bürgerspital* is an indication that she may have been a citizen in good standing.
[33] Eire, *War*, 68.

vandalism, not blasphemy. Zedler's *Universal Encyclopedia*, published in Halle and Leipzig between 1732 and 1754, reflects educated Protestant opinion on the cusp of the Enlightenment. The article on "Blasphemy" sums up the Protestant point of view: "according to Papist law it constitutes blasphemy when someone dares to push over crucifixes or throw them on the ground, or to foul images of saints with feces, and so on. They [the Catholics] punish this much more harshly than [blasphemy] with words. With us, this kind of disorderly behavior [is punished at the discretion of the judge], but by no means is punished as blasphemy."[34] Protestantism, religion of the word, imagined blasphemy above all as a verbal crime, so it is not be surprising that no instances of suicidal iconoclasm have come to light in Protestant regions.

It is surprising, however, that this form of suicide by proxy seems to have been peculiar to Austria, and to Vienna in particular. It may well be that further research will reveal additional cases in other Catholic regions, but I have found no clear instances of suicidal iconoclasm outside of Habsburg lands. Vienna was certainly not the only capital where the intense religiosity of Baroque Catholicism suffused public life. Why have no cases emerged in other bastions of the Catholic Counter-Reformation like Bavaria, or the Bishoprics of Trier, Würzburg or Cologne? The remarkable, and seemingly unique, accumulation of cases in late seventeenth- and early eighteenth-century Vienna requires explanation. What was it about the religious and political environment in Austria generally, and in Vienna specifically, that encouraged this outbreak of suicidal iconoclasm? What did host desecration mean in Baroque Vienna?

When Magdalena N. bit into the crucifix in 1713, did she have some kind of Eucharistic symbolism in mind? What were her feelings toward the crucifix? Was her act an expression of rage against God for her hopeless situation? Or was she trying to commit a transgression so outrageous that she could be sure of reaching her goal of being executed? Or all of the above? We cannot know for sure, because the sources that recount this and other cases of suicidal iconoclasm in Vienna are more laconic than many interrogation records in murder cases that have been preserved in other regions, where the suicidal killers explained their motives, thoughts, and emotions. Instead of effusive ego documents, the available sources on suicidal iconoclasm are procedural. They include city protocols that recorded

---

[34] "Gottes-Lästerung," *Zedlers Universal Lexikon*, vol. 11, (Halle: Johann Heinrich Zedler, 1735), 399–403, Sp. 400.

5 MARY WITH THE AXE: THE CULT OF THE INJURED ICON IN BAROQUE... 219

expenses related to executions, internal memoranda concerning prison administration, legal commentary and legislative collections, newspaper reporting and execution pamphlets. The city government solicited medical reports on the perpetrators from the medical faculty of the University of Vienna, so the protocols of the medical faculty provide information on some perpetrators.

The richest and most unique source on criminal justice in early modern Vienna is the protocol of the "Imperial Arch-Confraternity of the Dead." Founded in 1638 at the initiative of the Dowager Empress Eleonora Gonzaga of Mantua, widow of Emperor Ferdinand II, the confraternity accompanied condemned criminals to their execution and buried their bodies in consecrated ground afterward, as an act of Christian charity. Eleonora managed to secure a papal bull authorizing the establishment of the confraternity as well as papal indulgences that members earned by participating in the confraternity's religious devotions. The confraternity benefitted from ongoing imperial largesse and patronage. Emperor Ferdinand III was the official founder of the confraternity. He granted it the title of "Imperial Arch-Confraternity" and housed it in St. Georg's Chapel within the court church, the Augustinian church immediately adjacent to the imperial palace. Members of the confraternity appeared at executions in long black habits and black leather capes emblazoned with the imperial eagle, their faces hidden under pointed black hoods. From 1702, protocols of the confraternity have survived, in which are recorded the names and offenses of the criminals the lay brothers accompanied to the scaffold. Many of Vienna's suicidal iconoclasts are among them.[35]

The law code in effect during this outbreak of suicidal iconoclasm was the *Landesgerichtsordnung für Österreich unter der Enns*, the criminal code for Lower Austria promulgated in 1656 during the reign of Emperor Ferdinand III, commonly referred to as the *Ferdinandea*.[36] Among the

---

[35] On the founding of the confraternity, see Ernst Tomek, "Das kirchliche Leben und die christliche Charitas in Wien," in *Geschichte der Stadt Wien*, ed. Alterthumsvereine zu Wien, vol. 5 (Vienna: Verlag des Altertums Vereines zu Wien, 1914), 160–330, p. 305. One protocol records executions from 1702 to 1761. ÖNB, Cod 8363. A second protocol provides a clean and redacted copy of the first protocol, and continues to record executions until 1833. WB, Handschriften, Lb 18013.

[36] Article 59 of the *Ferdinandea*, the "Landesgerichtsordnung für Osterreich unter der Enns," in *Codicis Austriaci ..., Das ist: Eigentlicher Begriff und Innhalt/ Aller Unter deß Durchleuchtigsten Ertz-Hauses zu Oesterreich ... ausgegangenen ... Generalien*, vol. 1 (Vienna: Leopold Voigt, 1704), 687–688.

serious felonies listed in the *Ferdinandea*, blasphemy appeared in first place, followed by magic, injury to majesty,[37] rebellion and treason, and then murder. This order is typical for early modern criminal codes. Based on a classification of crimes derived from the Decalogue and Deuteronomy, blasphemy topped the list.[38] Also standard was the *Ferdinandea*'s exhortation that authorities prosecute blasphemy zealously, "so that God Almighty did not punish negligent authorities and the entire land himself in his just wrath."[39] It was the duty of Christian authority to preserve God's honor.

The *Ferdinandea* distinguished between three levels or "degrees" of blasphemy, directing courts to punish blasphemy more leniently or more severely depending on the severity of the blasphemy. "An intentional well-thought-out blasphemy" constituted the highest degree. The flesh of such a blasphemer should be torn with red-hot tongs, and strips of flesh should be cut from his body. Then he should be dragged to the site of execution, where the hand that he used to blaspheme should be cut off, or in case of verbal blasphemy, his blaspheming tongue should be cut out, as far as it can be extracted from the mouth. Finally, he should be burned alive until only dust and ashes remained.[40] (The *Ferdinandea* consistently used the masculine pronoun to describe the blasphemer, something we will return to in a discussion of gender and blasphemy in the next chapter.) Blasphemy in the second degree was to blaspheme "directly (*unmittelbar*) against God and his purest Mother or other saints with dishonorable shameful words or deeds," but somehow less egregiously than in the first degree. A blasphemer in the second degree should be beheaded after the tongue or the member with which he committed the blasphemy was cut off. Finally, the third and least serious degree of blasphemy was swearing and cursing. Such an offender was to be imprisoned on a diet of water and bread, or, in more serious cases, be exposed on the pillory, or have his tongue cut out and be banished from the territory. In a section on aggravating circumstances that called for greater severity, the *Ferdinandea* directed that Jews should be punished more harshly than others, and it classified "blasphemy by deed" as more heinous than blasphemy with the tongue. The *Leopoldina*, the criminal code issued by Emperor Leopold I (r. 1658–1705) for the

---

[37] That is, *Majestätsbeleidigung*, or *lèse majesté*.
[38] Helga Schnabel-Schüle, *Überwachen und Strafen im Territorialstaat. Bedingungen und Auswirkungen des Systems strafrechtlicher Sanktionen im frühneuzeitlichen Württemberg* (Cologne: Böhlau, 1997), 202–204.
[39] *Ferdinandea*, Art. 50, § 11, 688.
[40] *Ferdinandea*, Art. 59, §7, *Codicis Austriaci* I, 687.

5 MARY WITH THE AXE: THE CULT OF THE INJURED ICON IN BAROQUE... 221

Archduchy of Upper Austria in 1675, and the *Josephina*, the criminal code for Bohemia, Moravia, and Silesia issued by Emperor Joseph I in 1707, imposed the identical penalties.[41]

The severity of these codes was not unique to Habsburg lands.[42] What is distinctive to Austria is that courts actually carried out these punishments. Habsburg authorities punished blasphemers with exemplary severity until well into the eighteenth century. Why?

PIETAS AUSTRIACA

Habsburg monarchs cultivated a particularly militant Catholicism during the era of the Counter-Reformation and the Baroque, fostering a distinctive religious culture in which acts of suicidal iconoclasm made sense. In her classic study *Pietas Austriaca*, Anna Coreth explains the significance of Catholicism for the self-identity and rulership of the Habsburgs. *Pietas austriaca*, a term coined in baroque panegyrics of the Habsburg dynasty, was the Habsburgs' governing ideology from the Counter-Reformation and the Baroque until the accession of the "enlightened despot" Joseph II to the throne in 1780.[43] During these years, particularly from the mid-seventeenth through the mid-eighteenth centuries, the stridency of Austrian Catholicism was unmatched in other German Catholic territo-

---

[41] The *Leopoldina*, the criminal code issued by Emperor Leopold I for the Archduchy of Upper Austria in 1675, used the same definitions and classifications of the different kinds of blasphemy and set identical penalties. *Der Römischen Käyserlichen ... Majestät Leopoldi, Ertzherzogens zu Oesterreich ... Neue Landgerichts Ordnung des Ertzhertzogthumbs Oesterreich ob der Ennß* (Linz: Caspar Freyschmid, 1677), 96–101. *Der Römischen Kayser- auch zu Hungarn und Boehaimb etc. Koenigl. Mayestaet Josephi deß Ersten, Ertz-Hertzogens zu Oesterreich, unsers allergnädigsten Herrens, Neue Peinliche Hals-Gerichts-Ordnung vor das Koenigreich Boehaimb, Marggraffthumb Maehren und Hertzogthumb Schlesien* (Prag: Gerzabkische Erben, 1708), 63.

[42] On imperial law, see Christoph Blumblacher, *Commentarius In Käyser Carl deß Fünfften, und deß H. Röm. Reichs Peinliche Halsgerichts-Ordnung: Worinnen vmbständlich, gründlich und klar außgeführet wird, Wie man Den gantzen Peinlichen Proceß so wohl mit Protocollirn, mit der Captur, Examiniern, Constituirn, Torquirn, und sonsten biß zu Ende ordentlich führen, als auch nach Abführ- und Schliessung desselben, allerhand Unthaten gebührlich straffen solle* (Salzburg: Johann Baptista Mayrs Erben, 1704), 208–212. For a survey of legislation in German territorial states and some European countries, see Christoph Heinrich Schweser, *Des Klugen Beamten auserlesener Criminal-Proceß...* (Nuremberg: Gabriel Nicolaus Raspe, 1766), 331–338.

[43] Joseph II became Holy Roman Emperor in 1765, and served as co-regent of hereditary Habsburg lands with his mother Maria Theresa until her death in 1780.

ries.⁴⁴ Even in Bavaria, another bastion of the Catholic Counter-Reformation in German lands, certain secularizing trends began to emerge among elites after 1650.⁴⁵ The use of religion as an ideology of state was common to all divine-right monarchies in the confessional age, but the Habsburgs were not to be outdone. As Charles Ingrao puts it, the Habsburgs practiced religious piety as a "dedicated instrument of political legitimation" in a way that was "*sui generis* in its emphasis on the role of Providence, the agency of Mary, and the employment of ritual simultaneously as a sincere manifestation of faith and an effective vehicle of social control."⁴⁶

In the Habsburgs' self-understanding, their lineage was blessed by special divine favor made evident in the accumulation of crowns held by their dynasty, most notably the Hungarian and Bohemian crowns. Though the office of Holy Roman Emperor was officially elective, the Habsburgs saw it too as a hereditary possession, the imperial crown yet another manifestation of the special grace God had bestowed on their dynasty. Heir to Constantine, the first Christian emperor, the Holy Roman Emperor exercised the highest office in Christendom, so his position was more exalted than that of other monarchs, and correspondingly greater was his obligation toward God.⁴⁷ The Habsburgs' conviction that they were doing battle for God on two fronts also fostered the particular militancy of Austrian Catholicism. Battling the Ottoman Empire, the Habsburgs saw themselves as bulwarks against Islam, Christendom's "hereditary enemy."

⁴⁴On Catholicism as an ideology of state in Habsburg lands, see Anna Coreth, *Pietas Austriaca* (West Lafayette, Ind: Purdue University Press, 2004).

⁴⁵Wolfgang Behringer sees such secularizing tendencies as early as the 1630s. He attributes a decline in witch-hunting in Bavaria in the early seventeenth century to "a general shift in mentalities" in which political moderates gained the upper hand over zealous witch-hunters. As a result, after 1630 "natural law and reason of state would limit the excesses of faith." Wolfgang Behringer, *Witchcraft Persecutions in Bavaria: Popular Magic, Religious Zealotry and Reason of State in Early Modern Europe* (Cambridge: Cambridge University Press, 1997), 321. David Lederer observes a similar shift a few decades later, after 1650, in the treatment of madness in early modern Bavaria: "a pronounced mood of skepticism among the ruling elite in Bavaria" contributed to a new understanding of mental illness as a medical disorder rather than a diabolical affliction. David Lederer, *Madness, Religion and the State in Early Modern Europe: A Bavarian Beacon* (New York: Cambridge University Press, 2006), 227.

⁴⁶Charles Ingrao, "Forward," in Coreth, *Pietas Austriaca*, vii.

⁴⁷On the Habsburgs' understanding of the sacred nature of their office see Franz Matsche, *Die Kunst im Dienst der Staatsidee Kaiser Karls VI. Ikonographie, Ikonologie und Programmatik des "Kaiserstils"* (Berlin: de Gruyter, 1981), vol. 1, 82–85.

Turkish forces besieged Vienna twice, in 1529 and 1683. At the same time, the Habsburgs acted as defenders of the true faith, Catholicism, against the "new Turks," the Lutherans and Calvinists.[48]

The Habsburgs extolled piety as the princely virtue that raised their dynasty above all others. From piety flowed "Justice and Mercy" (*iustitia et clementia*), two other princely virtues that the Habsburgs embraced as hereditary characteristics of their dynasty. In the Habsburgs' self-understanding, this triad of virtues shaped the essential nature of the House of Austria and their reign.[49] According to this governing ideology, there was no conflict between genuine piety and political utility. In fact, genuine piety *was* utilitarian because it ensured the continued divine favor that was the wellspring of Habsburg power. The Habsburgs and their lands would flourish only if they fulfilled the hereditary duty of their dynasty to promote the glory of God.

The main components of Habsburg piety were devotion to the Holy Trinity, adoration of the Eucharist, devotion to the cross and Marian piety. The Habsburgs' devotion to the Trinity was particularly well suited to their understanding of divine-right monarchy. The Trinity represented divine omnipotence. "The glory of the most blessed Trinity," writes Anna Coreth, "shone above all courtly grandeur; the Trinity was the embodiment of power and justice, wisdom and clemency, the archetype for all royalty. The image of the Trinity made visible at once every relation of God to the individual person and to humanity in general."[50] The Habsburg's dedication to the Trinity is visible today in Vienna's famous Trinity Column, located on the *Graben*, the main thoroughfare in the heart of the city that connects the imperial palace and St. Stephen's Cathedral, an axis linking secular and spiritual power. In 1679, as a devastating plague struck Vienna that ultimately would claim twelve thousand lives,[51] Emperor Leopold I vowed to erect a Trinity column to appease God's wrath and so bring an end to the epidemic. Since the plague was

---

[48] Karl Vocelka and Lynne Heller, *Die Lebenswelt der Habsburger. Kultur- und Mentalitätsgeschichte einer Familie* (Graz: Styria, 1997), 13–14, 18–19.

[49] Matsche, *Kunst*, vol. 1, 212–223.

[50] Coreth, *Pietas Austriaca*, 6.

[51] Around 20% of the Viennese population died during this plague. Andreas Weigl, "Frühneuzeitliche Bevölkerungswachstum, in Peter Csendes and Ferdinand Opll, *Wien. Geschichte einer Stadt*, eds. Peter Csendes and Ferdinand Opll (Vienna: Böhlau, 2003), 112.

seen as God's punishment for human sinfulness, "prayers were directed to a triune God who was both judge and savior."[52]

The iconography of the Trinity Column is perhaps the clearest expression of the Habsburgs' theocratic understanding of their rule and the sacred nature of their office. The monument expresses an analogy between the divine Trinity and Leopold's earthly reign. The Trinity is enthroned above a choir of angels, while Leopold kneels at midlevel, the connecting point between the divine and earthly realms. Angels hold the insignia of his reign, indicating that they are God-given. Leopold intercedes on behalf of his subjects and represents divine majesty on earth. Below, the plague, in the form of a withered old woman resembling the stereotypical witch,[53] tumbles backward defeated. The construction of the monument was delayed in part by the Siege of Vienna of 1683 and the ongoing Turkish wars, so by the time the column was completed in 1693 it was as much a monument to victory over the Turks as it was an *ex voto*. Viewers of the monument learned that Leopold had vanquished the plague, also a traditional symbol of heresy, by means of his virtuoso piety and unshakable faith. He defeated the Turks, and suppressed mortal sins that provoked divine chastisement[54] (Image 5.1).

The Habsburgs' devotion to the Eucharist, their *pietas eucharistica*, derived from family history. The Habsburgs promoted a foundation myth of their dynasty that celebrated the exemplary Eucharistic devotion of Rudolf of Habsburg (1218–1291), founding father of the dynasty. Rudolph, so the story goes, was riding though his lands with his courtiers when they encountered a priest on foot carrying the host, on his way to administer the *viaticum* to a dying person. Rudolph dismounted and offered his horse to the priest. "Out of reverence for the body of Christ," Rudolf abased himself by leading the horse like a footman. Shortly after this encounter, Rudolf unexpectedly ascended to the throne of the Holy Roman Empire. Habsburg panegyrics of the Baroque era interpreted this story, first told in 1340, to mean that Rudolf "was consecrated King through the holy Eucharist itself."[55]

---

[52] Coreth, *Pietas Austriaca*, 6.

[53] On contemporary images of witches as desiccated, infertile old women, see Lyndal Roper, *Witch Craze: Terror and Fantasy in Baroque Germany* (New Haven: Yale University Press, 2006), 160–178.

[54] Thomas Winkelbauer, *Ständefreiheit und Fürstenmacht. Länder und Untertanen des Hauses Habsburg im konfessionellen Zeitalter* (Vienna: Ueberreuter, 2003), 188–189.

[55] Coreth, *Pietas Austriaca*, 14–15.

5 MARY WITH THE AXE: THE CULT OF THE INJURED ICON IN BAROQUE... 225

Image 5.1 Trinity Column, Vienna, 1693 (Detail). Photo by author

Seventeenth- and early eighteenth-century Habsburg rulers publicly reenacted Rudolf's legendary Eucharistic devotion. Emperors Ferdinand III (r. 1637–1657) and Joseph I (r. 1705–1711) and their entourage fell to their knees in the street if they encountered a priest carrying a Eucharist. Joseph was known to sometimes accompany the priest bearing the Eucharist to his destination. Joseph's biographer Eucharius Gottlieb Rink, writing in 1712, told of one occasion when Joseph and a large group of courtiers followed a priest to a "miserable hut" in a Viennese suburb where the priest was delivering the Eucharist to a sick person "who then was showered with gifts."[56] A contemporary copperplate engraving commemorates this event. Joseph and his entourage and local commoners kneel before the priest bearing the host. In the heavenly sphere a papal figure, recognizable by his distinctive cross and tiara, is surrounded by Angels bearing a crown and an oval image of Rudolf I. In the oval inset, Rudolf, dismounted, leads the horse ridden by the priest bearing the Eucharist. In the larger image below, Joseph reenacts Rudolf's pious example, demonstrating the continuity of Eucharistic devotion of the House of Austria. Joseph's piety, the text beneath the image explained, would pacify a turbulent world and sustain the House of Austria[57] (Image 5.2).

Eucharistic processions played an indispensable role in the Habsburgs' campaign to recatholicize their lands. Protestants had abolished Corpus Christi processions. Martin Luther instructed Lutherans to "abandon the monstrances and Corpus Christi processions, because there is no need for them; they ... only dishonor the sacrament with gross hypocrisy and mockery."[58] Annual Corpus Christi processions in Austrian lands declined or ceased altogether during the years of the Reformation when much of the population became Protestant. In response, the Habsburgs reintroduced or expanded Eucharistic processions. Exposing the host for public veneration in Corpus Christi processions and Forty-Hour Devotions

[56] Coreth, *Pietas Austriaca*, 16–17.
[57] Copperplate engraving by Christoph Weigel, Augustus Germ: Hungariae q' Rex Iosephus I. die 13. Iuly e venatione redux, cum Sam. Eucharistiam cleferentem Sacerdotem obuium haberet ..., 1701. On the text see also Matsche, *Staatsidee*, vol. 1, p. 113. The text reads:

> Túrbatúm pietás olím pacáret ut órbem,
> firmavít manibús scéptra Rudólphe tuís,
> Réx Proavúm pietáte refért. Furor ómnia vértat,
> Aústriacam ávertét nón tamen ílle Domúm.

[58] Quoted in Nils Holger Petersen, "The Quarant'Ore: Early Modern Ritual and Performativity," in *Performativity and Performance in Baroque Rome,* eds. Peter Gillgren and Mårten Snickare, (Farnham, Surrey: Ashgate, 2012), 118.

5 MARY WITH THE AXE: THE CULT OF THE INJURED ICON IN BAROQUE... 227

Image 5.2 Emperor Joseph I Venerates the Sacrament, 1701. Engraving by Christoph Weigel (after Caspar Luyken). The ALBERTINA Museum, Vienna. Historische Blätter Wien 8, Joseph I

powerfully affirmed the Catholic belief that the miracle of the mass transformed the oblate into the body of Christ, making the same Christ who died on the cross in Palestine bodily present.[59] Repudiating Protestant doctrines on the Eucharist, the Council of Trent reaffirmed the sacrament of transubstantiation and the real presence of Christ in the consecrated host. The reintroduction of Corpus Christi processions in the late sixteenth century, heavily promoted by the Jesuit order, marked the beginning of the Counter-Reformation in Austria.[60]

---

[59] Diarmaid MacCulloch, *The Reformation* (New York: Viking Penguin, 2003), 25.
[60] Martin Scheutz, "Kaiser und Fleischhackerknecht. Städtische Fronleichnamsprozessionen und öffentlicher Raum in Österreich während der Frühen Neuzeit," in *Aspekte der Religiosität in der frühen Neuzeit*, ed. Thomas Aigner (St. Pölten: Diözesanarchiv, 2003), 70.

Following a decree of Emperor Ferdinand II (r. 1619–1637) in 1622, Habsburg monarchs participated personally in Corpus Christi processions, accompanied by members of their court.[61] "A triumphal procession of the transubstantiated God,"[62] Viennese Corpus Christi processions in the seventeenth and eighteenth centuries grew into opulent extravaganzas. The procession was intended to represent urban society in its entirety, rich and poor, men and women, clergy and lay people. All inhabitants of Vienna were expected to attend, either walking in the procession or lining the route as spectators. The city gates remained closed during the procession. Following thousands of marchers, at the heart of the procession, the bishop of Vienna carried the host, displayed in an ornate golden monstrance, shaped to resemble the rays of the sun. The bishop, flanked by clergy swinging incensoria, walked under a baldachin, a precious canopy known as *Himmel* (Heaven), held aloft by four knights. Immediately behind the host walked the archdukes and the emperor, bearing torches, bareheaded to express their humility before the glory of the host.[63]

Beginning at St. Stephen's Cathedral the procession passed through the Graben. When the host reached the Trinity Column the entire procession came to a halt, and everyone—the marchers, spectators and the emperor and his court—fell to their knees to receive the episcopal blessing, a performance that observers described as an exemplary display of princely piety.[64] An engraving from the 1724 gives an impression of the scale of the event. It shows the Corpus Christi procession passing through the Graben. The bishop bearing the host has passed the Trinity Column that lies behind to the left. To the right crowds line the parade route.

---

[61] Richard Groner, *Wien wie es war. Ein Auskunftsbuch über Alt-Wiener Baulichkeiten, Hausschilder, Plätze und Strassen, sowie über allerlei sonst Wissenswertes aus der Vergangenheit der Stadt* (Vienna: Verlag der Waldheim-Eberle A. G., 1919), 93–94.

[62] Ulrike Kammerhofer-Angermann, "Quellenvergleich zu den Fronleichnamsprozessionen in den Städten Graz und Salzburg vor und nach der Reformationszeit. Die Rolle der Corporis-Christi-Bruderschaften in der Fronleichnamsprozession," in *Volksfrömmigkeit. Referate der Österreichischen Volkskundetagung 1989 in Graz*, eds. Helmut Eberhart, Edith Hörander and Burkhard Pöttler (Vienna: Selbstverlag des Vereins für Volkskunde, 1990), 267.

[63] A Protestant observer, Johann Sebastian Müller, a member of the diplomatic delegation of Saxony-Weimar, gives a vivid account of the procession in 1660 in his travel journal. Katrin Keller, Martin Scheutz and Harald Tersch, ed., *Einmal Weimar—Wien und retour. Johann Sebastian Müller und sein Wienbericht aus dem Jahr 1660* (Munich: R. Oldenbourg Verlag, 2005), 100–105.

[64] Martin Scheutz, "Kaiser," 105.

Troops stand in formation to his left[65] (Image 5.3). As the host passed their position, troops fell to their knees in synchronized sequence. The processions advanced to martial sounds of musket salvos, drums, and trumpets, as well as to the more traditionally religious sounds of hymns and church bells.[66] The militaristic elements, absent from Corpus Christi processions before the Reformation,[67] illustrate to what extent rituals of state and church became intertwined in the era of confessional absolutism.

The cross, too, featured prominently in the Habsburgs' religious repertoire. Under the tutelage of their Jesuit confessors, Habsburg rulers had mystical experiences as they meditated upon the crucifix. According to family tradition, Emperor Ferdinand II, under threat by Protestant rebels in 1619, was praying on his knees in front of a cross, when the cross spoke to him: "I shall not desert you." Empress Maria Theresia (r. 1740–1780) later had this cross exhibited weekly to the public to be kissed.[68] Devotion to the Virgin Mary was equally militarily efficacious. When Ferdinand II waged war against Protestants, he called the Virgin Mary his "supreme commander."[69] When Leopold I (r. 1658–1705) and his court embarked on pilgrimages to the wonderworking image of the Virgin at Mariazell, Austria's national shrine, it had become customary for imperial pilgrims to address Mary as "the supreme commander of the Austrian family."[70]

This was the religious and political climate in which Vienna's suicidal blasphemers acted. Seventeenth-century legal commentaries described blasphemy as "crime against the Divine Majesty."[71] The intense piety cultivated by Austria's ruling dynasty, and the political significance of their devotions, meant that blasphemy, and particularly violent attacks upon the Eucharist and cross so venerated by the Habsburgs, constituted *lèse majesté* against the Habsburg dynasty as well. The House of Habsburg performed its identity through the practice of *pietas austriaca*, so that such

[65] G. D. Heumann (nach Salomon Kleiner): Prospect des Grabens, Kupferstich, 1724.
[66] Scheutz, "Kaiser," 102–103. On the "soundscape" of Baroque Corpus Christi processions see Alexander J. Fischer, *Music, Piety, and Propaganda. The Soundscapes of Counter-Reformation Bavaria* (Oxford: Oxford University Press, 2014), Chap. 5.
[67] Charles Zika, "Hosts, Processions and Pilgrimages in Fifteenth-century Germany," *Past and Present* 118 (1988), 25–64.
[68] Coreth, *Pietas Austriaca*, 39–40.
[69] Coreth, *Pietas Austriaca*, 52.
[70] Coreth, *Pietas Austriaca*, 57.
[71] "*Crimen laesae majestatis divinae.*" For example, Joost de Damhoudere, *Praxis rerum Criminalium. Gründliche und rechte Underweysung Welcher massen in Rechtfertigung peinlicher Sachen ... zu handeln* (Frankfurt a. M.: Nicolaus Basseus, 1581), 92–93.

Image 5.3 "Prospect des Grabens." Engraving by Georg Daniel Heumann after Salomon Kleiner, in Salomon Kleiner, *Vera Et Accurata Delineatio Omnium Templorum et Coenobiorum Quae tam in Caesarea Urbe ac Sede Vienna Austriae, quam in circumjacentibus Suburbys ejus reperiuntur.* Vol. 2, *Abbildung der keysserl. Burg und Lust-Häuser.* (Augsburg: Johann Adreas Pfeffel, 1725), plate 99

sacrilegious assaults by suicidal people constituted an attack upon the foundation of their rule.

Vulnerable and Potentially Miraculous

Injured icons were objects of popular devotion in Vienna around the turn of the eighteenth century, the very years when the cases of suicidal iconoclasm were becoming more frequent. One example is the cult of Maria of Grünberg, a Marian icon also known as "Mary with the Axe." She arrived in Vienna in 1603. "Mary with the Axe" was a crowned limewood statue of Madonna and Child, sculpted in Grünberg in Bohemia around 1450. According to the story circulating in eighteenth-century Vienna, this statue fell victim to Protestant iconoclasm during the Reformation. The Sternbergs, a noble family and rulers of Grünberg, converted to

Protestantism in 1575. Two Sternberg brothers ordered the destruction of the statue. Tossed into the flames, the statue reappeared the next day, miraculously unscathed, at its original location in the church. Next, the executioner attempted to demolish the statue with an axe. The Virgin punished this attempted sacrilege promptly and severely. The executioner's blow struck the Virgin in the shoulder. The executioner was overcome by weakness and died on the spot. His axe remained embedded in her shoulder. Human hands could not pry it loose. The two Sternberg brothers who had ordered the statue's destruction went mad. A third brother, wisely, reconverted to Catholicism. He took the statue with him during a military campaign against the Turks. With the Virgin's support he won a spectacular victory in 1603. Then he lost the statue in a game of cards. Its new owner transported it to Vienna—during transport a lame horse pulling the wagon with the statue was made whole—and donated it to the Franciscans in 1607. The Franciscans exhibited it in their newly constructed church of St. Hieronymus, where it remains today.[72]

The miraculous reputation of this Marian image who had vanquished both Protestants and Turks now firmly established, pilgrims sought her protection. The faithful purchased printed engravings of the statue. These devotional images had been touched physically to the statue so they became contact relics that could confer protection at a distance. The Franciscans gave the wonder-working image additional prominence by moving her to the high altar in 1672 where she stood until the altar was renovated in 1706 and the statue was moved to stand above the tabernacle, where it stands today. The Viennese prayed to Mary of Grünberg for help in illnesses. The Franciscans compiled miracle books recounting the Virgin's intervention on behalf of these supplicants.[73] Viennese folklorists have analyzed one such miracle book from 1740, to show that those supplicants prompted to make the pilgrimage by a dream or apparition saw this specific statue of the Virgin ten times more often than they saw the Virgin Mary herself, an indication of the significance of icons in Catholic

---

[72] Gustav Gugitz, *Österreichs Gnadenstätten in Kult und Brauch*, vol. 1. *Wien* (Vienna: Verlag Brüder Hollinek), 6–11. For more details on the attacks upon the icon and the misfortunes that befell the Sternberg brothers as punishment for their sacrilege, see the narrative by Testarello della Massa, a cathedral canon at St. Stephens from 1661–1693, in his History of the Churches of Vienna, completed 1685. ÖNB, Cod 8227, pp. 545–554.

[73] Gugitz, *Gnadenstätten*, 6–11.

religious imagination and experience.⁷⁴ Having withstood fire twice, Mary of Grünberg became the Vienna's patron saint against fire. The Viennese tossed printed devotional images of her, that has been previously touched to the statue and thus become contact relics, into the flames as a fire retardant.⁷⁵

The sacrilege that Mary of Grünberg had suffered at the hands of the Protestants made the Virgin reveal her wonder-working powers. According to legend, the axe that struck her remained permanently embedded in her shoulder, a sign of her new miraculous identity. When the icon first arrived in Vienna in 1603, however, there was no axe in Mary's shoulder. Engravings of her published at the time of her arrival depict her without the axe. As late as 1629 a broadsheet celebrating her cult at the Franciscan church made no mention of an axe. It reported that Protestant iconoclasts had tried to demolish the image and that damage resulting from this assault was visible on the statue, but the broadsheet did not specify how she was attacked or what particular injury she suffered. The broadside includes an engraving that shows Madonna and Child clothed—as icons often were, wearing robes of different colors according to the liturgical season—but there was no axe. The clothing obscured any damage that might have been visible in the icon.⁷⁶ Only in the late seventeenth century did Mary of Grünberg acquire the axe as an attribute and become "Mary with the Axe." Evidently, at this time the Franciscans who promoted her cult believed that focusing the attention of pilgrims on the exact nature of the injury she suffered and on the specific weapon that inflicted it would heighten her appeal. Pilgrims kneeling before her could now contemplate the axe like they contemplated the instruments of the passion, the *arma Christi* (Images 5.4 and 5.5).

---

⁷⁴ Edmund Frieß and Gustav Gugitz, "Zum gegenreformatorischen Bilderkult in Wien. Das Standbild Maria Grünberg oder Maria mit der Axt in der Franziskanerkirche," *Jahrbuch für Geschichte der Stadt Wien* 3–4 (1942): 105.

⁷⁵ In memory of the sacrilege done to her by Protestants, Austrian military commanders and Empress Maria Theresa herself appealed to Maria of Grünberg for support in their conflict with Prussian (Protestant) forces during the Seven Years' War (1756–1763). Maria Theresia attributed the Austrian victory over Prussia at the battle of Kollin (1757) to the Virgin of Grünberg's intervention. Gugitz, *Gnadenstätten*, 8. Frieß and Gugitz, "Bilderkult," 94–95.

⁷⁶ *Gründlicher Ursprung der gnadenreichen Bildnuß vnser glorwürdigsten Himmelkönigin Mariæ so in der Kirch deß H. Hieronymi zu Wienn bey den Franciscanern ... zu sehen* ([Vienna]: [1629]). The broadside has been digitized by the ÖNB: http://data.onb.ac.at/rec/AC06380986.

5 MARY WITH THE AXE: THE CULT OF THE INJURED ICON IN BAROQUE... 233

Vienna's churches were home to dozens of wonder-working images of the Virgin Mary, talking crucifixes, saints' statues, and relics.[77] A recurring motif in the mythologies surrounding these icons was their inviolability. A fragment of the true cross in the Habsburgs' relic collection miraculously survived a fire that burned down a wing of the imperial palace in 1668, a fire that was widely believed to have been set by Jews. Dowager Empress Eleonore[78] then founded an order dedicated to the veneration of this relic for ladies of the high nobility. Icons in the suburbs were prompted to reveal their powers after being desecrated by Turks.[79] Crucifixes, columns, and saints' statues stood in squares or intersections in and around Vienna, many with their own lore that told of violent and untimely deaths of unbelievers or blasphemers who profaned them.[80]

Vienna lay within a larger sacred landscape that extended across Austria, Bohemia, and southern Germany. Local pilgrimages, promoted by church and state but often also originating in more spontaneous popular cults, proliferated in the seventeenth and eighteenth centuries. Many could be reached within a day's walk. By 1750 there were around five hundred pilgrimage shrines with miracle-working icons in Lower Austria alone.[81] It was easy to bring the sacred home. After completing a pilgrimage, or even

---

[77] The most famous Marian icon in Vienna was Maria Pötsch, a painting of Madonna and Child named after the village Pócz in Hungary where it hung before Emperor Leopold I brought her to Vienna in 1698, because the Virgin shed thaumaturgic tears. Like Mary of Grünberg, she bore the mark of a sacrilegious touch. When a skeptical Protestant corporal touched the Virgin's tears an indelible black stain appeared on the Virgin's cheek. Unlike the axe-swinging executioner who tried to demolish Mary of Grünberg, the corporal survived the encounter, and promptly converted to Catholicism. Winkelbauer, *Ständefreiheit*, 195. Maria Pötsch remains in St. Stephens Cathedral today, but it was moved to a side aisle in 1945. Gustav Gugitz, *Die Sagen und Legenden der Stadt Wien* (Vienna: Verlag Brüder Hollinek, 1952), 90–91. Gugitz, *Gnadenstätten*, 39–46. Csendes and Opll, eds., *Wien*, 358–359, 469. For further miraculous icons of the Virgin Mary, see Josef Maurer and Georg Kolb, *Marianisches Niederösterreich. Denkwürdigkeiten der Marienverehrung im Lande unter der Enns* (Vienna: "St. Norbertus" Buch- und Kunstdruckerei, 1899). On talking crucifixes, see Gugitz, *Gnadenstätten*, 12.
[78] Widow of Ferdinand III.
[79] Gugitz, *Gnadenstätten*, 64–66.
[80] For example, the "Gablerkreuz" a roadside crucifix that was said to have bled when a Protestant struck it with an axe. Then the Protestant, gripped by despair, stabbed himself to death. Gerhard Robert Walther von Coeckelberghe-Dützele, *Geschichten, Sagen und Merkwürdigkeiten aus Wien's Vorzeit und Gegenwart* (Vienna: F. Hagenauer's Witwe, 1841), 139–142.
[81] Winkelbauer, *Ständefreiheit*, 213.

Image 5.4 Devotional image of the Marian icon Maria Grünberg. Engraving, early eighteenth century. *Das wundertthaetige Bildnis Maria bei den Franziskanern.* Volkskunde Museum Wien, Vienna. AÖMV13.888

if one had not been able to go, believers could purchase cheap, widely available printed devotional images. "Consecrated and touched" to the

Image 5.5 Maria Grünberg, or "Mary with the Axe", Marian icon above the high altar in the Franciskanerkircher, Vienna. Photo by author

"Image of Mercy," as inscriptions on the engravings attested, the cheap prints became contact relics and so were in themselves potentially miraculous.[82]

The availability of such prints and of images in devotional books provided another opportunity to commit suicidal iconoclasm. In 1710 Maria

[82] Gerhardt Kapner, *Barocker Heiligenkult in Wien und seine Träger* (Munich: R. Oldenbourg Verlag, 1978), 146. Gugitz, *Andachtsbilder*.

Anna N, a twenty-eight-year-old woman from Augsburg under arrest in Vienna for prostitution and theft, "dishonored" in some unspecified way a picture of the crucifix that had been "cut out," of a book, presumably, and then threw it on the ground. She received thirty lashes and was banished from Austria for life.[83]

Eucharistic Devotions in Popular Practice

We have seen how the Habsburgs made Eucharistic devotion the centerpiece of the ritualized piety of their dynasty. Over the course of the seventeenth century, the Eucharist also came to play a more prominent role in the daily lives of common people. In addition to compulsory public devotions such as Corpus Christi processions, the Eucharist also featured prominently in individuals' private lives. Ever since the Forth Lateran Council of 1215 it had been obligatory within Latin Christendom to perform the sacrament of confession and take communion at least once a year, traditionally at Easter, but before the Reformation there was little attempt to enforce this requirement. During the Counter-Reformation, state and church developed new mechanisms to ensure compliance. An imperial edict from 1660, for example, read from the pulpit and announced by town crier, ordered "every Catholic of requisite age, male or female to appear and perform confession and communion as required by the Christian Catholic Church." Communicants would then be provided with "confession certificates" (*Beichtzettel*) that they had to turn in to their head of household. Heads of households were required to deliver these confession certificates to their parish church by four weeks after Easter. Heads of households who neglected this duty faced punishment.[84] Parish priests kept confession and communion registers and turned over the names of those who failed to perform their "Easter duty" to secular authorities. Parishioners who refused to comply faced banishment.[85] Governments of Catholic territories throughout the Holy Roman Empire required lay people to show such confession certificates to ensure that

---

[83] "/daß selbe auch ein ausgeschnittenes Leyden-Christi verunehret/ und sodann auf den Boden geworffen/" WD, Nr. 704, May 2, 1710. She dishonored this image after unsuccessfully trying to convince authorities that she had committed infanticide.

[84] Guarient, *Codicis Austriaci*, vol. 2, 115–116, March 2, 1660, Oeffentlicher Rueff. The edict does not specify what punishments heads of households might face for failing to turn in confession certificates.

[85] Winkelbauer, *Ständefreiheit*, 140.

their subjects fulfilled the yearly confession and communion requirement.[86] In Vienna, the "deserving poor" who had been granted beggars' badges allowing them to beg within the city limits had to show their confession certificates to city guards upon request, or face confiscation of their badges and deportation.[87] And if the threat of worldly punishment was not enough, the government ordered priests to instruct parishioners in their sermons that failure to perform their Easter duty constituted a mortal sin resulting in excommunication and denial of a Christian burial in this world, and eternal damnation in the next.[88]

These enforcement measures were largely successful. By the late seventeenth century, the majority of people confessed and took communion at least once a year, and in many cases far more frequently.[89] Taking communion was not only a matter of coercion. There was considerable demand for it among lay people as well. Jesuits in particular encouraged frequent communion as a sacrament of consolation, and many lay people experienced it as such.[90] It became customary to give confession and take communion once a month, or at least once every three months.[91] In Vienna the upward trend is clear. Holy Communion was distributed in the Jesuit church 51000 times in 1638. By 1647 it was 69000.[92] By 1700 the Jesuits were dispensing communion around 100,000 times per year. In 1732 in St. Stephen's Cathedral alone 129,900 people took communion.[93] The population of the city and suburbs was 123,500 in 1700; by 1750 population had increased to around 190,000. Of course, every other religious

---

[86] Trevor Johnson, *Magistrates, Madonnas and Miracles: The Counter Reformation in the Upper Palatinate* (Farnham, England: Ashgate, 2009), 81; R. Po-chia Hsia, *Social Discipline in the Reformation: Central Europe 1550–1750* (London: Routledge, 1991), 40–44.

[87] Helmut Bräuer, *"... und hat seithero gebetlet." Bettler und Bettelwesen in Wien und Niederösterreich während der Zeit Kaiser Leopolds I* (Vienna: Böhlau Verlag, 1998), 66.

[88] Klaus Gottschall, *Dokumente zum Wandel im religiösen Leben Wiens während des Josephinismus* (Vienna: Institut für Volkskunde der Universität Wien, 1979), 152–153.

[89] Marc R. Forster, *Catholic Germany from the Reformation to the Enlightenment* (New York: Palgrave Macmillan, 2007), 148.

[90] Austrian Jesuits described receiving the Eucharist as *Seelenarzenei* (medicine for the soul), so that taking communion became, as David Lederer argues, a kind of "Eucharistic therapy." Lederer, *Bavarian Beacon*, 11–12.

[91] Robert Bireley, *The Refashioning of Catholicism, 1450–1700* (Washington, DC: Catholic University of America Press, 1999), 105.

[92] Bernhard Duhr S.J., *Geschichte der Jesuiten in den Ländern deutscher Zunge*, vol. 2 (Freiburg im Breisgau: Herderische Verlagshandlung, 1913), 45, fn. 1.

[93] Tomek, "Kirchliche Leben," 277, 294.

order and parish church in Vienna was administering the Eucharist as well. By the early eighteenth century, frequent communion was not just for the well-educated or the exceptionally devout. People also took communion on the road. Pilgrims to an "Image of Mercy" combined venerating the sacred image and taking communion. In Vienna, the pilgrimage church of Mariahilf, for example, distributed communion 97,662 times in 1733.[94] In the vicinity, Maria Taferl, a popular pilgrimage shrine about two day's walk from Vienna, had twenty-five priests on staff to provide communion to the pilgrims.[95]

Chance encounters with the Body of Christ also became more frequent. As part of the Counter-Reformation effort to give the Eucharist greater visibility, in 1616 Emperor Matthias (r. 1612–1619) ordered that priests called to administer last rites would now walk carrying "The Most Holy" under a baldachin just as they did in Corpus Christi processions. Altar boys walked before and behind the canopy bearing burning torches, even in broad daylight, "a practice which is observed to this day," wrote a priest at St. Stephens Cathedral in 1779.[96] These processions became more elaborate over time. By the early eighteenth century as many as a hundred lay people bearing torches accompanied the priest.[97] When people unexpectedly encountered such processions of "The Most Holy" in the streets, they had to drop what they were doing and show reverence to the host. In 1693 a decree publicized by town crier even threatened the death penalty against passersby who failed to uncover their heads when they came upon

---

[94] Gugitz, *Gnadenstätten*, 65.

[95] Karl Vocelka, *Glanz und Untergang der Höfischen Welt* (Vienna: Ueberreuter, 2001), 211. The development was similar in other Catholic regions. Jesuit communion registers from seventeenth-century Munich, for example, show the rising frequency: Jesuits alone gave communion 89,000 times in 1615, the equivalent of five communions per inhabitant in a city of 16,000; by 1690 they provided communion 147,247 times, or seven times per inhabitant in a city that had grown to 20,000. W. David Myers, *"Poor Sinning Folk:" Confession and Conscience in Counter-Reformation Germany* (Ithaca, NY: Cornell University Press, 1996), 189.

[96] "welches bis itzo noch beobachtet wird." Joseph Ogesser, *Beschreibung der Metropolitankirche zu St. Stephan in Wien* (Vienna: Ghelensche Erben, [1779]), 282. Csendes and Opll, *Wien* (Vienna: Böhlau, 2003), 329.

[97] Bishop Franz Ferdinand Freiherr von Rummel, named bishop in 1706, promoted the participation of lay torch bearers in these processions. In 1720 and 1722, the Bishop Sigismund Graf Kollonitsch gave even greater prominence to these processions by requiring that the priest administering last rites be accompanied by two additional priests. Tomek, "Kirchliche Leben," 283–284, 296.

the "Most Venerable" being carried to sick people.[98] An engraving by Salomon Kleiner from 1728 shows people's reactions during such an encounter. Passing in front of one of Vienna's many aristocratic residences in the inner city, the procession is about to turn down an alleyway. People have fallen to their knees as the host is carried past them. To the left a woman kneels and a worker has lowered his wheelbarrow and doffs his hat, while some men engaged in conversation and a man on horseback some distance away are still unaware of the approaching procession[99] (Image 5.6). Such processions might grow larger as they advanced through the streets, as passersby spontaneously joined to follow the priest to his destination—a God-pleasing act that the famed Augustinian court preacher Abraham a Sancta Clara promised would earn the believer earthly and heavenly reward: "when I see that someone most zealously accompanies the highest Good, as it is carried to a sick person, I want to say to him with certainty and to prophesize that he can hope for worldly and eternal happiness in the future."[100]

Writing about medieval host desecration accusations against Jews, Miri Rubin has observed that as the Eucharist came to play a more central role in Catholic belief and practice in the thirteenth century, anxieties about the vulnerability of the host grew: "new rituals around it—visitation of the sick (*viaticum*), processions—exposed it to the open air, to unpredictable surroundings of people's homes, streets and roads. Just as the Eucharist's power was emphasized and increasingly realized, the myriad dangers and mishaps which could befall the host became clear."[101] To guard against

---

[98] Quoted in Schlager, *Wiener Skizzen*, vol. 2, 121.

[99] Salomon Kleiner, *Wahrhafte und genaue Abbildung Einiger antiquen als modernen Kirchen, Ehren-Säulen ... welche ... in der Kayserlichen Resdienz-Stadt Wien ... anzutreffen* (Augsburg: Johann Andreas Pfeffel, 1728). Kleiner shows similar scenes in other engravings. In Kleiner's 1724 engraving of St. Stephen's, on the lower right of the image a priest returns to the cathedral from delivering the host to a dying parishioner. As usual he walks beneath a baldachin. Parishioners follow in procession, bearing torches though it is daytime. Passersby kneel as the host is carried past. https://archive.org/stream/gri_33125010855209#page/n10/mode/1up. Another such scene plays out in his 1724 engraving of the Holy Cross Church. Passersby drop what they are doing and kneel in the street as the procession passes by. https://archive.org/stream/gri_33125010855209#page/n22/mode/1up.

[100] Abraham a Sancta Clara, *Judas Der ErtzSchelm Für ehrliche Leuth Oder: Eigentlicher Entwurff und LebensBeschreibung deß Iscariotischen Bößwicht*, vol. 4 (Salzburg: Melchior Haan, 1695), 391.

[101] Miri Rubin, *Gentile Tales. The Narrative Assault on late Medieval Jews* (Philadelphia: University of Pennsylvania Press, 1999), 28–29.

Image 5.6 Priest leads procession bringing last rites to dying parishioner. "Prospect des Gräfflich Kaysersteinischen Hauses" (Detail). Engraving by J. A. Corvinus after Sal. Kleiner. In Salomon Kleiner, *Vera Et Accurata Delineatio Omnium Templorum et Coenobiorum Quae tam in Caesarea Urbe ac Sede Vienna Austriae, quam in circumjacentibus [circumiacentibus] Suburbijs [Suburbiis] ejus [eius] reperiuntur*. Vol 3. *Das florirende vermehrte Wien*. (Augsburg: Johann Adreas Pfeffel, 1733), plate 211

possible profanation by Jews, a church council in Vienna in 1267 issued a canon ordering Jews to remain indoors when a procession with the host approached.

After receding from public view for much of the sixteenth century, the Eucharist took center stage again with the implementation of the Counter-Reformation in the late sixteenth and early seventeenth centuries and the ascendancy of Baroque Catholicism in the later seventeenth and much of the eighteenth centuries. This greater exposure of the body of Christ again led to heightened anxieties about its vulnerability, resulting in similar precautionary measures. A "Regulation of Jews" from 1723 decreed: "if a Jew is in the street when the *Venerabile* is carried to a sick person ..., he should withdraw into the next house and wait there until the *Venerabile* has passed. Similarly, when the *Venerabile* is carried in the street or when a procession passes by, no Jew may look out the window, but must withdraw so that he cannot be seen from, nor can he see onto the street."[102] A "Regulation of Jews" from 1764 repeated this order and held Jewish heads of household responsible if members of their households did not

---

[102] "Judenordnung, 29 October 1723," in Sebastian Gottlieb Herrenleben, *Sammlung Oesterreichischer Gesetze und Ordnunge: Wie solche von Zeit zu Zeit ergangen und publiciret worden .../[4]: ... so viel deren vom Jahr 1721. Bis auf Höchst-traurigen Tod-Fall Der Römisch-Kayserlichen Majestät Caroli VI. aufzubringen waren* (Vienna: Trattner, 1752), 148.

withdraw, threatening fines, physical punishment or expulsion.[103] Concern about Jewish defilement of sacred items extended beyond the Eucharist, to include reliquaries and icons. Liquidations at bankruptcies often involved the sale at auction of privately owned crucifixes, icons, or reliquaries, often made of gold or silver or inlaid with precious stones. A decree from 1759 prohibited the sale of such items to Jews to guard against desecration at their hands.[104]

HOST DESECRATION IN HISTORY AND MEMORY: THE USUAL SUSPECTS

Vienna's suicidal iconoclasts acted within a religious culture characterized by a pervasive anxiety about defilement. Commemoration of historical acts of blasphemy and sacrilege played an important role in the city's civic culture. The memorialization of past desecrations, whether historical or mythical, shaped people's understanding of the meaning of blasphemy in their own time.

The public deployment of the Eucharist during the Counter-Reformation was intended to combat Protestantism, so it is not surprising that Protestants featured prominently among notorious blasphemers. Matthias Fuhrmann, a Paulist monk and author of a chronicle of Vienna published in 1738, related two historical instances of Protestant blasphemy. Both date from the sixteenth century, when the Habsburgs had not yet succeeded in suppressing Protestantism in the city. On Corpus Christi Day 1549, after the celebration of the mass at Saint Stephen's Cathedral, the priest at the head of the Corpus Christi procession emerged from the Cathedral carrying the monstrance displaying the "venerable host." He was attacked by a "heretical" (i.e., Protestant) apprentice baker from Franconia, a Lutheran region. The apprentice grabbed the monstrance out of the priest's hand, threw it to the ground, smashing "the

---

[103] Judenordnung, May 5, 1764, in Thomas Ignaz von Pöck, *Supplementum Codicis Austriaci, oder Chronologische Sammlung .../6: ... aller vom 1ten Jäner 1759. bis letzten Dezember 1770. als der ... Regierung ... Mar. Theresiae, ... Generalien, Patenten, Satz-Ordnungen...* (Vienna: Trattner, 1777), 569.

[104] WStLA, Zusammengelegte Akten 1700–1759, 124/1759. If the reliquaries or frames could be separated into component parts and sacred relics or images removed, then sale to Jews was permitted.

Holy of Holies."[105] King Ferdinand I, acting out of "zealous fear of God," ordered a column topped by a monstrance to be erected at the site so no one would ever walk on the ground made holy through contact with the host. An inscription in Latin and German recounted the "horrific blasphemy" that had occurred on this spot and described the execution of the blasphemer. After having his tongue cut out and his hand amputated, the apprentice baker was dragged to the site of execution on a cowhide and burned alive. This, the inscription concluded, "should serve as a warning to others."[106]

Twenty-one years later, in 1570, Conrad Haußler, another apprentice baker, disrupted the Corpus Christi procession. On this occasion, as Fuhrmann tells it, the apprentice from the Lutheran territory of Württemberg did not attack the Eucharist physically, but uttered verbal blasphemies against the host as it was carried by him in the procession. At that moment the devil appeared and snatched the apprentice from the ground, carrying him through the air and dropping him into a tree, from where he fell to the ground, "half-dead and speechless." Though Fuhrmann was writing in 1738, there is no hint of doubt in his narrative that this miraculous event actually occurred. He reports these events as fact, not legend, even citing a city protocol from 1598 that described the incident to emphasize the veracity of his account.[107] And, like the host desecration twenty years earlier, Haußler's blasphemy was memorialized in stone. In 1624, Fuhrmann reports, the city council ordered that this occurrence be commemorated by a plaque at the city hospital with an inscription that recounted the incident "word for word." Fuhrmann's

---

[105] Presumably it was the monstrance that shattered? Mathias Fuhrmann, *Alt- und Neues Wien, Oder Dieser Kayserlich- und Ertz-Lands-Fürstlichen Residentz-Stadt Chronologisch- und Historische Beschreibung*, vol. 2 (Vienna: Johann Baptist Prasser, 1739), 798–799.

[106] Fuhrmann describes the blasphemer as "ein Ketzerischer Becken-Junge Johannes Hayn." King Ferdinand refers to Archduke Ferdinand, King of Hungary and Bohemia, King of the Romans, and after the abdication of his brother Charles V in 1556 Holy Roman Emperor Ferdinand I. The column commemorating this incident came to be called "At the Green Wreath" (*Zum grünen Krantz*), because the monstrance fell to ground in front of a house of the same name. Fuhrmann, *Alt- und neues Wien*, 798–799. Anton Reichsritter von Geusau, *Geschichte der Haupt- und Residenzstadt Wien...*, vol. 3 (Vienna: Alberti, 1799), 254–255. Geusau quotes the text of the inscription.

[107] I have been unable to locate said protocol.

chronicle includes an engraving showing a winged demon carrying the stricken apprentice through the air while the Corpus Christi procession takes place below[108] (Image 5.7).

The most notorious act of blasphemy ever recorded in Vienna's civic histories occurred in 1642, by which time Protestantism in Austria had been largely quashed.[109] It involved a spectacular act of apostasy by the Jewish convert to Catholicism Ferdinand Franz Engelberger.[110] This case is unusual because Engelberger actually did commit blasphemy against a crucifix and perhaps he desecrated the host as well, in contrast to more familiar fictitious Jewish host desecration tales. The case attracted attention throughout Central Europe and was featured in several chronicles and broadsheets.[111] They all tell more or less the same story. Engelberger and two unbaptized Jewish accomplices were arrested for burglary and sentenced to death by hanging as common thieves. One broadsheet reports that two Jesuit priests ministered to the three condemned men as they awaited the day of their execution. The Jesuits attempted to instruct the two unbaptized Jews in the Catholic faith and to soften their "hard hearts" to convert them, but the two remained steadfast in their Jewish

---

[108] Fuhrmann, *Alt- und neues Wien*, vol. 2, 806–808. The apprentice baker was named Conrad Haußler. The plaque was attached to the *Bürger-Spital*, the city hospital.

[109] On surviving crypto-Protestantism in the countryside, see the essays in Rudolf Leeb, Martin Scheutz and Dietmar Weikl, eds., *Geheimprotestantismus und evangelische Kirchen in der Habsburgermonarchie und im Erzstift Salzburg (17./18. Jahrhundert)* (Vienna: Böhlau, 2009).

[110] The spelling of his last name varies between Engelberger and Engelberger. David Kaufmann, *Die letzte Vertreibung der Juden aus Wien und Niederösterreich. Ihre Vorgeschichte (1625–1670) und ihre Opfer* (Budapest: Athenaeum, 1899), 36–38. Moritz Bermann, *Alt- und Neu-Wien. Geschichte der Kaiserstadt und ihrer Umgebungen. Seit dem Entstehen bis auf den heutigen Tag und in allen Beziehungen zur gesammten Monarchie* (Vienna: A. Hartleben, 1880), 906–908.

[111] Georg Philipp Harsdörffer, *Der Grosse Schau-Platz jämmerlicher Mord-Geschichte* (Hamburg: Johann Nauman, 1656), reprint Hildesheim: Georg Olms Verlag, 1975. Story CXXXV, "Der gemarterte Jud," 464–467; *Theatrum Europaeum, oder außführliche und warhafftige Beschreibung aller und jeder denckwürdiger Geschichten. Vierdter Theil, die sich ... seithero Anno 1638 biß Anno 1643, exclusive begeben haben* (Frankfurt am Main: Johann Goerlin, 1692), 903–904; Johann Jakob Schudt, *Jüdische Merkwürdigkeiten*, vol. 2 (Frankfurt: s.n., 1714), 91–94.

244 K. STUART

Image 5.7 "Der aergerlicher Laesterer des Hochheiligsten Sacraments." Engraving. In Mathias Fuhrmann, *Alt- und Neues Wien, Oder Dieser Kayserlich- und Ertz-Lands-Fürstlichen Residentz-Stadt Chronologisch- und Historische Beschreibung*. Vol. 2. (Vienna: Johann Baptist Prasser, 1739), with p. 807

faith.[112] So the Jesuits attended to Engelberger, preparing him for his execution as Catholic "poor sinner." As customary, they heard his confession, granted absolution and administered the Eucharist the night before the scheduled execution. Engelberger, according to several chroniclers, made a show of exemplary penitence, hoping that his piety and his status as a convert would earn him a pardon. On the day the hanging was to take place, Engelberger and his two Jewish accomplices were taken to the courthouse where their sentence would be publicly proclaimed. The two Jews were bound together, but Engelberger walked alone, unbound, holding a crucifix, flanked by the two Jesuits who loudly prayed with him.[113] One broadside described how Engelberger, still hoping for a pardon, fervently kissed the crucifix he was holding and beat his breast proclaiming, "Oh my Lord Jesus, be merciful with me."[114] Then the final sentence of hanging was announced. Engelberger asked the Jesuits whether any hope for a pardon remained. When the Jesuits urged him to commend his soul to God, Engelberger announced that if he had to die, he wanted to die "a true Jew." He took the crucifix he had been carrying, and threw it on the ground where, according to some accounts, it broke into pieces. In one broadside's report, he then "spat on it, and like a rabid dog jumped on it with both feet."[115] Horrified, the Jesuits rebuked him: he had just received the Eucharist as a Catholic the night before. No, Engelberger declared, he had taken it out of his mouth, wrapped it in a handkerchief and thrown it into the latrine, according to one version, or into a chamber pot, according to another. Either way, the abused host was later found and retrieved.

Several accounts gleefully relate how one Jesuit exclaimed in righteous indignation, "It would be no wonder if one killed all the Jews!" Needing no further encouragement, the crowd attacked Jews who were present to witness the execution, grievously injuring some, killing others, and

---

[112] *Kurtzer Innhalt der Execution, So inn der Statt Wien den 22. Augusti dises Jahrs durch rechtmessiges Vrthail zween verzweifleten Juden so jünger: vnd darauff den 26. dessen, mit dem ältisten, wegen erbärmlicher vnd Gottschändiger MalefitzThat, auff den vier Plätzen benannter Stadt fürgenommen ist worden* [Vienna: 1642].

[113] *Kurtzer Innhalt der Execution.*

[114] *Eygentlicher Bericht/ Was massen der getauffte/ jedoch wider vom Christentumb abgefallene Jud/ zu Wien den 22. Augusti 1642...* (s.l., s.n, s.d.), HMW, Gerichtswesen 1642, IN 52093.

[115] *Eygentlicher Bericht.*

plundering Jewish homes.[116] "Horrified and distraught" to learn of Engelberger's blasphemies, the emperor ordered the execution of Engelberger to be postponed. The hanging of the two Jewish thieves proceeded as scheduled.[117] Fanning the flames of Christian outrage, several broadsides reported upon Engelberger's subsequent interrogation. Even while pretending to be a Catholic he had never actually consumed the host, Engelberger claimed, but had always surreptitiously taken it out of this mouth and disposed of it in the latrine, because the sacrament was as abhorrent to Jews as pork.[118]

Engelberger received a new sentence that was carried out four days later, on August 26, 1642. Engelberger's execution was the most brutal ever recorded in Vienna because of its cumulative use of all possible exacerbating penalties available in Austrian criminal law.[119] Broadsides gloatingly described Engelberger's death. The day of his execution was Saturday, the day of the Jewish Sabbath when, as noted in one broadside, Engelberger's fellow Jews "were performing their idolatrous devotions."[120] Vienna's civic militia was out in force to prevent further attacks on Jewish homes by the crowd.[121] Engelberger was transported on a high wagon to the four main squares of the city, where his chest was ripped with red-hot pincers and strips of flesh were cut from his back. Then he was placed on an ox hide and dragged to the scaffold beyond the city walls, where his hand was severed and his tongue was cut out. Finally, he was hung upside down—a historic form of Jewish execution that had mostly fallen into disuse by this time[122]—and burned alive. Even as the flames consumed him, Jesuits exhorted him to convert. But Engelberger remained

---

[116] *Theatrum Europaeum*, 903.

[117] *Eygentlicher Bericht*.

[118] *Warhafftiger Bericht so sich zu Wien in Oesterreich mit dreyen Juden zugetragen/ darunter einer/ so vor diesem ein vornnehmer Rabbi gewesen/ unnd sich vor etlichen Jahren zu Rackawitz in Poln tauffen lassen/ aber ... die Christenheit verleugnet .../ so geschehen zu Wien den 16/26 Augusti 1642* (s.l., 1642).

[119] Schlager, *Wiener Skizzen*, 124.

[120] *Eygentlicher Bericht*.

[121] *Kurtzer Innhalt der Execution*.

[122] Rudolf Glanz, "The 'Jewish Execution' in Medieval Germany," *Jewish Social Studies* 5 (1943): 3–26.

"obdurate."[123] His ashes were strewn into the Danube.[124] According to one report, his amputated tongue and hand were attached to the Jewish synagogue.[125] And so the profaned host and injured crucifix were avenged (Image 5.8).

The event was memorialized within the courthouse that stood on the High Market where the blasphemy occurred. To the right of the entrance of the courtroom, there were two marble plaques, separated by a crucifix. After giving a brief synopsis of Engelberger's act of blasphemy—"he furiously threw the holy Crucifix to the ground and blasphemed gruesomely against the Holy Trinity and the Holy Sacrament of the altar"—and his execution, the Latin inscription concluded: "May others of his kind be terrified, and his memory expunged, but God's honor and glory augmented."[126] Of course, the plaque ensured that his memory was not expunged. The crucifix that Engelberger had desecrated was restored and a Latin inscription was added to its base in which it stood when it was being used execution processions: "This crucifix was honored in various ways by a baptized Jew, but then, when he was condemned to death for enormous crimes, it was thrown to the ground and stepped on by the same August 16." The crucifix became a kind of relic that was incorporated into the ritual surrounding public execution in Vienna. From 1642 on, the Confraternity of the Dead carried this crucifix in formal procession

---

[123] *Kurtzer Innhalt der Execution.*

[124] *Eygentlicher Bericht*; *Warhafftiger Bericht*. An accounting of the expenses associated with Engelberger's execution listing each individual task the executioner performed shows that these sensational news reports did not embellish in their description of the execution. "Extract Aus der Statt Wienn Under Camer Ambts Raittungen, was auf Reparierung des Ambthaus, und Hinrichtung der Malefiz Persohnen ist ausgangen und bezahlt worden." WStLA, Handschriften A 19, fo 137–144. A contemporary jurist observed that Engelberger's punishment conformed "word for word" to the penalties prescribed in the *Ferdinandea* for the highest degree of blasphemy. WStLA, Handschriften A 320, Annotation Z to Art 59. § 7, p. 65. This source is a 1673 edition of the *Ferdinandea* in which an unnamed jurist, most likely a Viennese local, but in any case, someone who was very familiar with Viennese cases, had glued additional pages with handwritten annotations to the code. On this source, see Michaela Laichmann, "Notizen zur Rechtsgeschichte im 17. Jahrhundert. Eine Handschrift der Ferdinandeischen Landgerichtsordnung im Wiener Stadt- und Landesarchiv," *Jahrbuch des Vereins für Geschichte der Stadt Wien* 67/68 (2011/2012), 41–60.

[125] *Kurtzer Innhalt der Execution.*

[126] The German and Latin text is given in Schudt, *Jüdische Merkwürdigkeiten*, 93–94. For description and location of the plaques, see Wilhelm Kisch, *Die Alten Strassen und Plaetze Wiens und ihre historisch interessanten Haeuser* (Vienna: M. Gottlieb's Verlagsbuchhandlung, 1883), 39, fn. 1.

Image 5.8 *Eygentlicher Bericht/Was massen der getrauffte/ jedoch wider vom Christenthumb abgefallene Jud/ zu Wien den 22. Augusti 1642...verurtheilt/...wegen der grausamen Gotteslästerung/... vollzogen worden.* Photo: Wien Museum, Gerichtswesen 1642, IN52093 M. 790

when they accompanied condemned criminals to the scaffold. The condemned were made to kiss it prior to their execution.[127]

Twenty-seven years after Engelberger's execution, in 1669, the plaques commemorating Engelberger's deed were cited as evidence in a lawsuit between Johann Christoph Holzner, former mayor of Vienna, and a Jewish merchant. Holzner presented a petition to the Lower Austrian government in which he first presented economic grievances against the Jews of Vienna but then launched into a diatribe against Jewish blasphemy. After accusing Jews of habitual verbal blasphemy against Jesus and Mary, he writes: "not to mention the horrific crimes and bloody miracles that the cursed Jews commit with the Most Holy Sacrament of the altar and with the blood of innocent Christian children, as is described in the many

---

[127] "Hic crucifixus a Judaeo baptizato varie cultus, deinde ab eodem ob enormia scelera ad mortem damnato in terram prostrates et conculcatus fuit Augusti 16." Bermann, *Alt- und Neu-Wien*, 906. This crucifix and its stand with the inscription can be viewed at https://www.online.landessammlungen-noe.at/objects/102861/standkruzifix-aus-der-armsunderzelle-des-wiener-landesgerich.

monuments .... We need look no further than the marble inscription at the courthouse to read about the shameful vice and crime committed in our own times."[128]

Like Jews, witches, too, were stereotypical blasphemers. Witch-hunting came late to most Austrian lands and remained moderate compared to the "heartland of the witch-hunt," southwestern and southeastern Germany, Franconia and Switzerland, where persecutions peaked between 1560 and 1630.[129] Only the western territories of Further Austria fell within this core area of the hunt. They experienced the most intense witch-hunts in Austrian territories.[130] In Tyrol witch-hunting remained limited, peaking between 1600 and 1630. Witch-hunting spread from west to east. In Vorarlberg in Anterior Austria the last witch was executed in 1651, whereas the largest witch-hunts in the Prince Archbishopric of Salzburg, an independent territory that did not come under Habsburg rule until 1803, happened between 1675 and 1690. Between 1531, the date of the earliest documented witch execution in Salzburg, and 1675 about two dozen people were executed for witchcraft. In the following fifteen years, 1675–1690, the so-called Sorcerer-Jack trials (*Zauber-Jackl Prozesse*) led to the execution of around 200 people. Sorcerer-Jack, a vagrant skinner's son at the center of the trials, was never caught. He was believed to be the leader of a band of witches comprised mostly of young male vagrants. More than two thirds of the victims of the Sorcerer-Jack trials were male,

---

[128] Ivo Cerman, "Anti-Jewish Superstitions and the Expulsion of the Jews from Vienna in 1670," *Judaica Bohemia* 26 (2000): 20-22. Cerman provides an extract of Holzner's petition in his appendix, 31.

[129] This discussion is limited to German-speaking Habsburg lands that lie within the boundaries of modern Austria, that is, the Archduchies above and below the Enns River, that is, Upper and Lower Austria, and the Inner Austrian Duchies of Styria and Carinthia, as well as the Prince-Archbishopric of Salzburg. The territories of Anterior Austria include Vorarlberg and, within the boundaries of modern Germany, the Sundgau, Breisgau and Freiburg, and several small territories in Swabia where witch-hunting war particularly intense. Edmund M. Kern, "Habsburg Territories," in *Europe 1450–1789. Encyclopedia of the Early Modern World*, ed. Jonathan Dewald, vol. 3 (New York: Scribner Thomson Gale, 2004), 113–119.

[130] These numbers are drawn from the statistics compiled by Martin Scheutz for Vorarlberg, Swabian Austria, and Vorderösterreich. Martin Scheutz, "Raub, Magie und Hexerei im frühneuzeitlichen Österreich. Das Fallbeispiel Oberösterreich," in *Räuber, Mörder, Teufelsbrüder. Die Kapererbande 1649–1660 im oberösterreichischen Alpenvorland*, eds. Martin Scheutz, Johann Sturm, Josef Weichenberger and Franz Xaver Wimmer (Linz: Oberösterreichisches Landesarchiv, 2008), 292. See also Johannes Dillinger, *"Evil People:" A Comparative Study of Witch Hunts in Swabian Austria and the Electorate of Trier* (Charlottesville: University of Virginia Press, 2009).

and under twenty-one.¹³¹ The Sorcerer-Jack trials sparked persecutions in neighboring territories of Tyrol, Styria, and Bavaria. In Tyrol, most witch-hunts happened before 1630, but a smaller series of trials occurred between 1670 and 1720, which involved mostly male vagrants.¹³² The age and gender profile of the victims of these hunts contrasts strongly with the general pattern of the European witch-hunt, where the bulk of the condemned were older women.¹³³ Across Europe 75–80% of all executed witches were women.¹³⁴ The image of the witch changed over time, however. In southern Germany at the height of the witch-hunt in the late sixteenth and early seventeenth centuries, Lyndal Roper finds a "shocking predominance of old women" among executed witches. By the late seventeenth and early eighteenth centuries, however, when witch trials in this core region of the witch-hunt had become far less frequent, a new witch stereotype emerged.¹³⁵ By the late seventeenth and early eighteenth centuries, children were increasingly caught up in witch trials, and, more than ever before, witch trials came to focus on male youths and young men. Witch-hunts in southeastern Germany, as Wolfgang Behringer has shown, influenced by the Sorcerer-Jack trials, focused increasingly on so-called boy-sorcerers, bands of vagrant male youths.¹³⁶

In Inner Austria major witch-hunts started in the mid-seventeenth century. In Carinthia young male beggars made up the majority of the victims. About 57% of executed witches were male.¹³⁷ In Styria, too, the witch-hunt focused on vagrants, but here women still made up the majority of the accused, though less so than in core witch-hunting regions at the height of the hunt: 58% of accused witches whose sex was specified were

---

¹³¹ One third of the victims were younger than fifteen. Winkelbauer, *Ständefreiheit*, 279–280.

¹³² Scheutz, "Raub, Magie, Hexerei," 291.

¹³³ Brian P. Levack, *The Witch-Hunt in Early Modern Europe* (Harlow: Pearson Longman, 2006), 141–151.

¹³⁴ Roper, *Witch Craze*, 18.

¹³⁵ Roper, *Witch Craze*, 181.

¹³⁶ A trial in the Prince Bishopric of Freising in 1720–1722, for example, resulted in the execution of eight "boy-sorcerers" aged fourteen to twenty-three, while old women among the accused were set free. Behringer, *Witchcraft Persecutions*, 337.

¹³⁷ Winkelbauer, *Ständefreiheit*, 282.

female.[138] Witch-hunting in Upper Austria peaked around 1680. More than two thirds of the accused were men.[139]

Lower Austria and its capital Vienna experienced few witch-hunts. Witch-hunting peaked between 1570 and 1630, much earlier than in neighboring territories. During these years, the majority of victims were female, as was generally the case during this phase of the European witch-hunt. In eighteenth-century cases, however, none of which resulted in execution, the majority of the accused were male.[140] An edict by Emperor Leopold I in 1679 requiring the participation of a commissioner of the Lower Austrian government in all witch trials in the Archduchy led to a decline in witch-hunting in the territory and an early end to executions.[141] This conforms to a general pattern historians of witchcraft have observed: greater control by central governments, particularly in the later phases of the witch-hunt, had a restraining effect on witch-hunting.[142] Vienna itself experienced only a handful of trials. Only two witch executions are known to have taken place in the city.[143]

One reason witch-hunts began late in much of Austria is that the elaborated concept of witchcraft that made diabolism instead of harmful magic the essential element in the crime—a precondition for large witch-hunts—was not widely accepted in Austria before the mid-seventeenth century. Earlier trials for witchcraft often focused on individual cases of harmful magic rather than on a widespread demonic conspiracy. With the promulgation of the *Ferdinandea* in 1656 the elaborated concept of witchcraft began to influence judicial practice in Austria. Article 60, which immediately follows the article on blasphemy, focused the attention of interrogators on diabolical aspects of the crime, directing them to investigate how the witch entered into a demonic pact with the Evil Enemy.[144] By the

---

[138] Of 675 accused witches in Styria, 394 were female; 281 were male. For an additional 145 accused witches the sex is not documented. Scheutz, "Raub, Magie, Hexerei," 290–291.

[139] According to Scheutz, in Upper Austrian trials men made up 68.8%, women made up 20.3%; for 10.4% of the accused no gender is documented. Scheutz, "Raub, Magie, Hexerei," 292; Winkelbauer, *Ständefreiheit*, 274.

[140] Scheutz, "Raub, Magie, Hexerei," 291.

[141] Winkelbauer, *Ständefreiheit*, 281.

[142] Levack, *Witch*-Hunt, 96–97.

[143] Edmund Kern, "Vienna," in *Encyclopedia of Witchcraft. The Western Tradition*, ed. Richard M. Golden (Santa Barbara: ABC-CLIO, 2006), 1168–1169.

[144] *Ferdinandea*, Art. 60, § 4, 689.

1680s the *Ferdinandea* had become an authoritative legal source in other Austrian lands as well.[145]

With the adoption of the elaborated concept of witchcraft, concern about host desecration by witches increased. The *Ferdinandea* instructed officials to search the homes of suspected witches for hosts, along with human bones, poisons, and other incriminating materials.[146] Helfried Valentinitsch has studied the incidence of host desecration accusations in Inner Austrian witch trials. Inner Austria experienced two waves of witch-hunting. A first small wave happened between 1580 and 1600. The second wave was much larger, and started around 1650 and reached its peak between 1670 and 1690. About 60% of all witch trials documented in Inner Austria from the late fifteenth century on happened after 1650. The concentration of witch-hunting in the second half of the seventeenth century is even clearer when focusing on the number of accused: of all the people accused from the late fifteenth century through the mid-eighteenth century, three quarters were brought to trial between 1650 and 1699.[147]

Accusations of host desecration did not arise in Inner Austrian witch trials until after 1600, and most occurred after 1650 during the peak period of the witch-hunt in Austria. Demonologists had been concerned with magical abuse of the host from the beginning of the European witch-hunt. As early as 1487, the *Malleus Maleficarum* warned that witches took communion but did not swallow, secretly taking the host out for their mouths to use later for magical purposes. To forestall such abuse, the *Malleus* instructed priests to make sure that women opened their mouths completely and extended their tongues when receiving the host.[148] But at this time the concerns of the demonologists did not catch on.

The first mention of host desecration in an Austrian witch trial occurred in 1602, just two years after the publication of the Jesuit Martin Delrio's influential witch-hunting manual, *Disquisitionum magicarum libri sex*, in 1600, in which he drew on the *Malleus* to warn of host desecration by witches. At that time Delrio was a theology professor at the University of Graz, but it is not known whether he was personally involved in this trial. In any case, this 1602 trial was one of a few isolated trials. It was not until

---

[145] Winkelbauer, *Ständefreiheit*, 271.

[146] *Ferdinandea*, Art. 60, § 2, 688.

[147] Helfried Valentinitsch, "Der Vorwurf der Hostienschändung in den innerösterreichischen Hexen- und Zaubereiprozessen (16.-18. Jahrhundert), *Zeitschrift des historischen Vereines für Steiermark*," 78 (1987): 6-7.

[148] Valentinitsch, "Hostienschändung," 5.

after 1650 that accusations of host desecration became a regular feature of Austrian witch trials. In other words, accusations of host desecrations coincided with the peak period of witch-hunting in Austria. Defendants now admitted to using the host in benign magic, such as butter-making, healing livestock or reconciling enemies. Soldiers and poachers were known to use the host in weapons magic in a technique known as "healing in" (*Einheilen*).[149] They inserted a host or a fragment of the host into a self-inflicted wound. When the wound healed, enclosing the host within the body (!), it made the person impervious to injury and increased physical strength and courage. Witches also confessed to mixing hosts into witches' salve that enabled them to fly to the Sabbath, to using hosts to whip up storms, to desecration of the host at witches' sabbaths, and to selling the hosts to Jews for host desecration.[150]

Valentinitsch attributes the rising prominence of host desecration in Austrian witch trials after 1650 to the Counter-Reformation campaign by church and state to promote the adoration of the Eucharist. Corpus Christi processions and other devotions and the combined pressure of church and state to participate in these rituals meant that common people were brought into contact with the host more than ever before. By 1650 Protestantism had been defeated, reduced to crypto-Protestant enclaves in remote mountainous regions of Upper Styria and Upper Carinthia. The Counter-Reformation had triumphed. The absolutist state now focused its agenda of social discipline on the lower orders and the poor, and particularly on beggars, vagrants, and other marginal groups—precisely the population served by the Vienna house of correction. As part of this offensive, a new generation of Catholic reformers shifted their attention from squelching Protestant heresies to extirpating superstitious abuses in popular culture that a previous generation of Catholic clerics had been more willing to tolerate.[151]

One trial that graphically illustrates the role of host desecration in Austrian witch trials and underlines the role of *men* in these sacrilegious acts is the notorious Kaperger trial that took place in Upper Austria

---

[149] On weapons magic, see B. Ann Tlusty, "Bravado, Martial Magic, and Masculine Performance in Early Modern Germany," in *Rethinking Europe: War and Peace in the Early Modern German Lands*, eds. Gerhild Scholz Williams, Sigrun Haude, and Christian Schneider (Leiden: Brill, 2019), 9–38.
[150] Valentinitsch, "Hostienschändung," 7.
[151] Valentinitsch, "Hostienschändung," 9.

between 1657 and 1659.[152] The prosecution focused on the "Kaperger gang," named after its leader the tavern-keeper Hans Kaperger. This was a large gang of highwaymen that terrorized Upper Austria in a series of robberies, home invasions and murders from 1650 until their arrest in 1657. In addition to murders and robbery, gang members now confessed to witchcraft, denial of the Holy Trinity, magical abuse of the host, including "healing in," the use of the host to raise storms and to remain undetected during burglaries, and the burial of the host in mud and feces. These sacrileges culminated in a collective act of host desecration. In a kind of satanic inversion of the last supper Hans Kaperger cut up the host and distributed fragments to the assembled gang members to confirm their bond and group contract with Satan. Fragments of the host were delivered to absent gang members. This element of the story is reminiscent of the Jewish host desecration accusation in Enns in 1420 that led to a pogrom that destroyed the Jewish community in Vienna, known in Jewish historiography as the *Wiener Geserah*, and to the expulsion of Jews from Austria.[153]

According to the legend surrounding the Enns case, the Jews who procured a stolen host distributed fragments of it to Jews throughout Austria so they could participate in the desecration.[154] The fragmentation of the host in the Enns narrative and in the Kaperger gang's confessions made "perfect sense in Eucharistic terms," as Miri Rubin explains: "after all, at every consecration of the host, Christ's very body, the historical body which suffered on the cross, was realized, unlimited in quantity or location. Even a single host could be infinitely broken down, and each of its crumbs would be fully Christ."[155] The host bled during the Kaperger gang's group desecration, as was also *de rigeur* in Jewish host desecration narratives. One highwayman-witch confessed: "Where it was cut the Holy Host became red, like blood, and wet as if it were sweating."[156]

---

[152] This case has been meticulously reconstructed by a group of historians, archivists, and art historians in a richly illustrated microhistory that also includes a selection of primary sources. Scheutz et al., eds., *Räuber, Mörder, Teufelsbrüder*.

[153] Eveline Brugger et al., *Geschichte der Juden in Österreich* (Vienna: Ueberreuter, 2006), 221–224.

[154] Rubin, *Gentile Tales*, 118.

[155] Rubin, *Gentile Tales*, 54.

[156] Johann Sturm, "Die Schlierbacher Ketzerbilder," in *Räuber, Mörder, Teufelsbrüder*, eds. Scheutz et al., 73.

After the execution of Kaperger gang members in 1658,[157] the prosecutor commissioned a painting to commemorate "the torture of the most Venerable from which blood flowed."[158] The image is subdivided into twenty-five separate images with explanatory captions, each showing a separate episode beginning with Satan's initial seduction of the highwaymen-witches and concluding with their executions. One image shows the collective desecration of the host by the gang. The gang members are assembled around a table in a manner reminiscent of images of the last supper. Their chief wields the knife that he has just used to cut the host, from which blood spills forth. The devil lurks behind his right shoulder. The caption reads: "They cut the H[oly] Host twice, from which H[oly] Blood flowed. The old Kaperger gave each a PARTICLE to confirm their denial of divine omnipotence."[159] The table shown in this image was brought to the Benedictine Abbey of Kremsmünster, where it was venerated as a contact relic[160] (Image 5.9).

In the second half of the seventeenth century such prosecutions of host desecration by witches coincided with a resurgent anti-Judaism and a renewal of host desecration and ritual murder charges against Jews.[161] Deteriorating demographic and economic conditions in the second half of the seventeenth century and the resulting rise in poverty and vagrancy brought a wave of property crime, and Catholic churches made easy targets. Church robbery was punishable by death. The *Constitutio Criminalis Carolina*, the 1532 criminal code of Emperor Charles V, set death by fire for the theft of sacred items such as monstrances, whether they contained hosts or not, since this constituted the crime of sacrilege. But the *Carolina* did not draw a connection between sacrilegious church robbery and magical or malicious abuse of the host. The assumption was that church robbers intended to sell these valuable items for profit; the sacrilege was incidental to the property crime, though it still deserved to be punished by death.[162] The Styrian criminal code of 1574 followed the *Carolina* in

---

[157] Josef Weichenberger, "Die Kapergerbande," in *Räuber, Mörder, Teufelsbrüder*, eds. Scheutz et al., 160–168.
[158] Sturm, "Ketzerbilder," p. 63.
[159] "Zerschneiden Zweymahl die Hl. Hostia, worauß das H: bluet geflossen, der Alte Kaperger gibt jeden einen PARTICUL, zuer bekräftigung der Verlaugnung Göttlicher Allmacht." Sturm, "Ketzerbilder," 63.
[160] Sturm, "Ketzerbilder," 63–74.
[161] Valentinitsch, "Hostienschändung," 9.
[162] Valentinitsch, "Hostienschändung," 5.

Image 5.9 *Zerschneiden Zweymahl die Hl. Hostia...* Kaberger-Ketzerbilder, 18th century. Stiftarchiv Schlierbach, Image 10. Photo: OÖLKG/Ernst Grilnberger

setting death as the penalty for sacrilegious church robbery, and like the *Carolina*, it did not associate church robbery with magical abuse of the host. But by the mid-seventeenth century jurists drew a new connection between sacrilegious theft and magical abuse of the host. The *Ferdinandea* of 1656 explicitly associated church robbery with magic. Judges were instructed to question thieves whether they had desecrated the host or used it for magic.[163] The *Ferdinandea* also gives expression to rising hostility and suspicion toward Jews, threatening church robbers who sold

[163] Valentinitsch, "Hostienschändung," 11.

monstrances and hosts to Jews with exacerbated penalties that would precede their death by fire, that is, ripping the flesh with red-hot tongs, amputation of the hands, and so on. The "Jews and sorcerers" who bought them should be tried separately. For Jews "the aforementioned penalty should be sharpened as appropriate."[164]

All these accusations came together in a large trial in 1657 against a gang of church robbers. Members of the gang confessed to magical abuse of the host. They pulverized the hosts in a bowl, urinated on them, and kneaded this mixture into dough. They then made little dough balls that they threw up into the air to conjure up a hail storm. They also confessed to selling hosts to Jews.[165] The rising anti-Judaism reflected in such witchcraft and church robbery trials culminated ultimately with the expulsion of Jews from Vienna and Lower Austria in 1670.[166]

A host desecration trial from 1749 involving three Austrian soldiers undoubtedly would have precipitated a full-blown witch trial had it happened a few decades earlier, but by the mid-eighteenth century the witch-hunt was, mostly, over. This case shows that the decline of witch-hunting did not diminish concern over defilement of the Eucharist, and it possibly even strengthened the symbolic association of Jews and blasphemy, now that the threat to the sacrament posed by witches (and Protestants and Turks) seemed more remote. No actual Jews were involved in this case, but as the title of the pamphlet recounting the crime illustrates, the word "Jewish" became a kind of generic descriptor of blasphemy. The pamphlet, entitled *Most Gruesome and Horrific Deed ... by Three Common Soldiers ... who Practiced Sorcery with The Most Holy Sacrament and Jewishly Stabbed It*,[167] reports on the crime of three soldiers in an Upper Austrian infantry regiment based in Linz that had fought in the War of Austrian Succession (1740–1748) and was currently stationed in Luxemburg, under Austrian Habsburg rule since 1715.[168]

---

[164] *Ferdinandea*, Art 85, § 8–11, p. 720.
[165] Valentinitsch, "Hostienschändung," 11–14.
[166] Circumstances surrounding the expulsion will be discussed in Chap. 6.
[167] *Höchst grausame und entsetzliche That ... durch drey vermessene gemeine Soldaten in der Stadt Lutzenburg. Welche ... das Hochwürdigste Gut zur Zauberey gebraucht und Jüdisch durchstochen* (Mainz: Buchdruckerey des Hospit. St. Rochi, 1749).
[168] Viktor Grois, *Geschichte des k.k. Infanterie-Regiments Nr. 14. Grossherzog Ludwig III. von Hessen und bei Rhein von der Errichtung 1733 bis 1876: Auf Befehl des k. k. Regiments-Commandos* (Linz: J. Feichtinger's Erben, 1876).

"The Jews crucified Christ to satisfy their lust for revenge," the pamphleteer wrote, but these perpetrators were Catholic. Around All Saints' Day (November 1) 1748 the three soldiers tried to devise a way to get rich quick. One of the soldiers went to a Jesuit church and gave confession and took communion, but instead of swallowing the host he smuggled it out of the church in his handkerchief. Taking the host to a deserted garden, the soldiers pinned it to a tree, and did the "Jewish work" of piercing it with a needle. "If you are the true God, then bring the devil here to give us money," they demanded. Satan failed to materialize.[169] Disappointed, the soldiers decided to dispose of the host. The soldier who had already received the host in his mouth during his fraudulent communion ate the host—along with the needle that had pierced it, which had essentially become an instrument of the passion.

"According to the Holy Gospel nothing is so secret that it will not be revealed," the pamphleteer declared. And indeed, soon after, one of the soldiers began to feel tormented by his conscience. He confessed his deed to another soldier, who promptly reported him. In January 1749 a criminal investigation was launched. A court martial condemned the three soldiers to death. One soldier was sentenced to beheading. The other two were sentenced to be burned alive, and the soldier who stabbed the host would have "his sacrilegious hand" severed prior to being burned. When their sentence was announced to them, the pamphleteer reported, God in his mercy "so touched their hearts" that they willingly submitted and prepared themselves for death with a general confession, encouraging one another to endure their executions steadfastly.[170] During the beheading of the first soldier the executioner had to strike twice. Perhaps God made this happen so that the soldier would suffer more and thus do more complete penance before death, thus lessening his time in purgatory, the pamphleteer opined. Next, the soldier who stabbed the host had his hand struck off and then both soldiers were tied to the stake. The executioner lit the pyres. One soldier managed to free himself, and ran out of the flames "patiently and softly begging" to be strangled. To no avail. Tossed back into the flames head first, he finally expired. "Undoubtedly," the pamphleteer observed, this happened so he could more completely expiate his sin.[171]

[169] *Höchst grausame und entsetzliche That.*
[170] *Höchst grausame und entsetzliche That.*
[171] *Höchst grausame und entsetzliche That.*

5 MARY WITH THE AXE: THE CULT OF THE INJURED ICON IN BAROQUE... 259

There is little sign of the approaching Enlightenment in this narrative. The remarkably brutal executions are an indication of the severity with which blasphemy and sacrilege were punished in Habsburg lands in the mid-eighteenth century. The execution pamphlet recycled many of the motifs of medieval host desecration narratives, but there were certain "modern" elements that distinguished it from medieval Jewish host desecration tales, as well as from sixteenth- and seventeenth-century accounts of witchcraft. Satan was not an active agent in this story. Satan did not tempt the sacrilegious soldiers—as he invariably tempted witches. Jews would not need to be tempted since they were considered demonic by their very nature. In the soldiers' case, it was their failure to control their desires and passions that caused their downfall.

Most importantly, the abuse of the host did not produce a miracle. The host did not bleed when the soldier "Jewishly pierced" it. In medieval Jewish host desecrations legends Jewish men stabbed or cut the host in various ways. Jewish women were peripheral to the action. The abused host then invariably bled and usually gave some additional miraculous signs. Often a crucifix or a young child, representing the Christ Child, appeared. Frightened by such miraculous apparitions, the Jews tried to dispose of the evidence of their crime but they found that the host had become indestructible. The host continued give miraculous signs until the crime became manifest. The host desecration legend of Pulkau (1338), forty-eight miles northwest of Vienna, is typical: after the host bled and the Christ Child appeared, the Jews threw the host into a well but the water became blood red. The Jews retrieved the host and tried to feed it to a pig that refused to eat it and piously knelt before it. The pig's squeals alerted the Christian public to the crime.[172] Such narratives concluded with just punishment of the Jews and the "cultic triumph of the, now miraculous, host."[173] The abused host was rescued and exposed for adoration in a church or newly constructed shrine, where it continued to perform miracles and became the object of a pilgrimage. Lower Austria was the site of nine such host desecration accusations against Jews between 1290 and 1420.[174] Several of these, most famously the host desecration

---

[172] Mitchell B. Merback, "Fount of Mercy, City of Blood: Cultic Anti-Judaism and the Pulkau Passion Altarpiece," *The Art Bulletin* 87 (2005): 589–642.

[173] Rubin, *Gentile Tales*, 45, 1.

[174] Mitchell B. Merback, *Pilgrimage and Pogrom: Violence, Memory, and Visual Culture in the Host-Miracle Shrines of Germany and Austria* (Chicago: University of Chicago Press, 2012), 72.

accusations of Kornneuburg (1305) and Pulkau, led to the establishment of major Eucharistic pilgrimages.

These stories were not ancient history in 1749. Flourishing pilgrimages to Holy Blood shrines in the later seventeenth and eighteenth centuries kept medieval Jewish host desecration narratives familiar and pertinent. Holy Blood shrines remained enormously popular in the eighteenth century. The pilgrimage shrine in Deggendorf in Bavaria, for example, drew 140,000 pilgrims in 1737.[175] Illiterate pilgrims could learn about the desecration of miraculous hosts in paintings displayed at the shrines. In 1652 and 1660 the pilgrimage shrines of Pulkau and of Korneuburg each commissioned a series of paintings portraying the desecration of their respective miraculous hosts. The paintings showed the legends from the fourteenth century, but kept the action relevant for seventeenth-century pilgrims by showing Jews in contemporary dress.[176] Miracle books compiled at the various shrines recorded the miracles the abused hosts were currently performing. Printed versions of the miracle books were widely available in the seventeen and eighteenth centuries. Devotional literature, often richly illustrated, publicized the desecration stories, describing the host desecrations step by step.[177] Small engravings of the miracle-working hosts could be purchased at the shrines and from vendors of devotional materials. One eighteenth-century engraving, for example, shows the miraculous hosts of Wolfsberg in Carinthia, where Jews were accused of desecrating hosts in 1338, the same year as Pulkau. Hosts in a monstrance bathed in miraculous light float in clouds surrounded by angels. Inset images depict the details of the Jewish desecration and miraculous recovery of the hosts. An inscription on the engraving guaranteed that the image had been "blessed and touched" to the miraculous hosts (Image 5.10).

The sacrilegious soldiers who tried to conjure the devil by means of a consecrated host in 1748 were undoubtedly familiar with and presumably inspired by such tales and images of miracle-working hosts. But at their

---

[175] Manfred Eder, Wallfahrten, eucharistische, publiziert am 22.02.2010; in: Historisches Lexikon Bayerns, URL: http://www.historisches-lexikon-bayerns.de/Lexikon/Wallfahrten,_eucharistische (10.04.2022).

[176] Brugger et al., *Geschichte der Juden*, 323.

[177] For example: *Warhaffte History, Was sich mit dem Hochwürdigsten Sacrament des Altars zu Deggendorff, durch unmenschliche geübte Boßheit der Juden, verloffen: Mit schönen Kupffern geziehret* (Regensburg: Lang, 1716). Engravings show the entire desecration story. http://daten.digitale-sammlungen.de/~db/bsb00002741/images/.

5 MARY WITH THE AXE: THE CULT OF THE INJURED ICON IN BAROQUE... 261

Image 5.10 "Abbildung der wunderbaren H. Hostien zu Wolfsberg in Kaernten." Engraving. Volkskundemuseum Wien, Vienna, AÖMV/13.808

hands the Body of Christ did not respond to its desecration—a jarring element in the narrative that the pamphleteer evidently felt the need to explain: "Divine blessing and his gifts and goods can only be achieved through humble prayer," he instructed his readers. In contrast to medieval host desecration tales, the disposal of the offended host also did not present a problem. The soldier who had obtained the host by fraudulently taking communion simply swallowed it, and the needle. The abused host was therefore unavailable as an object of devotion. God did produce miracles to make the desecration manifest, but by the mid-eighteenth century, God employed more subtle means than he had in the fourteenth century. Now God tormented the conscience of the desecrator until he unwittingly betrayed himself. God then acted to bring about the desecrators' ultimate salvation, first by softening their hearts so that they could confess and willingly submit to their penance, and then by prolonging their agony during their executions so they could more fully expiate their sin.

When Vienna's suicidal blasphemers stabbed the host, did they expect it to bleed? There can be no doubt that the suicidal individuals who assaulted crucifixes and desecrated hosts had some familiarity with the lore surrounding bleeding hosts and wounded icons who avenged their desecration. These stories were such an integral part of their culture that there was no escaping them. The host was, as Miri Rubin writes, "the most precious symbol of Christian community and identity."[178] This was as true for Catholics around 1700 as it had been in 1400. The adoration of the host was enforced by the state. Divine and worldly power intersected in it. To desecrate the host was a horror crime, worse than murder, associated with the enemies of Christendom in their various manifestations. When suicidal iconoclasts chose to desecrate the host or its associated symbol, the crucifix, they committed a quintessentially "Jewish" act, knowing it would bring down upon them the combined might of state and church, if not the wrath of God. In the next chapter we turn to the specific context in which most cases of suicidal iconoclasm occurred and the measures the government took to prevent them, as well as to the tactics and responses of the perpetrators.

[178] Rubin, *Gentile Tales*, 1.

CHAPTER 6

The Injured Crucifix: The Emperor's Conscience and Prisoners' Defiance

Most cases of suicidal iconoclasm in Vienna from the late seventeenth through the mid-eighteenth century took place in Vienna's prison-workhouse. This was a relatively new institution that opened for operation in 1673. It was located in the former Jewish quarter, the *Judenstadt*, now renamed Leopoldstadt after Emperor Leopold I. The Judenstadt had been founded in 1625 when Emperor Ferdinand II (r. 1619–1637) compelled Jews to move from the old city to a newly designated Jewish quarter in a marshy, sparsely populated suburb by the banks of the Danube northeast of the old city. The medieval Jewish quarter clustered around the Judenplatz in the heart of the old city had been destroyed when the host desecration trial of Enns sparked the *Wiener Geserah* in 1421, leading to the massacre of many of Vienna's Jews and the banishment of the survivors. Jews began to resettle in Lower Austria and Vienna in the early sixteenth century.

Following Emperor Ferdinand's decree establishing a new ghetto, Vienna's Jews resided in the Judenstadt until Emperor Leopold I ordered their expulsion from Vienna and Lower Austria in 1670. On March 1, 1670, a public proclamation ordered all Jews to vacate the city by Corpus Christi Day, for the "greater glory of God."[1] A contemporary broadside,

---

[1] David Kaufmann, *Die letzte Vertreibung der Juden aus Wien und Niederösterreich. Ihre Vorgeschichte (1625–1670) und ihre Opfer* (Budapest: Athenaeum, 1899), 123–126.

"Jewish News about the March from Vienna," celebrates the expulsion and gleefully describes the anguish of the Jews. In laborious rhyme it thanks the emperor for freeing the city from the Jewish scourge (Image 6.1):

Dang da da dang dang da da dang/	Ding dong, ding dong, ding dong,
Lebe unser Kayser lang/	May our Emperor live long,
Der den Greuel von sich schafft/	He has expelled the abomination,
So in Juden Herzen hast/	The hatred in the Jewish heart,
Singet Christen dang da dang/	Ding dong ding Christians sing,
Aus ists mit der Juden Schlang.	The Jewish snake has lost its sting.[2]

After the departure of the Jews from the Judenstadt, Viennese citizens moved in. Taking possession of the synagogue they declared: "We find ourselves in the place where Christ and the Immaculate Mother has been cursed thousands and thousands of times by impious Jews."[3] The synagogue was razed, and a new Christian church dedicated to St. Leopold, patron saint of Austria and namesake of the emperor, was erected in its place. Emperor Leopold himself symbolically laid the corner stone. A commemorative golden coin weighing half a pound was placed in the foundation. The inscription on the coin celebrated Leopold's role in purifying a defiled space and making it sacred: "The most majestic Emperor Leopold of Austria, after expelling the perfidious Jews and removing from this building the name synagogue has cleansed it of a den of thieves and consecrated it as a temple of God."[4]

In 1671 Emperor Leopold granted the Vienna city government an imperial privilege authorizing it to convert three buildings vacated by Jews

---

[2] *Jüdische neue Zeitung vom Marsch aus Wien...* (s.l., s.d) HMW, Inventar Nr. 199 198, M 791/1670, SN 23.225, Vertreibung der Juden aus Wien 1671 (Flugblatt).

[3] Ivo Cerman, "Anti-Jewish Superstitions and the Expulsion of the Jews from Vienna in 1670," *Judaica Bohemia* 26 (2000), 23.

[4] Anton Reichsritter von Geusau, *Geschichte der Haupt- und Residenzstadt Wien in Österreich, in einiger Verbindung mit der Geschichte des Landes; von den ältesten bis auf gegenwärtige Zeiten*, vol. 4 (Vienna: Alberti, 1793), 52–53. According to Geusau the coin weighed thirteen *Loth*. According to *Zedler's Universal-Lexikon*, one *Loth* equals half an ounce, so the coin weighed six to seven ounces. *Zedler's Universal-Lexikon*, vol. 18 (Halle: 1738), Sp. 497. The inscription on one side of the coin dedicates the church to Jesus Christ and St. Leopold. The inscription on the other side reads:Augustiss. ImperatorLeopoldus AustriacusPost ejectam IudaeorumPerfidiamAbolito ex his aedibusSynagogae nomineSpeluncam LatronumMundavit in Templum Dei,Et. D. LeopoldoAustria MarchioniAc PatronoRitu catholico consecrariFecitM.D.C.LXX

Image 6.1 *Jüdische neue Zeitung vom Marsch aus Wien...* (s.l., s.d). Vertreibung der Juden aus Wien 1670. Copperplate Engraving. Photo: Wien Museum. In. Nr. 199198

to a house of correction. The imperial privilege, written in fine calligraphy, was signed by Emperor Leopold personally.[5] It was adorned by a watercolor. The image, a glorification of Leopold as a Catholic monarch, has a rich iconographic program that gives expression to the ideology of his reign (Image 6.2). Leopold and his wife Empress Margarita Teresa ride in a golden chariot driven by the personification of Charity, a chastely dressed woman, shown, as she frequently was, with children, the most deserving object of the virtue she represents (Image 6.3). Charity bounces a happy naked baby on her lap. A second naked toddler stands at her feet looking out at the viewer.[6] Leopold is shown in full armor, bearing a scepter and wearing the collar of the Order of the Golden Fleece. Margarita Teresa's role was that of "Mother of the Land," who embodied piety and charity and provided refuge to the poor and weak.

[5] WStLA, Hauptarchivsakten, Privilegien 77.
[6] On portrayals of Charity feeding or caring for young children, see Maria Wellershoff-von Thadden, Art. "Caritas", *Reallexikon zur Deutschen Kunstgeschichte*, vol. 3 (Stuttgart: J.B. Metzler, 1954), 351.

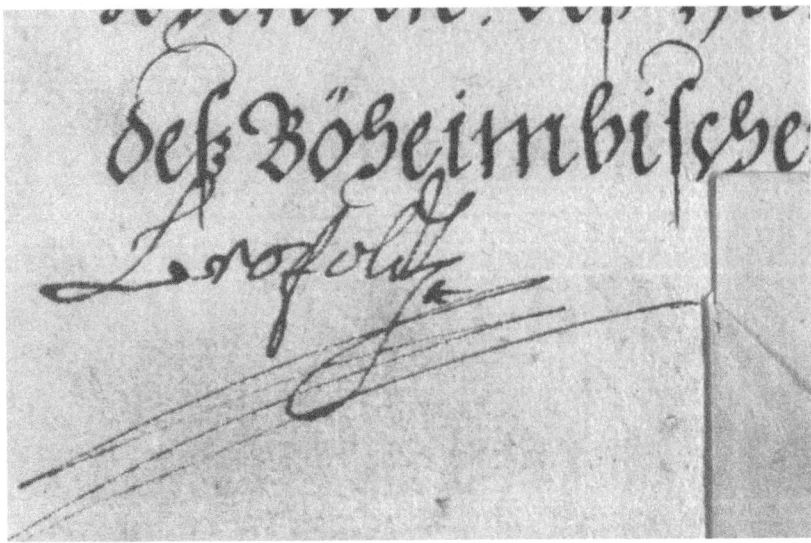

Image 6.2 Emperor Leopold I's signature under the imperial privilege founding the house of correction, 1671. Wiener Stadt und Landesarchiv, Hauptarchivsakten, Privilegien 77, f. 13

Her presence in the image was perhaps also a nod to the role she had played in the expulsion of the Jews. Leopold faced a succession crisis when his only child, Archduke Ferdinand Wenzel, died in 1668 when he was a little over three months old. Though Margarita Teresa gave birth to a girl a year later, Ferdinand Wenzel's death and a series of illnesses within the royal family raised fears of Jewish curse. Margarita Teresa believed that she would not give birth to a prince as long as Jews resided in the city. When she suffered a miscarriage on February 25, 1670, her fears were confirmed. The very next day the Imperial Privy Council issued the decree expelling the Jews from Vienna.[7] The Paulist monk Matthias Fuhrmann described the event in his city chronicle: Jews had long committed various "outrages," but bribery and illicit connections allowed them to go unpunished. Finally, however, "when Empress Margaretha suffered a miscarriage she made a vow to God. After recovering from her illness, out of

---

[7] Cerman, "Anti-Jewish Superstitions," 16–17.

Image 6.3 Apotheosis of Emperor Leopold I. Frontispiece to 1671 imperial privilege authorizing the founding of the house of correction. Wiener Stadt und Landesarchiv, Hauptarchivsakten, Privilegien 77

God-pleasing service and gratitude, she achieved with her pleas to the emperor ... that all Jews were expelled from Vienna and all of Austria."[8]

In the watercolor celebrating the founding of Vienna's house of correction, the double-headed eagle, symbol of the empire, is embossed in the backrest of the chariot just behind the royal couple. Perched on the backrest above them is a single eagle, wings outspread, a symbol of victory.[9] Leopold is victorious over sin, symbolized by the three figures crushed under the wheels of his chariot, representing three of the seven deadly sins. The first is Gluttony, on the left, a shirtless young man, whose elaborately groomed mustache gives him the appearance of a dandy. Drunk, he vomits copiously, a standard motif in representations of gluttony.[10] On the right, Lust is a half-naked young woman, breasts bared, arms thrown back, looking suggestively at the viewer. Both Gluttony and Lust are partially covered by a bright red drapery that frames and draws the eye to the figure between them. This is a Jew, representing the sin of avarice. He is clearly identifiable as a Jew by his dress and beard, resembling the Jews portrayed in the broadsheet celebrating their expulsion shown above. Jewish men in seventeenth- and eighteenth-century Central Europe typically wore black cloaks and hats, usually a flat round barrette but sometimes also the kind of three-cornered hat he is wearing here.[11] His hat mostly obscures the Jew's red hair. His most distinctive feature is his fiery red beard. The Jew clutches a moneybag, a standard attribute in the depiction of Jews. A number of coins spill out, including some red ones that bring out the color of his beard. In medieval and early modern folktales and art the color

---

[8] Matthias Fuhrmann, *Alt- und neues Wien, oder, Dieser Kayserlich- und Ertz-Lands-Fürstlichen Residentz-Stadt chronologisch- und historische Beschreibung*, vol. 2 (Vienna: Johann Baptist Prasser, 1739), 955.

[9] Art: "Adler," *Conversations-Lexikon für bildende Kunst*, vol. 1 (Leipzig: Emil Graul, 1845), 72. The eagle is an attribute of the ruler in the iconography of apotheosis. Clemens Sommer, Art: "Apotheose", *Reallexikon zur deutschen Kunstgeschichte* (Stuttgart: J.B. Metzler, 1937), 847.

[10] On gluttony, drunkenness, and vomiting, see B. Ann Tlusty, *Bacchus and Civic Order. The Culture of Drink in Early Modern Germany* (Charlottesville: University of Virginia Press, 2001), 62–67, 70–72.

[11] By this time the yellow Jewish hat and badge imposed on Jews in late medieval and Renaissance sumptuary law were no longer used. Ze'ev Yeivin, Alfred Rubens, and Miriam Nick, "Dress," *Encyclopaedia Judaica*, ed. Michael Berenbaum and Fred Skolnik, Vol. 6. 2nd ed. (Detroit: Macmillan Reference USA, 2007), 15. His hat also resembles the hats Jews are wearing in the illustration in Paul Christian Kircher, *Jüdisches Ceremoniel oder: Beschreibung derjenigen jüdische Gebräuche....* (Frankfurt: Gerhard, 1726), frontispiece.

red often served as a stigma symbol to mark people who were somehow morally suspect. Red hair in particular was a sign of immorality, treachery, and malice. When the devil took human form he often had red hair and beard. Red-haired women were vulnerable to witchcraft accusations, and paintings of Judas Iscariot often portrayed him with red hair and beard.[12] Similarly, depictions of Jewish men often show them with red hair and beards, as a sign of their moral turpitude.[13] These were the vices over which Leopold had triumphed—with the expulsion of the Jews—and would triumph over with the construction of the house of correction. The new institution would punish sinners, particularly sexually loose women, for their "Godless life." The establishment of the workhouse provided "the Christian opportunity to suppress all sorts of vice and disobedience and to implant a virtuous life and conduct."[14]

Having crushed the vices under the wheels of the chariot, the driver, Charity, points toward a triumphal arch still under construction. Stonemasons are hard at work, perhaps representing the kind of industriousness the house of correction was intended to inculcate. The arch is dedicated to Emperor Leopold, "the pious, fortunate, august ... Father of the Fatherland, Conqueror of Vice and Protector of the Poor."[15] The Holy Trinity watches over the proceedings from above. Christ, holding the Cross in his left hand, holds a laurel wreath over Leopold's head in his right as Leopold passes beneath.

---

[12] Rolf Wilhelm Brednich, "Rothaarig," *Enzyklopädie des Märchens. Handwörterbuch zur historischen und vergleichenden Erzählforschung*, ed. Rolf Wilhelm Brednich, vol. 11 (2004). Elisabeth Tucker, "Farben, Farbsymbolik," *Enzyklopädie des Märchens*, vol. 4 (1984), 802.

[13] Jews were shown with red hair and beards in intentionally defamatory images as well as in more matter-of-fact descriptive illustrations. For an example of the latter see the water color of a Jewish man from Worms from the second half of the sixteenth century from the chronicle of the Heidelberg jurist Markus von Lamm, although even in a descriptive image of a Jew the moneybag as attribute was *de rigeur*. This image from about a century earlier than the water color in the imperial privilege shows the Jew wearing the yellow badge that still was required at this time. Frederick G. Crofts, "Visualizing Germanness through Costumes in the Sixteenth Century," *The Historical Journal* 64 (2021): 1223.

[14] "durch solches Mittel eine fuegliche Christliche Gelegenheit gewunnen wirdt allerhandt Laster und...ungehorsamb abzustöllen, und dargegen Tugendsambes leben, und Wandel einzupflanzen." WStLA, Hauptarchivsakten, Privilegien 77, fol. 4v, 6r.

[15] The barely legible inscription contains a number of abbreviations: "Leopoldo Imp[eratori] Pio Fel[ici] Aug[usto] [illegible] P[atri] P[atriae] Domitori Viciorum et Pauper[um] Protect[ori]." Thank you to Helmut Zäh for helping to decipher it. See also Stekl, *Österreichs Zucht- und Arbeitshäuser, 1671–1920. Institutionen zwischen Fürsorge und Sozialdisziplinierung* (Vienna: Verlag für Geschichte und Politik, 1978), 295.

Renovations to the three buildings vacated by the Jews, including the addition of a chapel dedicated to St. Anthony of Padua, were complete in 1673, and the workhouse opened for business. A Latin plaque at the entrance read: "Emperor Leopold and Councilman Daniel Springer ... erected this house of correction (*Disciplinarium*) of the senate and people of Vienna. 1673."[16] An inscription above the entrance read "*Labore et Fame*" (Work and Hunger).[17] The prison's intended clientele was "masterless and able-bodied beggars, disobedient servants of male and female sex, undisciplined journeymen and other bad riffraff, and especially immoral women and their procuresses." Inmates would be compelled to work "with the greatest severity."[18] Upon their arrival, prisoners' personal possessions were confiscated, and they were given a prison uniform. Some if not all prisoners had their head shaven, an additional humiliation.[19] Incoming prisoners were then subjected to a "reception treatment" (*Emphangs-Tractament*) of a whipping, to be repeated at the time of their release.[20] This practice, common in German houses of correction, was known as "Welcome and Farewell" (*Willkomm und Abschied*). These public whippings in the presence of the assembled prisoners often left scars, a

---

[16] The Latin plaque read: "Imperante Leopoldo et consule Daniele Lazaro Springer S.C.M.C. Disciplinarium hoc Senatus Populusque Viennensis errexit. MDCLXXIII." Mathias Fuhrmann, *Historische Beschreibung Und kurz gefaste Nachricht Von der Römisch. Kaiserl. und Königlichen Residenz-Stadt Wien, Und Ihren Vorstädten* Part 2, vol. 2 (Vienna: Krauß, 1767), 721–721.

[17] Stekl, *Österreichs Zucht- und Arbeitshäuser*, 88–89.

[18] Zucht-Hauses Auffrichtung, [Leopoldus]. 12. Jan 1671. Franz Anton Gaurient, ed., *Codex Austriacus: Das ist: Eigentlicher Begriff und Innhalt Aller Unter deß Durchleuchtigsten Ertz-Hauses zu Oesterreich; Fürnemblich aber Der Allerglorwürdigisten Regierung Ihro Röm. Kayserl. ...Königl. Majestät Leopoldi I, Ertz-Hertzogens zu Oesterreich... Außgangenen und publicirten ... Generalien* (Vienna: Voigt, 1704), vol. 2, 546.

[19] A decree from 1771 orders the shearing of the prisoners' hair. Martin Scheutz, "'Hoc disciplinarium...errexit.' Das Wiener Zucht und Arbeitshaus um 1800—eine Spurensuche," in *Strafe, Disziplin, Besserung. Österreichische Zucht- und Arbeitshäuser von 1750 bis 1850*, eds. Gerhard Ammerer and Alfred Stefan Weiss, 70, 89, fn. 55. A decree from October 14, 1707, forbidding the "discipline master" to sell inmates' hair, indicates that such forced hair shearing was happening in the early eighteenth century as well. WStLA, Archivbehelfte 27/13 B. unpaginated, under heading Zuchthaus. It is unclear if both male and female inmates already had their heads shaved early in the century, as they would later. In the late eighteenth century, Emperor Joseph II ordered that inmates should have their hair shaved regardless of sex, an extremely stigmatizing measure. Emanuel Höggard, *Die entehrende Tonsur für exemplarische Büßerinnen unter der Regierung Josephs des Zweyten* (Vienna: C. Gerold, 1782).

[20] Stekl, *Österreichs Zucht- und Arbeitshäuser*, 201–202.

permanent visible stigma that made illusory the idea that such prisoners could be reintegrated into normal society upon release.[21] For men, prison labor consisted of sawing lumber, cutting marble, and breaking stone. Women spun and carded wool. Prisoners were supposed to maintain silence during work hours, although singing religious songs was allowed. Guards punished idle chatter or insubordination with additional labor, a diet of bread and water, withdrawal of food for twenty-four hours, chaining or whipping (Image 6.4).[22]

The priest of the parish of St. Leopold was responsible for the pastoral care of the inmates, assisted by Franciscans and after 1726 by Jesuits.[23] A second chapel was added during an expansion in the 1720s and dedicated to St. Lorenz.[24] In overtly religious language ordinances referred to inmates as "penitents" (*Büssende*). As in Hamburg's carceral institutions, religious indoctrination in the Viennese prison was unrelenting. According to instructions from 1723, inmates were catechized and required to attend sermons three times a week. The daily regimen included morning, noon, and evening prayers. In the morning and afternoon devotional literature was read aloud as inmates worked.[25] In 1728 the workhouse hired a priest fulltime. He read mass daily and catechized inmates on Sundays and holidays.[26] A set of instructions from 1769 for the workhouse in Innsbruck gives an idea of the intensity of religious instruction in Austrian houses of correction. On Sundays, inmates awoke between 5 and 6, depending on the season, and engaged in prayer, read devotional literature, gave

---

[21] Alfred Stefan Weiß, "'Karbatsch=Streiche zur künftigen Besserung.' Das Klagenfurter Zucht- und Arbeitshaus 1755–1813," in *Strafe, Disziplin und Besserung. Osterreichische Zucht- und Arbeitshäuser von 1750 bis 1850*, eds. Gerhard Ammerer and Alfred Stefan Weiß (Frankfurt am Main: Lang, 2006), 176. Eckhardt Meyer-Krentler, *Willkomm und Abschied: Herzschlag und Peitschenhieb: Goethe-Mörike-Heine* (Munich: W. Fink, 1987), 39–54.

[22] Scheutz, "Hoc disciplinarium," 67. Sebastian G. Herrenleben, ed., *Sammlung Oesterreichischer Gesetze und Ordnungen: Wie solche von Zeit zu Zeit ergangen und publiciret worden .../[4]: ... so viel deren vom Jahr 1721. Bis auf Höchst-traurigen Tod-Fall Der Römisch-Kayserlichen Majestät Caroli VI. aufzubringen waren* (Vienna: Johann Thomas Trattner, 1752), vol. 4, August 16, 1723, "Errichtung des Zuchthauses," 139.

[23] Stekl, *Österreichs Zucht- und Arbeitshäuser*, 159.

[24] Scheutz, "Hoc disciplinarium," 66.

[25] 16 August 1723, Errichtung des Zucht-Hauses, in Herrenleben, ed., *Sammlung Oesterreichischer Gesetze*, vol. 4, 138.

[26] Leopold Matthias Weschel, *Die Leopoldstadt bey Wien. Nach Quellen und Quellenschriftstellern, in Verbindung mit einer Skizze der Landesgeschichte, historisch dargestellt* (Vienna: A. Strauss, 1824), LXXXVII–LXXXIX.

Image 6.4 Vienna's House of Correction. Water coloring, c. 1850. Photo: Wien Museum. In. Nr. 15069, C. N. 231 (= Leopoldgasse Nr. 32) (Das alte Zuchthaus)

confession, and attended mass. Catechism instruction started 8–9 and continued until lunch and prayer 11–12, followed by catechism instruction 12–1, religious exercises, that is, the rosary and litanies starting 1–2 until dinner 6–7, followed by a devotional service 7–8.[27] This was the environment authorities intended to create for the inmates. In reality, however, conditions most likely fell short of this "ideal." Financing schemes for Vienna's workhouse failed to live up to expectations, and the institution suffered from chronic underfunding. Hygienic conditions were so bad that a 1723 decree ordered the prison director to maintain basic cleanliness or face dismissal. The decree noted that several inmates had died because of filthy conditions at the prison.[28]

It is not surprising that some inmates longed for death as an escape from this bleak and regimented existence. As the discussion of prisons in

---

[27] Stekl, *Österreichs Zucht- und Arbeitshäuser*, 222.
[28] 16 August 1723, Errichtung des Zucht-Hauses, in Herrenleben, ed., *Sammlung*, 140.

Hamburg has shown, suicide by proxy in its classic form of child murder was not an uncommon occurrence in German houses of correction. Viennese convicts were also familiar with this option. In 1713 twenty-year-old Theresia N., imprisoned in the house of correction, attempted to cut the throat of her little sister with a shoemaker's knife, leaving a gash a finger long in the girl's neck. For this attempted murder, she received thirty lashes, known as "a whole Schilling," and was banished from Austria for life.[29] As in Hamburg, there were plenty of children living in Vienna's house of correction. Vienna did not have a specialized orphanage before 1743. Until then Vienna's orphans were housed in the prison-workhouse.[30]

In addition to such wards and orphans, juvenile offenders held in the house of correction were also available as victims. On April 20, 1750, the prison inmate Johann Georg Hallmann, twenty-three, "out of weariness with life" decided to beat to death a twelve-year-old fellow prisoner, presumably a beggar boy.[31] Hallmann was a former cellar boy, Catholic, and a native of Pressburg, then capital of Hungary and site of Habsburg imperial coronations, about fifty miles to the east of Vienna.[32] Hallmann had been in and out of Vienna's house of correction since he was eighteen. Arrested for vagrancy and theft five times between 1745 and 1750, each time he was placed in the house of correction, whipped, and deported to his birthplace. He kept coming back. During his fifth imprisonment Hallmann formulated his murder plan. He struck the twelve-year-old over the head with a board "with full force." Amazingly, the boy escaped with only a concussion, though Hallmann insisted in his confession that it had been his intent to kill him. Attempted murder did not merit the death penalty, however, so Hallmann did not escape the workhouse. Instead, on June 6, 1750, he was sentenced to an additional two years of labor in chains. Every three months he would be exhibited on a public stage with a sign detailing his crime of attempted murder and whipped, as deterrence to his fellow inmates. Upon completion of his sentence he would be banished from all Austrian hereditary lands for life.

---

[29] *WD*, Nr. 1024, May 24–26, 1713, Theresia N.
[30] Friedrich Hartl, *Das Wiener Kriminalgericht. Strafrechtspflege vom Zeitalter der Aufklärung bis zur österreichischen Revolution* (Vienna: Böhlau, 1973), 127.
[31] ÖNB, Signatur 303.950-B Alt-Adl 9, *Wohlverdientes Todtes-Urtheil einer Ledigen Manns-Person Nahmens Johann Georg H.* (Vienna, [1752]). *WD*, Nr. 54, July 8, 1752. WB, Handschriften 18013, p. 30.
[32] Today this is Bratislava, capital of Slovakia.

At the time of his sentencing Hallmann had to swear an oath of *Urfehde*, an oath of peace. Convicted felons had to swear that they would not seek revenge against their judges for the torture or punishments they suffered at the hands of the authorities and that they would abide by the terms of their sentence.[33] With members of Vienna's criminal court as witnesses, banished felons swore a "bodily oath" to let memory of their punishment "fade into eternal oblivion" and to stay out of Austrian lands "in perpetuity." The formulaic *Urfehde* included the acknowledgment that they would be prosecuted for perjury, a capital offense, if they broke the oath. Convicts who were literate signed the oath with their own hand; otherwise, they made their mark. Below the convicts' sign or signature, members of the court affirmed with their signatures that banished felons had sworn this oath "willingly and gladly" after the terms had been explained to them "in great clarity."[34]

Hallmann's new sentence had barely started in the summer of 1750 when he came down with an unspecified "evil disease," presumably venereal disease. He was transferred to St. Marx Hospital and poorhouse, where workhouse inmates, along with the mentally ill, people with contagious diseases, pregnant women, and foundlings were cared for.[35] From here, he managed to escape, though not for long. Between October 1750 and May 1752 the cycle of arrest, sentencing, oath of *Urfehde*, imprisonment, hospitalization, and escape happened twice. Arrested an eighth time in May 1752 in the company of a "loose" (*liederliche*) woman who had previously been an inmate too, he finally received the sentence he had longed for two years earlier. Condemned to death as a perjurer who had broken his oath of *Urfehde* three times, he was beheaded on July 7, 1752. The woman was deported to Temeswar in Hungary.[36] Few sources docu-

[33] *Urfehde* meant literally "end of feud" (*ur* = away from; *Fehde* = feud). W. Sellert, "Urfehde," in *HRG*, vol. 5 (Berlin: Erich Schmidt Verlag, 1998), 562–570.

[34] This description of the ritual of *Urfehde* as practiced in Vienna is based on the surviving *Urfehde* of Nicolaus Stark on 20 April 1750. Nicolaus Stark was a fellow inmate of Hallman's in the house of correction. Stark attacked a crucifix a few months before Hallmann tried to murder the twelve-year-old. Stark's case is discussed below. Stark swore, "bey meinem cörperlichen Eid... [to place any injury he suffered] in ewige Vergessenheit stellen." He would be prosecuted as a "meineidge urphed-brecher" if he broke his oath. This all Stark swore "nach...ihme ganz deutlich vorgehaltener urphed willig und gern." WStLA, Handschriften A 17, fo. 6r–7v.

[35] Karl Weiss, *Geschichte der öffentlichen Anstalten, Fonde und Stiftungen für die Armenversorgung in Wien* (Vienna: Selbstverlag des Gemeinderathes, 1867), 91–96.

[36] ÖNB, Signatur 303.950-B Alt-Adl 9, *Wohlverdientes Todtes-Urtheil einer Ledigen Manns-Person Nahmens Johann Georg H.* (Vienna, [1752]). *WD*, Nr. 54, July 8, 1752. WB, Handschriften 18013, p. 30.

menting the day-to-day operation of the prison-workhouse have survived, so it is impossible to know how often such murders or attempted murders occurred there. Cases of child murder associated with suicide by proxy were fairly common in the city at large, as will be developed in Chap. 7, but surviving sources mention only one other suicidal murder in a Viennese prison.

In 1739 Johann K., twenty-two, was in lock-up in a military prison awaiting transport to the Hungarian border where he was sentenced to six years of hard labor. "Letting the spirit of despair take possession of his heart," as his execution pamphlet put it, he sought to escape his deportation by striking a priest who was a fellow inmate over the head with a piece of marble. Johann K. was broken on the wheel.[37] It seems that Vienna's suicidal prison inmates generally chose iconoclasm over murder as means to escape their fate. Or perhaps, cases of suicidal iconoclasm and blasphemy left more of an imprint in surviving records because authorities viewed them as more heinous crimes than suicide by proxy in its classic form of murder.

GOVERNMENTAL RESPONSES

The ability of the absolutist state to police its subjects and to enforce its decrees inevitably fell far short of rulers' lofty goal to realize a "Christian ideal state" in which God's honor reigned supreme.[38] The only area in which authorities might conceivably come close to exercising the domination to which they aspired was when administering criminal justice to offenders already in their custody. "The early modern state was not totalitarian, because it could not realize its all-encompassing will to regulate," historian Uwe Danker writes, but during an inquisitorial trial, in the torture chamber, or when preparing a condemned malefactor for execution, "when an individual prisoner was completely at the mercy of this will to

---

[37] "Er ließ Verzweiflungs-Geist in seinem Hertzen walten...." WB, 39975, *Wohl-verdientes Todtes Urtheil Einer ledigen Manns-Persohn Nahmens Johann K, Catholischer Religion, und 22 Jhar alt, von hier gebürtig* (s.l.: s.d.).

[38] I take the expression "Christian ideal state" from Bernd Roeck, "Christlicher Ideal Staat und Hexenwahn. Zum Ende der europäischen Hexenverfolgungen," *Historisches Jahrbuch* 108 (1988): 379–405.

discipline, the state could achieve total domination."[39] The extent to which governments could exercise control over the individual psyche of a prisoner is particularly evident in the transformation that authorities typically effected in condemned criminals awaiting execution, from obdurate malefactors to penitent "poor sinners" who thanked the authorities for a merciful judgment and went eagerly to the ravenstone, "as if to a wedding."[40] The inquisitorial trial and the theater of execution, as historian Richard van Dülmen has suggested, were the most spectacular expressions of the sovereignty of the early modern state.

Leopold I conceived of Vienna's new house of correction as a similar manifestation of his sovereignty and rule, as is evident in the apotheosis adorning the founding privilege of the prison-workhouse that showed him crushing the vices under the wheels of his chariot. This same founding document instructed the Vienna city government to display a special sign outside the prison-workhouse that marked it as an especially protected space, guaranteed by the authority of the state. Authorities commonly designated certain spaces, such as areas around courthouses, as "privileged" protected places. A sign with distinctive symbols, a *Salvegarde*, alerted the public that any breach of peace within the area would be punished with special severity.[41] Such places were often sites of power, representative of and imbued with the power of sovereignty, as was the case with Vienna's house of correction.

The sign that Leopold ordered to be affixed at the prison would show a man's outstretched arm bearing an unsheathed sword.[42] The message of the sign with its graphic display of the power to punish was not subtle, and it would seem to go without saying that violence within the prison would be dealt with harshly. This sign was not directed at the inmates being disciplined there, however. The sign's message illustrated for the broader

---

[39] Uwe Danker, *Räuberbanden im Alten Reich um 1700. Ein Beitrag zur Geschichte von Herrschaft und Kriminalität in der frühen Neuzeit* (Frankfurt a.M.: Suhrkamp, 1988), 172–173.

[40] Kathy Stuart, *Defiled Trades and Social Outcasts: Honor and Ritual Pollution in Early Modern Germany* (Cambridge: Cambridge University Press, 1999), 134.

[41] B. Ann Tlusty, *The Martial Ethic in Early Modern Germany: Civic Duty and the Right of Arms* (New York: Palgrave Macmillan, 2011), 60–61. "Salvegarde," *Zedler's Universallexikon*, vol. 33, (Leipzig: 1742), 1244–1245.

[42] The decree ordered the city government "das Sye zu männigliches wissen, und offentlichen Zaichen selbigen orths Freyheit...einen ausgestreckten Manns Armben, in der Handt ein bloßes Schwerd führendt, mahlen und anschlagen lassen sollen." Zuchthausprivileg 1671, WStLA, Hauptarchivsakten, Privilegien 77.

public and potential future inmates the reach of the disciplining power of the state. It served to reinforce "the image of prisons in peoples' minds, their symbolic meaning in society," that, historian Pieter Spierenburg suggests, had a greater impact on society than the state's actual capacity to confine deviants.[43] And yet, it was precisely within this symbolically marked space that an outbreak of suicidal iconoclasm began in the late seventeenth century, at the same time as Hamburg authorities struggled to quash suicidal child murders in their prisons. How galling it must have been for authorities that their disciplinary regime within the prison-workhouse, the institution specifically conceived to remold willful and defiant miscreants into docile subjects, went so horribly awry and produced such horrific defiance. How did authorities respond when faced with such suicidal blasphemy committed by this new breed of iconoclast who was neither Protestant nor Turk, neither witch nor Jew?

Authorities prosecuted all cases of suicidal iconoclasm as blasphemy in the second degree as defined in the *Ferdinandea* of 1656. This was blasphemy "directly against God and his purest Mother or other saints with dishonorable shameful words or deeds" that did not rise to the level of "blasphemy in the highest degree" due to some mitigating circumstances. Blasphemy in the highest degree would have been punished by burning alive, usually in combination with some additional exacerbating penalties such as tearing the flesh with hot tongs and amputations, as illustrated in the cases of the Jewish host desecrator Franz Engelberger in 1642, the highwaymen-witches in the Kaperger gang in 1659, and the host-desecrating soldiers in 1749. In contrast, none of Vienna's suicidal iconoclasts were burned at the stake. As blasphemers in the second degree, the *Ferdinandea* set their penalty at beheading after amputation of the offending member.[44] How was the *Ferdinandea* applied in practice?

Early cases of suicidal iconoclasm fell within the reign of Emperor Leopold I, who died in 1705.[45] The *Ferdinandea* required local courts, in this case the city court (*Stadtgericht*) of Vienna, to forward cases to the Lower Austrian government for review. Government officials and in some cases the emperor himself would then confirm, mitigate, or increase the

---

[43] Spierenburg argues against Foucault's "great confinement" thesis. Pieter Spierenburg, *The Prison Experience: Disciplinary Institutions and their Inmates in Early Modern Europe* (New Brunswick: Rutgers University Press, 1991), 10.
[44] *Ferdinandea*, Article 59, § 7–8, in Gaurient, *Codex Austriacus*, vol. 1, 687.
[45] Leopold II (1640–1705, r. 1658–1705).

sentences.[46] These records have not survived,[47] so there is no way to know the extent of Leopold's or his officials' involvement in the sentencing of Vienna's suicidal iconoclasts. It is likely that he did personally review some of these cases. In 1713 Leopold's biographer Eucharius Gottlieb Rink described the emperor's involvement with capital cases. "Justice and Mercy" (*iustitia et clementia*), as shown in the last chapter, were virtues traditionally associated with the House of Austria that derived from the Habsburg's fabled piety. In balancing these virtues, Rink wrote, Leopold was guided by a Habsburg handbook on government handed down by his father and grandfather, the *Princeps in Compendio* (Instruction of a Prince). In the German translation of this handbook the Latin *clementia* was rendered as *Sanftmut*, "tenderness" or "tender-heartedness." The foremost duty of the prince was to promote the honor of God. Therefore, under the heading "The Prince's Tenderness and Justice," the handbook advises the prince to "be kindhearted (*gütig*), but in the right measure: for being too merciful commonly leads to greater crimes. If the subjects know that the prince always forgives the greatest sins …, they take this mercy for granted and become ever more sinful …. If sin is not punished, the good is suppressed."[48] Accordingly, while extolling Leopold's tender-heartedness toward his subjects, Rink emphasized that in the name of just governance the emperor had to suppress his personal desire to pardon. "At the beginning of his reign," Rink wrote, "various offenders were granted life, though they should have lost it according to the letter of the law."[49] But when Leopold saw that such mercy only increased vices, he experienced "pangs of conscience about issuing pardons that deviated from laws estab-

---

[46] On this process of judicial review, see Andrea Griesebner, "'In via gratia et ex plenitudine potetatis.' Strafjustiz und landesfürstliche Gnadenakte im Erzherzogtum Österreich unter der Enns des 18. Jahrhunderts," *Frühneuzeit-Info* 11 (2000): 13–27.

[47] The bulk of early modern court records for Lower Austria were destroyed in a fire at the Palace of Justice (Justizpalast) that broke out during street fighting between Austrofascists and Social Democrats in 1927.

[48] I am quoting here from an abridged version of the *Compendio in Princeps* that Rink includes in his biography of Leopold. Eucharius Gottlieb Rink, *Leopolds des Grossen Röm. Käysers wunderwürdiges Leben und Thaten*, vol. 1 (Cologne: s.n., 1713), 50. According to Rink, Leopold ordered the imperial librarian Peter Lambeck to have a new edition printed in 1668 (p. 44). This appeared as *Princeps in compendio, hoc est, Puncta aliquot compendiosa, quae circa gubernationem Reipub. observanda videntur* (Vienna: Cosmerovius, 1668). The German version reproduced by Rink (pp. 44–74), is entitled "PRINCEPS IN COMPENDIO, Oder einige Puncta So bey der Regierung eines Lands zu beobachten."

[49] Rink, *Leopolds des Grossen*, vol. 1, 171.

lished by the Divine Majesty alone. Henceforth no criminal was granted life, as much as our pious monarch would have wanted that all might live."[50] It was not uncommon for rulers to experience pangs of conscience when weighing the just measure of mercy and severity in the administration of criminal justice. As late as 1785, Duke Karl Eugen of Wuerttemberg, a Protestant state, requested theological opinions from two of his court preachers on whether he could commute the death sentences of a father and daughter convicted of incest without burdening his conscience.[51] Until the administration of criminal justice was fully secularized, rulers, both Catholic and Protestant, were wary of disregarding the precepts of the Decalogue.

Early suicidal iconoclasts were executed, of course, but—perhaps in an exercise of imperial "tender-heartedness"—in a more lenient form than the *Ferdinandea* prescribed. When the twenty-one-year-old Franz Wunderlich attacked a Marian icon and ran the Christ Child through with his dagger in 1688 after blaspheming against the Holy Trinity and all the saints, beating his mother, and committing fornication, he was simply beheaded, without additional refinements.[52] Wunderlich was apparently not an inmate in the house of correction. The first documented case of suicidal iconoclasm in the prison-workhouse happened in 1697. Maria Anna Rossenberger, a nineteen-year-old from Styria, was beheaded on the High Market "for committing blasphemy against the Holy Host in the house of correction."[53] Meanwhile, at the same time that inmates of the prison-workhouse were committing suicidal iconoclasm, other suicidal individuals beyond the prison walls committed suicide by proxy in its classic form, child murder, or, in a related practice, accused themselves of infanticide, as will be detailed in Chap. 7. Two further cases of suicidal iconoclasm as well as three suicidal child murders happened in the last six years of Leopold's reign. Beginning in 1700 authorities began to follow the sentencing guidelines of the *Ferdinandea* in some cases of suicidal

---

[50] Rink, *Leopolds des Grossen*, vol. 1, 172.

[51] Helga Schnabel-Schüle, *Überwachen und Strafen im Territorialstaat. Bedingungen und Auswirkungen des Systems strafrechtlicher Sanktionen im frühneuzeitlichen Württemberg* (Cologne: Böhlau, 1997), 128–129. One court preacher argued against a pardon, while the other recommended life-long imprisonment at forced labor as an alternative. The sentence was commuted.

[52] J. E. Schlager, *Wiener Skizzen aus dem Mittelalter* (Neue Folge) (Vienna: Carl Gerold, 1842), vol. 2, 126–127.

[53] Schlager, *Wiener Skizzen*, 127.

iconoclasm and imposed amputation prior to beheading. That year the twenty-two-year-old thief Johann Carl Formstreith was beheaded after amputation of his right hand because he "inhumanly blasphemed against God during his imprisonment."[54] This brief entry in the city protocol does not specify how he blasphemed against God, but it is clear that this was a case of iconoclasm rather than verbal blasphemy, since his hand rather than his tongue was cut off. The *Ferdinandea*, after all, called for the amputation of the offending member. In 1702, Anna Rosina was beheaded after amputation of her right hand because she "cut up The Most Venerable with a knife in the house of correction."[55] After Leopold died on May 5, 1705, Maria Francisca Rosenburgerin was the first suicidal iconoclast executed during the reign of Leopold's son and successor Joseph I (r. 1705–1711). Rosenburgerin, eighteen or nineteen years old, was beheaded on May 12, 1705, because, as the *Wiennerisches Diarium* reported, she had taken the host out of her mouth after receiving communion, and then while she was imprisoned at the house of correction (presumably during her trial for this host desecration) she took a crucifix from the wall and jumped on it.[56] After two further executions for suicidal child murders within the city at large,[57] the next execution for suicidal iconoclasm took place on February 17, 1707. Maria Catherina N., an unmarried woman of twenty-four was beheaded because, as the *Wiennerisches Diarium* reported, "several years ago after receiving communion she cut up the Holy Host,

---

[54] Schlager, *Wiener Skizzen*, 127.
[55] The executioner botched her execution terribly. He had to strike four times before he completed her beheading. "…hat der freymann Hans Georg 4 mahl gehauet, Ihr Nahm war Anna Rosina hat ds Hochwürdige mit dem meßer zerschniten, in dem Zuchthaus.". ÖNB, Cod 8363, p. 1, Nr. 1, 23 June 1702. A second Protocol of the Confraternity of the Dead in the Wien Bibliothek records her crime and execution without mentioning the executioner's failures. WB, Handschriften 18013, p. 1, 23 June 1702. Schlager, *Wiener Skizzen*, 127.
[56] The report in the *Wiennerisches Diarium* does not make clear whether she was already an inmate in the house of correction. It identifies her as a nineteen-year-old unmarried woman. *WD*, Nr. 186, May 13, 1705. The "Protocol of the Confraternity for the Dead" identifies her as Maria Francisca Rosenburgerin. ÖNB, Cod 8363, p. 3, Nr. 16, 13 May 1705. The *Stadtprotokoll* cited by Schlager identifies her as Maria Rastenberger, 18, from Upper Austria. Schlager, *Wiener Skizzen*, 128.
[57] A woman was beheaded for cutting the throat of a farm laborer's child. *WD*, Nr. 257, January 19, 1706. The "Protocol of the Confraternity of the Dead" identifies her as Sidonia. ÖNB, Cod 8363, p. 4, Nr. 22, January 19, 1706. Another woman was beheaded for strangling the daughter of a stockman on January 4, 1707. Anna Maria N., *WD*, Nr. 357, January 4, 1707. The "Protocol of the Confraternity of the Dead" identifies her as Maria Susanna. ÖNB, Cod 8363, p. 4, Nr. 23, 4 January 1707.

and last year she stepped on a crucifix with her feet." Her earlier host desecration had not resulted in a death sentence—perhaps because of her youth? Presumably, she received an extended sentence in the house of correction, prompting a second, and possibly a third blasphemous deed. The entry recording her execution in the Protocol of the Confraternity of the Dead reported that she kicked a crucifix twice and cut the Holy Host with a knife.[58]

The following year, Elisabeth Stainin, twenty-three, from Lower Austria, was beheaded on March 16, 1708, after prior amputation of her right hand. She had dishonored the host and afterward broke a crucifix, the *Wiennerisches Diarium* reported. As the Protocol of the Confraternity of the Dead recounted, she "assaulted God twice." The city protocol recorded that after receiving communion she took the host out of her mouth and threw it on the ground. Then, in the city courthouse, presumably while on trial for host desecration, she threw a cross to the ground, stepped on it, and finally jumped on it.[59] In June 1709 Hans Georg Fritsch, a forty-seven-year-old man from Eger in Hungary, was beheaded for verbal blasphemy. He had previously been arrested for blasphemy and sentenced to forced labor, but he persisted in cursing "not only the sun, moon, and the saints of God, but also the Most Holy Trinity and Mother of God."[60]

On November 6, 1709, the *Wiennerisches Diarium* reported a far more uplifting event in a very different social milieu: "Today it happened that his Imperial Majesty wanted to go hunting. He met a priest returning from a sick person carrying the Most Venerable. Whereupon his Imperial Majesty descended from his carriage and accompanied the priest on foot back to St. Stephen's Cathedral. Only then, after receiving a blessing, did

---

[58] *WD*, Nr. 370, 17 February 1707. ÖNB, Cod 8363, p. 4, Nr. 24, 17 [month missing] 1707. The *Stadtprotokoll* cited by Schlager gives her name as Chaterina Graf. Schlager, *Wiener Skizzen*, 128. None of these three sources mentions that she committed the deed within the prison. Since the records usually do mention that detail, it seems likely that this case of suicidal iconoclasm happened outside the prison.

[59] "...welche sich zweymahl an got vergriffen...." The Protocol identifies her as Elizabeth. ÖNB, Cod 8363, addendum at end of volume, "pertinent ad Folium 5." The *Wiennerisches Diarium* identifies her only as N.N. *WD*, Nr. 482, March 16, 1708. The *Stadtprotokoll* excerpted by Schlager identifies her as Elisabeth Stainin. Schlager, *Wiener Skizzen*, 128.

[60] *WD*, Nr. 611, 11 June 1709. The Protocol of the Confraternity of the Dead gives his name as Hans Georg Fris. ÖNB, Cod 8363, p. 5, Nr. 33, 11 June 1709. Schlager, *Wiener Skizzen*, 128.

he go hunting."⁶¹ Just over a month later, on December 10 of that year Elizabeth N., a thirty-one-year-old vagrant sentenced to the house of correction, was beheaded after amputation of her right hand for taking a crucifix from an altar and demolishing it. In the past, she had been arrested multiple times, whipped, and banished from Austria three times, swearing an *Urfehde* each time. When she was arrested again she was condemned to beheading as a perjurer who had broken her oath of *Urfehde*, but "out of inborn benevolence and mercy" the emperor commuted her sentence to imprisonment in the house of correction. She responded by breaking the crucifix out of "weariness with her life and the length of her sentence."⁶² In 1710 three more women committed suicidal iconoclasm. Maria Anna Kaufleuthner, a twenty-eight-year-old woman from Linz was beheaded for breaking a crucifix. It is not clear whether this happened in the workhouse or in the city at large.⁶³ Maria Anna N., a twenty-eight-year-old widow from Augsburg imprisoned for prostitution, was whipped and banished for "dishonoring" a picture of a crucifix, after previously unsuccessfully trying to convince authorities that she had committed infanticide.⁶⁴ In a clear sign that suicidal iconoclasm was spreading beyond the prison, Rosina Wagnerin, a supervisor in the city hospital, committed some form of *blasphemia realis*. In contrast to the suicidal blasphemers within the workhouse, Wagnerin received medical treatment for melancholy and did not face criminal prosecution.⁶⁵

The first full year of the reign of Emperor Charles VI (r. 1711–1740)—1712—was the year suicidal iconoclasm really caught on. In that year, seven people demolished crucifixes or desecrated the host. Clearly bucking the general trend identified by Gerd Schwerhoff that physical punishments for blasphemy in German territories and in most of Europe became more lenient after 1650, all of these suicidal blasphemers suffered the exacerbated execution of having their right hand cut off before their beheadings. Further amplifying the infamy of their executions, their amputated hands were attached to a pole at the ravenstone to

---

⁶¹ WD, Nr. 654, November 6, 1709. This was Emperor Joseph I. This episode is similar to the incident commemorated in the engraving discussed in Chap. 5. See Image 5.2: Emperor Joseph I Venerates the Sacrament, 1701. Engraving by Christoph Weigel (after Caspar Luyken). Albertina, Vienna. Historische Blätter Wien 8, Joseph I.
⁶² *WD*, Nr. 663, 10 December 1709. ÖNB, Cod 8363, p. 6, Nr. 34, 10 December 1709.
⁶³ Schlager, *Wiener Skizzen*, 129.
⁶⁴ 2 May 1710, Maria Anna N. *WD*, Nr. 704.
⁶⁵ WStLA, B6-2, Decretenbuch 1703–1711, fol. 357r-v, 18. October 1710.

6 THE INJURED CRUCIFIX   283

Image 6.5 Execution of Catherina Jacobin, Vienna, 1769. Engraving. In *Todesurtheil einer ledigen Weibperson, Namens Catherina J....* Wienbibliothek im Rathaus, C-39975/1769

remain exposed indefinitely (Image 6.5). On June 7, 1712, Johann Posch, nineteen, from Lower Austria was executed "because he flagrantly and Godlessly dishonored a crucifix."[66] On July 12 Anna Catherina Köpflerin, eighteen, from Mödling, a market town about ten miles south of Vienna, suffered the same penalty "because she insolently attacked a crucifix in the local house of correction, and threw it to the ground so that it broke into pieces."[67] On August 30 Clara Dorothea Jancovitschin, twenty-three, from Pressburg, imprisoned for prostitution, was executed because she "brazenly threw a crucifix to the floor and then jumped on it with her

---

[66] "ein Crucifix-Bild höchstvermessentlich und gottloser Weis zuverunehren sich unterfangen." *WD*, Nr. 923, 7 June 1712. ÖNB, Cod 8363, p. 6, Nr. 44, 7 June 1713. Schlager, *Wiener Skizzen*, 129. It is unclear where he committed his blasphemous act.

[67] "um selbige sich höchst vermessen in dem alhiesigen Zucht-Haus mit einem Crucifix-Bildnus vergriffen/ und solches zur Erden geworffen/ daß selbiges in etliche Stuk zersprungen." *WD*, Nr. 933, 12 July 1712. The *Stadtprotokoll* excerpted by Schlager gives her name as Katherina Köplflerin. Schlager, *Wiener Skizzen*, 129. The Protocol of the Confraternity of the Dead in the ÖNB identifies her as Anna Köpflerin. ÖNB, Cod 8363, p. 7, Nr. 45, 12 July 1712. A second version of the protocol in the Vienna city library identifies her as Anna Catjherina. WB, Handschriften 18013, p. 10, Nr. 49, 12 July 1712.

feet."[68] On September 27 two suicidal iconoclasts were beheaded on the same day. Maria Susanna Grallin, nineteen, and Maria Magdalena Zechirlin, twenty, both from Vienna, seem to have conspired to commit their act of blasphemy together, in a similar way that women inmates in Hamburg's house of correction teamed up to commit suicidal child murder. As the *Wiennerisches Diarium* reported, they "attacked a crucifix, demolished it and broke it over their knees and threw it to the ground."[69] On November 17, 1712, Maria Elisabeth N., twenty, a prostitute and thief from Lower Austria, was beheaded for "committing a blasphemous deed against a crucifix."[70] And finally, one week later, on November 23, 1712, Benigna Rosina Weninger, seventeen, from Vienna, imprisoned for prostitution and theft, was executed because she "committed a highly blasphemous deed against a crucifix, and, when she last went to Holy Communion, she took the Holy Host out of her mouth with a handkerchief and tore it up."[71]

This accumulation of cases within a few months, resulting in seven executions from June through November 1712, brings to mind the "epidemics" of demonic possession and witchcraft accusation in institutional

---

[68] "ein Crucifix-Bild höchstvermessen auf die Erden geworffen/ folgends mit Füssen darauf gesprungen." *WD*, Nr. 947, 30 August 1712. ÖNB, Cod 8363, p. 7, Nr. 46, 30 [no month given] 1712. WB, Handschriften 18013, p. 10, Nr. 50, 30 August 1712. Schlager, *Wiener Skizzen*, 129. This case was also reported in Johann Xaver Meyer, *Das Neueste von der Zeit Oder Allerneueste Nachrichten Von den vornehmsten und merckwürdigsten Begebenheiten* (Frankfurt: Buggel u. Seitz, 1732), 185–186.

[69] "um willen selbige sich dahin vermessentlich unterfangen... sich an einer Crucifix-Bildnus zu vergreiffen/ selbige zu zerschlagen/ über die Knye zu zerbrechen/ und sodan auf die Erden zu werffen." The *Wiennerisches Diarium* identifies them as Maria Susanna N. and Maria Magdalena N. *WD*, Nr. 955, 27 September 1712. The Protocol of the Confraternity of the Dead identifies them as Susanna Grallin and Maria Magdalena Zechirlin. ÖNB, Cod 8363, p. 7, Nr. 47, 27 September 1712. The *Stadtprotokoll* excerpted by Schlager gives the names as Marai Magdalena Zechiellitz and Susanna Kralin. Schlager, *Wiener Skizzen*, 129. It is unclear whether they were workhouse inmates or not.

[70] "ein Gottslästerliche That an einem Crucifix verübet." *WD*, Nr 970, 17 November 1712. This case is not listed in either Protocol of the Confraternity of the Dead or in the *Stadtprotokoll*.

[71] "an einer Crucifix-Bildnus ein höchst Gottslästerliche That verübet/ nicht weniger/ als sie letztlich zum Heil. Nachmal gangen/ die hochheilige Hostie mit ihrem Fürtuch aus dem Mund genommen/ und solche zerrissen." The Wiennerisches Diarium gives her name as Benigna Rosina N. WD, Nr. 972, 23 November 1712. The *Stadtprotokoll* excerpted by Schlager identifies her as Rosina Weninger. Schlager, *Wiener Skizzen*, p. 129. The case is not listed in either version of the Protocol of the Confraternity of the Dead.

settings that sometimes sparked large-scale witch-hunts. Such outbreaks were common, as historian Wolfgang Behringer has observed, in "institutions where children, 'fools' and old people were concentrated: orphanages, educational institutions of all kinds."[72] One notorious example is the mass hunt within the city hospital of Würzburg between 1627 and 1629, resulting in the execution of 160 people, including 41 children.[73] In the early seventeenth century a spate of such cases erupted in Jesuit schools and orphanages in south Germany. Perhaps a similar dynamic was at work in the outbreak of suicidal iconoclasm in Vienna's house of correction.[74] The difference, of course, is that in contrast to earlier cases of witchcraft these physical acts of blasphemy were not occult crimes. Vienna's suicidal iconoclasts acted publicly. The *corpus delicti*, demolished crucifixes or desecrated hosts, was readily at hand.

The rash of cases in 1712 prompted the Lower Austrian government to order the Vienna city government to investigate and report on the conditions in the prison-workhouse. Written on October 8, 1712, ten days after the double execution of Susanna Grallin and Maria Magdalena Zechirlin, the directive noted that most blasphemers who had been executed for this "horrific crime," as well as offenders currently being tried, testified that they had committed blasphemy in order to escape the unbearable conditions in the prison. The mission of the house of correction was not only to incarcerate criminals but also to punish them, the directive noted. However, prisoners should not have to languish in hunger and misery to the point that they fell into despair and tried to hasten their deaths by committing such horrific crimes. The city government was instructed to ensure that prison personnel did not whip inmates beyond measure or without proper authorization. Something should be done to clear out the "almost unbearable stench," and prisoners should be fed enough "to sustain life."[75]

---

[72] Wolfgang Behringer, *Witchcraft Persecutions in Bavaria: Popular Magic, Religious Zealotry and Reason of State in Early Modern Europe* (Cambridge: Cambridge University Press, 1997), 167.

[73] Lyndal Roper, *Witch Craze: Terror and Fantasy in Baroque Germany* (New Haven: Yale University Press, 2004), 25.

[74] Behringer, *Witchcraft Persecutions*, 167–168.

[75] "...sovill nahrung, als zu erhaltung des lebens nöthig." WStLA, Alte Registratur, 1.2.1.A1—Zusammengelegte Akten/1700–1759 92 ex 1712, A 1–18. 7. 8ber [October] 1712.

These measures did not suffice to prevent further cases of suicidal iconoclasm. Between February and August 1713 two further prison inmates, Maria Magdalena N., eighteen,[76] and Stefan Maurer, sixteen,[77] broke crucifixes and suffered the same penalty—amputation of the hand, beheading, affixing the hand at the ravenstone—as had their fellow image-breakers the year before.[78] One more case occurred beyond the prison walls. On May 30 Anna Maria Elisabetha Werthaim received thirty lashes and was banished from Austria in perpetuity for host desecration. She had previously been in prison for prostitution and pickpocketing. Perhaps she learned about the practice of suicidal blasphemy there. Now free, she went to church and took Holy Communion without prior confession, that is, she took communion in an unworthy state. She then took the host out her mouth and hid it in a handkerchief, but "she did not lay a violent hand upon The Most Holy Host." Did she lose her nerve? She turned herself in at the courthouse, presumably presenting the soggy host as evidence of her crime.[79]

The government responded to these ongoing cases with legislation that increased penalties for blasphemy. This was a fairly typical response by

---

[76] Maria Magdalena N., executed 8 February 1713. *WD*, Nr. 994. It is not clear whether this is the same woman as the one listed in the Protocol of the Confraternity of the Dead, Barbara Weiglin, executed on the same day. ÖNB, Cod 8363, p. 7, Nr. 49, 8 February 1713. Under executions in 1713, the *Stadtprotokoll* excerpted by Schlager lists the crucifix-breaker Barbara Weidlerin, eighteen, without specifying the date of her execution. Schlager, *Wiener Skizzen*, 130.

[77] Stefan Maurer, 9 August 1713. *WD*, Nr. 1046. The *Wiennerisches Diarium* identifies him as Stafan N., 17. The Protocol of the Confraternity of the Dead lists his execution under 8 August 1713, identifying him as Stefan Maurer. ÖNB, Cod 8363, p. 7, Nr. 51, 8 August 1713. The *Stadtprotokoll* excerpted by Schlager identifies him as Stefan Maurer, 16. Schlager, *Wiener Skizzen*, 130. This case is also discussed in Johann Baptist Suttinger, *Additiones Consuetitudinem Austriacarum Renovatae* (Nuremberg: Martin Endter, 1718), 9–13, where he is identified as Stefan Maurer, 16.

[78] The first was Maria Magdalena N., executed on February 8, 1713. *WD*, Nr. 994. It is not clear whether this is the same woman as the one listed in the Protocol of the Confraternity of the Dead, Barbara Weiglin, executed on the same day. ÖNB, Cod 8363, p. 7, Nr. 49, 8 February 1713. Under executions in 1713 the *Stadtprotokoll* excerpted by Schlager lists the crucifix-breaker Barbara Weidlerin, eighteen, without specifying the date of her execution. Schlager, *Wiener Skizzen*, 130.

[79] "jedoch an der Hoch-Heiligen Hosty kein gewaltthätige Hand angeleget." Anna Maria Elizabetha [Werthaim], 30 May 1713. The *Wiennerisches Diarium* identifies her as Anna Maria Elisabetha N. *WD*, Nr. 1025. The *Stadtprotokoll* excerpted by Schlager identifies her as M. Anna Werhaim. Schlager, *Wiener Skizzen*, 130.

early modern governments. If authorities perceived that a certain offense was becoming more frequent, this meant that current penalties did not provide sufficient deterrence. The answer was to punish these crimes more harshly. The same dynamic played out in Hamburg, as we have seen, as authorities struggled to suppress suicidal child murders there. Indeed, the government of Lower Austria had responded in the same way to the growing number of child murders associated with suicide by proxy. An edict of 1706 ordered that such murderers should have their hands amputated prior to beheading, and their hand should be attached to the scaffold, as opposed to simple beheading.[80]

An imperial edict, dated July 28, 1713, imposed new harsher penalties for suicidal iconoclasts:

> We Charles VI etc.... have learned with the greatest displeasure how the horrific sin of blasphemy, or *Blasphemiae realis in Deum* [physical blasphemy against God], mostly by dishonoring, breaking or demolishing the holy images of our crucified Savior, has become all too common, and is becoming especially rampant in our capital city of Vienna. This horrible crime, as the many criminal trials of such offenders demonstrate, is mostly committed by young people who became accustomed to crime during childhood. After being repeatedly punished for their shameful life of sin by the courts, they form the ... sinful intent to be freed of their life by a single blow of the sword. We intend to punish this direct assault on the Highest Divine Majesty, and sacrilege against GOd, the hallowed body of our Savior, the dear saints, the holy cross, and other sacred images with the greatest severity, and thus avenge the violated honor of God.

Therefore, blasphemers would suffer extra punishment in addition to the penalty set in the *Ferdinandea* of beheading after amputation of the hand and its post-mortem display. Henceforth such offenders would be publicly whipped for three days prior to their execution. It was left to the judge's discretion whether to increase or reduce the punishment according to the particular circumstances of the case, although in this horrific sin of blasphemy judges should tend toward severity rather than leniency, "so that this great crime does not go unpunished, and the just wrath of God, which, alas!, we are currently experiencing, does not continue to afflict the

---

[80] "Wie es mit Bestrafung des Kinder-Mords zu halten," 22 March 1706, *Codicis Austriaci* III, 511–512.

land and people."⁸¹ Vagrant children and youths roaming cities and countryside were to be handed over to local authorities in their place of birth who would be responsible for their upkeep and instruction until they were old enough to work. Otherwise, they would fall into bad company and become mired in sin and vice.

The current manifestation of the wrath of God that the edict referred to was a plague epidemic then raging in Vienna. The great plague of 1679 was still a living memory when this new contagion approached Vienna from the east. A plague epidemic started in Hungary in 1709, peaked in 1712, and spread to Vienna by December. The contagion peaked in Vienna in July through December 1713. By the time the epidemic ended in February 1714, around 8000 people in the city had died.⁸² In addition to imposing travel restrictions and hygiene regulations, the authorities also organized collective religious exercises to combat the plague. The Paulist monk Matthias Fuhrmann described these religious countermeasures in his chronicle of Vienna. The government proclaimed general days of penance and fasting, and as a daily exercise and general call to prayer, church bells rang for fifteen minutes each morning and evening, and "everyone, without distinction, within houses as on the public streets, fell to their knees. United in prayer, they fervently called upon the Almighty God to mercifully avert the scourge he had imposed."⁸³ As the plague continued, Charles VI followed the example of his father Leopold I, who had vowed to construct the Trinity Column during the plague of 1679. On October 22, 1713, Charles VI headed a penitential procession that included the assembled citizenry, clergy, and imperial court. The miracle-working image of Maria Pötsch as well relics of St. Charles Boromeo were carried from the court church of the Augustinian Eremites to St. Stephen's Cathedral. At St. Stephen's, Charles knelt before the High Altar and publicly made the solemn vow to build a church dedicated to St. Charles once the plague ended.⁸⁴

---

⁸¹ Sebastian G. Herrenleben, ed., *Sammlung Oesterreichischer Gesetze, und Ordnungem: Wie solche von Zeit zu Zeit ergangen und publiciret worden …/[3]: … So viele deren über die in Parte I & II Codicis Avstriaci eingedruckten bis auf das Jahr 1720. weiter aufzubringen waren* (Leipzig: Zacharias Heinrich Eisfeld, 1748), 714–715.

⁸² Karl Vocelka, *Glanz und Untergang der Höfischen Welt. Repräsentation, Reform und Reaktion im Habsburgischen Vielvölkerstaat* (Vienna: Ueberreuter, 2001), 324.

⁸³ Fuhrmann, *Alt- und neues Wien*, vol. 2, 1330.

⁸⁴ Fuhrmann, *Alt- und neues Wien*, vol. 2, 1338–1339. In fulfillment of this vow, St. Charles Church was constructed between 1716 and 1737.

In this atmosphere of general crisis and heightened religious anxiety, the suppression of blasphemous image-breaking in Vienna's house of correction undoubtedly took on added urgency. Twelve days after the promulgation of the edict that increased penalties for blasphemy, the next execution of a suicidal iconoclast took place. Stefan Maurer, a sixteen-year-old beggar and pickpocket from Ofen in Hungary who demolished a crucifix in the house of correction, was executed on August 9, 1713.[85] Maurer had been orphaned "in his earliest childhood," but this fact apparently did not prompt imperial "tender-heartedness" in Charles VI when he was briefed about the case. Charles personally confirmed Maurer's sentence.[86] Because Maurer committed his crime before the new harsher penalties were decreed, he suffered the old penalty, that is, severing of his hand, beheading, and display of this hand on the ravenstone. He was spared the three days of public whippings that the 1713 edict imposed. Authorities used the occasion of his execution to publicize the new increased penalties, however. The court scribe read the edict aloud from the courthouse balcony after announcing Maurer's sentence to the crowd gathered in the square below. Confessors and clergy were instructed to announce the new penalties in their sermons, especially in sermons following public executions. Preachers were instructed to exhort the crowds attending executions to imagine: "how great a sin it is, in and of itself, when someone tries to shorten their own life. The sin is even greater if someone tries to achieve that end by knowingly and intentionally committing a capital crime. But when this crime is committed against GOd, the holy body of our Savior, the dear saints, the holy cross or other sacred images ... the crime and sin is increased incomprehensibly."[87]

This publicity offensive and the new harsher penalties still did not deter suicidal iconoclasts. In a worrisome development for the authorities, cases continued to spread beyond the house of correction. Three weeks after Stefan Maurer's execution, a fifteen-year-old girl who attacked a crucifix in a homeless shelter was executed on August 31 according to the old procedure, presumably because she committed the crime before the new

---

[85] See footnote 77 above.

[86] "/und haben Ihre Kayserl. Majest. über den deroselben gehorsamst beschehenen Vortrag resolviert/das/soviel die von dem Stefan Maurer beschehene Verunehrung des Crucifix, and dardurch begangene Gottslästerung betrifft/ die ihme Maurer geschöpfte Urthel mit Abschlagung Kopf- und Hand/ auch Aufsteckung der hand an einer Stangen vollzogenen werden solle." Suttinger, *Additiones*, 9.

[87] Suttinger, *Additiones*, 10.

penalties were announced.[88] The first suicidal iconoclast to suffer the new increased punishment was the nineteen-year-old Magdalena N., who broke and bit a crucifix. The newspaper report on her execution simply describes her as an unmarried woman rather than a prison inmate, so this was likely another case within the city at large. For three days prior to her execution she was chained to a column on a public platform for an hour with the whip hanging around her neck with which she was subsequently flogged. Then, on October 20, two days before Charles VI processed with the weeping mother of Maria Pötsch to St. Stephen's Cathedral to implore God to end the plague, Magdalena was beheaded after amputation of her hand. Three more suicidal iconoclasts were executed in the same manner in 1714: a twenty-six-year-old local married woman, apparently not an inmate, was executed on March 2 for committing "a blasphemous deed against a crucifix"[89]; on March 24 a twenty-year-old woman from Swabia who broke a crucifix and threw it on the floor in a homeless shelter was executed[90]; a nineteen-year-old woman from Vienna was executed on August 8. Not an inmate, she attacked a crucifix and appeared at the courthouse, broken crucifix in hand, demanding her punishment. Held in the house of correction during her trial, she apparently felt that her execution was too long in coming, so she attacked another crucifix in the prison to expedite her case.[91]

On March 20, 1715, the criminal court requested a medical evaluation of Maria Sabina Paumbgartnerin, a pensioner in the city hospital, who had committed physical blasphemy and believed herself to be possessed by a demon. University medical doctors examined her and concluded that "her fixed impression that she was possessed by the Evil Spirit" was a symptom of a "strong melancholy delirium" that afflicted her. They recommended that she be held in a quiet place where she was not vexed by other people and given proper medical care.[92] Three more suicidal iconoclasts were

---

[88] Theresia N. *WD*, Nr. 1052, 31 August 1713

[89] "an einer Crucifix-Bildnus ein Gottslästerliche That verübet." Anna Maria [Baumgartnerin], 26. *WD*, 1104. 2 March 1714. ÖNB, Cod 8363, p. 7, Nr. 53, 2 March 1714.

[90] Maria Johanna [Weberin], *WD*, Nr. 1111, 24 March 1714. ÖNB, Cod 8363, p. 7, Nr. 54, 24 March 1714, Johanna Maria Weberin. The *Stadtprotokoll* excerpted by Schlager identifies her as Maria Weberin from Swabia. Schlager, *Wiener Skizzen*, 130.

[91] Maria Anna Justina [Ziereiter], WD, Nr. 1150, 8 August 1714. Schlager, *Wiener Skizzen*, 130.

[92] UAW, AFMV VIII, fol. 345r–345v.

criminally prosecuted, suffering exacerbated executions between March and June 1715. They committed blasphemies both within the house of correction and in the city at large. Their acts were becoming more brazen and violent. A seventeen-year-old boy in the workhouse bit the crucifix and then placed it on the floor and demolished it with a stick, while at the same time committing "horrific blasphemies with words."[93] A twenty-two-year-old woman broke a crucifix into several pieces in a Viennese suburb.[94] A fifteen-year-old boy smashed one crucifix with a stone and cut up a second one with a knife, all the while verbally blaspheming God.[95]

A THEOLOGICAL-JUDICIAL LOOPHOLE ALLOWS A CHANGE IN GOVERNMENT TACTICS

By early August 1715, the authorities reached the conclusion that their efforts to quash suicidal iconoclasm by increasing the severity of executions had failed. On the basis of expert opinions, presumably from the law and theological faculties of the University of Vienna, they devised a new policy, outlined in an imperial resolution of August 6, 1715. This resolution was then published as an imperial patent within Austria on August 30, 1715.[96] People who committed blasphemy "out of faint-heartedness, melancholy, and weariness with life, *without the intent to directly blaspheme or insult God*," would now no longer be executed.[97] The question of intent was crucial. It provided authorities with the legal and theological justification to deviate from the Decalogue and not impose the death penalty in these cases. The blasphemous act was merely a means to an end and thus

---

[93] Andre N., *WD*, Nr 1216, 27 March 1715. The Protocol of the Confraternity of the Dead gives his age as 16. ÖNB, Cod 8363, pp. 7–8, Nr 58, 27 March 1715. He is identified as Andreas Mühlbacher, 17, in the *Stadtprotokoll* excerpted by Schlager, *Wiener Skizzen*, 131.

[94] Maria N. *WD*, Nr. 1218, 3 April 1715. The *Totenbruderschaftsbuch* identifies her as Maria Anna Wälnerin. ÖNB, Cod 8363, p. 8, Nr. 59, 3 April 1715. Annotations at the end of the protocol (unpaginated) indicate that her body was delivered for anatomical dissection. The *Stadtprotokoll* identifies her as Maria Waller. Schlager, *Wiener Skizzen*, 132.

[95] It is not clear whether he was an inmate or not. Adam N., *WD*, Nr. 1239, 18 June 1715. The *Stadtprotokoll* identifies him as Adam Hirschbeck, 15. Schlager, *Wiener Skizzen*, 131.

[96] The imperial patent of August 30, 1715, cites the Imperial Resolution of August 6, 1715. Herrenleben, *Sammlung Oesterreichischer Gesetze*, vol. 3, 801. The difference between the Imperial Resolution and Imperial Patent was that a Resolution might be limited to local decisions, whereas an Imperial Patent was widely publicized and distributed within Austria.

[97] "absque animo Deum directe blasphemandi aut iniurandi." Emphasis mine. 30 August 1715, Herrenleben, ed., *Sammlung Oesterreichischer Gesetze*, vol. 3, 801.

incidental to the true purpose of the crime. Suicidal blasphemers therefore lacked *dolus*, the malice and willful intent to blaspheme that was an essential component of criminal guilt,[98] so it became possible to justify penalties short of death.

The decree directed courts to take the blasphemers' age and mindset into account. Perpetrators under sixteen who committed the deed without special malice, but rather "out of faint-heartedness, melancholy, and weariness with life," would be imprisoned at the prison-workhouse, held in chains, and subjected to a series of public whippings depending on their age and status until improvement was observed. Then they would be released, without subsequent banishment from Austrian lands. A more severe penalty applied to a blasphemer over sixteen, or to a younger offender who exhibited particular malice, and had sufficient reason to be fully cognizant of the evil nature of the act: "Such a criminal, male or female, should not be condemned to death, as he (*sic*) wishes and demands, even though he would fully deserve it, specifically so he does not achieve the goal of his early death, and so that others like him are deterred."[99] After performing "a public expiation of their crime,"[100] such offenders would be imprisoned for three to five years in the prison-workhouse. They would be subjected to periodic whippings on a public stage. The nature of their offense would be announced to the viewing public to provide the necessary deterrence to "similar ill-intentioned people." After completing their sentence and swearing an oath of *Urfehde*, such offenders would be banished from Austria for life.

The edict also addressed the possibility of recidivist blasphemy, as had already occurred on a number of occasions. Offenders who returned to Austria without committing any other crime would be punished for breach of *Urfehde* with a whipping of thirty lashes ("a full Schilling") and renewed banishment from Austria. If, however, they returned to Austria "and, against hope, repeated the horrific sin of blasphemy by breaking or

---

[98] Legal commentaries use the Latin *dolus* and the German *Vorsatz* or *vorsätzlich* interchangeably. E. Kaufmann, "Vorsatz," *HRG*, V (Berlin: Erich Schmidt Verlag, 1998), 1061–1066.

[99] "ein dergleichen Ubelthäter, mann oder weiblichen Geschlechts, solle zu dem Tod, welchen er wünschet...nicht verurtheilet." The use of the male pronoun results from the noun der *Übelthäter*, a masculine noun. Herrenleben, *Sammlung Oesterreichischer Gesetze*, vol. 3, 802.

[100] "...praevia publica expiation sceleris...", Herrenleben, *Sammlung Oesterreichischer Gesetze*, vol. 3, 801–802.

dishonoring the crucifix or other sacred images, out of weariness with life," they would still not get the death penalty that they so amply deserved. After performing a public expiation, men would receive a whipping of thirty lashes on the ravenstone and then be sentenced for life to row in the galleys. Women, after performing the same expiation and receiving the same whipping, would be sentenced to labor in chains in the prison-workhouse for life and be subjected to periodic public whippings. The expiation such offenders were required to perform would take place on the ravenstone where the whipping would be administered. Offenders would kneel on a platform erected next to a crucifix statue adjacent to the ravenstone. Here they would publicly proclaim their penitence, beg God for forgiveness, and ask the crowd of spectators to forgive their outrageous act. They would publicly declare that they deserved death for their sinful deed, but that they would suffer a slow punishment instead, to which they willingly submitted (Image 6.6).[101]

The decree also ordered preventative measures. Inmates should be provided with sufficient food and with religious instruction and spiritual comfort. Prison guards should carefully supervise despondent people and deprive them of any opportunity to attack sacred images or to kill themselves or another person. Commenting on the youth of many such perpetrators, the decree noted that several offenders were "abandoned young people" who committed blasphemy after being placed in the house of correction for begging, vagrancy, sexual immorality, or minor thefts. To forestall such blasphemy the government ordered better education, with special emphasis on catechism instruction, as well as the establishment of hospitals and manufacturers in the countryside to provide young beggars with work and a means of subsistence. The decree concluded by exhorting local authorities to tend toward severity rather than leniency in punishing the horrific sin of blasphemy.

This measure, too, failed to quash further acts of suicidal iconoclasm. First, in a telling example of the distance that often separated aspiration from implementation in absolutist public policy, it proved remarkably difficult to ensure that suicidal inmates actually received pastoral care. Inculcating correct religious belief in inmates was a crucial element of the government's disciplining agenda, as we have seen. The Franciscans were responsible for religious instruction in the house of correction until 1726, when the Jesuits took over this duty. Despite repeated government

[101] Herrenleben, *Sammlung Oesterreichischer Gesetze*, vol. 3, 802.

Image 6.6 The ravenstone outside the Scottish Gate, c. 1760. Anonymous Pen and Ink Drawing. The ALBERTINA Museum, Inv. 7377, Ansichten (Vues) Wien, äussere Bezirke 2: Das Hochgericht gegen die Rossau hin

directives to comfort and catechize suicidal inmates, the Franciscans showed little zeal in ministering to prisoners. Indeed, it was difficult to get them even to show up. A government decree of October 1716 issued a stern reprimand: Not only had the friars failed to catechize the prisoners, contrary to previous government orders, they had not even bothered to visit them at all. Now the government threatened financial penalties to force the mendicants to perform their pastoral duties. The Franciscans would provide catechism lessons to prison inmates at set times in the presence of a prison official. The friars would have to provide written verification that catechism lessons had really taken place or they would lose their customary tax exemption on wine. Here the government used the same bureaucratic technique to enforce obedience from recalcitrant clergy that they normally used on their subjects to make them comply with the requirement of annual confession. As shown in Chap. 5, lay people had to present "confession receipts" to local authorities. Ironically, it was often mendicants, Franciscans in particular, who filled out such confession receipts.[102]

It was also not easy to keep religious icons out of the hands of suicidal inmates, as the case of Joseph Zeitler, a sixteen-year-old burglar who attacked a crucifix in the house of correction sometime in the spring of 1715, illustrates. In February 1715, Zeitler, then fifteen, son of a Viennese shoemaker, committed a major burglary in a tavern, stealing 2000 Florin and some jewels from a guest's room. Arrested *in flagranti*, he was held in chains in the house of correction during his trial. He was sentenced to deportation to Naples to row in the galleys, a punishment often imposed in lieu of the death penalty. Upon learning his sentence, Zeitler purchased a small brass crucifix from an elderly fellow inmate. Personal possessions of inmates were confiscated when they arrived at the house of correction, but apparently prisoners were allowed to keep devotional objects. Or possibly the crucifix was circulating as contraband? In any case, at some point in the spring of 1715 Zeitler got his hands on the crucifix and demolished it with a brick. He did this, he testified, "so that another sentence would be pronounced against him. He would rather die, than be sent to the galleys." But Zeitler was not sentenced to death. He received a new sentence of three years in the house of corrections with periodic public whippings.[103]

During Joseph Zeitler's imprisonment in the house of correction at least two other suicidal blasphemers were also in custody, the fifteen-year-old Rosina Plankhin and the somewhat "older" Johanna Frankenhauserin. By August 1715, Plankhin had broken a crucifix twice. For this, she was sentenced to five years in the house of correction, where she would be

---

[102] WStLA, Zusammengelegte Akten, 1700–1759, 106/1715, decree of 17. October 1716.

[103] StiftAL, Criminalia 377, 1719 Joseph Zeitler, Gütiges Examen September 15, 1719. Zeitler testified to the physical blasphemy he committed in Vienna when he was tried for church robbery by the district court of the Upper Austrian Benedictine monastery of Lambach in 1719. The circumstances of Zeitler's 1715 burglary are described in a letter from Vienna's city court to the court in Lambach, 20. September 1719. More on Zeitler's second criminal trial for church robbery below. On the sentence of deportation to Naples to row in the galleys, see Friedrich Maschek von Maasburg, *Die Galeerenstrafe in den deutschen und böhmischen Erbländern Oesterreichs: ein Beitrag zur Geschichte der heimischen Strafrechtspflege* (Vienna: Manzsche k. k. Hof-Verlags- und Universitätsbuchhandlung, 1885).

held in chains at moderate labor. She would be whipped three times a year on a public stage, bearing a placard detailing the nature of her offense.[104] Frankenhauserin, a local shoemaker's daughter and apparently a first-time crucifix-breaker, committed her blasphemous deed sometime before mid-July 1715, because the university medical faculty submitted a report on her case to the criminal court on August 22, 1715. Physicians had previously examined her at the courthouse in the presence of the city judge. Her temperament and physical condition, notably that she had suffered numerous diseases including the plague, indicated that she was afflicted by a severe hypochondriacal disease. She did not break the crucifix out of malice, the doctors determined, "but out of fearfulness due to continuous misery and the most extreme deprivation."[105]

Authorities completely disregarded this medical finding. Frankenhauserin's interrogations showed that she was of sound mind and fully cognizant of the evil nature of her deed, the court found. On August 13, 1715, she was sentenced to three years' labor in the house of corrections with periodic public whippings. Subsequently, she would be banished from Austria for life after swearing an *Urfehde*.[106] Meanwhile other suicidal blasphemers were still being executed, albeit with different legal justification. In December 1715, the seventeen-year-old Andre Frisch was beheaded after prior amputation of his tongue. He had previously been whipped and banished from Austria three times, which means that by returning to Austria he had perjured himself three times, which was punished by death. When he was arrested he committed "shameful and outrageous blasphemous deeds" and also uttered verbal blasphemies during his trial.[107]

---

[104] The imperial decree that mentions these two prisoners does not give their exact ages and simply describes Plankhin as "younger" and "Frankenhauserin as "older." WStLA, 1.5.1.B6-3 Decretenbuch 1712–1713, fol. 289, 13 August 1715. Plankhin's age is given in a newspaper report of the same date. *WD*, Nr. 1305, 13. August 1715.

[105] "das Selbe... mit einer starkhen malo hypochondriaco behafftet seye, mithin sie die Zerbrechung des Crucifix nicht ex malitia, sondern ex pusillanimitate wegen kontinuierlichen Miserien und äussersten Elend vorgenommen habe." UAW, Med. 1.8., AFMV VIII, fo. 352r–352v. That Frankenhauserin was the daughter of a Viennese shoemaker is mentioned in a later criminal trial of her fellow inmate Joseph Zeitler. StiftAL, Criminalia 377, Joseph Zeitler, 1719.

[106] WStLA, 1.5.1. B6-3 Decretenbuch 1712–1713, fo. 289, 13 August 1715.

[107] Andre N., 16. *WD*, Nr. 1291, 13 December 1715. ÖNB, Cod 8363, p. 8, Nr. 60, 13 December 1715, Andre Frisch.

A few weeks later Rosina Plankhin, serving her sentence in the house of correction, attacked a crucifix a third time. An imperial decree of January 4, 1716, reprimanded the Vienna city government for not properly supervising such despondent prisoners, and Rosina Plankhin in particular.[108] Sentenced at some point in February 1716 to a renewed five years in the house of correction, she was taken to a statue of the *Pieta* beyond the city walls near the ravenstone, where she again performed a public expiation, though she was not whipped. From there she was taken back to the prison-workhouse to serve out her sentence. On April 27, 1716, in celebration of the birth of a male heir two weeks earlier—the short-lived Archduke Leopold Johann, last in the male line of the Habsburg dynasty—Emperor Charles VI granted partial amnesty to five suicidal blasphemers, four women and one man, currently imprisoned in the house of correction. Among them, Joseph Zeitler and Johanna Frankenhauserin had their sentences shortened by a year. Rosina Plankhin who had been sentenced to five years just two months earlier for recidivism (*ob relapsum criminis*) had her sentence reduced by two years.[109]

A sixth woman, Polixena Helmin, "who broke a crucifix" in 1714, had already been diagnosed by the university medical faculty as melancholic in April of that year.[110] Over two years later, in May 1716, the government determined that she was suffering from hypochondriacal melancholy and therefore not criminally liable. Since her longstanding melancholy made her incapable of supporting herself, she was transferred to a city hospital "where those kind of people are cared for ... to prevent further harm."[111]

Among the imprisoned crucifix-breakers, Rosina Plankhin remained defiant. If the authorities had hoped that her reduction in sentence would

---

[108] WStLA, 1.2.1. A1, Zusammengelegte Akten/ 1700–1759, 15/1716, 4 January 1716.

[109] Plankhin was still fifteen years old in February 1716. The *Stadtprotokoll*, giving only the year 1716, recorded: "Die Rosina Blankin, 15 Jahr alt, ... vor das Schottenthor zu der Station der Schmerzhaften Mutter Gottes geführt umb allda Rey und Leyd ihrer begangenen Myssethat zu bekennen, hernach aber in das Zuchthaus gebracht." Schlager, *Wiener Skizzen*, 132. The decree granting imperial amnesty refers to Plankhin's most recent sentencing two months earlier. Decree of 27 April 1716. WStLA, Zusammengelegte Akten, 1700–1759, 64/1716. The imprisoned suicidal iconoclasts were Eleonora Knollin, Polixana Helmin, Maria Anna Frankenhauserin, Eva Sabina Kraurassin, Rosina Plankhin (her second offense), and Joseph Martin Zeitler. The crown prince, Archduke Leopold Johann, lived less than seven months (April 13, 1716-November 4, 1716). http://www.kaisergruft.at/kaisergruft/leojohann.htm.

[110] UAW, Med. 1.8, AFMV VIII, fo. 327r, 12. April 1714.

[111] WStLA, 1.5.1. B6-3, Decretenbuch 1712–1716, fo. 331r–331v, 5 May 1716.

elicit compliance, they were disappointed. Instead of patiently submitting to her punishment, she escaped from the prison-workhouse. Quickly recaptured, she bitterly complained that she had been forbidden to attend Mass. An imperial decree of August 22, 1716, again chastised the Vienna city government for insufficient supervision and for not providing spiritual comfort to despondent workhouse inmates, again singling out Rosina Plankhin in particular.[112] But the prison staff was simply not up to the task of keeping Plankhin from attacking the crucifix. In October 1716 she was on trial for breaking the crucifix again. Now she threatened to desecrate the host as well. An imperial decree of October 17, 1716, announced Plankhin's new sentence. She would certainly have deserved the penalty prescribed in the imperial edict of 1715, that is, after thirty lashes at the ravenstone after public expiation, life sentence in chains in the house of corrections, and public whippings three times a year. However, because she was afflicted with a severe despondency, her sentence had to take into account her depression as well as her malice. Therefore, she would be treated with compassion to prevent greater harm. Accordingly, she would be whipped on a platform in front of the house of corrections instead of on the ravenstone. This change of venue spared her the formal legal infamy that a public whipping at the ravenstone would have conferred. She would be held in the workhouse in chains and given appropriate work, until further notice. Meanwhile, staff should comfort her, assuring her that if she showed sufficient penitence and good behavior she might yet receive clemency. Before and after her whipping and during her imprisonment clergy should minister to her and explain the gravity of her sin and make her understand that she would have deserved a far harsher penalty. The decree exhorted the city government to ensure that she did not find any further opportunity to commit other crimes. Until her "conversion," crucifixes and saints' images should be kept out of her reach. The word "conversion" in this context meant a spiritual renewal the authorities hoped to effect in her by intensive religious instruction.[113] Since Plankhin had threatened to desecrate the host, she should not be admitted to Holy

[112] WStLA, 1.2.1. A1, Zusammengelegte Akten/ 1700–1759, 101/1716, 22 August 1716.
[113] David Luebke, "Introduction. The Politics of Conversion in Early Modern Germany," in *Conversion and the Politics of Conversion in Early Modern Germany*, eds. David M. Luebke, Jared Poley, Daniel C. Ryan, and David Warren Sabean (New York: Berghahn Books, 2012), 2. On the varying meanings of the word "Bekehrung" in early modern German usage, see Luebke's introduction, and the entire volume.

Communion until the clergy determined that she no longer posed a threat.[114]

Clearly the government was experimenting with a carrot-and-stick approach. Other suicidal iconoclasts held in the house of corrections were warned that they would suffer additional whippings and longer sentences "if they repeat this horrific sin." If they demonstrated true penitence and moral improvement, however, they would be treated with "mercy and mildness."[115] This new mercy offensive was put into practice when Joseph Zeitler petitioned the government to be spared his scheduled public whipping in October 1716. Zeitler's prison sentence had already been shortened during the imperial group amnesty granted to celebrate the birth of a male heir the previous April. Now the government remitted Zeitler's upcoming whipping as a reward for good behavior and promised "if he shows further penitence and improvement of his life by consistent good behavior, he might receive further mercy in the future."[116]

The government continued to fine-tune its response to suicidal iconoclasm. On October 25, 1716, five days after the government had announced Rosina Plankhin's new sentence, Anna Margaretha N., a twenty-six-year-old woman from Moravia and former prison inmate, was beheaded. She had previously been sentenced to the house of correction three times for prostitution. During her imprisonment she "taught another woman inmate how to commit a blasphemous deed with a crucifix." That one workhouse inmate "taught" another how to commit suicidal iconoclasm shows to what extent this practice had become endemic within an entrenched prison culture. It is a further example of female inmates conspiring to commit suicide by proxy, as also happened in the Hamburg house of correction. For this complicity Anna Margaretha N. was banished from Austria for life after swearing an *Urfehde*. She "perjuriously" returned to Austria twice. Each time she was whipped with thirty lashes and banished again after repeating the oath of *Urfehde*. When she returned

---

[114] WStLA, 1.2.2. A1—Zusammengelegte Akten, 1700–1759, 106/1715, decree of 17 October 1716.

[115] WStLA, 1.2.2. A1—Zusammengelegte Akten, 1700–1759, 106/1715, decree of 17 October 1716.

[116] WStLA, 1.5.1. B6-3, Decretenbuch 1712–1716, fo. 347r, 20 October 1716. The previous April, Zeitler's prison sentence had already been shortened during the imperial group amnesty granted in celebration of the birth of a male heir. The remaining three and half years that remained of his original were shortened by one year. Decretenbuch, fo. 330r–330v, 27 April 1716.

a third time she was sentenced to death. Again, it was her repeated perjuries associated with her breach of *Urfehde*, not suicidal iconoclasm, that provided legal justification of her death sentence.[117]

The government held out the promise of mercy for some suicidal blasphemers, but they punished others harshly. In March 1718 Regina N., eighteen, who had attacked a crucifix twice in the house of correction, was taken to the crucifix statue near the ravenstone, where she demonstrated her "heartfelt penitence." Then she was handed over to the executioner who administered a whipping of thirty lashes on the ravenstone, whereupon she was returned to the Prison-workhouse where she would serve out a life sentence in chains, and be whipped every four months on a public stage displaying a placard describing her crime.[118] A contemporary legal commentator praised Charles VI, who demonstrated with this sentence that he was ever "a great zealot for the honor of God, and a severe punisher of blasphemers."[119] In November 1718 the Protocol of the Confraternity of the Dead recorded the execution of Anna Maria Nitzlin, who "broke the crucifix." She was beheaded after amputation of her hand.[120] In the same year Polixena Helmin, the melancholy crucifix-breaker, whom the court had placed in the city hospital to be cared for in 1716, committed another blasphemous deed, but again she was spared criminal prosecution and remained at the hospital.[121] In April 1719 five men, whose ages ranged from nineteen to fifty, were deported to Naples to row in the galleys for a combination of thefts, "blasphemous deeds," and broken oaths of *Urfehde*.[122] On June 11, 1720, the Protocol of the Confraternity of the Dead recorded the execution of another suicidal

---

[117] "sie ein andere in dem Zuchthaus inhaftierte Weibs-Person zu der an einer Crucifix-Bildnus verübt-Gotteslästerlichen That angelernet." *WD*, 25 October 1716.

[118] Regina N., *WD*, Nr. 1530, 31 March 1718.

[119] "Ihro Kayserl. Jetzt glorwürdigst-regierende Majestät Carolus Sextus seynd ein grosser Eiferer der Ehr Gottes/ und strenger Bestraffer der Gottes-Lästerer." Johann Valentin Kirchgeßner, *Tribunal Nemesis iuste iudicantis. Oder: Richter-Stuhl der recht richtenden Gerechtigkeit* (Nuremberg: Johann Christoph Lochner, 1720), 358.

[120] ÖNB, Cod 8363, unpaginated annotations at end of volume, "pertinent ad Fol. 9."

[121] UAW, Med. 1.8, AFMV VIII, fo. 476r–476v, 24. Sept 1725. This entry from 1725 refers to her earlier examinations "ex capite blasphemia realis" in 1714 and 1718.

[122] *WD*, Nr. 1640, 19 April 1719. The report does not identify them by name but simply describes them as criminals (*Missethäter*).

blasphemer. A woman was beheaded after amputation of her hand, "because she blasphemed God and bit through a Crucifix."[123]

Why were Anna Maria Nitzlin and the unnamed woman who bit through the crucifix executed in 1718 and 1720 respectively? Was there some combination of offenses that legally justified their executions? Or was the imperial decree of 1715 being inconsistently applied? Or did they manage to convince authorities that in their hearts they fully and knowingly intended to blaspheme God? Then the blasphemy would not simply have been a means to an end but rather the true purpose of the crime, in which case the legal and theological rationale for the 1715 edict that justified not executing suicidal blasphemers would not apply. Did the women lie in order to compel authorities to execute them? If so, this would have been a risky strategy. The whole point of suicide by proxy, after all, was to ensure and expedite salvation by dying in a state of grace, cleansed of sin. If suicidal iconoclasts misled authorities about their true motives, if they achieved their death sentence under false pretenses, they would compromise their true penitence, putting their very salvation at risk. But then, perhaps the circumstances of their lives caused these women to feel such despair and rage that it had been their willful, knowing intent to blaspheme. Then they could still repent, after all, and achieve salvation.

Whatever the legal justification for their death sentences, these two women were among the last people to be executed for suicidal blasphemy. After 1720 the number of reported cases of suicidal iconoclasm declined significantly, perhaps because the message was slowly getting through that suicidal people would not succeed in precipitating their executions by breaking icons. A report in the *Wiennerisches Diarium* emphasized this point. On March 13, 1722, Johann N., a twenty-one-year-old man who broke a crucifix twice and also blasphemed verbally, performed a public expiation prior to being whipped on the ravenstone and transported back to the prison-workhouse where he awaited deportation to row in the galleys in Naples for ten years, a sentence he was unlikely to survive. The *Wiennerisches Diarium* described his motive: he did not blaspheme "out of rage or revenge against God Almighty, but so that he could be freed from the house of correction to which he had been condemned." Two days later the newspaper reported his deportation to Naples along with four other criminals, again emphasizing that his blasphemy was not

---

[123] "weilen sie Gott gelästert und dz Crucifix zerbissen." ÖNB, Cod 8363, p. 9, Nr. 74.

inspired by "any revenge or rage against God."[124] By emphasizing the incidental nature of Johann N.'s blasphemy, the *Wiennerisches Diarium* justified the government's policy of not executing such offenders.

What became of the suicidal blasphemers who remained hospitalized or in prison? The melancholy crucifix-breaker Polixena Helmin who committed physical blasphemy twice, in 1714 and 1718, remained troubled. She was still in custody at St. Mark's Hospital when the city court requested another medical evaluation of her condition in September 1725, though the nature of her new offense is unclear. Did she commit a third blasphemous act? The medical faculty reported that fearfulness and a hypochondriacal-hysterical constitution contributed to episodes of melancholy delirium precipitated by the movements of the moon.[125]

Prison inmates Joseph Zeitler, the young burglar, and Maria Anna Frankenhauserin were released shortly after the partial imperial amnesty of April 1716. Their sentences of banishment from Austrian lands after the completion of their prison terms were also remitted. Shortly after their release Joseph Zeitler and Maria Anna Frankenhauserin got married. Possibly they had known each other before their imprisonment. They were both from Vienna. Both of their fathers were shoemakers. In any case, their shared experience of blasphemy and the punishment that followed brought them closer. Zeitler found work as a journeyman shoemaker. They had a baby.

There was no happy ending for the young couple, however. After six months of making shoes, Zeitler "returned to robbery ... in order to make an easier living," he confessed after he was arrested again three years later.[126] Their baby died. Zeitler joined a gang of highwaymen operating in Lower and Upper Austria and Carinthia. Abandoned, his wife remained in

---

[124] "eine ledige Manns-Person... um willen sich selbe bereits das andertemal mittels Zerbrechung eines Crucifix wider Gott lästerlich vergriffen/ anbey auch verschiedene andere Gottslästerliche Wort ausgestossen/ welch ein und anderes aber nicht aus einem Zorn/ oder Rach gegen Gott dem Almächtigen/ sondern damit er aus dem Zucht-haus/ alwohin er das erstemal verurtheilet worden/ gebracht werden möchte." WD, Nr. XXI, 3 March 1722. The next issue reports his deportation and identifies him as Johann N., twenty-one, and emphasizes that the blasphemy happened "ohne eintziger Rach/ oder Zorn gegen Gott." WD, Nr. XXX, 15 April 1722.

[125] "Conclusit Facultas, hanc foeminam laborare delirio melancholico per certas periodos, praecipue circa lunae motum redeunte et arguit 1: ex constitutione ipsius hypochondriaco hysterica, 2do ex depravata victus ratione, et continuis ad D: Marcum tempore paroxismi habitis disturbijs, 3tio: ex pusillassimitate." UAW, Med. 1.8, AFMV VIII, fol. 476r–476v.

[126] StiftAL, Criminalia 377, Joseph Zeitler, 1719.

Vienna alone. In February 1719 Zeitler was taken into custody as a suspicious character wandering through the territory of the Benedictine Abbey of Lambach in Upper Austria in the company of a vagrant woman. By this time Zeitler clearly no longer wanted to die. He gave a false name and steadfastly denied involvement in any robberies. Finally, after judicial torture, he revealed his true identity and confessed to a series of highway and church robberies. The judge in Lambach inquired with authorities in Vienna, who informed him of Zeitler's earlier burglary, as well as his physical blasphemy against the crucifix. Among the numerous robberies Zeitler confessed to, the prosecution focused on a church robbery in the Viennese suburb of Gumpenbach because corroborating witnesses made conviction unproblematic. Zeitler had broken open the collection box. He had stolen a chalice and paten from the sacristy and sold them to a Jew. The paten and chalice were consecrated Eucharistic vessels that held the elements of bread and wine when they were transformed into the body and blood of Christ during the sacrament of the mass. The judge showed no particular interest in learning more about the sale of these sacred items to a Jew. Jews often acted as fences for stolen goods, so this element of Zeitler's confession was entirely plausible.[127] By 1719 the association of the theft of sacred items with magical abuse and host desecration was not as close as it had been during the peak period of Austrian witch-hunting during the second half of the seventeenth century.[128] And so the court imposed the standard penalty for sacrilegious theft, without additional refinements. Zeitler was sentenced to be hanged on a temporary gallows erected above a pyre. He would then be burned with the gallows, and his ashes disposed of in flowing water, so that no trace of him remained.[129] The court scribe included a drawing of the gallows surrounded by stacked wood in Joseph Zeitler's file (Image 6.7).

The incorrigible Rosina Plankhin and other recidivist blasphemers remained incarcerated. An imperial decree from 1726 seems to indicate that they were not able to maintain their defiance indefinitely. The decree ordered that inmates in the house of correction who were imprisoned for

---

[127] Otto Ulbricht, "Criminality and Punishment of the Jews in the Early Modern Period," in *In and Out of the Ghetto. Jewish-Gentile Relations in Late Medieval and Early Modern Germany*, eds. R. Po-chia Hsia and Hartmut Lehmann (Cambridge: Cambridge University Press, 2002), 59.
[128] See Chap. 5.
[129] OÖLA, Stadtarchiv Freistadt, Seyringer Rechtsgutachten, Hs. Nr. 1101, pp. 238–251, Joseph Zeitler, 24 October 1719.

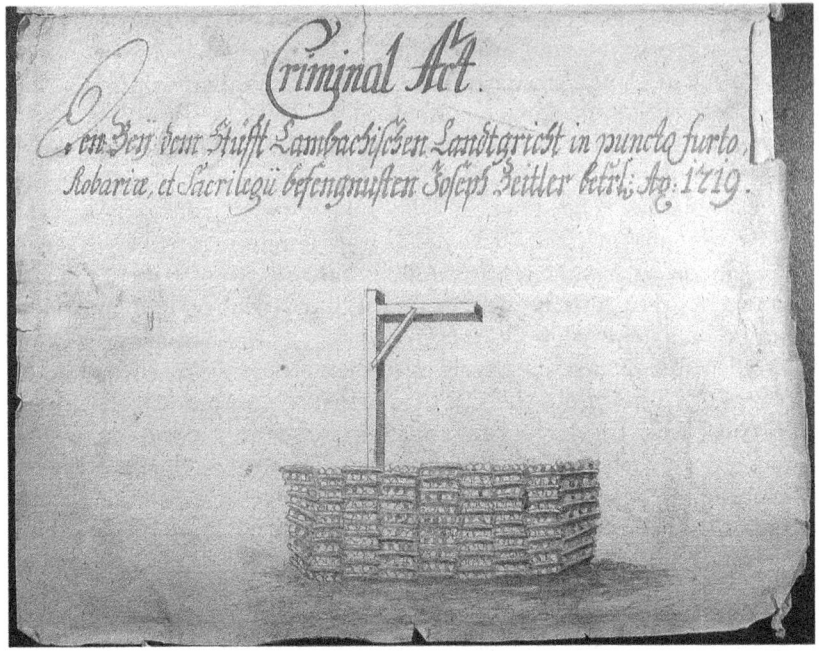

Image 6.7 Drawing of instruments of execution included in court records concerning Joseph Zeitler, executed 1719 in the territory of the Benedictine Abbey of Lambach for church robbery. Stiftarchiv Lambach, Criminalia 377, Joseph Zeitler, 1719

begging or minor crimes be separated from serious felons. Small-time offenders would be transferred to the newly constructed workhouse wing within the house of correction. Among the felons incarcerated in the prison at this time were several "female crucifix-breakers" (*Crucifix-Brecherinnen*) who had been "condemned several years ago." They were now working industriously at spinning and knitting, and according to reports by the prison director and clergy, their conduct had "notably improved." Holding out the possibility of transfer of these inmates from the prison wing to the workhouse wing, the decree ordered the prison administration to deliver quarterly reports to the imperial court, "so that his imperial majesty can mercifully shorten their sentences or remit their banishment" that would have followed completion of their prison terms. "Incorrigible offenders," however, should be treated with the appropriate harshness.¹³⁰ The fact that the emperor wished to be kept informed of the progress of these suicidal iconoclasts is an indication of the consternation these cases had caused at the highest levels of government.

In a commentary on the *Ferdinandea* published in 1751, the jurist and imperial councilor Franz Joseph Bratsch described the outbreak of suicidal iconoclasm as a thing of the past. Under the heading "The Injured Crucifix," Bratsch explained the evolving imperial policy toward suicidal blasphemers. Approximately thirty years ago, Bratsch wrote, blasphemies had become so "rampant" that the emperor had felt compelled to increase the penalty for such crimes in 1713. The new harsh penalties failed to deter these blasphemers, however, motivated as they were by their "yearning" for death. Indeed, they had the "opposite effect, as sad experience showed."¹³¹ So the emperor changed the penalty again in 1715, ruling out death in such cases and imposing long prison sentences instead, but this, too, proved unsuccessful. Authorities were now confronted with recidivist blasphemers who "did not demonstrate any repentance or improvement, since such persons who were condemned for life could not hope for an end to their misery, causing them to commit even greater crimes." Responding to a "particular case"—most likely Rosina Plankhin?—the emperor issued a new directive. Such blasphemers would be instructed that the only way to secure mercy from his Imperial Majesty as their sovereign was to demonstrate sufficient penitence and improved conduct.¹³²

The policy Bratsch described here seems to have been largely successful. Only a few cases of suicidal blasphemy were recorded over the next decades. In June 1728 Barbara Catharina B., twenty-two, committed a "blasphemous deed," apparently not in the prison-workhouse. She performed public expiation and was whipped on the ravenstone before being placed in the house of correction to serve a two-year sentence in chains and subsequently be banished for life from Austrian lands.¹³³ In April 1730, a sixty-eight-year-old widow, Anna Maria Sp., also apparently not a prison inmate, performed public expiation and was sentenced to labor in chains for four years in the house of correction, where she would be whipped twice a year on a public stage bearing a placard detailing her

---

¹³⁰ Herrenleben, *Sammlung Oesterreichischer Gesetze*, vol. 4, 395.
¹³¹ Bratsch, *Anweisungen*, 148–150.
¹³² The section is entitled "Das verletzte Crucifix." Bratsch, *Anweisungen*, 148–150.
¹³³ *WD*, Nr. 57, 17 July 1728.

crime.[134] It is hard to imagine that she survived this sentence for long. In July 1731 Anna Maria N., twenty-five, who broke the crucifix twice, performed expiation and received a life sentence of labor in chains in the house of correction with twice-yearly whippings.[135] In April 1732, two unmarried women, aged nineteen and twenty-two, apparently not workhouse inmates, performed an expiation for blasphemy at the crucifix statue by the ravenstone. Was this another case of women teaming up to commit blasphemy? The two women were sentenced to one year in the house of correction, where they would each receive a "welcome" and "farewell" of twelve lashes, before being banished to their birthplace.[136]

The last case of suicidal iconoclasm in Vienna that I have been able to document happened in 1750. Nicolaus Stark, twenty, broke a crucifix in the house of correction. Sources have survived that make it possible to reconstruct his life in some detail. His biography will have to stand for all the others of whom we know only their name and age at the time of their executions.

Nicolaus Stark (c. 1729–1757)

The earliest mention of Nicolaus Stark in Vienna's criminal records dates from March 1746. Stark, then seventeen, a native to Pressburg, was arrested as a "suspicious drifter."[137] Placed in the house of correction, he received twelve lashes upon arrival as "welcome" and would receive another twelve lashes as his "farewell" before his release, and then be expelled from Vienna's jurisdiction.[138] This marked the beginning of Stark's entanglement with Vienna's criminal justice system that would ultimately lead to his execution by beheading eleven years later. Stark's criminal career began even before his first arrest in Vienna. In the entry on his execution in the Protocol of the Confraternity of the Dead, we learn that his hometown authorities in Pressburg had already nabbed him as a pickpocket in 1745 when he was fifteen or sixteen. Arrested in Pressburg for the same offense again the following year, he was whipped, exposed at the pillory, and banished. This was quite a serious penalty for a seventeen-

---

[134] *WD*, Nr. 30, 15 April 1730.
[135] *WD*, Nr. 54, 7 July 1731.
[136] Their expiation took place on April 3, 1732. *WD*, Nr. 28, 5 April 1732.
[137] "…wegen verdächtig herumziehen." WStLA, Handschriften A 17, fol. 152r–153v.
[138] WStLA, Handschriften A 17, fol. 152r–153v.

year-old. Exposure at the pillory conferred formal legal infamy that effectively precluded return to a normal life. This discipline did not "bear fruit," however, as the scribe of the Protocol observed. Instead, he now joined a band of "shiftless thieving youths" and made the trek to Vienna with them.[139]

In June 1746, three months after his first arrest in Vienna, suffering from some unnamed malady, Stark was transferred from the prison-workhouse to St. Marx Hospital. Two months later he had recovered enough to escape during transport back to the prison-workhouse. But his freedom was short-lived. In November 1746 he was arrested again, for theft, and sentenced to one year in the house of corrections. Still only seventeen, he had already acquired a street name, "Zaun Dörre," presumably describing his emaciated physique (from *zaundürr*, thin as a fencepost).[140] Official use of his street name indicates that he was now a known member of the disreputable vagrant underworld that city authorities were trying to police.[141]

Two weeks into his second prison term he was sent back to St. Marx Hospital. Again, he must have escaped, because in April 1747 Stark, now eighteen, was arrested a third time, again for theft, and sentenced to yet another year in the house of correction. In January 1748 the court handed him over to the military as a recruit. He apparently deserted at the earliest opportunity because the following June Stark, now nineteen, was arrested for theft for the fourth time. Sentenced to the house of correction for another year, upon completion of his prison term he would be escorted to the territorial border, under threat never to return to Viennese territory. In November 1748, he was hospitalized at St. Marx again, from where he managed another escape.

In June 1749 Stark, now twenty, was arrested a fifth time for illegal return to Viennese territory and suspicious conduct. Sentenced to yet another year in the workhouse with twelve lashes "welcome" and "farewell," he would be deported to his "fatherland," that is, Pressburg. Less than a month later he was readmitted to St. Marx for scabies—and made his escape from there two months later. This time he only managed to

---

[139] WB, Handschriften 18013, pp. 42–45.
[140] *Grimms Wörterbuch*, vol. 31, 415.
[141] On the significance of nicknames in the criminal milieu and in popular culture in general see Norbert Schindler, *Rebellion, Community and Custom in Early Modern Germany* (Cambridge: Cambridge University Press, 2002), 48–92.

elude authorities for a week. Late in September 1749 he was arrested a sixth time and delivered to the prison-workhouse to complete his sentence. In January 1750, less than three months into his sixth prison term, he destroyed a crucifix.[142]

The authorities now initiated a full-fledged criminal trial against Stark for *blasphemia realis*. During his trial he was hospitalized at St. Marx again for ulcerated feet. Under better guard, or perhaps simply too debilitated, he was not able to escape this time. In April 1750 he was sentenced according to the guidelines of the 1715 edict. After performing the customary rite of expiation at the crucifix statue by the Ravenstone where he would publicly profess his heartfelt penitence for his crime, he would be imprisoned in the house of correction. He would be held in chains for three years. Every six months he would be exhibited on a public stage wearing a sign that described his crime and be whipped. Upon sentencing, Stark swore an oath of *Urfehde*. The young vagrant was literate enough to sign his "bodily oath" in his own hand. On the same day that Stark signed his *Urfehde*, April 20, 1750, Johann Georg Hallmann, another young thief from Pressburg, imprisoned in the house of correction at the same time as Stark, made his suicidal murder attempt on a twelve-year-old fellow inmate (Image 6.8).[143]

Two months into his new three-year sentence Stark was readmitted to St. Marx, only to be sent back to the workhouse just ten days later because he had threatened a guard and attempted to break through a wall. During the next year and a half he was hospitalized several times, still suffering from "open feet." Finally, in February 1752 during his fifth hospital stay he managed to break through a wall and escape.[144] By 1754 he was in Viennese custody once again. In December 1754 Vienna's criminal court sentenced him for perjury—by setting foot in Austrian lands he had he broken his oath of *Urfehde*—and for complicity in highway robbery. His sentence was harsh. Taken to the ravenstone, he received "a whole Schilling," that is, thirty lashes administered by the executioner or skinner. He was then branded on his back with "the customary symbol of

---

[142] WStLA, Handschriften A 17, fol. 152r–153v. Another source describes him as twenty years old at the time of his sentencing for blasphemy, 20 April 1750. WStLA, Handschriften A 19, fol. 138r–v.

[143] *Wohlverdientes Todtes-Urtheil einer Ledigen Manns-Person Nahmens Johann Georg H* (Vienna: s.d). ÖNB, 303.950-B.Alt-Adl. 9.

[144] WStLA, Handschriften A19, fol. 137–143.

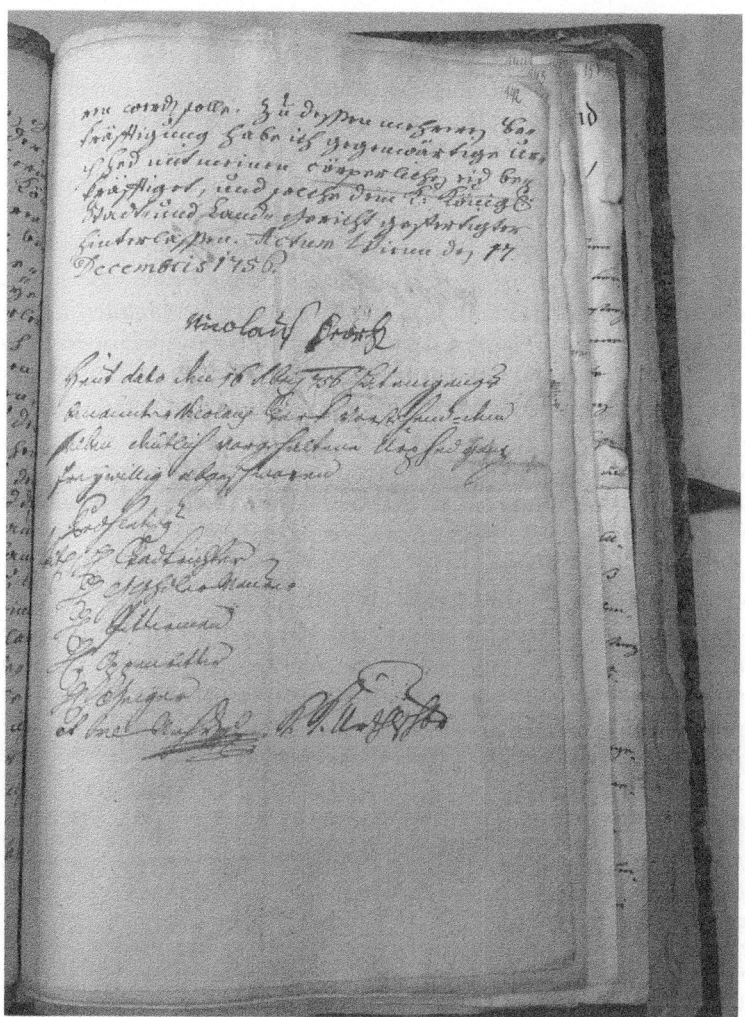

Image 6.8 Nicolaus Starck's signature under his *Urfehde* of 17 December 1756. Wiener Stadt und Landesarchiv, Handschriften A 19, fol. 142r

banishment."[145] This was typically the letter "R" for *relegatio* (banishment). The wound was then rubbed with gunpowder to increase the visibility of the brand.[146] Following the branding he was again banished from all Austrian hereditary lands for life. Once again, Stark's second criminal trial concluded with his ritual swearing of *Urfehde*. Added to the standard formula was Stark's acknowledgment that he would be harshly punished for two-fold perjury should he break his oath.

Stark did not stay away. In December 1756 he was under arrest again for his second breach of *Urfehde* and for attempted theft. He was sentenced to another thirty lashes on the ravenstone and branded a second time. He swore the *Urfehde* a third time and was again banished for life. He now returned to hometown of Pressburg, where he was arrested for theft, whipped, branded, and once again banished from Pressburg's jurisdiction. This discipline, too, "failed to bear fruit," as the scribe of the Protocol of Confraternity of the Dead commented in his entry on Stark's execution.[147] In September 1757 Stark was arrested in Vienna again, in the company of a "suspicious female," tools for picking locks in his possession. Convicted of his third breach of *Urfehde*, he was condemned to death. Placed in a high wagon, he was transported to the ravenstone where he was beheaded on October 22, 1757. He was twenty-eight. A procession consisting of two Augustinian friars and sixty lay brothers of the Confraternity for the Dead followed the wagon to the ravenstone and attended his beheading. They then accompanied Stark's body to the "Poor Sinners' Graveyard," where he was laid to rest.[148]

---

[145] Banishment for Austrian hereditary lands automatically conferred legal infamy. *Constitutio criminalis Theresiana oder der Römisch-Kaiserl. zu Hungarn und Böheim ... Majestät Mariä Theresiä ... peinliche Gerichtsordnung* (Vienna: Johann Thomas Edlen von Trattnern, 1769), 19, § 13.

[146] Imperial decrees from 1736 and 1751 aimed to increase the information these brands communicated by including the initials of the territory from where the person had been banished, that is, someone branded in Vienna would be marked with the letters "A.I." for *Austria infra* or Lower Austria in addition to the "R." Bratsch, *Anweisungen*, 121–125. However, this refinement seems not to have been introduced in practice. Schlager, *Wiener Skizzen*, 28–32.

[147] WB, Handschriften 18013, fol. 42–43.

[148] Stark's execution is described in three Viennese execution protocols: WB, Handschriften 18013, fo. 42–43; WB, Handschriften 67116, 1757, 22. October, unpaginated. ÖNB, Cod 8363, p. 25, Nr. 150. His sentence was also published in an official execution announcement: *Todes-Urtheil Einer ledigen Manns-person, Namens: Niclas St... Welches... den 22. Oct. 1757. allhier in Wien vollzogen wird* ([Vienna]: 1757).

An Ongoing Problem?

When Stark broke a crucifix in 1750, thirty years had passed since the last recorded execution for suicidal blasphemy in Vienna. Suicidal iconoclasm was not altogether a thing of the past, however. It was still enough of a problem in 1769 for Empress Maria Theresa (r. 1740–1780) to address the practice in a set of secret instructions distributed to judges and local governments regarding the implementation of her new criminal law code, the *Constitutio Criminalis Theresiana*, published in that year.[149] The *Theresiana* showed few influences of the Enlightenment, although it did effectively end witch-hunting in Austrian lands. The *Theresiana* included verbatim an earlier "Article on Sorcery," first promulgated in 1766. The article did not question the existence of witchcraft or the possibility of diabolical pact in principle, emphasizing instead the suppression of superstition and fraud, and condemning the credulity of common people that had led to excessive witch-hunts in the past. By requiring local courts to submit all witchcraft prosecutions to the central government for review, the *Theresiana* established the kind of judicial centralization that contributed to the decline of witch-hunting in other parts of Europe as well.[150] In other ways the *Theresiana* remained entirely traditional, beginning with its classification of crimes. "Among the sins, blasphemy is the first and most heinous," the *Theresiana* declared. It was listed first among the felonies, as it had been in the *Ferdinandea*.[151] The new code preserved the entire traditional repertoire of punishments to the body characteristic of the "theatre of horror" of early modern criminal justice,[152] imposing the same

---

[149] *Constitutio Criminalis Theresiana, oder der Römisch-Kaiserl. ... Majestät Maria Thersia, Erzherzogin zu Oesterrich, peinliche Gerichtsordnung* (Vienna: Johann Thomas Edlen von Trattnern, 1769).

[150] Edmund M. Kern, "An End to Witch Trials in Austria: Reconsidering the Enlightened State," *Austrian History Yearbook* 30 (1999), 159–185. Fritz Byloff, *Hexenglaube und Hexenverfolgungen in den österreichischen Alpenländern* (Hamburg: Severus Verlag, 2011), 238–239. This is a new edition of Byloff's classic survey of Austrian witch-hunts, first published 1934. On the role of judicial centralization in the decline of witch-hunting, see Brian Levack, "The Decline and End of Witchcraft Prosecutions," in *Witchcraft and Magic in Europe: The Eighteenth and Nineteenth Centuries*, eds. Bengt Ankarloo and Stuart Clark (Philadelphia: University of Pennsylvania Press, 1999), 13–19.

[151] *Theresiana*, Art. 56, § 1, p. 162.

[152] Richard van Dülmen, *Theatre of Horror: Crime and Punishment in Early Modern Germany* (Cambridge, UK: Polity Press, 1990).

penalties for blasphemy as had the *Ferdinandea*.[153] It sanctioned the practice of judicial torture, even providing helpful illustrations on how such torture was best applied.[154]

The "Secret Notes" (*Geheime Anmerkungen*) to the *Theresiana* give an idea of how seriously authorities took the stagecraft of early modern executions.[155] A limited number of copies of the "Secret Notes" were printed for distribution exclusively to superior courts and local lordships endowed with high justice. To prevent the leaking of this confidential document the "Notes" threatened punishment for unlicensed reprints.[156] The foreword explained that the empress, motivated by "motherly love for her subjects," had promulgated this new unified law code for all Austrian hereditary lands. Successful implementation of the *Theresiana* required that certain additional instructions "should not be known to common people, but should be communicated secretly."[157] Evoking the hereditary mercy of the House of Austria,[158] the "Notes" instructed judges to avoid imposing penalties that induced despair in the condemned, thus endangering his or her salvation, notably burning alive or breaking with the wheel from the bottom up. This mercy should not be made public, however. Both penalties should be included in the public text of the law, so as not to diminish the terror associated with them. However, the executioner should be instructed to strangle the condemned secretly as he was lighting the flames and, for safe measure, to hang a bag of gunpowder around the criminal's neck. This directive did not represent a humanitarian innovation of the Enlightenment, but rather it codified what had been common practice in many witchcraft cases since the second half of the seventeenth century. In the case of breaking with the wheel from the bottom up, the death sentence should be publicized in its full severity, the "Notes" instructed. Then, at the last moment, at the ravenstone, a representative of the court

---

[153] *Theresiana*, Art. 56, § 9, p. 164–165.

[154] *Theresiana*, Art. 38, pp. 115–116. The illustrations are included in the appendix (Beylagen), XIII-XLVIII.

[155] *Geheime Anmerkungen ad Constitutionem nostrum criminalem Theresianam, oder zu Unser neuen peinlichen Gerichtsordnung für Unsere Teutsch-erbländische Malefiz-Obergerichten, und die mit peinlichen Gerichtsbarkeit begabte unmittelbare Länderstellen*, p. 1. I am citing a text bound with a copy of the *Theresiana*, digitized by google: http://books.google.com/books?id=1HyVyBDaP0YC&pg=RA1-PA1#v=onepage&q&f=false.

[156] *Geheime Anmerkungen*, 19.

[157] *Geheime Anmerkungen*, 1.

[158] *Geheime Anmerkungen*, 2.

should announce that her Imperial Majesty had granted the poor sinner the "stroke of mercy," that is, the executioner would administer the first blow of the wheel to the neck of the condemned man, killing him before mangling the rest of the body with the wheel. In Austria, as in most of the Holy Roman Empire, though not in Hamburg, this penalty of breaking by the wheel was imposed almost exclusively on men. Only criminals who demonstrated true repentance would be granted the "stroke of mercy." Impenitent sinners would be punished according to the letter or the law.

Instruction Nr. 8 addressed the practice of suicidal iconoclasm. Entitled "Concerning blasphemies prompted by weariness with life," the instruction read:

> Unfortunate experience has repeatedly shown that certain people habituated to idleness and vice ... out of depression and weariness with their miserable, usually sinful life ... in order to end it with a rapid blow of the sword, have made the desperate decision to commit a capital crime, mostly blasphemous acts of breaking or demolishing crucifixes or other sacred images. They commit these desecrations knowingly and intentionally, and have achieved their ultimate goal in this manner.

To ensure that such sinners were punished in the way most painful to them and to prevent such evildoers "to whom death is a pleasure" from realizing their goal, the secret instruction imposed the same penalties laid out in the imperial patent of 1715. In addition, to prevent the problem of recidivist blasphemies, the instruction held out the possibility of mercy, as had the imperial decree of 1716: "so that people condemned to life-long punishment who have no hope for an end to their misery do not become obdurate in their malice and commit further crimes," they should be told at the time of their sentencing and repeatedly thereafter that their only hope for mercy from their sovereign lay in true penitence and moral improvement.[159]

The instruction essentially reaffirmed the legislative status quo vis-à-vis suicidal blasphemy that had been in effect since 1716. The fact that Maria Theresa's government did this via a secret instruction and not in a widely publicized imperial patent, such as the one promulgated by her father Charles VI in 1715, shows that authorities had gone through a learning

---

[159] "In Betreff der aus Ueberdruß des Lebens beschehenen Gotteslästerung." *Geheime Anmerkungen*, 18–19.

experience in dealing with this type of offender. Public condemnation of suicidal iconoclasm in proclamations and execution sermons was counterproductive. Far from deterring people from committing such acts, publicity seemed to inspire imitators, as Charles VI and his government had learned in the wake of fifteen-year-old Stefan Maurer's execution in 1713. Maria Theresa's government concluded that secrecy was the better policy.

Austrian government officials were still drawing on lessons learned during Vienna's outbreak of suicidal iconoclasm more than six decades later. In a report from 1781, Josef Ferdinand Ritter von Holger (1706–1783), one of three jurists tasked by Emperor Joseph II (r. 1765–1790) to work out how to implement a reduction or abolition of the death penalty, referred back to a case of suicidal iconoclasm from 1715. Holger was grappling with the question of what would be the appropriate penalty to replace execution for traditionally capital offenses. After pointing out that under the *Theresiana* felons whose death sentences were commuted were sentenced instead to ten years of hard labor—a punishment "closest to the penalty of death" (*ad poenam morti proximam*)—but not longer, Holger warned that simply replacing the penalty of death with life imprisonment posed risks. He cited the governmental decree on suicidal iconoclasm from August 30, 1715, as an example. The decree had imposed a life sentence of labor in chains with periodic public whippings on recidivist female crucifix-breakers. Male recidivist blasphemers were deported to Naples to row in the galleys for life. As we saw above, the government quickly learned that suicidal offenders facing life sentences were simply driven to repeat their violent blasphemies—in Rosina Plankhin's case, again, and again, and again. In Holger's report we learn that recidivist blasphemers who failed to achieve their execution and were sentenced to life imprisonment instead might also turn to murder to finally reach their goal: "Such a life sentence always causes despair, and adverse consequences. For example, one such female offender, for no other reason than to free herself from this onerous and lifelong punishment, beat another woman to death in her sleep." Based on this experience, the government had quickly reversed course, offering suicidal iconoclasts leniency in return for good behavior in prison. Holger urged Joseph's government to bear this experience in mind. Life sentences should be imposed rarely, and when they were, authorities should take precautions to prevent such despair-driven acts of violence, by either holding out the hope of pardon for these prisoners or holding them tightly confined in chains at all hours.[160] Interestingly, Holger never raised the possibility that such prisoners might be driven to commit suicide. We should not deduce from this that Holger was indifferent to that possibility—after all, if a prisoner escaped the government's grasp by committing suicide, this would undermine one of the governing principles of Enlightenment criminal justice reforms: punishment should be certain and inescapable. Instead, it seems that in 1781 Holger, who began his judicial career in 1730, still saw suicide by proxy and other acts of violence as a greater threat to the smooth operation of criminal justice than suicide.[161]

Why did Nicolaus Stark and other suicidal individuals persist in breaking sacred images decades after authorities stopped executing suicidal blasphemers? As long as rulers saw their foremost duty as protecting the honor of God, and avenging it if it had been violated, the practice of suicidal iconoclasm made sense. In Austria this remained the case until the accession of Joseph II to throne as sole ruler after his mother's death in 1780. Criminal codes from the *Ferdinandea* through the *Theresiana* set death as the appropriate penalty for blasphemy. Blasphemy remained on the books as a capital offense in Austria until the promulgation of Joseph II's criminal code, the *Josefina*, in 1787. In the *Josefina*, blasphemy, no longer first among felonies, was now grouped under "Crimes that lead to a Decline in Morals." Depending on the circumstances, blasphemers might be placed in an insane asylum, whipped, exposed on the pillory, or imprisoned. It was no longer a capital offense.[162]

For much of the eighteenth century, however, blasphemers were put to death with some regularity, reinforcing commonsense, and experiential knowledge that blasphemy was punished by death. A particularly tragic example of the extraordinary severity with which blasphemy was treated in

---

[160] Holger's report, dated March 16, 1781, is reprinted in the appendix of Gerhard Ammerer, *Das Ende für Schwert und Galgen? Legislativer Prozess und Öffentlicher Diskurs zur Reduzierung der Todesstrafe im Ordentlichen Verfahren unter Joseph II (1781–1787)* (Vienna: Studienverlag, 2010), 445–484, quotation, 460–461. See also Ammerer's discussion of this report, 138–139.

[161] Ammerer, *Ende für Schwert und Galgen*, 138–139. On Holger's career, 117–118.

[162] "Von den Verbrechen, die zum Verderbnisse der Sitten führen." *Allgemeines Gesetz über Verbrechen, und derselben Bestrafung* (Vienna: Johann Thomas Edlen von Trattnern, 1787), § 61–66, 109–111. Siegfried Leutenbauer, *Das Delikt der Gotteslästerung in der Bayerischen Gesetzgebung* (Cologne: Böhlau Verlag, 1984), 225–226.

Austrian courts involved the trial of Johann Georg Pilberger from Freistadt in Upper Austria in 1716–1717. In November 1716 Pilberger's wife gave birth to twins. Both babies died before a priest arrived to baptize them. Drunk on brandy, Pilberger vented his rage in blasphemy. God was not a good shepherd for letting his children die before baptism, he said, and cursed and swore at God for half an hour before collapsing in tears at his wife's bedside. His grief and drunkenness did not mitigate his sentence. He was beheaded in April 1717.[163]

In 1728 Charles VI personally increased the sentence of a blasphemer. The sentence, excerpted in Bratsch's 1751 commentary on the *Ferdinandea*, does not describe the nature of the blasphemy. Guilty of "injury of the divine majesty" in the highest degree, the blasphemer was condemned to be burned alive, with the addition that he should be secretly strangled by the executioner if he went penitently to his death. The emperor also reprimanded the lower court that had proposed a lesser sentence for unjustifiable leniency.[164] In 1731 Matthias N., a forty-eight-year-old man who committed "horrific blasphemies," was beheaded in Schwadorf, southeast of Vienna, after his tongue was cut out "as far as it is possible to bring it out of the mouth," as a warning to others accustomed to cursing and swearing.[165] In 1749 Maria Theresa sentenced a blasphemer to beheading—after remitting his original sentence to be burned alive.[166] In 1761 she personally confirmed the sentence of a soldier for repeated "gruesome blasphemy." After performing an expiation before a crucifix at execution site and begging God and the public for forgiveness, "his tongue, extended from his mouth, should be cut off," followed by his beheading.[167] In these cases, the opposite dynamic was at work than in many witchcraft cases. The involvement of central government in the later phases of the witch-hunt led to lesser sentences or a suspension of

---

[163] Suzanne Hehenberger, "Entfremdung von Gott? Gotteslästerung und Kirchendiebstahl vor weltlichen Gerichten im 18. Jahrhundert," in *Ermitteln, Fahnden und Strafen. Kriminalitätshistorische Studien vom 16. bis 19. Jahrhundert*, eds. Andrea Griesebner and Georg Tschannett (Vienna: Erhard Löcker Gmbh, 2010), 141–163.

[164] Bratsch, *Anweisungen*, 151–152.

[165] *WD*, Nr. 84, 19 October 1731.

[166] Ernst von Kwiatkowski, *Die constitutio criminalis Theresiana; ein Beitrag zur theresianischen Reichs- und Rechts- Geschichte* (Innsbruck: Wagner, 1904), 46.

[167] Georg Joseph Kögl von Waldinutzy, *De iure civili, et criminali Austriaco-bellico tractatus practicus....*, vol. 1 (Pressburg: Johann Michael Landerer, 1772), 95.

trials altogether. This effect was very clear in Lower Austria after 1679 when Leopold I ordered local courts to consult a commissioner of the Lower Austrian government in all witch trials. A marked decline in witchcraft convictions followed.[168] Maria Theresa's "Article on Sorcery" from 1766 effectively ended witch-hunting in Austrian lands.[169] In blasphemy cases, however, the imperial government confirmed the harshest penalties or increased them. Conversely, greater remoteness from the central government might translate into greater leniency toward blasphemers: The city of Freiburg im Breisgau, in Habsburg Outer Austria, executed no one for blasphemy during the early modern period, though the city had experienced a major witch-hunt in the late sixteenth and early seventeenth centuries. In Freiburg blasphemers faced fines, banishment, and occasionally, amputations.[170]

Frequent executions for church robbery, labeled *Sakrilegium* in early modern German criminal codes, also drove home the message that blasphemy merited death. By the eighteenth century, church robbery cases were for the most part no longer conflated with witchcraft and host desecration accusations, as they had been in the second half of the seventeenth century. Nonetheless, until the late eighteenth century church robbers who stole consecrated items such as monstrances or ciboria, even if they did not contain hosts, continued to suffer exacerbated executions that expressed the blasphemous nature of their crime. In 1772 the church robber Melchior G. was executed in the same manner as Joseph Zeitler had been in 1719. Melchior G. was hanged on special gallows erected above a pyre. After his hanging, his body was burned. His ashes were strewn in the Danube.[171]

---

[168] Thomas Winkelbauer, *Ständefreiheit und Fürstenmacht. Länder und Untertanen des Hauses Habsburg im konfessionellen Zeitalter* (Vienna: Ueberreuter, 2003), 281.

[169] Kern, "End to Witch Trials in Austria."

[170] Georg Schindler, *Verbrechen und Strafen im Recht der Stadt Freiburg im Breisgau von der Einführung des neuen Stadtrechts bis zum Übergang an Baden (1520–1806)* (Freiburg: Kommissionsverlag der Fr. Wagnerschen Universitätsbuchhandlung, 1937), 207–211.

[171] *Todesurtheil einer verheuratheten Mannsperson, Namens Melchior G...., welches...den 24. September 1772 allhier in Wien vollzogen wird.* (s.l., s.d.). This was the penalty set for church robbery in both the *Ferdinandea* and the *Theresiana*. At least thirteen people were executed for church robbery in Vienna between 1703 and 1750. Susanne Hehenberger, " 'Die beleidigte Ehre GOttes auf das empfindlichste zu rächen, in allweg gesonnen.' Blasphemie und Sakrileg im 18. Jahrhundert," in *Wien und seine WienerInnen. Ein historischer Streifzug durch Wien über die Jahrhunderte. Festschrift für Karl Vocelka zum 60. Geburtstag*, eds. Martin Scheutz and Vlasta Valeš (Vienna: Böhlau Verlag, 2008), 187.

The authorities distinguished between these kinds of blasphemers and those who blasphemed with suicidal intent. But would spectators at executions have understood this distinction? Would they have followed the nuanced logic that a blasphemer motivated by rage and a desire for revenge against God or a blasphemous church robber deserved death but one who blasphemed as a means to an end, with the goal of bringing about his or her own execution, did not?

Popular attitudes toward witchcraft after decriminalization may shed some light on this question. Owen Davies has studied the continuity of witchcraft beliefs in England after parliament passed the Witchcraft Act of 1736. The Act denied the existence of witchcraft as a real crime and instead threatened people who pretended to have magical abilities with prosecution for fraud. People's fear of witchcraft did not evaporate when authorities disengaged from witch-hunting, of course, and common people practiced vigilante justice against suspected witches in their communities for much of the nineteenth century. In addition to such self-help, however, Davies finds that people, "over a hundred years after the passing of the Witchcraft Act, still considered agents of state authority as allies in the continuing popular struggle against witchcraft. In the popular mind, witchcraft remained a crime against the individual and community ... Therefore, ... it was perceived that the state was obliged to act against it."[172] Davies provides numerous examples of people approaching local justices of the peace in the mid-nineteenth century, demanding government prosecution of witches. In a similar way, common people in eighteenth century Austria had traditional expectations of the role and duty of government in the prosecution of blasphemy. People committed suicidal blasphemy because they believed that government was under an obligation to act against blasphemy. They believed that government would be compelled to execute them, and they claimed their executions as their right. The authorities' subtle distinctions between different kinds of blasphemy most likely failed to make a dent in this worldview.

Blasphemy had not been a capital offense for fifty-nine years when Anna Zotter attacked a crucifix in 1846. A twenty-one-year-old syphilitic prostitute imprisoned in Vienna's workhouse, Zotter vented her rage and despair in a blasphemous act. In the presence of other inmates, she took a wooden crucifix down from the wall in the women's dormitory and cursed

---

[172] Owen Davies, *Witchcraft, Magic and Culture, 1736–1951* (Manchester: Manchester University Press, 1999), 100, 101–106.

it. According to her own confession and the testimony of witnesses, she said: "Get lost, you bloody rogue! You have to come down. You're not worth anything. There is no Christ in the workhouse." Then she broke the crucifix over her knee and threw the broken pieces out the window into the courtyard below. Prison officials were unable to retrieve the broken parts. Zotter had first been arrested four years earlier for practicing prostitution while knowingly infected with a venereal disease. She was arrested several more times for prostitution and then briefly imprisoned for a failed suicide attempt in 1845. She was arrested for prostitution again in 1846. She had served three months in the workhouse when she committed her blasphemous act. She testified that she broke the crucifix in anger because she was unhappy about being locked up and did not know when she would be released. She regretted her blasphemous words and deed wholeheartedly and asked for a merciful sentence. If she did blaspheme with suicidal intent, no mention of it was made in her trial records. She was convicted of "disturbance of religion" (*Religionsstörung*) and sentenced to six months in prison.[173]

Gender and Age of Suicidal Blasphemers

One thing will have become clear from the preceding descriptions of individual cases of suicidal blasphemy: the majority of such offenders were young women or girls. In thirty-seven of fifty-three clear cases of suicidal blasphemy documented in Vienna between 1697 and 1750, or 69%, the perpetrators were female. Of the forty-three image-breakers whose age is known, twenty-one were under the age of twenty. Another twelve were under twenty-five. The average age of Vienna's suicidal iconoclasts was just under twenty-four years.

The predominance of women among suicidal blasphemers is particularly noteworthy, considering that the majority of prisoners held in Vienna' house of correction were most likely male. No statistics are available on the sex ratio of the inmates until the late eighteenth century. However, men and boys made up the majority of vagrants and beggars in and around Vienna, and this was the population specifically targeted by the house of correction. Of all beggars listed in Viennese registers between 1665 and 1680, 56% were male. Among vagrant youths under the age of nineteen

---

[173] WStLA, 1.2.3.3. A1, Untersuchungen und Verurteilungen/ 1797–1850, 11 Z 1846 (Anna Zotter). Friedrich Hartl, *Wiener Kriminalgericht*, 349.

the percentage of males seems to have been much higher. Within this group, boys and male youths made up close to 90% of those whose sex was documented. The majority of these were begging illegally,[174] so their risk of ending up in the house of correction was high. Of course, the sex ratio of inmates in the workhouse need not have corresponded to the sex ratio of illegal beggars on the streets, but it seems likely that men made up a majority of the prison population.[175] For the late eighteenth century we know this to be true. When the British prison reformer John Howard visited Vienna's house of correction in 1778 he found 159 men and 140 women imprisoned there.[176]

The gender profile of Vienna's suicidal blasphemers contrasts with the gender pattern of early modern blasphemy prosecutions in general. The majority of blasphemy prosecutions throughout Europe involved men.[177] In Sweden, for example, of the 117 people prosecuted for blasphemy between 1680 and 1789, only 9 were women.[178] In France, blasphemy was particularly common in the hypermasculine milieus of the army and navy.[179] German sources also show blasphemy to be a mostly male offense, related, as Gerd Schwerhoff argues, to codes of masculinity and male patterns of sociability and conflict. A "gesture of virile challenge," blasphemy typically happened when men came together to drink and gamble.[180] The minority of women brought up on blasphemy charges were doubly stigmatized, first for their blasphemous transgression and then because they

[174] Helmut Bräuer, *"...und hat seithero gebetlet."* Bettler und Bettelwesen in Wien und Niederösterreich während der Zeit Kaiser Leopolds I* (Vienna: Böhlau Verlag, 1996), 82–86.

[175] Lack of sources makes it difficult to establish the sex ratio of inmates in early modern prison-workhouses generally. Numbers are available for late seventeenth and early eighteenth-century Danzig, where women made up 27% of workhouse inmates. Dariusz Kaczor, "Herrschaft und Verbrecher. Der Danziger Strafvollzug in der frühen Neuzeit," in *Kulturgeschichte Preussens königlich polnischen Anteils in der Frühen Neuzeit*, eds. Sabine Beckmann and Klaus Garber (Tübingen: Max Niemeyer Verlag, 2005), 154.

[176] John Howard, *The State of the Prisons in England and Wales, with Preliminary Observations, and an Account of Some Foreign Prisons*, 3rd edition. (Warrington: Cadell, 1784), 103.

[177] Richard van Dülmen, "Wider die Ehre Gottes. Unglaube und Gotteslästerung in der Frühen Neuzeit," *Historische Anthropologie* 2 (1994): 34.

[178] Soili-Maria Olli, "Blasphemy in Early Modern Sweden—An Untold Story," *Journal of Religious History* 32 (2008): 466.

[179] Alain Cabantous describes soldiers and sailors as "emblematic swearers." *Blasphemy: Impious Speech in the West from the Seventeenth to the Nineteenth Centuries* (New York: Columbia University Press, 2001), 81–96.

[180] Schwerhoff, *Zungen wie Schwerter*, 282.

engaged in a behavior that was gendered male.[181] In Spain, too, blasphemy occurred most frequently among men at the gaming table. "Women don't commonly lose themselves in swearing," a sixteenth-century Dominican friar observed. Crying and complaining, historian Maureen Flynn suggests, was the "socially appropriate form of contest for women."[182]

Early modern authorities viewed blasphemy as a male behavior, as is evident in the prescriptive language of early modern law codes. As we have seen, the *Ferdinandea*, for example, consistently referred to blasphemers by the male pronoun. This use of the male pronoun was not simply generic. As historian Andrea Griesebner has shown, for crimes that authorities viewed as gender neutral the code used both male and female forms, and for crimes specifically associated with women the code used the female pronoun exclusively. The code referred to a magician as the masculine *Zauberer* or the feminine *Zauberin* (*-in* is the feminine suffix); a procurer might be a *Kuppler* or *Kupplerin*, whereas a perpetrator of abortion or infanticide was referred to as "she."[183] In contrast to the article on blasphemy in the *Ferdinandea*, eighteenth-century legislation on suicidal iconoclasm specifically addressed "both sexes" (*beyderley Geschlechts*) or "the evildoer, of male or female sex."[184]

The extent to which early modern jurists understood blasphemy in general to be a masculine transgression is also reflected in visual images of blasphemy. The *Praxis rerum criminalium* by the jurist Joos de Damhouder included engravings showing blasphemers *in flagranti*. A widely used legal compendium published in multiple editions after 1554, the *Praxis* appeared in German translation 1565. Damhouder's legal manual influenced European criminal practice well into the eighteenth century. The engravings accompany Damhouder's discussion of "injury of the divine majesty." The engraving an edition from 1571 shows men in the foreground mocking and threatening a crucifix statue. A blasphemous deed seems imminent. The image of an edition from 1581 features verbal blasphemy (Image 6.9). Three men are gambling around a table. One of them

---

[181] Schwerhoff, *Zungen wie Schwerter*, 265.

[182] Maureen Flynn, "Blasphemy and the Play of Anger in Sixteenth-Century Spain," *Past and Present* 149 (1995): 49, 53.

[183] Andrea Griesebner, *Konkurrierende Wahrheiten. Malefizprozesse vor dem Landgericht Perchtoldsdorf im 18. Jahrhundert* (Vienna: Böhlau Verlag, 2000), 55–56.

[184] The 1713 edict refers to "junge Leute, beyderley Geschlechts." The 1715 edict refers to "ein dergleichen Übelthäter, mann- oder weiblichen Geschlechts." Herrenleben, *Sammlung Oesterreichischer Gesetze*, vol. 3, 714–715, 801–802.

points toward God the Father appearing in the sky in the far left, whom he has just blasphemed. In the background to the right, a man is worshipping the devil (Image 6.10).[185]

Protestant iconoclastic riots were also dominated by men. Usually groups of men, often armed—from the Catholic perspective a "mob"— forced their way into a church where they demolished what they perceived as the idolatrous images within.[186] They might also act as individuals, as we have seen in the two notorious sixteenth-century cases involving Protestant blasphemers in Vienna discussed in the last chapter. Host desecration, too, was often associated with men acting alone or in groups, whether Jews or highwaymen-witches. During the heyday of the witch-hunt female witches were also believed to desecrate the host at witches' sabbaths, but witch-hunting in Austrian lands after 1650 focused largely on men.

---

[185] Joos de Damhoudere, *Praxis rerum Criminalium. Gründliche und rechte Underweysung Welcher massen in Rechtfertigung peinlicher Sachen ... zu handeln* (Frankfurt am Main: Johannes Wolffius, 1571), 102v. Damhouder, *Praxis* (Frankfurt am Main: Nicolaus Basseus, 1581), 92. On Damhouder, see Rik Opsommer and Jos Monballyu, "Damhouder, Joos de." *Lexikon zur Geschichte der Hexenverfolgung*, eds. Gudrun Gersmann, Katrin Moeller and Jürgen-Michael Schmidt, in: historicum.net, URL: http://www.historicum.net/no_cache/persistent/artikel/1588/. That Damhouder's *Praxis* was used in criminal prosecutions in Vienna is evident in a late seventeenth-century anonymous commentary on the *Ferdinandea* that discusses Viennese and Lower Austrian cases. The *Praxis* is cited as an authoritative legal source. WStLA, Handschriften, A 320, fol. 2v.

[186] On iconoclasm as a male practice, see Christian von Burg, "'Das Bild vnsers Herren ab dem esel geschlagen.' Der Palmesel in den Riten der Zerstörung," in Peter Blickle and André Holenstein, eds., *Macht und Ohnmacht der Bilder: reformatorischer Bildersturm im Kontext der europäischen Geschichte.* (Munich: Oldenbourg, 2002), 117–141, and Lee Palmer Wandell, "Bildersturm im Elsaß," in ibid., 165–175, p. 165. Lucas Burkart, "Aus der Fastnacht in den Bildersturm: Knaben und junge Männer schänden und verbrennen das Kruzifix aus dem Basler Münster," in Cécile Dupeux, Peter Jezler and Jean Wirth, eds., *Bildersturm. Wahnsinn oder Gottes Wille? Austellungskatalog.* (Zürich, NZZ Verlag, 2000). Puritan iconoclasm in England was also "largely a male activity." Julie Spraggon, *Puritan Iconoclasm During the English Civil War: The Attack on Religious Imagery by Parliament and Its Soldiers.* (Woodbridge: Boydell & Brewer, 2003)., xii. Dutch iconoclasm also grew out of a "cultural world of male sociability," according to Peter J. Arnade. Even when women were involved in iconoclastic crowds, Arnade finds " a gendered division of labor in iconoclasm .... In which men do the physical destruction and women pilfer the goods." Peter J. Arnade, *Beggars, Iconoclasts, and Civic Patriots: The Political Culture of the Dutch Revolt.* (Ithaca: Cornell University Press, 2008), 110–112.

6 THE INJURED CRUCIFIX 323

Image 6.9 Depiction of blasphemy in Joos de Damhouder, *Praxis rerum criminalium: Gründlicher Bericht und anweisung, Welcher massen in Rechtfärtigung Peinlicher sachen, nach gemeynen beschribenen Rechten vor und in Gerichten ordentlich zuhandeln* (Franckfurt am Mayn: Johann Wolfius, 1571), 102v. Bayerische Staatsbibliothek München, 4 Crim. 41

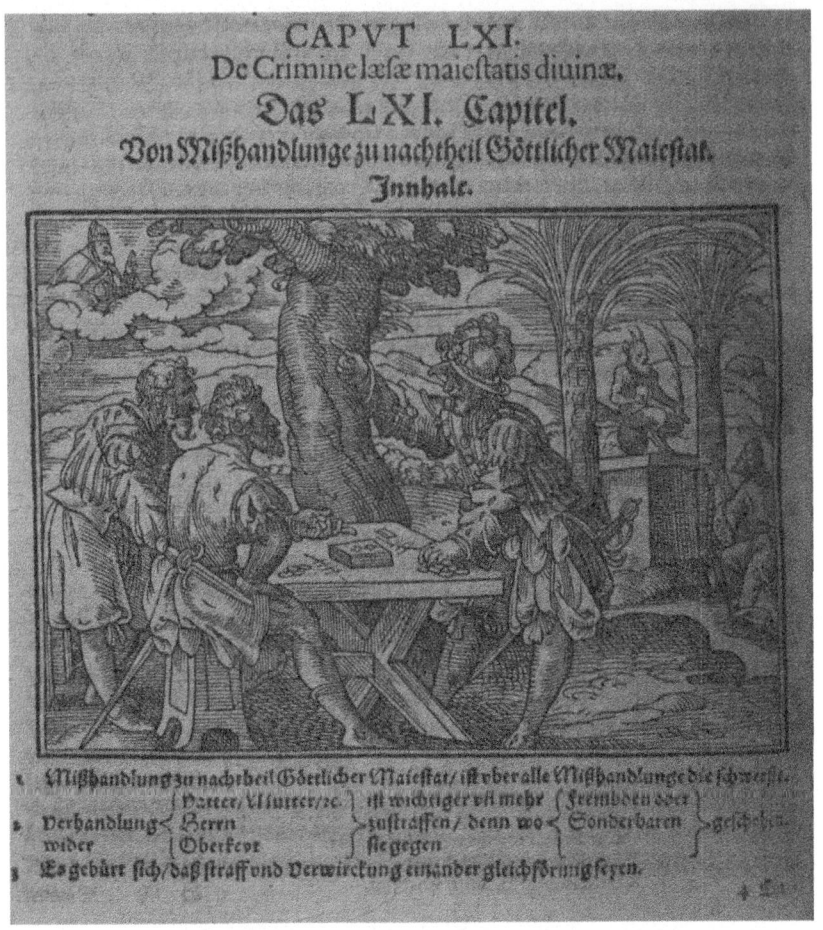

Image 6.10 Depiction of blasphemy in Joos de Damhouder, *Praxis rerum criminalium: Gründlicher Bericht und anweisung, Welcher massen in Rechtfärtigung Peinlicher sachen, nach gemeynen beschribenen Rechten vor und in Gerichten ordentlich zuhandeln* (Franckfurt am Mayn: Nicolaus Basseus, 1581), 92. Staatliche Bibliothek Regensburg, 999/2 Jur.353.

In any case, both verbal blasphemy and the violent destruction of icons, whether as deliberate blasphemy or a Protestant attack on idolatry (Catholics did not make this distinction, of course), were understood as male crimes. Church robbers, too, were mostly men. So the prevalence of women among Vienna's suicidal iconoclasts ran counter to traditional expectations and patterns of prosecution for blasphemy and sacrilege. Intriguingly, all cases of suicidal blasphemy in Vienna that involved verbal blasphemy—either by itself or in combination with iconoclasm—were committed by men. I have found no case where a woman blasphemed verbally. Women resorted exclusively to physical attacks, sometimes of a quite violent nature, as we have seen. This predominance of women among suicidal iconoclasts represents the same pattern already observed among suicidal child murders. When committing suicide by proxy women trespassed onto what was traditionally a masculine terrain.

In addition to the gender of the perpetrators it is necessary to consider the gender of the target of blasphemous assaults. With one exception, all suicidal iconoclasts attacked either the crucifix or the host, or both. In other words, the target of these attacks was Jesus. Even in the one case where a blasphemer attacked a statue of the Virgin Mary instead of the host or crucifix, his target was Jesus. In 1688 when Franz Wunderlich assaulted a Marian icon, he ran through the Christ child with his dagger, not the Virgin.[187] The *Ferdinandea* and subsequent codes defined the capital offenses of blasphemy in the first or second degree as blaspheming "directly against God and his purest Mother or other saints with dishonorable shameful words or deeds."[188] So demolishing an icon or image of the Virgin would certainly also have been an effective means of coercing one's execution. Given the centrality of the cult of the Virgin Mary in Counter-Reformation piety, and the many wonder-working images of the Virgin on display in the city, the question arises why Mary never became the target of suicidal iconoclasts. Was it simply a question of availability and ease of access, or was there a deeper, symbolic reason at play? I argue in the next chapter that there was a symbolic correspondence between the host, the

---

[187] Schlager, *Wiener Skizzen*, 126–127.
[188] Article 59 of the *Ferdinandea*, the "Landesgerichtsordnung für Osterreich unter der Enns," in *Codicis Austriaci ..., Das ist: Eigentlicher Begriff und Innhalt/ Aller Unter deß Durchleuchtigsten Ertz-Hauses zu Oesterreich ... ausgegangenen ...Generalien*, vol. 1 (Vienna: Leopold Voigt, 1704), 687–688.

crucifix, the Christ Child, and the child victims of suicide by proxy. However, gender symbolism, too, may have influenced suicidal iconoclasts' choice of target. I have argued that suicide by proxy was on a fundamental level a psychological response to social disciplining. Social discipline was imposed and enforced by patriarchal authority. By contrast, the Virgin Mary represented mercy and intercession, not the judgment and punishment suicidal iconoclasts sought.

When suicidal blasphemers attacked an icon or desecrated a host, what did they think and feel? None of Vienna's suicidal iconoclasts seem to have feared that they would be struck down by God on the spot, the recurring motif in so many legends and folktales surrounding blasphemy and sacrilege. But then, in storytelling about blasphemy such direct divine punishment tended to occur when this-worldly justice was not available or not forthcoming. In contrast, the Viennese blasphemers were already in the hands of the state, or they turned themselves in.

Clearly, they were instrumentalizing religious icons, just as suicidal murderers instrumentalized the children they killed. But how did suicidal iconoclasts feel about the crucifix or host they abused? Were they indifferent to it? Did they objectify it? Perhaps this was the case for the crucifix-breaker turned church robber, Joseph Zeitler. After all, he did not hesitate to steal and sell consecrated Eucharistic vessels after his release from Vienna's house of correction, so one wonders how much reverence he felt for the crucifix he demolished. Nonetheless, he felt the prohibition against committing direct suicide strongly enough that he chose the detour via suicidal blasphemy. Other suicidal iconoclasts seem to have experienced more profound spiritual anguish. Maria Sabina Paumbgartnerin, who committed physical blasphemy in the city hospital in 1715, was convinced that she was possessed by a demon. Rosina Plankhin, after destroying the crucifix three times and threatening to desecrate the host in 1715–1716, protested bitterly when she was denied access to Holy Communion. The fact that such blasphemers instrumentalized sacred objects does not preclude that many also believed that God was truly present in the host or crucifix they abused. Perhaps this is why Anna Maria Elisabetha Werthaim was unable to go through with desecrating the host in 1714, after she obtained it by means of fraudulent communion. Her hesitation resembles the vacillation and change of heart many child killers experienced before they ultimately succeeded in killing their intended victim. For suicidal child killers the murdered child was a means to an end. In many cases, however, the killers developed an emotionally intense relationship with the child they murdered, identifying with and effacing personal boundaries between themselves and their child victims. Did suicidal blasphemers have a similarly emotionally intense relationship to the sacred icon or host they defiled? The excessive violence with which some suicidal iconoclasts demolished the crucifix would seem to indicate that they did.

History and Memory

It is a historical irony that Vienna's house of correction was established in buildings vacated by Jews. A site where Viennese citizens imagined Jews perpetrating blasphemies became a place where Catholics actually did commit blasphemies. In contrast to blasphemies attributed to Jews—the actual desecration by the notorious Ferdinand Franz Engelberger, or the mythical medieval host desecrations Jews were accused of—the blasphemies committed by suicidal iconoclasts did not become the object of historical commemoration. Suicidal blasphemies did receive plenty of publicity at the time that they happened. The blasphemers' sentences were read publicly from the courthouse balcony on the day of their execution. They arrived at the ravenstone in dramatic public processions, accompanied by members of the Confraternity of the Dead. Priests excoriated their blasphemies in sermons addressed to the crowds that witnessed their executions. Indeed, as we have seen, this publicity seems to have inspired others to commit similar crimes, leading the authors of the *Theresiana* to treat these cases more discreetly. Historically, however, these blasphemers were effaced from memory. Instances of host desecration and sacrilege produced miracles and were worthy of commemoration only if they were perpetrated by the enemies of the true faith—Protestants, Jews, Turks, or witches. In Catholic storytelling, defilement by religious enemies led to miracles that resulted either in the conversion of the perpetrators, or in their exposure and exemplary punishment and death. The defiled host or icon emerged victorious to the greater glory of God. By contrast, the acts of Vienna's suicidal iconoclasts could not be woven into a triumphal narrative. These desperate perpetrators were not motivated by any competing faith or enmity toward Christendom. They were Catholics, already within the fold. There was not even a dramatic moment of discovery, when an occult crime became manifest. Suicidal blasphemers committed their deeds in public or made their act public by turning themselves in. This kind of blasphemy did not merit historical mention, let alone have miraculous effect. To Viennese authorities, these suicidal blasphemies were disturbing, frustrating, embarrassing, and inconvenient, best swept under the rug. And so, these desecrations were neither memorialized by any plaque or monument, nor recorded in Vienna's civic histories. This effacement from historical memory also held true for the practice of suicide by proxy more generally, as we shall see.

CHAPTER 7

Crime and Justice in a Sacred Landscape: Vienna, 1668–1786

Suicidal child murders happened contemporaneously to the outbreak of suicidal iconoclasm in late seventeenth- and early eighteenth-century Vienna, and continued for long after authorities developed the legal-theological rationale that allowed them to end executions of suicidal host desecrators and crucifix breakers. In this chapter I present the stories of some of Vienna's child murderers, and embed them in the physical spaces in which both the murders and the subsequent executions took place. Both killers and government authorities acted within a cityscape in which the sacred topography of Baroque Catholicism and the city's judicial infrastructure often overlapped, or even merged. These physical spaces framed and gave meaning to the ritual performances of both killers and authorities. Public executions in Vienna were imbued with Catholic ritual. Executions in early modern Europe were always dramatic spectacles. In Vienna, the tragic pomp was heightened further by the participation of the Imperial Arch-Confraternity of the Dead. This organization was created by the imperial dynasty, and presents a clear example of the melding of imperial sovereignty and salvific prowess that gave capital punishment in Vienna its distinctiveness. Criminal justice provided one more arena where Habsburg rulers put the *pietas austriaca* on display. These performances proved irresistibly alluring to many suicidal people in Vienna. Once again women stood out among the perpetrators of suicidal murders.

© The Author(s), under exclusive license to Springer Nature
Switzerland AG 2023
K. Stuart, *Suicide by Proxy in Early Modern Germany*, World
Histories of Crime, Culture and Violence,
https://doi.org/10.1007/978-3-031-25244-0_7

In preceding chapters, it has become clear how public execution became a religious resource that perpetrators of suicide by proxy exploited for their own personal salvation. In this chapter I expand the focus beyond suicidal perpetrators to consider the meaning public execution held for the broader Catholic public. Not only the salvation of the condemned criminal was at stake. Public execution also figured in the salvation strategies and devotions of ordinary Catholic lay folk, most of whom would never personally become a target of criminal justice. The Catholic doctrine of purgatory shaped religious ritual surrounding public execution in Vienna, and featured prominently in the pastoral care of condemned criminals. Belief in purgatory formed the basis of a salvific exchange between condemned criminals, who consented to play the role of penitent poor sinners on the scaffold, and the Catholic public. Government officials, clergy, and lay people invested significant resources to support the salvation of condemned criminals, an indication of the ideological significance of what amounted to a comprehensive societal effort. Catholics performed devotions on behalf of condemned criminals, in the hopes that they would benefit spiritually from the criminal's salvation. Their devotions in turn encouraged suicidal people to seek death on the ravenstone.

Surviving sources allow for greater insight into the individual circumstances as well as the subjectivity and motives of Vienna's suicidal child killers than it is possible to achieve for the city's suicidal iconoclasts. A number of printed execution notices, so-called Poor Sinner's Pamphlets, of these murderers have survived. These were cheap ephemeral prints, typically two to three pages long, that sometimes included engravings and moralizing poems. Sold before and during executions, these pamphlets were the product of close cooperation between criminal courts and the printers who published them. Printed with official approval, they provide detailed summaries of the confessions of the condemned.[1] As the eighteenth century progressed, the entries in the Protocols of the Confraternity of the Dead became more extensive. The *Wiennerisches Diarium* continued to report on suicidal child killings, as it had on blasphemy cases, though the newspaper became less interested in crime reporting after 1760, an indication of changing tastes and sensibility of the reading public

---

[1] Gerhard Ammerer and Friedrich Adomeit, "Armsünderblätter," in *Repräsentationen von Kriminalität und öffentlicher Sicherheit. Bilder, Vorstellungen und Diskurse vom 16. bis 20. Jahrhundert*, eds. Karl Härter, Gerhard Sälter and Eva Wiebel (Frankfurt a. M.: Vittorio Klostermann, 2010), 276.

in the later eighteenth century. Various news compendia and chronicles, such as the *Theatrum Europaeum*, also contained accounts of suicidal child murders.[2] Of course, in all of these sources the killers' narratives were condensed and filtered through the moralizing lens of religious and government authorities.

Early Cases

The earliest documented likely case of suicidal child murder in Vienna happened in 1668. On the evening of October 12, a soldier in the Viennese guard stabbed a six-year-old boy to death in the fields outside the city. Then he severed the boy's right hand and took it with him.[3] The severing of the boy's hand makes this case unique among suicidal child murders in Vienna, or for that matter within Germany writ large. Nothing similar occurred in any other case of suicide by proxy that I have identified. To the twenty-first-century reader this post-mortem dismemberment brings to mind the trophies some modern serial killers take from their victims' bodies, and raises the question whether this murder was a sadistic psycho-sexual killing, rather than a suicide by proxy.[4] However, in the seventeenth-century context, another explanation is more plausible. The soldier did not take the boy's hand as a souvenir. After the murder he went directly to the courthouse and turned himself in. Confessing to the murder, the soldier faced an incredulous judge who thought the soldier was a foolish person making a false confession. Several other early perpetrators of suicide by proxy faced similar incredulity. Then the soldier presented the judge with the boy's severed hand. Now the *corpus delicti* was established, and the soldier's identity as the perpetrator was not in doubt. By presenting the judge with his victim's hand, the soldier performed a medieval judicial ritual that had become archaic in most German territories by the seventeenth century. The ritual was related to the "Justice of the Street" that was still being performed in Hamburg. A "Suit with the dead Hand" was a means of establishing that a

---

[2] On the *Theatrum Europaeum*, see Hermann Bingel, *Das "Theatrum Europaeum", ein Beitrag zur Publizistik des 17. und 18. Jahrhunderts* (Berlin: E. Ebering, 1909).

[3] Wolfgang Jacob Geiger, *Theatrum Europaeum, oder außführliche und warhafftige Beschreibung aller und jeder denckwürdiger Geschichten ... von dem 1665sten Jahr biß in Anno 1671 ...* (Frankfurt a. M.: Matthäus Merian, 1677), 980.

[4] On the psychological meaning of serial killers taking trophies, such as personal possessions or body parts, from their victims, see Ronald M. Holmes and Stephen T. Holmes, *Profiling Violent Crimes: An investigative Tool* (Thousand Oaks, Calif: Sage, 2002), 136–137.

killing had taken place. The victim's hand, instead of the entire corpse, served as the *corpus delicti*.[5] The soldier's suicidal intent was clear. Before the murder, he had received the Eucharist without prior confession, that is, he received the sacrament in an unworthy state. Perhaps he planned a host desecration? He also attempted to drown himself, and to stab himself, before he murdered the boy.[6] The soldier was beheaded in January 1669, after the severing of his right hand.[7]

By contrast, an attempted suicide by proxy in 1692 was unsuccessful, for want of a *corpus delicti*. Anna Wadlin Cellensis appeared at the court house "desiring to die." She confessed to an infanticide she had committed eighteen years earlier. Authorities arrested her, but her confession alone was insufficient for conviction. The court requested an evaluation from the medical faculty of the University of Vienna. The physicians concluded that she was suffering from hypochondriacal melancholy and surmised that her confession resulted "from desperation and weariness with life." They recommended that she be whipped in the house of correction and released.[8]

Three years later, in 1695, a servant woman cut the throat of an eight-year-old boy as he lay sleeping. The jurist Johann Franz Maldoner attended her execution and wrote a brief account of the case. After the murder, the servant woman approached the executioner personally, instead of turning herself in at the courthouse, as most other suicidal child murderers did. She demanded from the executioner "that justice be done unto her." This

---

[5] D. Werkmüller, "Klage mit dem Toten Mann," *HDR*, vol. 2, 849–851. Heinrich Brunner, "Die Klage mit dem toten Mann und die Klage mit der toten Hand," *Zeitschrift der Savigny-Stiftung für Rechtsgeschichte: Germanistische Abteilung* 31 (1910): 235–252. In unsolved cases, victims' hands were preserved by the court as material evidence. For an example, see https://www.landesmuseum-mv.de/exponate/stadtgeschichtliches-museum-wismar/totenhaende-leibzeichen-in-gedrechselter-holzschale-aus-st.-georgen-wismar/index.html.

[6] Johann Constantin Feige, *Wunderbarer Adlers-Schwung oder Fernere Geschichts-Fortsetzung Ortelii redivivi & continuati das ist: Beschreibung von Staatshändeln* (Vienna: Leopold Voigt, 1693), 122.

[7] Anon., *Das Ehmals gedrückte/ vom Türken berückte/ nun Trefflich erquickte Königreich Hungarn/ samt dessen Ströme-Fürsten/ der Weltberühmten Donau* (Frankfurt: Christoff Riegel, 1688), 263.

[8] "Anna Wadlin Cellensis ratione sui infanticidii masculi ... ante 18 annos perpetrati spontanee se ipsam in tribunali caesareo denuntiat atque in arrestum ponit, mori desiderans." She confessed "ex desperatione ac taedio vitae." UAW, Med 1.7, AFMV VII, f. 104r, May 12, 1692.

case brings to mind a similar case in Hamburg in 1639, when journeyman shoemaker Johann Körner also went directly to the executioner to confess to a murder he had committed seven years earlier.[9] Just as the Hamburg executioner initially turned Körner away, the Viennese executioner suspected that the woman before him demanding her execution was deranged. He sent her to seek solace in church. In 1695 suicide by proxy was apparently not so common in Vienna that the executioner recognized the type of offender he was dealing with. The woman went to church and performed her devotions. Then she publicly announced her crime to other worshippers and requested a father confessor. In an odd twist, a highborn lady was also attending services in the church at that time. The lady decided to save the servant woman. She conveyed the self-accused child murderer across the Danube, presumably by carriage, three or four hours from Vienna. We know nothing of the lady's motivation or why she felt compelled to help a child killer. Her rescue attempt raises fascinating questions about how the public viewed criminal justice and what kind of emotional connection or sympathy people felt for criminal defendants. Or, was the highborn lady usurping a clerical role, since Catholic priests frequently granted asylum to felons facing capital punishment, or even facilitated their escape?[10] In any case, the lady's efforts were in vain. She transported the serving woman so far from Vienna "that she would have been free and clear, as far as the body is concerned," Maldoner wrote, but the servant woman, "of her own volition," walked all the way back to the city. Again, she went directly to the executioner. This time she was arrested. Justice was swift. She arrived in Vienna on Monday. The following Friday she was beheaded after her hand was struck off. Maldoner watched her conduct closely, an indication of how attuned observers were to the emotional states of criminals facing execution. Even as she listened to the reading of her death sentence and was led out to the site of execution, Maldoner reported, she did not change color or turn pale. "Rather, she bloomed like a rose."[11]

Vienna, like Hamburg, experienced cases in clusters. In 1704, for example, three women committed child murder in less than a month. On July 14, Maria Johanna Neuhofferin, a twenty-seven-year-old married

---

[9] See Chap. 3.
[10] See Chap. 2.
[11] Johann Franz Maldoner, *Synopsis militaris: Oder kurzer Begriff über die Kayserliche Kriegs-Articul* (Nuremberg: Johann Christoph Lochner, 1724), 222.

woman, whose husband regularly beat her, cut the throat of her three-month-old baby daughter. She was beheaded on the High Market ten days later, on July 24, 1704.[12] The executioner botched her beheading, striking her in the shoulder. Finally, as she sat, restrained, on the ground, the executioner succeeded in decapitating her with his second blow.[13] Neuhofferin's botched beheading did not dissuade the next killer. Eleven days later, on September 4, 1704, Susanna Weiglhofferin, twenty-five, a childminder for a roofer, cut his baby's throat as it slept in its crib. Four days later, on September 8, Maria Barbara Zächerlin, cut the throat of her neighbor's seven-year-old son.[14] Weiglhofferin and Zächerlin were beheaded together nine days later, on September 17, 1704. Zächerlin was sentenced to have her hand struck off prior to beheading, and attached to the pillory, but this additional penalty was remitted by imperial pardon.[15] Just over two months after this double execution, on November. 24, 1704, the *Wiennerisches Diarium* reported that a woman attempted to murder her child by slashing its throat "yet again."[16]

Susanna Weiglhofferin (c. 1679–1704): Murder as Pilgrimage?

Susanna Weiglhofferin's unusually detailed execution pamphlet gives insight into the mindset of one of these killers.[17] Her case exemplifies how some perpetrators attempted to incorporate religious devotions into their suicide by proxy. For Lutherans this involved praying with and over their victim, just prior to the murder, as several women inmates in the Hamburg house of correction did.[18] For Catholics this could mean embedding their ritual murder within the sacred landscape of Baroque Catholicism. Weiglhofferin cut the throat of her employer's child at home in its crib, but this was not her first choice of victim, or place. She would have preferred to commit the murder in a religiously more meaningful setting.

---

[12] *WD*, Nr. 99, 12–16 July, 1704. *WD*, Nr. 102, 23–25 July, 1704.
[13] ÖNB, Cod 8363, p. 2, Nr. 10, 24 July 1704, Johanna.
[14] *WD*, Nr. 114, 3–6 September 1704. *WD*, Nr. 115, 6–10 September 1704. *WD*, Nr. 118, 17–20 September.
[15] *WD*, Nr. 118, 17–20 September.
[16] "Eodem wurde abermal ein Weibs-Bild …/welches ihrem Kind in den Halß geschnitten/ und umbringen wollen/ gefänglich eingezogen." *WD*, Nr. 137, 24 November 1704.
[17] *WD*, Nr. 118, 17 September 1704.
[18] See Chap. 4.

Three months prior to the killing, Weiglhofferin began to suffer from depression. Tormented by "fantasies" that God had condemned her to die by the sword, she felt compelled to kill someone. "She availed herself of various spiritual aids," her execution pamphlet reported, but she found no relief. She decided to go to the suburb of Hernals, about a two-hour walk northwest of the city. There she planned to kill the first child she could lay hands on.

Hernals was one of several sacred destinations within walking distance of the city. A Way of the Cross led from the Corpus Christi altar in St. Stephen's Cathedral at the heart of the city to the parish church of Hernals where a Holy Sepulcher was constructed in 1639. Seven almost life-size Stations of the Cross were erected along the way. The distance between the Corpus Christi Altar and the Holy Sepulcher was believed to correspond exactly to the length of the *Via Dolorosa* in Jerusalem. Processions to Hernals played a prominent role in the performative piety of the Habsburgs.[19] Many of the stations and the sepulcher itself were damaged during the Turkish siege of 1683, a sacrilege that likely increased the statues' charisma, given the contemporary cult of injured icons. Processions to Hernals continued in the late seventeenth and early eighteenth centuries, even before construction began on a new pilgrimage church featuring a monumental Mount Calvary in 1709.[20] During a pilgrimage to Hernals in 1698, for example, participants carried images and acted out scenes of the passion during the procession.[21]

Why did Weiglhofferin choose Hernals? Perhaps she believed that the murder would be easier to carry out in the less densely populated suburb than in the city. Her later choices, however, make it likely that her decision

---

[19] ÖNB, Cod 8227, 241–249. Gustav Gugitz, *Österreichs Gnadenstätten in Kult und Brauch*, vol.1 (Vienna: Verlag Brüder Hollinkek, 1955), 92–95.

[20] Giovanni Salvadori, *Die Minoritenkirche und ihre Älteste Umgebung. Ein Beitrag zur Geschichte Wiens* (Vienna: Congregation der Italienischen Nationalkirche, 1895), 193. Neta Bodner, *Walking to "Jerusalem" from Vienna: A Seventeenth-Century Way of the Cross* (Jerusalem: Spectrum, The Hebrew University of Jerusalem, 2013), 26.

[21] Janet K. Page, *Convent Music and Politics in Eighteenth-Century Vienna* (Cambridge: Cambridge University Press, 2014), 156. The Benedictine monk Casimir Freschot describes Hernals in his travel memoirs, published 1705: "Il y a près de l'Eglise du lieu un sepulcre bâti dans la forme, & avec les mesures de celui de nôtre Seigneur, & le chemin qui y conduit de la Ville est semé de Chapelles, où les Mysteres de la Passion sont representez. Le Peuple ne manque pas de les visiter assez souvent." Casimir Freschot, *Memoires de la cour de Vienne: contenant les remarques d'un voyageur curieux sur l'état present de cette cour, et sur ses intérêts* (Cologne: Guillaume Etienne, 1705), 36.

to commit the murder at this sacred location was no coincidence. Weiglhofferin purchased a knife for five *Kreuzer* and set off to Hernals. Then, as today, Vienna was surrounded by vineyards. In Hernals she encountered a vintner with six young children. She asked for shelter. She stayed at the vintner's home for two days. She chose a particular child as her victim. She never found a suitable occasion to carry out the murder, however. Finally, she gave up and returned to Vienna. Now she contemplated an alternate setting. Again, she chose a sacred destination. She planned to travel to Mariazell, Austria's national pilgrimage shrine, a four to five day walk from Vienna along the *via sacra*, the "Holy Road," Austria's oldest pilgrims' trail. She would have had opportunity to worship at several miraculous shrines along the way, and before committing the murder, she likely planned to take communion at Mariazell, as more than 120,000 pilgrims did at the shrine every year.[22]

Did Weiglhofferin envision offering up the murdered child to the wonderworking icon, the Merciful Mother of Mariazell, a sacrifice in exchange for her salvation? In the context of her culture this would have made sense. Indeed, in a ritual performance of the *pietas austriaca*, Emperor Charles VI and his spouse Empress Elizabeth acted on a similar idea just over a decade later. On the Feast of the Holy Trinity 1715, which in that year fell on June 16, the royal couple made a pilgrimage to Mariazell to pray for the birth of an heir. On April 13, 1716 Archduke Leopold Johann was born. The imperial government celebrated the birth of this heir, as shown in Chap. 6, by granting amnesty to a number of suicidal iconoclasts then imprisoned in Vienna's house of correction. When Leopold Johann died six months later, his parents made a votive offering to the Virgin of Mariazell. They donated a statue of their infant son in pure gold, of the same weight as the baby had weighed in life. An accompanying inscription read: "Their son Leopold, prayed for in [Maria]Zell and returned to Heaven, whom they could not dedicate in life, Charles and Elizabeth give back in gold of the same weight, in eternal devotion." This votive statue of their dead child, styled as the voluntary offering of their first-born son in a kind of analogy to the Christ Child, demonstrated the royal couple's willingness to sacrifice, and their humble submission to the Virgin of

---

[22] Between 120,000 and 150,000 pilgrims took communion at Mariazell yearly during the eighteenth century. Jean Bérenger, "The Austrian Church," in *Church and Society in Catholic Europe of the Eighteenth Century*, eds. William James Callahan and David Higgs (Cambridge: Cambridge Univ. Press, 1979), 102.

Mariazell. In exchange for their offering, they could hope for continued divine blessing for the House of Austria. Their votive offering was celebrated as an exemplary act of devotion.[23] Of course, had Weiglhofferin acted on her idea to murder a child in Mariazell, it would certainly have been viewed as a particularly dastardly and sacrilegious crime, as she herself came to realize: "it came into her mind that such a deed was not appropriate at such a pilgrimage shrine."[24]

"In this state of indecision" the idea came to her to carry out the murder in the Viennese suburb of Hietzing. Southwest of the city, Hietzing was also a well-known pilgrimage site. The parish church of Hietzing, just outside the gardens of Schönbrunn Palace, housed a miracle-working icon of the Virgin Mary. It gained popularity after miraculously saving four peasants from invading Turks in 1529. A path with twelve Stations of the Cross, built in 1667, led from Schönbrunn Palace to the shrine.[25] Weiglhofferin's execution pamphlet does not explain whether she had this sacred setting in mind when she picked her destination. In any case, first she needed a new knife. She had lost the knife she purchased before her unsuccessful excursion to Hernals, so she spent another six *Kreuzer* on a shaving knife, and set out for Hietzing. On the road, she encountered several children whom she tried to persuade to come away with her. They all refused. Finally, she came across a boy, about six years old, sitting by himself on a rock. Promising to buy him some plums she managed to lure him some distance away. She reached into her bag for her shaving knife,

---

[23] The Latin inscription accompanying the votive offering read "Votum & Quem Coelis impetratum, Coelis resitutum, Vivum sister non possunt, LEOPOLDUM FILIUM Foecunditatis primitatias in auro aequi libri reddunt CAROLUS ET ELIZABETHA AETERNUM DEVOTI. Anon., *Wunderwürdiges Leben und Groß-Thaten Ihro Jetzt-Glorwürdigst-Regierenden Kayserl. und Catholischen Majestät Caroli des Sechsten* (Nuremberg: Buggel und Seitz, 1721), 314–315. For context, see Franz Matsche, *Die Kunst im Dienst der Staatsidee Kaiser Karls VI. Ikonographie, Ikonologie und Programmatik des "Kaiserstils,"* vol. 1 (Berlin: de Gruyter, 1981), 180–181. Empress Maria Theresa performed a similar, if less tragic devotion on April 20, 1757, when she made a votive offering in gold of her youngest son, Archduke Maximilian Franz (1756–1801), then four months old. Cölestin Wolfsgruber, *Geschichte der Loretokapelle bei St. Augustin in Wien* (Vienna: Alfred Hölder, 1886), 27.

[24] WD, Nr. 118, 17 September 1704.

[25] Augustinus Ristl, *Maria voll der Gnaden zu Hietzing, das ist, ausführlicher Bericht von dem Uralten Gottes-Haus der Regulirten Chor-Herren des H. Aug. zu Hietzing ohnweit Wienn* (Vienna: Gregor Kurtzböck, 1738), 112–117. Gugitz, *Österreichs Gnadenstätten*, 84–86.

but before she could cut the boy's throat she cut her finger. The boy escaped. Weiglhofferin walked on, in search of another victim.

Finally, she decided to go home and kill her employer's baby. She planned to kill the baby the next morning after the roofer left for work while the mother was at Mass. After the mother left for church, she entered the room where the child slept, believing that the father had left too. Just as she reached for her knife, the father came in. Concealing her intent, she managed, "against her inclination," to act cheerfully throughout the day, to avoid suspicion. She carried the baby around in her arms, lovingly caressing it. The next morning, September 4, 1704, the baby's mother was again at Mass, and the father really had left for work. Weiglhofferin cut the child's throat and went directly to the courthouse to turn herself in.[26]

The Government Responds, and Fails to End the Killings

Sixteen months after the beheadings of Weigelhofferin and Zächerlin, Vienna staged another double execution of two women. On January 19, 1706, Sidonia, thirty-four, was beheaded for cutting the throat of a vintner's child with a bread knife, in Hernals, a month earlier. Helena, twenty-two, was executed for aborting her unborn child.[27] This accumulation of cases prompted new legislation that addressed classic infanticide as well as suicidal child murder, both by mothers who killed their older children and by "strangers and unrelated people acting out of extreme malice, or also weariness with life." Entitled "How Child Murder Should be Punished," the edict was publicized by town crier within the city and distributed to criminal courts throughout lower Austria.[28] The edict was promulgated in upper Austria in 1712 (Image 7.1).[29]

Mothers "who premeditatedly killed their older children," that is, likely perpetrators of suicide by proxy, as well as infanticidal mothers who killed

---

[26] *WD*, Nr. 118, 17–20 September.

[27] *WD*, Nr. 257, 19 January 1706. ÖNB, Cod 8363, p. 4, Nr 22, 19 Januray 1706.

[28] "Wie es mit Bestrafung des Kinder-Mords zu halten," 22 March 1706, *Codicis Austriaci* III, 511–512. J. E. Schlager, *Wiener-Skizzen aus dem Mittelater*. Neue Folge (Vienna: Carl Gerold, 1842), vol. 2, 273. An example of the distribution of the edict to Lower Austrian criminal courts, see Archiv der Marktgemeinde Perchtoldsdorf, Patente, Karton 344.

[29] On 23 August 1712. Georg Joseph Kögl von Waldinutzy, *De iure civili, et criminali Austriaco-bellico tractatus practicus*, vol. 1 (Preßburg: Johann Michael Landerer, 1772), 184.

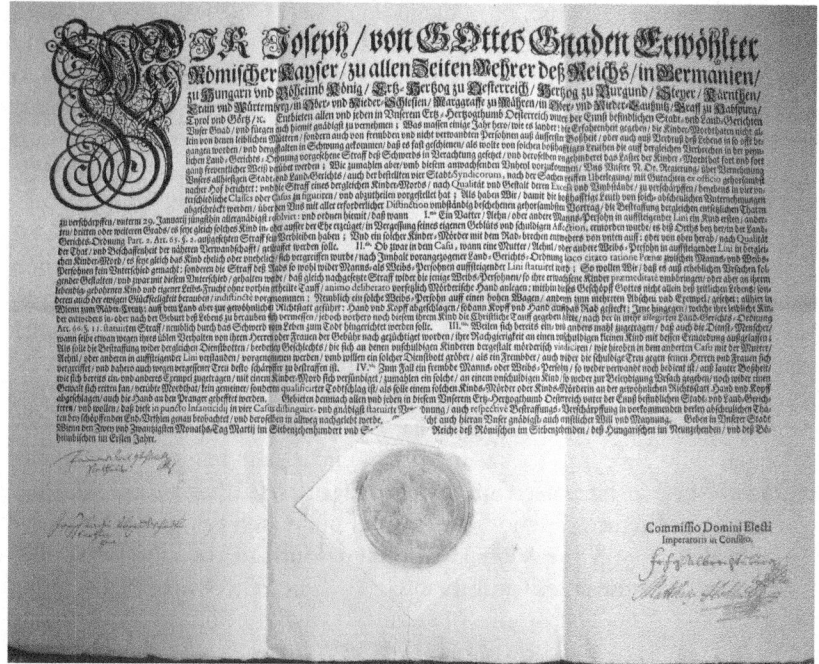

Image 7.1   Edict on Child Murders. "Wie es mit Bestrafung des Kinder-Mords zu halten," 22 March 1706. Archiv der Marktgemeinde Perchtoldsdorf, Patente, Karton 344

their newborn children "without prior baptism …, thus robbing the child not only of temporal life but also of eternal salvation" would both be beheaded after prior severing of the hand. Head and hand would remain exposed on the wheel by the ravenstone. Women who murdered their children during or just after birth, but baptized them first, would merely be beheaded. Wayward servants who sought revenge for punishment by their master or mistress by murdering their employers' children would suffer the same punishment as blood relatives, because their guilt was compounded by the breach of loyalty that they owed their masters. Finally, there were "strange men or women, who are neither related nor in service" who committed child murder "out of pure malice." This was a murder "with special circumstance" because the victim was an innocent child incapable of giving offense, or of defending itself.[30] Such murderers would be beheaded after their hand was severed. Subsequently the hand would be attached to the pillory. In the subtle calculus of infamy according to which early modern authorities meted out capital punishment, strangers suffered a slightly less severe penalty than blood relatives and wayward servants, since only the hand, not head and hand, would be exposed. The hand would be exposed at the pillory rather than the wheel by the ravenstone, a slightly less dreaded location.[31]

Viennese authorities, like their counterparts in Hamburg, soon learned that more brutal executions did not deter suicidal child murderers. Vienna's rulers would repeat this lesson a few years later when harsher executions also failed to quell suicidal iconoclasm, as shown in Chap. 5. The government first implemented the new edict in 1708, during the execution of Eva N., a thirty-six-year-old widow, who had thrown her newborn child alive into the latrine "in an unchristian manner." The court sentenced her to be placed on a high wagon, "so that people like her would mirror themselves and be revolted," and taken to the ravenstone at the Wheel Cross on the Vienna Mountain south of the city, just under three miles from the city's Carinthian Gate.[32] The Wheel Cross was a stone Pieta (Image 7.2). The origins of statue's name are obscure. Most likely the statue came to be known as the Wheel Cross because the bodies of executed felons were placed on wheels atop posts immediately adjacent to the Pieta, to be consumed by the elements. A short distance further, at the crest of the Vienna Mountain, stood the city's massive stone gallows. Nearby stood the *Spinnerin am Kreuz*, a gothic column erected in 1452 by Hans Puchsbaum, one of the architects of St. Stephen's Cathedral, featuring scenes of the passion of Christ. Here malefactors stopped to pray on their way to the gallows.[33] The elevated location made the gothic column and the gallows the first structures travelers saw as they approached

---

[30] *Codicis Austriaci* III, 512.

[31] On the calculus of honor and infamy in criminal justice see Stuart, *Defiled Trades*, 121–148.

[32] *WD*, Nr. 501, 22 May 1708, Eva N.

[33] Achim Timmermann, *Memory and Redemption: Public Monuments and the Making of the Late Medieval Landscape* (Turnout: Brepols, 2017), 51–54, 64–68. Walter Sturm, "… außer der Linie" Favoriten am Wienerberg: Beiträge zur Topographie und Siedlungsgeschichte im Raum des heutigen Wiener Gemeindebezirks Favoriten," *Favoritner Museumsblätter* 30 (2004).

7 CRIME AND JUSTICE IN A SACRED LANDSCAPE: VIENNA, 1668–1786

Image 7.2 Anonymous photo of the "Wheel Cross" (Räderkreuz), Column with Pieta adjacent to execution site on the Wienerberg, taken 1868 prior to its demolition. "Mariensäule an der Triesterstraße vor der Matzleinsdorfer[linie] b[eim] Richtplatz." Photo: Wien Museum, Inv. Nr. 78.369/1, 10

the city from the south, and they were visible from across the city (Image 7.3).[34]

Eva N.'s execution procession did not continue all the way up to the gallows at the hilltop, but stopped at the ravenstone by the Wheel Cross, where she was beheaded after severing of her hand. Head and hand remained exposed on a wheel by the ravenstone.[35] A detailed examination of Vienna's physical infrastructure of criminal justice and how the theater of punishment played out in urban space will follow below. For now, suffice it to point out a feature of Eva N.'s execution that distinguished it from all previous documented executions of infanticidal mothers, suicidal child murderers and suicidal iconoclasts. Up until this point all known executions of such perpetrators had taken place either within the city walls on the High Market, the large square where Vienna's city courthouse stood, or at the ravenstone just outside the city wall beyond the Scottish Gate. To be executed at the Wheel Cross, as Eva N. was, meant that members of the Confraternity of the Dead did not accompany her to her execution, nor did they give her a Christian burial afterward. The Protocols of the Confraternity show that its members never participated in executions on the Vienna Mountain. Male criminals who died here on the gallows or were beheaded or broken by the wheel on the ravenstone at the Wheel Cross were simply left exposed to the elements, but this was considered unseemly for female corpses. Eva N.'s body was most likely interred in a shallow grave nearby.[36] A parcel map from 1831 shows such a burial site next to the Pieta.[37]

The heightened infamy of Eva N's execution did not deter Rosalia N., eignteen, from cutting the throat of the eight-year-old son of a manservant. She was executed in the same location six weeks later. The severity of

---

[34] As pilgrims knelt before the crucifix at the Hernals Mount Calvary they could see the gallows and Spinnerin am Kreuz on the horizon. "Prospekt des Calvari Bergs zu Hernals," engraving by Georg Daniel Heumann after Salomon Kleiner, in Salomon Kleiner, *Vera Et Accurata Delineatio Omnium Templorum et Coenobiorum Quae tam in Caesarea Urbe ac Sede Vienna Austriae, quam in circumjacentibus Suburbys ejus reperiuntur*, vol. 1 (Augsburg: Johann Andreas Pfeffel, 1724), plate 67. In high resolution here: https://hdl.handle.net/2027/gri.ark:/13960/t5j99022h?urlappend=%3Bseq=67.

[35] *WD*, Nr. 501, 19–22 May, 1708, for Tuesday, 22 May 1708, Eva N.

[36] A report on execution of the child murder Anna Margaretha H., beheaded at the Wheel Cross in 1732, indicates that this was the standard practice for criminals executed at this location. *WD*, 25 October 1732, Nr. 86, 24 October 1732, Anna Margaretha H.

[37] Anton Lang, "Hochgericht und Räderkreuz: Die Hinrichtungsstätten am Wienerberg," *Favoritner Museumsblätter* 28 (2002): 48.

7 CRIME AND JUSTICE IN A SACRED LANDSCAPE: VIENNA, 1668–1786   343

Image 7.3 Parcel map showing execution sites on the Vienna Mountain, c. 1730. Wiener Stadt- und Landesarchiv, Pläne und Karten: Sammelband, P1, Pläne und Karten, 50, Gegend vor der Martleinsdorfer Linie

Rosalia's sentence exceeded the requirements of the 1706 decree. For three days in a row she stood on a stage at the New Market, one of Vienna's busiest market places. The knife with which she committed the murder hung around her neck. Here she received fifteen lashes, "a half Schilling," daily. On the day of her execution, she was placed on a high wagon and taken to the ravenstone at the Wheel Cross, where she died like Eva N. before her.[38]

The following year Vienna's criminal court sentenced another female child murderer to tortures more common in the executions of condemned witches during the heyday of the witch-hunt. On June 29, 1709, Catherina N., a thirty-eight-year-old married woman, cut her own child's throat "almost half way through" at "the White Cross," a roadside cross that stood along the River Wien. Her choice to commit the murder in public at a roadside cross is another example of a perpetrator embedding her murder within a sacred landscape. Seventeen days later she was executed at the Wheel Cross, like Rosalia N. before her. But first she was to endure additional agonies. From the High Market, where her sentence was proclaimed, she was to be placed in a high wagon, taken to the New Market, where her right breast would be ripped with red-hot pincers. Then she would be taken to the scene of the murder "at the White Cross," where her left breast would be ripped.[39] Witches, notorious for their attacks on fertility and on children, often suffered tearing of their breasts during their execution processions.[40] In Catherina N.'s case, the symbolism in the sentence to rip the breasts of this murderous mother was not subtle. In the end, she was spared these extra torments. "His Imperial Majesty, out of in-born most laudable mercy," remitted the tearing of her breasts.[41]

Viennese authorities prosecuted seven further cases between 1713 and 1720. All of the murderers were women, ranging in age from eighteen to

---

[38] *WD*, Nr. 516, 11 July 1708, Rosalia N.

[39] *WD*, Nr. 621, 16 July 1709, Catharina N.

[40] Lyndal Roper, *Oedipus and the Devil: Witchcraft, Sexuality and Religion in Early Modern Europe* (London: Routledge, 1994), 199–225. Lyndal Roper, *Witch Craze: Terror and Fantasy in Baroque Germany* (New Haven: Yale University Press, 2004), 65.

[41] *WD*, Nr. 621, 16 July 1709, Catharina N.

thirty-six.⁴² The first documented suicidal child murder by a *male* perpetrator since 1668 happened on May 13, 1723. Around six in the morning, Martin N., a twenty-five-year-old soldier, approached an eight-year-old boy outside a chapel. The soldier gave the boy a small coin and lured him into a nearby building. There, the *Wiennerisches Diarium* cryptically reported, the soldier ordered the boy to remove his "*Flor*," whereupon he cut his throat. *Flor* refers to a choral ruff or embroidered surplice, a clerical vestment worn by altar boys. Did the soldier wait by the chapel for Mass to end so he could abduct an altar boy? This would have made an ideal sacrificial victim. Attending as the priest performed the sacrament of transubstantiation, an altar boy would have received the Eucharist himself. Martin N. was beheaded three months after the murder at the military execution site outside the Carinthian Gate, after his hand had been severed.⁴³

⁴² Eva Maria N., a thirty-four-year-old married woman, executed 28 March 1713, for cutting her child's throat. *WD*, Nr. 1007. Theresa N., a twenty-year-old single woman, flogged and banished, 26 May 1713, for attempting to cut her little sister's throat. *WD*, Nr. 1024. Maria Catherina N., thirty-six, executed June 2, 1713, for cutting the throat of her two children. *WD*, Nr. 1026. The two versions of the Protocol of the Confraternity of the Dead give her name either as Peidlerin, ÖNB, Cod 8363, p. 7, Nr. 50, June 2, 1713, or as Pfladlerin, WB, Handschriften Lb 18013, f. 11. Nr. 55, June 2, 1713. Eva Maria Walnerin, twenty-four or twenty-five, executed 23 November 1714, for cutting the throat of a seven-month-old baby boy. *WD*, Nr. 1180. The entry in the Protocol of the Confraternity of the Dead identifies her as Eva Maria Walnerin. ÖNB Cod 8363, p. 7, N. 56, 23 November 1714. Maria Eleonora N., eighteen, executed 16 June 1716, for cutting the throat of the five-year-old daughter of a city guard. *WD*, Nr. 1343. Anna Maria Spenigen, an unmarried woman, who cut the throat of an unknown little boy, examined by medical faculty on 13 May 1719. UAW, Med.1.8, f. 417v. Anna Maria N. from Moravia//., around thirty, executed 11 June 1720 for cutting the throat of a four-year-old child "with a knife she had sharpened specifically for that purpose." *WD*, Nr. 1759.

⁴³ *WD*, Nr. 71, September 4, 1723. ÖNB, Cod 8363, p. 10, Nr. 86, September 2, 1723, "ein Statt Guardi Soldat." On *Flor*, see *Flohr*, in *Zedler's Universal-Lexikon*, vol. 9, 1269–70.

Vienna prosecuted an additional five women for suicidal child murder or attempted murder over the next fifteen years.[44] Then, in 1739, the city executed a second male murderer. His execution pamphlet, inadvertently, disseminated the logic of suicide by proxy. Johann K., twenty-two, a recidivist thief, had been imprisoned in the house of corrections twice. He had broken his oath of *Urfehde* three times, a capital offense. Instead of death, Johann K. received a sentence of six years forced labor at the Hungarian border. Awaiting transport in a military prison, he bludgeoned a priest, a fellow prisoner, over the head with a piece of marble, "in order to escape his six-year sentence."[45] In the absence of a suitable child victim, killing an ordained priest was the next best option. Johann K.'s execution pamphlet included a moralizing poem. Johann's "despair" prompted the murder:

> *Er ließ Verzweiflungs-Geist in seinem Hertzen walten.*
> *... O mörderische That! O schröckliches Beginnen!*
> *Muß eines andern Blut dir eine Kühlung seyn?*
> *Muß deine Verzweiflung so/ihr End und Zihl gewinnen?*

> He let the spirit of despair take possession of his heart.
> ... Oh, murderous deed! Oh, horrific intent!
> Must the blood of another be a balm to you?
> Must your despair in this manner achieve its goal and purpose?

---

[44] Catherina Pumin, who murdered a child on 13 October 1723, and "desired death," was diagnosed with hypochondriacal melancholy. UAW, Med 1.8, fol. 459r. Catherina Franckin attempted to kill a child, found *non compos mentis*, 21 April 1725. UAW, Med 1.8, fol. 471r–471v. Maria Magdalena Nastlin, beheaded for breach of *Urfehde* 28 March 1732, had previously attempted to cut the throat of a three-month-old baby in Vienna's house of correction. WD, Nr. 26, 29 March 1732. Anna Margaretha H., a servant woman, around thirty, cut the throat of her employer's two-year-old daughter on 30 September 1732, beheaded at the Wheel Cross after the severing of her hand on 24 October 1732. WD, Nr. 86, 25 Oct. 1732. Margaretha Dessingerin, twenty-four, married, beheaded after severing of her hand, March 5, 1738, for cutting the throat of her one-year-old goddaughter. *Das Von Sünden und Lastern abhaltende Beyspiel, bestehend in einer Todtes-Straff, Welche vollzogen wird heute Mittwoch den 5. Martij 1738. an einer verheyrathen Weibs-Persohn, Nahmens Margaretha D.* (Vienna: Johann Baptist Schilgen, 1738). The Protocol of the Arch-Confraternity of the Dead gives her name as Margaretha Dessingerin. ÖNB, Cod 8363, p. 13, Nr. 110. March 2, 1738 [*sic*].

[45] The *Wiennerisches Diarium* explained Johann K's motive. He killed the priest "um solch seiner 6.jährigen Straf-Zeit zu entgehen." WD, Nr. 90, 11 November 1739, p. 983.

Placed on a high wagon, Johann K. was transported to the Vienna Mountain where he was broken by the wheel from the top down, the only instance when a Viennese perpetrator of suicide by proxy suffered this particularly brutal form of execution. His body was braided into the wheel and exposed to the elements. And yet, despite the infamy of his death, Johann could expect salvation, as his execution poem promised:

bey Gottes-Thron all Gnad thut offen stehn/
Und selbe thut dir gwiß das ewig Heyl verkünden/
Wann du Bereuter wirst zu deiner Straffe gehn.

from God's Throne all Mercy is still open
And proclaims to you with certainty your everlasting salvation,
If you go to your punishment with repentance.[46]

Killings continued through the 1760s. Between 1744 and 1767 Vienna executed an additional eight women and one man for suicidal murder.[47]

---

[46] Anon., *Wohl-verdientes Todtes-Urtheil Einer ledigen Manns-Persohn Nahmens Johann K, Catholischer Religion, und 22 Jhar alt, von hier gebürtig* (Vienna: Johann Baptist Schilgen, [1739]).

[47] 1744, Catharina Hallenstettin. *Wohl-verdientes Todtes-Urtheil, Einer Ledigen Weibs-Persohn, Nahmens Catharina H.: Welche ... den 11. September 1744 ..., durch das Schwerd samt Kopf- und Hand-Abschlagung hingerichtet wird* (Vienna: Maria Eva Schilgen, 1744). 1749, Dorothea Hermlohrin. *Wohl-verdientes Todtes-Urtheil, So ... den 29. Julij An. 1749 an ... Dorothea H: ... vollzogen wurde* (Vienna: Maria Eva Schilgen, [1749]). 1756, Joseph Gött. *Todes-Urtheil Einer verheyrateten Manns-person, Namens: Joseph G: ...; Welches ... den 11. September 1756. alhier in Wien vollzogen wird* ([Vienna]: s.n., 1756). 1759, Clara K. *Todtes-Urtheil Einer ledigen Weibs-person, Namens: Clara K ...: Welches ... den 24. November 1759. alhier vollzogen wird* ([Vienna]: s.n., 1759). 1760, Maria Anna Gritschin. *Wolverdientes Todes-Urtheil Einer ledigen Weibs-person, Namens: Maria Anna G: ...; Welches ... den 27. Junii 1760 ... in Wien vollzogen wird* ([Vienna]: s.n., 1760). 1760, Regina Glanzin. *Todes-Urtheil Einer ledigen Weibs-Person, Namens Regina G ...: Welches ... den 24. October 1760, ... in Wien vollzogen wird* ([Vienna]: s.n., 1760). 1760, Anna Maria Bäuerin. *Wol-verdientes Todes-Urtheil Einer ledigen Weibs-Person, Namens: Anna Maria: ...; Welches ... heute den 31. Octob. 1760 ... in Wien vollzogen wird* ([Vienna]: s.n., 1760). 1764, Anna Maria Neumayrin. *Todes-Urtheil, einer verwittibten Weibs-person Namens: Maria Anna N: ...; Welches ... den 31. Augusti 1764 ... in Wien vollzogen wird* ([Vienna]: s.n., 1760). 1767, Elizabeth Wurmin. *Todes-Urtheil Einer verheuratheten Weibs-person, Namens: Elisabeth W ...: Welches ... den 30sten Jänner 1767 ... vollzogen wird* ([Vienna]: s. n., 1767).

Unmoored, Dispossessed, Out for Revenge: Women Vagrants as Serial Killers?

In 1769 Viennese authorities executed a woman they believed to be one of the most monstrous child murderers they had ever encountered, due to the sheer number of child killings she allegedly committed over several years. It was also one of the most legally problematic trials. In their horror at her confession, the judges threw judicial caution to the wind. Catharina Jacobin, twenty-four, was a vagrant from the village of Kovanec in northern Bohemia, almost three hundred miles from Vienna. In early 1767, "driven by her own conscience," she appeared at the courthouse in Vienna and made an elaborate confession to a series of child killings.[48] Her murderous rampage allegedly began in her home village. Seeking revenge on fellow villagers who had wronged her, she drowned two children in 1763 and 1764. In a deviation from the script of suicide by proxy, she did not turn herself in, but staged the drownings as accidents. Leaving her village, she lived as a vagrant. Over the next three years, she drowned, bludgeoned, and stabbed four more children, she claimed, each time concealing the murder or fleeing, as she continued her trek to Vienna (Image 7.4).[49]

This tale of horrors earned Jacobin a death sentence. Was this a case of multiple abortive attempts to commit suicide by proxy? Did Jacobin murder a child, and then lose the nerve to turn herself in, and then try, try again? Or, was this a particularly extravagant false confession? In any case, the Viennese court applied a lower standard of proof than was usually required to convict. It was a long-established legal principal that confession alone was insufficient to establish the *corpus delicti*, without some corroborating evidence. In previous cases when self-accusers presented themselves at the courthouse in the absence of a dead body or other evidence, Viennese jurists had proceeded cautiously.[50]

---

[48] Her execution pamphlet does not provide the date when she turned herself in. However, at the time of her execution in February 1769, a newspaper reported that the trial had lasted two years. *Bayreuther Zeitung*, Num. 24, 25 February 1769.

[49] Anon., *Todesurtheil einer ledigen Weibsperson, Namens Catharina J ... Welches ... den 10. Februarii 1769. allhier in Wien vollzogen worden* ([Vienna], [s.n.], 1769). Her execution pamphlet identifies her only as Catharina J. Two execution chronicles identify her as Catharina Jacobeckin or Catharina Jacobin. WB, Handschriften, Lb 18013, f. 81–88, 16 February 1769, Catharina Jacobeckin. WB, Handschriften, Lc 67116, f. 9r–9v, 16 February 1769, Catharina Jacobin.

[50] For example, the self-accusations of Anna Wadlin Cellensis in 1692 discussed above, and Maria Anna N., May 2, 1710, *WD*, Nr. 704. See also this discussion of standards of proof in Chap. 2.

7 CRIME AND JUSTICE IN A SACRED LANDSCAPE: VIENNA, 1668–1786   349

Image 7.4 Execution of Catherina Jacobin, Vienna, 1769. Engraving. In *Todesurtheil einer ledigen Weibperson, Namens Catherina J....* Wienbibliothek im Rathaus, C-39975/1769

Criminal courts usually went to great lengths to ascertain that alleged crimes had actually occurred, as Viennese prosecutors attempted to do in Jacobin's case. They inquired with authorities in Bohemia and Hungary where the murders supposedly occurred, but the evidence was inconclusive. This accounts for the somewhat defensive tone of her execution pamphlet: "Even though not all of the gruesome murders ... that the delinquent has confessed to could be legally proven," two child drownings and one head injury could be confirmed. But were these really murders, or accidents that Jacobin implicated herself in after the fact? Jacobin's execution pamphlet concluded, weakly: since the drownings and head injury had been confirmed, "it is all the more believable, that the delinquent committed all the other murderous crimes that she confessed to, especially since she manifested a particularly malicious and cruel demeanor during her imprisonment."[51] Jacobin's judges saw in her a vicious vagrant whose tales of murder were entirely plausible, given the Viennese court's extensive experience with child-murdering women over the previous seven decades. Jacobin did her utmost to persuade the Viennese court that she deserved death. "Whenever she laid eyes on a child and found the opportunity, she killed it right away," she testified, "because she lusted for the blood of children."[52] Jacobin was beheaded on the ravenstone outside the Scottish Gate. Her hand remained attached there.[53]

After Jacobin's execution the pace of prosecutions slowed. In 1773 a tailor's wife strangled her five-year-old stepson and turned herself in at the courthouse.[54] A decade later the city prosecuted the last documented case of suicidal child murder. Prosecutors again faced a vagrant woman who accused herself of serial child murder. On March 11, 1783, Adelheid Zieglerin, twenty, from Swabia, turned herself in after strangling and bludgeoning Katherina, her landlord's seven-year-old foster child.[55] Three years earlier, in 1780, she had drowned the baby daughter of another vagrant woman near Lake Constance. Her purpose, Zieglerin explained, was revenge, not against the baby's mother, but against Zieglerin's own family, from whom she was estranged. She wanted the infamy of her

---

[51] Anon., *Todesurtheil ... Catharina J* ....

[52] "in ihrer selbest eygener vernünfftigen Geständnus sagete sie wenn sie nur ein Künde zu sehen bekam und die Gelegenheit gefunden selbes gleich umgebracht hätte, weilen sie ... Künds Blueth begierig ware." WB, Handschriften, Lc 67116, "Relationen über Hinrichtungen," ff. 9r–9v, 16 February 1769, Catharina Jacobin.

[53] WB, Handschriften, Lb 18013, ff. 81–88, 16 February 1769, Catharina Jacobeckin,

[54] The outcome of that case is unknown. *WD*, Nr. 32, 21 April 1773.

[55] She accused herelf of killing four children. Only two murders could be proven. The journalist Josef Pfundheller published an account of Adelheid Zieglerin's case, entitled "A Swabian Medea," in his multivolume collection of true crime stories. He includes excerpts of trial records that have since been lost. His excerpts of the few records that have survived are accurate, an indication that his account of the case is reliable. Josef Pfundheller, *Die schwarze Bibliothek. Eine Sammlung interessanter Criminalgeschichten*. Neue Folge, vol. 1 (Vienna: Im Selbstverlag, 1664), 537–623. Surviving archival sources on Zieglerin's trials are WStLA, Handschriften A 20-1, p. 10; December 5, 1783 (562), p. 16; December 20, 1783 (765), p. 28; January 13, 1784 (247), p. 29; January 13, 1784 (249), p. 29; January 14, 1784 (278), p. 32; January 26, 1784 (539), p. 36; February 25, 1784 (1256), p. 115; April 24, 1786 (3028), p. 120; May 30, 1786 (4024). See also Friedrich Hartl, *Das Wiener Kriminalgericht. Strafrechtspflege vom Zeitalter der Aufklärung bis zur österreichischen Revolution* (Vienna: Böhlau, 1973), 317.

execution to dishonor her relatives. Zieglerin demanded her execution repeatedly, but she never explicitly articulated her suicidal intent. Her death would have been incidental to the revenge she desired. A quest for revenge was a motif in the confessions of several women who committed suicidal child murder.[56]

After the drowning, Zieglerin went directly to church and confessed the murder to the priest—who ordered her to flee! The priest's surprising response was likely motivated by fear of irregularity. Had he alerted authorities, or even advised Zieglerin to turn herself in, he would have been instrumental in bringing about a criminal trial that would ultimately have led to her execution. As shown in Chap. 1, Catholic clergy shunned any involvement in felony criminal trials before conviction, to avoid contributing in any way to a sentence that would result in the shedding of human blood. Only after conviction, did Catholic clergy become involved in capital cases, ministering to condemned felons in the days before and during their executions.

Wanted for murder, Zieglerin eluded capture for the next two years. In early 1782 she surrendered to authorities in Munich, demanding "the justice that I am due." The court found her mentally deranged, and therefore, not criminally liable. Ordered to return to her family, Zieglerin soon absconded, vowing to murder another child to cause her relatives even greater dishonor. In Vienna she made good on her threat. During her eleven-month trial for the murder of seven-year-old Katherina, Zieglerin attempted to hang herself three times. Evidently, her child murders were not motivated by religious prohibition of direct suicide. For her, as for several perpetrators in late eighteenth-century Hamburg, child murder had become a conventional suicidal gesture, a default mode of self-destruction, an established cultural practice that required no further reflection or explanation.

In January 1784 Zieglerin was sentenced to beheading and severing of her hand for her "various infanticides and repeated suicide attempts." Her sentence was commuted to life imprisonment in the house of correction.[57] Two years into her life-sentence, Zieglerin, now twenty-three, made her final attempt to commit suicide by proxy. She was angry about new prison

---

[56] For example, in Hamburg, the tailor's wife in 1686, or Catharina Maria Keonig in 1809. Chap. 4.

[57] "ex capite variorum infanticidorum et iterati propricidii." WStLA, Handschriften A 20-1, pp. 28–29, 13 January 1784 (247); 13 January 1784 (249); 14 January 1784 (278).

regulations that reduced rations and prohibited inmates from attending mass on weekdays, as she had been accustomed to do once, or even twice, daily. This was likely a Josephine directive to maximize inmate labor. Zieglerin briefly considered murdering a fellow inmate. This would have been an adult woman. After the establishment of a city orphanage in 1745, Empress Maria Theresa had ordered orphans previously cared for in the house of correction to be transferred to the new institution, so few potential child victims would have been available to Zieglerin within the prison.[58] She committed blasphemy instead. She received her Easter communion the morning of April 23, 1786. Later she announced that she had desecrated the host. She surreptitiously let the host fall from her mouth into her open prayer book, she claimed. Alone in her cell, she scraped the soggy host off the page with an amulet, and threw the host, amulet and prayer book into the chamber-pot. The prison priest searched the chamber-pot. He retrieved the amulet and the prayer book, but found no trace of the host. The priest was unconvinced that a host desecration had taken place. Surrounded by witnesses during communion, it would have been difficult for Zieglerin to remove the host from her mouth unobserved. Her self-accusation stemmed from mental derangement, he argued. She really enjoyed murdering children, she told him, and desired to do so again. She demanded her execution.

In the absence of the host, there was no *corpus delicti* to support a charge of host desecration. Zieglerin was unquestionably guilty, the court noted, of throwing consecrated objects, the amulet and the prayer book, into the chamber-pot, in themselves blasphemous deeds. A wicked and blasphemous person, she deserved the punishment laid out in law, the court declared when sentencing Zieglerin for the second time on May 30, 1786. Just six months later, on January 1, 1787, the *Josefina*, the new criminal code issued by Emperor Josef II, would downgrade blasphemy from a felony and potentially capital crime to an offense against decency. The *Josefina* famously also abolished the death penalty in Austrian lands for all crimes. During Zieglerin's trial, however, the *Theresiana*, the criminal code issued by Maria Theresa in 1769, was still the law of the land. The statuary penalty for first-degree blasphemy was death, although the edict of 1715 and the "Secret Instruction" of the *Theresiana* that punished suicidal blasphemers with life imprisonment and yearly public whippings

---

[58] Karl Weiß, *Geschichte der öffentlichen Anstalten, Fonde und Stiftungen für die Armenversorgung in Wien* (Vienna: Wilhelm Braumüller, 1867), 176.

instead of death, remained in effect.⁵⁹ Zieglerin was spared these whippings. She was a "crazed and desperate person" of "melancholy bilious temperament," physicians reported.⁶⁰ The court simply reinstated Zieglerin's original sentence from 1784 for her "various" child murders, that is, life imprisonment while performing labor in chains. Zieglerin was transferred from Vienna's house of correction to the Schlossberg, the prison-workhouse in Graz, where criminal courts throughout Austrian lands sent their worst offenders. Here she labored in chains until 1802. She received an imperial pardon on August 10, 1802, and died less than three months later, on All Souls Day (November 2), 1802.⁶¹

EXECUTION RATES AND GENDER

Where did Vienna's suicidal perpetrators fit within the general history of capital punishment in Vienna? At least 375 executions took place in Vienna between 1702 and 1786. This is likely a significant undercount. I have arrived at this number by drawing on execution chronicles compiled by the Confraternity of the Dead, supplemented by crime reporting in the *Wiennerisches Diarium*, and chance survivals of printed official death sentences and execution pamphlets.⁶² Executions in Vienna ended, temporarily, in 1786, a year before Joseph II officially abolished capital punishment in all Austrian lands in 1787.

375 documented executions between 1702 and 1786 means that Viennese authorities executed a minimum of four to five people per year during these eighty-five years. Of course, the executions did not take place at the same pace throughout the period. As one might expect, more

---

⁵⁹ See Chap. 5, pp.
⁶⁰ Pfundheller, "Medea," 593–594. WStLA, Handschriften A 20-1, pp. 118–120, 24 April 1786 (3028); 30 May 1786 (4024).
⁶¹ Pfundheller, "Medea," 612, 622.
⁶² The execution chronicles of the Confraternity of the Dead only recorded eexecutions of offenders who received a Christian burial. Executions at the Wheel Cross or gallows on the Vienna Mountain have left few sources. The *Wiennerisches Diarium* is available online at the ÖNB: http://anno.onb.ac.at/cgi-content/anno?aid=wrz. Missing years at the ÖNB, and can be viewed online at the Center for Research Libraries: https://dds.crl.edu/crldelivery/17908. Susanne Hehenberger of the Institut für Geschichte at the University of Vienna has compiled a database on crime reporting in the *Wiennerisches Diarium*, an indispensable resource for criminal justice history in Vienna: http://homepage.univie.ac.at/susanne.hehenberger/kriminaldatenbank/. The Wien Bibliothek owns a collection of printed execution notices: http://www.digital.wienbibliothek.at/nav/classification/466442?s=date.

executions were documented early in the eighteenth century than in later decades:

1702–1709: 62 executions, 7.75 per year.
1710–1719: 73 executions, 7.3 per year
1720–1729: 63 executions, 6.3 per year
1730–1739: 30 executions, 3 per year
1740–1749: 52 executions, 5.2 per year
1750–1759: 30 executions, 3 per year
1760–1769: 29 executions, 2.9 per year
1770–1779: 30 executions, 3 per year
1780–1786: 6 executions, 0.85 per year

The state of the sources makes it impossible to know to what extent these figures reflect the actual rate of decline, but the general downward trend is unmistakable. This decline in executions in the second half of the century was part of a larger European trend. As Helga Schnabel-Schüle has observed, executions slowed throughout the empire around 1760. In Vienna and Austria, the number of executions decreased most dramatically after 1780, the year Joseph II took over as sole ruler after the death of his mother Maria Theresa. Executions in Vienna decreased even though the population grew considerably throughout the century. Vienna had a population of 90000 in 1700. By 1740 the population had grown to 120000.[63] At the time of Vienna's first official census in 1754 the population of city and suburbs had grown to 174403. The population grew to almost 192971 by 1772 and to 207014 by 1790.[64]

The types of crimes and the kind of offenders punished by death also changed over the course of the century. One of the most striking features of criminal justice in eighteenth-century Vienna is the high number of women who suffered capital punishment. Of the 375 people executed in Vienna between 1702 and 1786, 253 were men and 122 were women, a sex ratio of 68% male and 32% female. By comparison: women made up 2.1% of all persons executed in the United States between 1973 and

---

[63] Karl Gutkas, "Die österreichischen Länder im Zeitalter des Hochbarocks," in *Prinz Eugen und das barocke Österreich*, ed. Karl Gutkas (Salzburg: Residenz Verlag, 1985), 167–178, p. 167.

[64] Wien Wiki Geschichte: Bevölkerung. https://www.wien.gv.at/wiki/index.php?title=Bev%C3%B6lkerung.

2012.⁶⁵ This sex ratio of roughly 2/3 men and 1/3 women among Vienna' executed criminals did not stay constant over the course of the century. Early in the century, the proportion of female offenders who died on the ravenstone was much higher, while toward the end of the century the number of women executed declined dramatically:

1702–1709: 62 executions, 37 women (60%), 25 men (40%)
1710–1719: 73 executions, 38 women (52%), 35 men (48%)
1720–1729: 63 executions, 19 women (30%), 44 men (70%)
1730–1739: 30 executions, 6 women (20%), 24 men (80%)
1740–1749: 52 execution, 8 women (15%), 44 men (85%)
1750–1759: 30 executions, 6 women (20%), 24 men (80%)
1760–1769: 29 execution, 6 women (21%), 23 men (79%)
1770–1779: 30 executions, 2 women (7%), 28 men (93%)
1750-1759: 30 executions, 6 women (20%), 24 men (80%)
1760-1769: 29 execution, 6 women (21%), 23 men (79%)
1770-1779: 30 executions, 2 women (7%), 28 men (93%)
1780–1786: 6 executions, 0 women, 6 men (100%)

The shift in the gender profile of executed criminals reflected a change in the types of crimes people were executed for. Between 1702 and 1719, women made up 55% of executed criminals in Vienna. These were precisely the years when Vienna's outbreak of suicidal iconoclasm was at its peak. Of the 135 people executed between 1702 and 1719, twenty-seven people, twenty-one women and six men, committed suicidal iconoclasm.⁶⁶ Another eleven women committed suicidal child murder. In other words, thirty-eight of 135 executions, or 28%, were cases of suicide by proxy. The predominance of women among the perpetrators of suicide by proxy during these years is particularly striking. In Vienna, as in Hamburg, suicide by proxy was initially almost exclusively a female strategy, that men adopted later, once it had become a familiar pattern.

The practice of suicide by proxy clearly contributed significantly to the predominance of women among executed criminals in early eighteenth-century Vienna. Even among people executed for other crimes the proportion of women was high. Of ninety-seven people executed for crimes unrelated to suicide by proxy, there were fifty-two men and forty-five women, that is, women made up 46% of these offenders. Many female offenders were executed for prostitution and theft, often in combination with breach of the oath of *Urfehde*. These were not first-time offenders. However, arrests for relatively minor offenses, such as begging, vagrancy,

⁶⁵ http://www.deathpenaltyinfo.org/women-and-death-penalty.
⁶⁶ Cases of suicidal iconoclasm that did not end in execution are not counted here.

fornication, prostitution, and petty theft, launched women on a trajectory that often ended with their execution.

Some of these women were remarkably young at the time of their execution. Anna Maria Paulin, an unmarried woman "from Austria," that is, not Vienna, was twenty when she was beheaded on the High Market for sizable thefts and prostitution on December 2, 1705.[67] Anna Rosina from Silesia was twenty-three when she was beheaded on December 11, 1705. Arrested and punished several times for unspecified offenses, she was sentenced to a "whole Schilling" and banished twice. She returned to Vienna and was executed for breach of *Urfehde*.[68] Three women were executed for bigamy, at once a sexual and religious crime since it violated the sacrament of marriage. Other women were executed as first-time offenders for abortion and infanticide. Helena, twenty-two, was executed for abortion on January 19, 1706.[69] Sabina N., nineteen, was beheaded on the ravenstone on January 4, 1707, for disposing of her newborn unbaptized baby in the latrine.[70] Sabina was one of ten women executed for infanticide between 1703 and 1719.[71]

When authorities started deporting male offenders to row in the galleys in Naples, or to perform forced labor on the Hungarian border, this contributed to decline in the number of men executed in Vienna. For the year 1726, for example, the *Wiennerisches Diarium* reported seven executions. Four women were executed, two for infanticide, one for theft and bigamy, and one for breach of *Urfehde*. Three men were executed, two for theft and breach of *Urfehde*, and one for adultery and attempted murder. Six women were flogged for breach of *Urfehde* and theft. Twenty men were

---

[67] *WD*, Nr. 244, 2–4 December 1705.
[68] *WD*, Nr. 246, 9–11 December 1705.
[69] *WD*, Nr. 257, 16–19 January 1706. ÖNB, Cod 8353, p. 4, Nr. 22, 1706 a 19. Januarius. WB, Handschriften Lb 18013, f. 5, Nr. 23, Ano 1706, January 19.
[70] *WD*, Nr. 357, 1–4 January 1707. WB, Handschrift Lb 18013, f. 6, Nr. 26, January 4, 1707.
[71] Helena. *WD*, Nr. 257, 16–19 January 1706. Maria. ÖNB, Cod 8363, p. 1, Nr. 6, June 28, 1703. Catherina. ÖNB, Cod 8363, p. 5, Nr. 26, April 20, 1707. Eva N, May 22, 1708. *WD*, Nr. 501, May 22, 1708. Apollonia. *WD*, Nr. 584, March 6, 1709. Anna Maria N. *WD*, Nr. 612, June 14, 1709. Maria Magdalnea N. *WD*, Nr. 703, April 29, 1710. Anna Maria N. *WD*, Nr. 738, 29 August 1710. Elisabeth N. *WD*, Nr. 798, 27 March 1711. Catharina P. *WD*, Nr. 2, January 3, 1726. Maria Elizabetha N. *WD*, Nr. 84, 18 October 1726. On June 6, 1727, Anna Maria E. *WD*, Nr. 46, June 6, 1727. On October 18, 1750, Anna Maria Eker. *WD*, Nr. 66, 19 August 1750.

deported to Naples or the Hungarian border.[72] Of course, such forced labor typically amounted to a death sentence too, albeit a slower death devoid of ritual trappings. However, in the early eighteenth century the fact that more men were now being punished elsewhere out of sight of the Viennese public, meant that women became more prominent among poor sinners dying in Vienna. The visibility of women on the ravenstone in these years meant that women in the audience, fantasizing about dying such a death themselves, had plenty of role models to follow.

In the 1720s the proportion of women among executed offenders dropped from over 50% for first two decades of the eighteenth century to 30%. The government's decision to punish suicidal iconoclasts by imprisonment rather than execution certainly contributed to this decline. The number of women executed for infanticide also declined sharply. There is no way to know whether a high number of unsolved cases, as in Hamburg, or a shift to punishing infanticidal mothers by lengthy prison sentences rather than execution, or both, contributed to this decline. From the 1730s through the 1760s the proportion of women among executed offenders ranged between 15% and 21%. After 1770 there were no further documented executions of women. The majority of male offenders were executed for theft and breach of *Urfehde*, followed by robbery, desertion, murder, and church robbery.

Sharing in a Blessed Death: Leveraging Salvation on the Ravenstone

Perpetrators of suicide by proxy were not the only ones to exploit the salvific potential of public execution. Regular Catholics sought to participate in the salvation of poor sinners, whose deaths were choreographed as the willing self-sacrifice of martyrs. The relationship between condemned criminals, and perpetrators of suicide by proxy in particular, and the broader Catholic public was reciprocal. The Catholic public incorporated condemned criminals into their own salvation strategies. Their enormous investment, in time, emotions, and money, in the salvation of condemned criminals created the culture in which suicide by proxy proliferated.

Secular criminal courts and the Catholic church operated hand in glove in crafting the execution ritual. Although the prospect of irregularity

---

[72] https://homepage.univie.ac.at/susanne.hehenberger/kriminaldatenbank/ for the year 1726.

prevented Catholic clerics from participating in interrogations during criminal trials, they spared no effort after sentencing to provide condemned criminals with a blessed death. Jesuits exercised an effective monopoly over pastoral care to condemned criminals in Vienna. They secured this prerogative when the order first arrived in Vienna in 1551 at the invitation of King Ferdinand, to combat the spread of Protestantism in Habsburg lands. Petrus Canisius, who later wrote the Large and Small Catechism that became the standard Catholic catechism in Counter-Reformation Germany, personally staked out the Jesuits' claim to the ministry to incarcerated criminals. "Today we gained access to the prisoners, ... who languish in spiritual as well as physical chains," he wrote in a letter of April 8, 1552. "I want ... to be their shepherd. With Christ's help, I will free them from the chains of sin, and lead them to the pasture ... where they will be replenished by the word of God."[73] Jesuits provided prisoners with rosaries, catechized them, took confession and provided the Eucharist. Canisius personally prepared a condemned criminal for death in 1553 and accompanied him to his execution, "comforting and encouraging him," a fellow Jesuit reported, "so that the crowd of spectators was quite moved." It was a point of pride for Jesuits that the very same priests who preached at the imperial court to members of the Habsburg dynasty also heard the confession of criminals and accompanied the condemned to their execution.[74] Jesuits jealously and successfully guarded their claim to the ministry of condemned criminals against encroachment by other religious orders for over two centuries. Only in 1773, when the Society of Jesus was dissolved, did this duty fall to the Augustinian Eremites, who had first attempted to seize this ministry from the Jesuits almost 150 years earlier.

The Discalced ("barefoot") Augustinians, the observant branch of the Augustinian Eremites, first tried take over the ministry to condemned criminals in the 1630s, when their church became the headquarters of the

---

[73] Bernhard Duhr S.J., *Geschichte der Jesuiten in den Ländern deutscher Zunge*, vol. 1 (Freiburg im Breisgau: Herderische Verlagshandlung, 1907), 72–73, 45–47.
[74] Duhr, *Jesuiten*, vol. 1, 516–517.

newly formed Imperial Arch-Confraternity of the Dead.[75] The most visible public function of this confraternity, described in its founding charter, was to "bury those persons who have been condemned to death for crimes they have committed," provided their death sentence allowed for a Christian burial. Empress Eleonora Gonzaga of Mantua (1598–1655), spouse of Emperor Ferdinand II (r. 1619–1637), was the driving force behind the formation of the new confraternity. Eleonora lived in Mantua until she was twenty-two, so she was undoubtedly familiar with Italian confraternities that cared for condemned criminals, the so-called *compagnia di giustizia* (companies of justice) or *conforterie* (comforting societies).[76] The Florentine society, formed in 1336, was known as the "Neri" (the Blacks) because of the black hoods and gowns the brothers wore as the habit of their society.[77] The Roman society, the "Arch-Confraternity of St. John the Beheaded," was founded in 1490. Mantua's *Compagnia della Morta* (Company of the Dead), one of the oldest, formed in the late thirteenth century and remained active until 1786.[78] Italian confraternity brothers accompanied condemned criminals to their executions and buried them in consecrated ground afterward, just like their counterparts in Vienna would also do. Burying repentant condemned criminals and care for the dead more generally came to be understood as the seventh canonical work of mercy, an expansion of the original six

---

[75] Claudia Resch, "Die Totenbruderschaft von St. Augustin und ihre Totenkapelle(n)— geziert, gemalt und gedruckt für die Ewigkeit ...," in *Bruderschaften als multifunktionale Dienstleister der Frühen Neuzeit in Zentraleuropa*, eds. Elisabeth Lobenwein, Martin Scheutz and Alfred Stefan Weiß (Vienna: Böhlau, 2018), 373–393. Claudia Resch, "Die kaiserlich-königliche Totenbruderschaft in Wien. 'Bündnuß und höchst Lob-würdige Alliantz' zum Heil der Seelen ...," in *Bündnisse. Politische, Soziale und Intellektuelle Allianzen im Jahrhundert der Aufklärung*, eds. Franz M. Eybl, Daniel Fulda, and Johannes Süssmann (Vienna: Böhlau, 2019), 183–194. Claudia Resch is directing a project for the Austrian Center for Digital Humanities to digitize early prints associated with the Confraternity of the Dead: "ÖAW: Confraternity Prints Digital": https://www.oeaw.ac.at/acdh/projects/completed-projects/confraternity-prints-digital, as well as the writings of one of the confraternity's most famous members, the grandiloquent preacher Abraham a Sancta Clara. "ÖAW: Austrian Baroque Corpus (ABaC:us)": https://acdh.oeaw.ac.at/abacus/.

[76] Adriano Prosperi, "Consolation or Condemnation: The Debates on Withholding the Sacraments from Prisoners," in *The Art of Executing Well. Rituals of Execution in Renaissance Italy*, ed. Nicholas Terpstra (Kirksville, MI: Truman State University Press, 2008), 102.

[77] Konrad Eisenbichler, "Lorenzo de' Medici and the Confraternity of the Blacks in Florence," *Fides et Historia* 26 (1994): 85–98, p. 89.

[78] Alessandro Agri, *La Giustizia Criminale a Mantova in Età Asburgica: Il Supremo Consiglio di Giustizia* (1750–1786), vol. 1 (Rome: Historia et Ius, 2019), 145–146.

canonical works of mercy enjoined by Christ in Matthew 24:34–35, that is giving food, drink, clothing, and housing the poor, and visiting the sick and those languishing in prison. Thus, Christians accumulated their inheritance in heaven.[79] In other words, when lay brothers buried the condemned, they contributed to their own salvation. Membership in Italian companies of justice included high government officials. Lorenzo de Medici and Michelangelo, for example, were at least nominal members of their local comforting societies. This meant that some of the same individuals who imposed death sentences in their official capacity, subsequently donned black hoods and gowns to accompany the condemned to their deaths.[80]

The new Viennese confraternity was modeled after these older Italian societies. Emperor Ferdinand II and Empress Eleonora launched the new Viennese Confraternity of the Dead unofficially in 1634, but the emperor died before the foundation was formalized, so this task fell to his son and successor Ferdinand III (r. 1637–1657).[81] In February 1638 Eleonora secured the approval of Pope Urban VIII for the Viennese confraternity. The Viennese Confraternity of the Dead was incorporated into the long-standing Roman Confraternity of Saint John the Beheaded, which meant that Vienna's confraternity would participate in the substantial papal indulgences that the Roman confraternity had accumulated over the centuries. The Roman and Viennese confraternities were now members of an alliance, a solidary salvific community in which both confraternities shared in the spiritual rewards earned by the meritorious good works performed by their respective members, leveraging and multiplying earned merit.[82]

[79] Prosperi, "Consolatio," 102.

[80] A unique feature of Italian Companies of Justice was that in addition to burial, lay brothers also provided most spiritual care for the condemned, a task that elsewhere in Europe was performed by clergy. Nicholas Terpstra, "Introduction: The Other Side of the Scaffold," in *The Art of Executing Well*, 1. Samuel Y. Edgerton, Jr., *Pictures and Punishment: Art and Criminal Prosecution during the Florentine Renaissance* (Ithaca: Cornell University Press, 1985), 165–179.

[81] Anon., *Hoch-feyerliches Saeculum oder erstes Jahr-Hundert Einer Hochlöblichen ... Todten-Bruderschafft bey denen PP. Augustinern Baarfüssern ...* (Vienna: Maria Theresia Voigt, 1738), unpaginated.

[82] Urban VIII's papal bull states that it was issued in response to a petition by Eleonora. The text of the bull and the incorporation of the Viennese confraternity into the Roman confraternity is included in Anon., *Regulen und andächtige Ubungen/ Der in der Statt Wienn ... /erhöbter ... Löbl. Bruderschafft* (Vienna: Matthäus Cosmerovius, 1650), 1–20. On the idea of alliance, see Resch, "Kaiserlich-königliche Totenbruderschaft," 188.

Once papal approval and incorporation of the new society into the Roman confraternity was official, Ferdinand III promulgated an imperial "privilege" formally establishing the Viennese confraternity in June 1638. He placed the confraternity and all its members under imperial protection. He granted the confraternity the right to use a crest in its official correspondence, replete with imperial heraldry and *memento mori* motifs. It consisted of the imperial double eagle wearing the imperial crown, with open wings, against a yellow background. On the right wing was written in golden letters "F. II." for Ferdinand II, on the left wing was written "E." for Eleonora, to honor the original founders of the confraternity. Between the talons of the imperial eagle were two crossbones and a skull (Image 7.5). Ferdinand II, Eleonora, and Ferdinand III also personally became members.

A pamphlet published by the confraternity in 1738 to celebrate the centenary of its founding proudly listed twenty-one members of the Habsburg dynasty who had joined the society. Emperor Charles VI, for example, who approved the death sentences of so many perpetrators of suicide by proxy whom the confraternity accompanied to their executions and then buried, joined in 1720.[83] Membership of the confraternity included lower social estates as well, such as merchants, goldsmiths, and even shoemakers, but officers of the confraternity were typically courtiers and high government officials.[84] As in Italy, then, some of the same individuals responsible for criminal prosecution of the condemned likely also buried them.

Ferdinand II and Eleonora installed the new Confraternity of the Dead in the Augustinian Church, immediately adjacent to the imperial palace, another sign of the confraternity's high prestige. The imperial family cultivated a particularly close relationship with this Augustinian monastery and church. In 1630 Ferdinand II ousted the Calced ("shoe-wearing") Augustinians, in residence in the monastery since the fourteenth century, whose moral laxness was a poor fit for the emperor's counter-reforming agenda. He bestowed the monastery upon the stricter reformed Barefoot Augustinians. In 1634, the same year as the unofficial launch of the

---

[83] Anon., *Hoch-feyerliches Saeculum*, unpaginated.
[84] On artisans and merchants among the members, Resch, "Kaiserlich-königliche Totenbruderschaft," 189. On aristocratic office holders, Anon., *Origo, Progressus, Et Memorabilia Ecclesiæ Cæsareæ S. P. Augustini Viennæ* (Vienna: Johannes Baptist Schilgen, [1730]), 45–48.

Image 7.5 Frontispiece, in "Verzeichnis deren von einer Hochlöblichen Privilegierten Kays. Königl. Todtenbruderschaft übernohmenen Malleficanten." Wienbibliothek im Rathaus, HIN-19008

confraternity, Ferdinand designated the Augustinian Church as imperial court church.

At the center of the main nave of the Church stood the Loreto Chapel, a prime location for the performance of the *pietas austriaca*, and a site of the Habsburgs' distinctive mortuary ritual. The hearts of deceased members of the dynasty were encrypted here.[85] In close proximity to this sanctum of the Habsburg dynasty, to the right of the nave, stood the St. George Chapel, consecrated in 1341. Originally the meeting place of a medieval knightly order that had since died out, Emperor Ferdinand II awarded this Chapel to the newly formed Confraternity of the Dead. Henceforth it was known as the "Chapel of the Dead."[86] The confraternity decorated the chapel with frescoes representing the torments of the poor souls in purgatory. Paintings portrayed edifying stories of the dead appearing to the living, requesting prayers, and, subsequently, coming to the aid of those who had prayed for them.[87] Many thousands of Holy Masses for the dead were celebrated here throughout the year, in order to achieve "the only and foremost purpose of this confraternity," which was "to lend a helping hand to the penitent souls in purgatory, to ease their painful suffering, to shorten the time of their punishment, and to open the Gates of Heaven ... by means of Christian works of charity."[88] The poor souls in purgatory cried out for such works of love and mercy by the living because their pain was in every way equal to the agony endured by the damned in hell, with the one crucial distinction that their punishment was temporary and not eternal. The confraternity was empowered to come to their aid by the generous indulgences that the pope had bestowed not only on the

---

[85] Wolfsgruber, *Loretokapelle*, 73.

[86] ÖNB, Cod. 8227, p. 1115. The close proximity of the Chapel of the Dead, a side chapel to the right of the nave, and the Loreto Chapel, is shown on a city map from 1710, reproduced in Günther Buchinger und Doris Schön, "'... jene, die ihre hände hilfreich zum bau erheben ...': Zur zeitlichen Konkordanz von Weihe und Bauvollendung am Beispiel der Wiener Augustinerkirche und Georgskapelle," *RIHA Journal* 20 (2011). https://doi.org/10.11588/riha.2011.0.69099, Image 19.

[87] This description of artwork in the chapel draws on Johannis Matthias Testarello della Massa, a cathedral canon at St. Stephen's, who discusses the confraternity and its chapel in his late seventeenth-century history of Viennese churches. ÖNB, Cod 8227, 1121–1122. These frescoes and paintings were destroyed by the renovation of the Augustinian Church ordered by Joseph II in 1784. A fresco of a skeleton with a scythe at the entrance of the chapel survived only because it was hidden beneath paint at the time of the Josephine renovations. A photo is included in Resch, "Totenbruderschaft von St. Augustin," 391.

[88] Anon., *Hochfeyerliche Begängnuß*, unpaginated.

confraternity itself, but also upon the chapel where the members performed their devotions. For every Mass celebrated at the "privileged" crucifix altar, the central altar in the Chapel of the Dead, one soul was freed from purgatory.[89] One requiem Mass after another was celebrated here when confraternity members convened in the chapel for their weekly services on Mondays. On All Souls Day (November 2), the high feast day of the confraternity, devotions extended for eight days. Members of the royal family were often in attendance.[90]

A poor soul in purgatory "suffers more in one moment... than in a thousand years on earth."[91] An early handbook of the confraternity of the Dead by the Augustinian friar Vincentius a Sancta Eleonora, flourishingly entitled *Purgatory's Probatic Pool, that lies between Austrian Mountains, from which Bright Clear Waters, and God-pleasing Works of Love and Mercy Flow, Bringing Refreshment to the Poor Souls Suffering the Bitter and Cruel Pains of Purgatory*, includes a frontispiece that vividly portrays the confraternity's mission of rescuing poor souls, while also paying homage to its imperial founders. It shows the Austrian eagle perched on a mountain top, beneath a bible verse, *Deus ab Austro Veniet* (Habacuc 3:3), an obvious wordplay on the House of Austria.[92] From the eagle's talons flow mercy, charity, and piety, providing relief to the poor souls languishing in the flames of purgatory below. Angels carry liberated souls toward heaven (Image 7.6).[93]

Living confraternity members alleviated the suffering of poor souls by performing religious devotions and acts of charity, and in so doing they

---

[89] Anon., *Hochfeyerliche Begängnuß*, unpaginated.

[90] Rohling, "Exequial and Votive Practices," 265–278. Harald Johannes Mann, "Die Barocken Totenbruderschaften," *Zeitschrift für Bayerische Landesgeschichte* 39 (1976): 132.

[91] A manual of the Viennese Arch-Confraternity of the Holy Trinity, published in 1705, warned "Allhier [i.e., in purgatory] leydet man mehr in einem Augenblick, als auff der Welt in tausend Jahren." Quoted in Rohling, "Exequial and Votive Practices," 290–291.

[92] "Deus ab austro veniet et Sanctus de monte Pharan." "God will come from the south, and the holy one from mount Pharan." Vulgate Bible, Habacuc 3:3.

[93] Vincenzo di Santa Eleonora, *Probatico Piscina del Purgatorio Situata Fra li Sacri Monti Austriaci: Onde Li scaturiscono limpide acque di pie, caritatiue, e misericordiose opere, per le quali l' afflitte anime sono refrigerate nelle loro acerbe, e crudeli pene, che patiscono* (Vienna: Maria Rittia Vedova, 1638.) Vincentius de S. Eleonora, *Des Fegfewers Probier Teuch So Zwischen Oesterreichischen Gebürgen liget/ Aus welchem gar klare und helle Wasser/ Gottseliger Werck der Lieb und Barmherzigkeit haraus fliessen/ dardurch die Betrübte Seelen in den Bittern und grausamen Peynen des Fegfewers gelabt und erquickt werden* (Vienna: Matthäus Formica, 1638).

Image 7.6 Frontispiece, in *Probatica Piscina del Purgatorio Situata Fra Li Sacri Monti Austriaci* (Vienna: Maria Rittia Vedova, 1638). National Library of the Czech Republic, Prague, Shelf Mark 36 E 000081

also helped themselves. Service to the dead was a practice of reciprocity. The Habsburg founders of the confraternity themselves hoped to benefit from this solidarity. "We and our entire venerable House of Austria hope to participate in their merit, supplication, and good works, through God's grace," Ferdinand III wrote in the confraternity's founding privilege.[94] The dead practiced similar reciprocity. The boundary between the living and the dead was permeable. Teaching the same lesson as the paintings in the Chapel of the Dead, Abraham a Sancta Clara wrote: even as the dead "expect help from us, in the same manner we will not go without the aid and gratitude" of the dead.[95] Confraternity brothers and sisters, living and dead, provided mutual aid in the face of death, to ensure a blessed death for living members, and an expedited exit from purgatory and entry into paradise for the deceased.[96] Repentant executed criminals participated in this salvific exchange and became powerful advocates for the living. The execution pamphlet of Margaretha D., beheaded in 1738 for cutting the throat of a shoemaker's child, included a moralizing poem written in the first person that offered such advocacy, in exchange for the prayers of the living: "I request of young and old, please keep me in your prayers. Come to aid of my soul today, as I face God's judgement. There I will plead to God on your behalf."[97]

---

[94] Guarient, *Codicis Austriaci*, 340.

[95] Abraham a Sancta Clara, *Lösch Wien/Das ist: Ein Bewögliche Anmahnung zu der Kays. Residentz-Statt Wienn in Oesterreich* (Vienna: Peter Paul Vivian, 1680), 214, quoted in Resch, "Kaiserlich-königliche Totenbruderschaft," 188. Resch, "Totenbruderschaft von St. Augustin," 374.

[96] Rupert Klieber, *Bruderschaften und Liebesbünde nach Trient. Ihr Totendienst, Zuspruch und Stellenwert im kirchlichen und gesellschaftlichen Leben am Beispiel Salzburg (1600–1950)* (Frankfurt: Peter Lang, 1999), 26–27. Mann, "Totenbruderschaften," 130.

[97] "thue ich mich befehlen jung und alt in euer Gebet, kommt zu hülf heut meiner Seelen, die hier furs G'richt Gottes geht, ich werd für euch Gott dort bitten, so viel mir wird möglich seyn." *Das von Sünden und Lastern abhaltende Beyspiele/ ... Todtes-Straff/ ... 5. Martii 1738 ... Margaretha D.* (Vienna: Johann Baptist Schilgen, [1738]).

"How to Comfort Poor Sinners, who will be Executed for their Misdeeds, and Dispose them Well for Death."[98]

Jesuits successfully defended their historical claim to the pastoral care of condemned criminals in Vienna against interlopers from the Confraternity of the Dead and the Barefoot Augustinians. They secured the support of the prince-bishop of Vienna in 1639 and 1640,[99] and presumably, the Habsburg patrons of the Confraternity of the Dead also did not want to offend Jesuit priests who served as their father confessors. The confraternity's involvement in criminal justice remained limited to providing Christian burial to executed criminals. Even in this restricted role, however, the Confraternity of the Dead became one of the most prominent confraternities in Vienna.[100]

Regardless of who provided the spiritual care, the religious instruction of Catholic condemned criminals on the eve of their execution remained remarkably constant from the Renaissance until the late eighteenth century.[101] The description of the Catholic pastoral care below is drawn from four German clerical handbooks authored by regular clergy from four different orders: (1) Vincentius' handbook for the Confraternity of the Dead, *Purgatory's Probatic Pool* (1638); (2) the *Large Handbook for the Sick* (1686) by the celebrated Capuchin preacher and author Martin von

---

[98] Vincentius, *Fegfewers Probier Teuch*, 373: "Wie man den armen Sündern; so wegen ihre begangene Missethaten gericht werden/ zusprechen/ und zum Wolsterben disponieren soll."

[99] Ernst Tomek, "Das kirchliche Leben und die christliche Charitas in Wien," in *Geschichte der Stadt Wien*, ed. Alterthumsvereine zu Wien, vol. 5 (Vienna: Verlag des Alterthumsvereines zu Wien, 1914), 305.

[100] Martin Scheutz, "Bruderschaften in Visitationsprotokollen und im Wiener Diarium. Quellen zu einer Geschichte der frühneuzeitlichen Bruderschaften in Österreich," *Acta historiae artis Slovenica*, 23 (2018): 258.

[101] On pastoral care to condemned criminals by Renaisance Italian confraternities, see Nicholas Terpstra, "Confraternities and Capital Punishment: Charity, Culture, and Civic Religion in the Communal and Confessional Age," in *A Companion to Medieval and Early Modern Confraternities*, ed. Konrad Eisenbichler (Leiden: Brill, 2019), 215–216. Nicholas Terpstra, "Comforting by the Books: Editorial Notes on the Bolognese Comforters Manual," in *The Art of Executing Well. Rituals of Execution in Renaissance Italy*, ed. Nicholas Terpstra (Kirksville, Missouri: Truman State University Press, 2008), 183–192.

Cochem;[102] (3) the *Fruitful Practice* (1723), a handbook for the sick and dying by the Viennese Jesuit Franz Partinger;[103] and (4) the *Handbook for the Sick* (1744) by Philibert Wellner, a Franciscan from the Austrian province and former military chaplain.[104] All four works were general meditations on the *ars moriendi*, the art of dying well. Each included a chapter on pastoral care for condemned criminals. Based on their instructions, the preparation for the execution, and the execution itself, would, ideally, have unfolded as follows.

Secular judicial personnel informed the prisoner of his or her death sentence. The priest remained out of sight during this announcement. This insulation was necessary, so that the condemned criminal would not feel hostility toward the cleric. Only after the malefactor's first fits of rage or despair had passed, did the priest enter the prison cell. He expressed sympathy and compassion, encouraging the poor sinner to see him as an ally. The priest bowed before any religious icon on display in the poor sinner's cell. In Vienna, the poor sinner's crucifix, venerated as an injured icon since it was desecrated by the apostate Jew Ferdinand Franz Engelberger in 1642, stood in the cell, between two candles. Later, on the day of execution, this crucifix was affixed to a pole. Augustinan friars carried it, as they headed the procession of the Confraternity of the Dead that accompanied the poor sinner to the ravenstone.[105] Upon entering the prison cell, the priest asperged the poor sinner and others present with holy water. The poor sinner was provided with various consecrated items.[106] This would certainly have included a rosary, but probably also amulets, a scapulary, devotional images, and prayer book. The priest encouraged the poor sinner to be grateful to God for allowing her to purge her sin by execution, thus preparing for eternal life more quickly and easily than if she had died at home, or in an accident. God had given her the gift of knowing the hour of her death. This was far preferable to dying of illness, desperately clinging to life, hoping for a cure, and missing

---

[102] Martin von Cochem, *Das Grössere Krancken-Buch/* ... (Frankfurt a. M.: John Melchior Bencard, 1689). The chapter on preparing condemned criminals was entitled "Weiß und Manier/mit den Malefitz-Personen umbzugehen," 419–454.

[103] Franz Partinger, *Praxis Fructuose* ... (Augsburg: Veith, 1723).

[104] Philibert Wellner, *Hand-Buch deren Krancken* (Vienna: Christoph Joseph Hueth, 1744).

[105] Lang, *Hochgericht*, 7.

[106] Wellner, *Handbuch*, 107.

7 CRIME AND JUSTICE IN A SACRED LANDSCAPE: VIENNA, 1668–1786

the opportunity to confess and repent, thus losing not only temporal life but also suffering eternal damnation.[107]

The priest reminded the criminal of the example of Dismas, the good thief crucified to Christ's right, to whom Christ said, "Today you will be with me in paradise." (Luke 23:43) Like Dismas, the poor sinner could hope to enter heaven immediately. "There is no better way to escape the pain of purgatory, than by such a shameful death," wrote the Franciscan Wellner. By willingly submitting to a violent death, the poor sinner made a pleasing sacrifice. "Certainly, a poor sinner, who so willingly accepts death, and offers it to God ... is cleansed of his sins still in this world, so that directly after death he enters eternal bliss."[108] To bypass purgatory entirely placed executed criminals in exalted company. Only the apostles, Christian martyrs and saints entered paradise directly. Baptized children, too, if they died before the age of reason, went to Christ immediately.[109] To join this community of saints the poor sinner would have to perform her scripted role perfectly, however.

The condemned criminal had to show "visible signs of true repentance and pain." Public weeping was encouraged.[110] After a convincing demonstration of repentance, the priest administered the sacrament of confession and granted absolution. If possible, the poor sinner attended Mass, offering up his life and death for Christ's sake, to wash off his sin, for the greater honor and glory of God, as an example to his neighbors. Then the priest provided the poor sinner with the Eucharist. The priest directed the execution ritual like a passion play.[111] He taught the poor sinner to understand his death as an imitation of Christ. The prisoner's last walk was like the Way of the Cross. When guards escorted the poor sinner to the courthouse for the public proclamation of the death sentence, the priest said:

---

[107] Vincenzo, *Probier Teuch*, 375–380.

[108] "Ein solcher armer Sünder kan nicht leichter entgehen den Peynen des Fegfeuers, als eben durch einen solchen schmählichen Tod." "Dann gewiß ein armer Sünder, welcher also gutwillig den Tod annimmt, Gott aufopffert, ... noch in dieser Welt von seinen Sünden gereiniget wird, daß solcher gleich nach dem Tod in die ewige Freuden übersetzet wird." Wellner, *Handbuch*, 96–97.

[109] Peter Jezler, "Jenseitsmodelle und Jenseitsvorsorge—Eine Einführung," in *Himmel, Hölle, Fegefeuer. Das Jenseits im Mittelalter*, ed. Peter Jezler (Munich: Wilhelm Fink Verlag, 1994), 18.

[110] Vincenzo, *Probier Teuch*, 385.

[111] For an analysis of the Italian execution ritual as passion play, see Kathleen Falvey, "Scaffold and Stage. Comforting Rituals and Dramatic Traditions in Late Medieval and Renaissance Italy," in *Art of Executing Well*, ed. Terpstra, 13–30.

"Think of Good Friday and Christ's bitter death for you. Follow his example now and die a bitter death for him."[112] At the sentencing, the priest exhorted the malefactor to accept the sentence, like Christ accepted his, and say: "Lord Jesus! Willingly and obediently I want to go like a patient lamb to my sacrificial altar, naming, praising, adoring the name of my God."[113]

What if the condemned criminal refused to submit and repent, because he was innocent of the charges? What if he claimed that he only confessed because he could not withstand judicial torture? This should not present an obstacle to the prisoner's ultimate conversion and transformation into a penitent poor sinner. Surely, he was guilty of some other hidden sins, that God was holding him accountable for now, the priest should ask. If he was truly innocent, his death would be an even more precious, God-pleasing sacrifice, if he offered it willingly. Christ was incapable of any sin, and yet he died an infamous death on the cross. If the poor sinner was executed innocently, his death would be even more Christ-like, and correspondingly greater would be his glory in heaven.[114]

Much of this ministry took place in the private space of the poor-sinner's cell, but on the day of execution the salvific drama played out in public. This day determined the poor sinner's fate for all eternity. Would the priest succeed in shepherding his charge through the dangerous transition to the afterlife? During the procession the poor sinner held a crucifix, fervently kissing it during the execution procession.[115] He also wore a rosary and other consecrated items on his person. The priest recited prayers that the prisoner repeated, as call and response, loudly and clearly so spectators could hear. Periodically, the poor sinner was offered a draught of wine, though not too much. It was well-known that the devil wanted to get the poor sinner drunk, because he knew how important it was to die in full possession of one's reason. To fend off the stalking devil, the priest spoke a benediction over the wine: "Lord Jesus Christ, who drank salt and vinegar on the cross, bless this wine, so it may be a comfort to the soul of this prisoner, against all assaults by evil spirits."[116]

Every discrete step in the execution process was marked by an appropriate prayer, explicitly making the connection between the stage of the execution and the stations of the cross. Initially the malefactor, prompted by

---

[112] Martin von Cochem, *Krancken-Buch*, 424–425.
[113] Partinger, *Praxis*, 256.
[114] Wellner, *Handbuch*, 92–94.
[115] Partinger, *Praxis*, 257.
[116] Martin von Cochem, *Krancken-Buch*, 440.

the priest, spoke these prayers herself, but at a certain point the priest assumed the role of mouthpiece for the dying poor sinner, reciting prayers in the first person. Once the ravenstone was in sight, prisoner and priest fell to their knees three times, in imitation of Christ who fell three times while carrying the cross. At the ravenstone prisoner and priest knelt, and the priest took confession a last time. The priest took his time, performing the sacrament with zeal. Moments before the execution, the priest spoke: "With this death, you pay for your grave sins. The dear angels are present who will carry your soul to heaven." Demonic forces were also lurking. Under no circumstances would the priest allow the executioner's men to remove any consecrated items the poor sinner was wearing. These were essential to protect the poor sinner from stalking demons.[117] Finally, in the case of beheading, the prisoner's neck was bared. The priest discreetly stepped out of the way, and said, "Let us pray 'Our Father.'" As priest and crowd prayed, the executioner swung his sword. The priest concluded the ceremony with another collective "Our Father," and a sermon.

From Mount Calvary to Poor-Sinners' Graveyard

The execution ritual played out in an urban space where the judicial infrastructure and the sacred topography of Baroque Catholicism blended into one another.[118] The malefactor's spiritual preparation for execution took place in the "Government House" (*Amtshaus*) in Rauhenstein Alley, a five-minute walk three alleyways south of St. Stephen's Cathedral. Located across the street from the Himmelpfort Convent of the Augustinian Canonesses, where many aristocratic families placed their daughters for schooling, this prison was popularly known as the "House of Felons and Rogues" (*Malefizspitzbubenhaus*). A dungeon at this location was first documented in 1445.[119] Prisoners were held in chains in underground cells that extended beneath neighboring buildings. Rebuilt in the early seventeenth century, a plaque on the new building commemorated the

---

[117] Wellner, *Handbuch*, 135–136.

[118] For the sacralization of the Viennese cityscape and the patronage of sacred architecture by the Habsburg dynasty as a political project, see Helmut Halb, "Zur Sakralisierung von frühneuzeitlichem Stadtraum amd Beispiel Wien," in *Sakralisierung der Landschaft. Inbesitznahme, Gestaltung und Verwendung im Zeichen der Gegenreformation in Mitteleuropa*, eds. Werner Telesko and Thomas Aigner (St. Pölten: Diözesanarchiv St. Pölten, 2019), 74–90.

[119] WStLA, Paul Harrer, "Wien: Seine Häuser, Menschen und Kultur," vol. 5, Part I. Unpublished manuscript (1955), 157. "Amtshaus," in Felix Czeike, *Historisches Lexikon Wien*, vol. 1, (Vienna: Kremayr & Scheriau/Orac, 2004), 94.

occasion: "In the Name of Christ's Blood and in Honor of the Most Sacred Trinity, Augustinus Hafner ... City Judge of Vienna, built it, 1608."[120] Serious felons were imprisoned here. This was also where the executioner performed judicial torture. The executioner did not have far to go on such occasions, since he resided within the prison.[121] The prison had its own chapel "To the Holy Cross."[122] The building was topped by a small bell-tower with the Poor-Sinner's Bell that rang when a malefactor was being led out.[123] This bell also rang when an inmate died in the prison, summoning the public to assemble outside to pray for the prisoner's soul.[124]

In 1721 this building was torn down and replaced by a new prison that could accommodate more prisoners. The Bishop of Vienna consecrated a new chapel "To the Holy Cross."[125] The British prison reformer John Howard visited this prison during on his tour of Vienna's carceral institutions in 1778: "The front of the great prison, *Lá Maison de Bourreau* [house of the executioner], is remarkable for a very striking representation of our *Saviour* and the two thieves on mount *Calvary*. In this prison are many horrid dungeons."[126] The elaborate Mount Calvary that John Howard described is shown in an engraving by Salomon Kleiner from the 1720s (Image 7.7). Rough-hewn boulders jut out from the building, framing the main entrance and two barred windows on the ground floor, giving them a grotto-like appearance. The boulders extend to the second floor to form the Mount Calvary where the crucifixion scene unfolds. Above the main entrance the central crucifixion group consists of Christ

---

[120] "Sub Titulo Sanguinis Christi ad Sanctissimae Trinitatis Laudem Augustinus Hafner secundum Consul, Regiae Maj. Praetor Viennensis aedificavit. 1608." Karl August Schimmer, *Ausführliche Häuser-Chronik der innern Stadt Wie: mit einer geschichtlichen Uebersicht sämmtlicher Vorstädte und ihrer merkwürdigsten Gebäude* (Vienna: Kuppitsch, 1849), 177.

[121] Gustav Adolph Schimmer, *Das alte Wien:* ... (Vienna: L.C. Zamarski, 1854), 19. Johann Basilius Küchelbecker, *Allerneueste Nachricht vom Römisch-Käyserlichen Hofe: nebst einer ausführlichen historischen Beschreibung der kayserlichen Residentz-Stadt Wien* ... (Hannover: Förster, 1730), 644–646.

[122] Anon., "Ein Rundgang durch das alte Wien zur Zeit des Steinhausen'schen Stadtplanes," *Berichte und Mittheilungen des Alterthums-Vereins zu Wien* 25 (1889): 32–68, p. 53.

[123] Schimmer, *Wien*, 20.

[124] This according to a caption on a water coloring of the prison from 1750. The caption is from a later date since it mentions the demolition of the building in 1785. HMW, I-N 61.354.

[125] Harrer, "Wien," 5.I, 158.

[126] Italics in the original. John Howard, *Appendix to the State of the Prisons in England and Wales* ... (Warrington: William Eyres, 1780), 31.

7 CRIME AND JUSTICE IN A SACRED LANDSCAPE: VIENNA, 1668–1786   373

Image 7.7 Execution Procession departing from Vienna's prison, Engraving by Johann August Corvinus after Salomon Kleiner, in Salomon Kleiner, *Vera Et Accurata Delineatio Omnium Templorum et Coenobiorum Quae tam in Caesarea Urbe ac Sede Vienna Austriae, quam in circumjacentibus Suburbys ejus reperiuntur*, vol. 1. (Augsburg: Johann Adreas Pfeffel, 1724), plate 41

on the cross, St. John the Baptist, the Virgin Mary and Mary Magdalene embracing the cross. Crucified to the right the good thief looks toward Christ; the bad thief, to the left, turns away from Christ. The Mount Calvary on the prison was completed just seven years after the Mount Calvary in the suburb of Hernals, built between 1709 and 1714.[127] These two Viennese installations were part of a wave of Mount Calvary constructions within the larger sacred landscape of the Baroque. Of the 109 Mount Calvaries documented in Austrian lands, most were built between 1650 and 1750.[128]

In this building, that was at once dungeon and monument to the Passion of Christ, Vienna's sacred and judicial topography became one. Salomon Kleiner's engraving gives an idea of how people engaged with such sacred installations. The image captures an early scene in the unfolding theater of punishment. Three malefactors have been led out of the

---

[127] Felix Czeike, *Wien. Kunst und Kultur Lexikon. Stadtführer und Handbuch* (Munich: Süddeutscher Verlag, 1976), 104–105. On the Mount Calvary at Hernals, see Gugitz, *Österreichs Gnadenstätten*, 92–94.

[128] Martin Lehmann, "Die Kalvarienberganlagen im Donauraum," in *Festschrift Franz Loidl zum 65. Geburtstag*, ed. Victor Flieder, vol. 1 (Vienna: Verlag Brüder Hollinkek, 1970), 113–159, pp. 128, 141–147.

prison, each accompanied by two Jesuits. A crowd has formed. Armed guards form a cordon separating the onlookers from the condemned criminals. The first poor sinner, in chains, kneels in prayer, the two priests kneeling at his side, facing the building and gazing up at the Mount Calvary. He holds a large crucifix as does the Jesuit to his right, who also holds a rosary. A guard kneeling behind the poor sinner, holding the poor sinner's chain, is also praying a rosary. A second condemned criminal also in chains, flanked by two priests, looks at the crowd, bewildered. Shortly he too will kneel to pray at the foot of the Calvary. A third malefactor who has just come out of the building looks back and up at the crucifix. Ahead to the left we see an armed man on horseback. This was the subordinate judge, who would preside over the execution.

From here the execution procession went north on Rauhenstein Alley, headed by a bailiff armed with a pike, the subordinate judge on horseback, the poor sinner flanked by Jesuits, the dungeon-master, and the executioner and his men.[129] It passed through "Poor Sinner's Alley," today Liliengasse, to arrive at St. Stephen's Cathedral.[130] At St. Stephen's everyone came to a halt to recite another prayer.[131] Then the procession continued the short distance to the High Market, where the formal public sentencing would take place. If St. Stephen's Cathedral was the center of Vienna's sacred topography, the High Market lay at the heart of its judicial topography. The High Market was Vienna's oldest and busiest market place. Since the early fourteenth century, if not earlier, it was also the

---

[129] This description is based on contemporary published accounts: Ferdinand Franz Engelberger flanked by Jesuits on his walk from the dungeon to the courthouse, prior to his sacrilege: *Kurtzer Innhalt der Execution, So inn der Statt Wien den 22. Augusti dises Jahrs durch rechtmessiges Urthail zween verzweifelten Juden so jünger: und drauff den 26. dessen/ mit dem ältesten/wgen erbärmlicher und Gottschändiger MalefitzThat/ ... fürgenommen ist worden* (s.l.: s.n., [1642]), 1r. SuStBA, 4 Jud 51-3. An account of a book burning in Vienna by the executioner in 1668 that emphasisizes that the court followed the same procedure used during the execution of a malefactor. Matthias Abele von und zu Lilienberg, Matthias. 1670. *Künstliche Unordnung: das ist: Wunder-Seltsame niemals in offentlichen Druck gekommene Gerichts- und ausser Gerichts- doch warhaffte Begebenheiten.* ([Nuremberg]: Endter, 1670), 315–316.
[130] "Armensündergassel," Czeike, *Historisches Lexikon Wien*, vol. 1, 158.
[131] Instruktion für Gefangenenseelsorger, undated (1770s?). WStLA, Handschriften A 21/1, p. 31,

location of Vienna's courthouse.¹³² The *Bürgerschranne*, literally the "Civic Bench," was the seat of the City and District Court of Vienna.¹³³ The court was an institution of the ducal government, not Vienna's city government, though part of its staff was recruited from the city council of Vienna. The "city judge" (*Stadtrichter*) presided over this court. Despite his title, he was appointed by the emperor and was responsible to the central government, though he was also a voting member of Vienna's inner council, the upper chamber of the city council. The city judge was assisted by twelve jurors, drawn from Vienna's large council, the lower chamber of Vienna's city council. Among his staff was the subordinate judge, whose duty it was to stage-manage public executions. This court held jurisdiction over criminal cases in Vienna and surrounding villages. Criminal sentences had to be confirmed by Vienna's city council, though ultimate authority lay with the emperor.¹³⁴

The iconography on and within the court house was replete with symbols of imperial sovereignty. Renovated in 1635, its façade featured statues of the imperial eagle and the Habsburg heraldic emblem, a lion with a golden crown, to the left and right of the main entrance. A statue of Justitia, richly decorated in gold, stood above. The architect's sketch shows that Justitia incorporated the same symbols of the Habsburg dynasty's imperial sovereignty as the ornamental statues on the façade. A female figure representing Justitia seated on a globe holds a scepter in her left hand. In her right hand she holds a sword supported by a standing lion. Justitia herself is crowned by an eagle.¹³⁵ Entering the building, a plaque to the left of the entrance to the courtroom read: "This building was renovated ... during the reign of the exalted Ferdinand II. Giving to all their just deserts, the might of the emperor punishes crime here with the sword. Reminded of the law, know justice."¹³⁶ To the right of the entrance were

---

[132] A medieval courthouse stood on the north-east corner of the market. When this building burned down in 1437, the city built a new courthouse on the southwest corner. The city court was located here from 1440 to 1839. Harrer, "Wien," vol. 1, Part 2 (1951), 400. Perger, *Hohe Markt*, 31.

[133] In Austrian lands here the courthouse was called the Schranne, from the old high German scranna, bench. Deutsches Rechtswörterbuch (DRW): Schranne. http://drw-www.adw.uni-heidelberg.de/drw-cgi/zeige?index=lemmata&term=schranne.

[134] On the organization of Vienna's court, see Richard Perger, "Die Baugeschichte des Wiener Schrannengebäudes nach schriftlichen Quellen," *Studien zur Wiener Geschichte. Jahrbuch des Vereins für Geschichte der Stadt Wien* 57/58 (202): 270.

[135] Perger, "Baugeschichte," 282.

[136] Quoted in Perger, "Baugeschichte," 284.

the two red marble plaques, separated by a crucifix, that commemorated the desecration of the crucifix by the apostate Jewish convert Ferdinand Franz Engelberger in 1642.[137]

The main entrance to the courthouse was on the second floor, accessed by a broad staircase that led to large balcony. On days when "blood court" was held, city judge and jurors assembled here at eight in the morning. The courthouse bell, the "Poor-Sinner's Bell," tolled, to announce the impending execution. A red flag hung from the balcony.[138] When the procession with the condemned criminal arrived from the prison, the city judge was handed a silver-inlaid sword and staff, wrapped in black velvet. Not to be confused with the executioner's sword, this was a ceremonial sword that the city judge carried along with the staff as insignia of his office. They represented the right to exercise "blood justice," the "right of the sword" (*ius gladii*), bestowed upon him by the sovereign. Judges' swords often bore engravings and inscriptions, emblematic of the melding of worldly and divine justice. The sword of the city judge of Linz from 1659, for example, had an engraving of Justice bearing sword and scales and the word IUSTITIA on one side of the blade. On the other side was engraved a crucifix and a prayer: "Oh Jesus, I live for you; Oh, Jesus, I die for you; Oh Jesus, I am yours dead and alive. What are the four last things of man? These Four: 1. Death. 2. The Last Judgment. 3. Hell. 4. Heaven. Oh Man, think in all your actions of your last things, then you will never sin. In all your doings, freely pray to God to be your helper. Who can be against us when God is with us."[139] The sword in use in Vienna had been bestowed upon the city judge of Vienna by Emperor Rudolf II in 1580, and the staff was a gift from the imperial government in 1632.[140]

As the malefactor and his Jesuit comforters stood in square below, the city scribe loudly read a description of the crime from the balcony, so that the surrounding crowd could hear. Then the city judge addressed the malefactor, asking if this account was true. Typically, the malefactor answered yes. The court scribe then loudly proclaimed the sentence in the

---

[137] See Chap. 5.

[138] Harrer, "Wien," 1, II, 402–403.

[139] Quoted in Fritz Fellner, Gernot Kocher, Ute Streitt, eds., *Katalog: Schande, Folter, Hinrichtung. Rechtsprechung und Strafvollzug in Oberösterreich* (Linz, Oberösterreichisches Landesmuseum, 2011). 12–17. Examples of the staves and swords bourne by Austrian city judges can be viewed here: https://www.ooegeschichte.at/themen/politik-recht-und-gesellschaft/schande-folter-hinrichtung/recht-und-ordnung/die-hohe-gerichtsbarkeit/.

[140] WStLA, Handschriften, A 21/2, pp. 1–3.

name of the sovereign, specifying the manner and location of the execution, concluding with the formula "This as his well-deserved punishment, and to other of his ilk a gruesome deterrent and example. May God have mercy on his soul."[141] At this point the judge snapped a rod in two to symbolize the finality of the sentence.[142]

Now the poor sinner was remanded to the hands of the executioner. If the death sentence allowed for a Christian burial, the Confraternity of the Dead was in attendance. The brothers had processed dressed in the habit of their confraternity from the Augustinian Church to the High Market, where they awaited the arrival of the poor sinner from the prison.[143] The dramatic appearance of the Confraternity of the Dead contributed to the solemnity and spectacle of public executions in Vienna. They wore full-length black habits, with black belts with buckles made of bone. They wore black hats over pointed black hoods with openings only for the eyes, and waist-length capes emblazoned with the confraternity crest of the imperial double eagle astride the skull and crossbones.[144]

An engraving commemorating the execution of Count Ferenc Nádasdy, beheaded in 1671 for his part in a magnate conspiracy against Emperor Leopold I, shows the confraternity in action. Because of the politically explosive nature of his case, Nádasdy was beheaded in the private space of the courtyard of city hall, instead of in public at the ravenstone. After the execution, his body in its casket was displayed to the public. The Confraternity of the Dead was in attendance, waiting to carry the body away for burial. The engraving shows the lay brothers in the habit of their order, with masked faces. Standing among the masked confraternity members to the left are four figures with unmasked faces. These were the Augustinian friars who headed the procession. One of them holds the poor sinner's crucifix attached to a pole (Image 7.8).[145]

In the seventeenth century and in the early years of the eighteenth century most malefactors who were granted the mercy of a Christian burial were executed on the north-east corner of the High Market. A pillory had

[141] [August Richter], *Umständliche Doch in möglichster Kürtze verfaßte Historische Einleitung Uber den Criminal-Process* (Frankfurt: Johann Conrad Wohler, 1738), 300.
[142] Abele, *Künstliche Unordnung*, 315.
[143] Vincentius, *Fegfewers Probier Teuch*, 349–351.
[144] *Regulen Und andächtige Ubungen, Der in der Statt Wien ... Löbl. Bruderschafft* (Vienna: Leopold Voigt, 1672), 71–72.
[145] *"Warhaffte Bildnuß Francisco Nadasti welcher ... zu Wienn enthaubt worden, ... im Jahr 1671."* HMW, IN. 37.988, Gerichtswesen 1671, M 790. Detail.

Image 7.8 "Wahrhafte Bildnuß Francisci Nadasti wegen aufrührerischem Meineid in dem Rathaus zu Wien enthaupt den 30. April 1671." Engraving (Detail). Photo: Wien Museum. Inv. Nr. 37988

stood at this location since the late Middle Ages. Here felons were exposed to the public as an honor punishment, and floggings and brandings took place. Condemned criminals were beheaded on a raised wooden stage next to the pillory. The British physician Edward Brown witnessed an execution here in 1669: "In Treason and high Crimes they cut off the right Hand of the Malefactor, and his Head immediately after. I saw a woman beheaded sitting in a Chair, the Executioner striking off her Head with a Fore-blow, she behaved herself well, and was accompanied unto the Market-place by the Confraternity of the Dead who have a charitable care of such Persons."[146] After 1706 the pillory was moved to the ravenstone outside the Scottish Gate, and beheadings now took place here as well. The removal of the pillory from the High Market should not be read as a sign of emerging discomfort with the performance of bloody punishments within city walls. Such squeamishness would not develop before the mid-eighteenth century. Rather, the pillory was moved to make room for a grand new "Joseph's Fountain," also known as the "Nuptial Fountain" because it depicted the marriage of Mary and Joseph at temple. A votive

---

[146] Edward Brown, *An Account of Several Travels through a great part of Germany* (London: Benj. Tooke, 1677), 111.

offering by Emperor Leopold I, the Joseph's Fountain was second only to the Trinity Column in the Graben as a monument to the *pietas austriaca*.[147]

The relocation of beheadings to the ravenstone beyond the walls meant that execution processions now traversed more of the city. Participation by the Confraternity of the Dead made for an even more impressive event. The founding privilege of the confraternity originally limited the number of brothers who would attend executions to twelve.[148] Perhaps the number twelve represented the twelve apostles, given the explicit comparisons Catholic comforters made between public executions and the Passion of Christ. It is unclear if this limit was ever enforced. By the mid-eighteenth century, confraternity brothers walked in execution procession in far greater numbers, ranging from sixty to as many as 240. Nineteen-year-old Regina Glanzin, beheaded in 1760 for bludgeoning to death the six-month-old daughter of her employer, was accompanied by seventy lay brothers and two Augustinian friars. Catharina Jacobin, the self-accused Bohemian serial child murderer beheaded in 1769, was accompanied by 100 lay brothers and the two friars.[149] The brothers marched immediately behind the poor sinner, bearing the coffin on their shoulders.[150] They bore pilgrims' staves and torches, though it was broad daylight, to symbolize the light of Christ (Image 7.9).[151]

The route from the courthouse to the ravenstone was just over a mile from the High Market through the Freyung, a busy square in front of the Scottish Church, and then out the Scottish Gate onto the *glacis*. The *glacis* was an expanse of land that encircled the ramparts of the inner city, separating it from its suburbs. After the first Turkish siege of 1529 the area was kept clear of buildings to ensure the defense of the inner city. The

---

[147] This was the *Vermählungsbrunnen* (Nuptual Fountain) dedicated to the marriage of Mary and Joseph. An imperial decree from March 15, 1706 ordered the removal of the pillory to an alternate location, and directed the city to complete the work by feast day of St. Joseph (which falls on March 19). WStLA, B6-2, Decretenbuch 1703–1711, fo. 115r.

[148] "Todten-Bruderschaffts-Privilegium," June 5, 1638, in *Codicis Austriaci*, ed. Franz Anton von Guarient und Raall, vol. 2 (Vienna: Voigt, 1704), 340–341.

[149] WB, Handschriften, Lc 67116. Regina Glanzin, f. 5r, Catharina Jacobin, ff. 9r–9v.

[150] Karl Hofbauer, *Die Wieden mit den Edelsitzen Conradswerd, Mühlfeld, Schaumburgerhof und dem Freigrunde Hungerbrunn: historisch-topographische Skizzen zur Schilderung der Vorstädte Wiens* (Vienna: Gorischek, 1864), 168.

[151] Staves: Anon., *Hoch-feyerliches Saeculum*, unpaginated. Torches: Hofbauer, *Wieden*, 170.

Image 7.9 Procession of a Confraternity. "Prospect des Hoch-Gräffl. Traunischen Gebäudes in der Herren-Gassen." Engraving by J. A. Corvinus after Sal. Kleiner. In Salomon Kleiner, *Vera Et Accurata Delineatio Omnium Templorum et Coenobiorum Quae tam in Caesarea Urbe ac Sede Vienna Austriae, quam in circumjacentibus [circumiacentibus] Suburbijs [Suburbiis] ejus [eius] reperiuntur.* Vol 3. *Das florirende vermehrte Wien.* (Augsburg: Johann Adreas Pfeffel, 1733), plate 202

ravenstone stood here near the suburb of the Rossau.[152] Just before arriving at the ravenstone, the procession passed a pieta and a crucifix statue, where suicidal blasphemers performed their expiation, and poor sinners stopped to pray.[153]

The ravenstone was a rounded stone terrace, twelve to fourteen feet above ground level. Spectators standing below could view the beheading from all sides. An account by the British traveler Sir Nathanial William Wraxall, who witnessed the beheading of four men for robbery in 1778 or 1779, gives an idea of what they saw. "Many thousand spectators of all conditions were assembled to witness it; and I never saw any public ceremony performed with so much solemnity and awful decorum." Wraxall climbed onto a cart for a better view, "whence I could distinguish even the countenances and features of the criminals." The first malefactor was seated on a chair fixed to the ground, blindfolded and restrained to prevent movement. His neck was bared. Four monks, carrying a crucifix approached him, prayed, and took his confession. The executioner's man gathered up the malefactor's hair and pulled his neck upright. The

---

[152] See Chap. 6, Image 6.7. For another view of the ravenstone with the inner city in the background, see Johann Adam Delsenbach (Kupferstecher), "Prospect der Stadt Wien vor dem Schotten-Thor," 1719, HMW, Inv.-Nr. 78049/1, CC0 (https://sammlung.wienmuseum.at/objekt/145498/). The ravenstone is at the far right.

[153] See Chap. 6. Hartl, *Wiener Kriminalgericht,* 133. Wilhelm Deutschmann and Herbert Spehar, *200 Jahre Rechtsleben in Wien. Advokaten, Richter, Rechtsgelehrte* (Vienna: Museen der Stadt Wien, 1986), 14.

executioner "threw off his cloak, and being in his white waistcoat, he unsheathed the instrument of punishment. It was a strait, two-edged sword, of an equal breadth quite to the point, prodigiously heavy, broad, and sharp as a razor. Coming in flank of the prisoner, who was blindfolded and consequently ignorant of the precise moment of his approach, he took off the head at one stroke, with a dexterity and celerity exceeding imagination. The assistant held it up streaming with blood, and then laid it down on the ground; while the decapitated trunk was allowed to remain for some seconds in the chair, the blood spouting up at first to the height of three or four feet in the air." Wraxall was deeply moved by this "solemn sight." Compared to hanging, the common method of execution in England, "decapitation ... makes a far more awful and profound impression on the multitude, who are affected by the sight of the headless trunk .... The rapidity and precision with which the act itself is performed, constitute not the least wonderful part of it, and may be compared to the effect of lightning."[154]

If the malefactor had been granted a Christian burial, the Confraternity of the Dead now took center stage. They carried the poor sinner's casket for almost two miles to the "Poor Sinners' Graveyard." The funeral procession went around the inner city through the *glacis* to the suburb of Wieden outside the Carinthian Gate. The graveyard was established by the Confraternity of the Dead in 1639 within a preexisting graveyard belonging to the city hospital that had been located here since 1571. Previously known as "Graveyard of the City Hospital," it now became known as "Poor Sinners' Graveyard." Not only executed criminals were buried here. The composer Antonio Vivaldi was buried in the "Poor-Sinners' Graveyard" in 1741.[155] It is unknown whether the graves of executed criminals were segregated from the other dead. An engraving by Salomon Kleiner from 1737 of the Poor Sinners' Graveyard shows well-tended grounds and a chapel, dwarfed by the newly constructed St. Charles

---

[154] Nathanial William Wraxall, *Memoirs of the Courts of Berlin, Dresden, Warsaw, and Vienna, in the years 1777, 1778, and 1779*. 2nd edition (London: A. Strahan, 1800), 261–267.

[155] This "Graveyard of the City Hospital" (*Bürgerspitalsfriedhof*) was first established in 1571. When the Confraternity of the Dead began the practice of burying executed criminals here, it became known as the Poor Sinners' Graveyard. Deutschmann and Spehar, *200 Jahre Rechtsleben*, 14. Werner T. Bauer, *Wiener Friedhofsführer. Genaue Beschreibung sämtlicher Begräbnisstätten nebst einer Geschichte des Wiener Bestattungswesens* (Vienna: Falter Verlag, 1997), 36–38.

Image 7.10 The Poor Sinners' Graveyard. "Prospect des Bürgerl. Hospitals-Gotts-Acker nebst der Capelle St. Rochi, vor dem Kärnter Thor. a. S. Caroli Borromaei Kirche." Engraving by J. A. Corvinus after Sal. Kleiner. In Salomon Kleiner, *Vera Et Accurata Delineatio Omnium Templorum et Coenobiorum Quae tam in Caesarea Urbe ac Sede Vienna Austriae, quam in circumjacentibus [circumiacentibus] Suburbijs [Suburbiis] ejus [eius] reperiuntur.* Vol. 4. *Des florirenden vermehrten Wiens fernere Befolgung.* Plate 47

Church in the background. The graveyard is not desolate or forsaken. Decorative crosses, similar to those one sees in south German and Austrian graveyards today, mark individual graves. Two clergymen, one bearing a large crucifix, the other a rosary, process through the grounds. A woman in the foreground prays the rosary. Three others are heading into the chapel, as another parishioner leaves (Image 7.10)[156]. It was a dignified final

[156] Salomon Kleiner, *Des florierenden vermehrten Wiens Fernere Befolgung, oder, Wahrhafte und genaue Abbildung derer in dieser Kayserl. Residenz-Statt ... ausgeführten Gebäuden ...* (Augsburg: Johann Andreas Pfeffel, 1737), Vierter Theil. It was referred to as the *Armsündergottesacker* or the *Bürgerspitalfriedhof.* Kleiner's engraving mistakenly labels the chapel as St. Rochus. In fact, it was the Augustinkapelle, first founded by the Viennese citizen Augustin Hirneis in 1638, the same year the Confraternity for the Dead was founded. The chapel was destroyed during the Turkish siege of 1683, and replaced in 1701 by a larger chapel, as shown in Kleiner's engraving, though of course it appears quite diminutive next to St. Charles Church looming in the background. Gugitz, *Österreichs Gnadenstätten,* 58.

resting place for repentant executed criminals, fully reintegrated into society, albeit the society of the dead. Archeological evidence, unearthed during construction work at the site of the former graveyard in 1938, reveals that poor sinners were laid to rest wearing crucifixes, rosaries, and pilgrim's amulets, particularly those dedicated to the Virgin of Mariazell, to ease their passage into the afterlife.[157]

An Ideological Imperative: Eliciting the Poor Sinner's Compliance

Such comprehensive religious support persuaded most condemned criminals to play their assigned role of repentant poor sinner. The public took pleasure at particularly edifying performances. In 1772 the condemned thief Benedikt Bacher at first raged against his death sentence, but ultimately, he "so docilely disposed himself towards death," wrote the scribe of the Confraternity of the Dead, that the many thousand people who attended his execution "took the greatest pleasure in him." He urged spectators to confess their sins, and even recited a rhyme on the ravenstone:

> *O wie schön steht mir der Himmel offen.*
> *Da mein Seel tracht hinein.*
> *Weil ich heut muß ein Kind des Todes seyn.*
>
> Oh, how beautifully the gates of Heaven stand open to me.
> My soul longs to enter.
> Because today I must be a child of death.[158]

In the rare cases when a malefactor remained "obstinate," threatening to disrupt the smooth sequence of the execution ritual, authorities went to extraordinary lengths to elicit his or her compliance, an indication of the ideological significance of the poor sinner's consent. Faced with a recalcitrant malefactor, authorities postponed or even interrupted an execution. Anna Maria N., a twenty-eight-year-old vagrant, was sentenced to be beheaded on September 23, 1723, for breach of *Urfehde*. Escorted by the Confraternity of the Dead, the procession arrived at the ravenstone as

---

[157] Elke Doppler, Christian Rapp, and Sándor Békési, eds., *Am Puls der Stadt: 2000 Jahre Karlsplatz. [Sonderausstellung, Wien Museum Karlsplatz, 29. Mai–26. Oktober 2008].* (Vienna: Czernin, 2008), 305.

[158] WB, Handschriften, Lb 18013, f. 98–102, Nr. 192, April 4, 1772, Benedict Bacher.

scheduled. Once there, however, the *Wiennerisches Diarium* reported, "she absolutely did not want to die, nor did she want to wash off her sins through a penitent confession."[159] The chronicler of the Confraternity of the Dead described the dramatic scene: Anna Maria was already seated in the chair, restrained, awaiting her beheading that was to take place momentarily. Faced with her intransigence, however, the executioner asked the subordinate judge, presiding on horseback as master of ceremonies, how to proceed. The judge ordered the executioner to carry on with the execution. The executioner refused. In a dramatic gesture he lay down his sword. The executioner demanded that the judge ride back into town to seek further orders from higher authority. Undoubtedly the executioner was worried about the possibility of a botched beheading, which occurred with some regularity, an accident that would be all the more likely if the condemned criminal struggled as the executioner swung his sword. More importantly, the executioner likely also did not want to dispatch Anna Maria straight to hell, as would be expected for a recalcitrant malefactor who died unrepentantly. Faced with the executioner's defiance, the judge rode back into town and returned with a new order: Anna Maria N. would be granted a reprieve of one day, if she promised to comply the following day. She was untied and returned to the dungeon. She died the following day, September 24, "well disposed," after performing a voluntary public expiation. "Many thousand people" were in attendance.[160]

In 1757 the authorities went to even greater lengths to elicit a malefactor's compliance, unsuccessfully in this case. The beheading of Johann Adam Scharbaur, twenty-eight, convicted of various thefts and breaking his oath of *Urfehde* three times, was scheduled for Friday, December 16. In the days leading up to his execution Scharbauer refused to pray or give confession. On the appointed day he was led out to the ravenstone, escorted by the Confraternity of the Dead. The confraternity's chronicler described the event. "A very great crowd of people" was in attendance. Scharbaur refused to perform any expiation or to confess, even as he arrived at the ravenstone. At this point the dungeon-master read an order, obviously prepared in advance, that granted Scharbaur a delay of twenty-four hours, "to ensure his soul's salvation." He was driven back to town

---

[159] *WD*, Nr. 77, 24 September 1723, Anna Maria N.

[160] ÖNB, Handschriften, Cod 8363, pp. 10–11, Nr. 87, 1723, 13 September, Maria Anna. (There is a variation in dates. The *Wiennerisches Diarium* gives September 24 as the date of her execution.) *WD*, Nr. 77, 24 September 1723, Anna Maria N.

and returned to the dungeon. But Scharbaur remained obdurate. He was granted another reprieve. The city judge proclaimed that by imperial mercy the execution would be postponed until Monday, to provide Scharbaur every opportunity for his "conversion," that is, the internal spiritual transformation required to die a good death. The Jesuit poor sinner's priest made every effort to dissuade him from his obstinacy. Other members of the clergy and high-ranking lay people visited Scharbaur in the dungeon, urging him to repent. The Archbishop and Cardinal of Vienna, Count Christoph Anton Migazzi, personally visited Scharbaur. The Archbishop offered to stay by his side through the night and personally accompany him out to the ravenstone the next morning, if he would die repentantly. Despite all of these "fatherly admonitions" Scharbaur remained recalcitrant.[161] Finally, the authorities lost patience. The next morning, as thousands of people watched, the Jesuit priest led him out to the ravenstone a second time. When Scharbaur arrived at the ravenstone, the executioner addressed him, pointing out a coffin and the waiting members of the Confraternity for the Dead. Eighty lay brothers were in attendance, along with two Augustinian friars who led their procession. If he would convert, the executioner told him, he would be placed in this coffin and the Confraternity of the Dead would provide him with a Christian burial. But should he refuse, the knacker's wagon stood ready to cart him away like a dead animal. The executioner's words remained without effect. Scharbauer was led onto the ravenstone along with two priests and two executioners who beseeched him for another fifteen minutes to repent. Before his eyes were covered, one of the executioners showed him the unsheathed sword that would take his life, something that had "never been shown to anyone before," the scribe of the confraternity remarked, "so as not to terrify them, only to him alone." Even as the executioner touched the sword to his neck, Scharbaur refused to express repentance, insisting that he died innocently. Finally, a commissioner of the court gave a sign, and Scharbaur was beheaded. After the execution the members of the Confraternity of the Dead departed immediately. Scharbaur's head and body were placed on the skinner's cart. The skinner's men buried the body in a ditch where carrion was disposed of. According to an anonymous execution chronicle, "he was buried next to the Danube in unconsecrated ground, like an animal, as is fitting for such a Christian for whom all spiritual measures were taken, but who stubbornly turned away from

[161] ÖNB, Cod 8363, pp. 25–27, Nr. 150, 19 December 1757, Johann Adam Scharbaur.

the Catholic Church, which alone can bring salvation."[162] The extraordinary efforts by high-ranking clerics and lay people in the days before the execution, and by the executioners and four clergymen present at the ravenstone, to convince Scharbaur to go to his death willingly and repentantly are another indication of the ideological significance of the salvific drama of public executions in Vienna, even in the second half of the eighteenth century. In a remarkable example of the "simultaneity of the non-simultaneous," however, later that evening medical students retrieved the body from the carrion pit and transported it to the university's anatomical theater for dissection.[163]

In old-regime criminal justice, the blending of secular authority and religious ritual made public execution into a religious resource. Obviously, this was true for perpetrators of suicide by proxy who instrumentalized criminal justice for personal religious ends. It was also true for people far removed from any personal connection to crime, criminals, or the criminal justice system. Upstanding citizens desired to participate vicariously in the salvation of repentant malefactors. The devotions and charitable deeds of the Confraternity of the Dead are a clear example of the effort by respectable people to tap into the salvific charisma of condemned criminals. Individual Christians also sought to access this salvific resource by personally endowing Masses for the souls of condemned and executed criminals, or for their own souls, to be celebrated in the chapel most closely associated with capital punishment, the chapel in the Government House Prison. When performing religious devotions, location mattered. A Mass celebrated at a "privileged" altar endowed with indulgences, as, for example, the Crucifix Altar in the Chapel of the Dead, was more powerful than a Mass celebrated at a regular altar. In a similar way, Viennese donors endowed Masses to be celebrated in the Government House Chapel to benefit spiritually from the suffering of condemned criminals who confessed and received the Eucharist there shortly before their executions. In

---

[162] WB, Handscrhiften, Lc 67116, ff. [3r–3v].

[163] Jörn Leonhard, "Non-simultaneity," in: *Encyclopedia of Early Modern History Online*, Editors of the English edition: Graeme Dunphy, Andrew Gow. Original German Edition: Enzyklopädie der Neuzeit. Im Auftrag des Kulturwissenschaftlichen Instituts (Essen) und in Verbindung mit den Fachherausgebern herausgegeben von Friedrich Jaeger. Copyright © J.B. Metzlersche Verlagsbuchhandlung und Carl Ernst Poeschel Verlag GmbH 2005–2012. Consulted online on 27 July 2022 https://doi.org/10.1163/2352-0272_emho_COM_029268. ÖNB, Cod 8363, pp. 25–27, Nr. 150, 19 December 1757, Johann Adam Scharbauer. WB, Handscrhiften, Lc 67116, ff. [3r–3v].

1613, for example, Anna Khunigin, a Viennese citizen and owner of an apothecary, left an endowment of 800 *Reichstaler* to Vienna's criminal court. The funds were deposited with the treasury of the city of Vienna and yielded a yearly interest of 32 *Reichstaler*. The endowment required the Jesuit poor-sinners' priest to read a Mass every Friday in the prison chapel, unless one or more prisoners were scheduled to be executed that week, in which case the priest should perform the Mass on the day of execution. The next scheduled Mass would be celebrated specifically for the souls for the most recently executed criminals.[164] In 1697 Sigmund Pell and Eleonora Reichlin made a bequest of 450 *Reichstaler*. The yearly interest of eighteen *Reichstaler* would finance thirty Masses per year for their souls to be celebrated with assembled prisoners in the Government House chapel. In 1716 Wilhelm Sattler, a medical doctor, bequeathed 350 *Gulden* to the city government in Vienna, to be invested a 5% yearly interest. The interest would fund a Mass to be read for the soul of the poor sinner each time an execution took place.[165] Criminals awaiting their execution also made bequests for Masses to be read for their souls. A bequest in 1771 of fifty *Reichstaler* by two female inmates, Catharina Jakobeckin and Theresia Nachbahrin, yielded a yearly interest of two *Reichstaler*. The money would fund a Mass to be read on the anniversaries of their executions in the chapel of the Government House Prison.[166] Catharina Jakobeckin, *alias* Jacobin, was the self-accused serial child murderer discussed above, and Theresia Nachbahrin was an eighteen-year-old servant woman executed for setting her employer's barn on fire after her mistress had accused her of theft. The women's bequest is very modest compared to other endowments, and it seems that the monies of the two executed women had to be pooled to arrive at the sum of 50 *Reichstaler*. Catherina Jacobeckin was executed on February 16, 1769. Theresia Nachbahrin was executed on March 9, 1771, the date of the bequest.[167] Most likely Catherina Jacobeckin's funds deposited at the time of her execution were insufficient to fund a Mass, and were then combined with Theresia

---

[164] DAW, GF 21, G/S 1, Gerichts und Strafhäuser 2, Amtshauskapelle, 1588–1761, 24 July 1613, Stiftung Ana Khünigen.

[165] DAW, GF 21, G/S 1, Gerichts und Strafhäuser 2, Amtshauskapelle, 1588–1761, 17 September 1715, Wilhelm Sattler.

[166] DAW, KL/01, Barfüßer Augustiner Eremiten, Maria Loreto St. Augustin, 1637–1835. List of bequests for ministry to prisoners, dated 12 Christmonaths [i.e., December] 1782.

[167] WB, Handschriften Lb 18013, pp. 81–88, Nr. 189, 16 Feburary, 1769, Catharina Jacobeckin, and pp. 91–93, Nr. 191, March 9, 1771, Theresia Nachbahrin.

Nachbahrin's bequest. There is no indication that the two women knew each other. There were many similar endowments for soul Masses for poor sinners, both in the Government House Chapel and in other Viennese churches. The sums of money involved were substantial and interest accumulated over decades, if not centuries.[168] This financial entanglement between Vienna's criminal court and the Catholic Church formed a kind of judicial-ecclesiastical complex. It demonstrates the broad societal interest and investment in the salvation of condemned criminals, in the hope that others might benefit spiritually from penitent malefactors' entry into paradise.

The Demise of Old-Regime Criminal Justice

Decades before Joseph II initiated reforms that fundamentally transformed criminal justice, while simultaneously launching a frontal assault upon Baroque Catholicism, the upper echelons of society began to distance themselves from the traditional blood rites of early modern criminal justice.[169] A telling episode involved Joseph's mother. In 1747 Maria Theresa took a carriage ride from the imperial palace in town to her summer palace in Laxenburg. Her route passed close by the gallows on the Vienna Mountain. Distressed at the sight of several corpses hanging there, she ordered the removal of the execution sites on the Vienna Mountain.[170] It was "inappropriate," the governmental decree noted, that executions sites were located so close to the imperial summer residence in Schönbrunn. The central government ordered the city of Vienna to demolish both the gallows and the ravenstone by the Wheel Cross. In their place, the ravenstone outside the Scottish Gate would be expanded to accommodate all types of executions, including hangings and breakings by the wheel. Should the need arise, temporary gallows could be erected, but they would

---

[168] For numerous further examples, see WStLA, Handschriften A 21/2, pp. 222–227, and Handschriften A 21/3, pp. 198–229.

[169] Gerhard Ammerer, *Das Ende für Schwert und Galgen? Legislativer Prozess und öffentlicher Diskurs zur Reduzierung der Todesstrafe im Ordentlichen Verfahren unter Joseph II. (1781–1787)* (Innsbruck: StudienVerlag, 2010), 15. For a granular account of Joseph II's assault on Baroque Catholicism, see Klaus Gottschall, *Dokumente zum Wandel im religiösen Leben Wiens während des Josephinismus* (Vienna: Institut für Volkskunde der Universität Wien, 1979).

[170] Anton Lang, *Hochgericht und Räderkreuz. Die Hinrichtungsstätten am Wienerberg* (Vienna, Museumsverein Favoriten, 2002), 25–26.

be disassembled after each use. Henceforth the bodies of executed criminals would be removed shortly after execution, rather than "letting them hang on the gallows or lie on the wheel for such a long time."[171] A later Josephine decree specified that the body would remain hanging on the gallows or exposed on the wheel for no longer than twelve hours.

Changing editorial priorities by the publishers of the *Wiennerisches Diarium* are another sign of distancing by the reading public. In the later eighteenth century crime reporting declined precipitously. From 1730–1739, for example, the *Wiennerisches Diarium* published 123 reports of executions, floggings, banishments, and forced labor deportations. From 1760–1769 the newspaper published only six crime reports. It reported on just four executions over the course of the decade, without mentioning eighteen further executions that can be documented in other sources.[172] The newspaper's clientele apparently took less pleasure than in earlier decades in reading about public floggings or decapitations, even as they were still ongoing.

Authorities also lost interest in the sacred landscape. By 1768 the crucifix statue by the ravenstone outside the Scottish Gate, where so many suicidal iconoclasts had performed their expiation, had fallen into disrepair. Bureaucratic wrangling ensued over who should pay for its restoration. The Archbishopric of Vienna complained to the central government, which in turn tasked the criminal court of Vienna to determine who originally erected this crucifix, and whether funds had been set aside for its maintenance. Two years later the statue still had not been repaired. The crucifix lay toppled in the mud when the beheading of Catharina Jacobin, the self-accused serial child murderer, took place at the ravenstone in 1769. In 1770 the Viennese criminal court submitted its report. A local executioner had erected the crucifix "very many years ago." No monies had been set aside, and there was no one who could be held responsible

---

[171] "Demnach sich nicht geziemen will, daß in so naher Gegend dero Kais. Königl Residenz und Lustschloss Schönbrunn die Hochgerichter an und auf dem Wienerberg verbleiben sollen." Bodies should be removed quickly, "und nicht mehr auf dem Galgen hängen oder auf dem Rad so lange Zeit liegen gelassen werden sollen." WStLA Handschriften A 21/1, p. 319, Nr. 307, June 5, 1747.

[172] For crime reporting by the *Wiennerisches Diarium*, 1730–1739 and 1760–1769, see https://homepage.univie.ac.at/susanne.hehenberger/kriminaldatenbank/. For additional executions in these years, see ÖNB, Cod 8363. WB, Handschriften Lb 18013. WB, Handschriften Lc 67116, and the collection of printed execution notices in the Wien Bibliothek.

for its repair. It was essential, however, the city judge wrote, to repair the crucifix to avoid the ongoing public scandal of a holy icon lying in the muck. Furthermore, the crucifix would be needed if a blasphemer was ordered to perform a public expiation here, or if a condemned criminal was led by in the procession to the ravenstone.[173] The crucifix ultimately must have been restored, because it survives to the present day. After the temporary end of capital punishment in Austria in 1787, the ravenstone was razed in 1788. The crucifix was moved to the nearby Servite Church, where it hangs to the right of the high altar.[174] The pieta that stood at the ravenstone was lost.

In 1770 the central government attempted to end postponements of executions when condemned criminals "did not want to die" and refused to play their assigned role of penitent poor sinner. An imperial decree ordered that all executions in Austria proceed at their scheduled time, regardless whether the condemned criminal was well disposed to die or not.[175] This decree proved impossible to implement. Even in Vienna, under the nose of imperial authorities, the city's criminal court delayed executions on several occasions over the next decade to allow condemned criminals more time for their "conversion." However, the decree reveals the changed understanding of the role of government among high officials. They no longer considered ensuring the salvation of condemned criminals to be a government responsibility. Instead, their priority was to ensure the efficiency, predictability, and certainty of criminal punishment imposed by law. Furthermore, delaying the execution of an intransigent criminal by a day or two was pointless, even from a spiritual point of view. Attacking the central belief that motivated suicide by proxy, proponents of the Catholic Enlightenment, like their Protestant counterparts, rejected the idea that a lifetime of sin and crime could be expunged by a last-minute conversion on the ravenstone. "God does not allow himself to be mocked," Franz Giftschütz, theology professor at the University of Vienna, wrote in 1785."[176]

One of the criminals who was granted a delay in execution was Benedict Bacher, scheduled to be hanged for theft on April 2, 1772. He was granted

---

[173] WStLA, Handschriften A 21/1, pp. 8–9. Correspondence from November 9, 1768 and August 5, 1770.

[174] Czeike, *Wien*, 154.

[175] Ammerer, *Ende für Schwert und Galgen*, 44–45.

[176] "Gott läßt mit sich nicht spotten." Quoted in Ammerer and Adomeit, "Armsünderblätter," 282, fn. 38.

a two-day reprieve because he was unrepentant and uncooperative. He did come around, however, and delivered a particularly edifying performance on the ravenstone. Then 240 confraternity brothers carried his body in procession to the Poor Sinners' Graveyard, as throngs of spectators at the execution joined the funeral procession. This particularly extravagant display of bathos and pomp prompted the government to curtail the participation of the Confraternity of the Dead, and ultimately to abolish it.[177] An imperial decree established a new protocol, implemented at the next execution two months later. The confraternity would continue to escort condemned criminals to their execution as they always had done, but after the execution they would leave immediately. They would no longer carry the body to be buried. Without exception the body would remain at the ravenstone until evening. At nightfall the executioner's men, whom the public considered dishonorable, would lay the body in a simple casket without the presence of any clergyman or member of the confraternity, and transport it on a small wagon made specifically for this purpose pulled by one horse, without ceremony, to the gate of the Poor Sinner's Graveyard. There they would place the coffin on a table set up outside the gate, and leave. Four members of the Confraternity of the Dead waiting within the graveyard would then retrieve the body and store it in the mortuary overnight. The handoff was organized in this way to avoid any contact between the dishonorable executioner's men and the confraternity brothers. The next morning the confraternity brothers and two friars would appear at the graveyard and bury the malefactor in a simple ceremony.[178]

The point of this reform was to deny executed criminals the honor of a funeral procession that was often far grander than those of respectable citizens. Separating the execution from the religious rite of the burial lessened the aura of sanctity that attached to the penitent malefactor. Heightening the infamy of the execution would, the authorities hoped, increase its didactic, deterrent effect. In 1775 Joseph ended the participation of confraternity brothers in the execution entirely. Two Augustinian friars would attend the execution as representatives of the confraternity. Confraternity brothers were limited to appearing at the graveyard the next morning to perform the burial.[179] In 1783 the confraternity was dissolved, along with all other lay confraternities in Vienna.[180]

[177] April 4, 1772, Benedictus Bacher. WB, Handschriften, Lc 67116, ff. 9v–10r.
[178] WB, Handschriften, Lc 67116, ff. 10r–10v, June 12, 1772, Joseph Zahl Maister.
[179] February 23, 1775, Lorentz Hohen Möcker. WB, Handschriften, Lc 67116, ff. 12v–13r.
[180] Gottschall, *Dokumente*, 35–36.

At the same time that Joseph's government stripped away religious ritual surrounding criminal justice, the physical spaces where these rituals were performed were dismantled. 1784 was a pivotal year. Joseph II ordered the closure of all graveyards within Vienna's fortifications, as part of a larger hygiene offensive. In 1784 the Poor Sinners' Graveyard was shut down, and the chapel to St. Augustine razed.[181] After the dissolution of the Confraternity of the Dead, the Chapel of the Dead in St. Georg's Chapel in the Augustinian Church was repurposed. During a general renovation of the Church in 1784, the paintings and frescoes in the Chapel of the Dead showing the sufferings of the poor souls in purgatory and salvific exchanges between the living and the dead were removed or painted over. The Loreto Chapel with the heart crypt of the Habsburgs was moved to the now vacant Chapel of the Dead, and remains there today.[182] The Government House Prison in Rauhenstein Alley closed in 1784. The building was sold to a blacksmith, who tore it down and replaced it with the building that stands at this location today.[183] The Mount Calvary on the façade of the prison was dismantled. The figures of Christ, John the Baptist and the Virgin Mary at the center of the Mount Calvary were moved to of the pilgrimage church Mariahilf. The statues were displayed in an outdoor chapel attached to the church, where they stand today.[184]

The arrival of the crucifixion group at Mariahilf provided pilgrims with a new object of devotion. Most pilgrims to Mariahilf came to worship at the famous miracle-working icon of the Virgin of Mariahilf, but now the "Poor-Sinner's Crucifix" before which so many condemned criminals had prayed as they embarked on their last journey to the ravenstone, attracted pilgrims and acquired a miraculous reputation of its own. A Freemason and Josephine pamphleteer, Leopold Alois Hoffmann, described the scene in 1784: "Everyone will notice the large crucifix standing by the side entrance, because so much rabble throngs to it, where they perform a quite unusual devotion. Within a few minutes we saw several hundred people. After a short prayer, they kissed all the toes, felt the wounds on the feet with their hands and then wiped their eyes, presumably to treat eye pain. People also shaved off pieces from the foot of the cross and took them home as relics. To all excess, there are even *ex voto* images displayed

---

[181] Bauer, *Wiener Friedhofsführer*, 25–26.
[182] Wolfsgruber, *Loretokapelle*, 52–55
[183] Harrer, "Wien," vol. 5, Part 1, "Rauhensteingasse Nr. 10," 155–159, p. 159.
[184] Czeike, *Wien*, 104–105.

with it."[185] Perhaps pilgrims believed, in the kind of analogical thinking typical of early modern popular piety, that the Poor-Sinner's Cross would help with ailments of the eyes because so many condemned criminals had gazed upon it in their last hour, a kind of a transfer of the salvific gaze that brought spiritual benefit to the one who looked upon sacred objects. As R. Po-chia Hsia explains: "To see is to establish contact. For the laity, to behold the sacred was to create a direct bond between themselves and the sources of sanctity. "[186] When condemned criminals looked up at the Christ figure on the Mount Calvary on the wall of the dungeon they were just leaving, their gaze contributed to their salvation. And in a sense, their salvation rebounded back upon the crucifix. The Poor Sinner's Crucifix, sacred to begin with simply by virtue of being a crucifix, became doubly salvific as a kind of visual contact relic that let pilgrims who worshipped at Christ's feet participate in the salvation they believed that penitent poor sinners earned during their execution, as they died a martyr's death. The spontaneous development of this new popular devotion in 1784 shows that common people still longed for contact with the salvific charisma of condemned criminals, but criminal justice during and after the reign of Joseph II would no longer satisfy this desire.

After Joseph's death in 1790 the death penalty was reintroduced, in stages. First, in response to the French Revolution, an imperial decree reintroduced the death penalty for high treason in 1796. Then, in 1803, the "Law Code on Crimes and Serious Misdemeanors" reintroduced capital punishment more generally.[187] Executions remained rare, however, and the religious ritual surrounding public executions was markedly reduced. Malefactors were executed by hanging on a temporary gallows erected for each occasion on the Vienna Mountain by the Spinnerin am Kreuz, where the city's massive stone gallows once stood. Death by hanging was less appealing than the more honorific decapitation. Most importantly, executed criminals were now denied a Christian burial and interred near the execution site. Suicidal child murders did not resume. The practice of suicide by proxy was quickly forgotten.

---

[185] Quoted in Edmund Friess and Gustav Gugitz, "Die Mirakelbücher von Mariahilf in Wien (1689–1775)," in *Deutsche Mirakelbücher: Zur Quellenkunde und Sinngebung*, ed. Georg Schreiber (Düsseldorf: Schwann, 1938), 128.
[186] R. Po-chia Hsia, *The Myth of Ritual Murder: Jews and Magic in Reformation Germany* (New Haven: Yale University Press, 1988), 10.
[187] Ammerer, *Ende für Schwert und Galgen*, 195–198.

CHAPTER 8

Conclusion: The Decline of Suicide by Proxy and its Historical Effacement

The grief of the parents of the murdered children has remained invisible in this history of suicide by proxy. The sources are mostly silent on the matter. It was not legally relevant in determining the criminal culpability of the murderers. In the thousands of pages of trial records that I have read while researching this book, I have come across two brief mentions of the parents' response.

In 1704 Agnes Catharina Schickin, a Württemberg peasant, lured seven-year-old Hans Michael Furch, son of the cowherder Jacob Furch, into a nearby forest, where she cut his throat. When Hans Michael failed to come home that evening, Furch went searching for his son. In the meantime, his son was found. Upon learning what had happened, the father fainted. As Schickin's trial got underway, the cowherder remained "inconsolable over the loss of his pious little son."[1]

In 1761 Eva Lizlfelnerin, an upper Austrian peasant, tricked Barbara Ströblin, who lived by a waterfall on the River Traun, into leaving her house. Ströblin's son Matthias, who was almost two, was sleeping in his crib. Schickin took the boy and threw him into the waterfall, and left to turn herself in. When Ströblin returned home a few minutes later, she

---

[1] "...welcher sich über diesen erbärmlichen Verlust seines frommen Söhnleins nicht will trösten lassen." HStAS, A 209/1806, Agnes Catherina Schickin, 1704. Report dated 30 May 1704.

found her baby missing. Her husband Balthasar Ströbl, a fifty-eight-year-old carpenter employed at the nearby locks, rushed home when his wife's message reached him that a woman had stolen their son. This was their only child. The carpenter's first twenty-year marriage had been childless. After his first wife died five years earlier, he married Barbara, then thirty-four. Three years into their marriage she gave birth to Matthias.

No one had witnessed the murder, so the parents had no idea that their baby was dead. The carpenter went from house to house searching for his son. He finally arrived at Lizlfelnerin's farm, where he learned that she was in custody for throwing a baby into the waterfall. Hearing this, Ströbl crossed himself, "stunned as if he had seen the devil incarnate." He rushed home, where he found the bailiff waiting for him. Together they searched the rapids for his son, but no trace of the child was found.

When the bailiff left, Ströbl continued to search on his own. Three days later he found Matthias' body washed up among the reeds a mile downstream. He and his wife buried their son the next morning. Their child appeared "as beautiful as if he had died in the crib," Matthias' mother said.[2]

If the loss they would inflict on the parents of their child victims ever entered the murderers' minds, it did not deter them. Perpetrators of all forms of suicide by proxy focused on working the criminal justice system to achieve the outcome they desired. They were familiar with judicial procedures and made every effort to meet evidentiary requirements. When sixteen-year-old Maria Ostertag presented herself at the prison in Ellwangen in 1613 denouncing herself as a witch, she helpfully pointed out the devil's mark in her armpit, important material evidence in witchcraft cases.[3] In 1644 witchcraft self-accuser Catharina Schmid reminded city councilors in Reutlingen of the duties of their office, and their obligations under imperial law.[4] When courts stopped convicting self-accusers of witchcraft, bestiality, or past infanticides without additional corroborating evidence in the late seventeenth century, perpetrators of suicide by proxy adjusted their tactics. They provided the required material evidence by committing child murder, or iconoclasm or host desecration, instead of confessing to "occult" crimes that were difficult to prove. Some bestiality

---

[2] 18 February 1762, Testimony of Catherina Ströblin. "....das Kind... so schön gewesen, als wann es in der Wiegen gestorben." OÖLA, HA Puchheim, Schachtel 43, B60, Nr. 32, Eva Lizlfellnerin, 1762.
[3] Chapter 2.
[4] Chapter 2.

self-accusers, who may well have been guilty of the sexual transgression they turned themselves in for, anticipated disbelief by prosecutors and committed an add-on child murder to ensure that they achieved their desired execution.[5] In order to meet rising standards of proof, Vienna's first documented child murderer in 1668 went so far as to revive an archaic judicial practice, the "suit of the dead hand." By presenting the severed hand of the boy he killed to the court, he proved that he was indeed the murderer.[6]

Hamburg, a Lutheran republic, and Vienna, the Catholic imperial capital, both experienced high numbers of suicide by proxy. Despite confessional differences, ruling elites in both cities conceived of and exercised governmental authority in similar ways. The Hamburg senate and the Austrian government both cooperated closely with their respective state churches to enact rigorous morals policing and disciplining campaigns in the seventeenth century. Ironically, it was this very discipline that produced suicide by proxy. The houses of correction in the two cities, emblematic institutions of the confessional age, implemented essentially identical disciplinary regimes. Excessive discipline in the Lutheran and Catholic institutions backfired when desperate individuals responded by committing suicide by proxy. The Lutheran and Catholic confessional states reacted to the brazenness of these perpetrators by imposing ever more brutal forms of execution. But this type of offender could not be deterred by the traditional repertoire of old regime criminal justice.

Suicide by proxy was a malleable practice. Perpetrators incorporated devotions specific to their confession. The plasticity of the practice is particularly clear in the uniquely Catholic variant of suicide by proxy, suicidal host desecration and iconoclasm. Perpetrators responded to the intensity of Eucharistic devotions and the cult of images, promoted by church and state. In 1715 the Austrian government developed a genuinely novel response to the outbreak of suicidal blasphemy in Vienna in the late seventeenth and early eighteenth century. They made a creative judicial-theological argument. These suicidal actors were not true blasphemers,

---

[5] For example Hans Bützer's bestiality self-accusation and child murder in 1673, discussed in Chap. 2 as well as the very similar case of Micheal Fischer, who committed child murder in 1786 because he believed prosecutors would dismiss his self-accusation of bestiality. Anonym, "Verbrechen eines 63jährigen Mannes aus Gewissensunruhe über Vergehungen, die er im 17ten und 18then Jahre begangen hatte," *Annalen der Gesetzgebung und Rechtsgelehrsamkeit* 2 (1788): 65–76.
[6] See Chap. 7.

the government declared, because their blasphemy had been incidental, a means to an end, rather than an intentional assault upon God. This reasoning enabled authorities to circumvent the biblical and legal mandate to execute blasphemers. By imprisoning such offenders instead, Viennese authorities prevented them from achieving the execution they desired. Intractable Rosina Plankhin responded by mutilating a crucifix again, and again, and again.[7] Over time, suicidal perpetrators adapted to the changed legal landscape by committing child murder instead of blasphemy.

Just as suicidal people in Vienna exploited criminal justice to achieve their personal salvation, so too did ordinary Catholics. Their god-pleasing devotions on behalf of executed criminals improved their own prospects in the afterlife. By entering into a reciprocal spiritual relationship with repentant poor sinners, they hoped to gain an advocate in heaven.

Perpetrators of suicide by proxy showed remarkable tenacity and cunning. The trial of Eva Lizlfelnerin, twenty-five, who murdered baby Matthias in 1761, illustrates the challenge this type of offender posed to governmental authorities.[8] Lizlfelnerin's case was discussed in Chap. 2 as an example of Catholic reluctance to acknowledge suicidal ideation. In the leadup to the murder, Lizfelnerin had repeatedly told members of her family that she wanted to leave the world, yet no one saw any reason for alarm.[9] And so, Lizlfelnerin devised an exit strategy. Before she resorted to child murder, she first formulated an alternative plan to evade the eternal damnation that befell suicides. She purchased some arsenic. Her idea was to take enough poison so that she would ultimately die, but not so much that she would not be able to make it to a priest first. She intended to take the poison, give confession to a priest, receive absolution and last rites, and then die. She would have revealed her suicide to the priest under the seal of confession so no one would have been any the wiser. She would have ended her life, ensured her salvation, and maintained her and her family's honor in the bargain. This clever plan proved difficult to carry out in practice. She took some arsenic and became violently ill, but she did not feel close to death. When she recovered, she decided not to try again. She worried about getting the dosage right. If she took too much, she might die before she made it to a father confessor. Concluding that her original

---

[7] Chapter 6.
[8] OÖLA, HA Puchheim, Schachtel 43, Nr. 32, Eva Lizlfellnerin, 1762.
[9] Chap. 2.

plan of poisoning herself was too risky, she decided to murder a child instead.

How Lizlfelnerin set out to carry out the murder shows the level of deceit perpetrators of suicide by proxy regularly employed to gain mastery over, or access to, their intended victim. A week after her attempted poisoning, she went walking along the Ager River with the express purpose of finding someone to push in and drown. She encountered a "middling beggar boy." He was "as tall as a chair," a witness later testified. She asked the boy for directions and persuaded him to walk with her a while. The boy went willingly and was eager to please. There was a pear tree by the riverside. Lizfelnerin asked the boy to pick a pear from a branch hanging out over the bank. She held his hand and he leaned out over the water to reach for it. At that moment she let go. He plunged into the river. The boy had already been carried some distance downstream, she testified, when a local day-laborer came upon this scene. Fearful that the man would intervene or question her, she pulled the screaming boy out of the water. The boy fled.

The very next day she set out for a waterfall on the River Traun, where she intended to shove someone into the rapids. Arrived at the waterfall, she briefly considered jumping in herself, but she quickly "repented." She returned to her original murder plan. Waiting for a suitable victim, she saw a woman come out of her cottage to hang laundry. This was Ströblin, Matthias' mother. Lizfelnerin watched Ströblin hang baby clothes on the line. "There is a child in there," she thought. "I will see that I get it and... throw it into the waterfall."[10] (At this point in Lizlfelnerin's interrogation the scribe specified that these were her exact words, by adding *formalia*, and underlining the text.) Lizlfelnerin approached Ströblin's cottage and asked for water. She saw the sleeping baby. To get the mother out of the way, Schickin concocted an elaborate story. She had a message for a worker on the far side of the waterfall, but she was too afraid of heights to cross the narrow footbridge to the other side herself. She asked Ströblin to deliver the message for her. Grudgingly, Ströblin agreed.

---

[10] "...unter der aufgehenckten Wäsch ein Kinder Hemmetl wahr genohmen, folglich ihr gadacht, *formalia*: <u>Da ist ein Kind darin, das werde ich schauen, dz ichs krieg, und wills hinunter werffen in Fahl</u>." Urgicht Eva Lizlfelnerin, 8 July, 1762. The scribe emphasized that these were her exact words, by adding *formalia*, and underlining the text. OÖLA, HA Puchheim, Schachtel 43, Nr. 32, Eva Lizlfellnerin, 1762.

During her murder trial Lizlfelnerin did her utmost to preempt an insanity defense. Like many other perpetrators of suicide by proxy, she was familiar with the legal requirements to secure conviction. "I was in possession of myself when I drowned the child. I knew what I was doing," she insisted.[11] Again the scribe indicated that these were her exact words. Lizlfelnerin convinced her judges. After a seven-month trial she was beheaded after prior amputation of the hand.[12]

It was not until 1767 that a secular government developed a new approach. In that year the Duchies of Schleswig and Holstein and the kingdom of Denmark published an edict:[13]

> ....that, when someone ... wants to lay hands on an innocent child or an adult and kill them with the sole intention of committing a felony in order to forfeit his or her life, such an evildoer will not lose his or her life but instead... will be punished in the following manner: 1) The criminal will be publicly whipped and branded on the forehead and then cast in chains, and will be locked up for life at the hardest...and most shameful...labor.... 2) In order to make a greater impression on those who might have the same idea, once a year on a market day such criminals will be led from the penitentiary in a hideous outfit, with uncovered head, flying hair and with a rope around their necks, with hands bound and their feet in chains, with a board attached to their chest with this inscription: Murderer of an innocent child..., and led through town exposed on the skinner's cart. 3) When such a criminal dies, his or her body should be taken to the gallows by the executioner's servants, where the head and hand will be hacked off and the body exposed on the wheel, and head and hand nailed to a post.[14]

This legislation was at once traditional and innovative. It made full use of all the time-honored defamatory measures available in the traditional theater of punishment to maximize the convict's suffering and dishonor, including the practice of branding that had all but fallen out of use by the second half of the eighteenth century. At the same time, however, the law took the quite radical step of decoupling murder and capital punishment, thus abandoning the Old Testament demand of blood for blood in

---

[11] "...in formalibus, ich bin wohl bey mir selbst gewesen, wie ich das Kind getrencket, ich habe mich ganz gut verwust."

[12] 7 July 1762, Urtheil Eva Lizlfelnerin.

[13] This edict was issued contemporaneously in the Kingdom of Denmark. Krogh, *Lutheran Plague*, 137–155.

[14] Quoted in Lind, *Selbstmord*, 62–63.

murder cases. Such an innovative measure would not have been possible without a more general Enlightenment-inspired secularization of criminal justice in the later eighteenth century.[15] And yet this law, too, failed to bring an end to the practice of suicide by proxy. Cases of suicide by proxy continued to occur in Schleswig and Holstein throughout the eighteenth and well into the nineteenth century.[16]

In the 1770s and 1780s, Lutheran Hamburg and Catholic Vienna pared down the traditional "tragic pomp" that surrounded public executions to heighten the deterrent effect of capital punishment and make death on the ravenstone less alluring to their suicidal subjects. In Hamburg this meant secularizing capital punishment by banning the participation of clergy in execution processions and the execution itself.[17] In Vienna this meant ending spectacular execution and funeral processions put on by the Confraternity of the Dead. Joseph II dissolved this confraternity along with all others, as part of his comprehensive dismantling of Baroque Catholicism. Ultimately Joseph II took the revolutionary step of abolishing the death penalty, though this measure was short-lived. Even after the reintroduction of capital punishment in Vienna, however, suicidal child murders did not resume, or at least, they have left no trace in the archive. In Hamburg suicidal child murders slowed after the 1780s but cases continued into the early nineteenth century.

It took almost thirty years after Denmark and the Duchies of Schleswig and Holstein published the 1767 edict ending executions for suicidal child murder, for another state to enact similar legislation. In 1794 Prussia promulgated a new comprehensive law code, the *Allgemeines Landrecht*. Paragraphs 831 and 832 addressed suicidal murders:

---

[15] On the controversy surrounding the implementation of the 1767 edict in Denmark, see Krogh, *Lutheran Plague*, 137–155.

The debate about ending the death penalty for classic infanticide also centered on the question whether it was acceptable to disregard this Old Testament precept. Ulbricht, *Kindsmord*, 308–311.

[16] There was a case as late as 1832. Göttsch, "Mörderin," 47.

[17] Contemporaneously authorities in Berlin put into effect similar measures. The death sentences of several suicidal child murderers in Berlin specified that they would go to their executions unaccompanied by clergy. For example: *Umständliche Nachricht des zur Gerichts-Stätte geführten Delinquenten Namens: Peter Wilcke...* ([Berlin]: s.n, [1780]). *Trauriger Bericht von dem Delinquenten Namens: Christian Gottlieb Carl Schmidt...* ([Berlin]: s.n., [1785]).

If it is established that someone who is otherwise of sound mind commits a murder...with the intent of being executed, he should not achieve his goal. Instead he should be imprisoned for life in the narrowest confinement under close supervision and be whipped in public at regular intervals.[18]

Here too the legislation did not put a stop to suicide by proxy. Cases continued to occur in Prussia at least until 1829.[19]

Why did cases continue in Schleswig and Holstein and in Prussia after these states enacted legislation ending the execution of perpetrators of suicide by proxy? Most likely for the same reason that cases of suicidal iconoclasm continued in Vienna for several decades after authorities stopped executing such blasphemers. It took time for the public to understand that the legal ground had shifted. It is not surprising that Anne Rosine Dunkel, a maid servant in Berlin, on trial in 1795 for cutting the throat of her fifteen-month-old daughter, had never heard of the code enacted a year earlier. She expected and desired to be executed. Instead, she was sentenced to life imprisonment, though she was spared the periodic floggings due to mitigating circumstances.[20] Margarethe Eleonore Boldt may also have been unaware of the new code when she drowned her five-year-old son in Berlin in 1797, because her lover left her. She did not drown herself along with the boy, "because she did not want to escape the judge." She was sentenced to life in prison in 1799.[21]

The new legislation was inconsistently applied. In April 1796 Carolina Wilhemine Langen, a bed renter in Berlin who earned her living by spinning, became weary of her life and wished to die. She drowned the one-year-old grandson of her landlady. She was beheaded two months later. Her body was exposed on the wheel.[22] In 1800 Anne Chrstine Henkc, a prostitute in Berlin, was broken by the wheel for bludgeoning to death a

---

[18] *Allgemeines Landrecht für die Preußischen Staaten von 1794. Textausgabe* (Frankfurt am Main: Alfred Metzner Verlag, 1970), 699.

[19] Weber, "Selbstmord, 166–167.

[20] E.F. Klein, "Selbstmord durch Tödtung anderer; dargestellet in der Untersuchungssache wider die Anne Rosine Dunkel," *Annalen der Gesetzgebung und Rechtsgelehrsamkeit* 14 (1796): 220–248. GSAPK, I. HA GR, Rep. 49, H Nr. 139.

[21] Dr. Julius Freidrich Heinrich Abegg, *Untersuchungen aus dem Gebiete der Strafrechtswissenschaft* (Breslau: Josef Max u. Komp., 1830), 49–50. GSAPK, I. HA GR, Rep. 49, H Nr. 129.

[22] *Ausführlicher Bericht von der vorsätzlichen Mordthat der... Caroline Wihelmine Langen, ... Für welches Verbrechen dieselbe den 8ten Juni 1796. durch das Schwerdt gerichtet* ([Berlin]: s.n, 1796).

four-year-old boy in her care the previous year. She turned herself in at the constabulary right after the murder.[23]

A case in Tapiau in East Prussia in 1822 illuminates why suicidal child murderers continued to be executed, despite the legislation imposing life imprisonment on such perpetrators. Anna Maria Ebel, an inmate in the poorhouse, sought to escape the institution by accusing herself of having murdered a woman in Danzig. Authorities transported her to Danzig for the criminal investigation. There she briefly managed to escape but was recaptured. The court found no evidence to support Ebel's self-accusation and ordered her return to Tapiau. During her transport back, she told fellow prisoners and the gendarmes guarding them: "Now I don't know any other way to get out of the house that I hate so much than to grab the first brat I can lay hands on to cut its throat." Back at the poorhouse Ebel received a "severe welcome." A "welcome" was the initiatory flogging that new arrivals routinely received. Ebel was not new to the institution, of course. In her case, the flogging was punishment for her false self-accusation. She now told a fellow woman inmate, Gudaleweska, that she planned to either kill herself or someone else to escape the workhouse. Gudaleweska, too, was weary of life because she endured frequent whippings for failing to meet her required daily output of spinning. The two women discussed the matter for weeks, finalizing their murder plot while walking to church. Gudaleweska agreed to bring a child to Ebel, so that she could escape the poorhouse too, though she did not want to lay hands on the child herself. Ebel needed Gudaleweska's help, because her murder self-accusation made other inmates wary of her. They kept their children out of her reach. Gudaleweska selected a little girl, choosing "the most ugly child" in the workhouse. On two occasions Gudaleweska delivered the little girl to Ebel, but both times other people were nearby. Finally, the third time, Ebel was alone with the child long enough to cut her throat.[24]

---

[23] *Ausführliche Nachricht von der schrecklichen Mordthat eines Kindes der Anne Christine Hencken: welche den 19ten August 1800 zu Berlin von oben herunter gerädert und auß Rad geflochten worden* (Berlin: Zürngibl, [1800]). GSAPK, I. HA GR, Rep. 49, H Nr. 130.

[24] [Ober-Landes-Gerichts-Rath Seligo], "Votum des Correferenten in der Untersuchungssache wider die Häuslinge Anna Maria Ebel, genannt Caroline Lichnowska oder Lindenowska, und die Anna Catherina Birkhahn, genannt Gudalewska, in dem Land-Armen-Hause zu Tapiau, wegen Ermordung der Anne Marie Erszkus," *Zeitschrift für die Criminal-Rechts-Pflege in den Preußischen Staaten mit Ausschluß der Rheinprovinzen*, ed. Julius Eduard Hitzig. Drittes Heft. (Berlin: Ferdinand Dümmler, 1826), 69–110. Eduard Osenbrüggen, *Casuistik des Criminalrechts* (Schaffhausen: F. Hurter, 1854), 59–61.

This case reveals the difficulty of implementing articles 831 and 832 of the new Prussian code. Ostensibly, the legislation prohibited the execution of murderers who killed with the purpose of being executed. Murderers who killed either out of suicidal intent, or out of religious enthusiasm and yearning for heaven, were to be sentenced to life in prison with periodic floggings. However, judges had considerable discretion in how to apply the code, and how to assess the murderer's motives. In this case, it appears that the judges really wanted to execute Ebel, because they developed a convoluted argument why the articles did not apply. Neither women showed any signs of religious enthusiasm, the judges emphasized. Their possible execution was merely incidental to their primary purpose of escaping the institution. Since the murder motive was escape, and death merely the means of escape, articles 831 and 832 did not apply. Ebel was sentenced to be broken by the wheel from the top down, the statutory penalty for first-degree murder. As an accessory to murder, Gudaleweska was sentenced to life imprisonment.[25]

This murder also shows the effect of secularization on the centuries-old practice of suicide by proxy. Neither the prisoners nor the investigators suggested that religion played any role in the murder, a striking contrast to seventeenth- and eighteenth-century cases. The court records do not even mention Ebel's religious confession, though in all likelihood she was Lutheran. This silence on matters of religion was not simply a reflection of changing priorities of the judges. If the two women had articulated religious concerns, this would have been legally relevant, since the code explicitly raised the issue of religious enthusiasm. During their interrogations, the two women recounted their conversations in the leadup to the murder. Ebel made repeated suicide threats. Religious prohibitions against suicide (or murder) never entered into the conversation. The women seemed to see suicide or child murder as essentially equivalent and interchangeable. Ebel and Gudaleweska did not discuss questions of salvation or damnation, or even death. Their goal was to escape the institution. If death on the ravenstone was the only exit, so be it. In their account, there was no ritualization or sentimental attachment to their child victim, as seen in many earlier cases. When Agnes Catharina Schickin murdered the cowherder's son in 1704, she selected her victim among four "beautiful little boys." As she cut his throat, she said to him: "May God protect you,

---

[25] [Seligo], "Votum," 69–110.

you sweet angel, you are an angel before God."[26] Ebel and Gudaleweska saw the four-year-old girl they murdered as an ugly brat. Neither "martyr" nor "angel," she was simply a means to an end. This late case shows how a deviant cultural script, once established, could live on, even after the symbolic logic on which the script was originally based, had become brittle or irrelevant. For Ebel and Gudaleweska, child murder was a clichéd and conventional form of suicide. It required no explanation.

As the number of executions declined dramatically in the nineteenth century,[27] suicide by proxy waned, and quickly faded from public awareness. In contrast to the European witch-hunt, or the frequent executions of infanticidal mothers, suicide by proxy vanished from historical memory. One reason for this forgetting is that suicide by proxy was an uncomfortable topic. Witch-hunting and infanticide could more easily be incorporated into a triumphal narrative. Women who were executed for witchcraft were innocent and pitiable victims of religious fanaticism. Such benighted superstition had been overcome, however, by the Enlightenment and enlightened government. Due to these achievements, "the female sex can now grow old in peace," wrote Frederick II of Prussia.[28]

Debate over public policy towards infanticide occasioned an outpouring of journalistic and literary texts in the late eighteenth century. The tragic plight of infanticidal mothers was one of the favorite topics of the literary movement of the *Sturm und Drang*. The story of Gretchen in Goethe's *Faust* is the most famous example.[29] These women, too, were victims, first of the men who seduced and abandoned them, and then of societal prejudices and a cruel and barbarous criminal justice system. Such injustice was also a thing of the past, however. Enlightened and humane jurists had come to understand that these women were under such duress and so distraught when they committed infanticide that they were not culpable of intentional homicide. Indeed, they often acted in the throes of

---

[26] This case is discussed in Chap. 2.

[27] Richard J. Evans, *Rituals of Retribution: Capital Punishment in Germany 1600–1987* (Oxford: Oxford University Press, 1996), 228.

[28] Frederick II, *Ausgewählte Werke Friedrichs des Grossen. Ins Deutsche übertragen* (Würzburg: A Stuber, 1873), 207.

[29] Kirsten Peters, *Der Kindsmord als Schöne Kunst Betrachtet. Eine Motivgeschichtliche Untersuchung der Literatur des 18. Jahrhunderts* (Würzburg: Königshausen & Neumann, 2001).

puerperal madness.[30] Executions for infanticide declined sharply in the 1770s and 1780s. Infanticidal mothers were now more commonly punished by relatively brief prison sentences.[31]

In contrast to witches or infanticidal mothers, women who committed suicidal child murder were difficult to cast as victims. These women acted in their calculated self-interest, as they saw it. The murders involved premeditation and planning. The murderers lured in their child victims and deceived their parents. The "rationality" of their crime violated the prevailing gender ideology of the late eighteenth and nineteenth century, that saw women as passive, emotional, loving, maternal, and self-sacrificing. It was men who were believed to act aggressively and rationally to promote their self-interest.[32] The agency of these murderous women was less palatable to the nineteenth-century reading public than the pathetic helplessness of infanticidal mothers.

All perpetrators of suicide by proxy, men and women, made a mockery of governmental authority, another jarring element to the nineteenth-century public. Suicide by proxy was conveniently forgotten.

---

[30] Otto Ulbricht, *Kindsmord und Aufklärung in Deutschland* (Munich: R. Oldenbourg Verlag, 1990), 259–263.

[31] Evans, *Rituals*, 138–140.

[32] Karin Hausen, Die Polarisierung der 'Geschlechtscharaktere'—Eine Spieglelung der Dissoziaton von Erwerbs- und Familienleben," in *Sozialgeschichte der Familie in der Neuzeit Europas*, ed. Werner Conze (Stuttgart: Ernst Klett Verlag, 1976), 363–393.

BIBLIOGRAPHY

MANUSCRIPT SOURCES

ARCHIV DER MARKTGEMEINDE PERCHTOLDSDORF (AMP)

Patente, Karton 344. "Wie es mit Bestrafung des Kinder-Mords zu halten," 22 March 1706.
Kriminalakten 90/2, 1719 Maria Anna Umgeherin, 1719.

BAYERISCHES STAATSARCHIV NÜRNBERG (StAN)

52b Amts- und Standbücher, 209, 210, 225.
4A Verläße des inneren Rats, vols. 1456, 1457, 1509, 1510.

DIÖZESANARCHIV WIEN (DAW)

GF 21, G/S 1, Gerichts und Strafhäuser 2, Amtshauskapelle, 1588–1761.
KL/01, Barfüßer Augustiner Eremiten, Maria Loreto St. Augustin, 1637–1835.

FÜRSTLICH OETTINGEN-WALLERSTEINISCHES ARCHIV (FÖWAH)

Criminalsachen Zusum, VI. 115. 11, Katherina Häuslerin, 1786.

GEHEIMES STAATSARCHV PREUSSISCHER KULTURBESITZ (GSAPK)

I. HA GR, Rep. 49, H Nr. 139. Bestrafung der Dienstmagd Anne Rosine Dunckel wegen Ermordung ihres Kindes, 1795.
I. HA GR, Rep. 49, H Nr. 130. Strafe des Rades für die Christine Hencke in Berlin wegen Ermordung eines fremden Kindes, Dez. 1799 - Juli 1800.
I. HA GR, Rep. 49, H Nr. 129. Bestrafung von Margarethe Eleonre Boldt in Spandau wegen Ertränkung ihres Kindes, Jul. - Sept. 1799.

GERMANISCHES NATIONALMUSEUM, (GNM)

Handschriften, R. 3108: "Nachricht der Persohnen so zu Nürnberg sind hingericht worden."

INSTITUT FÜR STADTGESCHICHTE FRANKFURT (ISG)

Criminalia Akten 2453, Anna Maria Drechslerin, 1705.
Criminalia Akten 2812, Niklas Scheffer 1715.
Criminalia Akten 3822, Anna Elisabetha Seibelin, 1729.
Criminalia Akten 4085, Johannes Heinrich Schwach, 1732.

LANDESARCHIV BADEN-WÜRTTEMBERG, HAUPTARCHIV STUTTGART (HStAS)

Oberrat Kriminalakten

A 209/576, Barbara Seegräberin, 1612.
A 209 /166, Hans Bützer, 1673.
A 209/ 1120, Catharina Oberländer, 1623.
A 209/1179, Margaretha Mayrin, 1703.
A 209/1576, Hans Jacob Reylen, 1710.
A 209/1773, Ursula Waser, 1723.
A 209/1806, Agnes Catherina Schickin, 1704.

LANDESARCHIV SALZBURG (LAS)

Pfleggericht Golling, Criminalakt 2. Bund, Nr. 17, Kasten 137 (Criminalia 1731-1735/1), 1734 Thomas Hinteregger.

OBERÖSTERREICHISCHES LANDESARCHIV (OÖLA)

HA Puchheim, Schachtel 43, Nr. 32, Eva Lizlfellnerin, 1762.
Stadtarchiv Freistadt, Seyringer Rechtsgutachten, Hs. Nr. 1101.
HA Oberwallsee, Schachtel 24, II) 2/i. Gerichtswesen, Kindesmord 1711-1770, Joseph Vogler, 1770.

Österreichische Nationalbibliothek (ÖNB). Handschriften

Cod 8363, "Verzeichnis Deren Jenigen Delinquenten welche von einer Hochlöblichen Todten Bruderschaft zu der Erden seyend Bestattet worden von dem Jahr 1702."
Cod 8227, Johannis Matthias Testarello della Massa, "Historia ecclesiastica urbis Viennensis a conversion ad fidem christianum usque ad annum 1685."

Sächsisches Staatsarchiv, Hauptstaatsarchiv Dresden (HStAD)

30 Geheimer Rat/ Loc 9703/7, Martha Padigen, 1738.
10024 Geheimer Rat/ Loc 10118/8, Annen Marien Rößlerin, 1730.
10024 Geheimer Rat/ Loc 9723/7, Johann Georg Dinnebieren, 1779.
10079 Landesregierung/ Loc 12333, Johann Gottfried Gittlern, 1790.

Staatsarchiv Augsburg

Hochstift Augsburg NA, Akten 806. 1744-1745 Joseph Wachter.

Staatsarchiv Hamburg (StAH)

111-1, Senat, Cl.VII, Lit. Mb, No.3, Vol.1, 363. Kriminalurteile und Executionen.
111-1, Senat, Cl.VII, Lit. Mb, No.3, Vol.4a, Nachricht wie es bey der Ausführung eines zum Tode verurtheilten Delinquenten gehalten., 1700-1804.
111-1 Bd 73, Cl.VII Lit Ma No9 Vol. 1b, Strassenrecht.
111-1, Senat, Bd 75, Cl.VII Lit Mb No. 3 Vol. 4b, Acta wegen Abstellung der bisherigen Gewohnheit die Missethäter durch Prediger zur Gerichtsstätte begleiten zu lassen, 1784.
111-1, Senat, Cl.VII, Lit.M6, Nr.3, Vol.5. Acta über den Gebrauch vor der Hinrichtung eines Delinquenten das über denselben gesprochenen Todesurtheil dem jedesmahligen Herrn Seniori Reverendi Ministeri durch den Herrn Praetoren zu schicken zu laßen.
111-1 Senat, Cl.VII, Lit.Me, Nr.8, Vol.2b, Cl.VII, Lit.Me, Nr.8, Vol.2b, Fasc 1a, Strafe des Kindermords, 1724.
111-1 Senat, Cl.VII, Lit.Me, Nr.8, Vol.2b, Fasc 1b, Relatio cum voto in peinl. Sachen... ctra Engel Seldenschoen.
111-1 Senat, Cl.VII, Lit.Me, Nr.8, Vol.2b, Fasc 5, Relatio i. S. N. C. Carstens pto infanticidii, 1781.
111-1, Senat, Cl.VII, Lit. Me, Nr.8, Vol. 2b, Fasc 6b, Votum u. Sentenz i. S. Anton Lorenz Ammon pcto Infanticidii, 1786.
111-1, Senat, Cl.VII, Lit. Me, Nr.8, Vol. 2b, Fasc 6c, Votum in S. Elis. Jentzen pcto Infant., 1790.

111-1, Senat, Cl.VII, Lit.Me, Nr.8, Vol.16, Relation Urthel etc. in pein. Sachen wider Cath. Maria Koenig geb. Hartung, wegen Ermordung eines Kindes zum Schwerte verurtheilt, 1809.

242-1 I, A14, Bd 1-11. Gefängnisverwaltung I, Zuchthaus, Verwaltungsprotokoll.

242-1, I, A29, Bd.1, Gefängnisverwaltung I, Spinnhaus Verwaltungsprotokoll.

331-2, P-K, 1786, Nr. 2B, Anton Lorenz Ammon, Krautkrämergeselle: Untersuchung und Strafprozess wegen Mordes an seiner 8 Tage alten Tochter.

331-2, P-K, 1802, Nr.81. Untersuchung und Strafprozess gegen den Schiffszimmermann Johann Wilhelm Köhrse wegen Mordversuch an dem 8jährigen Johann Martin Heinrich Lembcke, (1774) 1802-1803.

STAATS- UND STADTBIBLIOTHEK AUGSBURG (SUSTBA)

2° Cod Aug 247, Bürgermeister Amtsinstruktion, II, 1653.

STADTARCHIV AUGSBURG (STADTAA)

Strafamt 107, Strafbuch 1654-1699.
Strafamt 162, Johann Bausch, "Vezeichnis der Maleficanten."
Strafamt 167, Verbrecherbuch 1700-1806.
Strafamt, Urgicht, Anna Peurin, 1560. VII, 23.
Strafamt, Urgicht, Susanna Schönin, 1572. I, 14-16.
Strafamt, Urgicht, Appollonia Mayrin, 1686 b, II, 22, V, 26. 1686.
Strafamt, Urgicht, Augustin Gerstecker, 1665. III, 20, V, 5.

STADTARCHIV LEIPZIG (STADTAL)

Richterstube Strafakten Nr. 719, Johannen Reginen Reißmannin. 1752.

STADTARCHIV LÜBECK (STADTALÜ)

8_1_725, fol. 229r. "Warnung an die ruchlose Weibspersonen, welche mit den Gedanken umgehen, unschuldige Kinder zu ermorden," 19. Juli, 1747.

STADTARCHIV NÜRNBERG (STADTAN)

B 14/IV Nr. 533. Bluturtheil. Susanna Brennerin (1745).

STADTBIBLIOTHEK NÜRNBERG (STADTBN)

Amb 307 2°, Malefizbuch.

Stiftarchiv Kremsmünster (StiftAK)

Gerichts Akten (Kriminal) 1721-1729, Georg Edlauer 1729.
Gerichtsakten (Kriminal) 1741-1750, Sebastian Schachermayr 1750.
Gerichtsakten (Kriminal) 1751-1760, Maria Anna Quittnerin 1756.
Gerichtsakten, XVII/5 18. Jhdt. Johann Zwirnsberger, 1758.

Stiftarchiv Lambach (StiftAL)

Criminalia 377, Joseph Zeitler 1719.
Criminalia 388, Margaretha Öttlin 1722.
Criminalia 393, Selbstmorde, 1607-1729.

University of Pennsylvania, Rare Book & Manuscript Library

Ms. Codex 1199, "Chronica perpetua, darinnen alle und jede Malefiz-Persohnen, zusamen getragen...", http://hdl.library.upenn.edu/1017/d/medren/4322016.

Unversitätsarchiv Wien. (UAW)

Cod. Med. 1.7, Acta Facultatis Medicae VII, 1677-1709.
Cod. Med 1.8, Acta Facultatis Medicae VIII, 1710-1725.

Universitätsbibliothek Augsburg, Oettingen-Wallersteinische Bibliothek (UBA, OWB)

Handschriften, III. 3. Fol. 24, Verzeichnis aller im Nürnbergischen vom J. 1298 bis 1739 hingerichteten Personen.

Wien Bibliothek (WB)

Handschriften 18013. Verzeichnis deren von einer Hochlöblichen Privilegirten Kays. Königl. Todten Bruderschaft übernohmenen Malleficanten. 1702-1833.
Handschriften 67116. Relationen über Hinrichtungen zu Wien vom 7. Juni 1753 bis 26. Februar 1783.

Wiener Stadt-und Landesarchiv (WStLA)

Archivbehelfte 27/13 B.

1.2.1.A1 Zusammengelegte Akten/ 1700-1759, 1/1713.
1.2.1.A1 Zusammengelegte Akten/ 1700-1759, 27 a-e/1703.

1.2.1.A1 Zusammengelegte Akten/ 1700-1759, 92/1712, A 1-18.
1.2.1.A1 Zusammengelegte Akten/ 1700-1759, 50/1701.
1.2.1.A1 Zusammengelegte Akten/ 1700-1759, 64/1716.
1.2.1.A1 Zusammengelegte Akten / 1700-1759, 15/1716.
1.2.1.A1 Zusammengelegte Akten/ 1700-1759, 101/1716.
1.2.1.A1 Zusammengelegte Akten/ 1700-1759, 106/1715.
1.2.1.A1 Zusammengelegte Akten/ 1700-1759, 193/1709.
1.2.1.A1 Zusammengelegte Akten/ 1700-1759, 124/1759.
1.2.3.3. A1, Untersuchungen und Verurteilungen/ 1797-1850, 11 Z 1846 (Anna Zotter).
1.5.1. B6-2 Dekretenbuch, 1703–1711.
1.5.1. B6-3. Dekretenbuch 1712-1716.
3.4. A.17. Handschriften. Stadt- und Landgericht Wien: Urfehden, 1750-1813.
3.4. A.19. Handschriften. Stadt- und Landgericht Wien: 'Miscellen', 1686-1786.
3.4.A.20.-5 – Handschriften. Annalen des Wiener Kriminal-Gerichtes, 1783-1842.
3.4.A.21.1-7 Handschriften. Memorabilien Wiener Kriminalgericht.
3.4.A.320 Handschriften, Neue Peinliche Landgerichtsordnung, 1656.
Hauptarchivsakten, Privilegien 77.

Printed Primary Sources

Abraham a Santa Clara. *Judas Der ErtzSchelm Für ehrliche Leuth Oder: Eigentlicher Entwurff und LebensBeschreibung deß Iscariotischen Bößwicht*. Vol. 4. Salzburg: Melchior Haan, 1695.

Abraham a Sancta Clara. *Lösch Wien/Das ist: Ein Bewögliche Anmahnung zu der Kays. Residentz-Statt Wienn in Oesterreich*. Vienna: Peter Paul Vivian, 1680.

Adelung, Wolfgang Heinrich. *Kurtze Historische Beschreibung der Uhr-Alten Kayserlichen und des Heil. Römischen Reichs Freyen An- See- Kauff- und Handels-Stadt Hamburg*. Hamburg: Conrad Neumann, 1696.

Allgemeines Gesetz über Verbrechen, und derselben Bestrafung. Vienna: Johann Thomas Edlen von Trattnern, 1787.

Allgemeines Landrecht für die Preußischen Staaten von 1794: *Textausgabe*. Frankfurt a. M.: Alfred Metzner Verlag, 1970.

Anderson, Christian Daniel. *Sammlung Hamburgischer Verordnungen. Eine Fortsetzung sowohl der Sammlung Hamburgischer Gesetze und Verfassungen als der Sammlung Hamburgischer Mandaten*. Hamburg: Carl Wilhelm Meyn, 1783.

Anon. *Ausführlicher Bericht über die hingerichteten Missethäter in Hamburg, welche mit dem Schwerte, Strange, Feuer, Rades, Guillotine und arquebusieret vom Leben zum Tode gebracht*. Hamburg: Heyde's Officin, [1858?].

Anon. *Das Ehmals gedrückte/ vom Türken berückte/ nun Trefflich erquickte Königreich Hungarn/ samt dessen Ströme-Fürsten/ der Weltberühmten Donau*. Frankfurt: Christoff Riegel, 1688.

Anon. *Das Von Sünden und Lastern abhaltende Beyspiel, bestehend in einer Todtes-Straff, Welche vollzogen wird heute Mittwoch den 5. Martij 1738. an einer verheyrathen Weibs-Persohn, Nahmens Margaretha D.* Vienna: Johann Baptist Schilgen, 1738.

Anon. *Der Stadt Hamburgk Gerichtsordnung und Statuta.* Hamburg: Frobenius, 1605.

Anon. "Die Dorothee Catharina Wilhelmine Kramerinn tödtet ein fremdes Kind aus Ueberdruß des Lebens." *Annalen der Gesetzgebung und Rechtsgelehrsamkeit.* Vol. 9. 1792.

Anon. *Die hingerichtete See-Räuber Störtebeck und Gödeke Micheel.* 1701. In Deutsches Textarchiv, http://www.deutschestextarchiv.de/nn_stoertebeck_1701.

Anon. *Die Hirten-Treue Christi, welche er an einem seiner verlornen Schafe, nemlich an Gertrude Magdalene Bremmelin, einer vorsetzlichen Kindermörderin, erwiesen.* 2nd edition. [Werningerode]: Waysenhaus, 1745.

Anon. *Gründlicher Ursprung der gnadenreichen Bildnuß vnser glorwürdigsten Himmelkönigin Mariæ so in der Kirch deß H. Hieronymi zu Wienn bey den Franciscanern ober dem hohen Altar zu sehen.* [Vienna]: [1629].

Anon. *Hoch-feyerliches Saeculum oder erstes Jahr-Hundert Einer Hochlöblichen... Todten-Bruderschafft bey denen PP. Augustinern Baarfüssern alhier, welche im Jahr 1738 den 16. Novembris wird celebriret warden.* Vienna: Maria Theresia Voigt, 1738.

Anon. *Höchst grausame und entsetzliche That...durch drey vermessene gemeine Soldaten in der Stadt Lutzenburg. Welche...das Hochwürdigste Gut zur Zauberey gebraucht und Jüdisch durchstochen.* Mainz: Buchdruckerey des Hospit. St. Rochi, 1749.

Anon. *Jüdische neue Zeitung vom Marsch aus Wien....* S.l., s.d.

Anon. *Kurtzer Innhalt der Execution, So inn der Statt Wien den 22. Augusti dises Jahrs durch rechtmessiges Vrthail zween verzweifleten Juden so jünger: vnd darauff den 26. dessen, mit dem ältisten, wegen erbärmlicher vnd Gottschändiger Malefitz That, auff den vier Plätzen benannter Stadt fürgenommen ist worden.* [Vienna]: 1642.

Anon. *Lutherisches Gesangbuch.* S.l., 1770.

Anon. "Maria Dorothea Bulsinn, eine unglückliche Versmacherinn." *Annalen der Gesetzgebung und Rechtsgelehrsamkeit* 2 (1788): 170–196.

Anon. "Mord aus Melancholie." In *Annalen der Gesetzgebung Napoleons*, edited by Franz Georg Joseph von Lassaulx, 261–263. Vol. 2. Koblenz, Pauli und Compagnie, 1808.

Anon. *Neu-Vollständigers Marggräfl. Brandenburgisches Gesang-Buch.* Bayreuth: 1672.

Anon. *Origo, Progressus, Et Memorabilia Ecclesiæ Cæsareæ S. P. Augustini Viennæ.* Vienna: Johannes Baptist Schilgen, 1730.

Anon. *Peinliches Urtheil... über Maria Anna Lauterin,... wegen der an Aloysius Pankratius Reich... verübter Mordthat, den 17. October 1772, ergangen...* (n.p, n.d.). SuStBA, 4 S 567-17.

Anon. *Peinliches Urtheil...über Maria Anna Mayrinn... wegen einer and einem dreijährigen Mädchen vorsäzlich verübten Mordthat den 8 Febr. 1783. ergangen...* (n.p, n.d). SuStBA, 4 S 567-2.

Anon. *Regulen und andächtige Ubungen/ Der in der Statt Wienn von Ihrer Päpstlichen Heiligkeit Urbano Dem Achten/ Auf Anhaltung Ihrer Kayserl: und Königl: Mayesthäten Ferdinandi Des Anderen...und Eleonorae, Dessen Geliebtesten Frawen Gemahlin/ erhöbter... Löbl. Bruderschafft.* Vienna: Matthäus Cosmerovius, 1650.

Anon. *Sammlung Oesterreichischer Gesetze und Ordnungen, wie solche vor Zeit zu Zeit ergangen und publicieret worden, So viele deren ueber die in Parte I & II Codicis Austriaci eingedruckten bis auf das Jahr 1720 weiter aufzubringen waren, gesammelt und in diese ordnung gebracht von S.G.H.* Leipzig: Zacharias Heinrich Eisfeld, 1748.

Anon. *Sammlung der älteren Kaiserlich-Königlichen Landesfürstlichen Gesetze und Verordnungen in Publico-Ecclesiasticis: erste Abtheilung vom Jahre 1518 bis 1740.* Vol. 1, II. Vienna: Johann Thomas Edlen von Trattnern, 1785.

Anon. *Theatrum Europaeum, oder außführliche und warhafftige Beschreibung aller und jeder denckwürdiger Geschichten. Vierdter Theil, die sich... seithero Anno 1638 biß Anno 1643, exclusive begeben haben.* Frankfurt am Main: Johann Goerlin, 1692.

Anon. *Theatrum novum politico-historicum, das ist eine gruendliche und ausfuerliche Erzehlung alles dessen was sich in dem 1686 Jahr auff diesem Kugelrunden Welt-Gebäu an allen Orten und Enden zu Wasser und Land denck- und schreibwürdiges zugetragen und begeben hat: worinnen nebst einer gantz genauen Entwerffung deß Koenigreichs Ungarn viel curiose und nutzbare Materien von polit. Staats-Gruenden u. klugen Sittenlehren ... zu finden seynd.* Würzburg: Quirinus Heyl, 1687.

Anon. *Todes-Urtheil Einer verheyrateten Manns-person, Namens: Joseph G: Eines gewesten Gartners, Alt 36. Jahr, Von hier gebürtig, und Catholischer Religion; Welches in Folge der bey dem alhiesigen Kaiserl. Königl. Stadt- und Land-gericht abgeführten Criminal-verfahrung ... heut den 11. September 1756. alhier in Wien vollzogen wird.* [s.l.]: 1756.

Anon. *Todes-Urtheil Einer ledigen Manns-person, Namens: Niclas St.: Ohne Profeßion, Alt 28. Jahr, Von Preßburg gebürtig, und Catholischer Religion; Welches zufolge der bey dem allhiesigen Kaiserl. Königl. Stadt- und Land-gericht abgeführten Criminal-verfahrung ... heut den 22. Oct. 1757. allhier in Wien vollzogen wird.* [Vienna]: 1757.

Anon. *Todesurtheil einer ledigen Weibsperson, Namens Catharina J...Welches...den 10. Februarii 1769. Allhier in Wien vollzogen worden.* [Vienna]: [s.n.], 1769.

Anon. *Todtes-Urtheil Einer ledigen Weibs-person, Namens: Clara K. Alt 29. Jahr. Von hier gebürtig, Catholischer Religion: Welches in Folge der bey dem alhiesig- Kaiserl. Königl. Stadt- und Land-gericht wider sie abgeführten Criminal-verfahrung ... an gleich benannter Clara K., einer Dienst-magd ... heut den 24. November 1759. alhier vollzogen wird.* [Vienna]: [S.n.], 1759.
Anon. *Todes-Urtheil Einer ledigen Weibs-Person, Namens Regina G. Alt 19. Jahr. Von Braunstorf nächst Hollabrunn in Unter-öster-reich gebürtig, Catholischer Religion : Welches in Folge der bey dem alhiesig-kaiserl. königl. Stadt- und Landgericht wider sie abgeführ-ten Criminal-verfahrung ... an gleich benannter Regina G. ... heute den 24. October 1760, alhier in Wien vollzogen wird.* [Vienna]: [s.n.], 1760.
Anon. *Todesurtheil einer verheuratheten Mannsperson, Namens Melchior G...., welches...den 24. September 1772 allhier in Wien vollzogen wird.* S.l., s.d.
Anon. *Todes-Urtheil Einer verheuratheten Weibs-person, Namens: Elisabeth W. Alt 37. Jahr. Allhier gebürtig, und catholischer Religion : Welches in Folge der bey dem allhiesig Kaiserl. Königl. Stadt- und Land-gericht abgeführten Criminalverfahrung ... den 30sten Jänner 1767. allhier vollzogen wird.* [Vienna]: [s.n.], 1767.
Anon. *Todes-Urtheil, einer verwittibten Weibs-person Namens: Maria Anna N : alt 26. Jahr, allhier auf dem Schottenfeld gebürtig, Catholischer Religion ; Welches in Folge der, über die mit ihr bey dem allhiesig- Kaiserl. Königl. Stadt- und Land-Gericht wegen begangener Ermordung eines 6. ein halbjährigen Knäbleins abgeführte Criminal-Verfahrung geschöpft ... heute den 31. Augusti 1764. allhier in Wien vollzogen wird.* [Vienna]: [s.n.], 1760.
Anon. *Warhaffte History, Was sich mit dem Hochwürdigisten Sacrament des Altars zu Deggendorff, durch unmenschliche geübte Boßheit der Juden, verloffen : Mit schönen Kupffern geziehret.* Regensburg: Lang, 1716.
Anon. *Warhafftiger Bericht so sich zu Wien in Oesterreich mit dreyen Juden zugetragen/ darunter einer/ so vor diesem ein vornnehmer Rabbi gewesen/ unnd sich vor etlichen Jahren zu Rackawitz in Poln tauffen lassen/ aber...die Christenheit verleugnet.../ so geschehen zu Wien den 16/26 Augusti 1642.* S.l., 1642.
Anon. *Wahrhaffter Entwurff einer...Mordthat, so ein...Handelsman mit Namen Bogner den 21. Mart. Anno 1747 vrybet, in deme er sein eigenes halbjähriges Kindt, ...mit einem Messer, und also aller väterlichen Liebe vergessen ermordet.* n.p.: n.d. SuStBA, Graphic 29/126.
Anon. *Wohl-verdientes Todtes-Urtheil, Einer Ledigen Manns-Persohn, Nahmens Johann K : Catholischer Religion, und 22. Jahr alt, von hier gebürtig, um weilen derselbe nach verschiedenen begangenen Diebstählen ... Als wird derselbe heute Dienstag den 10. November andern zum Beyspiel auf den hohen Wagen gesetzt, sodann auf den Wienner-Berg zur gewöhnlichen Richtstatt geführt, allda mit dem Rad von oben herab vom Leben zum Todt hingerichtet ...* Vienna: Johann Baptist Schilgen, [1739].

Anon. *Wohl-verdientes Todtes-Urtheil, Einer Ledigen Weibs-Persohn, Nahmens Catharina H., Catholischer Religion, 18. Jahr alt, allhier gebürtig : Welche heute Freytag, den 11. September 1744. anderen zum Beyspiel vor dem Schotten-Thor auf dasigen Raaben-Stein, durch das Schwerd samt Kopf- und Hand-Abschlagung hingerichtet wird*. Vienna: Maria Eva Schilgen, 1744.

Anon. *Wolverdientes Todes-Urtheil Einer ledigen Weibs-person, Namens: Maria Anna G : Alt 20. Jahr, Auf dem Maria-hülfer-grund alhier gebürtig, Catholischer Religion ; Welches in Folge der bey dem alhiesig- Kaiserl. Königl. Stadt- und Land-gericht wider sie abgeführten Criminal-verfahrung ... heute den 27. Junii 1760. alhier in Wien vollzogen wird*. [Vienna]: s.n.,1760.

Anon. *Wohl-verdientes Todtes-Urtheil, Einer Ledigen Manns-Person, Nahmens Johann Georg H : Catholischer Religion, zu Prespurg gebürtig, 25. Jahr alt ; Welcher Heut Dato den 7. Julii 1752. wegen dreymalig gebrochener Urphed halber vor dem Schotten-Thor auf der gewöhnlichen Richt-Statt mit dem Schwerdt von dem Leben zum Todt hingerichtet wurde ; Den Innhalt seines Verbrechens wird der geneigte Leser hierinnen finden*. Vienna: Maria Eva Schilgen, [1752].

Anon. *Wohl-verdientes Todtes-Urtheil, So heut Dato den 29. Julij An. 1749. an einer Ledigen Weibs-Persohn Nahmens Dorothea H : Gegen 21. Jahr alt, Dahier in dem alten Lerchenfeld gebürtig, Catholischer Religion, wegen an einem fremden 5.-jährigen Knaben begangenen Kindes-Mord ; vor dem Schotten-Thor auf dasigen Rabenstein der Kopf und die rechte Hand zugleich abgeschlagen, sodann die abgeschlagene Hand an dem daselbstigen Pranger angeheftet, vollzogen wurde.* Vienna: Maria Eva Schilgin, [1749].

Anon. *Wol-verdientes Todes-Urtheil Einer ledigen Weibs-Person, Namens: Anna Maria B : Alt 29. Jahr, Von Frauen-Haid unweit Oedenburg in Hungarn gebürtig, Catholischer Religion ; Welches in Folge der bey dem alhiesig- Kaiserl. Königl. Stadt- und Land-gericht wider sie abgeführten Criminal-verfahrung ... heute den 31. Octob. 1760. alhier in Wien vollzogen wird*. [Vienna]: s.n., 1760.

Anon. *Wohlverdientes Todtes-Urtheil einer Ledigen Manns-Person Nahmens Johann Georg H*. Vienna: s.n., [1752].

Anon. *Wohl-verdientes Todtes Urtheil Einer ledigen Manns-Persohn Nahmens Johann K., Catholischer Religion, und 22 Jahr alt, von hier gebürtig*. s.l.: s.d.

Anon. *Wunderwürdiges Leben und Groß-Thaten Ihro Jetzt-Glorwürdigst-Regierenden Kayserl. und Catholischen Majestät Caroli des Sechsten*. Nuremberg: Buggel und Seitz, 1721.

Augspurgisches Extra-Blatt. 1777.

Augspurgische Ordinari Postzeitung. 1777.

Bayreuther Zeitung. 1769-1777.

Baur, Gilbert. *P. Gilbert Baur Des Heil. Prämonstratenser-Ordens Chorherrn ... Viertägige Zubereitung Eines Zum Tode Verurtheilten Malefikanten.* Augsburg: Rieger, 1785.

Bahn, Nicolaus. *Das unschuldig vergoßne Blut Welches an statt einer Leichen-Predigt/... Bey Christlicher Beerdigung eines kleinen Kindes von 3. Jahren/ Nehmlich Daniel Zeibigs/ So von seinem leiblichen Vater/ Meister Daniel Zeibigen... Am 26. Junii... in der Wiegen schlaffend/ mit einem Scheer-Messer jämmerlich ermordet.../ vorgestellet.* Pirna: Georg Balthasar Ludewig, 1699.

[Beer, Johann Christoph]. *Historischer Rosen-Garten, bestehend in drey Hundert ausserlesenen ... Historien und Discursen, aus den berühmtesten Scribenten zusammen getragen.* Frankfurt: Michael Schmatz, 1710.

Beer, Johann Christoph. *Historisches Spatzier- und Conversation ... Büchlein, von 300. auserlesenen theils lust-und lehrreichen, theils schrecken-vollen Trauer-Geschichten ... In dreyen absonderlichen Theilen ... aus bewährten Autoren vorgestellet.* Nuremberg: Wolffgang Michahelles and Johann Adolph, 1701.

[Blank, Johan Friedrich]. *Sammlung der von E. Hochedlen Rathe der Stadt Hamburg so wol zur Handhabung der Gesetze und Verfassungen als bey besonderen Eräugnissen ... ausgegangenen allgemeinen Mandaten.* Vol. 2. Hamburg: J. C. Piscator., 1764.

Blumblacher, Christoph. *Commentarius In Käyser Carl deß Fünfften, und deß H. Röm. Reichs Peinliche Halsgerichts-Ordnung: Worinnen vmbständlich, gründlich und klar außgeführet wird, Wie man Den gantzen Peinlichen Proceß so wohl mit Protocollirn, mit der Captur, Examiniern, Constituirn, Torquirn, und sonsten biß zu Ende ordentlich führen, als auch nach Abführ- und Schliessung desselben, allerhand Unthaten gebührlich straffen solle.* Salzburg: Johann Baptista Mayrs Erben 1704.

Breuning, Johann Christian. *Rede Bei Der Zu Regensburg Durchs Schwerd Vollzognen Hinrichtung Der Anna Magdalena Schießlin: Auf Öffentlicher Richtsstatt Den 19. Mai 1774 Gehalten.* Regensburg: Keyser, 1774.

Brockes, Barthold Heinrich. *Herrn Barthold Henrich Brockes J.U.L. Verteutschter Bethlehemitischer Kinder-Mord des Ritters Marino: Nebst etlichen von des Herrn Ubersetzers Eigenen Gedichten.* Cologne: Benjamin Schillers Wittwe, 1715.

Brown, Edward. *An Account of Several Travels through a great part of Germany.* London: Benj. Tooke, 1677.

Carpzov, Benedict. *Peinlicher sächsischer Inquisition- und Achts-Proceß.* Leipzig: Johann Christoph Tarnov, 1673.

Carpzov, Benedict. *Practica Nova Imperialis Saxonica Rerum Criminalium.* Leipzig: Christian Kirchner, 1669.

Cochem, Martin von. *Das Grössere Krancken-Buch/ Denen Gesunden so wohl als Krancken sehr nutzlich und notwendig.... Wie man Denen Krancken die Sacramenten reichen und fürbetten/Denen in Zügen ligenden mit Litanyen und Psalmen zu Hülff kommen/Denen Sterbenden tröstlich zusprechen/ und bis zum Tod beystehen sole.* Frankfurt a. M.: John Melchior Bencard, 1689.

Constitutio criminalis Theresiana oder der Römisch-Kaiserl. zu Hungarn und Böheim ... Majestät Mariä Theresiä ... peinliche Gerichtsordnung. Vienna: Johann Thomas Edlen von Trattnern, 1769.

Damhouder, Joost de. *Praxis Rerum Criminalium: Gründliche und rechte Underweysung...in Rechtfertigung Peinlicher Sachen.* Frankfurt am Main: Bassee, 1575.

Damhoudere, Joost de. *Praxis rerum Criminalium. Gründliche und rechte Underweysung Welcher massen in Rechtfertigung peinlicher Sachen ... zu handeln.* Frankfurt a. M.: Nicolaus Basseus, 1581.

Damhoudere, Joos de. *Praxis rerum Criminalium. Gründliche und rechte Underweysung Welcher massen in Rechtfertigung peinlicher Sachen ... zu handeln.* Frankfurt am Main: Johannes Wolffius, 1571.

Der Post-tägliche Mercurius oder ein gantz besondere Post-tägliche Relation, von den wichtigsten in Europa vorgegangenen Novellen, mit couriosen Raisonemens und politischen Reflexionen untermenget. Vienna: Sedlmayer, 1703-1710.

Der Römischen Käyserlichen ... Majestät Leopoldi, Ertzherzogens zu Oesterreich... Neue Landgerichts Ordnung des Ertzhertzogthumbs Oesterreich ob der Ennß. Linz: Caspar Freyschmid, 1677.

Der Römischen Kayser- auch zu Hungarn und Boehaimb etc. Koenigl. Mayestaet Josephi deß Ersten, Ertz-Hertzogens zu Oesterreich, unsers allergnädigsten Herzens, Neue Peinliche Hals-Gerichts-Ordnung vor das Koenigreich Boehaimb, Marggraffthumb Maehren und Hertzogthumb Schlesien. Prague: Gerzabkische Erben, 1708.

Dreyhaupt, Johann Christoph von. *Pagus neletici et nudzici, oder ausführliche diplomatisch-historische Beschreibung des zum... Herzogthum Magdeburg gehörigen Saal-Kreyses.* Vol. 2. Halle: Verlag des Waysenhauses, 1755.

Erlanger Real-Zeitung. 1773.

Ernst, Jacob Daniel. *Die neu-auffgerichtete Schatz-Cammer vieler hundert anmuthiger und sonderbarer Erfindungen, Gedancken und Erzehlungen.* Altenburg: Gottfried Richters seel. Erben, 1696.

"Errichtung des Zuchthauses." August 16, 1723. In *Sammlung Oesterreichischer Gesetze und Ordnungen: Wie solche von Zeit zu Zeit ergangen und publiciret worden .../[4]: ... so viel deren vom Jahr 1721. Bis auf Höchst-traurigen Tod-Fall Der Römisch-Kayserlichen Majestät Caroli VI. aufzubringen waren,* ed. Sebastian G. Herrenleben. Vol. 4. Vienna: Johann Thomas Trattner, 1752.

Feige, Johann Constantin. *Wunderbarer Adlers-Schwung oder Fernere Geschichts-Fortsetzung Ortelii redivivi & continuati das ist: Beschreibung von Staatshändeln.* Vienna: Leopold Voigt, 1693.

Fleming, Hanns Friedrich von. *Der Vollkommene Teutsche Soldat.* Leipzig: Johann Christian Martini, 1726.

Freschot, Casimir. *Memoires de la cour de Vienne: contenant les remarques d'un voyageur curieux sur l'état present de cette cour, et sur ses intérêts.* Cologne: Guillaume Etienne, 1705.

Fritsch, Johann Christian. *Seltsame jedoch wahrhafftige Theologische/Juristische/ Medizinische und Physicalische Geschichten,* Vol. 3. Leipzig: Johann Friedrich Brauns sel. Erben, 1733.

Fuhrmann, Mathias. *Alt- und Neues Wien, Oder Dieser Kayserlich- und Ertz-Lands-Fürstlichen Residentz-Stadt Chronologisch- und Historische Beschreibung.* Vol. 2. Vienna: Johann Baptist Prasser, 1739.

Fuhrmann, Mathias. *Historische Beschreibung Und kurz gefaste Nachricht Von der Römisch. Kaiserl. Und Königlichen Residenz-Stadt Wien, Und Ihren Vorstädten.* Part 2. Vol. 2. Vienna: Krauß, 1767.

Geiger, Wolfgang Jacob. *Theatri Europaei. Das ist: Glaubwürdige Beschreibung Denckwürdiger Geschichten* .... Vol. 10. Frankfurt a.M: Johann Görlin, 1703.

Geiger, Wolfgang Jacob. *Theatrum Europaeum, oder außführliche und warhafftige Beschreibung aller und jeder denckwürdiger Geschichten... von dem 1665sten Jahr biß in Anno 1671....* Frankfurt a. M.: Matthäus Merian, 1677.

Geusau, Anton Reichsritter von. *Geschichte der Haupt- und Residenzstadt Wien in Österreich, in einiger Verbindung mit der Geschichte des Landes; von den ältesten bis auf gegenwärtige Zeiten.* Vol. 3. Vienna: Alberti, 1798.

Glawnig, D. "Fünftes Gutachten ueber den Zustand eines Kindermörders." In *Aufsätze und Beobachtungen aus der gerichtlichen Arzneywissenschaft*, vol. 8, edited by Johann Theodor Pyl, 263-268. Berlin: Mylius, 1793.

Goeze, Johann Melchior. *Gewissenhafte Erinnerungen zu der Schrift: Ueber die Gewohnheit, Missethäter durch Prediger zur Hinrichtung begleiten zu lassen.* Hamburg: Dieterich Anton Harmsen, 1784.

Goeze, Johann Melchior. *Johan Melchior Goezens, Pastoris zu St. Cathar. in Hamburg, Auszüge aus seinen Sontags-, Fest- und verschiedenen Wochen-Predigten des 1777 Jahres.* Hamburg: Dietrich Anton Harmsen, 1777.

Grass, Michael. *Collectionis novae consiliorum juridicorum Tubingensium.* Vol. 5. Tübingen: J. G. Cotta, 1733.

Grießheim, Christian Ludwig von. *Anmerk. u. Zugaben über den Tractat: die Stadt Hamburg nach ihrem politischen, oeconomischen und sittlichen Zustande.* Hamburg: Wilhelm Drese, 1759.

Griesheim, Christian Ludwig von. *Verbesserte und vermehrte Auflage des Tractats: die Stadt Hamburg in ihrem politischen, öconomischen und sittlichen Zustande: nebst Nachträgen zu diesem Tractate; und Beyträgen zu der Abhandlung : Anmerk. u. Zugaben über den Tractat die Stadt Hamburg, welche selbigen ebenfalls verbessern und gewisser machen.* Hamburg: Wilhelm Drese, 1760.

Grimm, Johann Melchior. *Als Margaretha Ursula Huberin Burgerliche Balln-Binderin allhier in Regensburg Wegen begangenen Kinder-Mords Nach Urtheil und Recht zum Tode verdammet/ Und darauf Den 21. Octobr. 1734. Durch das Schwerdt Vom Leben zum Todt hingerichtet worden.* Regensburg: Johann Caspar Memmel, 1734.

Guggenberger, Vitus. *Processe und vortreffliche Gutachten in Criminalibus.* Augsburg: Daniel Walder, 1722.

Harpprecht, Ferdinand Christoph. *Responsorum Criminalium et Civilium.* Vol. 4. Tübingen: August Metzler, 1706.

Harsdörffer, Georg Philipp. *Der Grosse Schau-Platz jämmerlicher Mord-Geschichte.* Hildesheim: Georg Olms Verlag, 1975. First published 1656 in Hamburg by Johann Nauman.

Johann Hieronymus Hermann. *Sammlung allerhand Auserlesener Responsorum.* Vol. 2. Jena: Johann Volckmar Marggraf, 1731.

Herrenleben, Sebastian Gottlieb. *Sammlung Oesterreichischer Gesetze und Ordnunge : Wie solche von Zeit zu Zeit ergangen und publiciret worden .../ [4]: ... so viel deren vom Jahr 1721. Bis auf Höchst-traurigen Tod-Fall Der Römisch-Kayserlichen Majestät Caroli VI. aufzubringen waren.* Vienna: Trattner, 1752.

Heß, Jonas Ludwig von. *Hamburg topographisch, politisch und historisch beschrieben.* Vol. 2. Hamburg: Selbstverlag, 1789.

Hess, Jonas Ludwig von. *Hamburg topographisch, politisch und historisch beschrieben*, 2nd ed. Vol. 2. Hamburg: Selbstverlag, 1811.

Heumann, Georg Daniel. "Prospekt des Calvari Bergs zu Hernals." Engraving. In *Vera Et Accurata Delineatio Omnium Templorum et Coenobiorum Quae tam in Caesarea Urbe ac Sede Vienna Austriae, quam in circumjacentibus Suburbys ejus reperiuntur*, by Salomon Kleiner. Vol. 1. Augsburg: Johann Andreas Pfeffel, 1724.

Heumann, G. D. (after Salomon Kleiner). *Prospect des Grabens.* Engraving. 1724.

Höggard, Emanuel. *Die entehrende Tonsur für exemplarische Büßerinnen unter der Regierung Josephs des Zweyten.* Vienna: C. Gerold, 1782.

Hommel, Karl Ferdinand. *Rhapsodia quaestionum in foro quotidie obvenientium, neque tamen legibus decisarum.* Vol. 5. Bayreuth: Joh. And. Lubeccium, 1779.

Horb, Jacob Daniel, and Jacobus Rhenferd. *Disputatio inauguralis de jure viarum circa clamorem violentiæ, vulgo Strassen Recht das mordgeschrey betreffend.* Franeker: Johannes Gyzelaar, 1699.

Howard, John. *Appendix to the State of the Prisons in England and Wales, &c. Containing a farther Account of the Foreign Prisons and Hospitals.* Warrington: William Eyres, 1780.

Howard, John. *The State of the Prisons in England and Wales, with Preliminary Observations, and an Account of Some Foreign Prisons.* 3rd ed Warrington: Cadell, 1784.

Joannes Vincentius a Sancta Eleonora. *Andächtige Gebetter: Für die Herren Brüder vnnd Schwestern, so in der Todten-Brüderschafft, in der Augustiner Parfusser Kirchen Einverleibt sein / Durch den Ehrwürdigen P. Fr. Ioan. Vincentium à S. Eleonora, geistlichen Vattern in obgemelter TodtenBruderschafft.* Vienna: Matthäus Cosmerovius, 1643.

Kircher, Paul Christian. *Jüdisches Ceremoniel oder: Beschreibung derjenigen jüdische Gebräuche, welche die Jüden so wol inn - als ausser dem Templ ... in acht zu nehmen pflegen: nunmehro aber bey dieser neuen Aufl. Mit accuraten Kupfern versehen ....* Frankfurt: Gerhard, 1726.

Kirchgeßner, Johann Valentin. *Tribunal Nemesis iuste iudicantis : oder Richter-Stuhl der recht richtenden Gerechtigkeit.* Nuremberg: Kranzfelder, 1720.
Klefeker, Johannes. *Sammlung der Hamburgischen Gesetze und Verfassungen in Bürger- und Kirchlichen, auch Cammer-, Handlungs- und übrigen Policey-Angelegenheiten und Geschäften samt historischen Einleitungen.* Vol. 1. Hamburg: J. C. Piscator, 1770.
Klefeker, Johannes. *Sammlung der Hamburgischen Gesetze und Verfassungen in Bürger- und Kirchlichen, auch Cammer-, Handlungs- und übrigen Policey-Angelegenheiten und Geschäften samt historischen Einleitungen.* Vol. 8. Hamburg: J. C. Piscator, 1770.
Klein, E. F. "Selbstmord durch Tödtung anderer; dargestellet in der Untersuchungssache wider die Anne Rosine Dunkel." *Annalen der Gesetzgebung und Rechtsgelehrsamkeit* 14 (1796): 220-248.
Klein, E. F. "Ueber die Brandstiftung der Eva Veronika Chillin, nebst einigen in die Gesetzgebung einschlagenden Bemerkungen, 1) über die Verbrechen, welche aus Ueberdruß des Lebens begangen werden..." *Annalen der Gesetzgebung und Rechtsgelehrsamkeit.* 7 (1791): 3-14.
Kleiner, Salomon. *Wahrhafte und genaue Abbildung Einiger antique als modernen Kirchen, Ehren-Säulen... welche... in der Kayserlichen Resdienz-Stadt Wien... anzutreffen.* Augsburg: Johann Andreas Pfeffel, 1728.
Kleiner, Salomon. *Des florierenden vermehrten Wiens Fernere Befolgung, oder, Wahrhafte und genaue Abbildung derer in dieser Kayserl. Residenz-Statt... ausgeführten Gebäuden....* Augsburg: Johann Andreas Pfeffel, 1737.
Kohler, Josef, and Willy Scheel, eds. *Die peinliche Gerichtsordnung Kaiser Karls V. Consitutio Criminalis Carolina.* Halle a. S.: Verlag Buchhandlung des Waisenhauses, 1900.
Krausold, Fridrich. *Friderici Krausoldi Discursus iuridico-politicus de miraculis et egregiis usibus S. Raspin.* Merseburg: Georg Christian Forberger, 1698.
[Kropatschek, Joseph. ed.] *Handbuch aller unter der Regierung des Kaisers Joseph des II. für die K. K. Erbländer ergangenen Verordnungen und Gesetze.* Vol. 1. Vienna: Joh. Georg Moesle, 1785.
Küchelbecker, Johann Basilius. *Allerneueste Nachricht vom Römisch-Käyserlichen Hofe: nebst einer ausführlichen historischen Beschreibung der kayserlichen Residentz-Stadt Wien, und der umliegenden Oerter, theils aus den Geschichten, theils aus eigener Erfahrung zusammen getragen und mit saubern Kupffern ans Licht gegeben.* Hannover: Förster, 1730.
"Landesgerichtsordnung für Osterreich unter der Enns." In *Codicis Austriaci..., Das ist: Eigentlicher Begriff und Innhalt/ Aller Unter deß Durchleuchtigsten Ertz-Hauses zu Oesterreich.... ausgegangenen...Generalien,* 659-728. Vol. 1. Vienna: Leopold Voigt, 1704.
Leopold I. *Princeps in compendio, hoc est, Puncta aliquot compendiosa, quae circa gubernationem Reipub. observanda videntur.* Vienna: Cosmerovius, 1668.

[Leopoldus]. "Zucht-Hauses Auffrichtung." 12. Jan 1671 In *Codex Austriacus: Das ist: Eigentlicher Begriff und Innhalt Aller Unter deß Durchleuchtigisten Ertz-Hauses zu Oesterreich; Fürnemblich aber Der Allerglorwürdigisten Regierung Ihro Röm. Kayserl. ...Königl. Majestät Leopoldi I, Ertz-Hertzogens zu Oesterreich... Außgangenen und publicirten ... Generalien*, edited by Franz Anton Gaurient, 545-547. Vol. 2. Vienna: Voigt, 1704.

Lilienberg, Matthias Abele von und zu. *Künstliche Unordnung: das ist: Wunder-Seltsame niemals in offentlichen Druck gekommene Gerichts- und ausser Gerichts- doch warhaffte Begebenheiten.* [Nuremberg]: Endter, 1670.

Linck, Georg Heinrich. *Consiliorum sive Responsorum.* Nuremberg: Johannis Georg Lochner, 1738.

[Lueger, Bonaventurea]. *Heilsame Ermahnung über die ausschweifende Liebe junger Leute in einer Sittenrede auf dem katholischen Gottesacker zu Augsburg vorgetragen..., als Maria Anna Mayrinn...den 8. Hornung des 1783 Jahrs durch das Schwert vom Leben zum Tod hingerichtet... wurde.* [Augsburg]: Johann Bernhard Stadelberer, [1783]. SuStBA, Aug 1477.

Luther, Martin. "Nun bitten wir den heiligen Geist." Hymnary.org. https://hymnary.org/text/nun_bitten_wir_den_heiligen_geist.

Luther, Martin. "We now Implore God the Holy Ghost." Hymnary.org. https://hymnary.org/text/we_now_implore_god_the_holy_ghost.

Luther, Martin. "Verleih uns Frieden Gnädiglich." Hymnary.org. https://hymnary.org/text/verleih_uns_frieden_gnadiglich.

Luther, Martin. "Verleih uns Frieden Gnädiglich," Bach Cantatas Website. http://www.bach-cantatas.com/Texts/Chorale169-Eng3.htm.

Lutherisches Gesangbuch (s.l., 1770).

Maldoner, Johann Franz. *Synopsis militaris: Oder kurzer Begriff über die Kayserliche Kriegs-Articul.* Nuremberg/Frankfurt a.M.: Johann Christoph Lochner, 1724.

Marino, Giambattista. *La strage degl'innocenti : poema.* Naples: Ottavio Beltrano, 1632.

Meyer, Johann Xaver. *Das Neueste von der Zeit Oder Allerneueste Nachrichten Von den vornehmsten und merckwürdigsten Begebenheiten: Welche sich in dem uns bekanntesten Theil der Welt, bis auf gegenwärtige Zeit, so wohl in Kriegs- und Staats-Angelegenheiten als in Bürgerlichen und Criminal-Händeln, ereignet und zugetragen haben; Wie auch was von neuen und raren Erfindungen in dem weitläufftigen Reich der Natur an verschiedenen Orten bekannt gemacht worden.* Frankfurt/Leipzig: Buggel und Seitz, 1732.

Mercurii Relation, oder wochentliche Reichs Ordinari Zeitungen, von underschidlichen Orthen. 1698.

Moser, Johann Jacob. *Seelige Letzte Stunden Einiger dem zeitlichen Tode übergebener Missethäter.* Stuttgart: Erhardt, 1767.

Nettelbladt, Christian von. *Thesaurus Iuris Provincialis Et Statutarii Illustrati Germaniae Oder Samlung zur Erläuterung derer Provinzial- und Statutarischen Rechte Teutschlandes, ...deren Erster Band dem Statuarischen Recht der*

Kayserlichen Freyen Reichs-Stadt Hamburg gewidmet worden. Giessen: Johann Christoph Schroeder, 1756.

Ogesser, Joseph. *Beschreibung der Metropolitankirche zu St. Stephan in Wien.* Vienna: Ghelensche Erben, 1779.

Olearius, Adam. *Continuirte Fortsetzung der hollsteinischen Chronica von Anno 1662 bis 1702.* Frankfurt: Georg Heinrich Öhrling, 1703.

Osiander, Andreas. *Ob es war vn[d] glaublich sey, daßdie Juden der Christen kinder heymlich erwürgen, vnd jr blut gebrauchen: ein treffenliche schrifft, auff eines yeden vrteyl gestelt.* [Nuremberg]: [Petreius], ca. 1530.

Partinger, Franz. *Praxis Fructuose, Et Ad Mentem S. P. Ignatii, atque ab eodem Institutae Societatis Assistendi Infirmis ac Moribundis, & reis Item juvandi diversos hominum status per Utilem Conversationem Ad majorem Jesu Christi Dei Hominis In terris cum hominibus conversantis atque In Cruce Morientis Gloriam & Honorem.* Augsburg: Veith, 1723.

Pfister, Ludwig. *Aktenmäßige Geschichte der Räuberbanden an den beiden Ufern des Mains.* Heidelberg: Gottlieb Braun, 1812.

Pfundheller, Josef. *Die schwarze Bibliothek. Eine Sammlung interessanter Criminalgeschichten.* Neue Folge. Vol. 1. Vienna: Im Selbstverlag, 1864.

Platner, Ernst. *Questiones Medicinae forensis et medicinae stadium octo semestribus descriptum.* Leipzig: s.n., 1797.

Pöck, Thomas Ignaz von. *Supplementum Codicis Austriaci, oder Chronologische Sammlung .../6: ... aller vom 1ten Jäner 1759. bis letzten Dezember 1770. als der fürwährend-weiteren angetretenen glorreichsten Regierung Allerdurchlauchtigst-Großmächtigsten Römischen Kaiserinn zu Hungarn und Böheim Königinn, ... Mar. Theresiae, ... Generalien, Patenten, Satz-Ordnungen....* Vienna: Trattner, 1777.

Praetorius, Johannes. *M. DC. LXVIII. Zodiacus Mercurialis eXpLICanDIssIMVs. Das ist: Jährige Europaeische Welt-Chronick, So in einem wohl-verfasseten Kurtzem Begriffe alle merckwürdige Begebenheiten vorbildet: Welche sich im verschienenen und zurückgelegten 1668.sten Wetter-Jahre, durch alle und einzählige Reiche des Erdbodens, zugetragen haben.* Jena: Johannes Nisius, 1669.

Reichs Post Reuter. Altona: s. n., 1777-1778.

Regulen Und andächtige Ubungen, Der in der Statt Wien von Ihrer päpstlichen Heiligkeit Urbano Dem Achten, Auff Anhaltung Ihrer Kayserl. und Königl. Mayestäten Ferdinand I ... Mit sonderbahren Freyheiten und Gnaden begabter ... Löbl. Bruderschafft. Vienna: Leopold Voigt, 1672.

[Richter, August]. *Umständliche Doch in möglichster Kürtze verfaßte Historische Einleitung Uber den Criminal-Process.* Frankfurt: Johann Conrad Wohler, 1738.

Rink, Eucharius Gottlieb. *Leopolds des Grossen Röm. Käysers wunderwürdiges Leben und Thaten.* Vol. 1. Cologne: s.n., 1713.

Ristl, Augustinus. *Maria voll der Gnaden zu Hietzing, das ist, ausführlicher Bericht von dem Uralten Gottes-Haus der Regulirten Chor-Herren des H. Aug. zu Hietzing ohnweit Wienn.* Vienna: Gregor Kurtzböck, 1738.

Schedel, Hartmut. *Weltchronik*. Nuremberg: Anton Koberger, 1493.

Schlüter, Matthäus. *Historisch- und Rechtsbegründeter Tractat von dem Verlassungs-Recht*. Hamburg: Zacharias Hertel, 1703.

Schmidt, Frantz. *The Executioner's Journal: Meister Frantz Schmidt of the Imperial City of Nuremberg*. Translated by Joel Harrington. Charlottesville: University of Virginia Press, 2016.

Schmid, Jacob. *Heiliger Ehren-Glantz Der Gefürsteten Graffschafft Tyrol/ Das ist: Geschicht Und Lebens-Verfassung Aller Der Jenigen Heiligen Seeligen Und Gottseeligen Personen Welche Mit Ihrem Scheinbaren Leben... Tyrol... Gezieret Haben*. Vol. 2. Augspurg: Matthias Wolff, 1732.

Schudt, Johann Jakob. *Jüdische Merkwürdigkeiten*. Vol. 2. Frankfurt: s.n., 1714.

Schweser, Christoph Heinrich. *Des Klugen Beamten auserlesener Criminal-Proceß: Worinnen von dem Ursprung der Criminal-Verordnung unter Kayser Maximiliano I. Wie auch von dem Criminal-Proceß überhaupt und insbesondere, und von denen Straffen nach dem Göttlichen, Römischen, alten Deutschen, Carolingischen, und vielen Landes-Gesetzen ... gehandelt wird : Nebst Beyfügung der hierzu nöthigen Peinlichen Halß-Gerichts-Ordnung Kayser Carls des Vten, samt denen Projecten*. Nuremberg: Gabriel Nicolaus Raspe, 1766.

Senfelder, Leopold. ed., *Acta Facultatis medicae Universitatis Vindobonensis*. VI. *1677-1724*. Vienna: Verlag des Wiener Medizinischen Doktorenkollegiums, 1912.

Staphorst, Nicolaus. *Historia ecclesiæ Hamburgensis diplomatica, das ist: Hamburgische Kirchengeschichte, aus Glaubwürdigen und mehrentheils noch ungedruckten Urkunden, so wol Kaiserlichen, Königlichen, Fürstlichen, Gräflichen, [et]c. ...gesammlet, beschrieben, und in Ordnung gebracht*. Vols. 1, 2. Hamburg: Theodor Christoph Felginern, 1725.

Staats-Relation Derer neuesten Europäischen Nachrichten und Begebenheiten. Regensburg: Bader, 1746-1754.

Steltzner, Michael Gottlieb. *Versuch einer zuverlässigen Nachricht von dem kirchlichen und politischen Zustande der Stadt Hamburg*. 3 vols. S. l.: s. n., 1733.

Struensee, Adam. *Die Zarte Liebe Jesu zu den Elenden, ...Bey Gelegenheit einer...Enthauptung einer Kinder-Mörderin*. Halle: Waysenhaus, 1736.

[Sturm, Christoph Christian]. *Ueber die Gewohnheit, Missethäter durch Prediger zur Hinrichtung begleiten zu lassen*. Hamburg: Gottlieb Friedrich Schniebes, 1784.

Suttinger, Johann Baptist. *Additiones Consuetitudinem Austriacarum Renovatae*. Nuremberg: Martin Endter, 1718.

Thomasius, Christian. *Ernsthaffte, aber doch Muntere und Vernünftige Thomasische Gedanken... über allerhand auserlesene Jusistische Händel*. Vol. 1. 2nd edition. Halle: Rengerische Buchhandlung, 1723.

"Todten-Bruderschaffts-Privilegium." 5 June 1638. In *Codicis Austriaci*, edited by Franz Anton von Guarient und Raall, 340-341. Vol. 2. Vienna: Voigt, 1704.

Troppanneger, D. Christian Gottlieb. *Decisiones Medico-Forensis.* Dresden: Gottlieb Christian Hilschern, 1733.
Ulrich, Johann Caspar. *Johann Caspar Ulrichs, Pfarrers zum Frauen-Münster in Zürich, Sammlung Jüdischer Geschichten welche sich mit diesem Volk in dem XIII. und folgenden Jahrhunderten bis auf MDCCLX. in der Schweitz von Zeit zu Zeit zugetragen.* Basel: [Nicolaus Kölner?], 1768.
Valentin, Samuel. *Ein...Rath der...Stadt Augsburg hat hiemit zu Urthel und Recht erkannt, daß Samstag den 11. January 1772, Leonhard Fels...wegen begangener Mord-That an seinem leiblichen Sohn...mit dem Schwerdt und blutiger Hand vom Leben zum Tod gebracht werden solle.* Augsburg: Brinhaußer, n.d.
Verein für Hamburgische Geschichte, ed. *Der Stadt Hamburg Gerichts-Ordnung und Statuta.* Hamburg: Perthes, Besser & Mauke, 1842.
Vincentius de S. Eleonora. *Des Fegfewers Probier Teuch So Zwischen Oesterreichischen Gebürgen liget/ Aus welchem gar klare und helle Wasser/ Gottseliger Werck der Lieb und Barmherzigkeit haraus fliessen/ dardurch die Betrübte Seelen in den Bittern und grausamen Peynen des Fegfewers gelabt und erquickt werden.* Vienna: Matthäus Formica, 1638.
Vincenzo di Santa Eleonora. *Probatico Piscina del Purgatorio Situata Fra li Sacri Monti Austriaci: Onde Li scaturiscono limpide acque di pie, caritatiue, e miseri¬cordiose opere, per le quali l' afflitte anime sono refrigerate nelle loro acerbe, e crudeli pene, che patiscono.* Vienna: Maria Rittia Vedova, 1638.
Waldinutzy, Georg Joseph Kögl von. *De iure civili, et criminali Austriaco-bellico tractatus practicus, das ist: Praktische Abhandlung deren in österreichischen Kriegsgerichten vor fallenden bürger- und peinlichen Rechtsentscheidungen eingerichtet nach...Maria Theresiae, Erzherzogin zu Oesterreich, neuen Kriegsartikeln.* Vol. 1. Pressburg: Johann Michael Landerer, 1772.
Weber, Veit [Leonhard Wächter]. *Sagen der Vorzeit.* Vol. 1 Berlin: Friedrich Maurer, 1787.
Weittenau, Felix Anton von. *Centuria Consiliorum Criminalium.* Augsburg: Mathias Rieger, 1763.
Weigel, Christoph, and Augustus Germ. *Hungariae q' Rex Iosephus I. die 13. Iuly e venatione redux, cum Sam. Eucharistiam cleferentem Sacerdotem obuium habaret....* 1701. Copperplate engraving.
Wellner, Philibert. *Hand-Buch deren Krancken.* Vienna: Christoph Joseph Hueth, 1744.
Weschel, Leopold Matthias. *Die Leopoldstadt bey Wien. Nach Quellen und Quellenschriftstellern, in Verbindung mit einer Skizze der Landesgeschichte, historisch dargestellt.* Vienna: A. Strauss, 1824.
"Wie es mit Bestrafung des Kinder-Mords zu halten." In *Codicis Austriaci Ordine Alphabetico Compilati....* Edited by Sebastian Gottlieb Herrenleben, 511-512. Vienna: Johann Thomas Trattner, 1752.
Wiennerisches Diarium. Vienna: Ghelen, 1703-1779.

Woltersdorff, Ernst Gottlieb. *Der Schächer Am Kreutz: Das Ist Vollständige Nachrichten von der Bekehrung und Seligem Ende Hingerichteter Missethäter.* 2 vols. Budißin: Deinzer, 1753-1760/66.
Wraxall, Nathanial William. *Memoirs of the Courts of Berlin, Dresden, Warsaw, and Vienna, in the years 1777, 1778, and 1779.* 2nd ed. London: A. Strahan, 1800.
Zach, Ignatius. *Ausführliche Beschreibung der Marter eines heiligen und unschuldigen Kinds Andreae von Rinn in Tyrol... : Welches von denen Juden aus angebohrnem Haß gegen Christum und gesambten seiner Christenheit grausam gequälet und ermordet worden.* Augsburg: Matthias Wolff, 1724.
Zedler, Johann Heinrich. *Grosses Universal-Lexikon aller Wissenschaften und Künste.* 68 vols. Halle and Leipzig: Johann Heinrich Zedler, 1731-1754.
Zoepfl, Heinrich, ed. *Die Peinliche Gerichtsordnung Kaiser Karl's V nebst der Bamberger und der Brandenburger Halsgerichtsordnung, sämmtlich nach den ältesten Drucken und mit den Projecten der Peinlichen Gerichtsordnung Kaiser Karl's V. von den Jahren 1521 und 1529, beide zum erstenmale vollständig.* Leipzig: C.F. Winter, 1883.

Secondary Sources

Anon. "Ein Rundgang durch das alte Wien zur Zeit des Steinhausen'schen Stadtplanes." *Berichte und Mittheilungen des Alterthums-Vereins zu Wien* 25 (1889): 32-68.
"Adler." In *Conversations-Lexikon für bildende Kunst*, 70-72. Vol. 1. Leipzig: Emil Graul, 1845.
Agri, Alessandro. *La Giustizia Criminale a Mantova in Età Asburgica: Il Supremo Consiglio di Giustizia* (1750-1786). Vol. 1. Rome: Historia et Ius, 2019.
Ammerer, Gerhard. *Das Ende für Schwert und Galgen? Legislativer Prozess und Offentlicher Diskurs zur Reduzierung der Todesstrafe im Ordentlichen Verfahren unter Joseph II (1781-1787).* Vienna: Studienverlag, 2010.
Ammerer, Gerhard, and Christoph Brandhuber. *Schwert und Galgen: Geschichte der Todesstrafe in Salzburg.* Salzburg: Verlag Anton Pustet, 2018.
Ammerer, Gerhard, and Friedrich Adomeit. "Armsünderblätter." In *Repräsentationen von Kriminalität und öffentlicher Sicherheit. Bilder, Vorstellungen und Diskurse vom 16. bis 20. Jahrhundert*, edited by Karl Härter, Gerhard Sälter and Eva Wiebel, 271-307. Frankfurt a. M.: Vittorio Klostermann, 2010.
Arnade, Peter J. *Beggars, Iconoclasts, and Civic Patriots: The Political Culture of the Dutch Revolt.* Ithaca: Cornell University Press, 2008.
Auler, Jost, ed. *Richtstättenarchäologie*, 3 vols. Dormagen: Archaeotopos-Buchverlag, 2008-2012.

Auslander, Diane Peters. "Victims or Martyrs: Children, Anti-Semitism, and the Stress of Change in Medieval England," in: *Childhood in the Middle Ages and the Renaissance: The Results of a Paradigm Shift in the History of Mentality*, ed. Albrecht Classen. Berlin: Walter de Gruyter, 2005: 105-134.

Bauer, Werner T. *Wiener Friedhofsführer. Genaue Beschreibung sämtlicher Begräbnisstätten nebst einer Geschichte des Wiener Bestattungswesens.* Vienna: Falter Verlag, 1997.

Barbagli, Marzio. *Farewell to the World: A History of Suicide.* Cambridge: Polity Press, 2015.

Behringer, Wolfgang. *Witchcraft Persecutions in Bavaria: Popular Magic, religious Zealotry and Reason of State in Early Modern Europe*, trans. J.C. Grayson and David Lederer. Cambridge: Cambridge University Press, 1997.

Beneke, Otto. *Hamburgische Geschichten und Sagen*, 2nd ed. Hamburg: Perthes, Besser & Mauke, 1854.

Beneke, Otto. *Von unehrlichen Leuten. Cultur-Historische Studien und Geschichten.* Hamburg: Perthes, Besser und Mauke, 1863.

Bérenger, Jean. "The Austrian Church." In *Church and Society in Catholic Europe of the Eighteenth Century*, edited by William James Callahan and David Higgs, 88-105. Cambridge: Cambridge University Press, 1979.

Berg, Johannes van den, and Martin Brecht. *Der Pietismus vom siebzehnten bis zum frühen achtzehnten Jahrhundert*. Göttingen: Vandenhoeck & Ruprecht, 1993.

Berger, Andreas. "Bodies in Pain: Early Modern Suicide by Proxy." *German History* 42/1 (2024).

Binder, Beate. *Illustriertes Recht. Die Miniaturen des Hamburger Stadtrechts von 1497.* Hamburg: Verlag Verein für Hamburgische Geschichte, 1988.

Bingel, Hermann. *Das 'Theatrum Europaeum', ein Beitrag zur Publizistik des 17. und 18. Jahrhunderts.* Berlin: E. Ebering, 1909.

Bireley, Robert. *The Refashioning of Catholicism, 1450-1700.* Washington, D. C.: Catholic University of America Press, 1999.

Blazek, Matthias. *Seeräuberei, Mord und Sühne. Eine 700-jährige Geschichte der Todesstrafe in Hamburg, 1292-1945.* Stuttgart: Ibidem Verlag, 2012.

Bode, Rechtsanwalt. "Die Kindestötung und ihre Bestrafung im Nürnberg des Mittelalters." *Archiv für Strafrecht und Strafprozess* 61 (1914): 430-481.

Bodner, Neta. *Walking to "Jerusalem" from Vienna: A Seventeenth-Century Way of the Cross.* Jerusalem: Spectrum, The Hebrew University of Jerusalem, 2013.

Brahmst, Claus. *Das Hamburgische Strafrecht im 17. Jahrhundert. Der Übergang vom städtischen zum gemeinen Strafrecht.* Hamburg: Ludwig Appel Verlag, 1958.

Bräuer, Helmut, '...und hat seithero gebetlet.' *Bettler und Bettelwesen in Wien und Niederösterreich während der Zeit Kaiser Leopolds I.* Vienna: Böhlau Verlag, 1998.

Brednich, Rolf Wilhelm. "Rothaarig." In *Enzyklopädie des Märchens. Handwörterbuch zur historischen und vergleichenden Erzählforschung*, edited by Rolf Wilhelm Brednich. Vol. 11. Berlin: de Gruyter, 2004.

Brietzke, Dirk. *Arbeitsdisziplin und Armut in der Frühen Neuzeit. Die Zucht- und Arbeitshäuser in den Hansestädten Bremen, Hamburg und Lübeck und die Durchsetzung bürgerlicher Arbeitsmoral im 17. Und 18. Jahrhundert.* Hamburg: Verein für Hamburgische Geschichte, 2000.

Briggs, Robin. *Witches and Neighbors. The Social and Cultural Context of European Witchcraft.* New York: Viking, 1996.

Brittain, Robert P. "Cruentation in Legal Medicine and in Literature." *Medical History* 9 (1965): 82-88.

Brunner, Heinrich. "Die Klage mit dem toten Mann und die Klage mit der toten Hand." *Zeitschrift der Savigny-Stiftung für Rechtsgeschichte: Germanistische Abteilung* 31 (1910): 235-252.

Brugger, Eveline, Martha Keil, Albert Lichtblau, Christoph Lind, Barbara Staudinger. *Geschichte der Juden in Österreich.* Vienna: Ueberreuter, 2006.

Buek, Friedrich Georg. *Hamburgische Alterthümer: Beitrag zur Geschichte der Stadt und ihrer Sitten.* Hamburg: Perthes-Besser & Mauke, 1859.

Burg, Christian von. "'Das Bild vnsers Herren ab dem esel geschlagen.' Der Palmesel in den Riten der Zerstörung." In *Macht und Ohnmacht der Bilder: reformatorischer Bildersturm im Kontext der europäischen Geschichte*, edited by Peter Blickle and André Holenstein, 117-141. Munich: Oldenbourg, 2002.

Burkart, Lucas. "Aus der Fastnacht in den Bildersturm: Knaben und junge Männer schänden und verbrennen das Kruzifix aus dem Basler Münster." In *Bildersturm. Wahnsinn oder Gottes Wille? Austellungskatalog*, edited by Cécile Dupeux, Peter Jezler and Jean Wirth. Zürich: NZZ Verlag, 2000.

Cabantous, Alain. *Blasphemy: Impious Speech in the West from the Seventeenth to the Nineteenth Centuries.* New York: Columbia University Press, 2001.

Cameron, Euan. *The European Reformation.* Oxford: Oxford University Press, 1991.

Cerman, Ivo. "Anti-Jewish Superstitions and the Expulsion of the Jews from Vienna in 1670." *Judaica Bohemia* 26 (2000): 5-30.

Coeckelberghe-Dützele, Gerhard Robert Walther von. *Geschichten, Sagen und Merkwürdigkeiten aus Wien's Vorzeit und Gegenwart.* Vienna: F. Hagenauer's Witwe, 1841.

Connell, William J., and Giles Constable. *Sacrilege and Redemption in Renaissance Florence: The Case of Antonio Rinaldeschi.* Toronto: Centre for Reformation and Renaissance Studies, 2005.

Czeike, Felix. "Amtshaus." In *Historiches Lexikon Wien.* Vol. 1. Vienna: Kremayr & Scheriau/Orac, 2004.

Czeike, Felix. "Armensündergassel." In *Historisches Lexikon Wien.* Vol. 1. Vienna: Kremayr & Scheriau/Orac, 2004.

Czeike, Felix. *Wien. Kunst und Kultur Lexikon. Stadtführer und Handbuch.* Munich: Süddeutscher Verlag, 1976.

Danker, Uwe. *Räuberbanden im Alten Reich um 1700. Ein Beitrag zur Geschichte von Herrschaft und Kriminalität in der frühen Neuzeit.* Frankfurt a.M.: Suhrkamp, 1988.

Darnton, Robert. *The Great Cat Massacre and other Episodes in French Cultural History.* New York: Basic Books, 2009.

Daur, Georg. "Goeze, Johann Melchior." In *Neue Deutsche Biographie* 6 (1964): 598-599 [Online-Version]; URL: https://www.deutsche-biographie.de/pnd118540386.html#ndbcontent.

Davies, Owen, and Francesca Matteoni. *Executing Magic in the Modern Era. Criminal Bodies and the Gallows in Popular Medicine.* Basingstoke: Palgrave Macmillan, 2017.

Davies, Owen. *Witchcraft, Magic and Culture, 1736-1951.* Manchester: Manchester University Press, 1999.

Davies, Owen. "Talk of the Devil: Crime and Satanic Inspiration in Eighteenth-Century England," Unpublished manuscript, 2007.

Death Penalty Information Center. "Women." http://www.deathpenaltyinfo.org/women-and-death-penalty.

Deutschmann, Wilhelm, and Herbert Spehar. *200 Jahre Rechtsleben in Wien: Advokaten, Richter, Rechtsgelehrte.* Vienna: Museen der Stadt Wien, 1986.

Dieselhorst, Jürgen. "Die Bestrafung der Selbstmörder im Territorium der Reichsstadt Nürnberg." *Mitteilung des Vereins für Geschichte der Stadt Nürnberg* 44 (1953): 58-230.

Diez, C. A. *Der Selbstmord; Seine Ursachen und Arten vom Standpunkte der Psychologie dargestellt.* Tübingen: H. Laupp'schen Buchhandlung, 1838.

Dillinger, Johannes. *"Evil People": A Comparative Study of Witch Hunts in Swabian Austria and the Electorate of Trier.* Charlottesville: University of Virginia Press, 2009.

Dillinger, Johannes. *Kinder im Hexenprozess. Magie und Kindheit in der Frühen Neuzeit.* Stuttgart: Franz Steiner Verlag, 2013.

Doppler, Elke, Christian Rapp, and Sándor Békési, eds. *Am Puls der Stadt: 2000 Jahre Karlsplatz. [Sonderausstellung, Wien Museum Karlsplatz, 29. Mai - 26. Oktober 2008].* Vienna: Czernin, 2008.

Duhr, Bernhard, S.J. *Geschichte der Jesuiten in den Ländern deutscher Zunge.* Vol. 2. Freiburg im Breisgau: Herderische Verlagshandlung, 1913.

Dülmen, Richard van. *Theatre of Horror: Crime and Punishment in Early Modern Germany.* Cambridge: Polity Press, 1990.

Dülmen, Richard van. *Kultur und Alltag in der Frühen Neuzeit.* Vol. 2, *Dorf und Stadt. 16.-18. Jahrhundert.* Munich: C. H. Beck, 1992.

Dülmen, Richard van. "Wider die Ehre Gottes. Unglaube und Gotteslästerung in der Frühen Neuzeit." *Historische Anthropologie* 2 (1994): 20-38.

Durkheim, Emile. *On Suicide.* London: Penguin Classics, 2007.

Eder, Manfred. "Wallfahrten, eucharistische." In *Historisches Lexikon Bayerns*, http://www.historisches-lexikon-bayerns.de/Lexikon/Wallfahrten,_eucharistische.

Edgerton, Samuel Y., Jr. *Pictures and Punishment: Art and Criminal Prosecution during the Florentine Renaissance.* Ithaca: Cornell University Press, 1985.

Eichler, Frank, ed. *Die Langenbeck'sche Glosse zum Hamburger Stadtrecht von 1497.* Hamburg: Mauke Schweitzer Gruppe, 2008.

Eire, Carlos M. N. *War against the Idols: The Reformation of Worship from Erasmus to Calvin.* Cambridge: Cambridge University Press, 1986.

Eisenbichler, Konrad. "Lorenzo de' Medici and the Confraternity of the Blacks in Florence." *Fides et Historia* 26 (1994): 85-98.

Erler, A. "Gottesurteil." *HRG* 1. Berlin: Erich Schmidt Verlag, 1971.

Evans, Richard J. *Rituals of Retribution: Capital Punishment in Germany, 1600-1987.* Oxford and New York: Oxford University Press, 1996.

Fanning, William. "Irregularity." *The Catholic Encyclopedia.* Vol. 8. New York: Robert Appleton Company, 1910. 29 Aug. 2022 <http://www.newadvent.org/cathen/08170a.htm>.

Falvey, Kathleen. "Scaffold and Stage: Comforting Rituals and Dramatic Traditions in Late Medieval and Renaissance Italy." In *The Art of Executing Well: Rituals of Execution in Renaissance Italy,* edited by Nicholas Terpstra, 13-30. Kirksville, MI: Truman State University Press, 2008.

Fellner, Fritz, Gernot Kocher, and Ute Streitt, eds. *Katalog: Schande, Folter, Hinrichtung. Rechtsprechung und Strafvollzug in Oberösterreich.* Linz: Oberösterreichisches Landesmuseum, 2011.

Fischer, Alexander J. *Music, Piety, and Propaganda: The Soundscapes of Counter-Reformation Bavaria.* Oxford: Oxford University Press, 2014.

Flynn, Maureen. "Blasphemy and the Play of Anger in Sixteenth-Century Spain." *Past and Present* 149 (1995): 29-56.

Forster, Marc R. *Catholic Germany from the Reformation to the Enlightenment.* New York: Palgave Macmillan, 2007.

Frank, Michael. "Die fehlende Geduld Hiobs. Suizid und Gesellschaft in der Grafschaft Lippe (1600-1800)," in *Trauer, Verzweiflung, Anfechtung: Selbstmord und Selbsmordversuche in mittelalterlichen und frühneuzeitlichen Gesellschaften,* edited by Gabriela Signori, 152-188. Tübingen: edition diskord, 1994.

Friess, Edmund, and Gustav Gugitz. "Die Mirakelbücher von Mariahilf in Wien (1689-1775)." In *Deutsche Mirakelbücher: Zur Quellenkunde und Sinngebung,* edited by Georg Schreiber. Düsseldorf: Schwann, 1938.

Frieß, Edmund, and Gustav Gugitz. "Zum gegenreformatorischen Bilderkult in Wien. Das Standbild Maria Grünberg oder Maria mit der Axt in der Franziskanerkirche." *Jahrbuch für Geschichte der Stadt Wien* 3-4 (1942): 73-125.

Fritz, Thomas. "Reutlingen - Hexenverfolgungen." In: *Lexikon zur Geschichte der Hexenverfolgung.* Edited by Gudrun Gersmann, Katrin Moeller and Jürgen-Michael Schmidt, in: historicum.net, URL: https://www.historicum.net/purl/jdzr3/.

Frommer, Hartmut H. "Jämmerliche Mordgeschichten. Vom Umgang des Rats 'mit gottlosen Raaben-Müttern welches ihre in Unehren erloffenen Kinder umzubringen sich unterstanden.'" *Mittheilung des Vereins für die Geschichte der Stadt Nürnberg*. 99 (2012): 121-149.

Gallois, Johann Gustav. *Hamburgische Chronik von den ältesten Zeiten bis auf die Jetztzeit*. Vols. 2-3. Hamburg: s.l., 1862.

Gemert, G. C. A. M. van. "Beer, Johann Christoph (1638-1712)." In *Killy Literaturlexikon. Autoren und Werke des deutschsprachigen Kulturraums*. Vol. 1. 2nd edition. Berlin/New York: De Gruyter, 2008.

Gernet, Herman Gustav. *Mittheilungen aus der älteren Medicinalgeschichte Hamburgs. Kulturhistorische Skizze auf urkundlichem und geschichtlichen Grunde*. Hamburg: W. Mauke Söhne, 1869.

Glanz, Rudolf. "The 'Jewish Execution' in Medieval Germany." *Jewish Social Studies* 5 (1943): 3-26.

Goldberg, Ann. *Sex, Religion, and the Making of Modern Madness. The Eberbach Asylum and German Society 1815-1849* (Oxford: Oxford University Press, 1999).

Göttsch, Silke. "Mörderin an ihrem unschuldigem Kinde aus Überdruß des Lebens." *Bayerisches Jahrbuch für Volkskunde* (1996): 43-49.

Gottschall, Klaus. *Dokumente zum Wandel im religiösen Leben Wiens während des Josephinismus*. Vienna: Institut für Volkskunde der Universität Wien, 1979.

Grebner, Gundula. "Die Judendarstellung am Frankfurter Brückentor als Schandbild. Funktionen Der Bekleidung im Bild." In *Kopf- und andere Tücher*, edited by Gisela Engel and Susanne Scholz, 87-102. Berlin: Trafo Verlag, 2005.

Griesebner, Andrea. "'In via gratia et ex plenitudine potetatis.' Strafjustiz und landesfürstliche Gnadenakte im Erzherzogtum Österreich unter der Enns des 18. Jahrhunderts." *Frühneuzeit-Info* 11 (2000): 13-27.

Griesebner, Andrea. *Konkurrierende Wahrheiten. Malefizprozessevor dem Landgericht Perchtoldsdorf im 18. Jahrhundert*. Vienna: Böhlau Verlag, 2000.

Grieshofer, Franz and Nora Witzmann. *Weihnachtskrippen: Spiegelbilder Vergangener Lebenswelten*. Vienna: Österreichisches Museum für Volkskunde, 2008.

Grois, Viktor. *Geschichte des k.k. Infanterie-Regiments Nr. 14. Grossherzog Ludwig III. von Hessen ind bei Rhein von der Errichtung 1733 bis 1876: Auf Befehl des k. k. Regiments-Commandos*. Linz: J. Feichtinger's Erben, 1876.

Groner, Richard. *Wien wie es war. Ein Auskunftsbuch über Alt-Wiener Baulichkeiten, Hausschilder, Plätze und Strassen, sowie über allerlei sonst Wissenswertes aus der Vergangenheit der Stadt*. Vienna: Verlag der Waldheim-Eberle A. G., 1919.

Gugitz, Gustav. *Die Sagen und Legenden der Stadt Wien*. Vienna: Verlag Brüder Hollinek, 1952.

Gugitz, Gustav. *Österreichs Gnadenstätten in Kult und Brauch*. Vol. 1. Vienna: Verlag Brüder Hollinek, 1955.

Gumpelzhaimer, Christian Gottlieb. *Regensburg's Geschichte, Sagen und Merkwurdigkeiten von den altesten bis auf die neuesten Zeiten*. Vol. 3. Regensburg: Friedrich Pustet, 1838.
Gutkas, Karl. "Die österreichischen Länder im Zeitalter des Hochbarocks." In *Prinz Eugen und das barocke Österreich*, edited by Karl Gutkas, 167-178. Salzburg: Residenz Verlag, 1985.
Gutkas, Karl. *Prinz Eugen und das barocke Österreich: Marchfeldschlösser Schlosshof und Niederweiden, 22. April bis 26. Oktober 1986*. Vienna: [Das Kuratorium], 1986.
Hagen, Friedrich von, and Michael Diefenbacher. *Die Henker von Nürnberg und ihre Opfer. Folter und Hinrichtungen in den Nürnberger Ratsverlässen 1501 bis 1806*. Nuremberg: Stadtarchiv, 2010.
Halb, Helmut. "Zur Sakralisierung von frühneuzeitlichem Stadtraum amd Beispiel Wien." In *Sakralisierung der Landschaft. Inbesitznahme, Gestaltung und Verwendung im Zeichen der Gegenreformation in Mitteleuropa*, edited by Werner Telesko and Thomas Aigner, 74-90. St. Pölten: Diözesanarchiv St. Pölten, 2019.
Härter, Karl. "Asyl für die Rechtsgeschichte," *Rechtsgeschichte Rg* 5 (2004): 235-243.
Harrington, Joel F. "Escape from the Great Confinement: The Genealogy of a German Workhouse." *The Journal of Modern History* 71 (1999): 308-345.
Harrington, Joel F. *The Faithful Executioner: Life and Death, Honor and Shame in the Turbulent Sixteenth Century*. New York: Farrar, Straus and Giroux, 2013.
Harrington, Joel F. *The Unwanted Child: The Fate of Foundlings, Orphans and Juvenile Criminals in Early Modern Germany*. Chicago: University of Chicago Press, 2009.
Harrington, Joel F., "The Strange Survival of the Bleeding Corpse," in: *Embodiment, Identity and Gender in the Early Modern Age*. Edited by Amy E. Leonard and David M. Whitford, 13-23. New York: Routledge, 2021.
Harster, Theodor. *Das Strafrecht der freien Reichstadt Speier*. Breslau: Verlag von M. & H. Marcus, 1900.
Hartl, Friedrich. *Das Wiener Kriminalgericht. Strafrechtspflege vom Zeitalter der Aufklärung bis zur österreichischen Revolution*. Vienna: Böhlau, 1973.
Hehenberger, Susanne. "'Die beleidigte Ehre GOttes auf das empfindlichste zu rächen, in allweg gesonnen.' Blasphemie und Sakrileg im 18. Jahrhundert," in *Wien und seine WiennerInnen: Ein historischer Streifzug durch Wien über die Jahrhunderte: Festschrift für Karl Vocelka zum 60. Geburtstag*, edited by Martin Scheutz and Vlasta Valeš, 179-201. Vienna: Böhlau Verlag, 2008.
Hehenberger, Suzanne. "Entfremdung von Gott? Gotteslästerung und Kirchdiebstahl vor weltlichen Gerichten im 18. Jahrhundert." In *Ermitteln, Fahnden und Strafen. Kriminalitätshistorische Studien vom 16. bis 19. Jahrhundert*, edited by Andrea Griesebner and Georg Tschannett, 141-163. Vienna: Erhard Löcker Gmbh, 2010.

Hehenberger, Susanne. *Unkeusch wider die Natur. Sodomieprozesse im frühneuzeitlichen Österreich.* Vienna: Löcker, 2006.
Hellerstedt, Andreas. "Ett stort bevis av Evangelii kraft och sanning. Suicidalmord, avrättningar och herrnhutisk teologi." *Historisk tidskrift* 131 (2011): 491–510.
Hennings, Elsa. *Das Hamburgische Strafrecht im 15. und 16. Jahrhundert und seine Verwirklichung.* Hamburg: Hansicher Gildenverlag, 1940.
Hinschius, Paul. *Das Kirchenrecht der Katholiken und Protestanten in Deutschland.* Vol. 1. Berlin: I. Guttentag, 1869.
Hofbauer, Karl. *Die Wieden mit den Edelsitzen Conradswerd, Mühlfeld, Schaumburgerhof und dem Freigrunde Hungerbrunn: historisch-topographische Skizzen zur Schilderung der Vorstädte Wiens.* Vienna: Gorischek, 1864.
Holmes, Ronald M., and Stephen T. Holmes. *Profiling Violent Crimes: An Investigative Tool.* Thousand Oaks, Calif: Sage, 2002.
Horodowich, Elizabeth. "Civic Identity and the Control of Blasphemy in Sixteenth-Century Venice." *Past & Present* 181 (2003): 3-33.
Hsia, R. Po-chia. *Social Discipline in the Reformation: Central Europe 1550-1750.* London: Routledge, 1991.
Hsia, R. Po-chia. *The Myth of Ritual Murder: Jews and Magic in Reformation Germany.* New Haven: Yale University Press, 1988.
Hsia, R. Po-chia. *Trent 1475: Stories of a Ritual Murder Trial.* New Haven, CT: Yale University Press, 1992.
Jacobi, Daniel Heinrich. *Geschichte des Hamburger Niedergerichts.* Hamburg: Gustav Edouard Nolte, 1866.
Jansson, Arne. *From Swords to Sorrow: Homicide and Suicide in Early Modern Stockholm.* Stockholm: Almqvist & Wiksell International, 1998.
Jansson, Arne. "Suicidal Murders in Stockholm." In *From Sin to Insanity: Suicide in Early Modern Europe,* edited by Jeffrey R. Watt, 81-99. Ithaca: Cornell University Press, 2004.
Jezler, Peter. "Jenseitsmodelle und Jenseitsvorsorge—Eine Einführung." In *Himmel, Hölle, Fegefeuer. Das Jenseits im Mittelalter,* edited by Peter Jezler, 13-26. Munich: Wilhelm Fink Verlag, 1994.
Jochmann, Werner, and Hans-Dieter Loose, eds. *Hamburg. Geschichte der Stadt und ihrer Bewohner.* Vol. 1. Hamburg: Hoffmann und Campe, 1982.
Johnson, Trevor. *Magistrates, Madonnas and Miracles: The Counter Reformation in the Upper Palatinate.* Farnham: Ashgate, 2009.
Jost, Jean E. "Loving Parents in Middle English Literature." in *Childhood in the Middle Ages and the Renaissance: The Results of a Paradigm Shift in the History of Mentality,* edited by Albrecht Classen, 307-328. Berlin: Walter de Gruyter, 2005.
Kaatzer, Dr. Pet. "Über den indirekten Selbstmord. Psychiatrisch-forensische Abhandung." Diss., Marburg: no publisher, 1872.

Kaczor, Dariusz. "Herrschaft und Verbrecher. Der Danziger Strafvollzug in der frühen Neuzeit." In *Kulturgeschichte Preussens königlich polnischen Anteils in der Frühen Neuzeit*, edited by Sabine Beckmann and Klaus Garber, 129-156. Tübingen: Max Niemeyer Verlag, 2005.

Kammerhofer-Angermann, Ulrike. "Quellenvergleich zu den Fronleichnamsprozessionen in den Städten Graz und Salzburg vor und nach der Reformationszeit. Die Rolle der Corporis-Christi-Bruderschaften in der Fronleichnamsprozession." In *Volksfrömmigkeit. Referate der Österreichischen Volkskundetagung 1989 in Graz*, edited by Helmut Eberhart, Edith Hörander and Burkhard Pöttler, 267-283. Vienna: Selbstverlag des Vereins für Volkskunde, 1990.

Kapner, Gerhardt. *Barocker Heiligenkult in Wien und seine Träger*. Munich: R. Oldenbourg Verlag, 1978.

Kapuzinergruft. "Kapuzinergruft." https://www.kapuzinergruft.com.

Kästner, Alexander. *Tödliche Geschichte(n): Selbsttötungen in Kursachsen in Spannungsfeld von Normen und Praktiken (1547-1815)* (Konstanz, UVK Verlagsgesellschaft, 2012).

Karant-Nunn, Susan. *The Reformation of Ritual: An Interpretation of Early Modern Germany*. London and New York: Routledge, 1997.

Kaufmann, David. *Die letzte Vertreibung der Juden aus Wien und Niederösterreich. Ihre Vorgeschichte (1625-1670) und ihre Opfer*. Budapest: Athenaeum, 1899.

Kaufmann, E. "Vorsatz." *HRG*. Vol. 5. Berlin: Erich Schmidt Verlag, 1998.

Keller, Katrin, Martin Scheutz and Harald Tersch, eds. *Einmal Weimar – Wien und retour. Johann Sebastian Müller und sein Wienbericht aus dem Jahr 1660*. Munich: R. Oldenbourg Verlag, 2005.

Kern, Edmund M. "Habsburg Territories." In *Europe 1450-1789: Encyclopedia of the Early Modern World*, edited by Jonathan Dewald, 113-119. Vol. 3. New York: Scribner Thomson Gale, 2004.

Kern, Edmund M. "Vienna." In *Encyclopedia of Witchcraft: The Western Tradition*, edited by Richard M. Golden, 1168-1169. Santa Barbara: ABC-CLIO, 2006.

Kisch, Wilhelm. *Die Alten Strassen und Plaetze Wiens und ihre historisch interessanten Haeuser*. Vienna: M. Gottlieb's Verlagsbuchhandlung, 1883.

Klammer, Peter. *Peinliche Ordnung. Von Giftmördern und anderen malefizigen Personen im Erzstift Salzburg*. Maria Pfarr: Peter Klammerer Verlag, 2010.

Kleinheyer, Gerd, and Jan Schröder. *Deutsche und Europäische Juristen aus neun Jahrhunderten eine biographische Einführung in die Geschichte der Rechtswissenschaft*. Tübingen: Mohr Siebeck, 2017.

Klieber, Rupert. *Bruderschaften und Liebesbünde nach Trient. Ihr Totendienst, Zuspruch und Stellenwert im kirchlichen und gesellschaftlichen Leben am Beispiel Salzburg (1600-1950)*. Frankfurt: Peter Lang, 1999.

Koch, Eduard Emil. *Geschichte des Kirchenlieds und Kirchengesangs der Christlichen, insbesondere der deutschen evangelischen Kirche*. Vol. 8. 3rd ed Stuttgart: Chr. Belser, 1876.

Kopitzsch, Franklin. "Zwichen Hauptrezeß und Franzosenzeit, 1712-1806." In *Hamburg. Geschichte der Stadt und ihrer Bewohner*, edited by Werner Jochmann and Hans-Dieter Loose, 351-414. Vol. 1. Hamburg: Hoffmann und Campe, 1982.

Koslofsky, Craig M. "Controlling the Body of the Suicide in Saxony." In *From Sin to Insanity: Suicide in Early Modern Europe*, edited by Jeffrey R. Watt, 48-63. Ithaca, N.Y.: Cornell University Press, 2004.

Koslofsky, Craig, and Dana Rabin. "The Limits of the State: Suicide, Assassination, and Execution in Early Modern Europe." In *Selbsttötung als kulturelle Praxis. Ansätze eines interkulturellen historischen Vergleichs*, edited by Andreas Bähr and Hans Medick, 45-63. Cologne: Böhlau Verlag, 2005.

Kounine, Laura. *Imagining the Witch: Emotions, Gender and Selfhood in Early Modern Germany*. Oxford: Oxford University Press, 2018.

Krogh, Tyge. A *Lutheran Plague: Murdering to Die in eht Eighteenth Century*. Leiden: Brill, 2012.

Krogh, Tyge. "Commentary on an article by Tine Reeh and Ralf Hemmingsen in Sjuttonhundratal 2018: 'Common Sense, No Magic: A case Study of Female Child Murderers in the Eighteenth Century', *1700-tal: Nordic Journal for Eighteenth-Century Studies*, 17 (2020): 229–232.

Kühnel, Florian. *Kranke Ehre? Adlige Selbsttötung im Übergang zur Moderne*. Munich: Oldenbourg, 2013.

Kunstmann, Helmut H. *Zauberwahn und Hexenprozeß in der Reichstadt Nürnberg*. Nuremberg: Stadtarchiv Nürnberg, 1970.

Kunze, Michael. *Highroad to the Stake. A Tale of Witchcraft*. Chicago: University of Chicago Press, 1980.

Kwiatkowski, Ernst von. *Die constitutio criminalis Theresiana; Ein Beitrag zur theresianischen Reichs- und Rechts- Geschichte*. Innsbruck: Wagner, 1904.

Laichmann, Michaela. "Notizen zur Rechtsgeschichte im 17. Jahrhundert. Eine Handschrift der Ferdinandeischen Landgerichtsordnung im Wiener Stadt- und Landesarchiv." *Jahrbuch des Vereins für Geschichte der Stadt Wien* 67/68 (2011/2012): 41-60.

Lang, Anton. *Hochgericht und Räderkreuz. Die Hinrichtungsstätten am Wienerberg*. Vienna: Museumsverein Favoriten, 2002.

Langbein, John H. *Torture and the Law of Proof. Europe and England in the Ancien Regime*. Chicago: University of Chicago Press, 1977.

Lappenberg, Johann Martin. *Hamburgische Rechtsalterthümer*. Vol. 1, *Die ältesten Stadt- Schiff- und Landrechte Hamburgs*. Hamburg: Johann August Meissner, 1845.

Lau, Thomas. "Müßigkeit is aller Laster Anfang? Sodomitenverfolgung im Zürich des 17. Jahrhunderts." *Frühneuzeit-Info* 21 (2010): 58-66.

Lederer, David. "Aufruhr auf dem Friedhof. Pfarrer, Gemeinde, und Selbstmord im frühneuzeitlichen Bayern," in *Trauer, Verzweiflung, Anfechtung: Selbstmord und Selbsmordversuche in mittelalterlichen und frühneuzeitlichen Gesellschaften*, edited by Gabriela Signori, 189-209. Tübingen: edition diskord, 1994.

Lederer, David. *Madness, Religion and the State in Early Modern Europe: A Bavarian Beacon*. New York: Cambridge University Press, 2006.
Lederer, David. "Wieder ein Faß aus Augsburg..." Suizid in der frühneuzeitlichen Lechmetropole." *Mitteilungen. Institut für Kulturgeschichte der Universität Augsburg* (2005): 47-72.
Leeb, Rudolf, Martin Scheutz and Dietmar Weikl, eds. *Geheimprotestantismus und evangelische Kirchen in der Habsburgermonarchie und im Erzstift Salzburg (17./18. Jahrhundert)*. Vienna: Böhlau, 2009.
Lehmann, Martin. "Die Kalvarienberganlagen im Donauraum." In *Festschrift Franz Loidl zum 65. Geburtstag*, edited by Victor Flieder, 113-159. Vol 1. Vienna: Verlag Brüder Hollinkek, 1970.
Leonhard, Jörn. "Non-simultaneity." In *Encyclopedia of Early Modern History Online*, edited by Graeme Dunphy and Andrew Gow. Heidelberg: J.B. Metzlersche Verlagsbuchhandlung und Carl Ernst Poeschel Verlag, 2005-2012.
Leutenbauer, Siegfried. *Das Delikt der Gotteslästerung in der Bayerischen Gesetzgebung*. Cologne: Böhlau Verlag, 1984.
Levack, Brian. "The Decline and End of Witchcraft Prosecutions." In *Witchcraft and Magic in Europe. The Eighteenth and Nineteenth Centuries*, edited by Bengt Ankarloo and Stuart Clark, 1-93. Philadephia: University of Penssylvania Press, 1999.
Levack, Brian P. *The Witch-Hunt in Early Modern Europe*. Harlow: Pearson Longman, 2005.
Lewis, Margaret Brennan. *Infanticide and Abortion in Early Modern Germany*. New York: Routledge, 2016.
Lieberwirth, R. "Gotteslästerung." *HRG*. Vol. 1. Berlin: Erich Schmidt Verlag, 1971.
Liliequist, Jonas. "Peasants against Nature: Crossing the Boundaries between Man and Animal in Seventeenth- and Eighteenth-Century Sweden," *Journal of the History of Sexuality* 1 (1991): 393-423.
Liliequist, Jonas. "Reverence, Shame and Guilt in Early Modern European Cultures," in: *The Routledge Companion to Cultural History in the Western World*. Edited by Allessandro Arcangeli, Jörg Rogge and Hannu Salmi. London: Routledge, 2020: 240-255
Lind, Vera. *Selbstmord in der Frühen Neuzeit. Diskurs, Lebenswelt, und kultureller Wandel am Beispiel der Herzogtümer Schleswig und Holstein*. Göttingen: Vandenhoeck & Ruprecht, 1999.
Lind, Vera. "The Suicidal Mind and Body." In *From Sin to Insanity: Suicide in Early Modern Europe*, edited by Jeffrey R. Watt, 64-80. Ithaca: Cornell University Press, 2004.
Lindemann, Mary. "Armen-und Eselbegräbnis in der europäischen Frühneuzeit." In *Studien zur Thematik des Todes im 16. Jahrhundert*, edited by Paul Richard Blum, 125-140. Wolfenbüttel: Herzog August Bibliothek, 1983.

Lindemann, Mary. "Fundamental Values: Political Culture in Eighteenth-Century Hamburg." In *Patriotism, Cosmopolitanism and National Culture: Public Culture in Hamburg, 1700-1933*, edited by Peter Uwe Hohendahl, 17-32. Amsterdam: Rodopi, 2003.

Lindemann, Mary. "Gender Tales: the Multiple Identities of the Maiden Heinrich, Hamburg 1700." In *Gender in Early Modern German History*, edited by Ulinka Rublack, 131-151. Cambridge: Cambridge University Press, 2002.

Lindemann, Mary. "Maternal Politics: The Principles and Practice of Maternity Care in Eighteenth-Century Hamburg." *Journal of Family History* 9 (1984): 44-63.

Lindeman, Mary. "Murder, Melancholy and the Insanity Defence in Eighteenth-century Hamburg." In *Medicine, Madness and Social History: Essays in Honour of Roy Porter*, edited by Roberta Bivins and John V. Pickstone, 161-172. Basingstoke: Palgrave Macmillan, 2007.

Lindemann, Mary. *Patriots and Paupers: Hamburg, 1712-1830*. New York/Oxford: Oxford University Press, 1990.

Lindemann, Mary. *The Merchant Republics Amsterdam, Antwerp, and Hamburg, 1648-1790*. Cambridge: Cambridge University Press, 2017.

Loetz, Francisca. *Mit Gott handeln: von den Zürcher Gotteslästerern der Frühen Neuzeit zu einer Kulturgeschichte des Religiösen*. Göttingen: Vandenhoeck und Ruprecht, 2002.

Lohsträter, Kai. "Hinter den Kulissen eines Schreckenstheaters: Der Fall Jastram und Snitger in der Theatrum-Literatur des 17. Jahrhunderts." In *Theatralität von Wissen in der Frühen Neuzeit*, edited by Nikola Roßbach and Constanze Baum. 2013. http://diglib.hab.de/ebooks/ed000156/id/ebooks_ed000156_article09/start.htm.

Loose, Hans-Dieter. "Das Zeitalter der Bürgerunruhen und der großen europäischen Kriege, 1618-1712." In *Hamburg. Geschichte der Stadt und ihrer Bewohner*, edited by Werner Jochmann and Hans-Dieter Loose, 259-350. Vol. 1. Hamburg: Hoffmann und Campe, 1982.

Loose, Hans-Dieter. *Barthold Heinrich Brockes (1680-1747): Dichter und Ratsherr in Hamburg ; neue Forschungen zu Persönlichkeit und Wirkung*. Hamburg, Hans Christians Verlag, 1980.

Lorenz, Maren. *Kriminelle Körper—Gestörte Gemüter. Die Normierung des Individuums in Gerichtsmedizin und Psychiatrie der Aufklärung*. Hamburg: Hamburger Edition, 1999.

Lott, Arno. *Die Todesstrafen im Kurfürstentum Trier in der frühen Neuzeit*. Frankfurt a.M.: Peter Lang, 1998.

Luebke, David. "Introduction: The Politics of Conversion in Early Modern Germany." In *Conversion and the Politics of Conversion in Early Modern Germany*, edited by David M. Luebke, Jared Oley, Daniel C. Ryan, and David Warren Sabean 1-13. New York: Berghahn Books, 2012.

Luef, Evelyne. "A Matter of Life and Death: Suicide in Early Modern Austria and Sweden (ca. 1650–1750)." Ph.D. diss., University of Vienna, 2016.
Lutz, Kristiane. "Der Stadtteil St. Georg im Wandel. Veränderungen im Wohnquartier aus der Sicht zweier Stadtteil-Vereine." M.A. Thesis, University of Hamburg, 2004. https://www.grin.com/document/47712.
Maasburg, Friedrich Maschek von. *Die Galeerenstrafe in den deutschen und böhmischen Erbländern Oesterreichs: ein Beitrag zur Geschichte der heimischen Strafrechtspflege*. Vienna: Manzsche k. k. Hof-Verlags- und Universitätsbuchhandlung, 1885.
MacCulloch, Diarmaid. *The Reformation*. New York: Viking Penguin, 2003.
Mährle, Wolfgang. "Ellwangen - Hexenverfolgungen." In *Lexikon zur Geschichte der Hexenverfolgung*. Edited by Gudrun Gersmann, Katrin Moeller and Jürgen-Michael Schmidt, in: historicum.net, URL: https://www.historicum.net/purl/jfzqr/.
Mann, Harald Johannes. "Die Barocken Totenbruderschaften." *Zeitschrift für Bayerische Landesgeschichte* 39 (1976): 127-151.
Marti, Susan, and Daniela Mondini. "Ich manen dich der brüsten min, Das du dem sünder wellest milte sin!": Marienbrüste und Marienmilch im Heilsgeschehen." In *Himmel, Hölle, Fegefeuer. Das Jenseits im Mittelalter*, edited by Peter Jezler, 79-90. Munich, Wilhelm Fink Verlag, 1994.
Martignoni, Andrea. "Langue Blasphématoire et Geste Iconoclaste. Blasphèmes et Pouvoirs dans la Terre Ferme Vénitienne à la fin du Moyen Age." *Studi Veneziani* 49 (2005): 79-112.
Martschukat, Jürgen. "Ein Freitod durch die Hand des Henkers. Erörterungen zurKomplementarität von Diskursen und Praktiken am Beispiel von 'Mord aus Lebens-Überdruß' und Todesstrafe im 18. Jahrhundert." *Zeitschrift für historische Forschung* 27 (2000): 53-74.
Martschukat, Jürgen. *Inszeniertes Töten. Eine Geschichte der Todesstrafe vom 17. bis zum 19. Jahrhundert*. Cologne: Böhlau, 2000.
Matsche, Franz. *Die Kunst im Dienst der Staatsidee Kaiser Karls VI.: Ikonographie, Ikonologie und Programmatik des "Kaiserstils."* Vol. 1. Berlin: de Gruyter, 1981.
Maurer, Josef and Georg Kolb. *Marianisches Niederösterreich; Denkwürdigkeiten der Marienverehrung im Lande unter der Enns*. Vienna: "St. Norbertus" Buch- und Kunstdruckerei, 1899.
Mayer-Pfannholz, Anton. *Die heilbringende Schau in Sitte und Kult*. Münster: Aschendorff, 1938.
Mecklenberg-Vorpommern Virtuelles Museum zur Landesgeschichte. "Totenhände (Leibzeichen) in gedrechselter Holzschale aus St. Georgen, Wismar." https://www.landesmuseum-mv.de/exponate/stadtgeschichtliches-museum-wismar/totenhaende-leibzeichen-in-gedrechselter-holzschale-aus-st.-georgen-wismar/index.html.
Meeder, W. L. *Geschichte von Hamburg, vom Entstehen der Stadt bis auf die neueste Zeit*. Vol. 2. Hamburg: J. J. S. Wörmer, 1839.

Merback, Mitchell B. "Fount of mercy, city of blood: cultic anti-Judaism and the Pulkau Passion Altarpiece." *The Art Bulletin* 87 (2005): 589-642.
Merback, Mitchell B. *Pilgrimage and Pogrom: Violence, Memory, and Visual Culture in the Host-Miracle Shrines of Germany and Austria.* Chicago: University of Chicago Press, 2012.
Meyer-Krentler, Eckhardt. *Willkomm und Abschied: Herzschlag und Peitschenhieb: Goethe-Mörike-Heine.* Munich: W. Fink, 1987.
Michalik, Kerstin. *Kindsmord. Sozial und Rechtsgeschichte der Kindstötung im 18. und beginnenden 19. Jahrhundert am Beispiel Preußen.* Pfaffenweiler: Centaurus Verlag, 1997.
Midelfort, H. C. Erik. "Religious Melancholy and Suicide: On the Reformation Origins of a Sociological Steriotype." *Graven Images* 3 (1996): 41-56.
Midelfort, H. C. Erik. *Witch Hunting in Southwestern Germany, 1562-1684. The Social and Intellectual Foundations.* Stanford, CA: Stanford University Press, 1972.
Miettinen, Riikka. *Suicide, Law, and Community in Early Modern Sweden.* Cham, Switzerland: Palgrave Macmillan, 2019.
Milka, Amy. "'Preferring Death': Suicidal Criminals in Eighteenth-Century England." *Eighteenth-Century Studies* 53 (2020): 685-705.
Nendza, Elena. "'Zerhaut, zerreißt, zerschmettert!' *Der Bethlehemitische Kindermord – ein interkonfessionelles Bindeglied in den europäischen Künsten,*" *Daphnis* 45 (2017): 250-273.
Nendza, Elena. *Der Bethlehemitische Kindermord in den Künsten der Frühen Neuzeit: Studien zu Intermedialen und Interkonfessionellen Popularisierungen und Austauschprozessen.* Berlin: Walter de Gruyter, 2020.
Myers, W. David. *'Poor Sinning Folk.' Confession and Conscience in Counter-Reformation Germany.* Ithaca: Cornell University Press, 1996.
Ogris, Werner, "Bahrprobe," in *Lexikon zur Geschichte der Hexenverfolgung*, edited by Gudrun Gersmann, Katrin Moeller und Jürgen-Michael Schmidt, in: historicum.net, https://www.historicum.net/purl/jfzna/.
Olli, Soila-Maria. "Blasphemy in Early Modern Sweden—An Untold Story." *Journal of Religious History* 32 (2008): 457-470.
Opsommer, Rik, and Jos Monballyu. "Damhouder, Joos de." In *Lexikon zur Geschichte der Hexenverfolgung*, edited by Gudrun Gersmann, Katrin Moeller and Jürgen-Michael Schmidt. http://www.historicum.net/no_cache/persistent/artikel/1588/.
Page, Janet K. *Convent Music and Politics in Eighteenth-Century Vienna.* Cambridge: Cambridge University Press, 2014.
Perger, Richard. "Die Baugeschichte des Wiener Schrannengebäudes nach schriftlichen Quellen." *Studien zur Wiener Geschichte. Jahrbuch des Vereins für Geschichte der Stadt Wien* 57/58 (202): 269-299.

Petersen, Chr. "Zioter (Zeter) oder Tiodute (Jodute), der Gott des Kriegs und des Rechts bei den Deutschen. Eine rechtsgeschichtliche und mythologische Untersuchung." In *Forschungen zur deutschen Geschichte*. Edited by Königlich Bayerische Akademie der Wissenschaften. Vol. 6. 1866.

Petersen, Nils Holger. "The Quarant'Ore: Early Modern Ritual and Performativity." In *Performativity and Performance in Baroque Rome*, edited by Peter Gillgren and Mårten Snickare, 115-133. Farnham, Surrey: Ashgate, 2012.

Pizzini, Meinrad. "Ursula Pöck – eine mittelalterliche Ritualmordlegende aus Lienz." *Veröffentlichungen des Tiroler Landesmuseums Ferdinandeum* 70 (1990): 219-234.

Postel, Rainer. "Obrigkeitsdenken und Reformation in Hamburg." *Archiv für Reformationsgeschichte* 70 (1979): 169-201.

Postel, Rainer. "Reformation und Gegenreformation, 1517-1618." In *Hamburg. Geschichte der Stadt und ihrer Bewohner*, edited by Werner Jochmann and Hans-Dieter Loose. Vol. 1. Hamburg: Hoffmann und Campe, 1982.

Prosperi, Adriano. "Consolation or Condemnation: The Debates on Withholding the Sacraments from Prisoners." In *The Art of Executing Well: Rituals of Execution in Renaissance Italy*, edited by Nicholas Terpstra, 98-117. Kirksville, MI: Truman State University Press, 2008.

Prosperi, Adriano. *Infanticide, Secular Justice, and Religious Debate in Early Modern Europe*. Turnhout: Brepols, 2016.

Puff, Helmut. *Sodomy in Reformation German and Switzerland*. Chicago: University of Chicago Press, 2003.

Reeh, Tine and Ralf Hemmingsen. "Common Sense, No Magic: A Case Study of Female Child Murderers in the Eighteenth Century." *1700-tal: Nordic Yearbook for Eighteenth-Century Studies* 15 (2018): 110-134.

Resch, Claudia. "Die kaiserlich-königliche Totenbruderschaft in Wien. 'Bündnuß und höchst Lob-würdige Alliantz' zum Heil der Seelen...." In *Bündnisse. Politische, Soziale und Intellektuelle Allianzen im Jahrhundert der Aufklärung*, edited by Franz M. Eybl, Daniel Fulda, and Johannes Süssmann, 183-194. Vienna: Böhlau, 2019.

Resch, Claudia. "Die Totenbruderschaft von St. Augustin und ihre Totenkapelle(n) - geziert, gemalt und gedruckt für die Ewigkeit...." In *Bruderschaften als multifunktionale Dienstleister der Frühen Neuzeit in Zentraleuropa*, edited by Elisabeth Lobenwein, Martin Scheutz and Alfred Stefan Weiß, 373-393. Vienna: Böhlau, 2018.

Resnick, Irven M. "Cruentation, Medieval Anti-Jewish Polemic, and Ritual Murder." *Antisemitism Studies* 3 (2019): 95-131.

Robisheaux, Thomas. *The Last Witch of Langenburg Murder in a German Village*. New York: W.W. Norton, 2009.

Rodegra, Heinrich, Mary Lindemann and Martin Ehwald. "Kindsmord und verheimlichte Schwangerschaft im 18. Jahrhundert." *Gesnerus* 36 (1978): 276-296.

Roeck, Bernd. "Christlicher Ideal Staat und Hexenwahn. Zum Ende der europäischen Hexenverfolgungen." *Historisches Jahrbuch* 108 (1988): 379-405.
Rogge, Roswitha. "Hexenverfolgung in Hamburg? Schadenzauber im Alltag und in der Justiz." *Geschichte in Wissenschaft und Unterricht* 46 (1995): 381-401.
Rogge, Roswitha. "Schadenszauber, Hexerei und die Waffen der Justiz im frühneuzeitlichen Hamburg." In *Hexerei, Magie und Volksmedizin. Beiträge aus dem Hexenarchiv des Museums für Völkerkunde Hamburg*, edited by Bernd Schmelz, 149-172. Bonn: Holos Verlag, 1997.
Rohling, Geraldine M. "Exequial and Votive Practices of the Viennese *Bruderschaften*: A Study of Music and Liturgical Piety." PhD diss., The Catholic University of America, 1996.
Röpe, Georg Reinhard. *Johann Melchior Goeze. Eine Rettung*. Hamburg: Gustav Eduard Nolte, 1860.
Roper, Lyndal. *Oedipus and the Devil: Witchcraft, Sexuality and Religion in Early Modern Europe*. London: Routledge, 1994.
Roper, Lyndal. *Witch Craze: Terror and Fantasy in Baroque Germany*. New Haven/London: Yale University Press, 2004.
Rowlands, Alison. "In Great Secrecy: The Crime of Infanticide in Rothenburg ob der Tauber, 1501-1618." *German History* 15 (1997): 179-199.
Rowlands, Alison. *Witchcraft Narratives in Germany: Rothenburg, 1561–1652*. Manchester/New York: Manchester University Press, 2003.
Rubin, Miri. *Gentile Tales: The Narrative Assault on late Medieval Jews*. Philadelphia: University of Pennsylvania Press, 1999.
Rublack, Ulinka. *The Crimes of Women in Early Modern Germany*. New York: Oxford University Press, 1999.
Rublack, Ulinka. *The Oxford Handbook of the Protestant Reformations*. Oxford: Oxford University Press, 2017.
Rublack, Hans-Christoph. "Lutherische Beichte und Sozialdisziplinierung." *Archiv für Reformationsgeschichte* 84 (1993): 127–155.
Ruff, Herbert. "Die Margaretha von Pforzheim - Geschichte, Legende, Tradition." In *Ängste und Auswege. Bilder aus Umbruchszeiten in Pforzheim*, vol. 1, edited by Gerhard Brändle, 139-170. Ubstadt-Weiher: Verlag Regionalkultur 2001.
Sabean, David Warren. *Power in the Blood. Popular Culture and Village Discourse in Early Modern Germany*. Cambridge: Cambridge University Press, 1992.
Sabean, David Warren. "Production of the Self during the Age of Confessionalism." *Central European History* 29 (1996): 1-18.
Salvadori, Giovanni. *Die Minoritenkirche und ihre Älteste Umgebung: ein Beitrag zur Geschichte Wiens*. Vienna: Congregation der Italienischen Nationalkirche, 1895.
Schär, Markus. *Seelennöte der Untertanen. Selbstmord, Melancholie und Religion im alten Zürich* (Zurich: Chronos Verlag, 1985).

Scheutz, Martin. "Bruderschaften in Visitationsprotokollen und im Wiener Diarium. Quellen zu einer Geschichte der frühneuzeitlichen Bruderschaften in Österreich." *Acta historiae artis Slovenica* 23 (2018): 245-261.
Scheutz, Martin. "'Hoc disciplinarium...errexit.' Das Wiener Zucht und Arbeitshaus um 1800 – eine Spurensuche." In *Strafe, Diszipline, Besserung. Österreichische Zucht- und Arbeitshäuser von 1750 bis 1850*. Edited by Gerhard Ammerer and Alfred Stefan Weiss, 63-95, 245-251. Frankfurt a.M.: Peter Lang, 2006.
Scheutz, Martin. "Kaiser und Fleischhackerknecht. Städtische Fronleichnamsprozessionen und öffentlicher Raum in Österreich während der Frühen Neuzeit." In *Aspekte der Religiosität in der frühen Neuzeit*, edited by Thomas Aigner, 62-125. St. Pölten: Diözesanarchiv, 2003.
Scheutz, Martin. "Raub, Magie und Hexerei im frühneuzeitlichen Österreich. Das Fallbeispiel Oberösterreich." In *Räuber, Mörder, Teufelsbrüder. Die Kapererbande 1649-1660 im oberösterreichischen Alpenvorland*, edited by Martin Scheutz, Johann Sturm, Josef Weichenberger and Franz Xaver Wimmer, 257-304. Linz: Oberösterreichisches Landesarchiv, 2008.
Schifferle, Rebekka. "Gotteslästerung in der Stadt Basel 1674-1798: ein Werkstattbericht." *Basler Zeitschrift für Geschichte und Altertumskunde* 105 (2005): 131-155.
Schild, Wolfgang. "Gerechtigkeitsbilder." In *Recht und Gerechtigkeit im Spiegel der europäischen Kunst*, edited by Wolfgang Pleister and Wolfgang Schild, 86-171. Cologne: DuMont Buchverlag, 1988.
Schimmer, Gustav Adolph. *Das alte Wien: Darstellung der alten Plätze und merkwürdigsten jetzt grösstentheils verschwundenen Gebäude Wien's nach den seltensten gleichzeitigen Originalen: Mit erläuternden Texte aus den bewährtesten Geschichtsquellen*. Vienna: L.C. Zamarski, 1854.
Schimmer, Karl August. *Ausführliche Häuser-Chronik der innern Stadt Wien: mit einer geschichtlichen Uebersicht sämmtlicher Vorstädte und ihrer merkwürdigsten Gebäude*. Vienna: Kuppitsch, 1849.
Schindler, Georg. *Verbrechen und Strafen im Recht der Stadt Freiburg im Breisgau von der Einführung des neuen Stadtrechts bis zum Übergang an Baden (1520-1806)*. Freiburg: Kommissionsverlag der Fr. Wagnerschen Universitätsbuchhandlung, 1937.
Schindler, Norbert. *Rebellion, Community and Custom in Early Modern Germany*. Translated by Pamela E. Selwyn. Cambridge: Cambridge University Press, 2002.
Schlager, J. E. *Wiener Skizzen aus dem Mittelalter (Neue Folge)*. Vol. 2. Vienna: Gerold, 1842.
Schmid, Alfred A., ed. *Die Schweizer Bilderchronik des Diebold Schilling*. Faksimile-Verlag: Luzern, 1981.
Schmidt-Kohberg, Karin. "'und hat sich selbesten an einen Strickhalfter hingehenckt...' Selbstmord im Herzogtum Württemberg im 17. und 18.

Jahrhundert." In *Zauberer—Selbstmörder—Schatzsucher. Magische Kultur und behördliche Kontrolle im frühneuzeitlichen Württemberg*, edited by Johannes Dillinger, 113-220. Trier: Kliomedia, 2003.

Schnabel-Schüle, Helga. *Überwachen und Strafen im Territorialstaat. Bedingungen und Auswirkungen des Systems strafrechtlicher Sanktionen im frühneuzeitlichen Württemberg*. Cologne: Böhlau, 1997.

Schramm, Percy Ernst. *Hamburg, ein Sonderfall in der Geschichte Deutschlands*. Hamburg: H. Christians Verlag, 1964.

Schuster, Peter and Andrea Bendlage, eds., *Die Letzten Tage der Zum Tode Verurteilten. Das Tagebuch des Nürnberger Gefangenenseelsorgers Johann Hagendorn 1605-1620*. Münster: Verlag für Regionalgeschichte, 2022.

Schuster, Peter. *Verbrecher, Opfer, Heilige eine Geschichte des Tötens 1200-1700*. Stuttgart: Klett-Cotta, 2015.

Schroubek, Georg R. "Andreas von Rinn. Der Kult eines 'heiligen Ritualmordopfers' im historischen Wandel," *Österreichische Zeitschrift für Volkskunde*, XLIX/98 (1995): 371-396.

Schwerhoff, Gerd. "Gott und die Welt herausfordern. Theologische Konstruktion, rechtliche Bekämpfung und soziale Praxis der Blasphemie vom 13. bis zum Beginn des 17. Jahrhunderts." Habilitationsschrift, Universität Bielefeld, 1996.

Schwerhoff, Gerd. *Zungen wie Schwerter. Blasphemie in alteuropäischen Gesellschaften 1200-1650*. Konstanz: Universitätsverlag Konstanz, 2005.

Sellert, W. "Urfehde." In *HRG*, 562-570. Vol. 5. Berlin: Erich Schmidt Verlag, 1998.

Sluhovsky, Moshe. *Becoming a New Self: Practices of Belief in Early Modern Catholicism*. Chicago: University of Chicago Press, 2017.

Sommer, Clemens. "Apotheose." In *Reallexikon zur deutschen Kunstgeschichte*, 842-852. Stuttgart: J.B. Metzler, 1937.

Sperling, Jutta. "Squeezing, Squirting, Spilling Milk: The Lactation of Saint Bernard and the Flemish Madonna Lactans (ca. 1430-1530)." *Renaissance Quarterly* 17 (2018): 868-918.

Sperling, Katja. "Christoph Murers Glasgemälde für den Rat und für Patrizierfamilien der Stadt Nürnberg." M.A. Thesis, Friedrich-Alexander-Universität Erlangen-Nürnberg, 1991.

Spierenburg, Pieter. *The Prison Experience: Disciplinary Institutions and their Inmates in Early Modern Europe*. New Brunswick: Rutgers University Press, 1991.

Spierenburg, Pieter. *The Spectacle of Suffering: Executions and the Evolution of Repression: From a Preindustrial Metropolis to the European Experience*. Cambridge: Cambridge University Press, 1984.

Spraggon, Julie. *Puritan Iconoclasm During the English Civil War: The Attack on Religious Imagery by Parliament and Its Soldiers*. Woodbridge: Boydell & Brewer, 2003.

Stekl, Hannes. *Österreichs Zucht- und Arbeitshäuser, 1671-1920. Institutionen zwischen Fürsorge und Sozialdisziplinierung.* Vienna: Verlag für Geschichte und Politik, 1978.
Stephens, Walter. *Demon Lovers: Witchcraft, Sex, and the Crisis of Belief.* Chicago: University of Chicago Press, 2003.
Stokes, Laura. *Demons of Urban Reform: Early European Witch Trials and Criminal Justice, 1430–1530.* New York: Palgrave Macmillan, 2011.
Stopp, F. J. "Verbum Domini Manet in Aeternum. The Dissemination of a Reformation Slogan, 1522-1904." In *Essays in German Culture and Society*. Edited by Siegbert S. Prawer, R. Hinton Thomas and Leonard Forster, 123-235. London, Institute of Germanic Studies, 1969.
Streng, Adolf. *Geschichte der Gefängnissverwaltung in Hamburg von 1622-1872.* Hamburg: Verlagnsanstalt und Druckerei Aktien-Gesellschaft, 1890.
Strom, Jonathan. *German Pietism and the Problem of Conversion.* University Park, USA: Penn State University Press, 2018.
Strom, Jonathan. "Pietist Conversion Narratives and Confessional Identity." In *Conversion and the Politics of Religion in Early Modern Germany*, edited by David M. Luebke, Jared Poley, Daniel C. Ryan and David Warren Sabean, 135-152. New York: Berghahn Books, 2012.
Stuart, Kathy. *Defiled Trades and Social Outcasts: Honor and Ritual Pollution in Early Modern Germany.* Cambridge: Cambridge University Press, 1999.
Stuart, Kathy. "Suicide by Proxy: The Unintended Consequences of Public Executions in Eighteenth-Century Germany," *Central European History* 41 (2008): 413-445.
Stuart, Kathy. "Melancholy Murderers: Suicide by Proxy and the Insanity Defense," in *Ideas and Cultural Margins in Early Modern Germany: Essays in Honor of H.C. Erik Midelfort.* Edited by Robin Barnes and Marjorie Plummer, 67-73. Aldershot, Hambleton: Ashgate, 2009.
Sturm, Johann. "Die Schlierbacher Ketzerbilder." In *Räuber, Mörder, Teufelsbrüder. Die Kapererbande 1649-1660 im oberösterreichischen Alpenvorland.* Edited by Martin Scheutz, Johann Sturm, Josef Weichenberger and Franz Xaver Wimmer, 93-168. Linz: Oberösterreichisches Landesarchiv, 2008.
Sturm, Walter. "...außer der Linie": Favoriten am Wienerberg; Beiträge zur Topographie und Siedlungsgeschichte im Raum des heutigen Wiener Gemeindebezirks Favoriten, *Favoritner Museumsblätter* 30 (2004).
Terpstra, Nicholas. "Introduction: The Other Side of the Scaffold." In *The Art of Executing Well: Rituals of Execution in Renaissance Italy.* Edited by Nicholas Terpstra, 1-9. Kirksville, MI: Truman State University Press, 2008.
Teter, Magda. *Blood Libel: On the Trail of an Antisemitic Myth.* Cambridge, Mass.: Harvard University Press, 2020.
Theopold, Wilhelm. *Das Kind in Der Votivmalerei.* Munich: K. Thiemig, 1981.
Timmermann, Achim. *Memory and Redemption: Public Monuments and the Making of the Late Medieval Landscape.* Turnout: Brepols, 2017.

Tlusty, B. Ann. *Bacchus and Civic Order: The Culture of Drink in Early Modern Germany.* Charlottesville: University of Virginia Press, 2001.

Tlusty, B. Ann. "Bravado, Martial Magic, and Masculine Performance in Early Modern Germany." In *Rethinking Europe: War and Peace in the Early Modern German Lands.* Edited by Gerhild Scholz Williams, Sigrun Haude, and Christian Schneider, 9-38. Leiden: Brill, 2019.

Tlusty, B. Ann. "Invincible Blades and Invulnerable Bodies: Weapons Magic in Early Modern Germany." *European Review of History* 22 (215): 658-679.

Tlusty, B. Ann. *The Martial Ethic in Early Modern Germany: Civic Duty and the Right of Arms.* New York: Palgrave Macmillan, 2011.

Tomasini, Floris. *Remembering and Dismembering the Dead: Posthumous Punishment, Harm and Redemption over Time.* London: Palgrave Macmillan, 2017.

Tomek, Ernst. "Das kirchliche Leben und die christliche Charitas in Wien." In *Geschichte der Stadt Wien.* Edited by Alterthumsvereine zu Wien, 160-330. Vol. 5. Vienna: Verlag des Altertums Vereines zu Wien, 1914.

Towers, S., et al, "Contagion in Mass Killings and School Shootings," *PLOS ONE* 10 (2015): e0117259.

Treue, Wolfgang. *Der Trienter Judenprozess. Voraussetzungen, Abläufe, Auswirkungen (1475-1588).* Hannover: Hahn, 1996.

Tschackert, Paul. "Sturm, Christoph Christian." In *Allgemeine Deutsche Biographie,* edited by Historische Kommission bei der Bayerischen Akademie der Wissenschaften, vol. 37 (1894): 4–5, https://de.wikisource.org/w/index.php?title=ADB:Sturm,_Christoph_Christian&oldid=-.

Troescher, Georg. "Weltgerichtsbilder in Rathäusern und Gerichtsstätten." *Westdeutsches Jahrbuch für Kunstgeschichte: Wallraf-Richartz Jahrbuch* 11 (1939): 139-214.

Trummer, Carl. *Vorträge über Tortur, Hexenverfolgungen, Vehmgerichte, und andere merkwürdige Erscheinungen in der Hamburgischen Rechtsgeschichte.* Vol. 1. Hamburg: Johann August Meißner, 1844.

Tucker, Elisabeth. "Farben, Farbsymbolik." In *Enzyklopädie des Märchens. Handwörterbuch zur historischen und vergleichenden Erzählforschung,* edited by Rolf Wilhelm Brednich, 840-863. Vol 4. Berlin: de Gruyter, 1984.

Tuczay, Christa Agnes. "Herzesser und andere Schurken. Medialer Transfer kriminellen Aberglaubens." *Medienimpulse* 59 (2021): 1-28.

Ulbricht, Otto. "Criminality and Punishment of the Jews in the Early Modern Period." In *In and Out of the Ghetto. Jewish-Gentile Relations in Late Medieval and Early Modern Germany,* edited by R. Po-Chia Hsia and Hartmut Lehmann, 49-70. Cambridge: Cambridge University Press, 2002.

Ulbricht, Otto. "Kindmörderinnen vor Gericht. Verteidigungsstrategien von Frauen in Norddeutschland 1680-1810." In *Mit den Waffen der Justiz. Zur Kriminalitätsgeschichte des späten Mittelalters und der frühen Neuzeit,* edited by Andreas Blauert and Gerd Schwerhoff, 54-85. Frankfurt a. M.: Fischer Taschenbuch Verlag, 1993.

Ulbricht, Otto. *Kindsmord und Aufklärung in Deutschland.* Munich: R. Oldenbourg Verlag, 1990.

University of Heidelberg. "Schranne." *Deutsches Rechtswörterbuch (DRW).* https://drw-www.adw.uni-heidelberg.de/drw-cgi/zeige?index=lemmata&term=schranne.

University of Vienna. "Kriminalität in und um Wien 1703 bis 1803. Eine Datenbank." Last modified 2010. https://homepage.univie.ac.at/susanne.hehenberger/kriminaldatenbank/.

Valentinitsch, Helfried. "Der Vorwurf der Hostienschändung in den innerösterreichischen Hexen-und Zaubereiprozessen (16.-18. Jahrhundert)." *Zeitschrift des historischen Vereines für Steiermark* 78 (1987): 5-14.

Vignau-Wolberg, Thea. *Christoph Murer und die "XL Emblemata Miscella Nova."* Bern: Benteli Verlag, 1982.

Vignau-Wilberg, Thea. "Zur Entstehung zweier Emblemata von Christoph Murer." *Anzeiger des Germanischen Nationalmuseums* (1977): 85-94.

Vitoduranus, Johannes. "Die Chronik des Minderbruders Johannes von Winthertur III." *Neujahrs-Blatt der Bürgerbibliothek in Winterthur* 22 (1861): 137-212.

Vocelka, Karl and Lynne Heller. *Die Lebenswelt der Habsburger. Kultur- und Mentalitätsgeschichte einer Familie.* Graz: Styria, 1997.

Vocelka, Karl. *Glanz und Untergang der Höfischen Welt. Repräsentation, Reform und Reaktion im Habsburgischen Vielvölkerstaat.* Vienna: Ueberreuter, 2001.

Wallman, Johannes. *Pietismus Studien. Gesammelte Aufsätze.* Vol. 2. Tübingen: Mohr Siebeck, 2008.

Wandell, Lee Palmer. "Bildersturm im Elsaß." In *Macht und Ohnmacht der Bilder. reformatorischer Bildersturm im Kontext der europäischen Geschichte,* edited by Peter Blickle and André Holenstein, 165-175. Munich: Oldenbourg, 2002.

Wasyliw, Patricia Healy. *Martyrdom, Murder, and Magic: Child Saints and their Cults in Medieval Europe.* New York: P. Lang, 2008.

Watt, Jeffrey R. *Choosing Death: Suicide and Calvinism in Early Modern Geneva.* Kirksville: Truman State University Press, 2001.

Weber, H von. "Selbstmord als Mordmotiv." *Monatsschrift für Kriminalbiologie und Strafrechtsreform* 28, no. 4 (1937): 161-181.

Wegert, Karl. *Popular Culture, Crime, and Social Control in 18th-Century Württemberg.* Stuttgart: Franz Steiner Verlag, 1994.

Weigl, Andreas. "Frühneuzeitliche Bevölkerungswachstum." In *Wien. Geschichte einer Stadt,* edited by Peter Csendes and Ferdinand Opll. Vienna: Bölau, 2003.

Weiß, Alfred Stefan. "'Karbatsch=Streiche zur künftigen Besserung.' Das Klagenfurter Zucht- und Arbeitshaus 1755-1813," in *Strafe, Disziplin und Besserung. Osterreichische Zucht- und Arbeitshäuser von 1750 bis 1850.* Edited by Gerhard Ammerer and Alfred Stefan Weiß, 167-194. Frankfurt am Main: Lang, 2006.

Weiß, Karl. *Geschichte der öffentlichen Anstalten, Fonde und Stiftungen für die Armenversorgung in Wien*. Vienna: Selbstverlag des Gemeinderathes, 1867.
Wellershoff-von Thadden, Maria. "Caritas," in *Reallexikon zur Deutschen Kunstgeschichte*, 543-356. Vol. 3. Stuttgart: J.B. Metzler, 1954.
Werkmüller, D. "Klage mit dem Toten Mann." In *HDR*. Vol. 2, 849-851.
Whaley, Joachim. *Religious Toleration and Social Change in Hamburg, 1529-1819*. Cambridge: Cambridge University Press, 1985.
Wiechmann, Ralf, Eilin Einfeldt, and Klaus Püschel. "'...Man soll ihnen ihre Köpfe abschlagen und sie auf einen Stock nageln.' Die Piratenschädel von Grasbrook." In *Klaus Störtebeker. Ein Mythos wird Entschlüsselt*, edited by Ralf Wiechmann, Günter Bräuer and Klaus Püschel, 79-118. Munich: Wilhelm Fink Verlag, 2003.
Wien Geschichte Wiki. "Spinnerin am Kreuz." Last modified April 4, 2022. https://www.geschichtewiki.wien.gv.at/index.php?title=Spinnerin_am_Kreuz&oldid=824866.
Wilflingseder, Franz. "Gestalten des heimischen Aberglaubens. Aus Kriminalakten der Herrschaft Spital am Pyhrn vom 16. Bis zum 18. Jahrhundert," *Jahrbuch der oberösterreichischen Musealvereines* 112 (1967): 117-60.
Wilhelm-Schaffer, Irmgad. *Gottes Beamter und Spielmann des Teufels. Der Tod im Spätmittelalter und Früher Neuzeit*. Cologne: Böhlau, 1999.
Wiltenburg, Joy. *Crime and Culture in Early Modern Germany*. Charlottesville: University of Virginia Press, 2012.
Winkelbauer, Thomas. *Ständefreiheit und Fürstenmacht: Länder und Untertanen des Hauses Habsburg im konfessionellen Zeitalter*. Vienna: Uebberreuter, 2003.
Witzmann, Nora. *Gnadenreiches Jesulein. Jesukindverehrung in der Andachtsgraphik*. Vienna: Österreichisches Museum für Volkskund, 1998.
Wolfsgruber, Cölestin. *Geschichte der Loretokapelle bei St. Augustin in Wien*. Vienna: Alfred Hölder, 1886.
Wosnik, Richard. *Beiträge zur Hamburgischen Kriminalgeschichte*. Hamburg: Selbstverlag, 1926.
Yeivin, Ze'ev, Alfred Rubens, and Miriam Nick. "Dress." In *Encyclopaedia Judaica*, edited by Michael Berenbaum and Fred Skolnik. Vol. 6. 2nd edition. Detroit: Macmillan Reference USA, 2007, 12-17.
Yildiz, Muhammed, et al, "Suicide Contagion, Gender, and Suicide Attempts among Adolescents," *Death Studies* 43 (2019): 365-371.
Zeder, Isabelle D. "'mit flehenlich bitten man soll ir einen tod anthüen': Selbstbezichtigungen während der frühneuzeitlichen Hexenverfolgung als 'suicide by trial'." MA Thesis, Universität Basel, Philosophisch-Historische Fakultät, 2018.
Zeder, Isabelle. "Selbstbezichtigungen während der Hexenverfolgung als 'suicide by trial.' Eine Fallstudie aus Reutlingen," *Reutlinger Geschichtsblätter* 60 (2021): 77-115.

Zika, Charles. "Cannibalism and Witchcraft in Early Modern Europe: Reading the Visual Images." *History Workshop Journal* 11 (1997): 77-105.

Zika, Charles. *The Appearance of Witchcraft: Print and Visual Culture in sixteenth-century Europe.* London/New York: Routledge, 2007.

Zika, Charles. "Hosts, Processions and Pilgrimages in Fifteenth-century Germany." *Past and Present* 118 (1988): 25-64.

Index[1]

A

Abortion, 46, 123, 321, 356
Abraham, 54
  See also Isaac
Abraham a Sancta Clara, 239, 359n75, 366
Absolution, 18, 19, 52, 158, 245, 369, 398
Adultery, 7, 9n24, 44, 99, 102, 123, 356
Allegory of good government, 1, 3, 5, 6, 19, 34
Amentia occulta, 203
Ammon, Anton Lorenz, 197–201, 200n188, 208
Amsterdam, 80, 147
Anderl of Rinn, 60–62
Anglicans/Anglicanism, 30
Anna Rosina, 215, 280, 280n55, 356
Aries, Philippe, 83
Ars moriendi, 368

Arson, 9, 9n25, 32, 47, 64n93, 106, 123, 168
Augsburg, 14, 16, 20, 42, 52n49, 52n50, 60, 62, 64n93, 73, 83–86, 88, , 91, 236, 282
Augustinian Eremites, 288, 358
  See also Discalced Augustinians
Austria, Lower, 22, 25, 219, 233, 249n129, 251, 257, 259, 263, 278n47, 281, 283, 284, 287, 302, 310n146, 317, , 338, 339
Austria, Upper, 16, 22, 46, 47, 74, 249n129, 251, 253, 254, 280n56, 302, 303, 316, 338

B

B., Barbara Catharina, 305
Bacher, Benedikt, 383, 390
Bamberg, 3

---

[1] Note: Page numbers followed by 'n' refer to notes.

© The Author(s), under exclusive license to Springer Nature Switzerland AG 2023
K. Stuart, *Suicide by Proxy in Early Modern Germany*, World Histories of Crime, Culture and Violence,
https://doi.org/10.1007/978-3-031-25244-0

Banishment, 46–48, 133, 158, 210,
213, 214, 236, 263, 292, 302,
304, 310, 310n145, 317, 389
Baptism, 54, 198, 316, 339
Basel, 23, 213
Bavaria, 3, 14–16, 22, 30, 143n6,
218, 222, 222n45, 250, 260
Beccaria, Cesare, 141
Beckensteinerin, Maria Elisabetha, 85
Beer, Johann Christoph, 124n87, 131,
132, 132n116
Beggars/begging, 12, 31, 41, 63, 64,
81, 149, 150, 237, 250, 253,
258, 270, 273, 289, 293, 304,
316, 319, 320, 355
Beheading, 7, 24, 25, 37, 38, 40, 49,
66, 80, 87, 89, 102, 107, 111,
113, 115, 119–121, 126, 133,
135, 155, 161, 166, 169, 172,
175, 176, 184, 188, 189, 195,
201, 205, 207, 209, 213, 258,
277, 280, 280n55, 282, 286,
287, 289, 306, 310, 316, 334,
338, 351, 371, 378–380,
384, 389,
Behnke, Marten, 144
Behont, Maria, 122, 123,
123n83, 145
Behringer, Wolfgang, 45, 222n45,
250, 285
Berger, Andreas, 23, 23n84
Berlin, 21, 30, 67n102, 71,
401n17, 402
Bertz, Jeremias, 84, 85n167
Bertzel, Hans, 63
Besche, Cord, 107, 108
Bestiality, 9, 23, 24, 30, 32, 37,
43–48, 43n21, 52, 52n50,
52n51, 53, 396, 397n5,
Beyn, Hans Jakob, 189–191
Bigamy, 123, 168, 356
Blasphemia realis, 215, 282, 308

Blasphemia verbalis, 215
Blasphemy, 30, 32, 95, 103, 109, 110,
110n51, 210–218, 212n5,
215n19, 220, 221n41, 229,
241–243, 246–248, 247n124,
251, 257, 259, 275, 277,
279–282, 284–287, 289–293,
295n103, 296, 301–303,
302n124, 305, 306, 308n142,
311–321, 324–328, 330, 352,
397, 398,
Bleken, Abelke, 106
Blood, 7, 13, 49, 54, 58, 59, 62,
65n95, 66, 69, 72, 77, 79,
87–89, 120, 122, 124–126, 130,
131, 163, 173, 184, 200, 201,
248, 254, 255, 259, 303, 339,
340, 350, 351, 381, 388, 400
Blood libel, 4, 33, 55, 58, 60, 62, 63,
80, 81, 121, 122, 122n82,
132, 132n116
Bohemia, 221, 230, 233, 242n106,
348, 349
Boldt, Margarethe Eleonore, 402
Brandenburg, 21
Bratsch, Franz Joseph, 305, 316
Breaking by the wheel, 87n171, 111,
145, 146, 155, 176, 184, 189,
207, 313, 389
Bremmelin, Gertrude Magdalena, 72,
84, 89n176
Briggs, Robin, 42, 43
Brockes, Barthold Heinrich, 55, 56
Brown, Edward, 378
Bruns, Maria, 169
Bugenhagen, Johannes, 94, 116,
116n67, 117, 137, 143n5,
190, 193
Bunzlau, 66
Burial, 12, 14–17, 35, 40, 117, 129,
141, 142, 143n5, 143n6, 144,
175, 177, 179, 181–183, 186,

189, 191, 198, 202, 237, 254,
342, 353n62, 359, 360n80, 367,
377, 381, 385, 391, 393
See also Funeral
Bützer, Hans, 48–50, 52, 397n5,

C

Calvinist, 23, 28, 32, 95n12,
216, 223
See also Reformed
Canisius, Petrus, 358
Capital punishment, 34, 38, 69, 71,
93, 113, 115, 132, 137, 329,
333, 340, 353, 354, 386, 390,
393, 400, 401
See also Executions
Carinthia, 249n129, 250, 260, 302
Carolina, 117, 124, 127, 139n1, 196,
255, 256
Carpents, Elisabeth Margareta, 162
Carpzov, Benedikt, 17, 44
Carstens, Johann Christian,
188, 189
Catechism, 155, 156, 185, 194, 272,
293, 294, 358
Catholic/Catholicism, 3, 5, 8, 10, 12,
13, 16, 18, 20, 22, 28, 31,
31n121, 32, 34, 35, 37–39, 42,
45, 46, 53n54, 54, 56, 57, 59,
60, 63, 64n93, 67–74, 76, 85,
93, 95, 95n12, 110, 117, 140,
143, 147, 148, 157, 192, 198,
198n184, 210–214, 216–218,
221, 222n44, 223, 227, 231,
233n77, 236, 238n95, 239, 240,
243, 245, 246, 253, 255, 258,
262, 265, 273, 279, 322, 325,
327, 329, 330, 333, 334, 351,
357, 358, 367, 371, 379,
386, 388, 388n169, 397,
398, 401

Cellensis, Anna Wadlin, 332,
332n8, 348n50
Ceremony, 13, 94, 99, 100, 125,
127–130, 131n111, 135–137,
139n1, 142, 164, 178–180, 186,
189, 196, 371, 380, 384, 391
See also Ritual
Charles V, Emperor, 9n24, 117,
242n106, 255
Charles VI, Emperor, 55, 282,
287–290, 297, 300, 313, 314,
316, 336, , 361
Child/children, 2, 37, 91, 140,
165–168, 181–189, 197–205,
208, 210, 211, 230, 265, 329,
395–401, 397n5,
401n17, 403–406
Christ, 19, 54, 57, 65n95, 67n102,
68, 85, 89, 103, 105, 116, 152,
163, 216, 224, 227, 240, 254,
258, 264, 264n4, 269, 303, 319,
340, 360, 367, 369–373, 379,
392, 393
Christ Child, 3, 54, 57, 57n66, 170,
215, 259, 279, 325, 326, 336
Church robbery, 255–257, 295n103,
303, 304, 317, 317n171, 357
Claessen, Johann, 176
Clauß, Rode, 107
Clergy, 27, 37, 53n54, 68–73,
70n110, 95, 95n12, 113–117,
126, 130, 131n115, 190–193,
201, 207, 228, 288, 289, 295,
298, 299, 304, 330, 351,
360n80, 367, 380, 385,
401, 401n17
Cologne, 213, 218
Communion, 157, 158, 160, 198,
215, 236–238, 237n90, 238n95,
252, 258, 262, 280, 281, 284,
286, 326, 336, 336n22, 352
See also Eucharist; Lord's Supper

Confession (denomination),
  18, 32, 65
Confession (judicial), 11, 18, 31, 37,
  46, 47, 58, 69, 70, 126, 127,
  303, 331, 348, 370
Confession (ritual or sacrament), 12,
  18, 68, 69, 127, 128, 157, 158,
  236, 237, 303, 331, 332,
  369, 371
Confraternity of the Dead, 34, 247,
  327, 342, 353, 353n62, 361,
  363, 364, 367, 368, 377–379,
  381, 381n155, 383–386, 391,
  392, 401
Conscience, 7n16, 31, 44, 48, 59, 70,
  120, 121, 258, 262–328, 348
Consilium/consilia, 32, 44, 45, 53,
  63n89, 79
Copenhagen, 23, 28
Cordes, Anneken, 133
Coreth, Anna, 221, 223
Corpus Christi procession, 79,
  226–229, 236, 238,
  241–243, 253
Corpus delicti, 44–47, 70, 128, 285,
  331, 332, 348, 352
Counter-Reformation, 35, 139, 221,
  227, 236, 238, 240, 241,
  253, 325
Crimen exceptum, 44–46
Crucifix, 20, 35, 48, 53, 75, 209–211,
  209n1, 215–218, 229, 233,
  233n77, 233n80, 236, 241, 243,
  245, 247, 248n127, 259,
  262–329, 342n34, 364, 368,
  370, 374, 376, 377, 380, 382,
  383, 389, 390, 392, 393, 398
Cruentation, 83, 125–127, 125n92,
  127n98, 129, 130n107, 131,
  132, 132n116
  See also Ordeal of the bier
Cult of images, 35, 211, 397

D

D., Margaretha, 366
Damhouder, Joos de, 17, 18, 321,
  322n185, , 323, 324
Damnation, 9, 12, 17–19, 33, 52, 93,
  113, 158, 167, 194, 208, 237,
  369, 398, 404
Danish, 26, 143n5, 145
Danker, Uwe, 275
Danzig, 213, 320n175, 403
Darnton, Robert, 180
Davies, Owen, 38n1, 318
Davis, Natalie Zemon, 83
Decapitation, 107, 109n48, 114, 165,
  166, 381, 389, 393
  See also Beheading
Decree, 70, 179, 180, 182, 187, 188,
  217n32, 228, 238, 241, 263,
  266, 270n19, 272, 275,
  276n42, 292–294, 296n104,
  297, 297n109, 298, 301,
  303, 304, 310n146, 313,
  314, 344, 379n147,
  388–391, 393
Deggendorf, 260
Delrio, Martin, 252
Demon/demonic, 8, 38, 39, 73, 99,
  101, 106, 243, 251, 259, 290,
  326, 371
Demonic possession, 284
Demonology/demonologists,
  216, 252
Denmark, 26, 28, 94, 94n9, 95n12,
  400, 401, 401n15
Deportation, 210, 237, 275,
  295, 295n103, 301,
  302n124, 389
Depression, 74, 182–184, 204, 298,
  313, 335
  See also Melancholy/melancholic
Desecration, 13, 15, 20, 35, 40, 42,
  62, 93, 102, 107, 117, 136,

140–144, 167, 172, 211, 216, 218, 239, 241–263, 260n177, 280, 281, 286, 303, 313, 317, 322, 327, 328, 332, 352, 376, 396, 397
Despair, 8, 41, 73, 91, 124, 125, 143, 143n6, 144, 146, 165, 176, 186, 188, 195, 203, 233n80, 275, 285, 301, 312, 314, 318, 346, 368
Dessau, 31
Deterrence, 13, 89, 99, 140, 177, 195, 273, 287, 292
Devil, 7, 8, 12, 13, 38, 38n1, 40–43, 49, 72–74, 106, 110, 131, 150, 158, 163, 171, 208, 242, 251, 255, 258, 260, 269, 322, 370, 396
  See also Evil enemy; Satan
Devil's pact, 42, 43
Diabolism, 101, 251
Dippoldiswalde, 48
Discalced Augustinians, 358
Discipline/disciplining/disciplinary, 10, 11, 13, 32, 38, 93, 103, 136, 140, 148, 152, 158, 161, 172, 207, 253, 276, 277, 293, 307, 310, 326, 397
  See also Policing
Dishonor, 16, 17, 149, 149n29, 160, 167, 177, 178, 189, 205, 226, 351, 400
Dismas, 68n104, 369
  See also Good thief
Dittmers, Anna Ilsabe, 173, 175
Donauwörth, 83
Dovings, Giesel, 111
Dreckmann, Hinrich, 117
Dresden, 147
Dülmen, Richard van, 276
Dunkel, Anne Rosine, 402
Durkheim, Emile, 27, 73

E

Ebel, Anna Maria, 403–405, 403n24
Edict, 24–26, 54, 75, 173, 175, 185, 187, 210, 236, 236n84, 251, 287–289, 292, 298, 301, 308, 338, 338n28, 340, 352, 400, 400n13, 401, 401n15
Edlauer, Georg, 74, 75
Eger, 281
Eilers, Engelen, 133
Eleonora Gonzaga of Mantua, 219, 359
Ellwangen, 39, 40, 45, 396
Emblin, Anna, 69, 70, 70n110
Endingen, 63, 64
Engelberger, Ferdinand Franz, 243, 243n110, 245–248, 247n124, 277, 327, 374n129
England, 22, 29, 30, 38n1, 76, 129, 318, 322n186, 381
Enlightenment, 30, 63, 97, 106, 140, 192, 218, 259, 311, 312, 315, 405
Enns, 254, 263
Enthusiasm, 147, 191, 205, 404
Eucharist, 18, 66, 115, 116, 157, 223, 224, 226, 227, 229, 236, 237n90, 238–242, 245, 253, 257, 332, 345, 358, 369, 386
Evil enemy, *see* Devil; Satan
Executioner, 4n8, 6, 7, 13, 14, 16, 34, 38, 57, 60, 69, 71, 82, 94, 101–103, 108, 111, 113, 114, 119–121, 124, 128, 129, 135, 139n1, 142, 143n5, 144, 147, 149, 155, 155n52, 158, 160, 160n68, 161, 164–167, 169n95, 173, 175, 177–182, 185, 186, 188, 195, 207–210, 231, 233n77, 247n124, 258, 280n55, 300, 308, 312, 313, 316, 332–334, 371, 372, 374, 374n129, 376–378, 380, 381, 384–386, 389, 391, 400

454 INDEX

Execution rates, 6, 93, 102, 103, 118, 137, 353–357
Executions, 4n8, 37, 91, 139, 209, 275, 329, 353–357, 397, 398, 401, 401n17, 402, 404–406
Ex voto, 62, 224, 392

F
Faltzer, David, 189
Faust, 405
Felons/felony, 6, 18, 35, 59, 94, 99, 101, 102, 106–110, 115, 116, 118, 123, 127–129, 136, 137, 139n1, 140, 149, 158, 159, 168, 179–181, 220, 274, 304, 311, 314, 315, 333, 340, 351, 352, 372, 378, 400
Ferdinand II, Holy Roman Emperor, 219, 228, 229, 263, 359–361, 363, 375
Ferdinand III, Holy Roman Emperor, 219, 225, 360, 361, 366
Ferdinandea, 219, 219n36, 220, 247n124, 251, 252, 256, 277, 279, 280, 287, 305, 311, 312, 315, 316, 321, 322n186, 325
Finck, Johann, 40
Finland, 23
Flor, Agnes Julia, 162–164, 162n76
Forgerin, Christina, 11, 11n28, 20n61
Formstreith, Johann Carl, 280
Fornication, 10, 44, 47, 95, 149, 161, 279, 356
Fourth Lateran Council, 126
France, 22, 42, 320
Franciscans, 7, 71n113, 231, 232, 271, 293, 295, 368
Franconia, 241, 249
Franke, August Hermann, 18
Frankenhauserin, Maria Anna, 297n109, 302

Frederick II of Prussia, 405
Frederick the Wise, 55
Freiburg im Breisgau, 249n129, 317
Freistadt, Upper Austria, 46, 316
Fresen, Anna, 145, 145n14
Freyin, Anna, 7, 7n15, 8, 11, 20n61, 38, 39, 57
Frisch, Andre, 216, 296
Fritsch, Hans Georg, 216, 281
Fuhrmann, Matthias, 241, 242, 242n105, 242n106, 266, 288
Funeral, 12, 13, 15, 65n95, 142, 198–200, 381, 391, 401
See also Burial
Furch, Hans Michael, 81, 395

G
G., Anna Maria, 176, 177, 184
G., Melchior, 317
Gallows, 14, 38, 101, 107, 108, 111, 113, 142, 173, 175, 177, 178, 181, 303, 317, 340, 342, 342n34, 343, 353n62, 388, 389, 393, 400
Garmers, Johann, 134, 135
Gaskill, Malcolm, 83
Gassenrecht, 99
See also "Justice of the Street"
Geier, Martin, 147
Gender, 9, 11, 75, 76, 106, 106n40, 118n76, 141, 170, 188, 205, 206, 211, 220, 250, 251n139, 319–327, 353–357, 406
Giftschütz, Franz, 390
Glanzin, Regina, 379
Goethe, Johann Wolfgang von, 405
Goeze, Johann Melchior, 116n67, 130, 131n111, 141, 182, 192–196, 201
Good thief, 68, 68n104, 194, 369, 373

INDEX 455

Gößler, Hinrich, 172
Götsch, Hermann, 179
Government/governmental/
 governance, 1, 2, 4–6, 8–10, 15,
 18, 19, 24, 25, 30, 33–35, 43,
 45, 47, 48, 51, 53, 57, 62, 63,
 69, 70, 71n113, 76, 89, 92–98,
 95n12, 102, 103, 105–109, 127,
 136, 137, 140–142, 144, 147,
 155, 175, 177–180, 182, 183,
 185, 187, 190–193, 195, 196,
 201, 207, 210, 212, 214,
 217n32, 219, 236, 237, 248,
 251, 262, 264, 275–306,
 276n42, 311, 313–318,
 329–331, 336, 338–347, 357,
 360, 361, 375, 376, 387–392,
 397, 398, 400, 405, 406
Grace, 12, 18, 35, 38, 40, 49, 65, 66,
 68, 72, 73, 108, 116, 143,
 163, 191, 194, 222,
 301, 366
Graf, Urs, 38, 39
Grallin, Maria Susanna, 284,
 284n69, 285
Graveyard, 12, 13, 15, 16, 70, 182,
 381–383, 391, 392
Graz, 353
Gretchen (*Faust*), 405
Griesebner, Andrea, 321
Griesheim, Christian Ludwig von,
 167n89, 190
Grüble, Bastian, 58, 60
Guarinoni, Hippolyt, 60
Gudaleweska, 403–405

H

Habsburg dynasty, 34, 35, 221, 229,
 297, 358, 361, 363,
 371n118, 375
Halle, 66, 218

Hallmann, Johann Georg, 273, 274,
 274n34, 308
Hamburg, 15, 20, 25, 27, 28, 31, 32,
 34, 38, 55, 56, 75, 89, 91–137,
 139–208, 213, 271, 273, 277,
 284, 287, 299, 313, 331, 333,
 334, 340, 351, 351n56, 355,
 357, 397, 401
Hansen, Barbara, 170
Harrington, Joel, 6, 6n13, 7n15, 197
Haußler, Conrad, 242, 243n108
Häuslerin, Katherine, 83, 84,
 84n162
Heß, Jonas Ludwig von, 113, 165n84,
 170, 170n100
Heidmanns, Maria Dorothea, 183
Hell, 8, 13, 18, 47, 53, 198, 363,
 376, 384
Helmin, Polixena, 297, 297n109,
 300, 302
Helmstädt, 81
Hemmingsen, Ralf, 28, 29
Hempels, Cissie, 110
Henrichs, Trine, 162–164, 162n76
Hermlohrin, Dorothea, 79
Hernals, 335–338, 335n21, 373
Hietzing, 337
High Market, 247, 279, 334, 342,
 344, 356, 374, 377–379
Hinteregger, Thomas, 52
Hoffmann, Leopold Alois, 392
Holger, Josef Ferdinand Ritter von,
 314, 315, 315n160
Hölsen, Catharina, 91, 92, 185,
 185n150, 186, 188
Holstein, 14, 21, 25–27, 76,
 77, 400–402
Holy Innocents, 54–57, 81
Holy Roman Emperor, 221n43, 222
Holy Roman Empire, 8, 22, 32, 92,
 110, 115, 147, 147n21, 178,
 206, 213, 224, 313

Holy Trinity, 109, 215, 216, 223,
  247, 254, 269, 279, 281,
  336, 364n91
Holzner, Johann Christoph,
  248, 249n128
Homicide, 8, 26, 27, 42, 80, 111,
  124, 160, 405
  See also Murder
Hommel, Karl Ferdinand, 9, 75
Honor, 152, 159, 179, 182, 220, 247,
  275, 278, 300, 315, 361, 369,
  378, 391, 398
Horb, Johannes, 130
Hörnlein, Georg, 57
Host, 20, 35, 40, 42, 48, 53, 62,
  68n105, 102, 209, 211,
  215–218, 224, 226–228,
  238–263, 239n99, 277,
  280–282, 284–286, 298, 303,
  317, 322, 325–327, 329, 332,
  352, 396, 397
  See also Eucharist
Host desecration, 20, 40, 42, 62,
  68n105, 102, 216, 218, 239,
  241–263, 280, 281, 286, 303,
  322, 327, 332, 352, 396, 397
House of correction, 48, 66, 67n102,
  71, 80, 119–121, 140, 144,
  147–158, 161, 162, 164, 165,
  169–172, 176, 177, 180, 207,
  210, 265, 268–270, 272, 273,
  276, 279–285, 289–291, 293,
  295–301, 303–308, 319, 320,
  332, 346, 351, 352
  See also Prison/prisons; Workhouse
Howard, John, 320, 372
Hsia, R. Po-Chia, 4, 85, 121,
  122, 393
Hue and cry, 34, 127–129, 128n100,
  131, 132, 134, 136, 139n1, 142,
  165, 173, 186, 196
Hügel, Johann Peter, 189, 190

Hungary, 22, 233n77, 242n106, 273,
  274, 281, 288, 289, 349
Huttmanns, Gesche, 111

I
Iconoclasm, 20, 23, 32, 35, 53, 210,
  211, 218, 219, 221, 230, 235,
  262, 263, 275, 277, 279, 280,
  281n58, 282, 285, 286, 291,
  293, 299–301, 305, 306, 311,
  313–315, 321, 322n186, 325,
  329, 340, 355, 355n66, 396,
  397, 402
Iconography, 2, 85, 106, 118, 136,
  224, 375
Icons, 57, 209–262, 295, 301, 325,
  326, 335–337, 390, 392
"Image of Justice," 1
"Image of Mercy," 235, 238
Images, 2, 4, 5, 35, 57, 62, 84–87,
  85n170, 99, 101, 105, 129, 211,
  216–218, 223, 226, 229,
  231–235, 236n83, 238, 239n99,
  250, 255, 260, 265, 266,
  269n13, 277, 287–289, 293,
  298, 313, 315, 321, 322, 325,
  335, 362, 368, 373, 392, 397
Incest, 44, 46, 47, 123, 279
Indirect suicide, 8, 23, 32, 33
Infamy, 93, 147, 167, 168, 171, 282,
  298, 307, 340, 342, 347,
  350, 391
  See also Dishonor
Infanticide, 9–11, 9n24, 20, 23, 24,
  26, 32, 33, 35, 42, 46–48, 53,
  69, 77, 83, 93, 118, 122, 123,
  132–137, 145, 159, 160, 169,
  169n95, 169n96, 175, 206,
  236n83, 279, 282, 321, 332,
  338, 351, 356, 357, 396,
  401n15, 405, 406

See also Neonaticide
Ingrao, Charles, 222
Injury to majesty, 214, 220
  See also Lèse majesté
Inmate, 32, 48n39, 66, 67n102, 71, 80, 120, 144, 145, 147–150, 152–155, 152n40, 157–166, 169–171, 176–179, 210, 217, 270–277, 270n19, 274n34, 279, 280n56, 284–286, 290, 293–295, 296n105, 298, 299, 302–306, 308, 318–320, 320n175, 334, 352, 372, 387, 403
Innocent/innocence, 1, 3, 3n5, 4, 19, 25, 46, 53, 53n54, 55, 63, 75, 85, 87, 88, 125, 126, 129, 131, 135, 136, 175, 187, 205, 248, 339, 370, 400, 405
Insanity, 7, 8, 16n44, 33, 47, 142, 143, 202, 205, 217, 400
  See also Madness
Insanity defense, 142–144, 146, 176, 186, 188, 200, 202, 204, 400
Institutoris, Heinrich, 101
Intent, 24, 28, 29, 32, 33, 38, 42, 51, 72, 74, 75, 89, 119, 123, 125, 133, 146, 175, 184, 187, 200–202, 206, 210, 216, 273, 287, 291, 292, 318, 319, 332, 338, 351, 402, 404
Irregularity, 68–71, 351, 357
Isaac, 54
  See also Abraham
Italy, 361

J

Jacobin, Catharina, alias Jakobeckin, 348–350, 348n49, 379, 387, 389, 390
Jancovitschin, Clara Dorothea, 283
Jansson, Arne, 26, 27, 29

Jastram, Cord, 96, 113–115
Jentzen, Elisabeth, 202, 205, 208
Jesuits, 40, 56, 60, 227, 229, 237, 237n90, 238n95, 243, 245, 246, 252, 258, 271, 285, 293, 358, 367, 368, 374, 374n129, 376, 385, 387
Jewish ritual murder, 2–4, 26, 60, 63, 85, 122
  See also Blood libel
Jew/Jewish, 1, 2, 4, 6, 19, 35, 54, 59–64, 60n82, 64n93, 80, 95n12, 122, 132, 211, 216, 220, 233, 239–241, 241n104, 243, 245–249, 253–260, 262–264, 266, 268–270, 268n11, 269n13, 277, 303, 322, 327, 368, 376
Josefina, 315, 352
Joseph I, Holy Roman Emperor, 221, 225, 227, 280, 282n61
Joseph II, Holy Roman Emperor, 64, 221, 221n43, 270n19, 314, 315, 353, 354, 363n87, 388, 388n169, 392, 393, 401
Josephina, 221
Justice, 2, 6, 6n13, 11, 27, 29, 34, 35, 49, 53, 69–71, 93, 94, 98, 99, 102–104, 109, 113, 117, 118, 129, 130n110, 137, 139–142, 149n29, 152, 159, 164, 177, 180, 181, 189, 190, 196, 197, 200, 207, 208, 219, 223, 275, 279, 306, 311, 312, 315, 318, 326, 329–393, 353n62, 360n80, 396–398, 401, 405
"Justice of the Street," 94, 99, 122–137, 127n98, 139, 139n1, 142, 145, 159, 161, 164, 165, 173, 186, 188–190, 196, 207, 331
  See also Hue and cry

K

K., Johann, 275, 346, 346n45, 347
Kaperger, Hans, 253–255, 277
Kaufleuthner, Maria Anna, 282
Khörse, Johann Wilhelm, 202, 203, 208
Khunigin, Anna, 387
Klefeker, Johann, 128, 158, 159n65, 167, 167n90, 182, 184
Kleiner, Salomon, 230, 239, 239n99, 240, 342n34, 372, 373, 381, 382, 382n156
Knau, Jobst, 57
Koblenz, 17
Koch, Ernst, 142, 143, 143n5
Koenig, Catharina Maria, 204, 205, 208
Kohl, Valentin, 119–121
Kohnaus, Barbara, 170
Königsberg, 79
Köpflerin, Anna Catherina, 283, 283n67
Kopitzsch, Franklin, 97
Körner, Johann, 120, 121, 130, 333
Kornneuburg, 260
Koslofsky, Craig, 29
Kösters, Liesche, 171
Kremsmünster, 74
Krögers, Anna Gertrud, 161, 162, 162n74
Krogh, Tyge, 21n67, 23, 23n82, 27–30, 67
Krohns, Ilsabe, 161
Kummerfeldt, Gerhardt, 181
Kunze, Michael, 59

L

Lambach, 47, 48n39, 295n103, 303
Langen, Carolina Wilhemine, 402
Längin, Maria Helena, 20n61, 80
Last Judgment, 105, 106, 116, 376

Lederer, David, 16, 222n45, 237n90
Legislation, 8, 24, 33, 109, 173–177, 187, 201, 212, 214, 217, 221n42, 286, 321, 338, 400–404
See also Decree; Edict
Leipzig, 47, 80, 89, 139n1, 203, 218
Leopold I, Holy Roman Emperor, 220, 221n41, 223, 224, 229, 233n77, 251, 263, 265, 268, 276, 277, 288, 317, 377, 379
Leopoldina, 220, 221n41
Leopoldstadt, 263
Lèse majesté, 229
See also Injury to majesty
Lessing, Gotthold Ephraim, 192
Liliequist, Jonas, 22, 23n80, 52n51
Lind, Vera, 21n67, 27, 29, 76, 76n129
Lindemann, Mary, 96
Linz, 48, 48n39, 257, 282, 376
Lippe, Principality of, 16
Liturgy, 37–89, 121, 137
Lizfellnerin, Eva, 74, 74n121, 395, 396, 398–400
Lord's Supper, 157, 158, 194, 197, 198
Lorraine, France, 42
Lübeck, 25, 75, 128, 139n1
Lutheran/Lutheranism, 1, 2, 5, 6, 8, 12, 13, 15, 16, 18, 20–22, 27, 28, 30–32, 34, 37, 41, 45, 48, 49, 55, 63, 65, 67, 67n102, 68n104, 69–73, 70n110, 92–95, 95n12, 131, 140, 141, 154, 155, 157, 165, 170, 182, 191, 192, 195, 198n184, 201, 213, 223, 226, 241, 242, 334, 397, 404
Luther, Martin, 13, 55, 72, 73, 94, 95, 155, 217, 226

M

Madness, 133, 143n6, 203–205, 222n45, 406
Magdeburg, 63
Magic, 4, 4n8, 40–42, 58, 64, 101, 102, 104, 106, 110, 220, 251, 253, 256
Maldoner, Johann Franz, 332, 333
Malice, 25, 33, 162, 164, 184, 269, 292, 296, 298, 313, 338
Malleus Maleficarum, 101, 252
Mantua, 219, 359
Margarita Teresa, Empress, 265, 266
Maria Anna (Vienna, 1710), 215, 235
Mariahilf, 238, 392
Maria Lactans, 5
　See also Virgin Mary
Maria of Grünberg, 230, 232n75
　See also Mary with the Axe
Maria Pötsch (Marian icon), 233n77, 288, 290
Maria Taferl (Marian icon), 238
Maria Theresa, Empress, 25, 70, 71n113, 229, 232n75, 311, 313, 314, 316, 337n23, 352, 354, 388
Mariazell, 229, 336, 336n22, 337, 383
Marino, Giambattista, 55
Martauschin, Johanna, 71, 72
Martinin, Anna Maria, 48
Martin von Cochem, 69, 367
Martschukat, Jürgen, 27, 98, 203
Martyrs/martyrdom, 2, 54, 60, 63, 64, 68, 81, 84, 85, 132, 132n116, 194, 357, 369, 393, 405
Mary with the Axe, 209–262
Massaus, Cicilia, 183
Mass (Catholic), 12, 68, 102, 227, 241, 271, 272, 303, 364, 369, 386, 387
Matthias, Holy Roman Emperor, 238
Matz, Valentin, 119–121, 121n81
Maurer, Stefan, 286, 289, 314
Mayrin, Appollonia, 42
Mayrin, Margaretha, 79n143, 82, 82n152
Mayrin, Maria Anna, 10, 73, 83
Mecklenburg, 82
Medicalization, 141
Meinart, Andreas, 63
Melancholy/melancholic, 15, 16, 24, 31, 44, 46–48, 51, 52n50, 53, 66, 73, 79n143, 91, 143, 143n5, 144, 146, 159, 175, 176, 182, 184, 186, 190, 202, 217, 282, 291, 292, 297, 300, 302, 332, 346n44
Mental illness, 28, 203, 222n45
　See also Insanity; Madness
Mevius, 44, 53
Meyer, Margaretha, 172
Meyers, Anna Rebecca, 181
Meyers, Lemken, 106–107
Midelfort, Erik, 73
Migazzi, Christoph Anton, 385
Milka, Amy, 29, 30
Miracle/miraculous, 62, 132, 211, 227, 230–236, 233n77, 242, 248, 259, 260, 262, 327, 328, 336, 392
Moilanen, Lauri, 23, 23n81
Monstrance, 75, 116, 226, 228, 241, 242, 242n105, 242n106, 255, 257, 260, 317
Moravia, 221, 299, 345n42
Moser, Johann Jacob, 65, 66, 66n96, 67n102
Mother of God, 216, 281
　See also Virgin Mary
Motive, 7, 11, 15, 21n64, 32, 33, 58, 74, 84, 123–125, 132, 175, 189, 201, 208, 210, 218, 301, 330, 404

Mount Calvary, 335, 371–382,
   392, 393
Munich, 59, 61, 79, 211,
   238n95, 351
Municipal code, Hamburg, 99,
   101–103, 109, 111, 117, 152
Murder, 2–4, 6–9, 9n24, 11, 11n28,
   12, 17–23, 23n80, 23n82, 25,
   26, 28–35, 37, 38, 40, 48, 49,
   51–53, 55, 56, 58–60, 62–64,
   65n95, 66, 72, 74, 75, 77,
   79–86, 79n143, 89, 91–94, 99,
   101–104, 106, 115, 118–129,
   124n87, 128n100, 132, 133,
   135–137, 139–140, 210, 211,
   218, 220, 254, 255, 262, 273,
   274n34, 275, 277, 279, 280,
   284, 287, 308, 314, 325, 329,
   331–339, 344–351, 350n55,
   353, 355–357, 393,
   396–406, 397n5
Murer, Christoph, 1, 2, 4, 6

N
N., Adam (Vienna, 1715), 216
N., Anna Margaretha (Vienna,
   1717), 299
N., Anna Maria, (Vienna, 1723),
   345n42, 383, 384
N., Anna Maria, (Vienna,
   1731), 306
N., Catherina, (Vienna, 1709), 344
N., Elizabeth (Vienna, 1709),
   282, 336
N., Eva (Vienna, 1708), 340,
   342, 344
N., Johann (Vienna, 1722), 301,
   302, 302n124
N., Magdalena (Vienna, 1713),
   209–211, 218, 286n78, 290

N., Maria Anna (Vienna, 1710), 236,
   282, 348n50
N., Maria Catherina (Vienna, 1707),
   280, 345n42
N., Maria Elisabeth (Vienna,
   1712), 284
N., Maria Magdalena (Vienna, 1713),
   286, 346n44
N., Martin (Vienna, 1723), 345
N., Matthias (Schwadorf, 1731), 316
N., Regina (Vienna, 1718), 300
N., Rosalia (Vienna, 1708), 342, 344
N., Theresia (Vienna, 1713), 25, 70,
   221n43, 229, 232n75, 273, 311,
   313, 314, 316, 352, 354, 388
Nachbahrin, Theresia, 387
Nádasdy, Ferenc, 377, 378
Naples, 210, 295, 295n103, 300, 301,
   314, 356, 357
Neonaticide, 20, 134, 135, 159, 169,
   181, 187, 204, 206
   See also Infanticide
Neubauer, Caspar, 145
Neuhofferin, Maria Johanna, 333, 334
Neujahr, Friedrich, 173
Nitzlin, Anna Maria, 300, 301
Nördlingen, 31, 78
Nuremberg, 1–8, 4n7, 4n8, 6n13, 11,
   13–16, 19, 20, 24, 25, 34, 38,
   39, 57, 60, 69, 77, 81, 131,
   175, 213

O
Oberhausen, 10, 62
Ordeal of the bier, 125–127, 129,
   131, 132
   See also Cruentation
Osiander, Andreas, 4
Ostertag, Maria, 40, 45, 51, 396
Öttlin, Margaretha, 47, 48n39

P

Pappenheimer family, 59
Partinger, Franz, 368
Passion of Christ, 85n170, 213, 216, 340, 343, 373, 379
Pastoral care, 35, 37, 65, 67, 68n104, 68n106, 70n110, 72, 93, 115–117, 180, 185, 190, 192, 193, 271, 293, 330, 358, 367, 367n101, 368
Paulin, Anna Maria, 356
Paumbgartnerin, Maria Sabina, 290, 326
Pell, Sigmund, 387
Petersen, Berte, 123
Peurin, Anna, 62
Pfister, Ludwig, 71
Pforzheim, 122n82, 132, 132n116
Pieta, 297, 340, 342, 380, 390
Pietas austriaca, 211, 221–230, 329, 336, 363, 379
Pietism, 27, 28, 31
Pilberger, Johann Georg, 316
Pilgrimage, 57, 60, 62, 229, 231, 233, 238, 259, 260, 335–337, 392
Pillory, 99, 109n48, 118, 133
Plankhin, Rosina, 295, 296n104, 297, 297n109, 298, 303, 305
Platner, Ernst, 203
Poison/poisoning, 58, 76, 101, 103, 106, 107, 110, 123, 158, 168n93, 213, 252, 398, 399
Poland, 22
Policing, 93, 103, 139, 397
    See also Discipline/disciplining/disciplinary
Poor sinner, 18, 19, 39, 65, 71, 72, 82, 113, 116, 122, 155, 190, 245, 276, 313, 330, 357, 368–371, 374, 377, 379–381, 381n155, 383, 385, 387, 388, 390, 393, 398
Poor Sinners' Graveyard, 310, 371, 381, 382n155, 391, 392
Postel, Rainer, 95
Posthumous punishment, execution, 107
Post-mortem punishment, execution, 107, 136
Prandsteter, Adam, 46
Pressburg, 273, 283, 306–308, 310
Prince-bishopric, 3, 38, 52
Prison/prisons, 32, 40, 69, 70, 70n110, 85, 92, 101, 106, 107, 109n48, 111, 117, 119, 120, 129, 140, 144, 147–150, 152, 158–172, 159n65, 176–179, 185, 190, 191, 193, 194, 201, 203, 205, 207, 208, 210, 212, 214, 217, 219, 270–273, 275–277, 279, 281n58, 282, 285, 286, 290, 293, 294, 298, 299, 299n116, 302, 304, 305, 307, 308, 314, 319, 320, 346, 351, 352, 357, 360, 368, 371–374, 372n124, 376, 377, 387, 392, 396, 402, 404, 406
Prostitutes/prostitution, 10, 79, 82, 149, 158, 165–168, 168n93, 172, 236, 282–284, 286, 299, 318, 319, 355, 356, 402
Protestantism, 27, 116, 218, 231, 241, 243, 243n109, 253, 358
Prussia, 26, 232n75, 401, 402, 405
Puchsbaum, Hans, 340
Pulkau, 259, 260
Purgatory, 12, 67, 68, 72, 148, 258, 330, 363, 364, 364n91, 366, 369, 392

R

Rabin, Dana, 29
R. Anna Elisabeth, 46
Rape, 118, 123
Rauhenstein Alley, 371, 374, 392
Ravenstone, 65, 67, 70, 109n48, 111, 113, 115, 116, 121, 132, 137, 142, 158, 161, 166, 168, 169, 172, 176–178, 190, 195, 276, 282, 286, 289, 293, 294, 297, 298, 300, 301, 305, 306, 308, 310, 312, 327, 330, 339, 340, 342, 344, 350, 355–366, 368, 371, 377–380, 380n152, 383–386, 388–392, 401, 404
Reeh, Tine, 28, 29
Reformation, 63, 94n9, 95, 116, 139, 192, 217, 226, 229, 230, 236
Reformed, 23, 213, 214, 217
Regensburg, 64, 67n102
Reichlin, Eleonora, 387
Rentzel, Peter, 159
Reutlingen, 41, 396
Revenge, 47, 125, 146, 146n18, 187, 200, 204, 205, 258, 274, 301, 302, 318, 339, 348, 350, 351
Rink, Eucharius Gottlieb, 226, 278, 278n48
Ritual, 2–4, 6, 18, 19, 26, 30, 33, 34, 37, 38, 60, 62, 63, 71, 79–89, 94, 98–100, 100n25, 108, 114–116, 118, 122, 125n92, 127, 128, 128n100, 129n105, 130, 132, 137, 139n1, 140–142, 158, 167, 168, 170, 177, 178n126, 179–181, 186, 189–191, 193–196, 207, 222, 229, 239, 247, 253, 255, 274n34, 310, 329–331, 334, 336, 357, 363, 369, 369n111, 371, 383, 386, 392, 393

Robbery, 59, 102, 103, 118, 123, 168, 254–257, 295n103, 302, 303, 308, 317, 317n171, 357, 380
Roper, Lyndal, 52n49, 74, 250
Rosenburgerin, Maria Francisca, 215, 280, 280n56
Rosenfeld, 49, 49n43
Rossenberger, Maria Anna, 215, 279
Rothenburg ob der Tauber, 31
Rowlands, Alison, 3
Rubin, Miri, 239, 254, 262
Rudolf II, Emperor, 376
Rudolf of Habsburg, 224

S

Sabean, David, 157
Sacralization of executions, 115
Sacrament, 12, 68, 69, 73, 115, 116, 157, 158, 226, 227, 236, 237, 246, 257, 303, 332, 345, 356, 369, 371
Sacred landscape, 35, 233, 329–393
Sacrifice, 27, 37, 54, 57, 60, 64, 68n104, 79–89, 122, 137, 170, 336, 369, 370
Sacrilege, 217, 231, 232, 232n75, 241, 254, 255, 259, 287, 325–327, 335, 374n129
See also Blasphemy; Iconoclasm
St. Augustine, 12, 392
St. Charles Boromeo, 288
St. Stephen's Cathedral, 223, 228, 233n77, 237, 238, 239n99, 241, 281, 288, 290, 335, 340, 364n87, 371, 374
Salvation, 9, 11, 17, 19, 28, 33, 42, 48, 60, 67, 72, 73, 87, 120, 147, 153, 158, 168, 194, 212, 262, 301, 312, 330, 336, 339, 347,

357–366, 384, 386, 388, 390, 393, 398, 404
Salvific gaze, 116, 393
Salzburg, 52, 64, 213, 214, 249
Satan, 7, 8, 12, 13, 38, 42, 43, 46, 47, 51, 52n50, 65, 106, 107, 110, 131, 251, 254, 255, 258, 259
See also Devil; Evil enemy
Sattler, Wilhelm, 387
Saxony, 22, 46, 65n95, 128n100, 147
Scaffold, 35, 68, 71, 72, 84, 87, 89, 93, 98, 113, 115, 120–122, 137, 141, 173, 175, 189, 195, 205, 208, 209, 219, 246, 248, 287, 330
See also Ravenstone
Scandinavia, 22, 30
Schachtner, Hans, 45, 53
Scharbaur, Johann Adam, 384–386
Scharenberg, Catharina, 159, 160
Scheffer, Niklas, 31
Schickin, Agnes Catharina, 9n23, 81, 81n150, 82, 82n151, 84, 395, 399, 404
Schirm, Margaretha, 41
Schleswig, 21, 25–27, 76, 77, 400–402
Schlüter, Matthäus, 105, 105n38
Schmans, Sophie, 171, 172n107
Schmid, Catharina, 41, 42, 396
Schmid, Jacob, 61, 62
Schmidt, Frantz, 6, 6n13, 57, 58, 60
Schmidts, Margaretha, 145
Schmied, Elisabeth, 89
Schnabel-Schüle, Helga, 354
Schölermann, Hein Clas, 183
Schönbrunn, 388
Schönin, Susanna, 62
Schramm, Percy Ernst, 97
Schröder, Johann Christian, 204
Schulz, Burckhardt, 17
Schutte, Jochim, 108
Schwabmünchen, 53

Schwach, Johannes Heinrich, 31, 31n121
Schwerhoff, Gerd, 214, 282, 320
Secularization, 33, 106, 401, 404
Self-accusation, 9n25, 24, 32, 37, 40, 42, 43, 45–48, 51–53, 52n50, 52n51, 59, 123n83, 145, 352, 397n5, 403
See also Self-confessed
Self-confessed, 46, 53, 71n113
Sellenschloen, Engel, 183, 184, 184n145
Siege of Vienna, 224
Silesia, 21, 66, 221, 356
Simon of Trent, 2, 55, 60, 63, 85, 122
Sin, 10, 12, 19, 52, 53, 85, 89, 121, 126, 130, 149, 166, 183, 194, 208, 237, 258, 262, 268, 278, 287–289, 292, 293, 298, 299, 301, 358, 368–370, 376, 390
Siners, Gretkin, 133
Snitger, Hieronymus, 96, 113–115
Social disciplining, 10, 38, 326
Sodomy, 9n25, 23, 24, 43–49, 52n50, 123, 168
Sorcerer-Jack trials, 249, 250
Sorcery/sorcerer/sorceress, 101, 103, 110, 111, 213, 257
Sottmann, Daniel, 175
Sovereignty/sovereign, 16, 42, 94–98, 94n9, 178, 182, 195, 211, 214, 276, 305, 313, 329, 375–377
Sp., Anna Maria, 305
Spandau, 67n102, 71
Speyer, 213
Spierenburg, Pieter, 23, 80, 277, 277n43
Spinnerin am Kreuz, 340, 343, 393
Spinnhouse, 140, 145, 147, 148, 156, 158–162, 165, 166, 170, 172, 176, 177, 180, 185n150, 202, 206, 207

Spirlings, Catharina, 145
Sprenger, Johann, 101
Springer, Daniel, 270
Stainin, Elisabeth, 215, 281
Stark, Nicolaus, 274n34, 306–308, 310, 310n148, 311, 315
Stations of the Cross, 335, 337, 370
   See also Way of the Cross
Steinhäuser, Albert Georg, 146, 177
Steinhäuserin, Catherina, 146, 159, 177, 184
Straßenrecht, 99
   See also Gassenrecht; "Justice of the Street"
Streng, Adolf, 119, 140
Ströbl, Balthasar, 396
Ströbl, Matthias, 395, 396, 398, 399
Ströblin, Barbara, 395, 396, 399
Strölin, Anna, 7, 7n15, 7n16, 8, 11, 20n61, 38n2, 57
Struensee, Adam, 66, 66n98, 67
Stubs, Margaretha, 161
Stüller, Niklaus, 57, 58
Sturm und Drang, 405
Sturm, Christoph Christian, 141, 191
Stuttgart, 51
Styria, 250, 251n138, 279
Suicide, 8–35, 9n24, 9n25, 16n44, 37–89, 91–94, 98, 100, 114, 117–123, 125, 130, 130n110, 132, 135–137, 139–146, 148, 155, 161, 167–169, 168n92, 171–173, 175, 177–179, 181–190, 205–208, 210, 211, 217, 218, 273, 275, 279, 287, 299, 301, 315, 319, 325, 326, 328, 330–334, 338, 346–348, 351, 355, 357, 361, 386, 390, 393, 395–406
Suicide, indirect, 8, 23, 32, 33
Swabia, 22, 249n129, 290, 350
Sweden/Swedish, 16n44, 23, 23n80, 24, 26, 27, 29, 43, 52n51, 76, 144n7, 212, 320
Switzerland, 23n84, 249

T

Taboo, 17, 136, 177–179, 208
Tapiau, 403
Taylor, John, 111, 113
Temeswar, 22n75, 274
Thaylfingen, 48
Theft, 23, 30, 46, 48, 85, 102, 106, 118, 123, 145, 168, 181, 236, 255, 256, 273, 284, 293, 300, 303, 307, 310, 355–357, 384, 387, 390
Theresiana, 25, 311, 312, 314, 315, 317n171, 327, 352
Thieves' candles, 57, 58
Thomasius, Christian, 63
Tlusty, Ann, 59
Torture, judicial, 11, 46, 58, 70, 303, 312, 370, 372
Transubstantiation, 227, 345
   See also Communion; Eucharist; Lord's Supper
Trarbach, 17
Trent, 2, 55, 59, 60, 63, 85, 122, 227
Trier, 130, 213, 218
Trinity Column, 223, 224, 228, 288, 379
Trogs, Margaretha, 161
Tübingen, University of, 41, 79n143
Turks, 6, 35, 211, 223, 224, 231, 233, 257, 277, 327, 337
Tyrol, 56, 60, 249, 250

U

Uhlin, Catharina, 66, 66n98, 66n99, 68n104, 71, 72, 88n172, 89n175
Ulbricht, Otto, 77

INDEX 465

University of Altdorf, 44
University of Tübingen, 41, 79n143
University of Vienna, 219, 291, 332, 353n62, 390
Unruhe, Hans, 46, 47
Urban VIII, 360, 360n82
Urfehde, 274, 274n33, 274n34, 282, 292, 296, 299, 300, 308, 310, 346, 346n44, 355–357, 383, 384

V

Vagrant/vagrancy, 31, 52, 59, 63, 64, 64n93, 160, 249, 250, 253, 255, 273, 282, 288, 293, 303, 307, 308, 319, 348–353, 355, 383
Valentinitsch, Helfried, 252, 253
Viaticum, 224, 239
Victim/victimology, 3, 9, 11, 13, 15, 19, 34, 40, 55, 58, 62, 73, 77, 79–85, 87, 88, 94, 99, 120–122, 122n82, 126–129, 128n100, 131, 132, 135–137, 139n1, 142–144, 143n6, 150, 161, 162, 170, 170n100, 179, 186, 188, 200, 208, 230, 249–251, 250n131, 273, 326, 327, 331, 331n4, 332, 332n5, 334, 336, 338, 339, 345, 346, 352, 396, 399, 404–406
Vienna, 8, 11, 19, 25, 31, 32, 34, 35, 47, 48, 57, 77, 79, 175, 209–211, 214, 215, 217–219, 223, 224, 227–233, 233n77, 235–241, 243, 246–248, 251, 253, 254, 257, 259, 262–264, 266, 268, 270, 272–278, 274n34, 283n67, 284, 285, 287–290, 295n103, 297, 298, 302, 303, 306–308, 310, 310n146, 311, 314, 317n171, 318–320, 322, 322n185, 325–393, 397, 398, 401, 402

Vincentius a Sancta Eleonora, 364
Violence, 6, 16, 26, 27, 33, 37, 55, 64, 74, 77, 79, 80, 83, 89, 96, 103, 152, 203, 213, 215, 276, 314, 315, 327
Virgin Mary, 5, 75, 212n7, 229, 231, 233, 325, 326, 337, 373, 392
Voß, Carsten Christopher, 204
Voßin, Anna Dorothee, 81
Völkner, Daniel, 82
von Rinn, Anderl, 63

W

Wachter, Joseph, 52
Wächter, Leonhard, 127, 127n98
Wagnerin, Rosina, 217, 217n32, 282
Walkersbrunn, 7
Walters, Adelgunda, 123, 124, 124n87, 127, 144–145
Wannier, Claudon, 42
Waserin, Ursula, 49, 51
Way of the Cross, 335, 369
  See also Stations of the Cross
Weariness with life, 7, 25, 41, 44–47, 53, 72, 92, 123, 139–140, 210, 273, 291–293, 313, 332, 338
Weiglhofferin, Susanna, 334–338
Wellner, Philibert, 368
Weninger, Benigna Rosina, 284, 285
Wernigeroda, 67n102, 72, 84
Werthaim, Anna Maria Elisabetha, 286, 326
Westphalia, 31, 31n121
Wheel Cross, 340, 342, 342n36, 344, 346n44, 353n62, 388
Wiener Geserah, 254, 263
Wiennerisches Diarium, 284, 346n45
Wilhelm-Schaffer, Irmgard, 130

Witch, 2, 4, 6, 19, 35, 38, 40–43, 45,
    51, 53, 58, 59, 70n110, 92, 99,
    101–103, 106, 107, 110, 118,
    137, 211, 216, 224, 249–253,
    251n138, 255, 257, 259, 277,
    317, 318, 322, 327, 344,
    396, 406
Witchcraft, 4, 4n7, 4n8, 11, 27, 31,
    32, 37, 39–45, 47, 48, 51–53,
    52n49, 52n50, 59, 93, 101, 103,
    106, 110, 111, 118, 122, 137,
    211, 249, 251, 252, 254, 257,
    259, 269, 284, 285, 311, 312,
    316–318, 396, 405
Witch-hunt, 3, 4, 10, 31, 35, 38, 39,
    45, 49, 51, 52, 57, 102, 106,
    110, 211, 213, 249–252, 257,
    285, 311, 316, 317, 322,
    344, 405
Wittenberg, Judith, 145, 145n13
Wolf, Franz, 161
Wölffin, Magdalena, 11, 12, 20n61
Wolfsberg, 260, 261
Woltersdorff, Ernst Gottlieb, 66,
    67n102, 68n104
Women, 5, 6, 9, 9n24, 10, 23, 33, 37,
    44, 47, 52, 57–60, 62–64,
    62n87, 64n93, 67n102, 72,
    75–77, 79, 80, 93, 94, 101–103,
    106, 110, 118, 123, 132, 133,
    136, 137, 141, 149, 150,
    159–165, 167–170, 167n89,
    169n96, 172, 175, 176, 181,
    185, 188, 199, 204–207, 211,
    224n53, 228, 250, 250n136,
    251n139, 252, 259, 269–271,
    274, 282, 284, 293, 297, 301,
    306, 318–321, 320n175,
    322n186, 325, 329, 333, 334,
    338, 339, 344, 346–357, 387,
    388, 396, 399, 403–406
Workhouse, 48n39, 66, 81, 119, 120,
    147–150, 149n27, 152, 152n40,
    153, 159, 160, 163, 164, 179,
    217, 269–274, 282, 291, 298,
    299, 304, 307, 308,
    318–320, 320n175
Wosnik, Richard, 28
Wraxall, Nathanial William, 380, 381
Wunderlich, Franz, 215, 279, 325
Württemberg, 21, 48, 49, 65, 82, 157,
    158, 242, 395
Würzburg, 3, 218, 285

Z
Zach, Ignatius, 60, 60n82
Zächerlin, Maria Barbara, 334, 338
Zauber-Jackl Prozesse, 249
    See also Sorcerer-Jack trials
Zechirlin, Maria Magdalena, 284,
    284n69, 285
Zedler, Isabelle, 27, 40, 41
Zeitler, Joseph, 295, 295n103,
    296n105, 297, 297n109, 299,
    299n116, 302, 303, 317, 326
Zetergeschrei, 128
Zieglerin, Adelheid, 350–353, 350n55
Zotter, Anna, 318, 319
Zurich, 23, 24, 63, 76, 214,
    215, 215n19
Zweiffelsberg, 46

The manufacturer's authorised representative in the EU is Springer Nature Customer Service Centre GmbH, Europaplatz 3, 69115 Heidelberg, Germany. If you have any concerns regarding our products, please contact ProductSafety@springernature.com

Printed and bound by CPI Group (UK) Ltd, Croydon, CR0 4YY

25/03/2026

02078179-0007